OTHER BOOKS BY JEFF SMITH

BONE

BONE Color Reprint Series
Bone Volume 1: Out from Boneville
Bone Volume 2: The Great Cow Race
Bone Volume 3: Eyes of the Storm
Bone Volume 4: The Dragonslayer
Bone Volume 5: Rock Jaw, Master of the Eastern Border
Bone Volume 6: Old Man's Cave
Bone Volume 7: Ghost Circles
Bone Volume 8: Treasure Hunters
Bone Volume 9: Crown of Horns
Bone Handbook

Bone: Rose
(written by Jeff Smith, painted by Charles Vess)

Bone: Tall Tales
(written by Jeff Smith and Tom Sniegoski, drawn by Jeff Smith)

Bone: Quest for the Spark Book 1
(written by Tom Sniegoski, illustrated by Jeff Smith)

Bone: Quest for the Spark Book 2
(written by Tom Sniegoski, illustrated by Jeff Smith)

Bone: Quest for the Spark Book 3
(written by Tom Sniegoski, illustrated by Jeff Smith)

Little Mouse Gets Ready

Available in fine bookstores and comic shops everywhere
For more information visit us at
www.boneville.com

Facebook: The Official Jeff Smith Page

Twitter: @jeffsmithsbone

For more information about the color series visit:
www.scholastic.com/bone

RASL

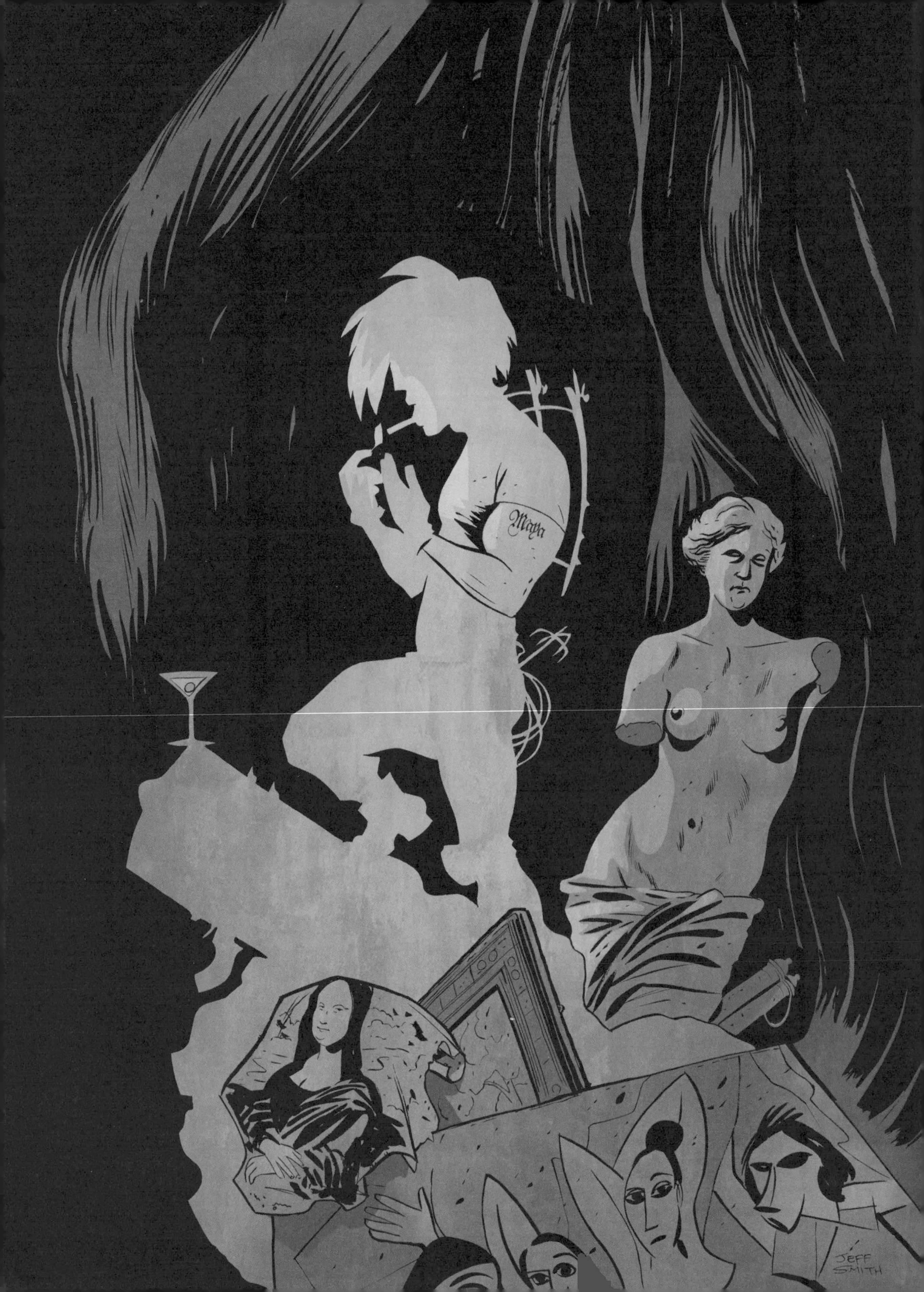
Maya
JEFF SMITH

RASL

BY
JEFF SMITH

CARTOON BOOKS
COLUMBUS, OHIO

THIS BOOK IS DEDICATED TO

Vijaya Iyer
for believing from the very beginning

and

Jennifer Gwynne Oliver
for telling me about the invisible ship

COLOR

JEFF SMITH   ART DIRECTION
STEVE HAMAKER   COLORIST
TOM GAADT   ADDITIONAL COLOR & DESIGN

COPYRIGHT © 2013 BY JEFF SMITH

PARTS OF THIS BOOK WERE ORIGINALLY SERIALIZED IN THE COMIC BOOK RASL
RASL™ IS © 2008 BY JEFF SMITH.

ALL RIGHTS RESERVED. PUBLISHED BY CARTOON BOOKS.
RASL, CARTOON BOOKS, AND ASSOCIATED LOGOS ARE TRADEMARKS AND/OR REGISTERED TRADEMARKS OF CARTOON BOOKS

COVER ART BY JEFF SMITH
COVER COLOR & LOGO/DESIGN BY STEVE HAMAKER

FOR CARTOON BOOKS:
VIJAYA IYER   PUBLISHER
KATHLEEN GLOSAN   PRODUCTION MANAGER
TOM GAADT   PRE PRESS / DESIGN

FOR INFORMATION WRITE:
CARTOON BOOKS
P.O. BOX 16973
COLUMBUS, OH 43216

13 DIGIT ISBN: 978-1-888963-37-3
10 DIGIT ISBN: 1-888963-37-9

10 9 8 7 6 5 4 3 2 1

PRINTED IN SINGAPORE

Table of Contents

Act One: The Drifter

Act Two: The Fire of St. George

Act Three: Romance at the Speed of Light

Act Four: The Lost Journals of Nikola Tesla

ACT ONE

THE DRIFTER

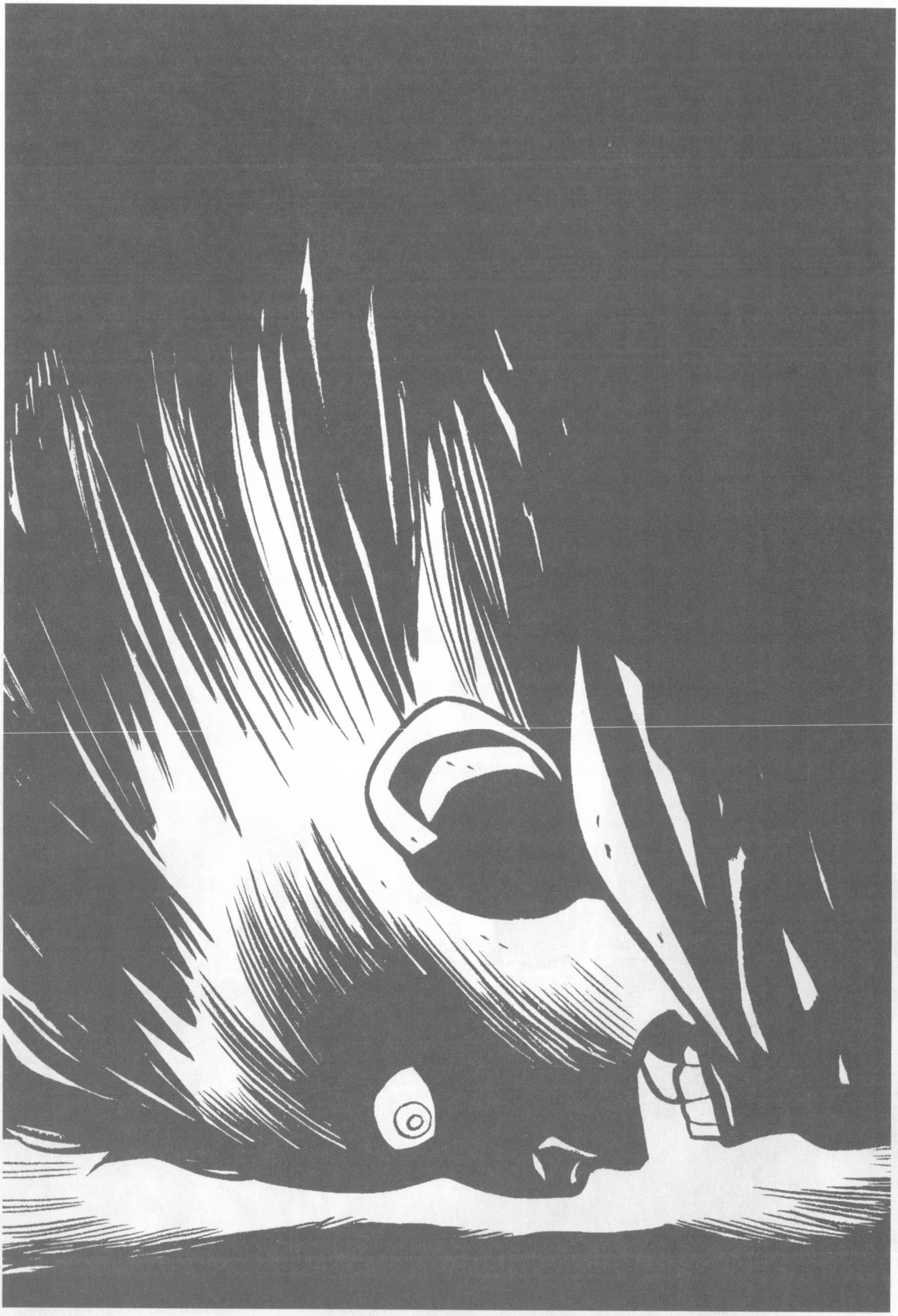

"Throughout space there is energy. Is this energy static or kinetic?
If static, our hopes are in vain; if kinetic – and we know it is, for certain – then it is
a mere question of time when men will succeed in attaching their machinery to the very
wheelwork of nature."

-Nikola Tesla

I
THE DRIFT

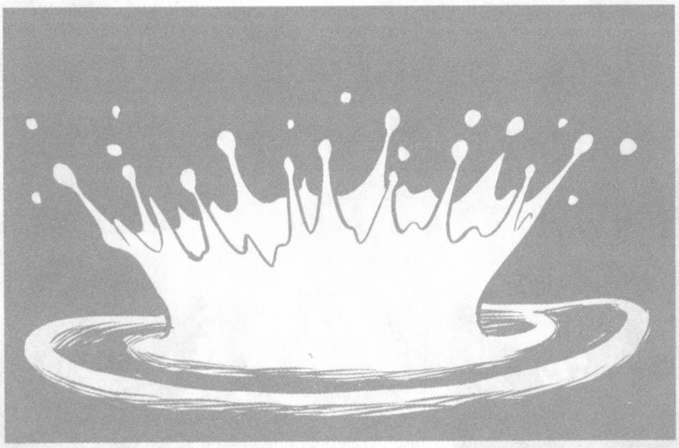

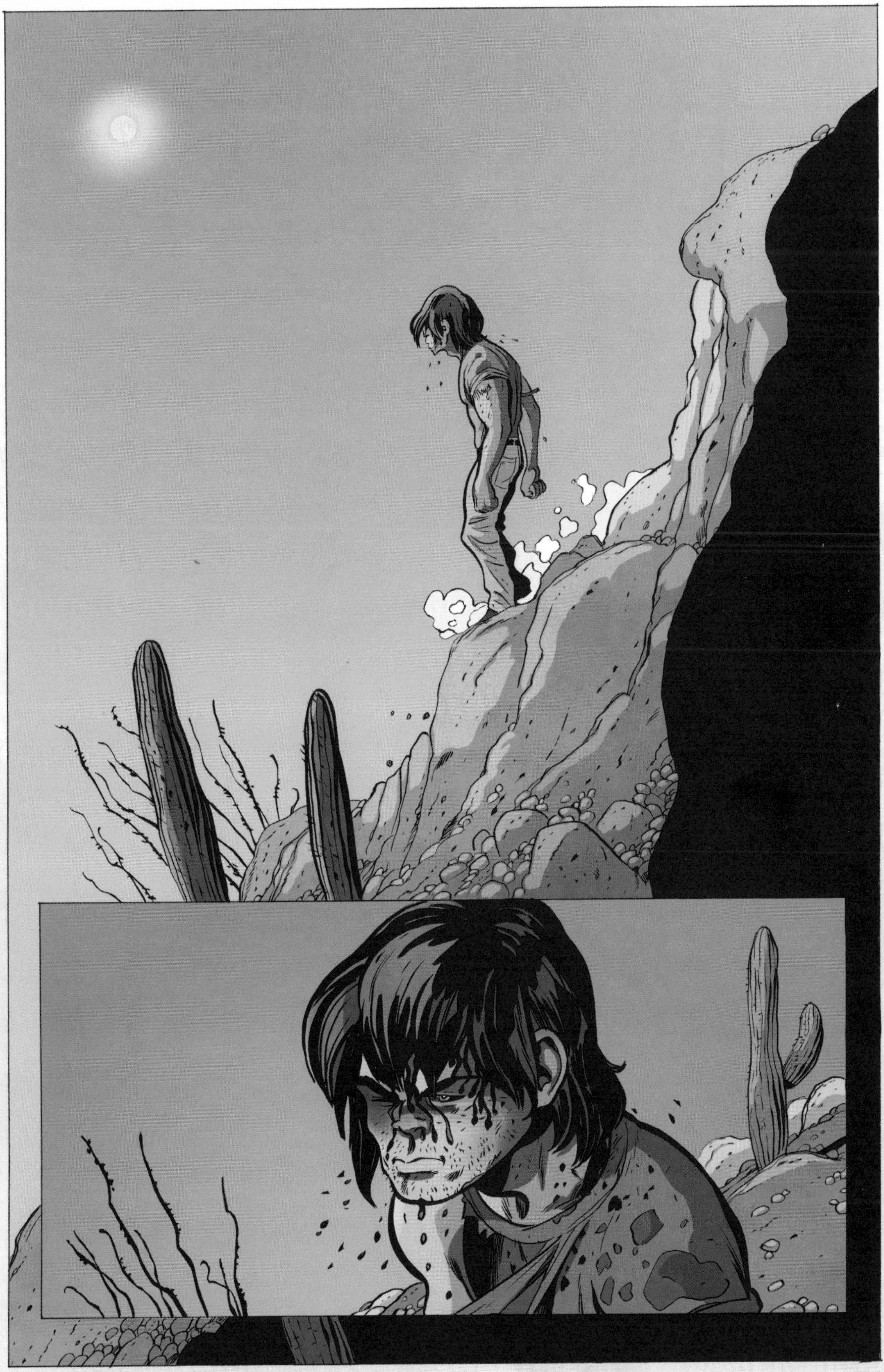

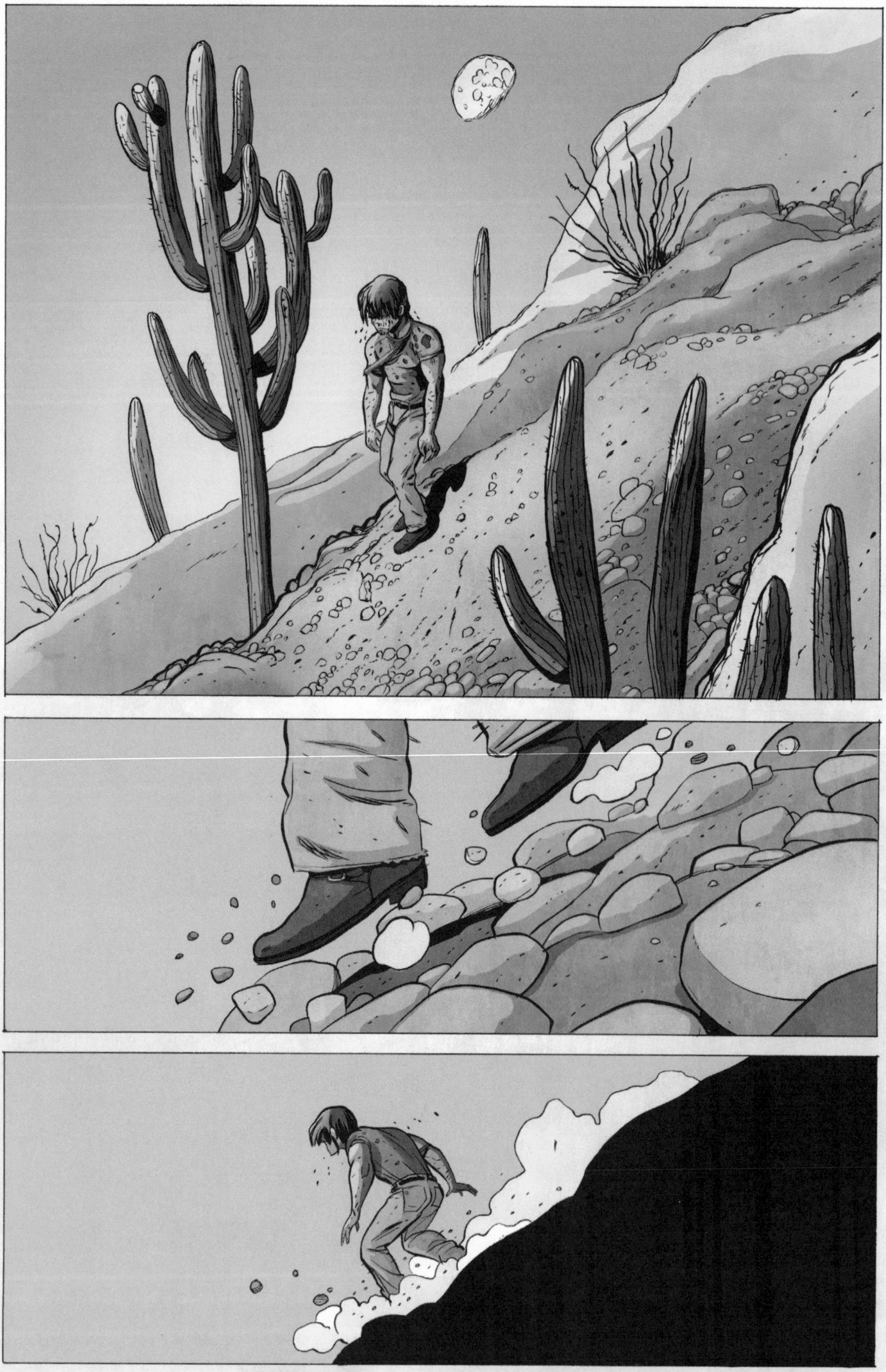

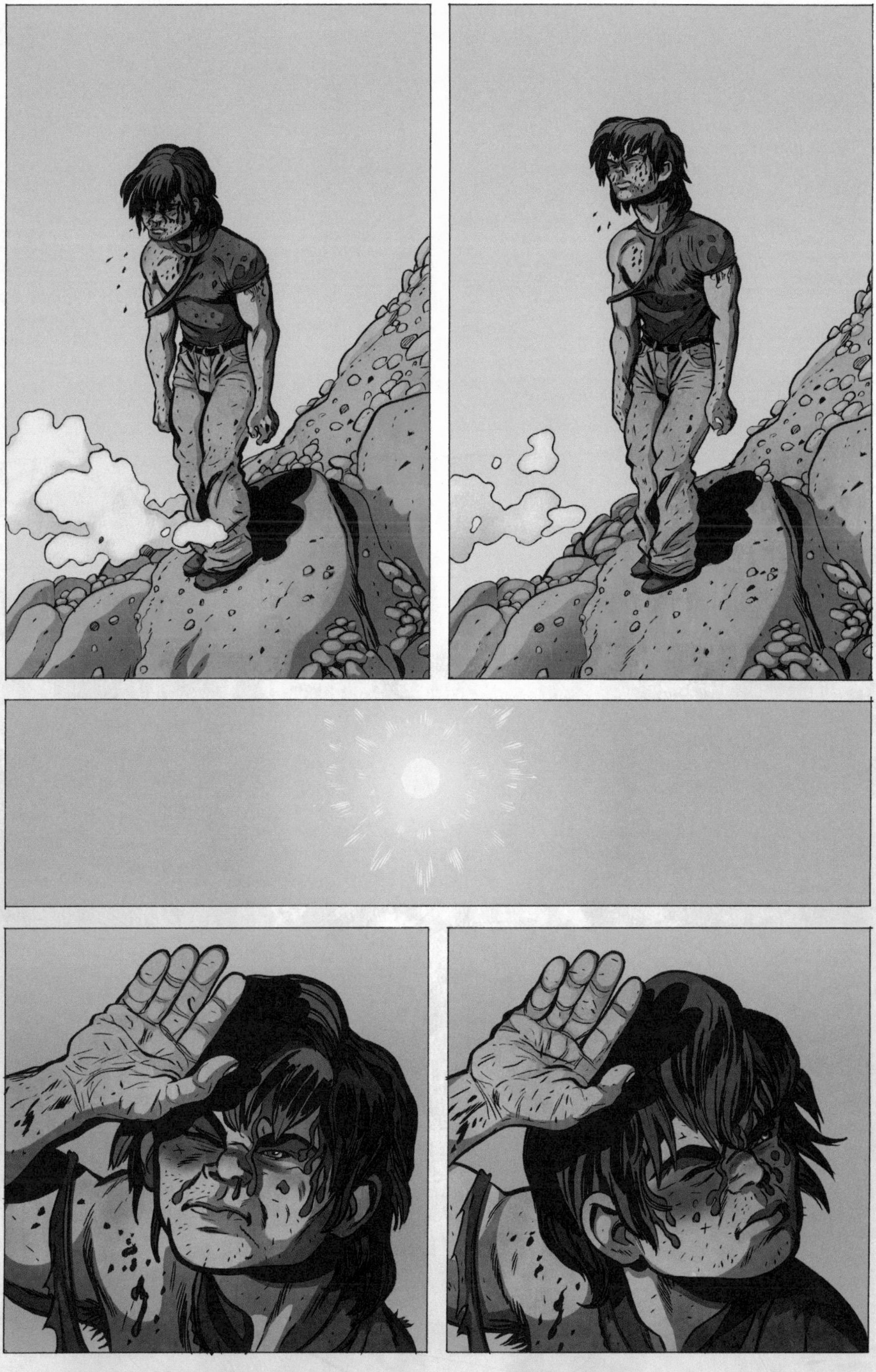

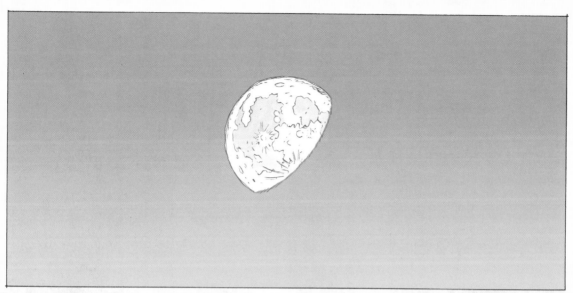

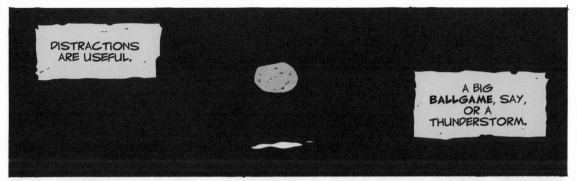

DISTRACTIONS ARE USEFUL.

A BIG BALLGAME, SAY, OR A THUNDERSTORM.

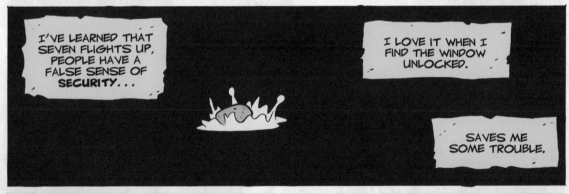

I'VE LEARNED THAT SEVEN FLIGHTS UP, PEOPLE HAVE A FALSE SENSE OF SECURITY...

I LOVE IT WHEN I FIND THE WINDOW UNLOCKED.

SAVES ME SOME TROUBLE.

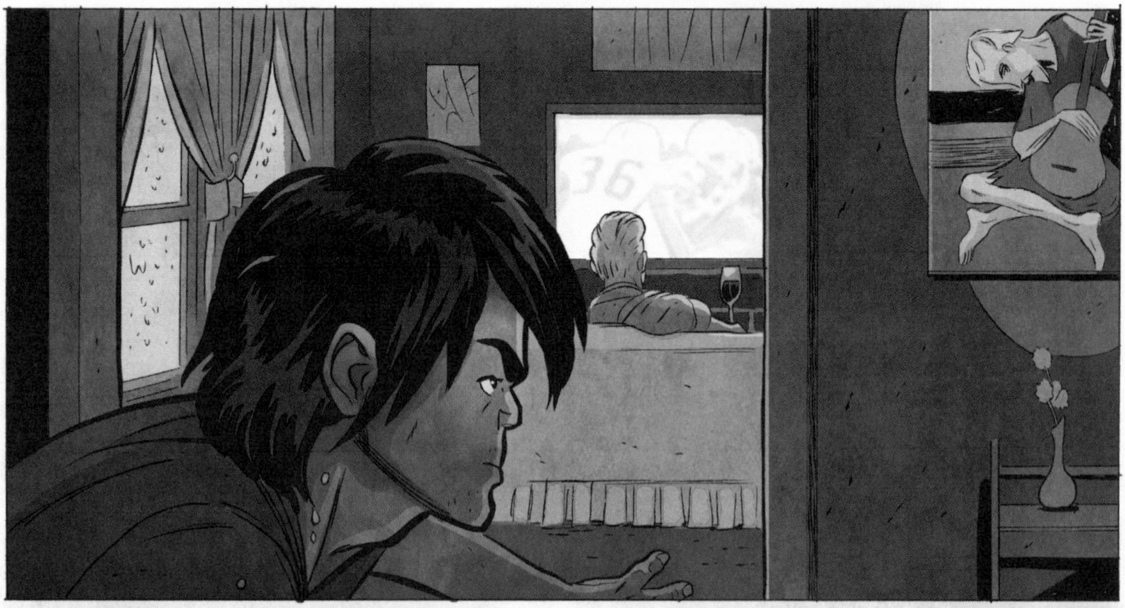

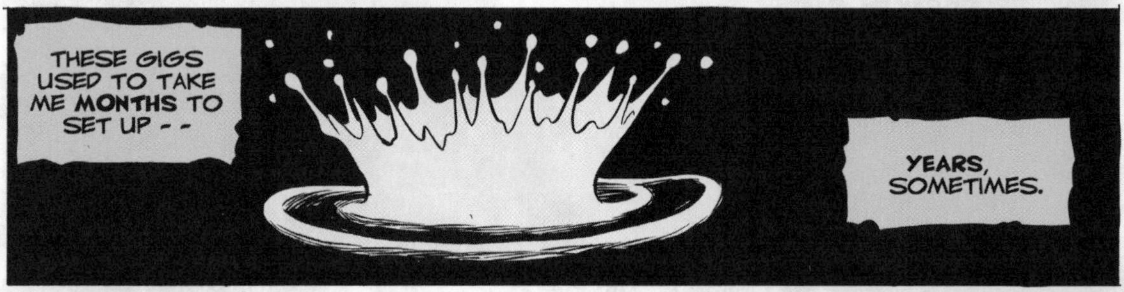
THESE GIGS USED TO TAKE ME MONTHS TO SET UP - -
YEARS, SOMETIMES.

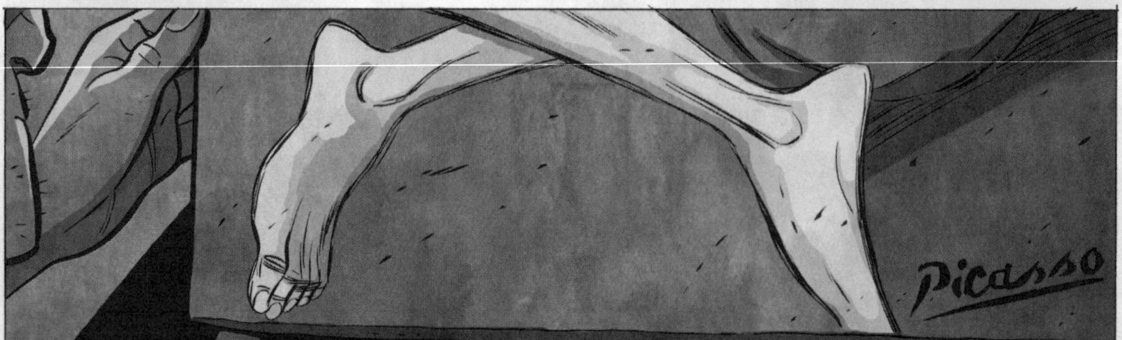
Picasso

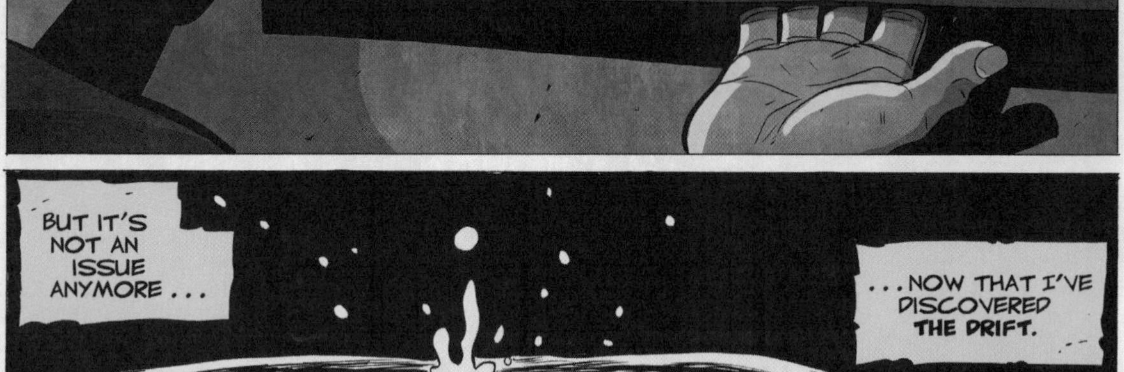
BUT IT'S NOT AN ISSUE ANYMORE . . .
. . . NOW THAT I'VE DISCOVERED THE DRIFT.

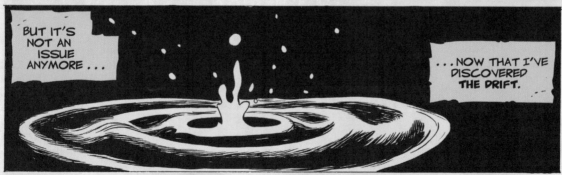

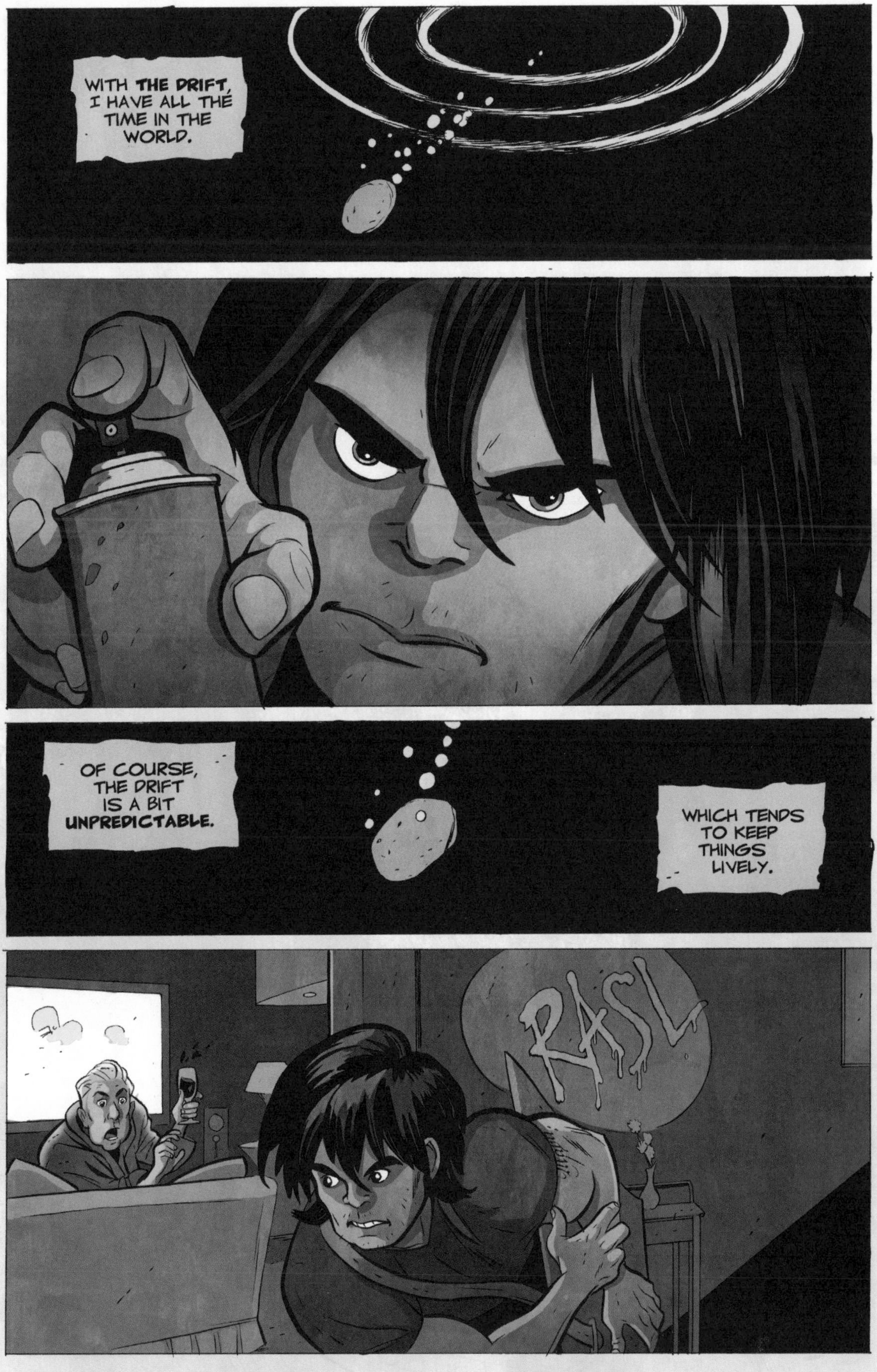

WITH THE DRIFT, I HAVE ALL THE TIME IN THE WORLD.
OF COURSE, THE DRIFT IS A BIT UNPREDICTABLE.
WHICH TENDS TO KEEP THINGS LIVELY.
RASL

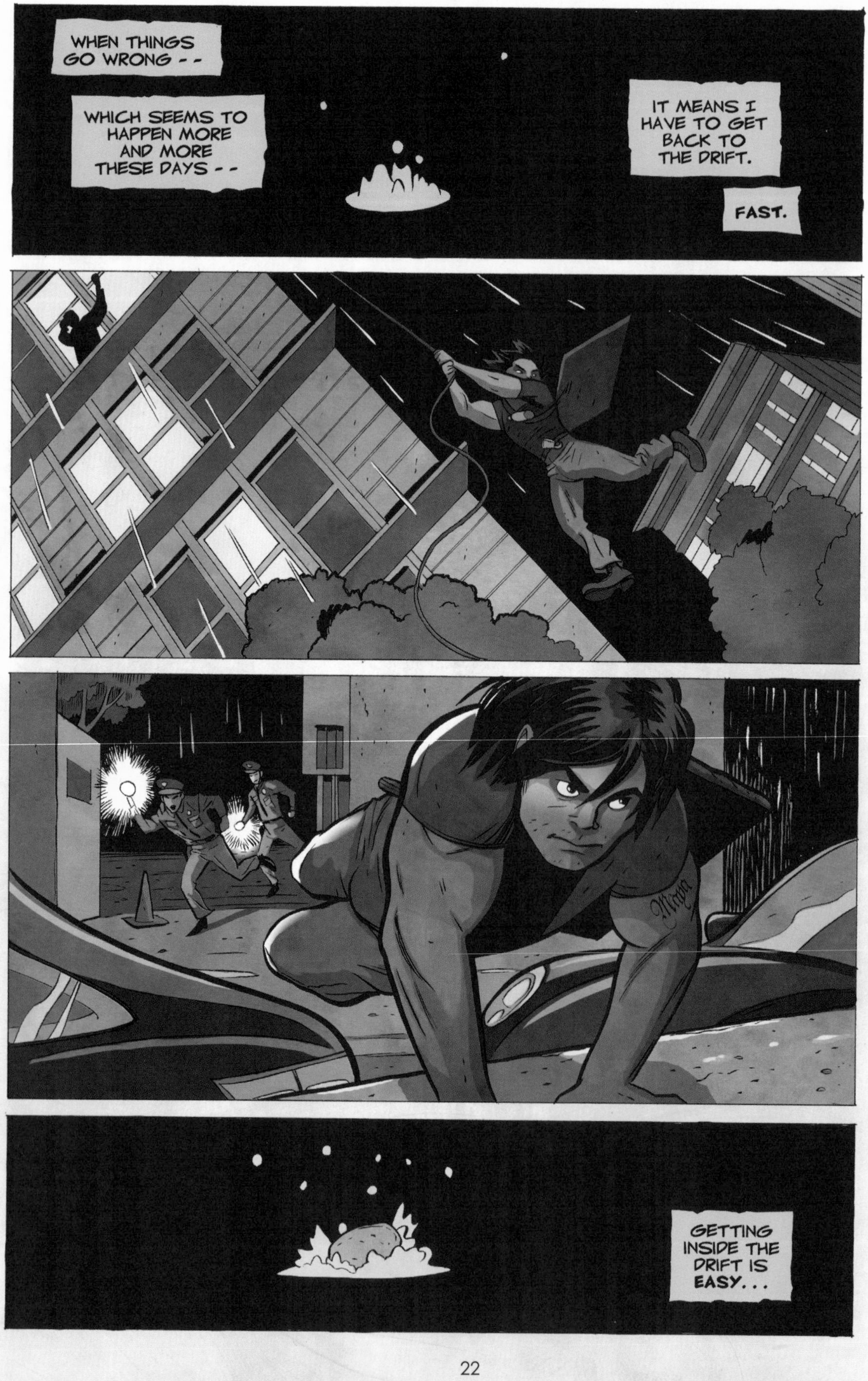
WHEN THINGS GO WRONG - -
WHICH SEEMS TO HAPPEN MORE AND MORE THESE DAYS - -
IT MEANS I HAVE TO GET BACK TO THE DRIFT.
FAST.
GETTING INSIDE THE DRIFT IS **EASY**...

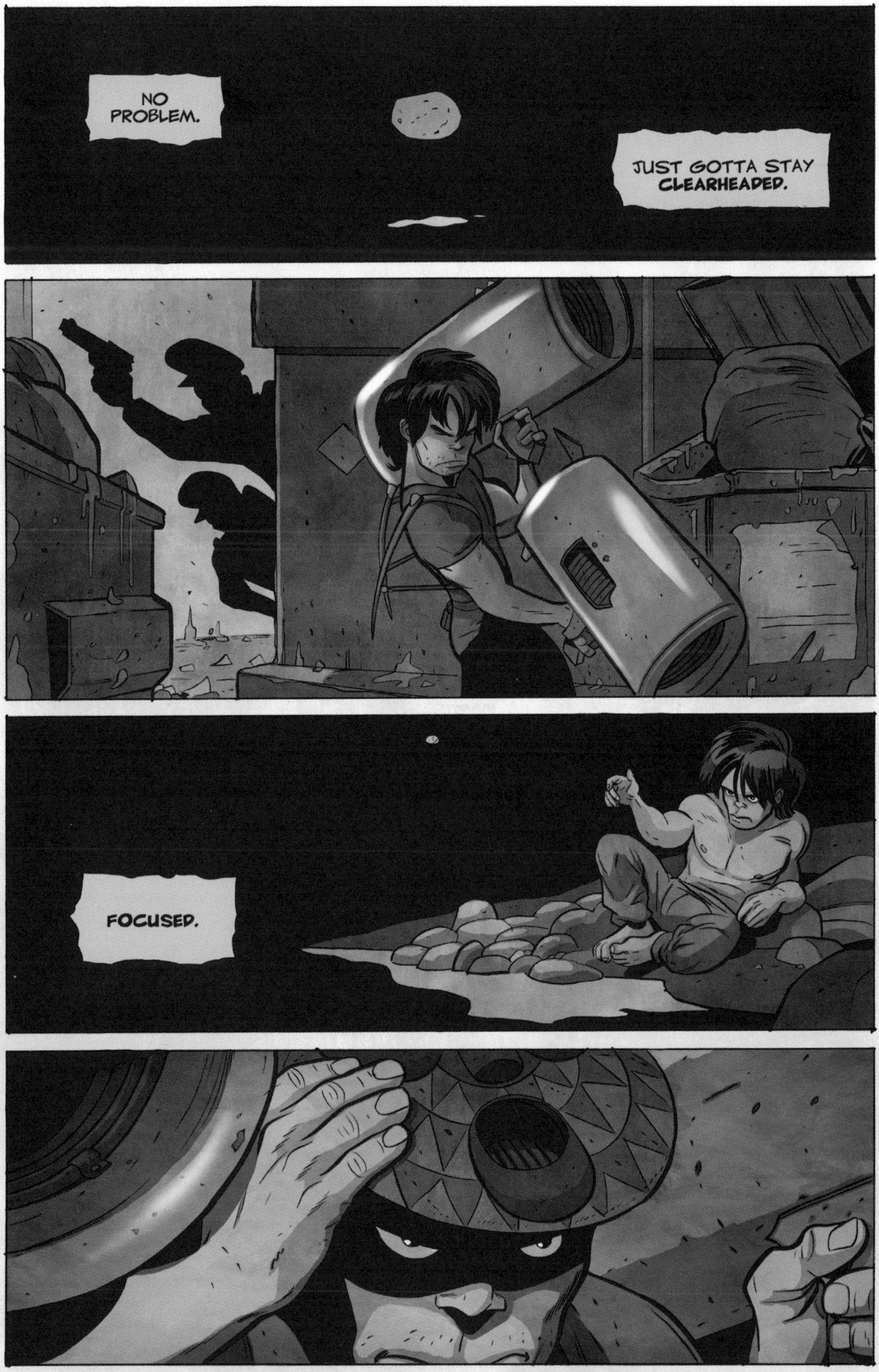
NO PROBLEM.
JUST GOTTA STAY CLEARHEADED.
FOCUSED.

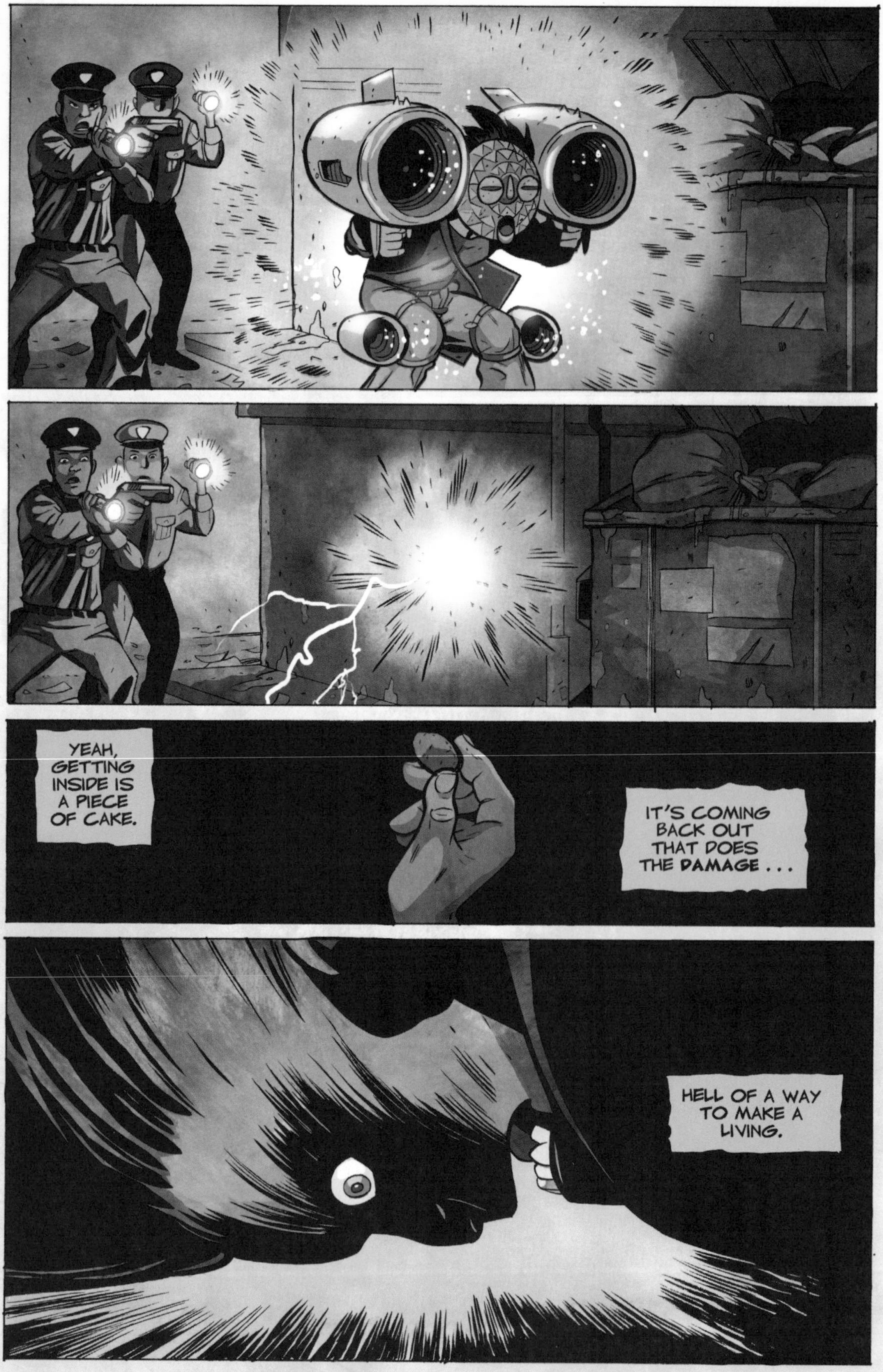
YEAH, GETTING INSIDE IS A PIECE OF CAKE.
IT'S COMING BACK OUT THAT DOES THE DAMAGE . . .
HELL OF A WAY TO MAKE A LIVING.

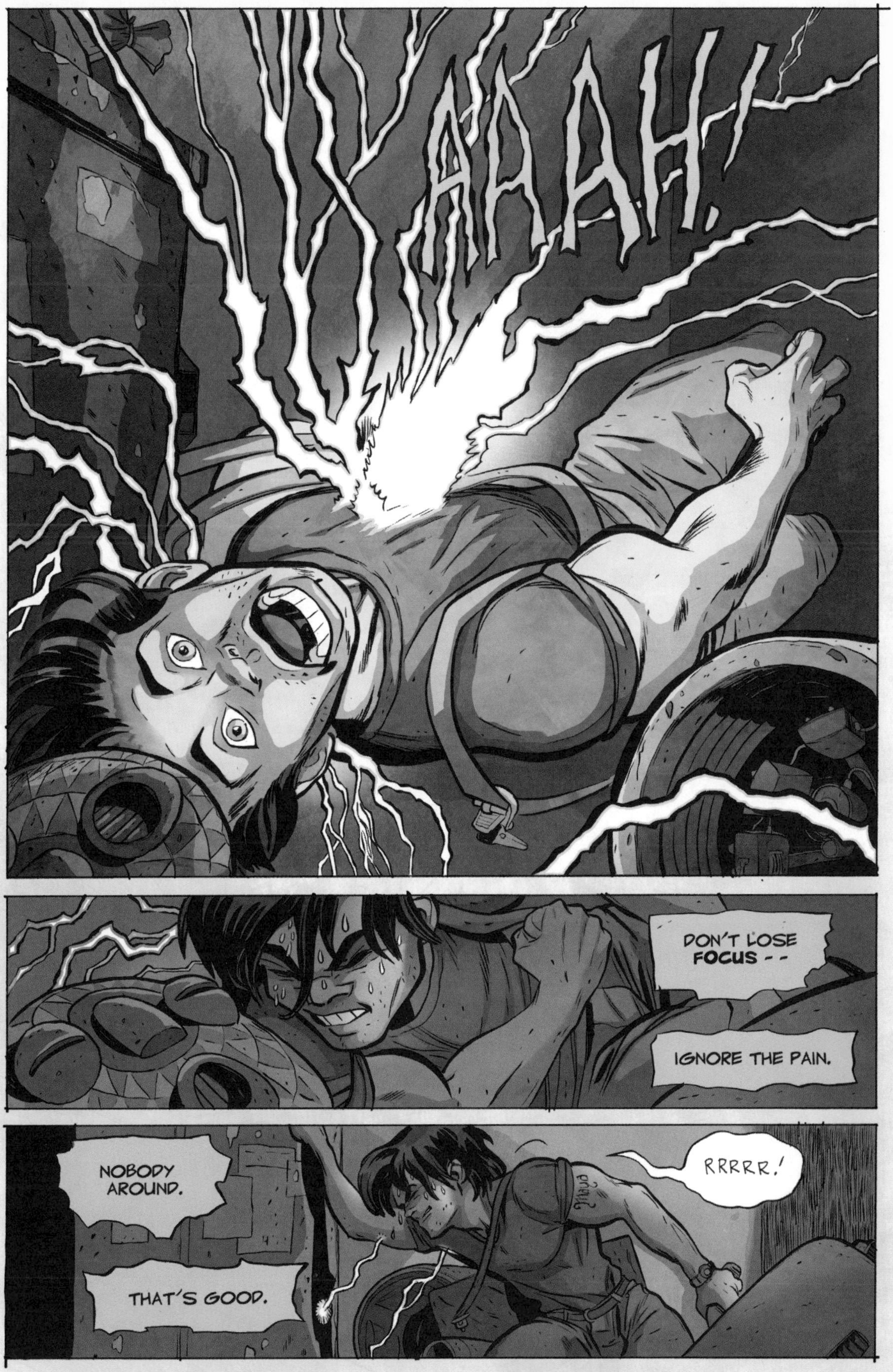
YYAAAH!
DON'T LOSE FOCUS --
IGNORE THE PAIN.
NOBODY AROUND.
RRRRR!
THAT'S GOOD.

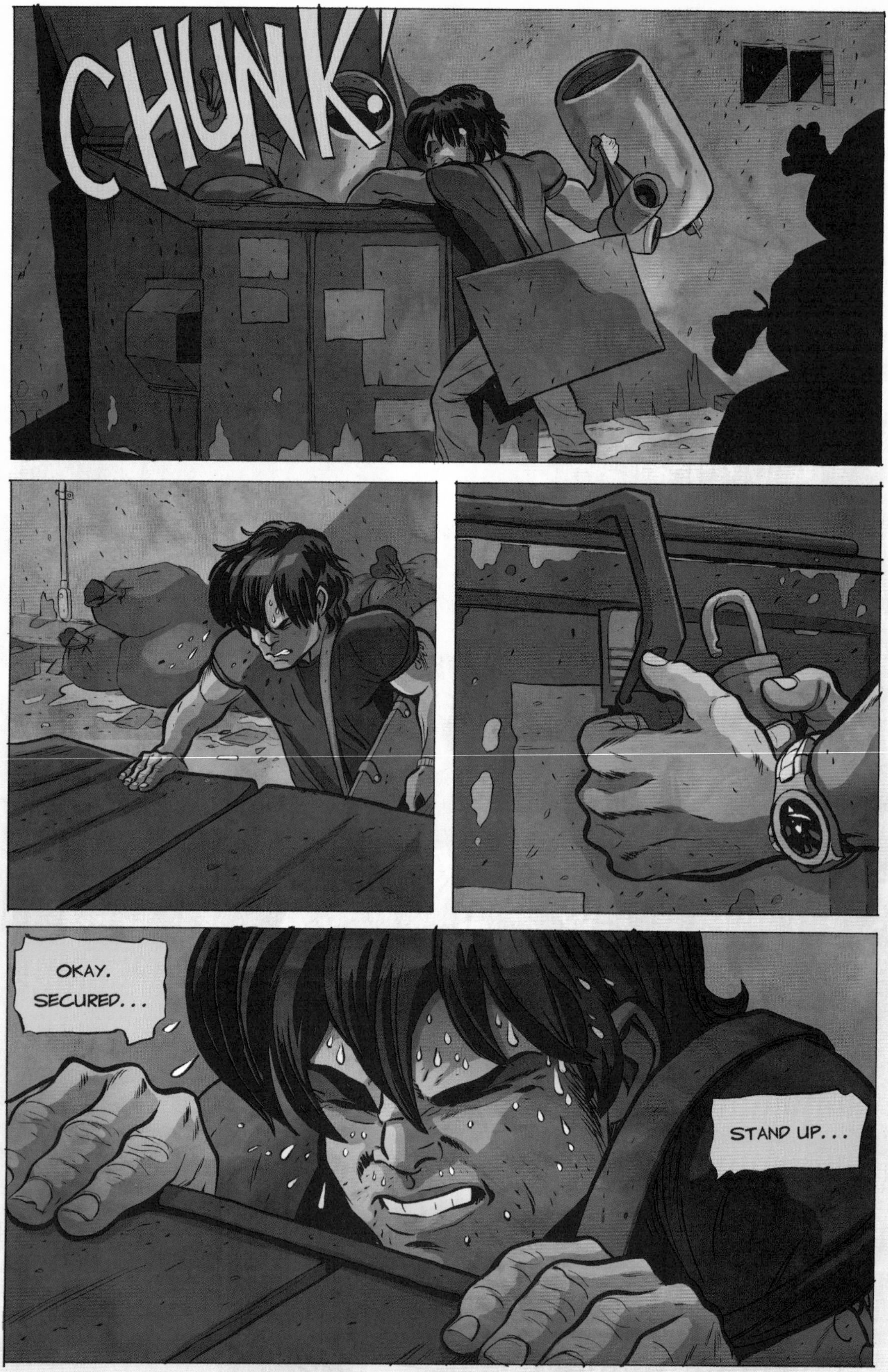
CHUNK!
OKAY. SECURED...
STAND UP...

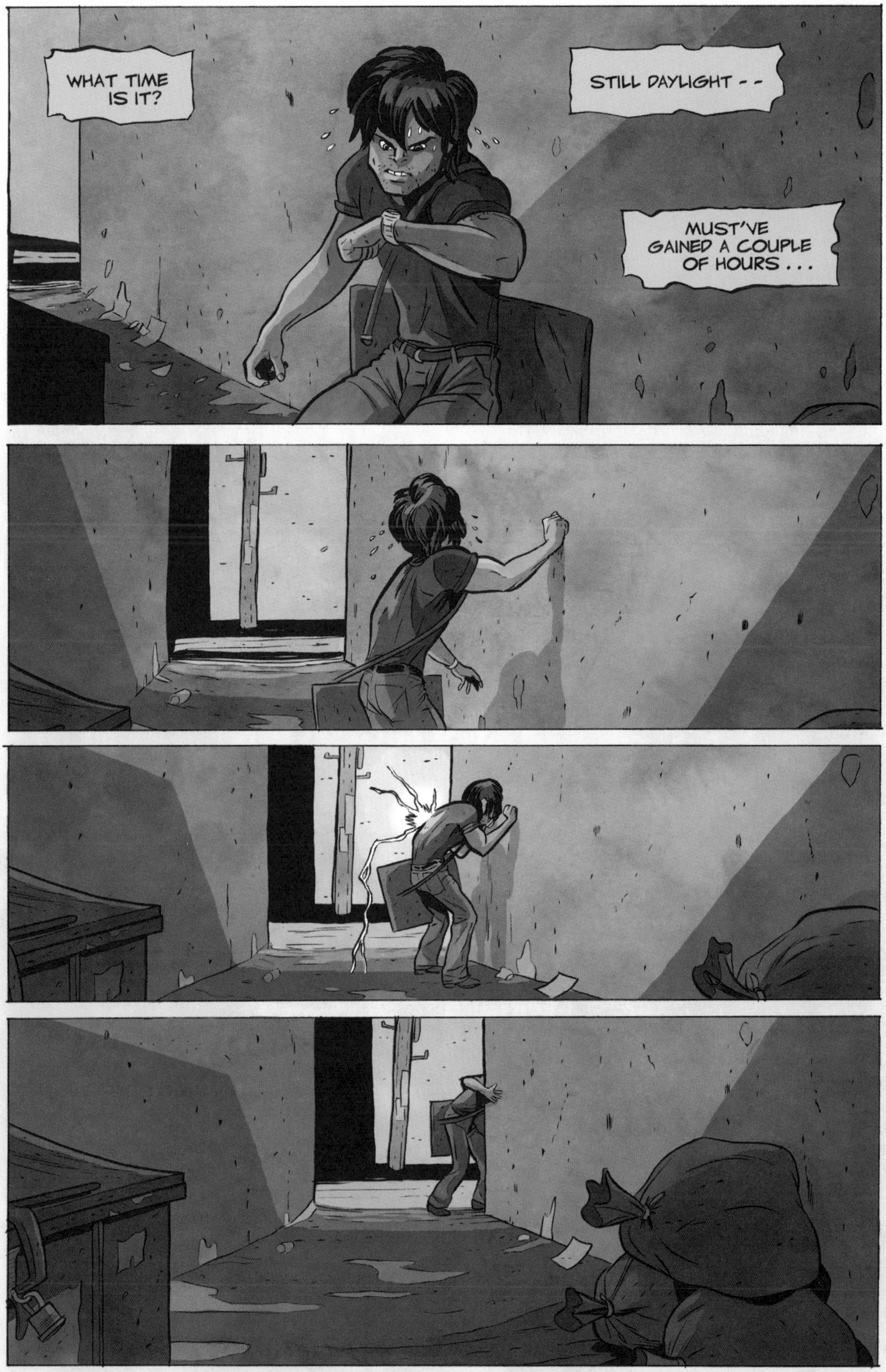
WHAT TIME IS IT?
STILL DAYLIGHT - -
MUST'VE GAINED A COUPLE OF HOURS . . .

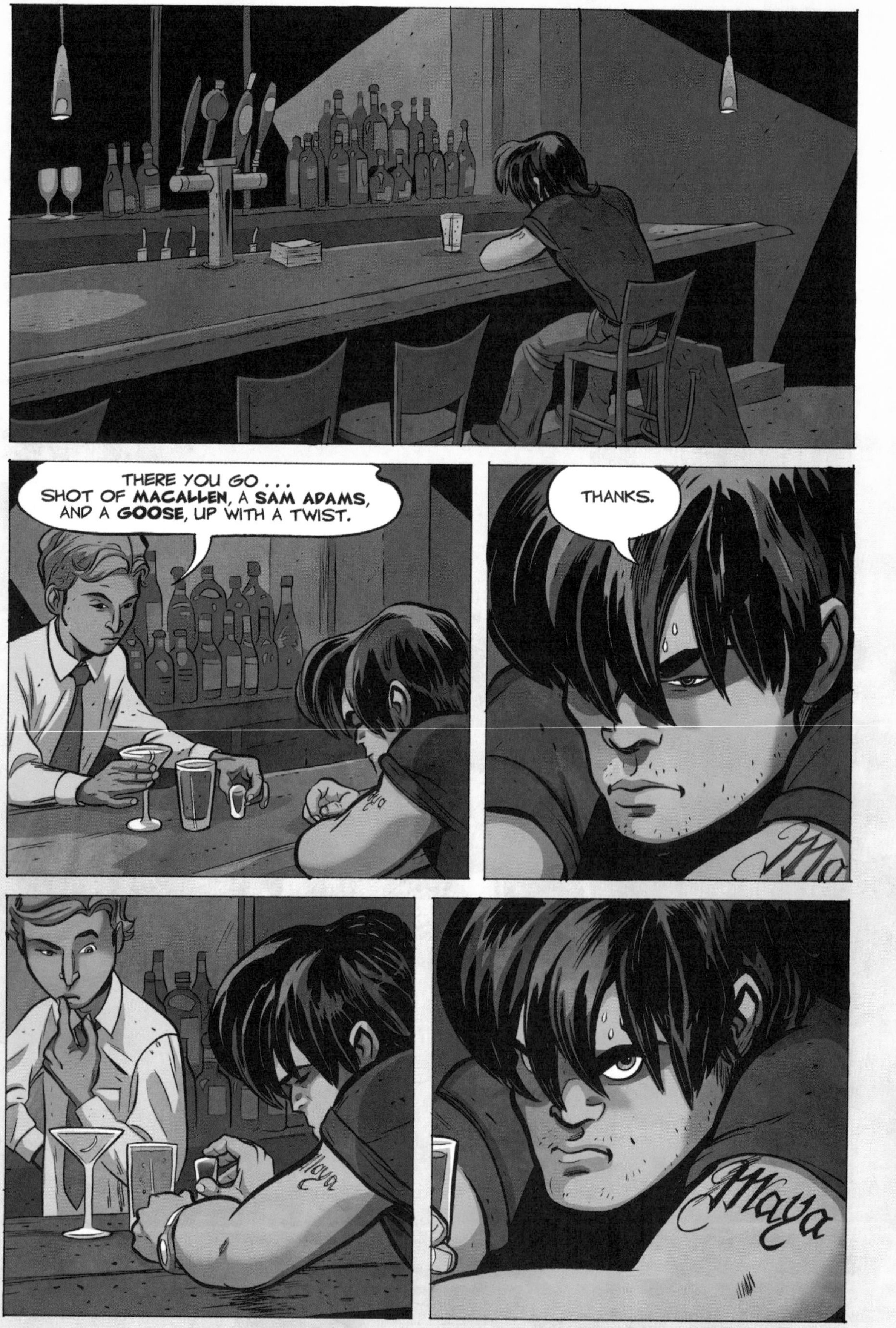
THERE YOU GO . . . SHOT OF **MACALLEN**, A **SAM ADAMS**, AND A **GOOSE**, UP WITH A TWIST.
THANKS.
Maya

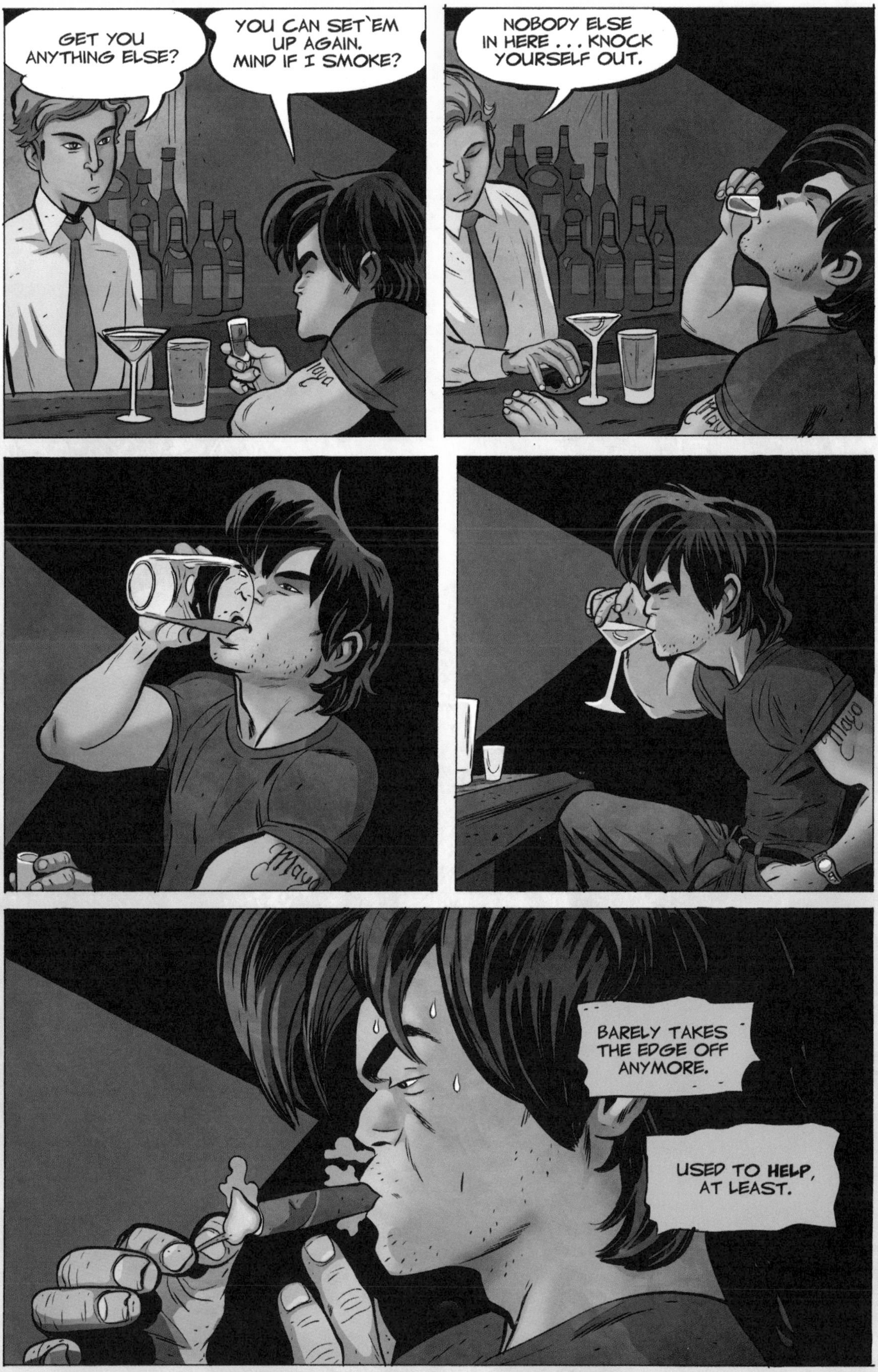
GET YOU ANYTHING ELSE?
YOU CAN SET`EM UP AGAIN. MIND IF I SMOKE?
NOBODY ELSE IN HERE . . . KNOCK YOURSELF OUT.
BARELY TAKES THE EDGE OFF ANYMORE.
USED TO **HELP**, AT LEAST.

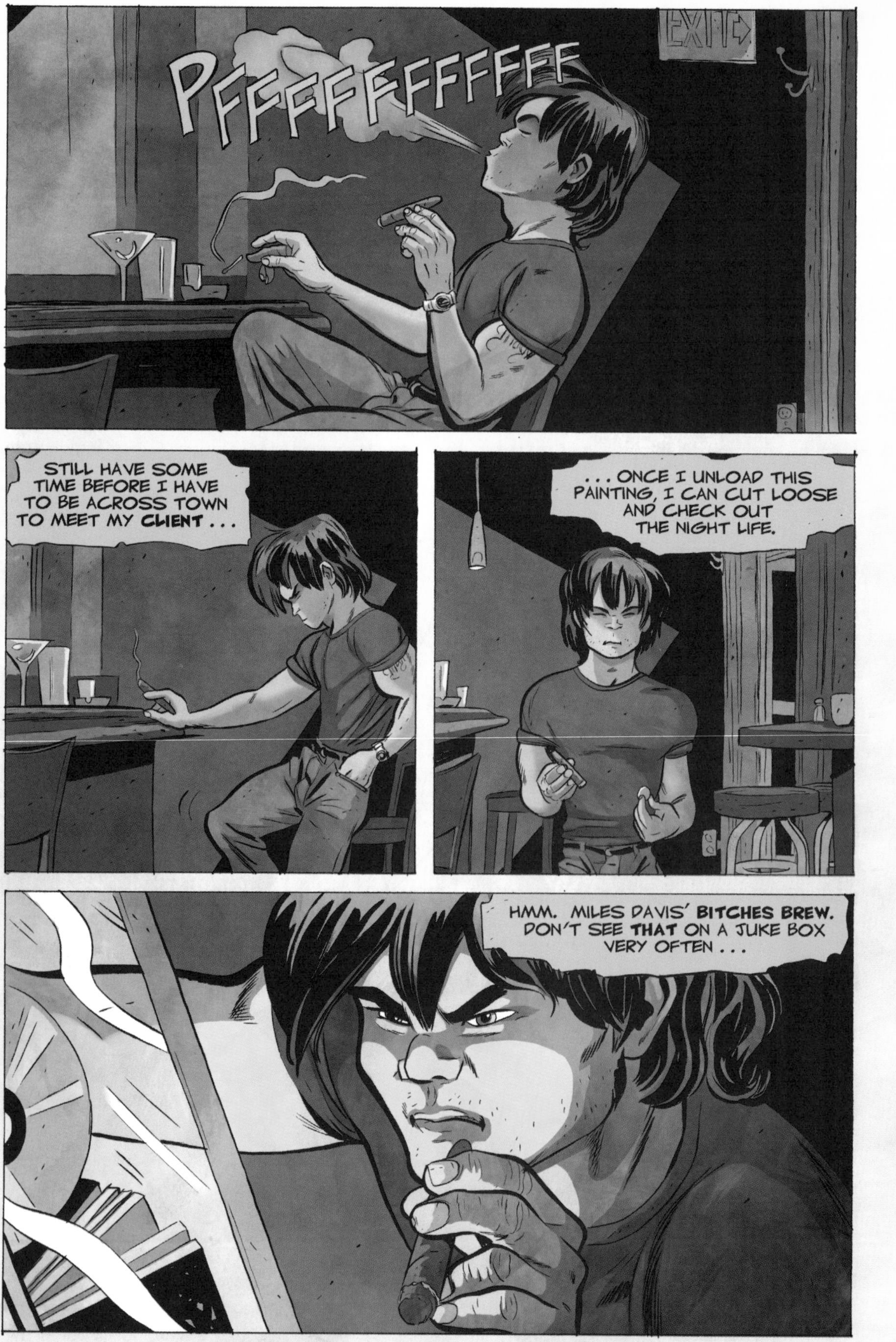
PFFFFFFFFFFF
EXIT
STILL HAVE SOME TIME BEFORE I HAVE TO BE ACROSS TOWN TO MEET MY CLIENT . . .
. . . ONCE I UNLOAD THIS PAINTING, I CAN CUT LOOSE AND CHECK OUT THE NIGHT LIFE.
HMM. MILES DAVIS' BITCHES BREW. DON'T SEE THAT ON A JUKE BOX VERY OFTEN . . .

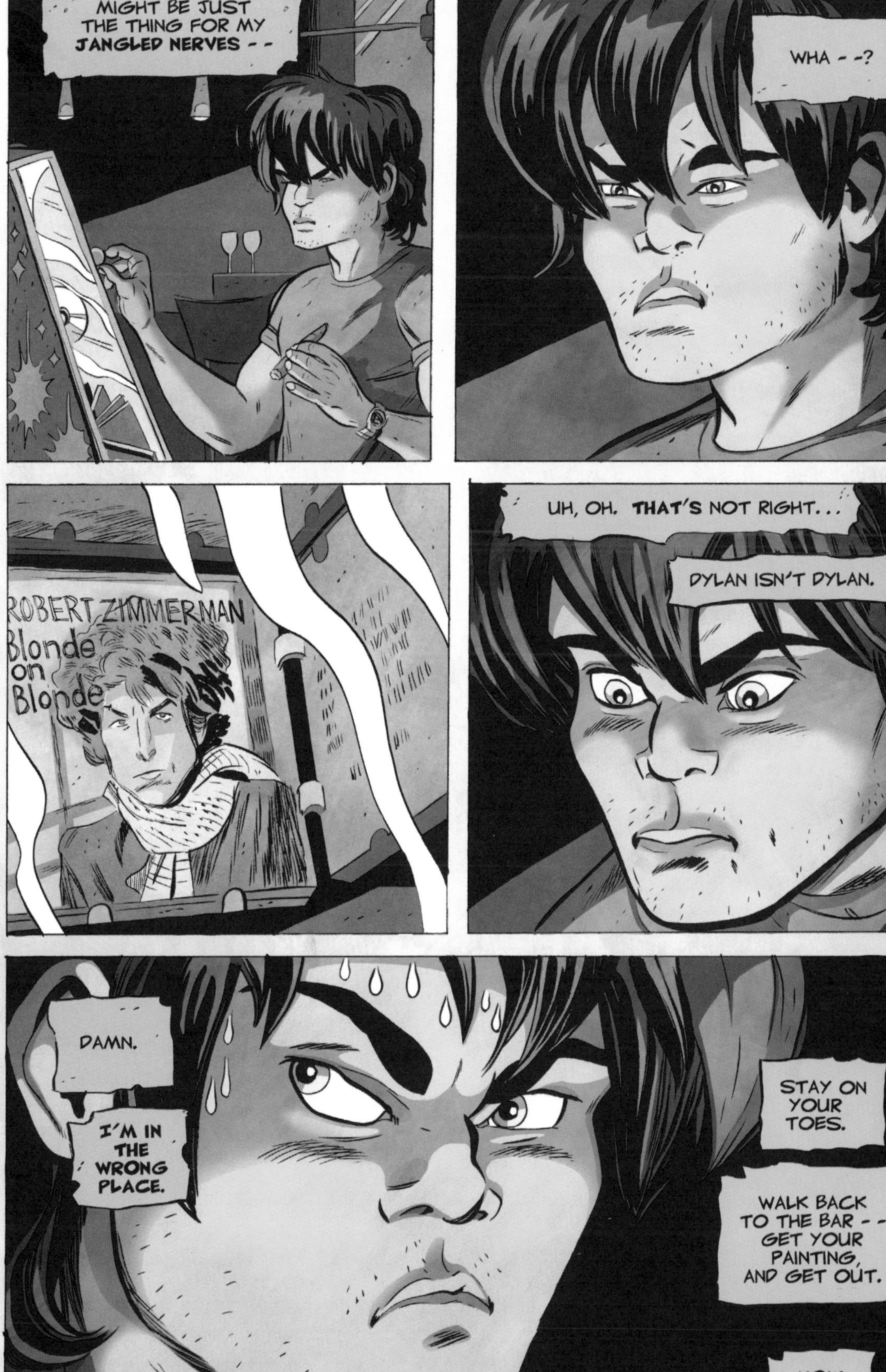
MIGHT BE JUST THE THING FOR MY JANGLED NERVES - -
WHA - -?
ROBERT ZIMMERMAN
Blonde on Blonde
UH, OH. THAT'S NOT RIGHT...
DYLAN ISN'T DYLAN.
DAMN.
I'M IN THE WRONG PLACE.
STAY ON YOUR TOES.
WALK BACK TO THE BAR - - GET YOUR PAINTING, AND GET OUT.
NOW.

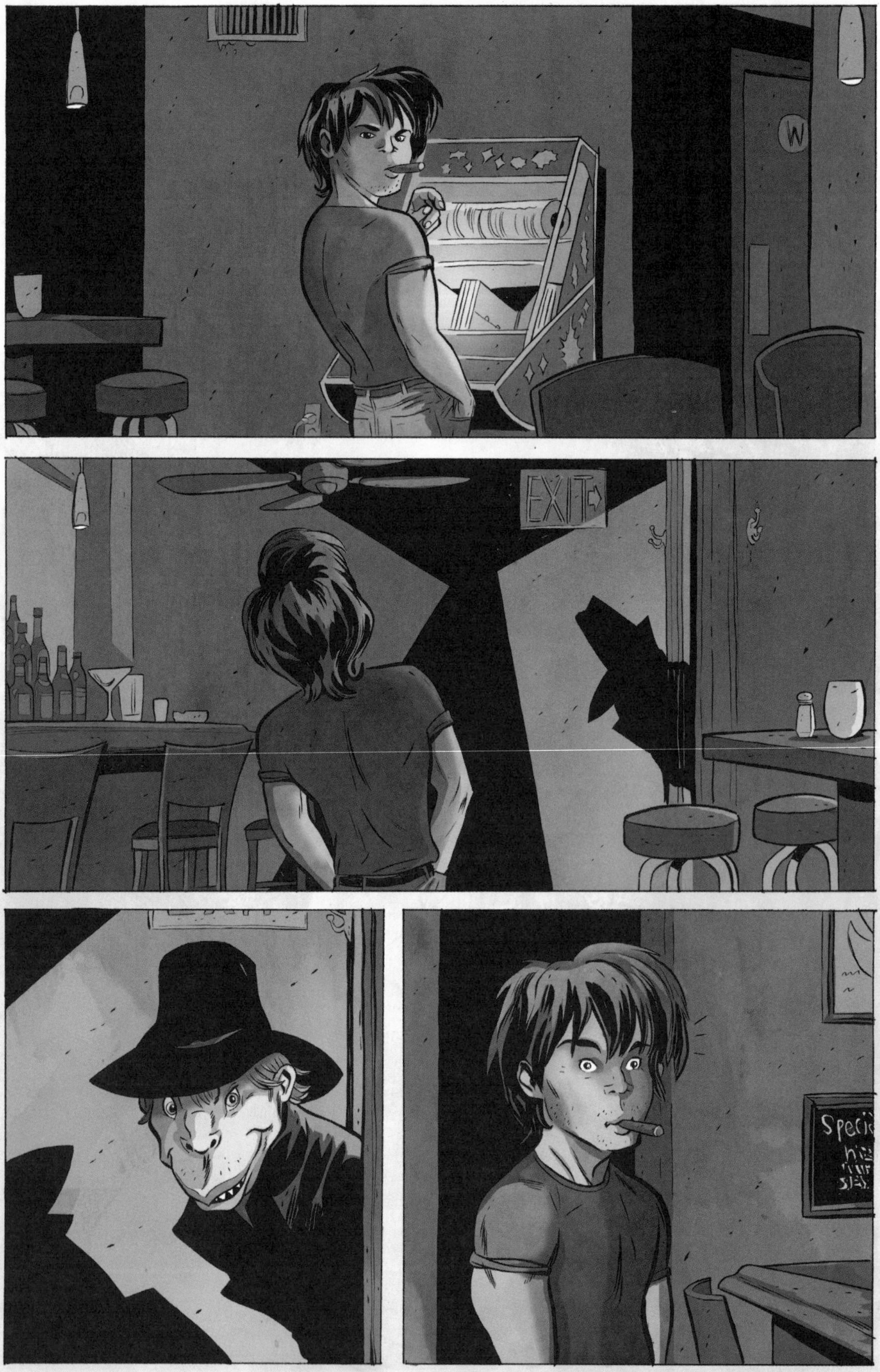
W
EXIT

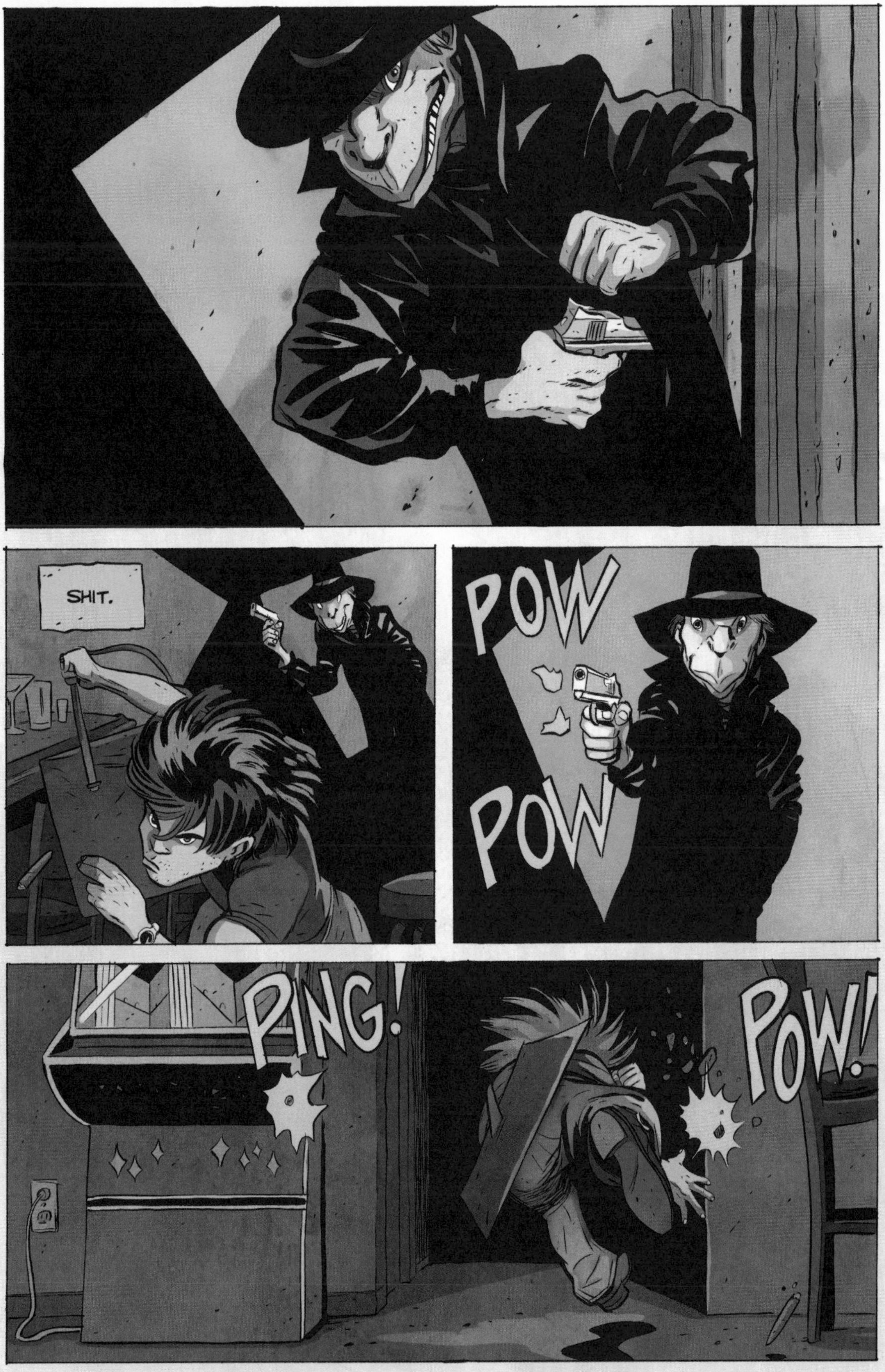
SHIT.
POW
POW
PING!
POW!

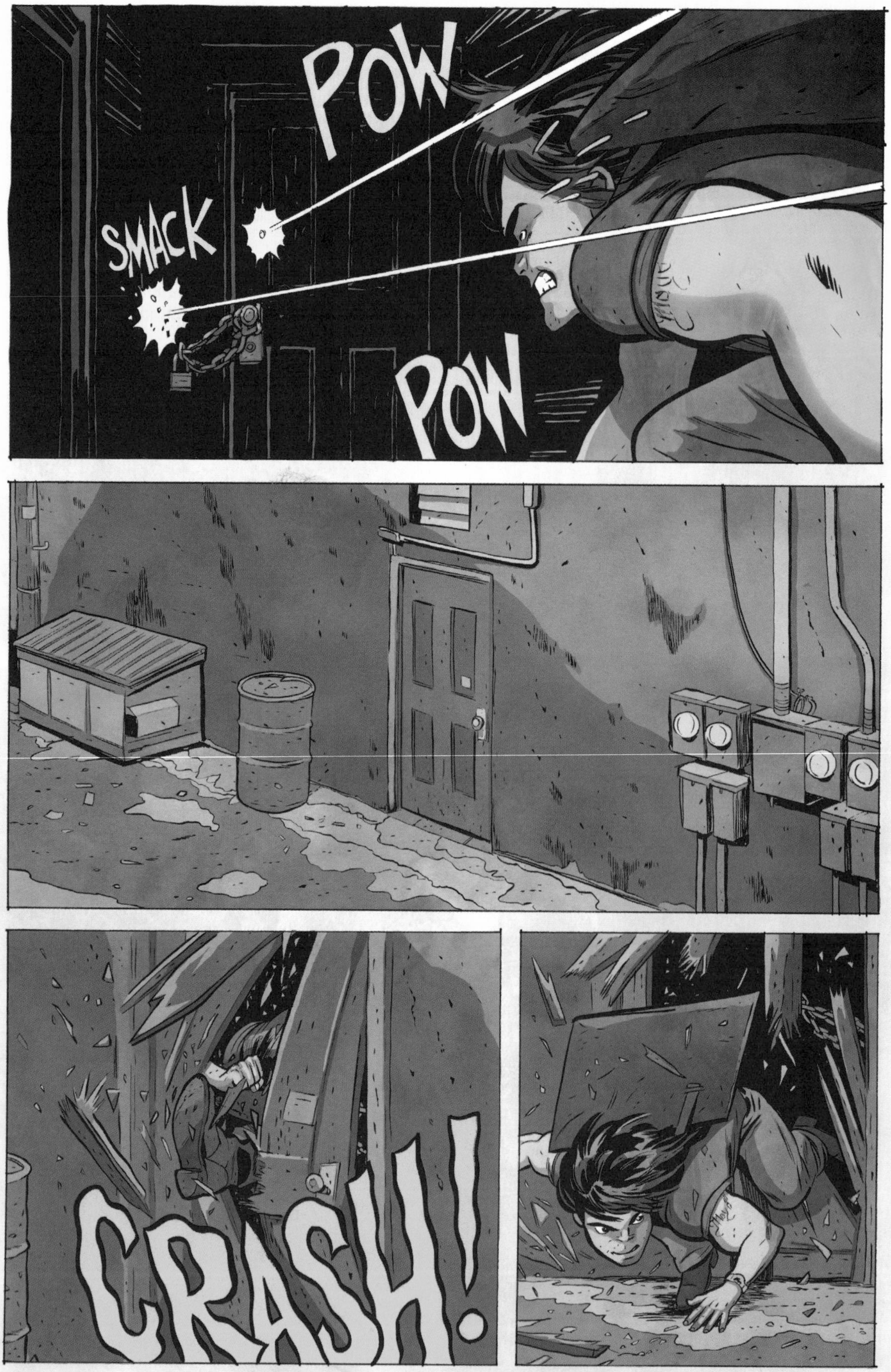
POW
SMACK
POW
CRASH!

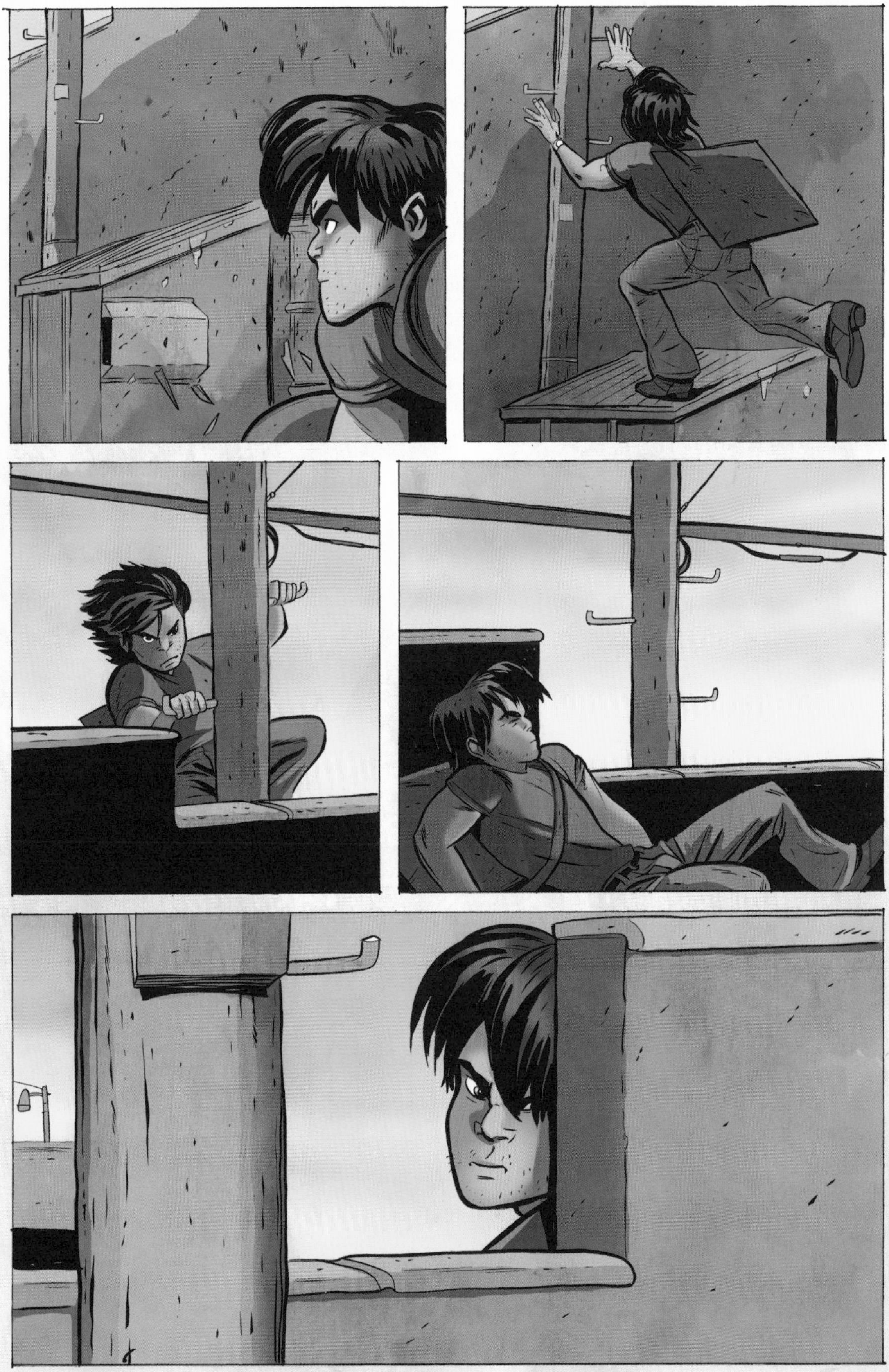

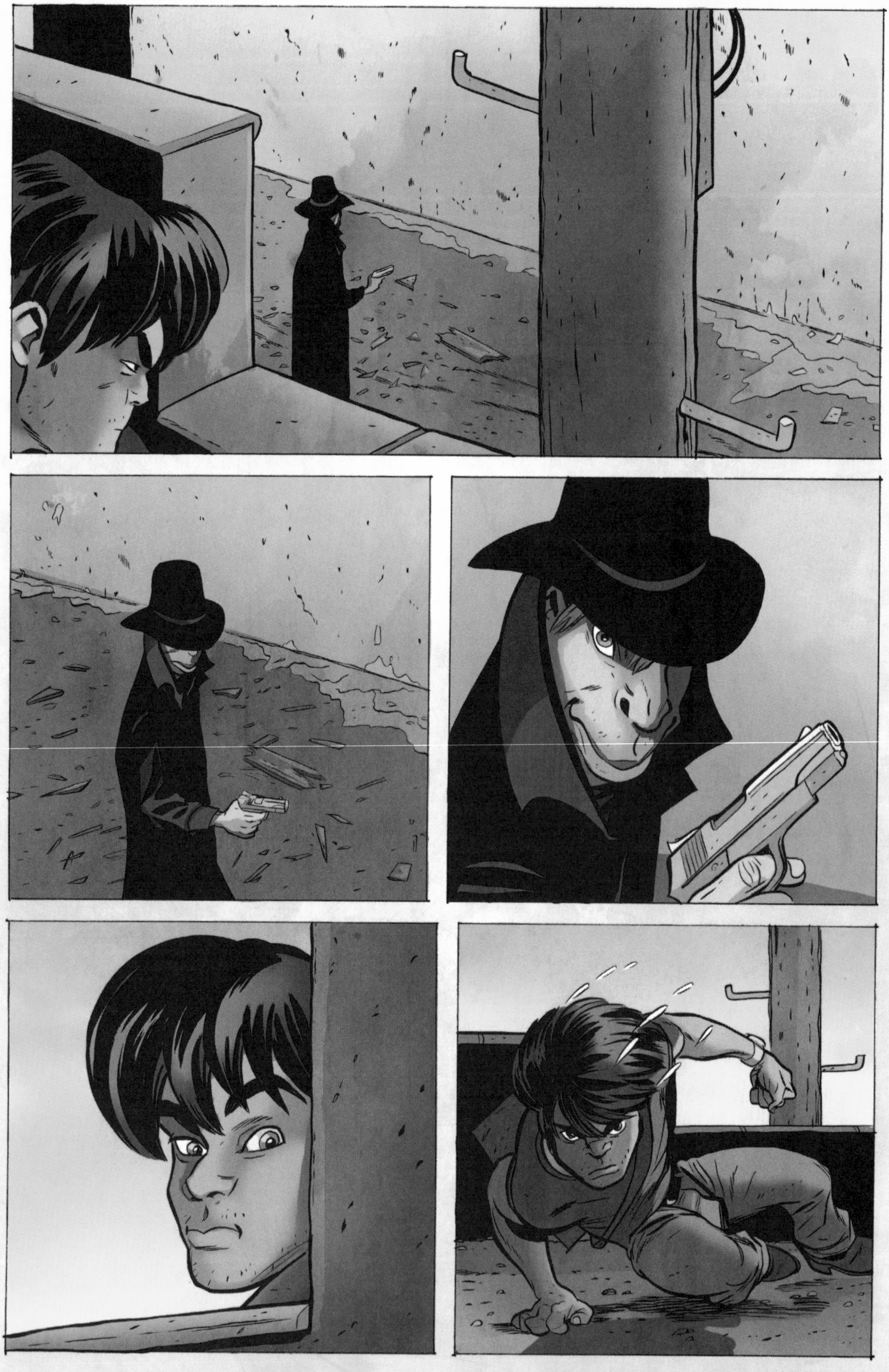

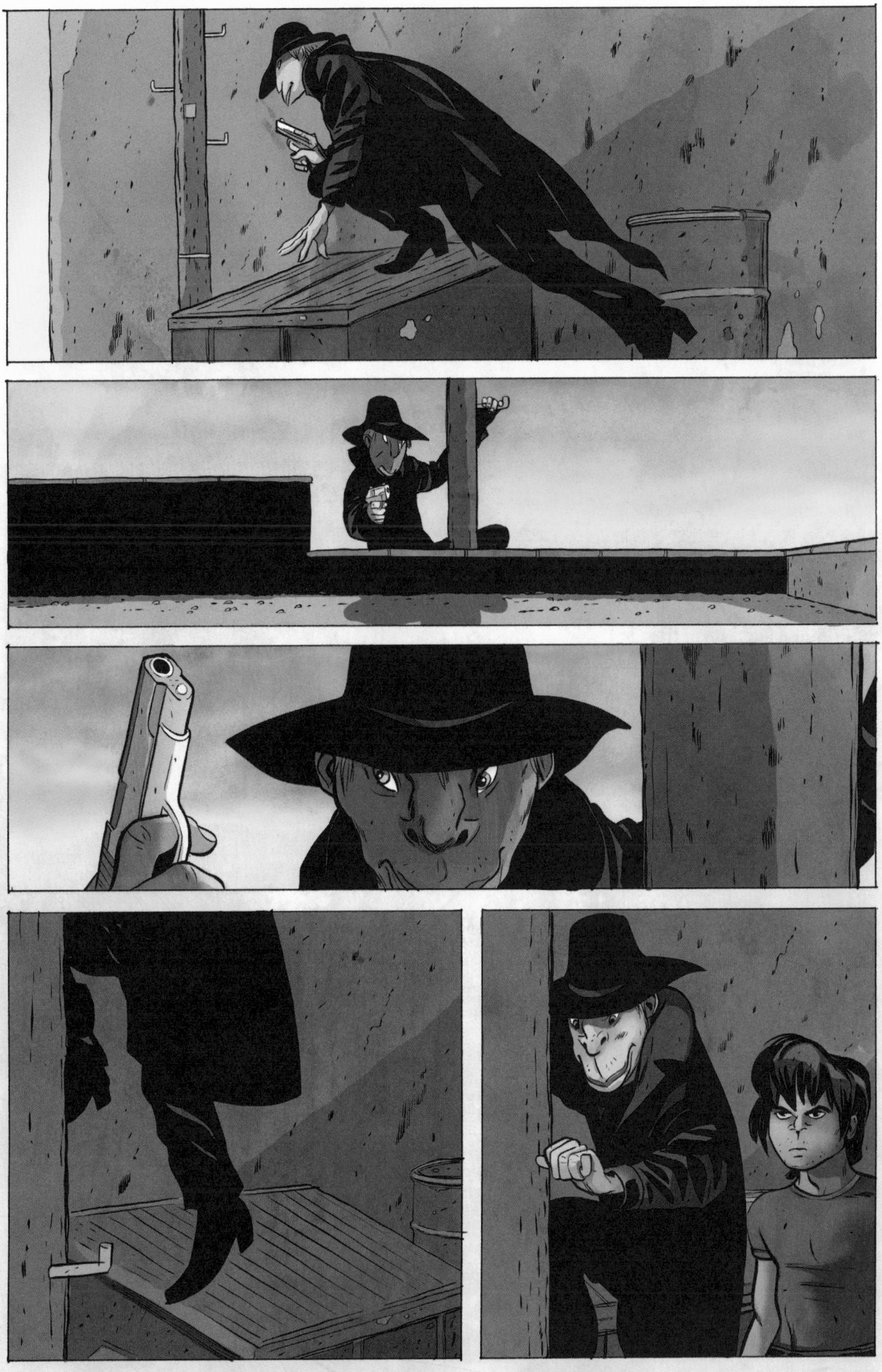

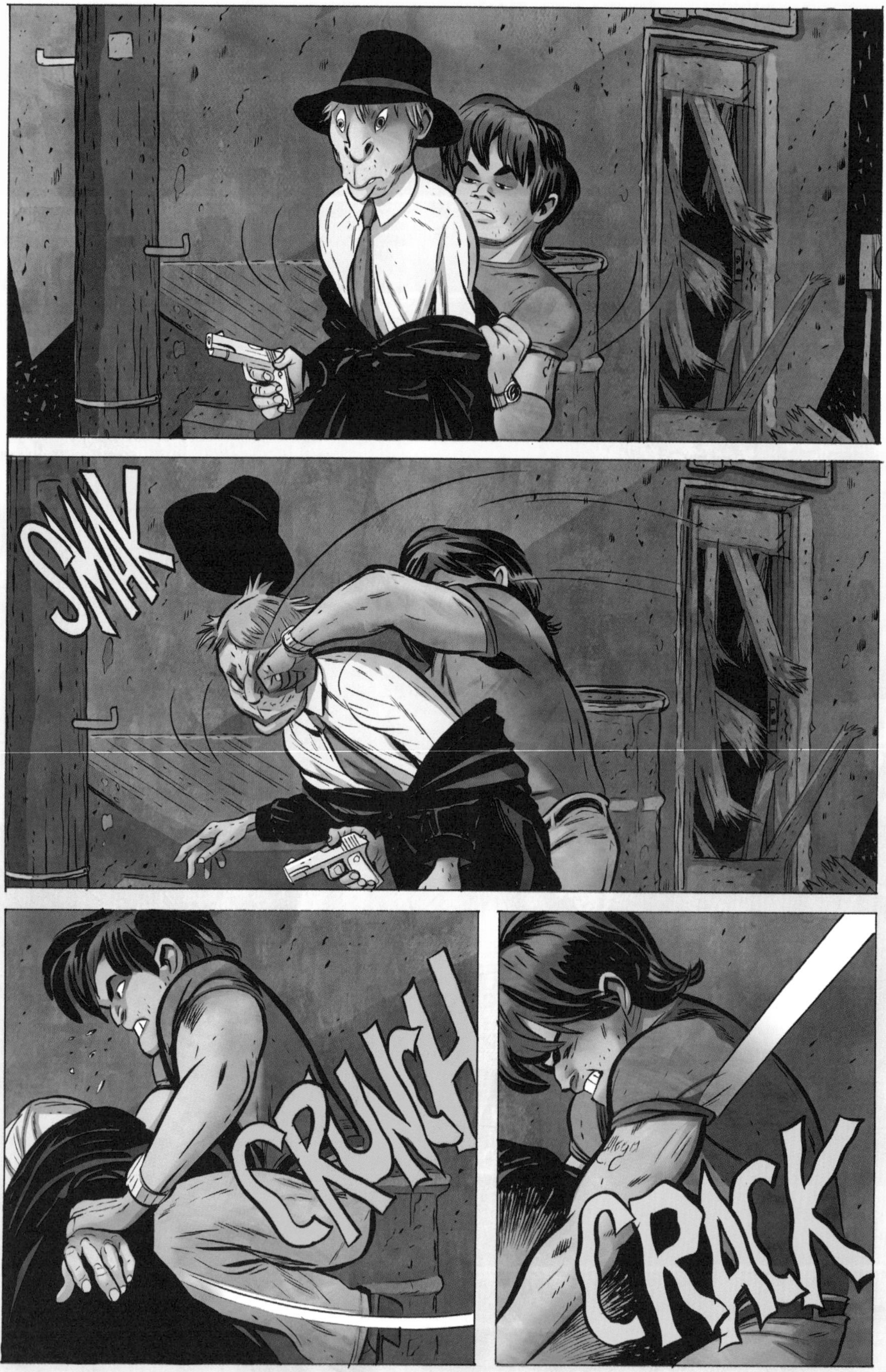
SMAK
CRUNCH
CRACK

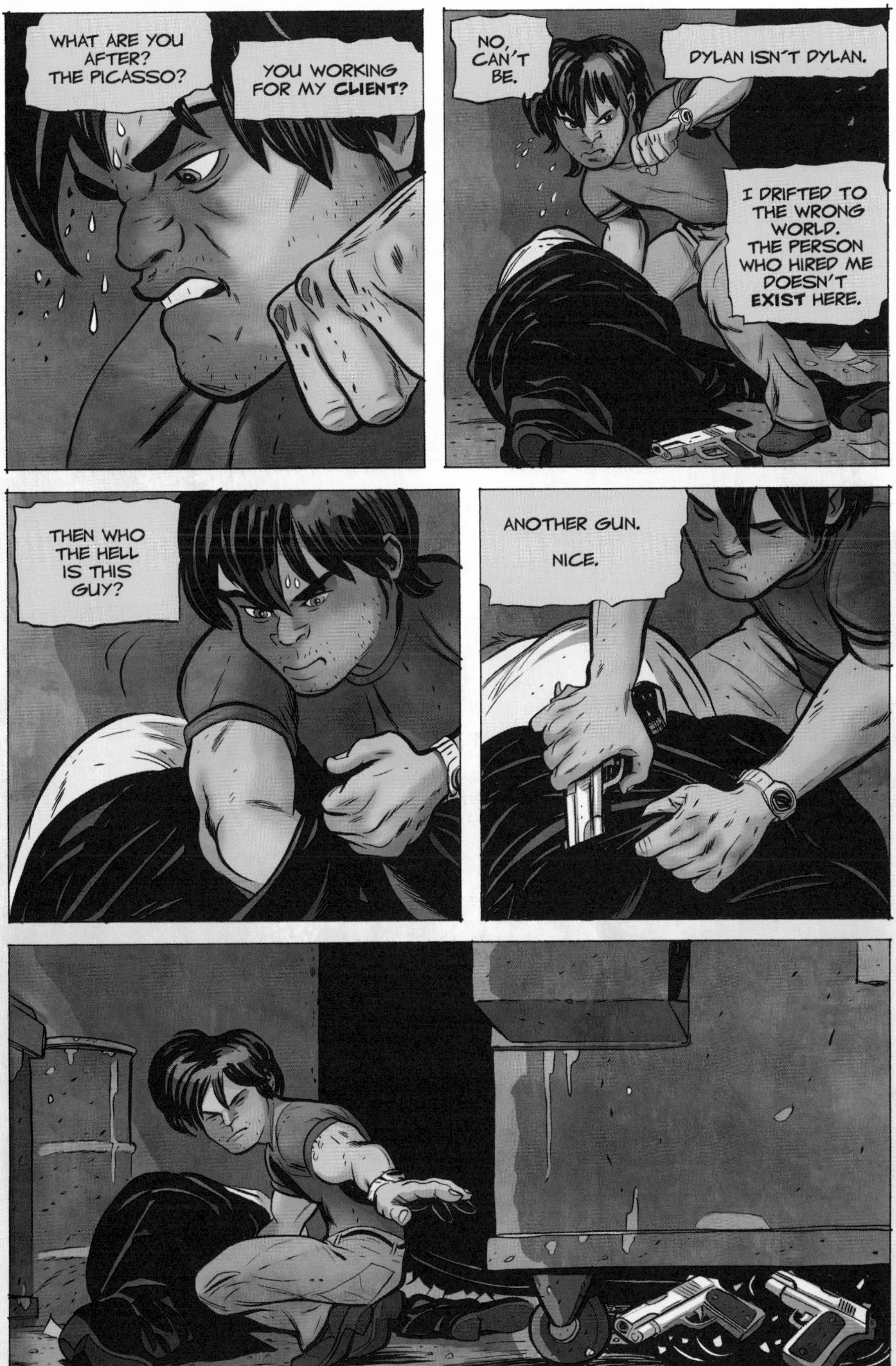
WHAT ARE YOU AFTER? THE PICASSO?
YOU WORKING FOR MY CLIENT?
NO, CAN'T BE.
DYLAN ISN'T DYLAN.
I DRIFTED TO THE WRONG WORLD. THE PERSON WHO HIRED ME DOESN'T EXIST HERE.
THEN WHO THE HELL IS THIS GUY?
ANOTHER GUN.
NICE.

NO WALLET.
NO I.D.

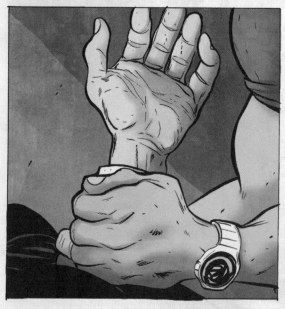

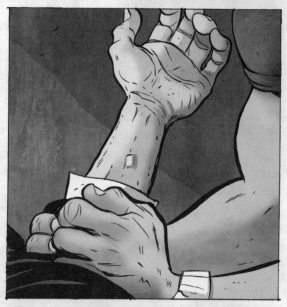

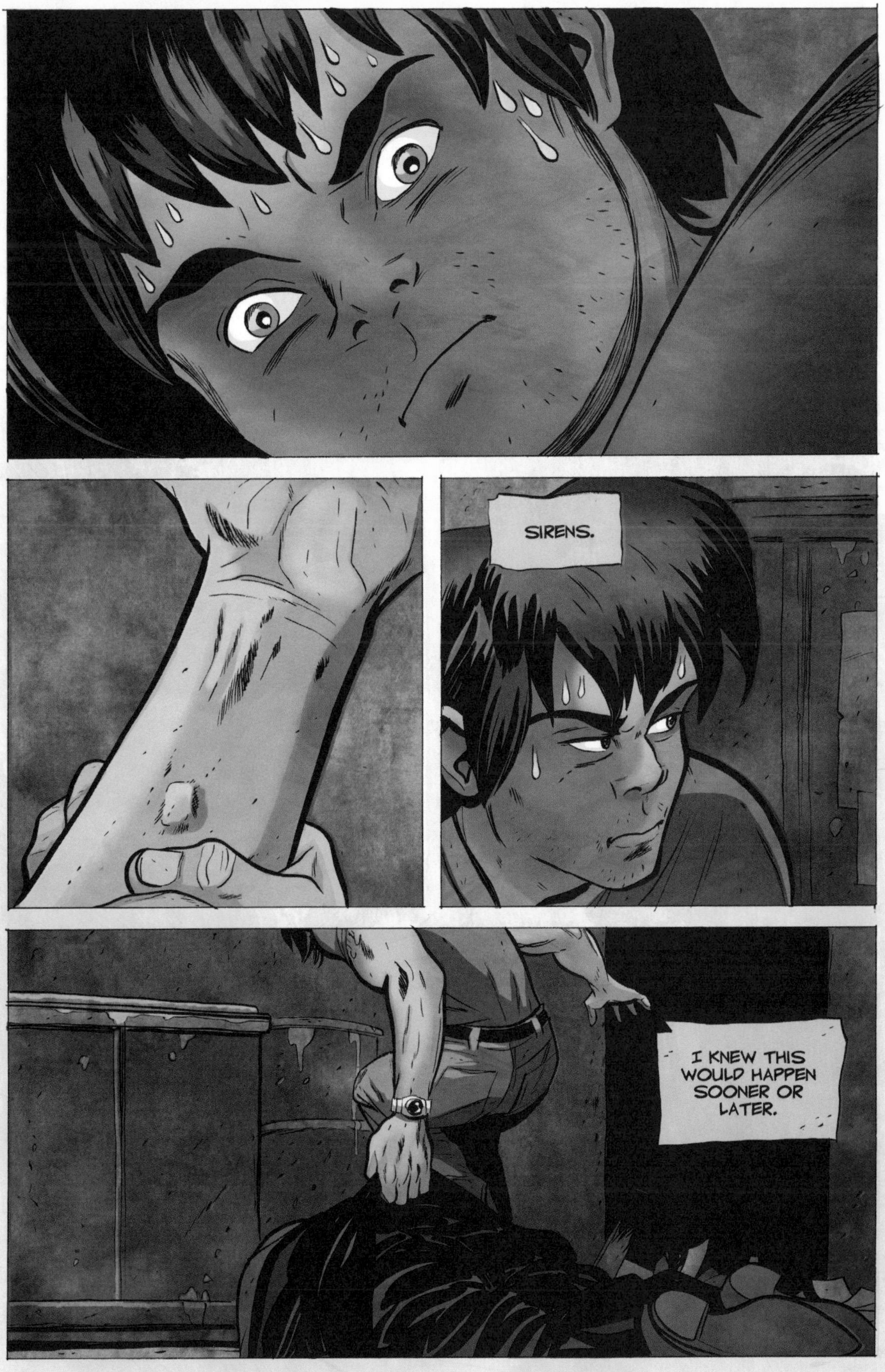
SIRENS.
I KNEW THIS WOULD HAPPEN SOONER OR LATER.

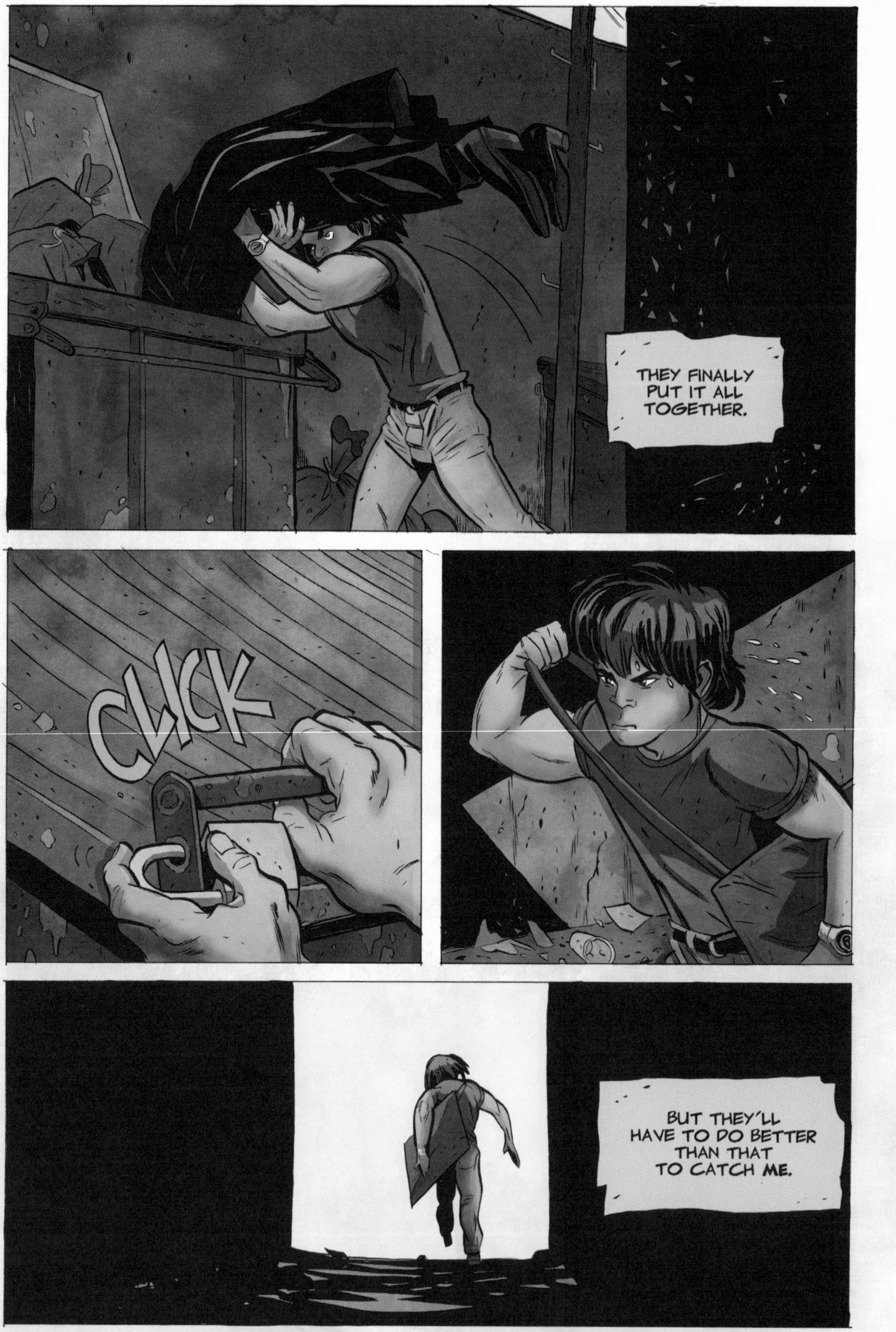
THEY FINALLY PUT IT ALL TOGETHER.
CLICK
BUT THEY'LL HAVE TO DO BETTER THAN THAT TO CATCH ME.

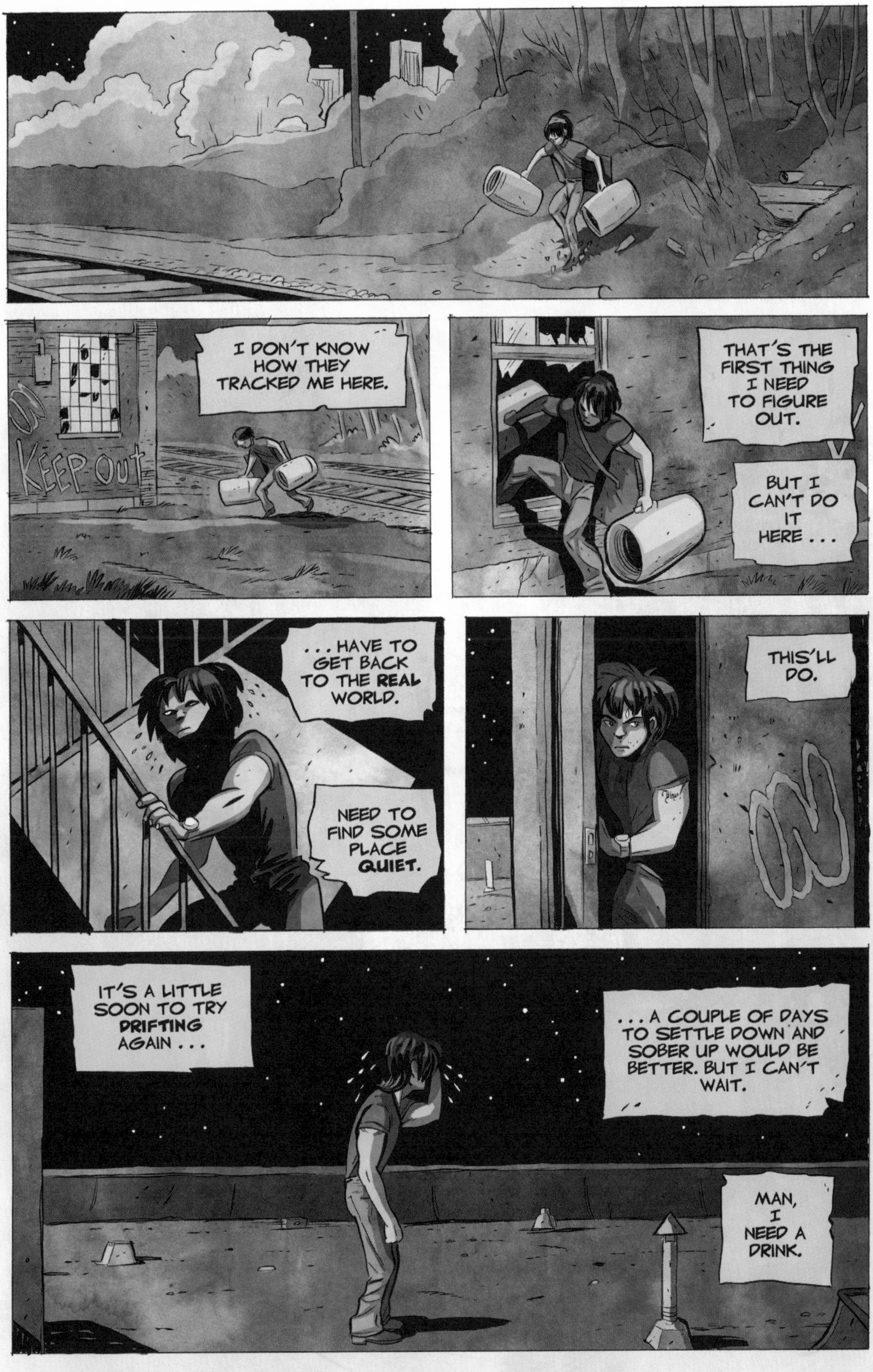
I DON'T KNOW HOW THEY TRACKED ME HERE.
KEEP OUT
THAT'S THE FIRST THING I NEED TO FIGURE OUT.
BUT I CAN'T DO IT HERE . . .
. . . HAVE TO GET BACK TO THE REAL WORLD.
NEED TO FIND SOME PLACE QUIET.
THIS'LL DO.
IT'S A LITTLE SOON TO TRY DRIFTING AGAIN . . .
. . . A COUPLE OF DAYS TO SETTLE DOWN AND SOBER UP WOULD BE BETTER. BUT I CAN'T WAIT.
MAN, I NEED A DRINK.

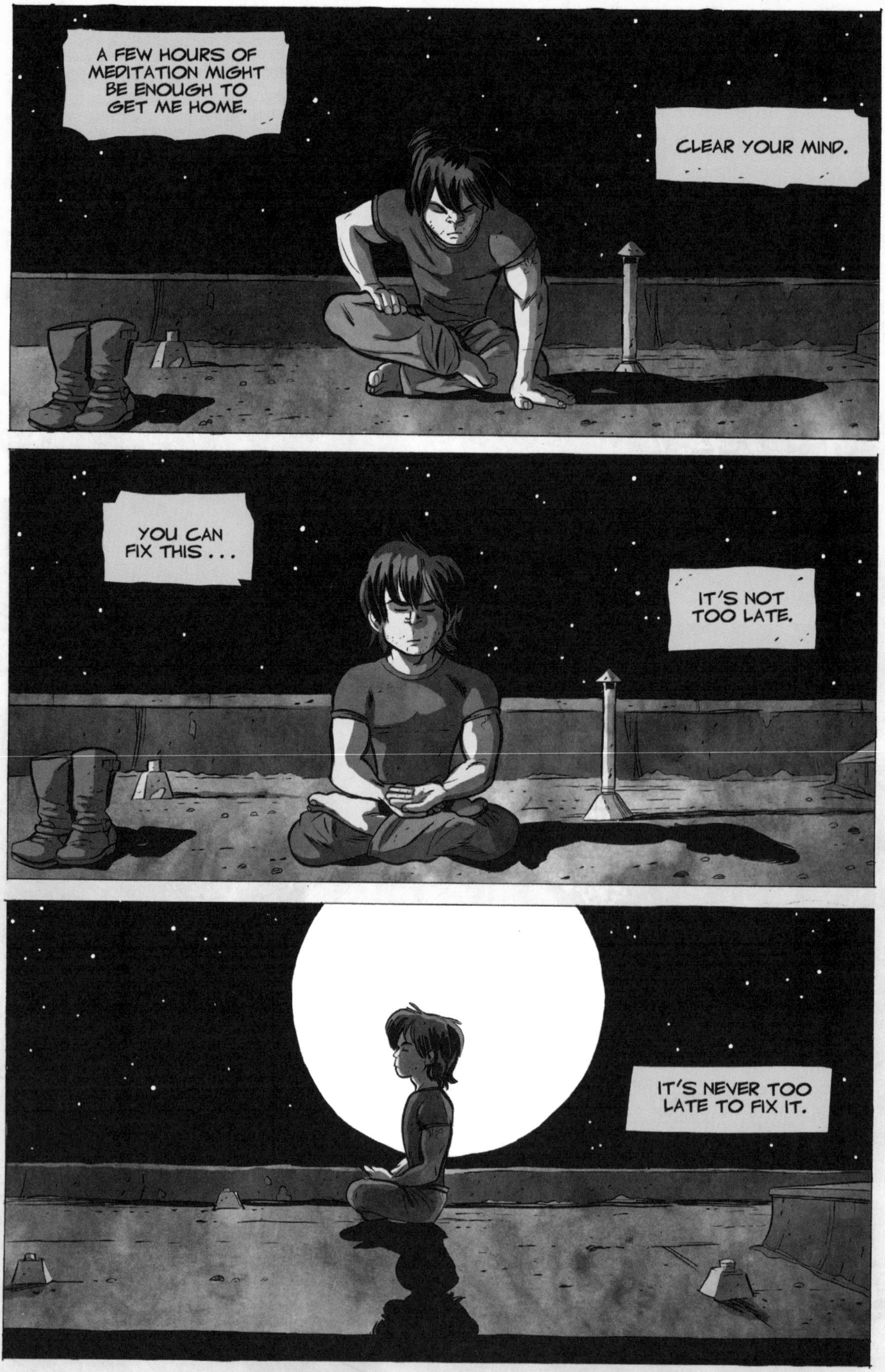
A FEW HOURS OF MEDITATION MIGHT BE ENOUGH TO GET ME HOME.
CLEAR YOUR MIND.
YOU CAN FIX THIS . . .
IT'S NOT TOO LATE.
IT'S NEVER TOO LATE TO FIX IT.

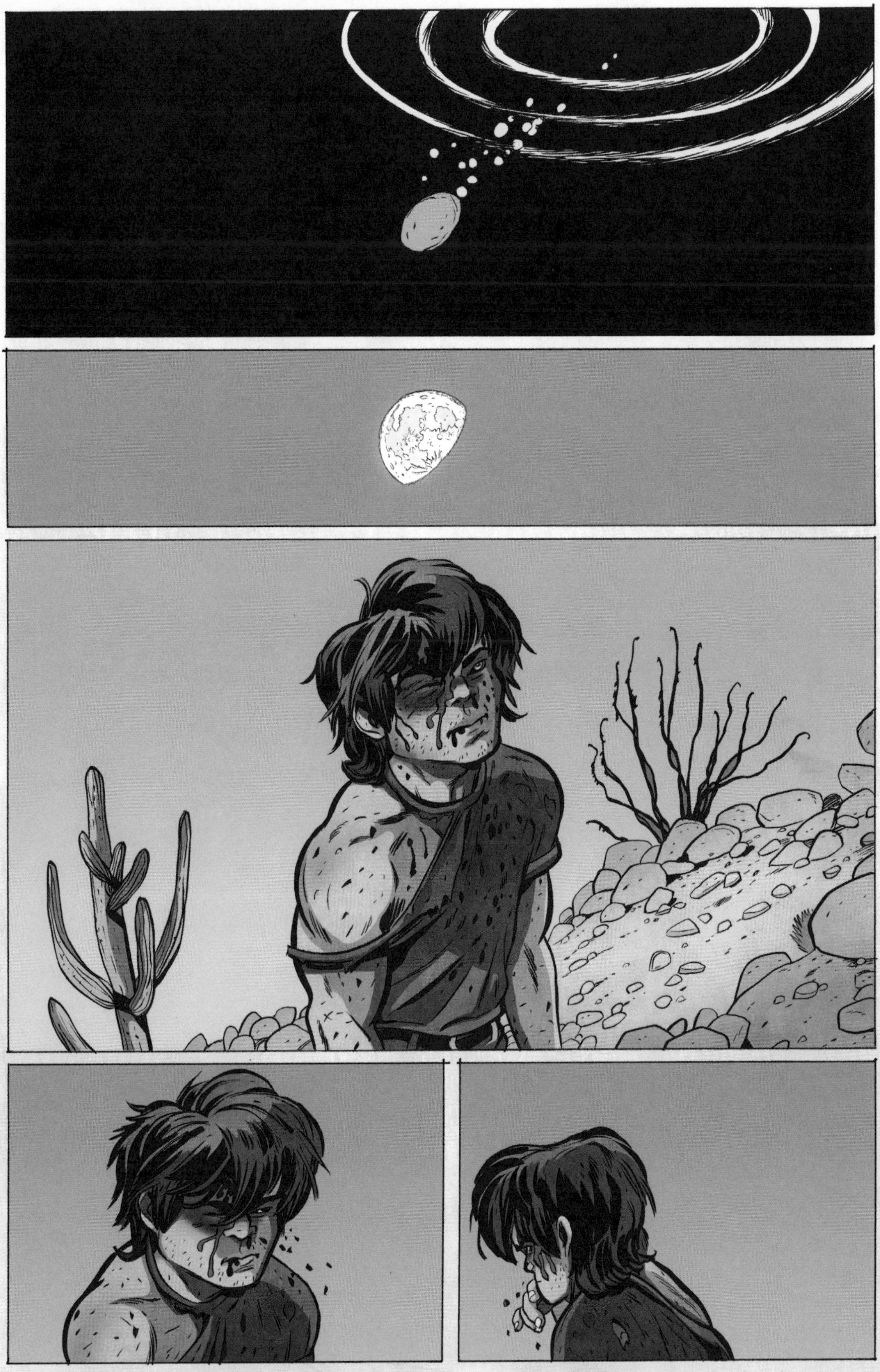

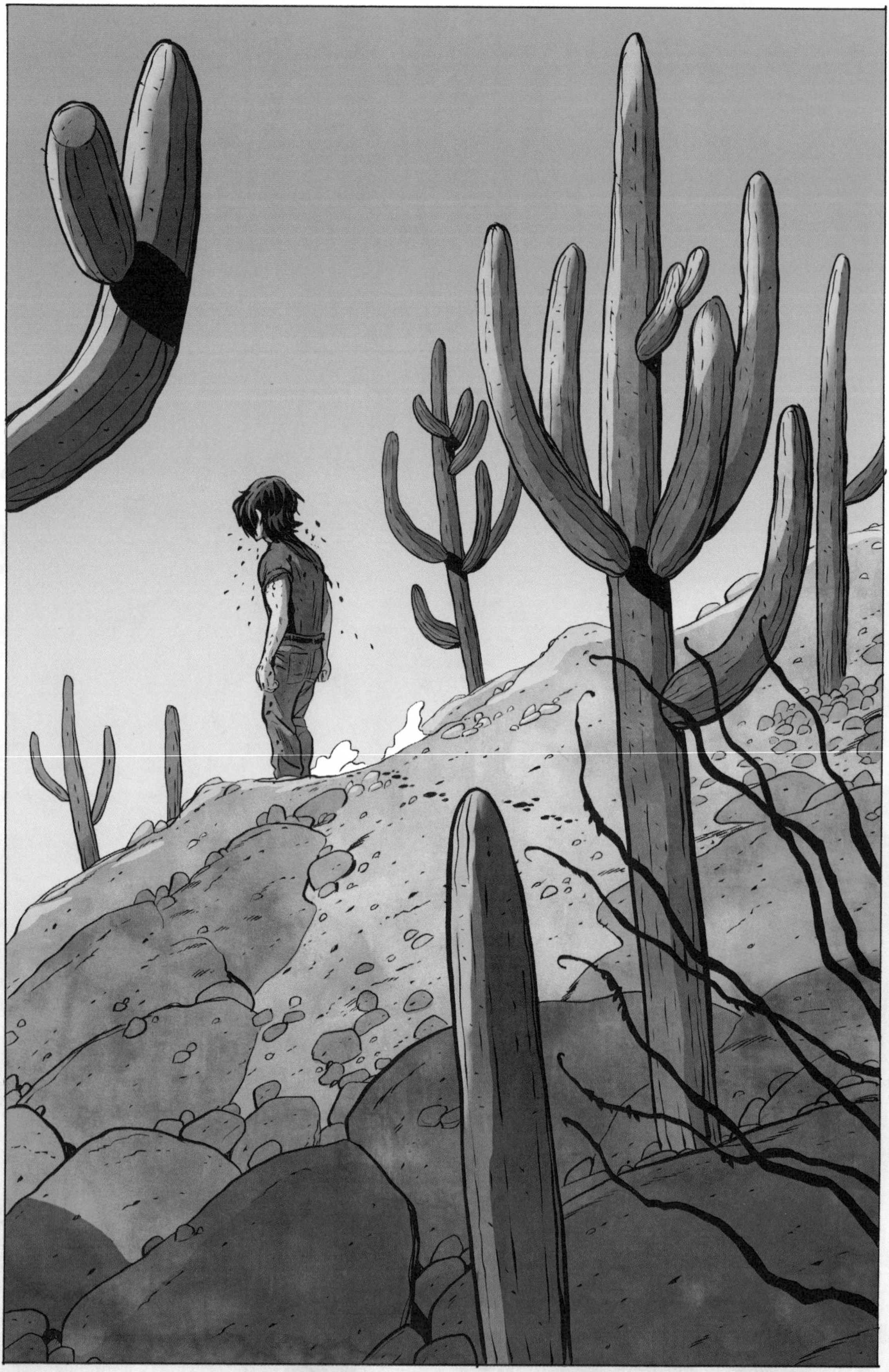

II

ANNIE

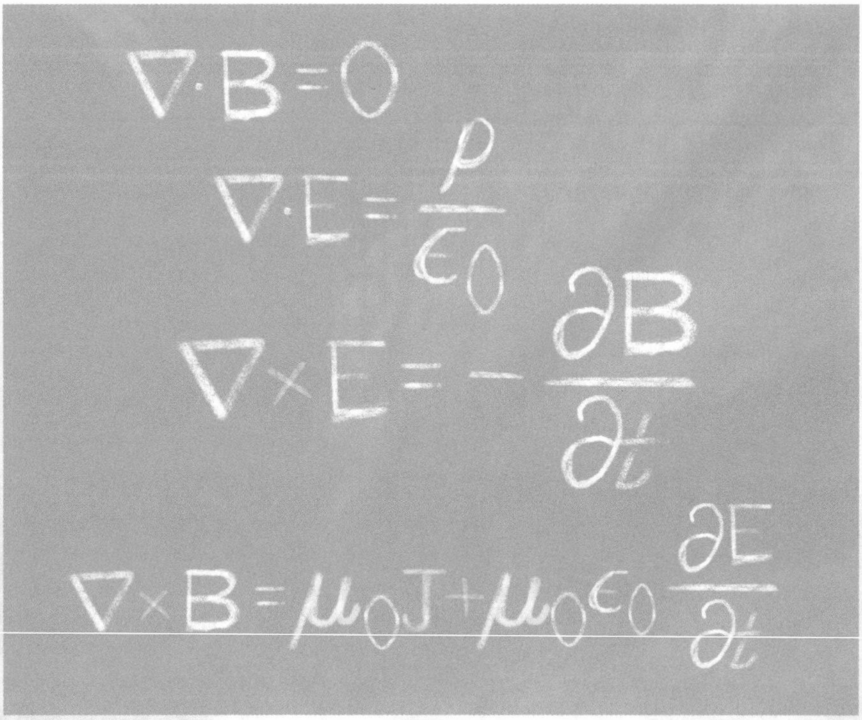
$\nabla \cdot B = 0$
$\nabla \cdot E = \frac{\rho}{\epsilon_0}$
$\nabla \times E = -\frac{\partial B}{\partial t}$
$\nabla \times B = \mu_0 J + \mu_0 \epsilon_0 \frac{\partial E}{\partial t}$

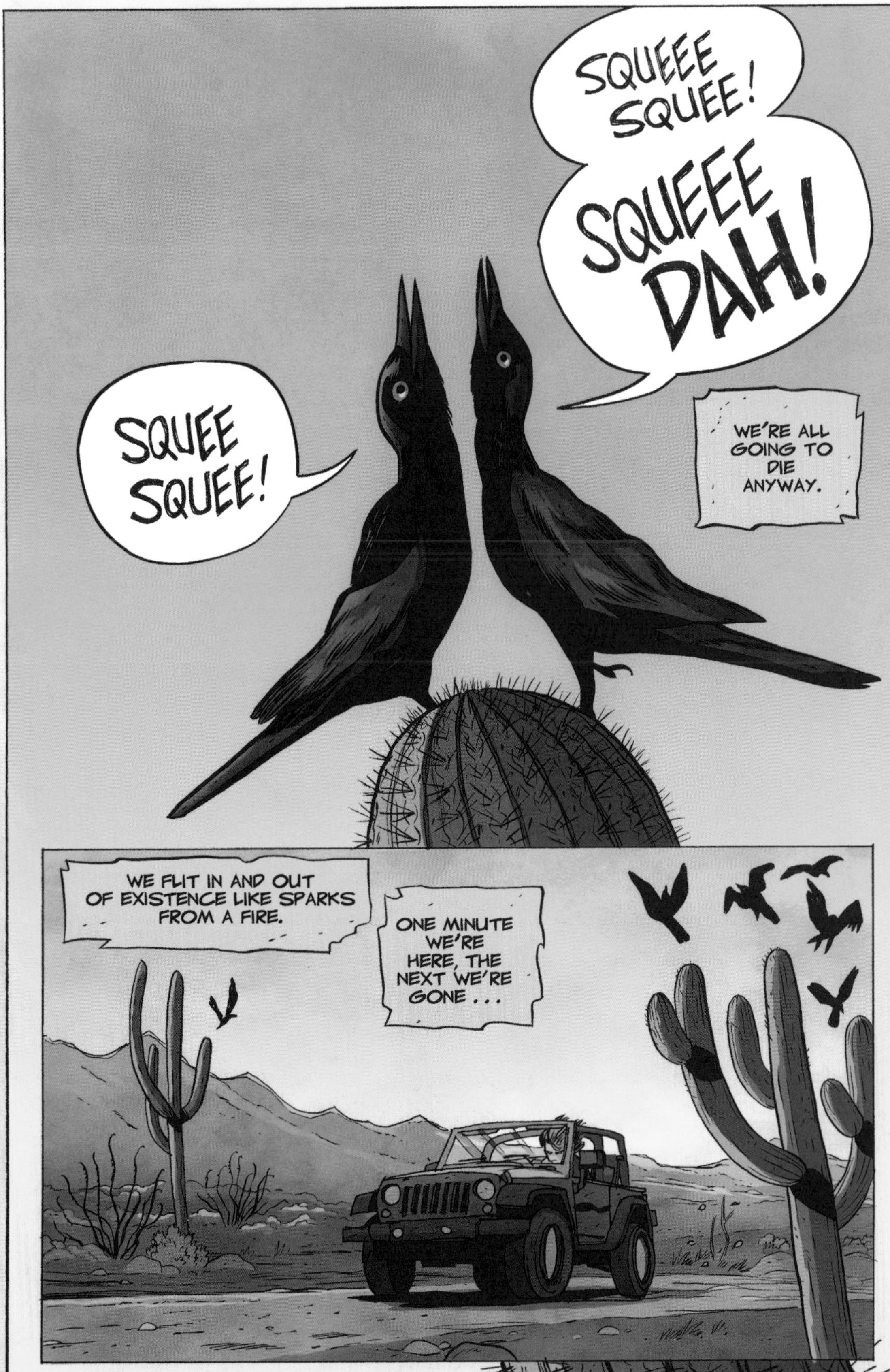
SQUEE SQUEE!
SQUEEE SQUEE!
SQUEEE DAH!
WE'RE ALL GOING TO DIE ANYWAY.
WE FLIT IN AND OUT OF EXISTENCE LIKE SPARKS FROM A FIRE.
ONE MINUTE WE'RE HERE, THE NEXT WE'RE GONE . . .

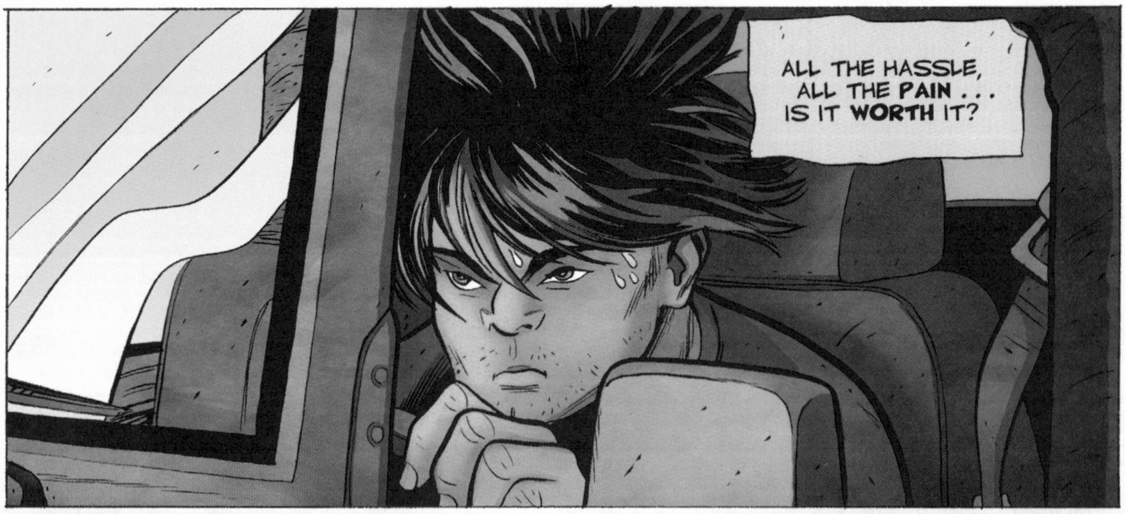
ALL THE HASSLE, ALL THE PAIN . . . IS IT WORTH IT?

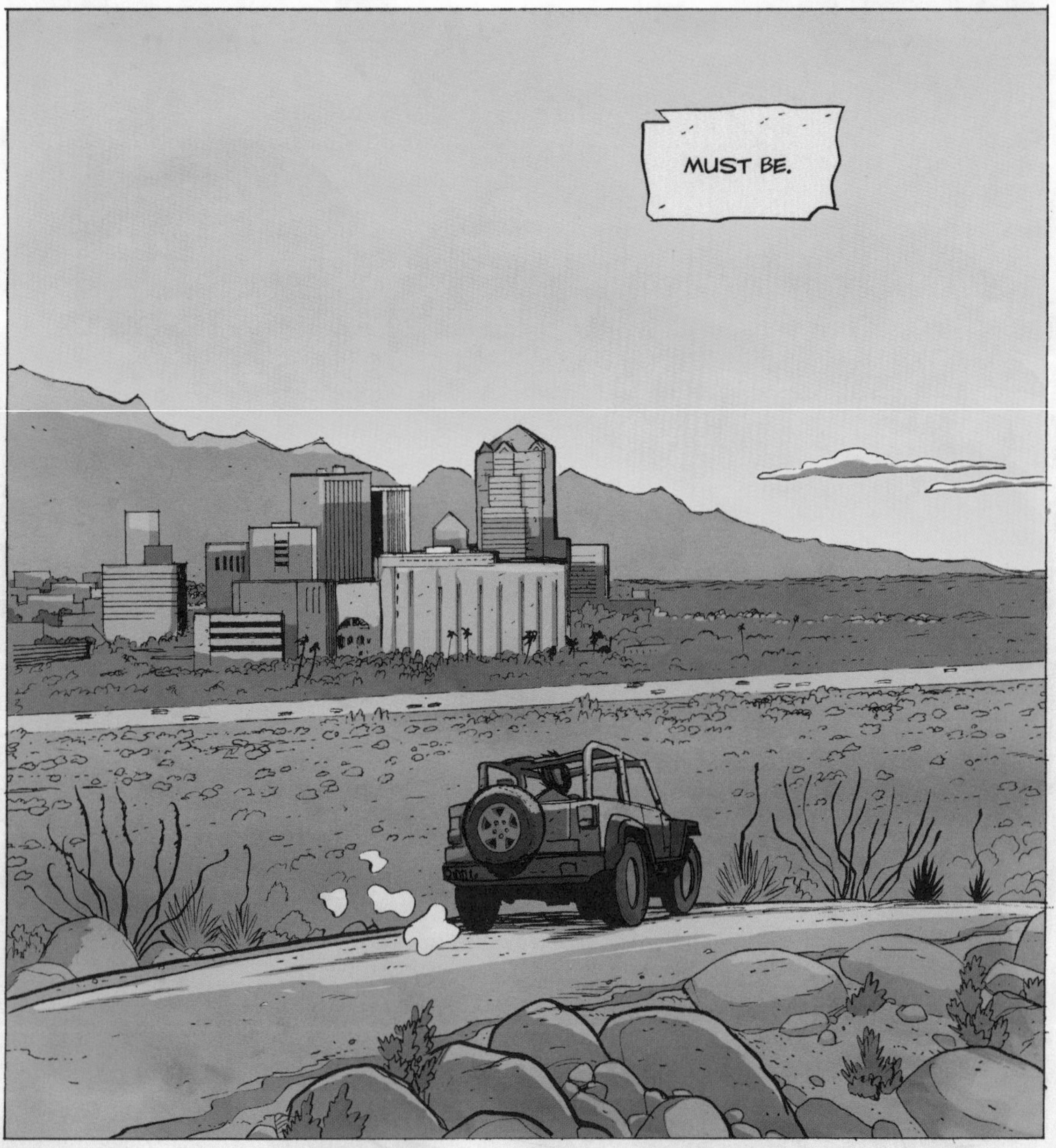
MUST BE.

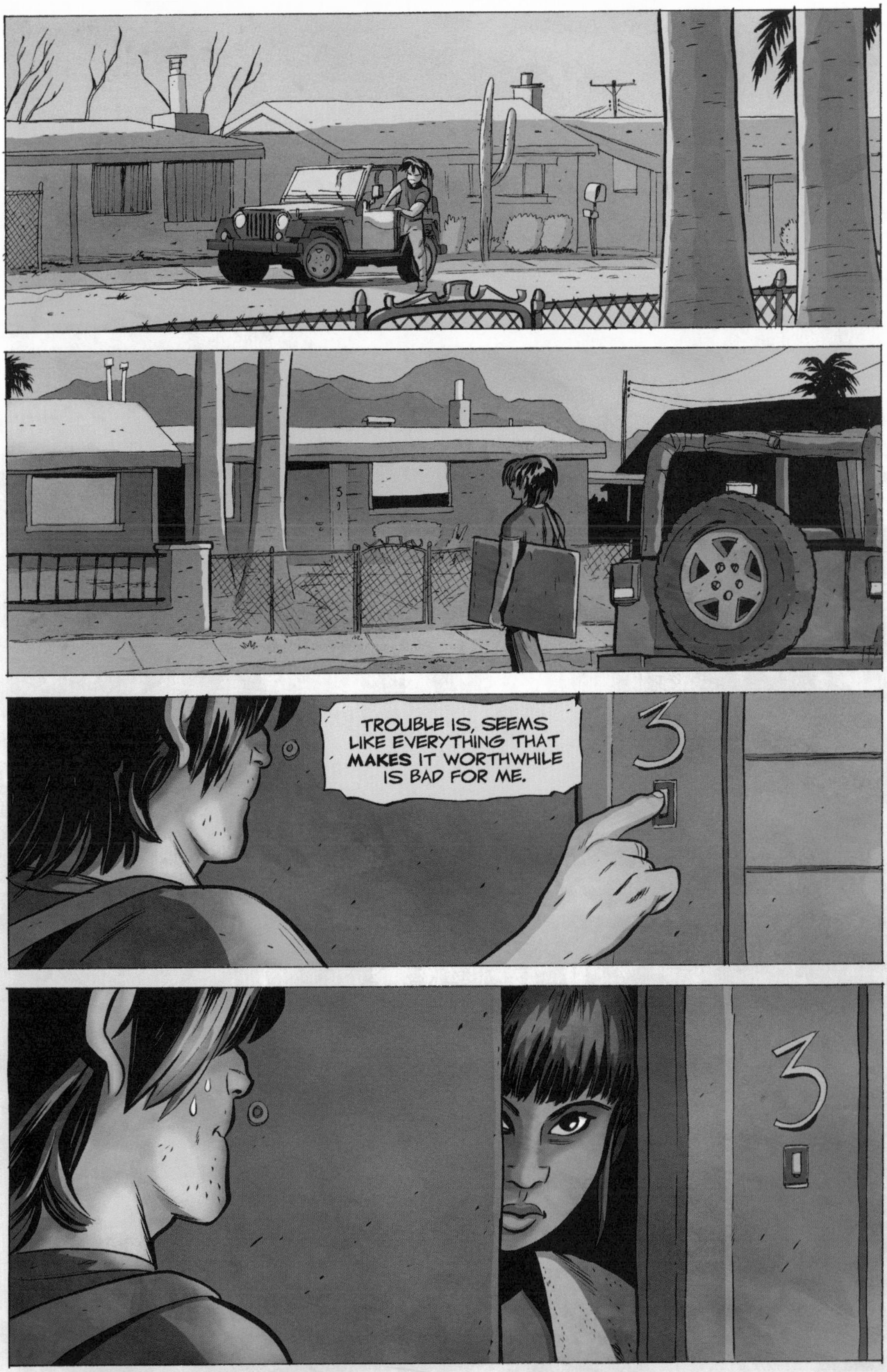
TROUBLE IS, SEEMS LIKE EVERYTHING THAT **MAKES** IT WORTHWHILE IS BAD FOR ME.

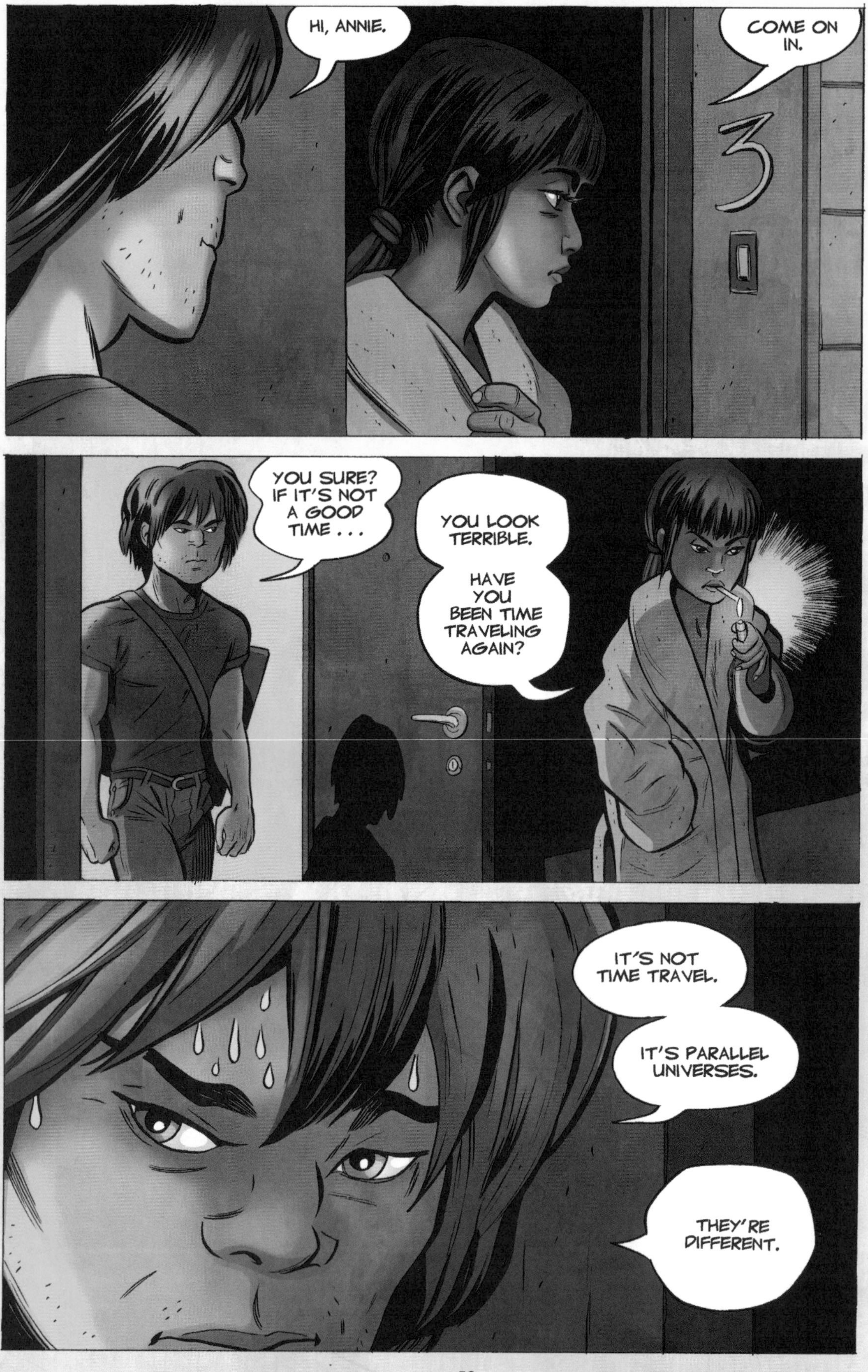
HI, ANNIE.
COME ON IN.
YOU SURE? IF IT'S NOT A GOOD TIME . . .
YOU LOOK TERRIBLE.
HAVE YOU BEEN TIME TRAVELING AGAIN?
IT'S NOT TIME TRAVEL.
IT'S PARALLEL UNIVERSES.
THEY'RE DIFFERENT.

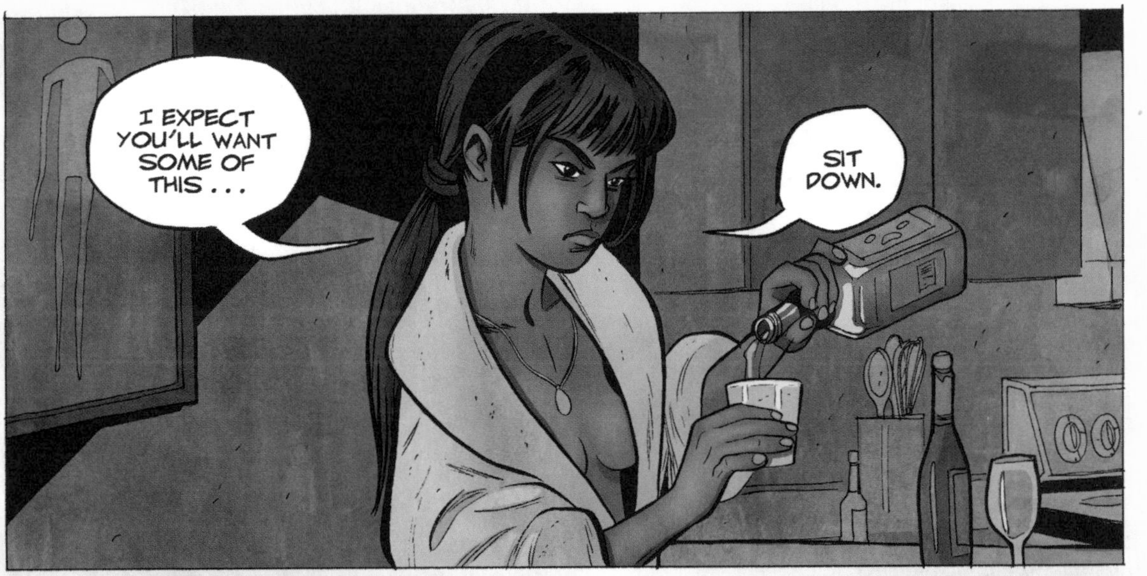
I EXPECT YOU'LL WANT SOME OF THIS . . .
SIT DOWN.

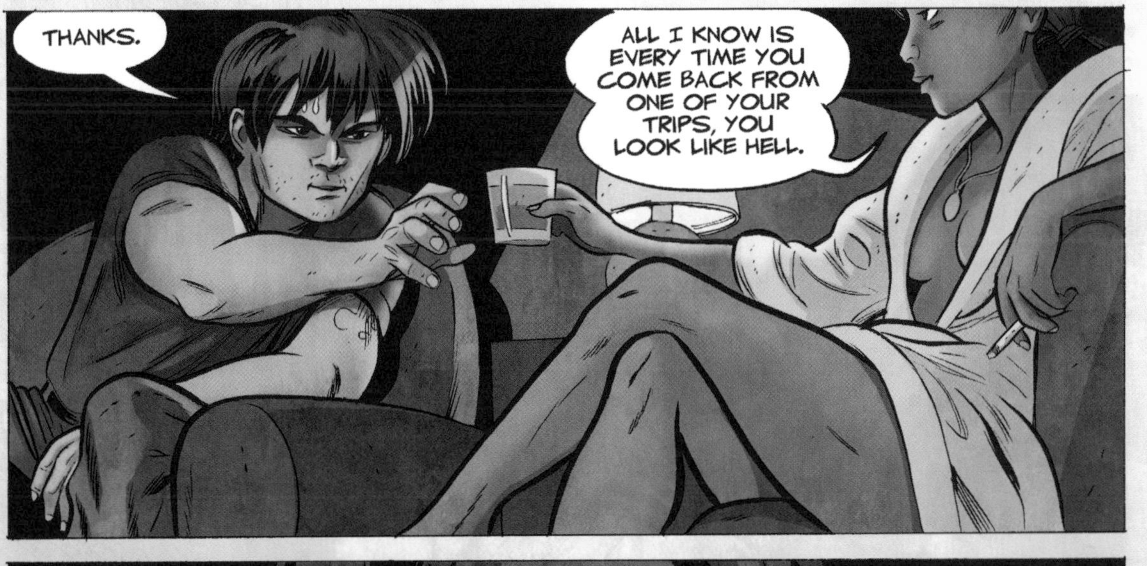
THANKS.
ALL I KNOW IS EVERY TIME YOU COME BACK FROM ONE OF YOUR TRIPS, YOU LOOK LIKE HELL.

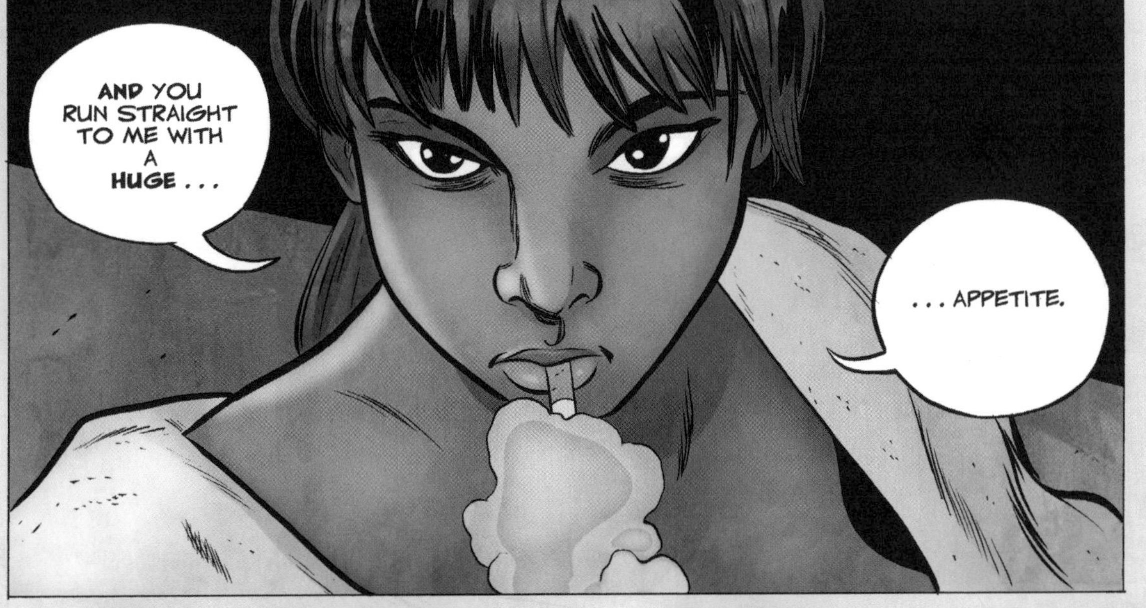
AND YOU RUN STRAIGHT TO ME WITH A HUGE . . .
. . . APPETITE.

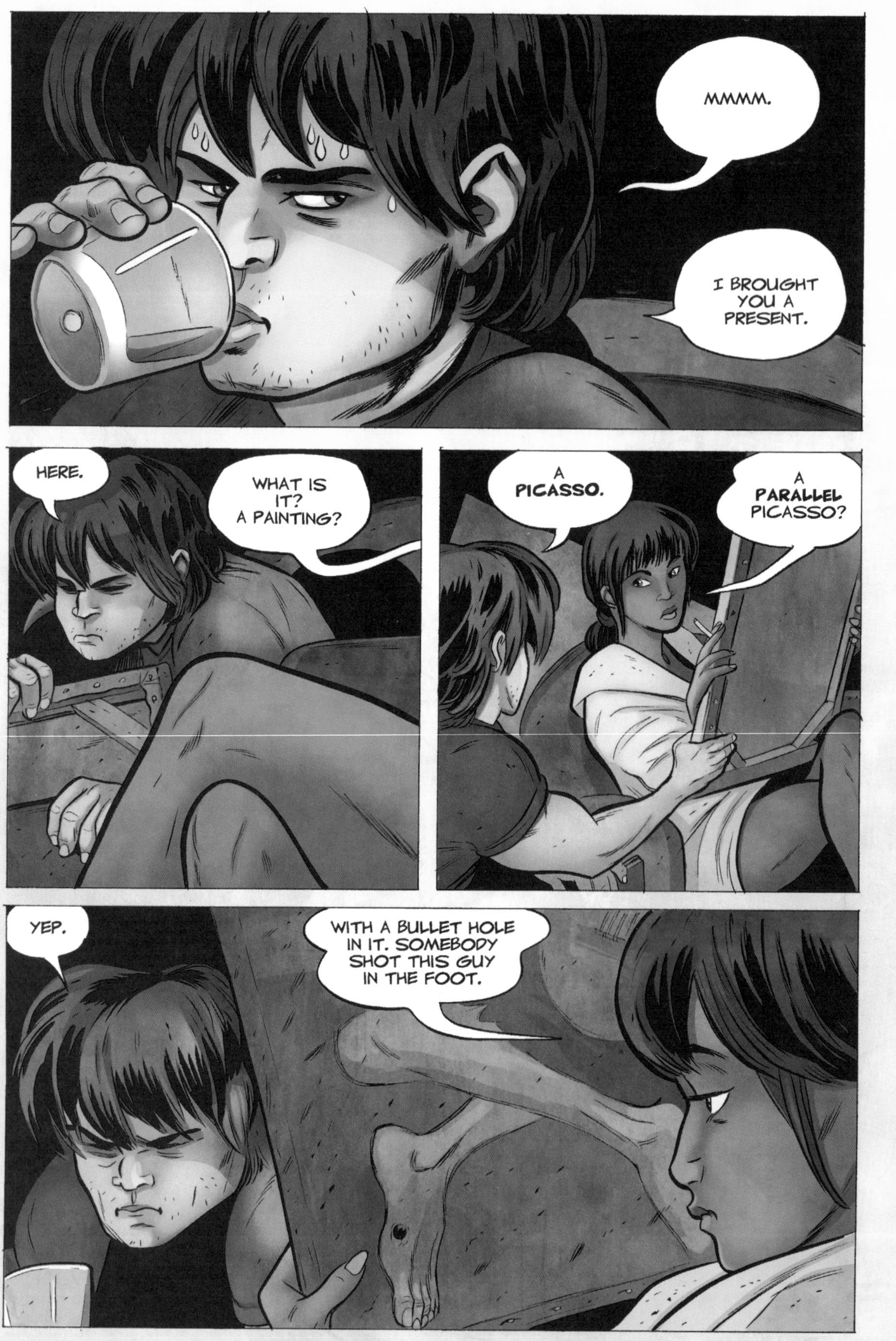
MMMM.
I BROUGHT YOU A PRESENT.
HERE.
WHAT IS IT? A PAINTING?
A PICASSO.
A PARALLEL PICASSO?
YEP.
WITH A BULLET HOLE IN IT. SOMEBODY SHOT THIS GUY IN THE FOOT.

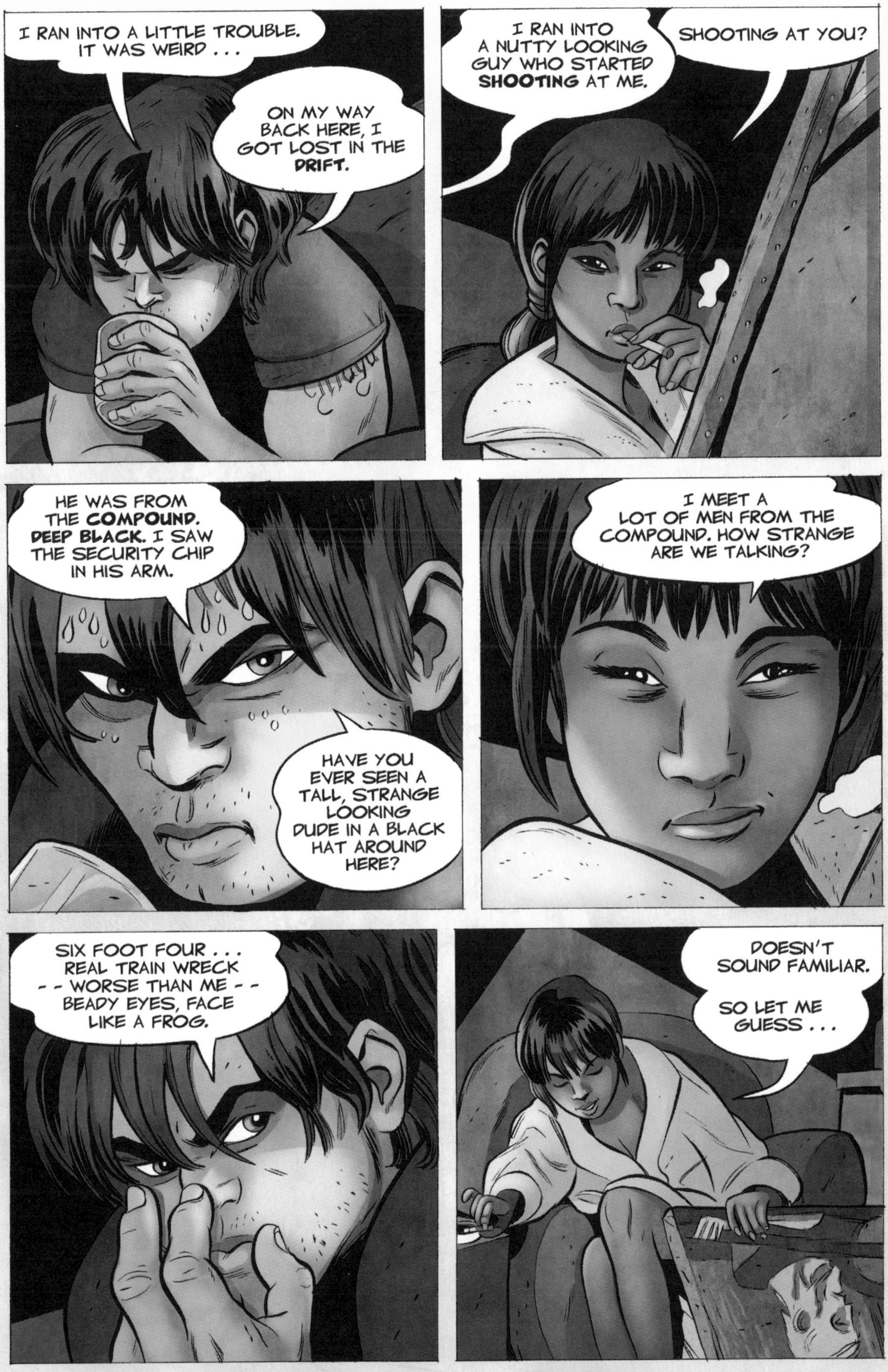
I RAN INTO A LITTLE TROUBLE. IT WAS WEIRD . . .
ON MY WAY BACK HERE, I GOT LOST IN THE DRIFT.
I RAN INTO A NUTTY LOOKING GUY WHO STARTED SHOOTING AT ME.
SHOOTING AT YOU?
HE WAS FROM THE COMPOUND. DEEP BLACK. I SAW THE SECURITY CHIP IN HIS ARM.
HAVE YOU EVER SEEN A TALL, STRANGE LOOKING DUDE IN A BLACK HAT AROUND HERE?
I MEET A LOT OF MEN FROM THE COMPOUND. HOW STRANGE ARE WE TALKING?
SIX FOOT FOUR . . . REAL TRAIN WRECK - - WORSE THAN ME - - BEADY EYES, FACE LIKE A FROG.
DOESN'T SOUND FAMILIAR.
SO LET ME GUESS . . .

...THE PAINTING IS RUINED, WHICH MEANS YOU DIDN'T GET PAID...

AND NOW YOU WANT TO FOOL AROUND ON CREDIT.

ON CREDIT? HOW ABOUT ON THE HOUSE? I JUST GAVE YOU A PICASSO.

A PICASSO WITH A BULLET HOLE IN IT THAT I CAN NEVER SHOW ANYONE.

CREDIT, THEN?

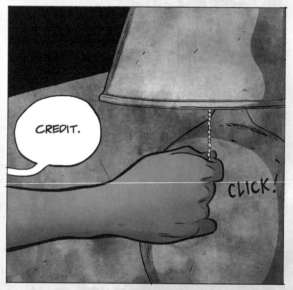

CREDIT.

CLICK!

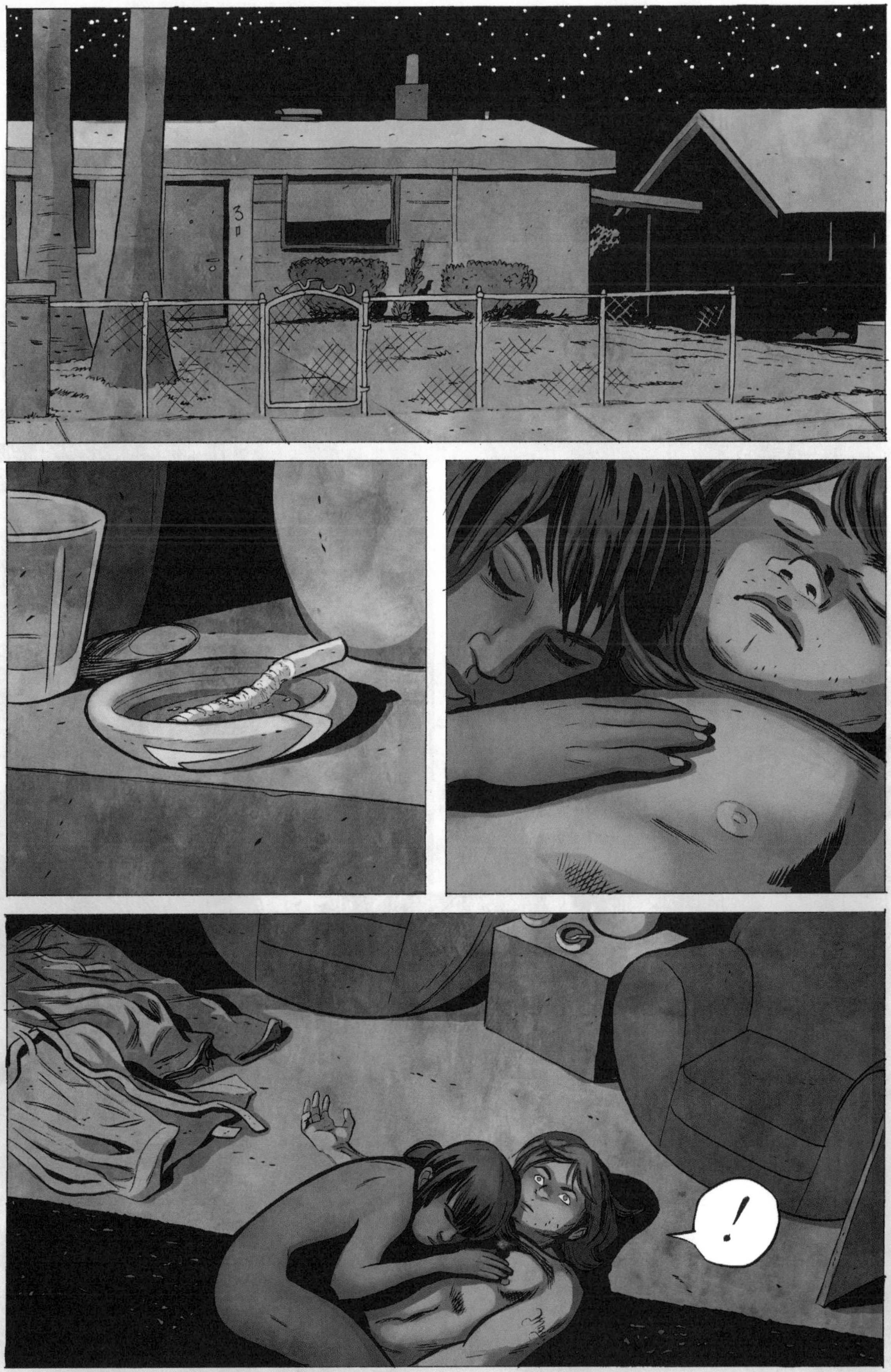
!

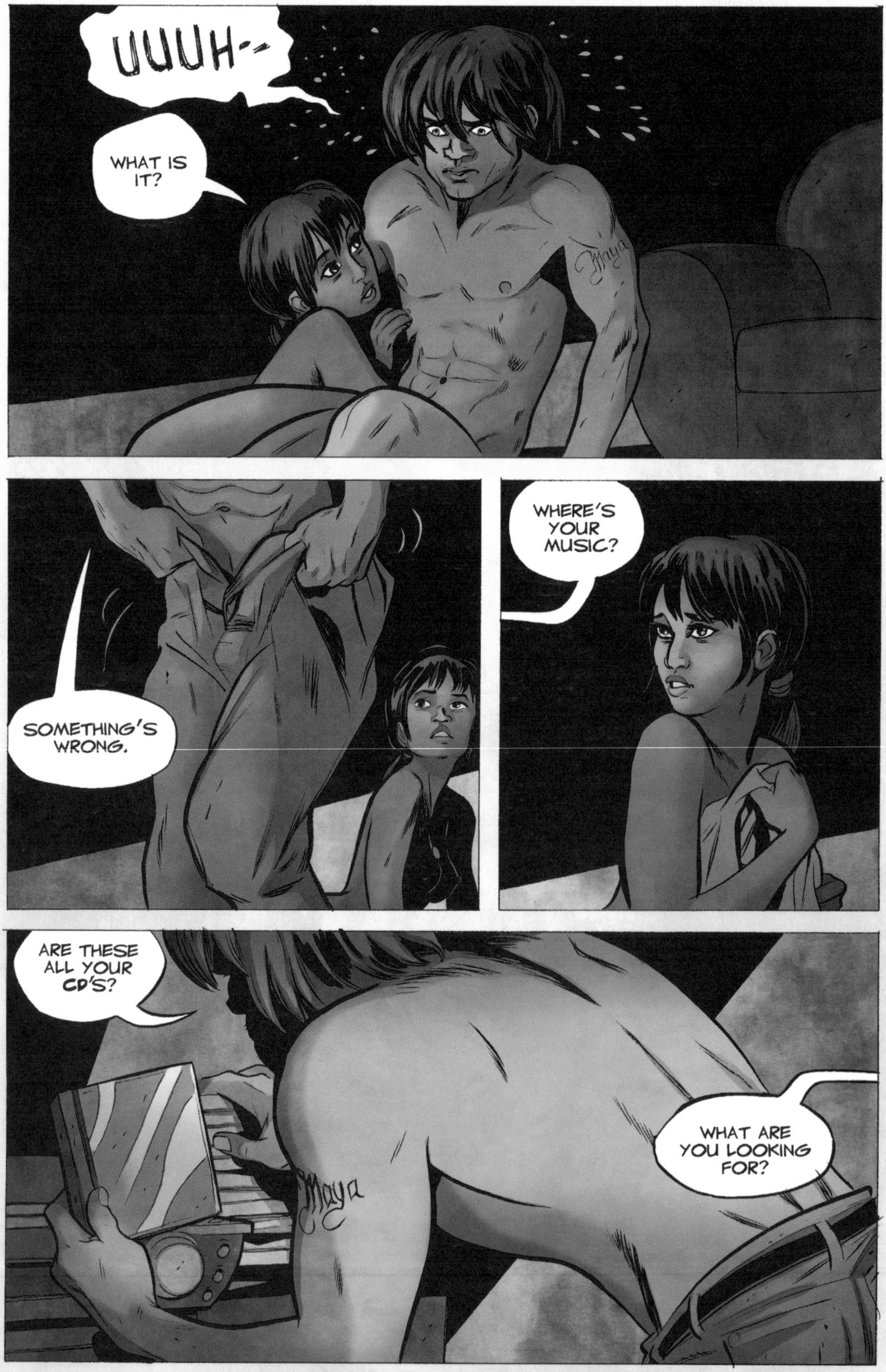
UUUH--
WHAT IS IT?
SOMETHING'S WRONG.
WHERE'S YOUR MUSIC?
ARE THESE ALL YOUR CD'S?
WHAT ARE YOU LOOKING FOR?

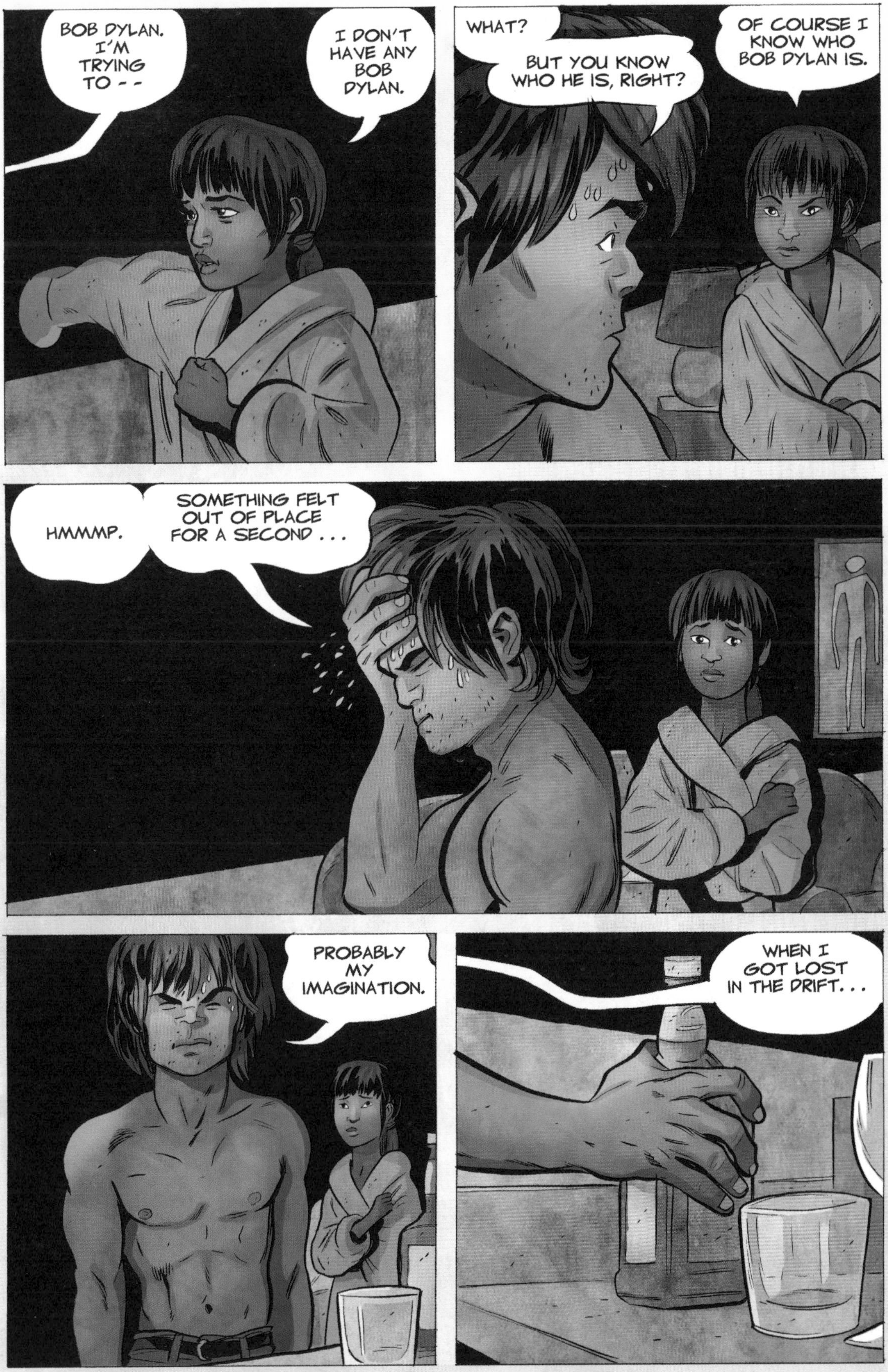
BOB DYLAN. I'M TRYING TO - -
I DON'T HAVE ANY BOB DYLAN.
WHAT?
BUT YOU KNOW WHO HE IS, RIGHT?
OF COURSE I KNOW WHO BOB DYLAN IS.
HMMMP.
SOMETHING FELT OUT OF PLACE FOR A SECOND . . .
PROBABLY MY IMAGINATION.
WHEN I GOT LOST IN THE DRIFT. . .

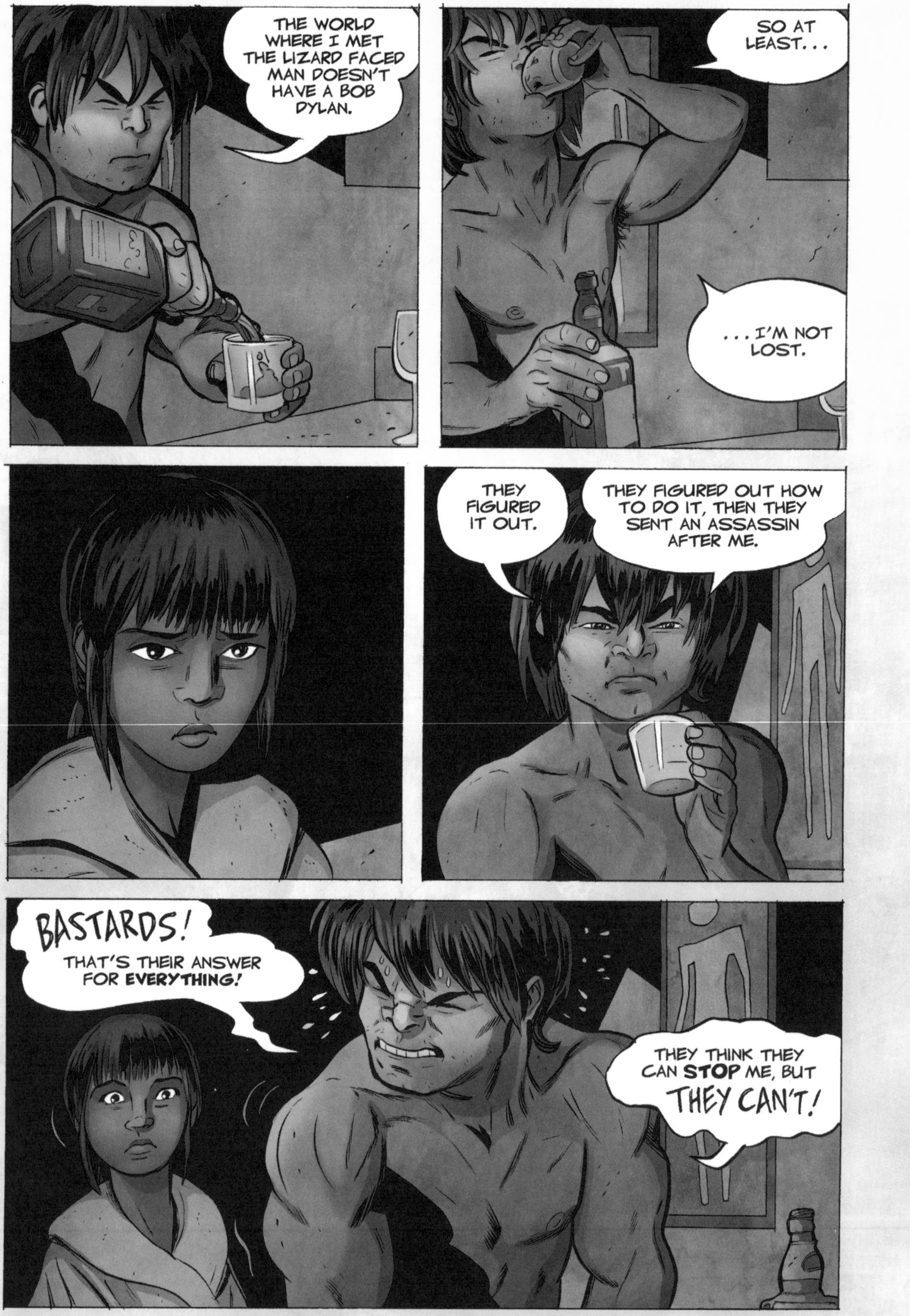
THE WORLD WHERE I MET THE LIZARD FACED MAN DOESN'T HAVE A BOB DYLAN.
SO AT LEAST...
...I'M NOT LOST.
THEY FIGURED IT OUT.
THEY FIGURED OUT HOW TO DO IT, THEN THEY SENT AN ASSASSIN AFTER ME.
BASTARDS!
THAT'S THEIR ANSWER FOR EVERYTHING!
THEY THINK THEY CAN STOP ME, BUT THEY CAN'T!

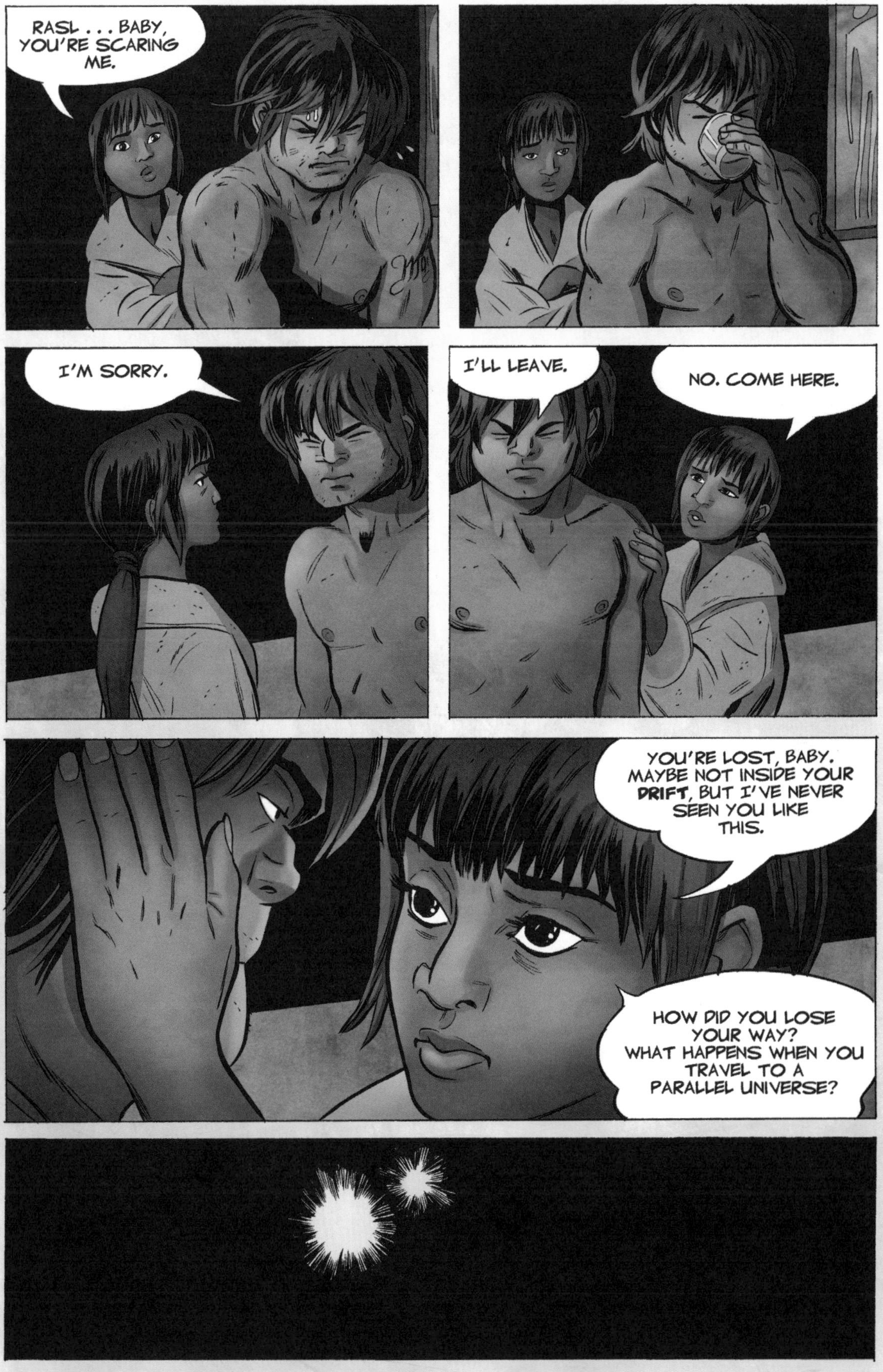
RASL . . . BABY, YOU'RE SCARING ME.
I'M SORRY.
I'LL LEAVE.
NO. COME HERE.
YOU'RE LOST, BABY. MAYBE NOT INSIDE YOUR DRIFT, BUT I'VE NEVER SEEN YOU LIKE THIS.
HOW DID YOU LOSE YOUR WAY? WHAT HAPPENS WHEN YOU TRAVEL TO A PARALLEL UNIVERSE?

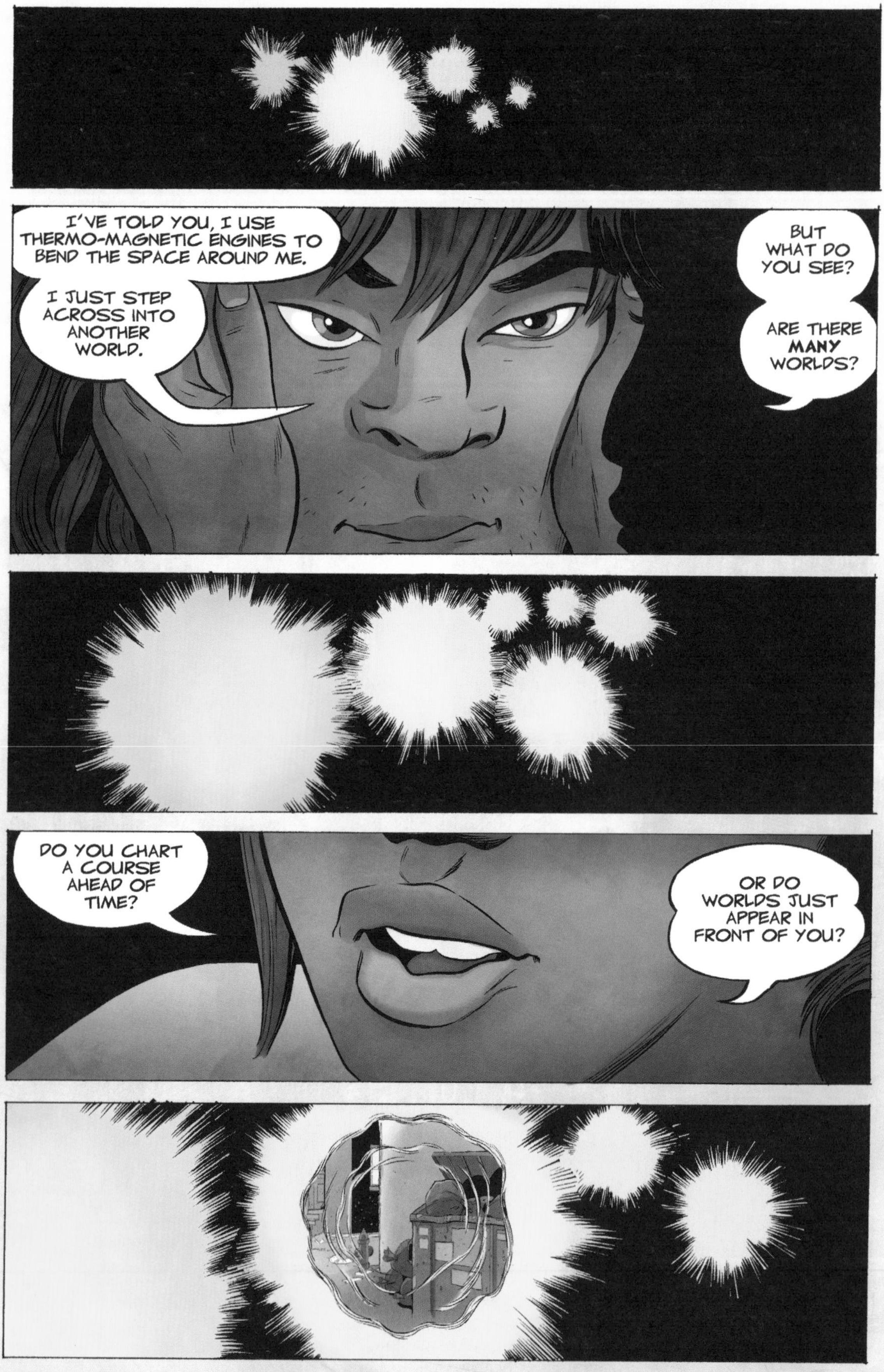
I'VE TOLD YOU, I USE THERMO-MAGNETIC ENGINES TO BEND THE SPACE AROUND ME.
I JUST STEP ACROSS INTO ANOTHER WORLD.
BUT WHAT DO YOU SEE?
ARE THERE MANY WORLDS?
DO YOU CHART A COURSE AHEAD OF TIME?
OR DO WORLDS JUST APPEAR IN FRONT OF YOU?

I SEE MULTIPLE WORLDS. EVENTUALLY ONE OF THEM COMES INTO FOCUS. THAT'S THE ONE I GO FOR.

INTERESTING. SO YOU DO NOT CHOOSE THE WORLD . . . IT CHOOSES YOU.

HMMM. NEVER THOUGHT OF IT THAT WAY. BUT ONCE A WORLD OPENS TO ME, I CAN ALWAYS FIND IT AGAIN.

WELL, SOMETHING WENT WRONG. WE'LL HAVE TO HEAL YOU.

HEAL ME? WHAT, YOU'RE A MEDICINE WOMAN, NOW?

DON'T BE SMART. HERE, LOOK.

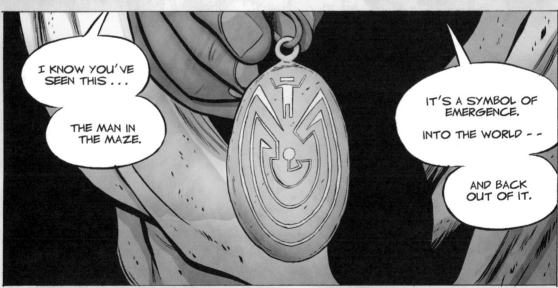

I KNOW YOU'VE SEEN THIS . . .

THE MAN IN THE MAZE.

IT'S A SYMBOL OF EMERGENCE.

INTO THE WORLD - -

AND BACK OUT OF IT.

63

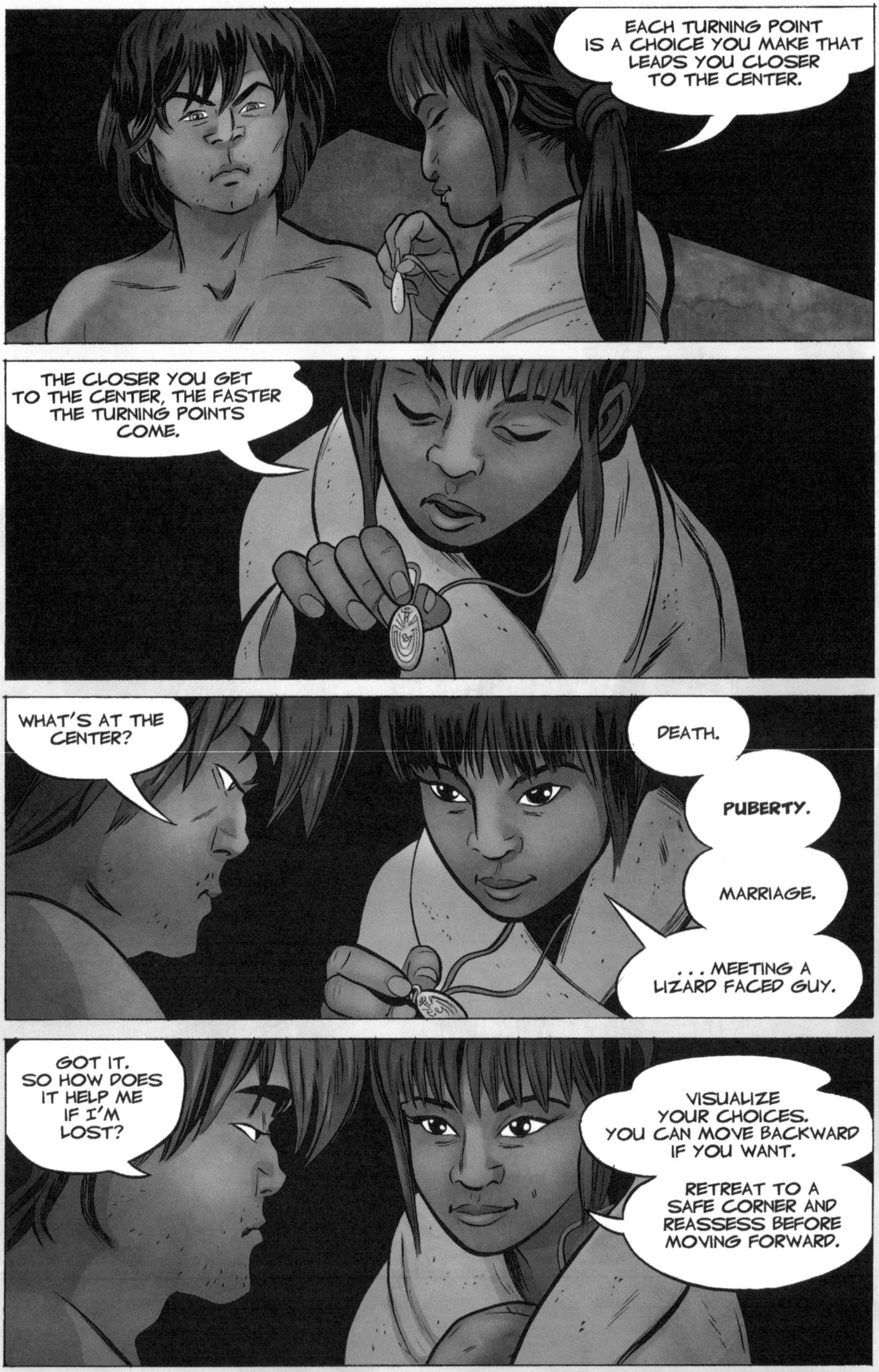
EACH TURNING POINT IS A CHOICE YOU MAKE THAT LEADS YOU CLOSER TO THE CENTER.
THE CLOSER YOU GET TO THE CENTER, THE FASTER THE TURNING POINTS COME.
WHAT'S AT THE CENTER?
DEATH.
PUBERTY.
MARRIAGE.
. . . MEETING A LIZARD FACED GUY.
GOT IT. SO HOW DOES IT HELP ME IF I'M LOST?
VISUALIZE YOUR CHOICES. YOU CAN MOVE BACKWARD IF YOU WANT.
RETREAT TO A SAFE CORNER AND REASSESS BEFORE MOVING FORWARD.

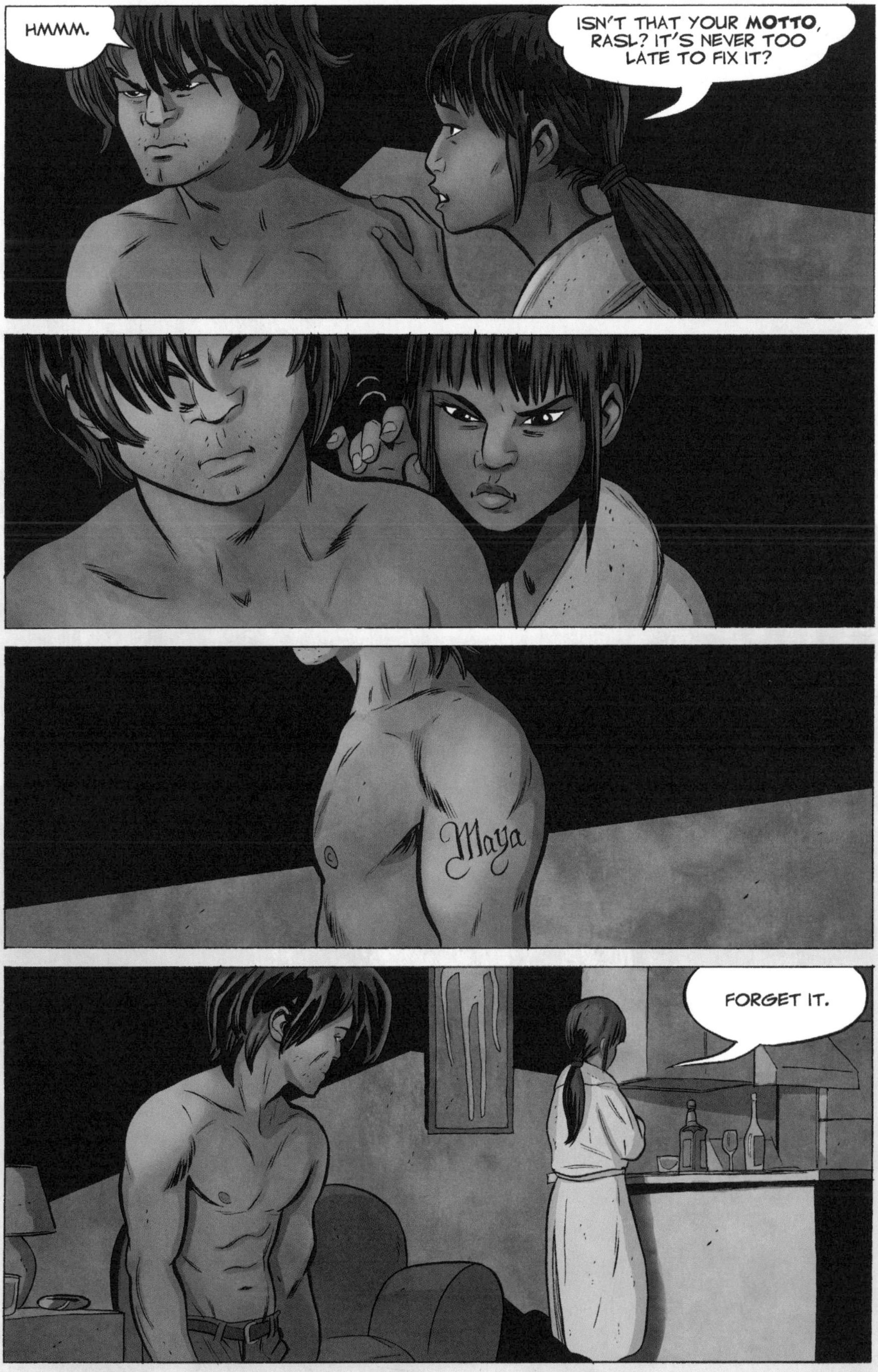
HMMM.
ISN'T THAT YOUR MOTTO, RASL? IT'S NEVER TOO LATE TO FIX IT?
Maya
FORGET IT.

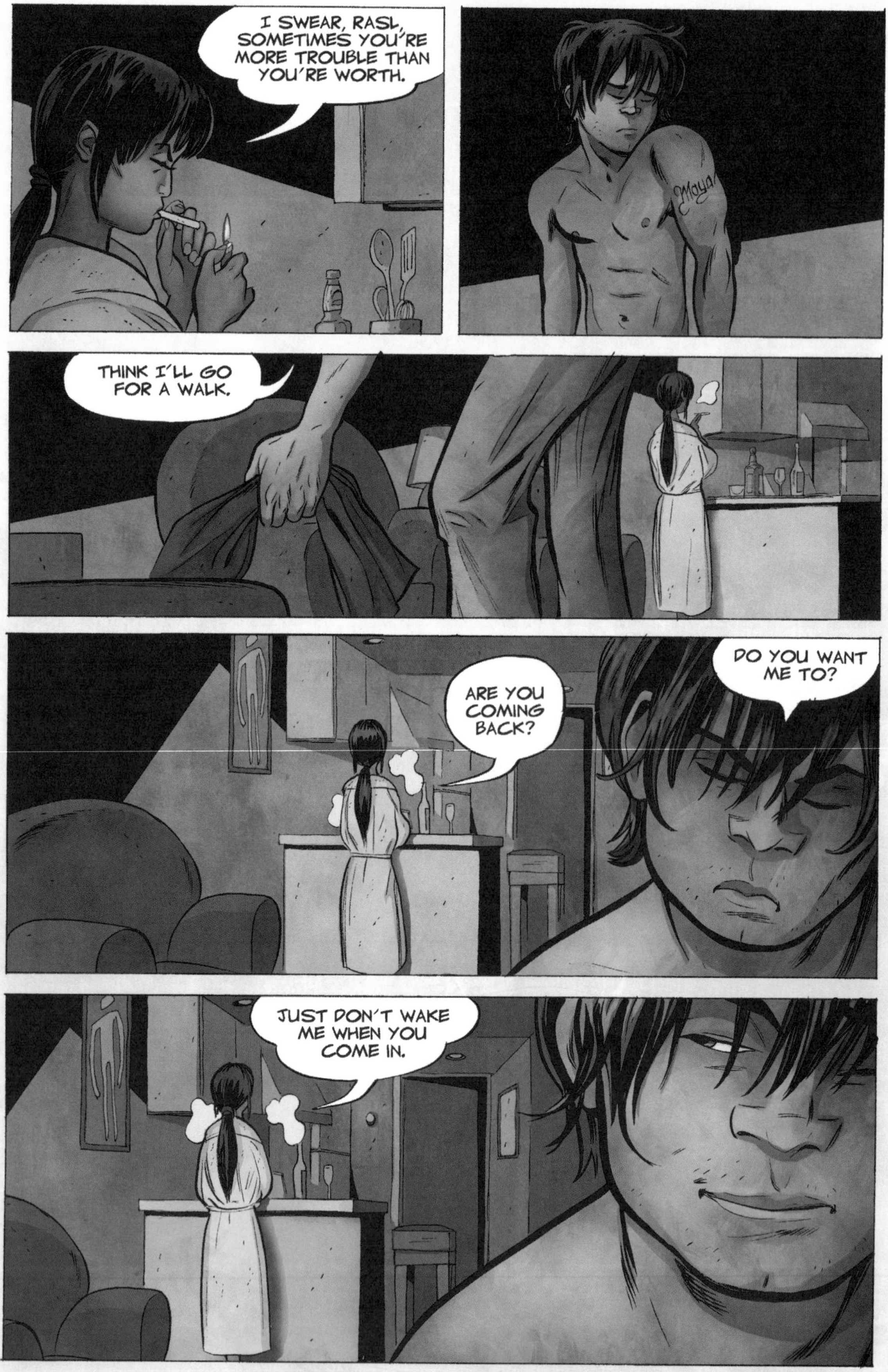
I SWEAR, RASL, SOMETIMES YOU'RE MORE TROUBLE THAN YOU'RE WORTH.
THINK I'LL GO FOR A WALK.
ARE YOU COMING BACK?
DO YOU WANT ME TO?
JUST DON'T WAKE ME WHEN YOU COME IN.

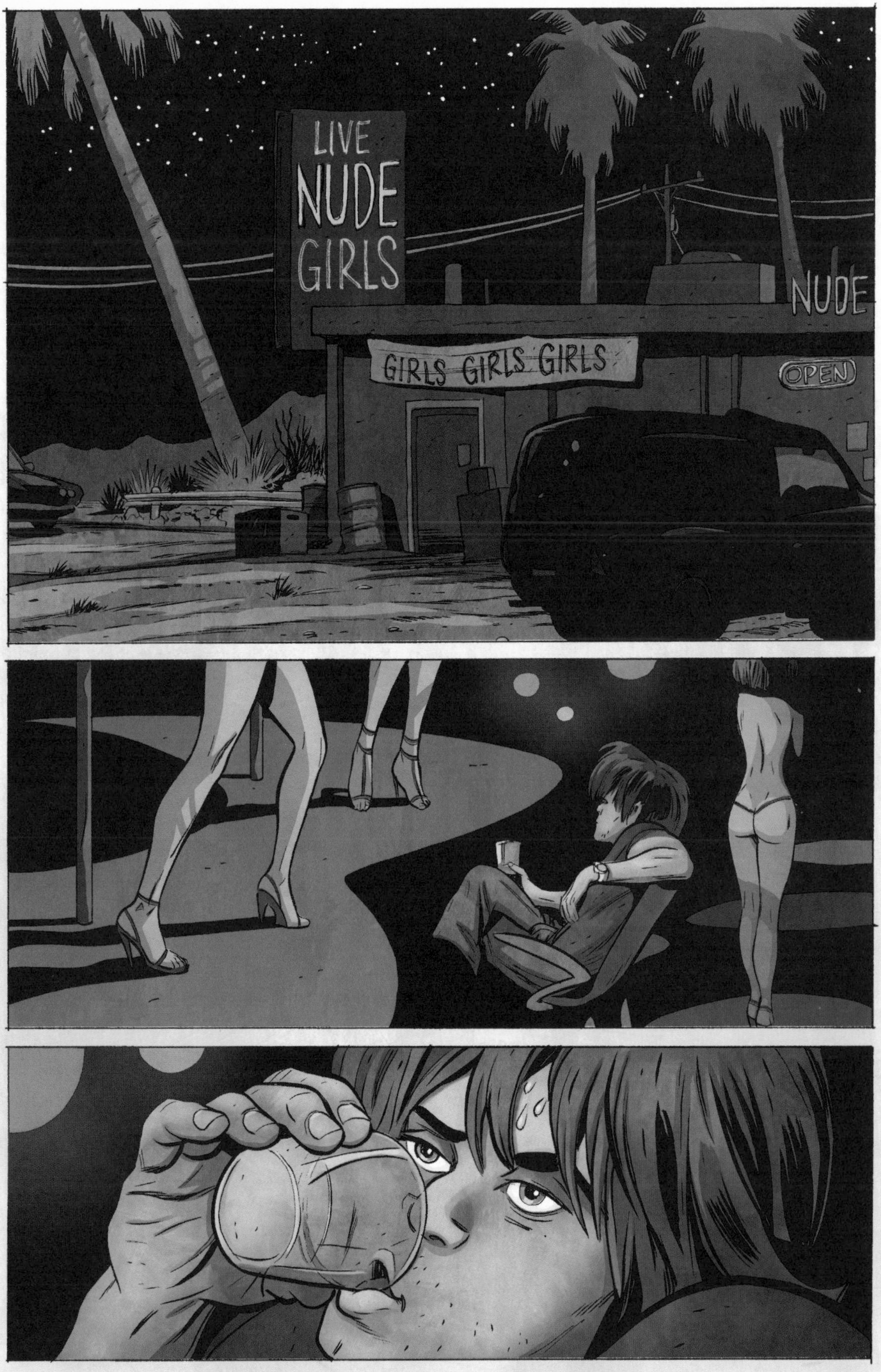
LIVE
NUDE
GIRLS
GIRLS GIRLS GIRLS
NUDE
OPEN

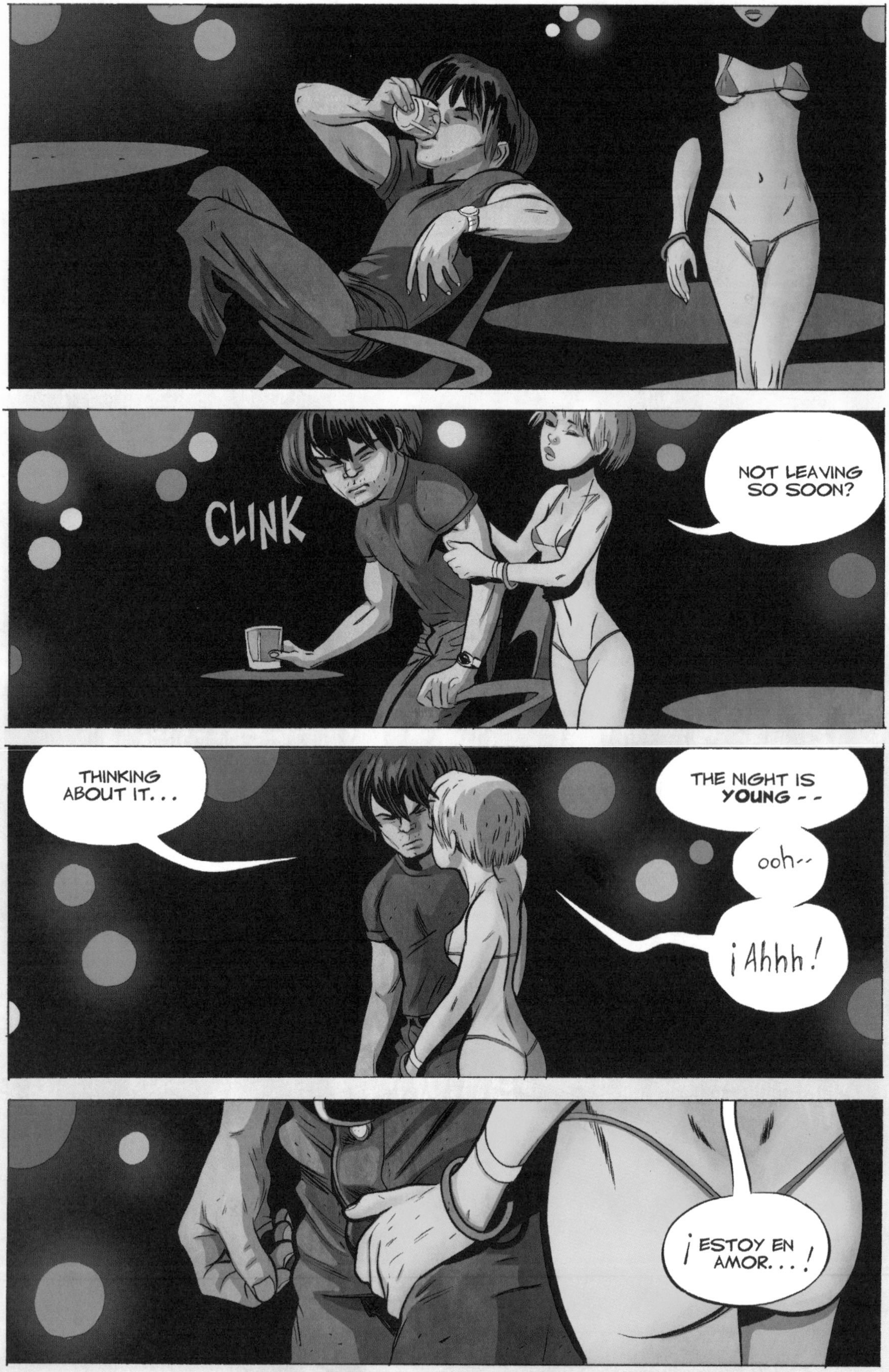
NOT LEAVING SO SOON?
CLINK
THINKING ABOUT IT...
THE NIGHT IS YOUNG --
ooh--
¡Ahhh!
¡ESTOY EN AMOR...!

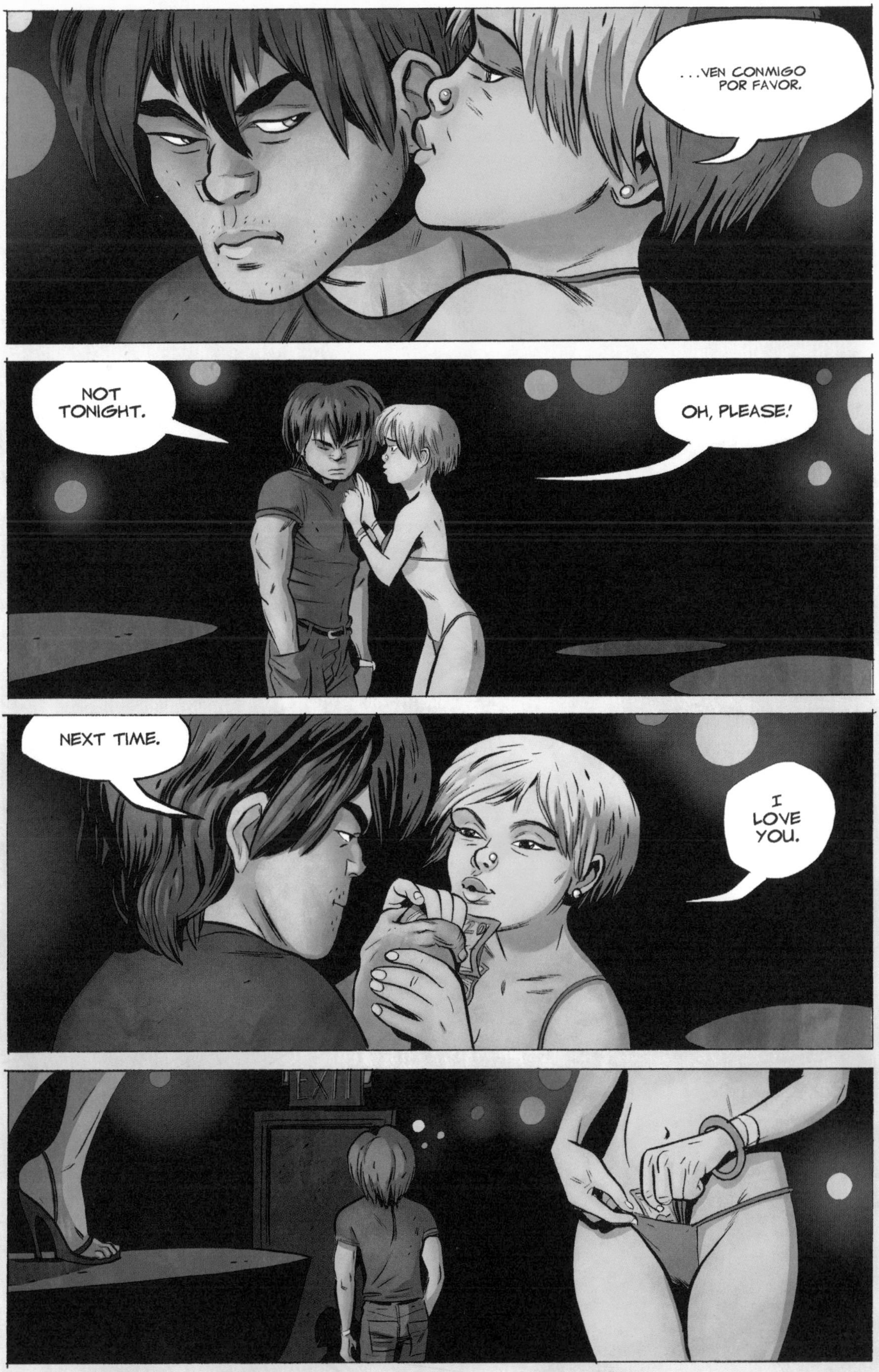
...VEN CONMIGO POR FAVOR.
NOT TONIGHT.
OH, PLEASE!
NEXT TIME.
I LOVE YOU.
EXIT

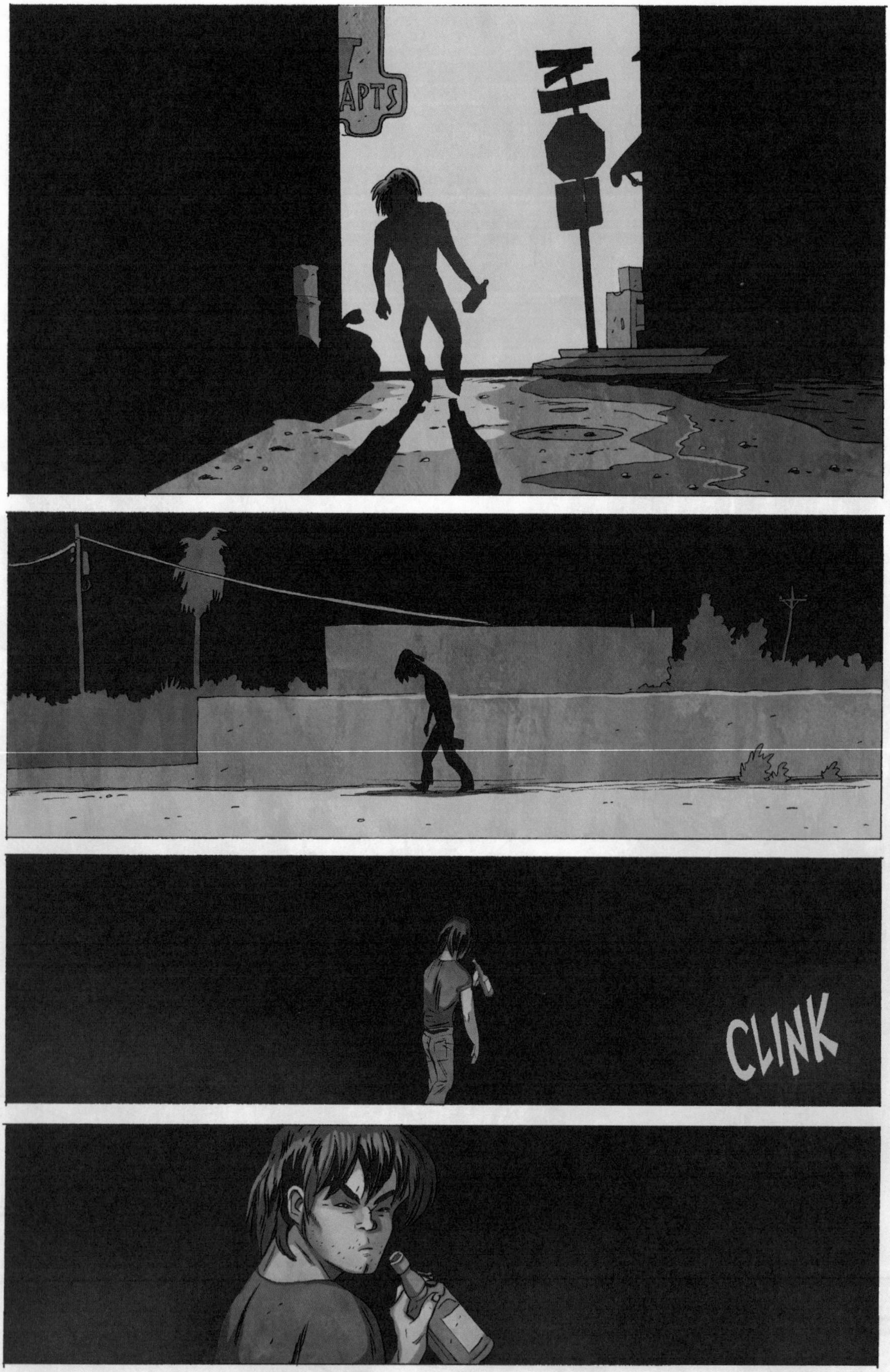
APTS
CLINK

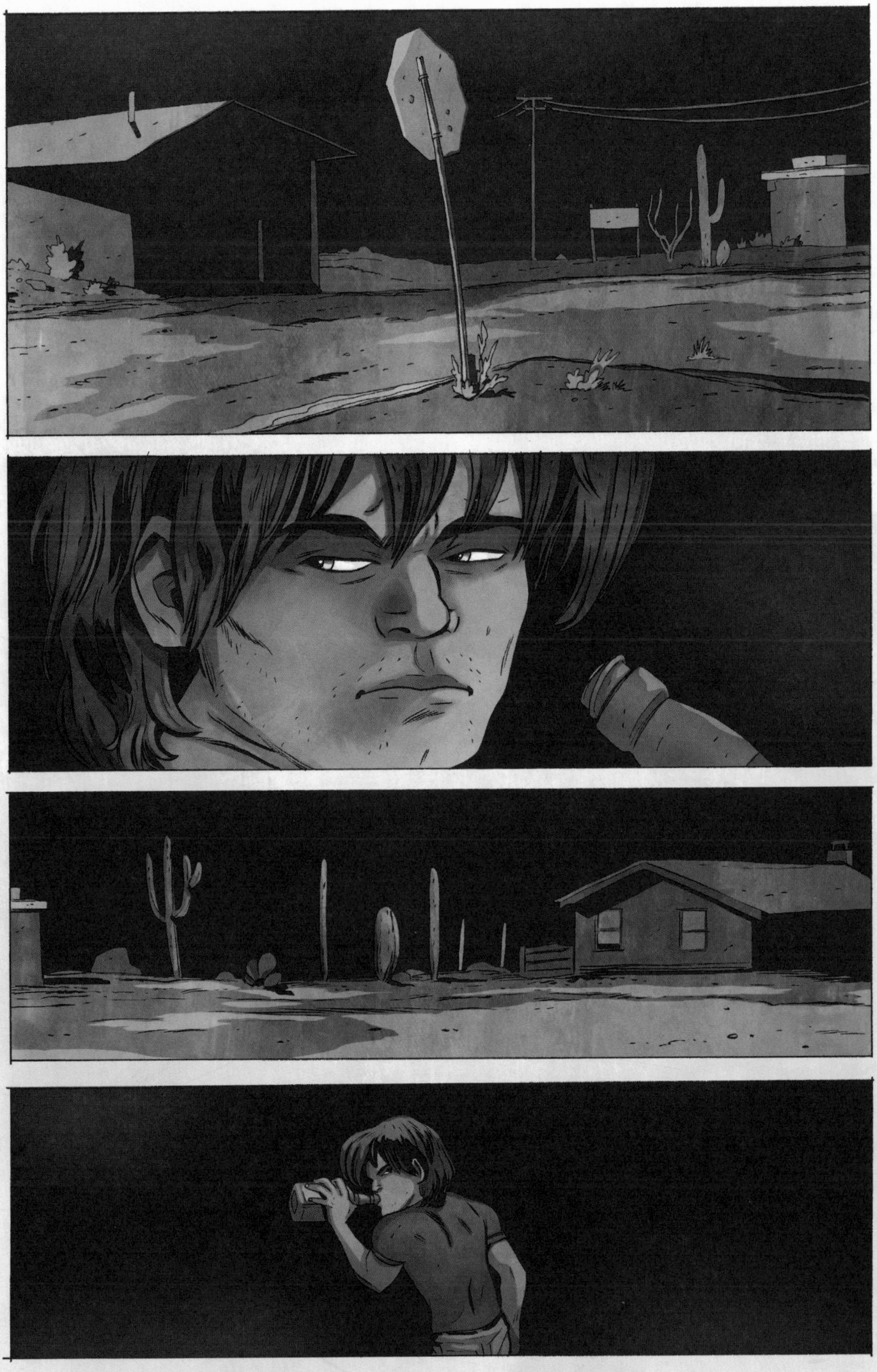

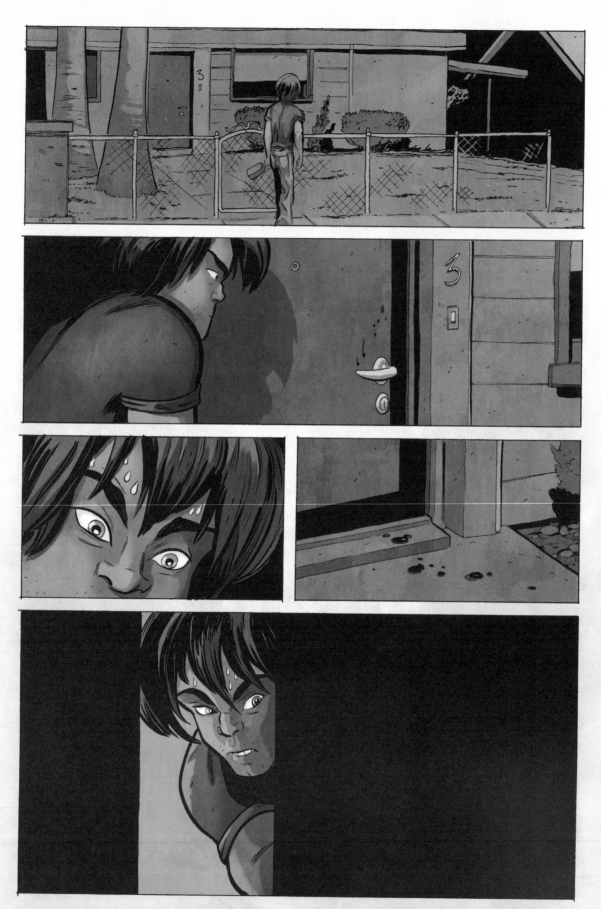

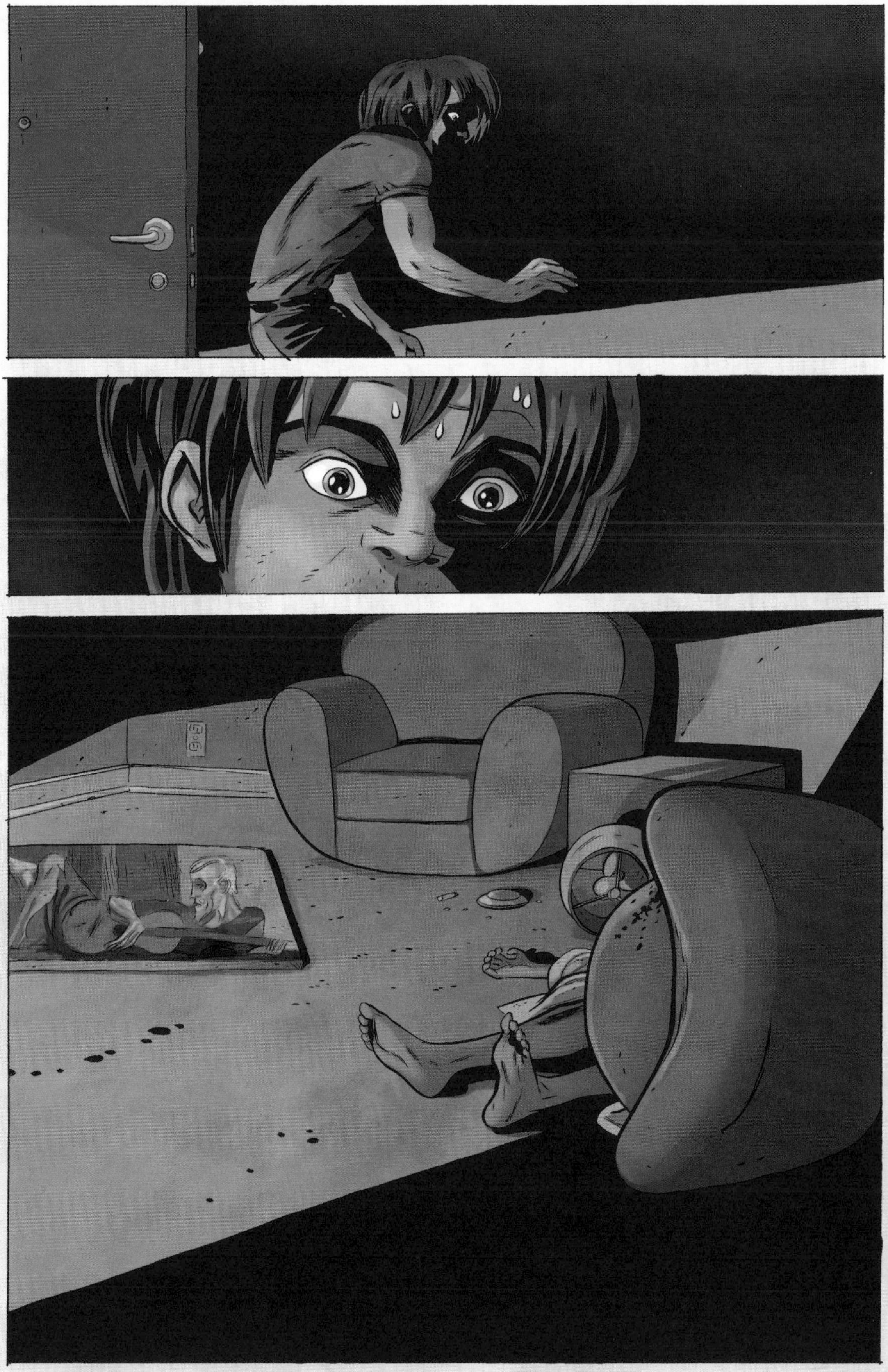

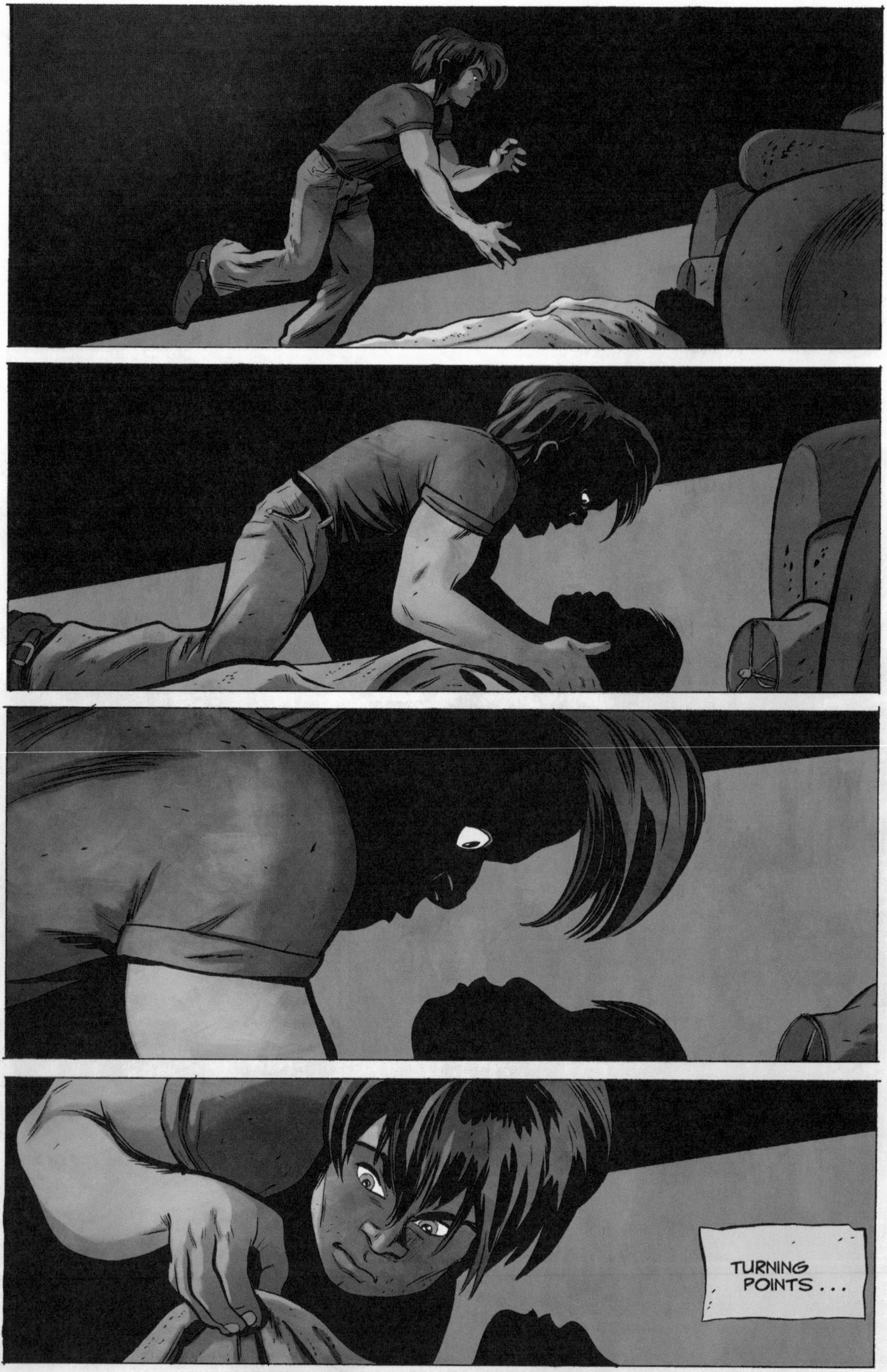
TURNING POINTS . . .

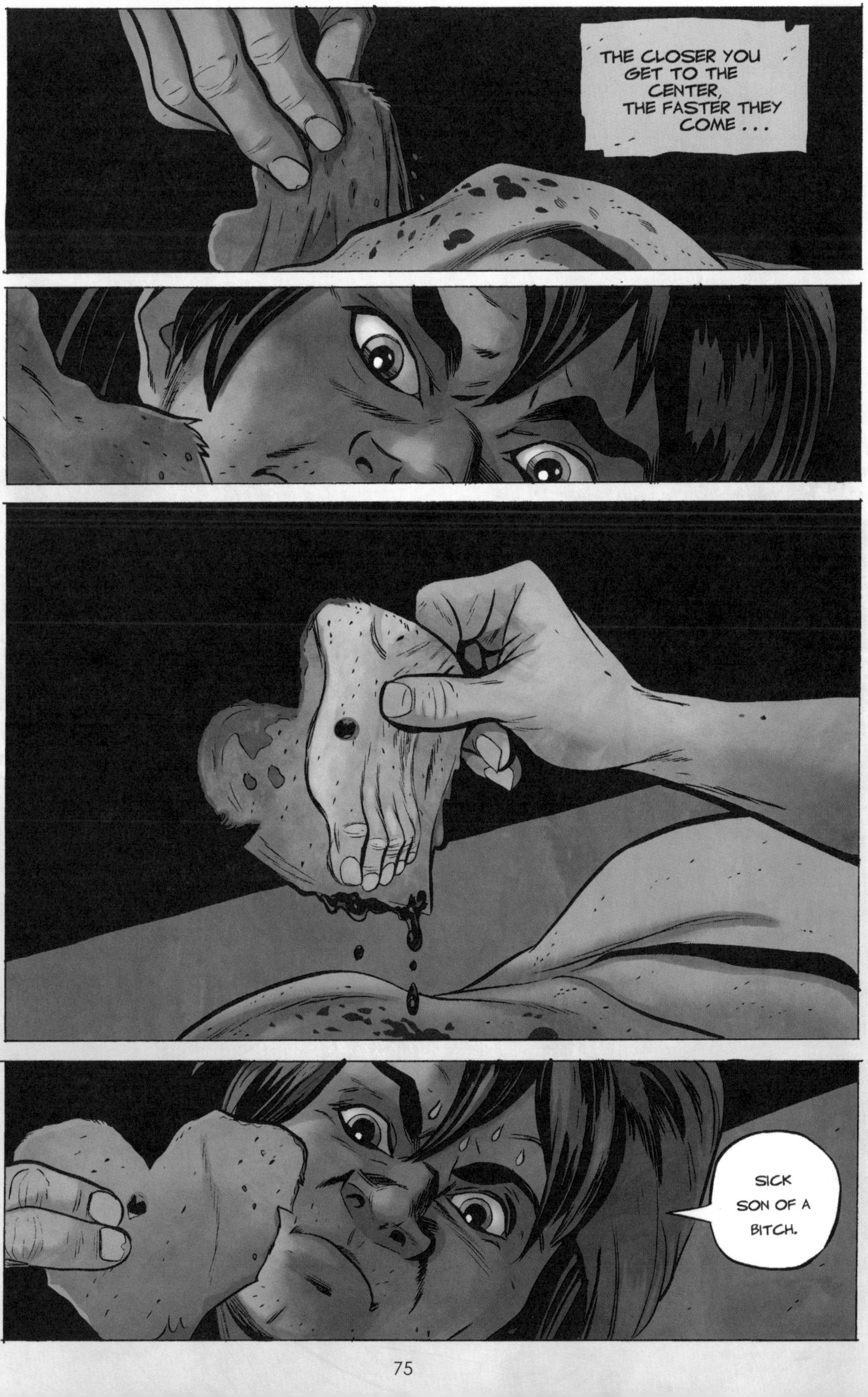
THE CLOSER YOU GET TO THE CENTER, THE FASTER THEY COME . . .
SICK SON OF A BITCH.

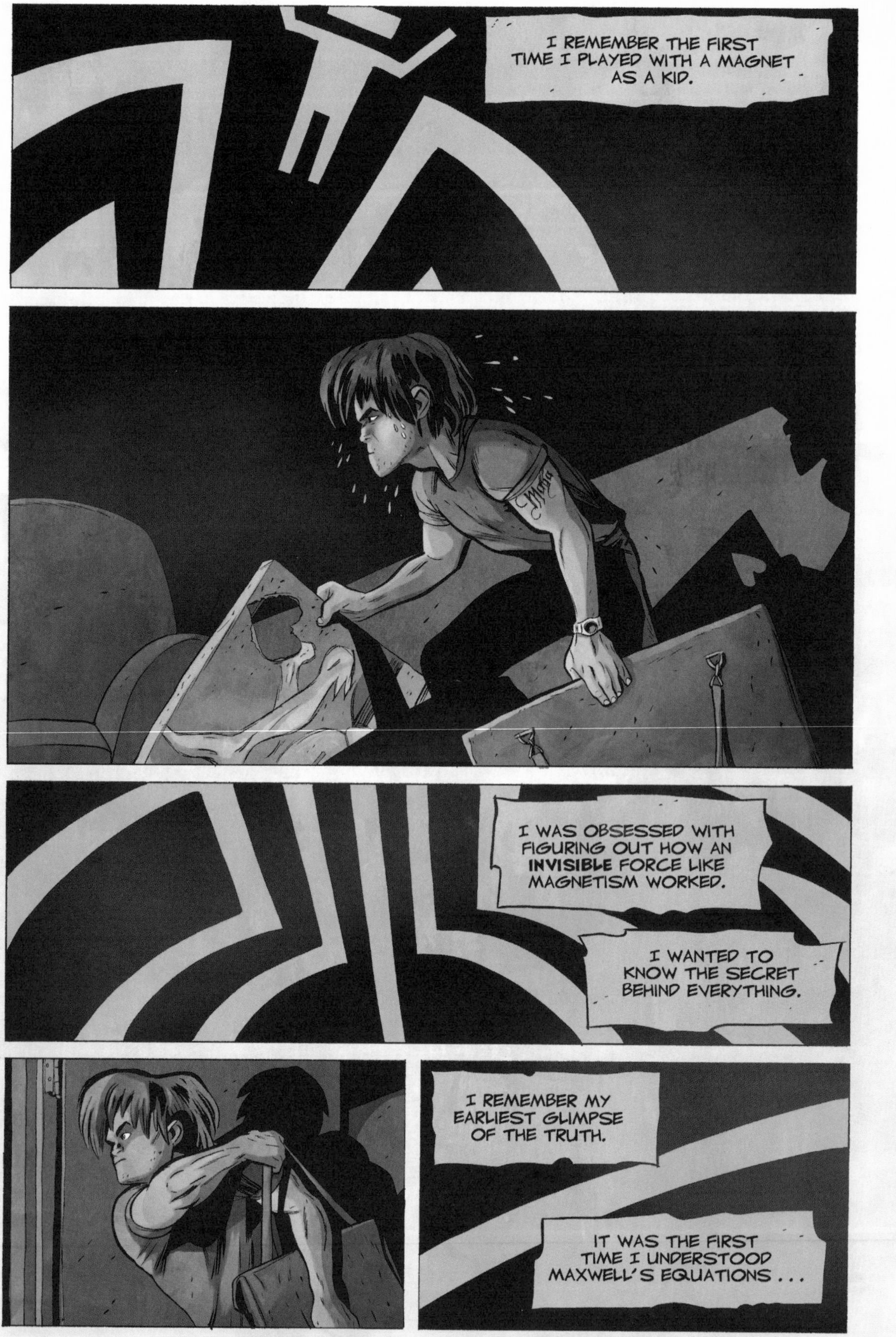
I REMEMBER THE FIRST TIME I PLAYED WITH A MAGNET AS A KID.
I WAS OBSESSED WITH FIGURING OUT HOW AN INVISIBLE FORCE LIKE MAGNETISM WORKED.
I WANTED TO KNOW THE SECRET BEHIND EVERYTHING.
I REMEMBER MY EARLIEST GLIMPSE OF THE TRUTH.
IT WAS THE FIRST TIME I UNDERSTOOD MAXWELL'S EQUATIONS . . .

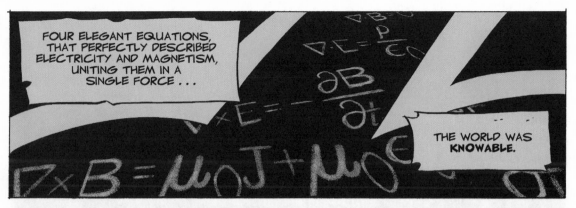

FOUR ELEGANT EQUATIONS, THAT PERFECTLY DESCRIBED ELECTRICITY AND MAGNETISM, UNITING THEM IN A SINGLE FORCE . . .

THE WORLD WAS KNOWABLE.

KEEP OUT

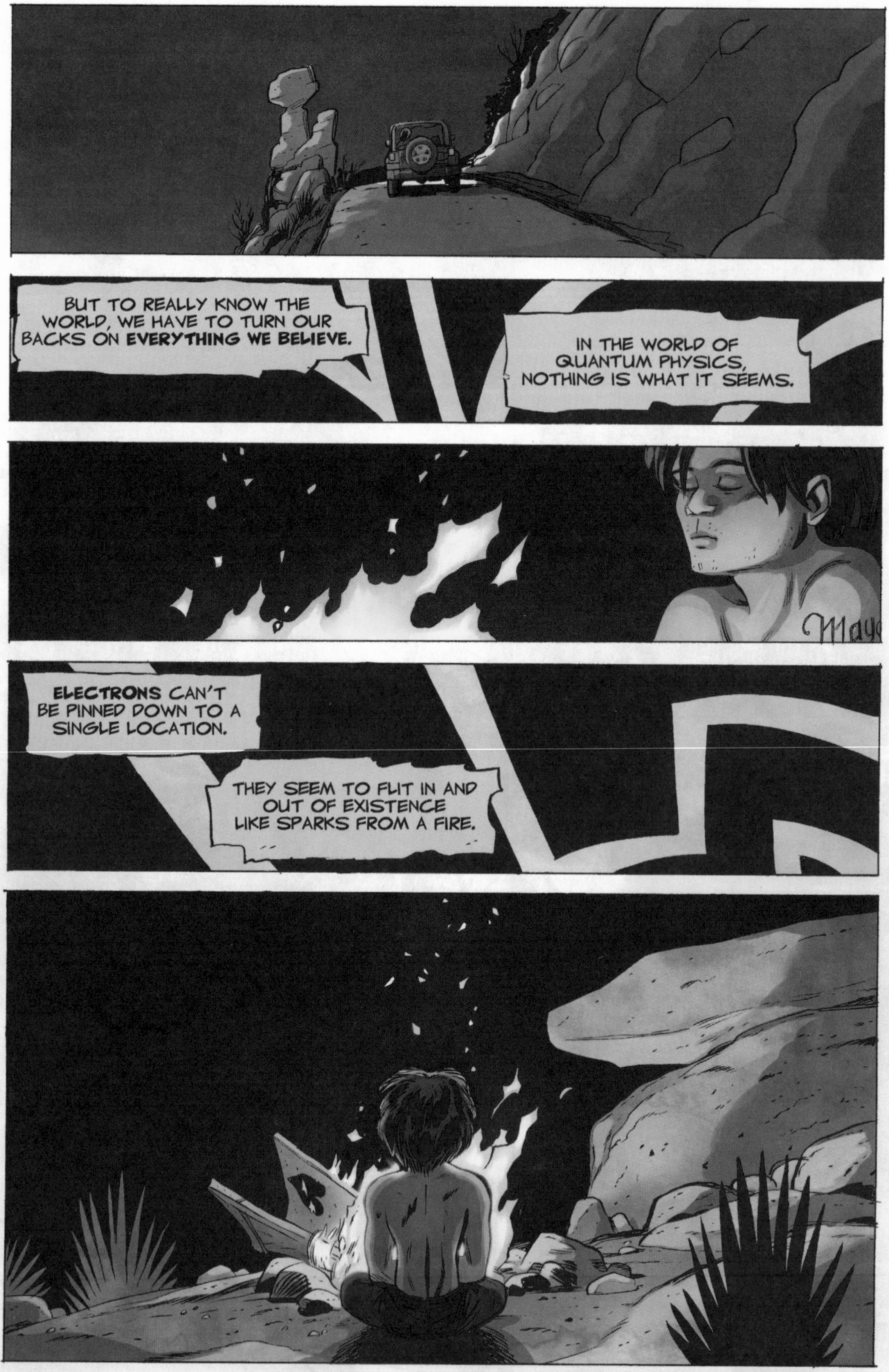
BUT TO REALLY KNOW THE WORLD, WE HAVE TO TURN OUR BACKS ON EVERYTHING WE BELIEVE.
IN THE WORLD OF QUANTUM PHYSICS, NOTHING IS WHAT IT SEEMS.
ELECTRONS CAN'T BE PINNED DOWN TO A SINGLE LOCATION.
THEY SEEM TO FLIT IN AND OUT OF EXISTENCE LIKE SPARKS FROM A FIRE.

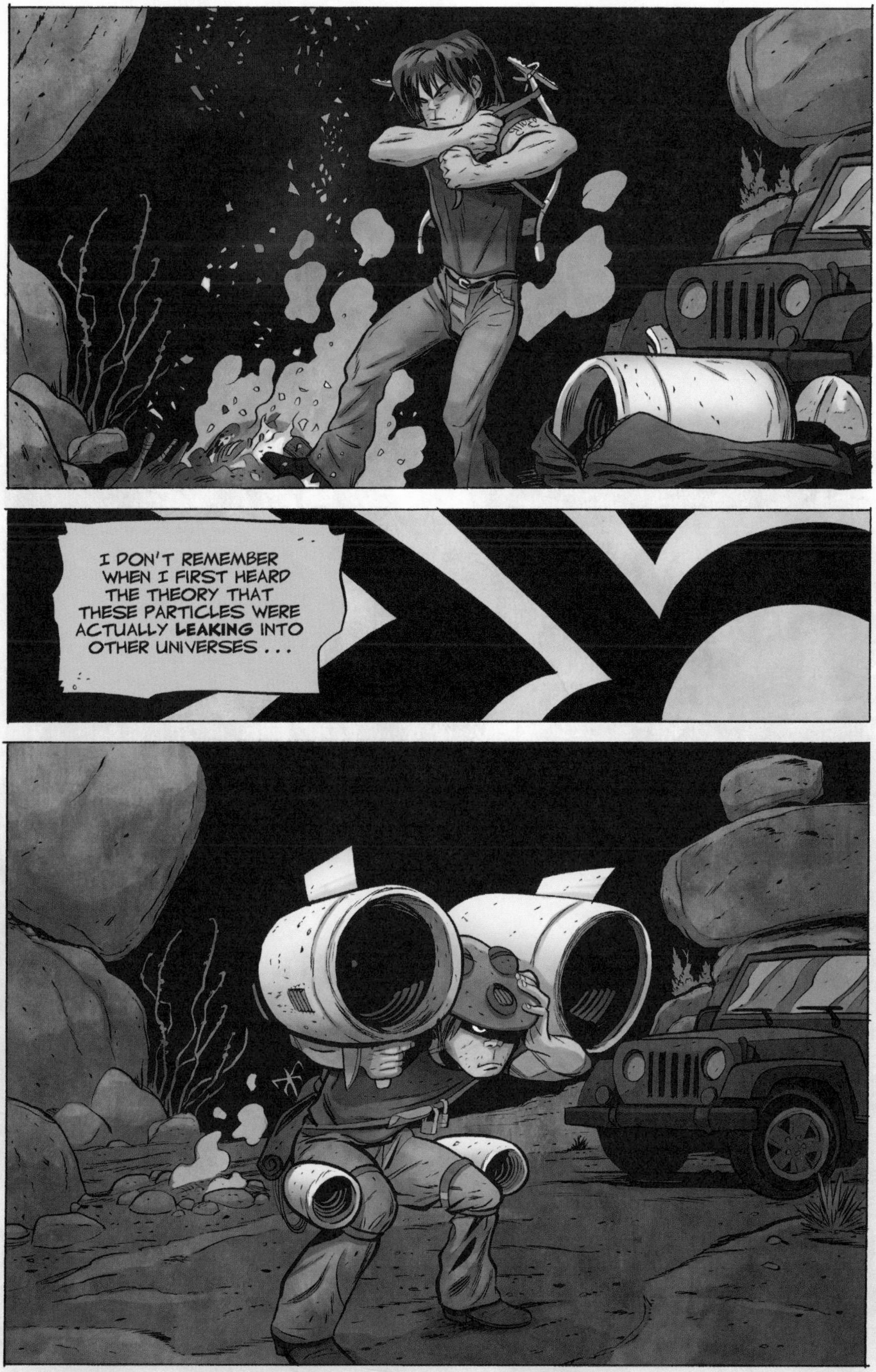
I DON'T REMEMBER WHEN I FIRST HEARD THE THEORY THAT THESE PARTICLES WERE ACTUALLY LEAKING INTO OTHER UNIVERSES . . .

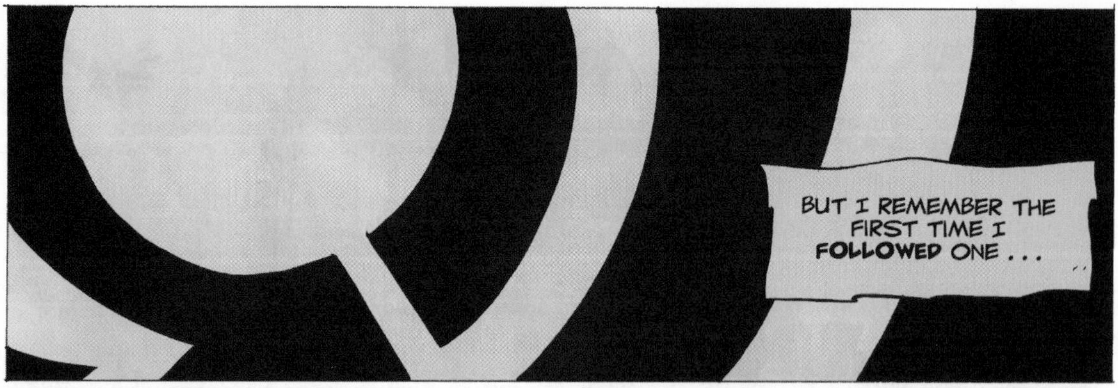
BUT I REMEMBER THE FIRST TIME I **FOLLOWED** ONE . . .

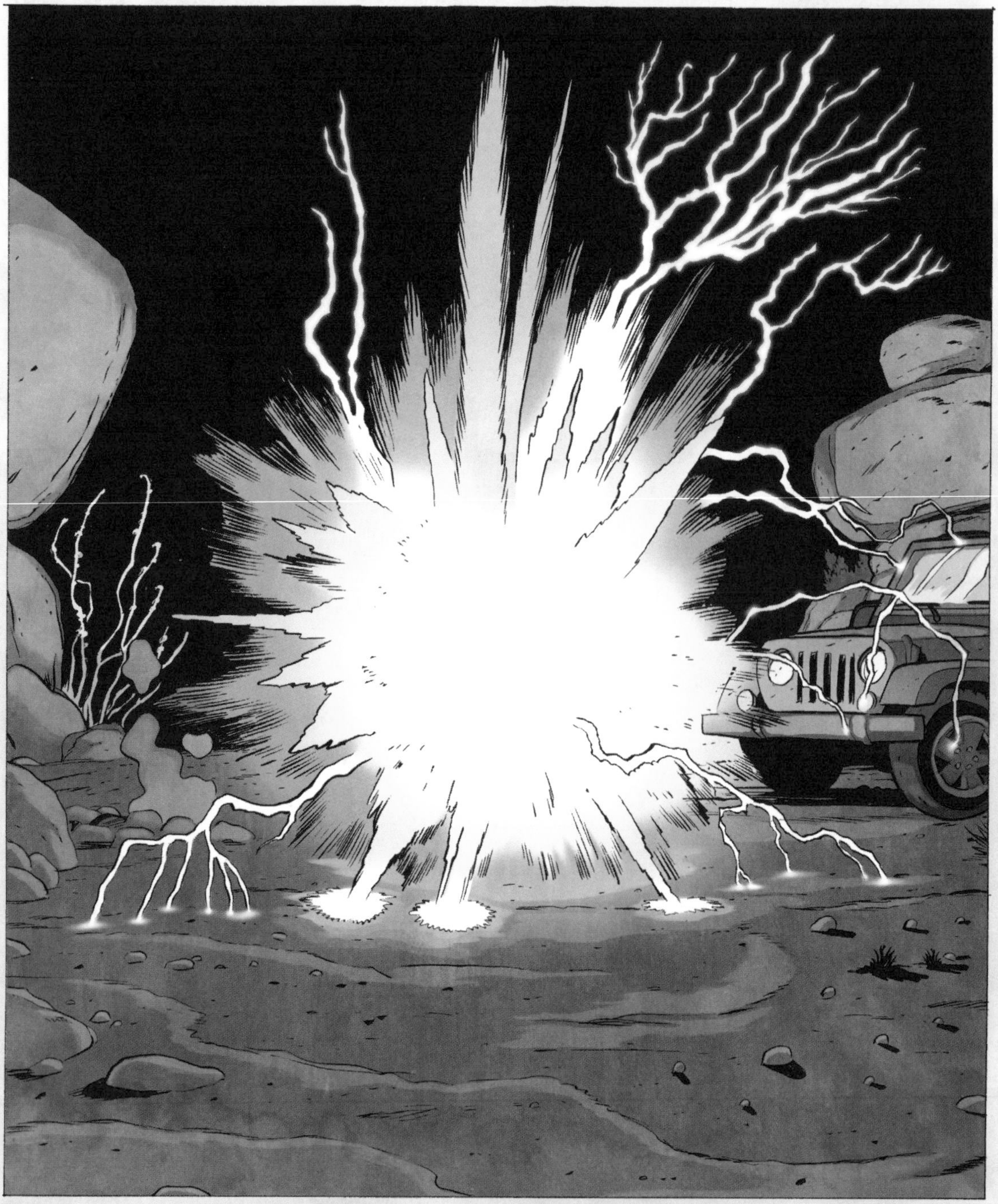

III

MAYA

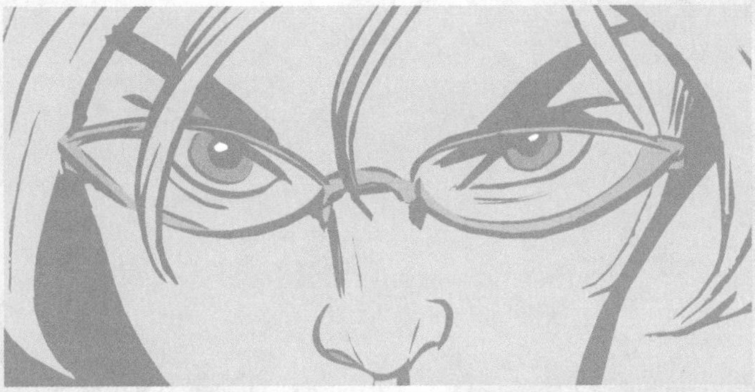

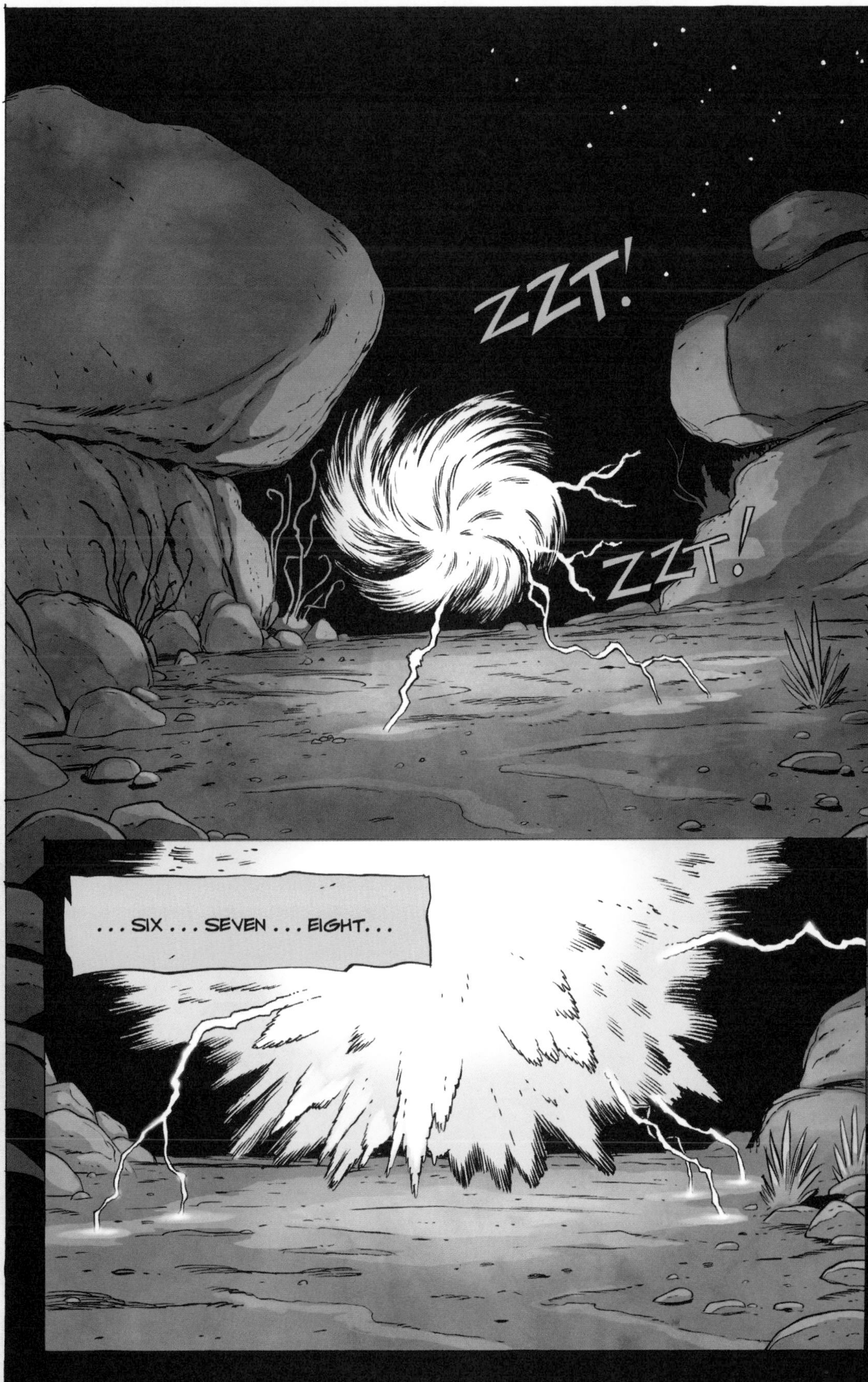
ZZT!
ZZT!
. . . SIX . . . SEVEN . . . EIGHT . . .

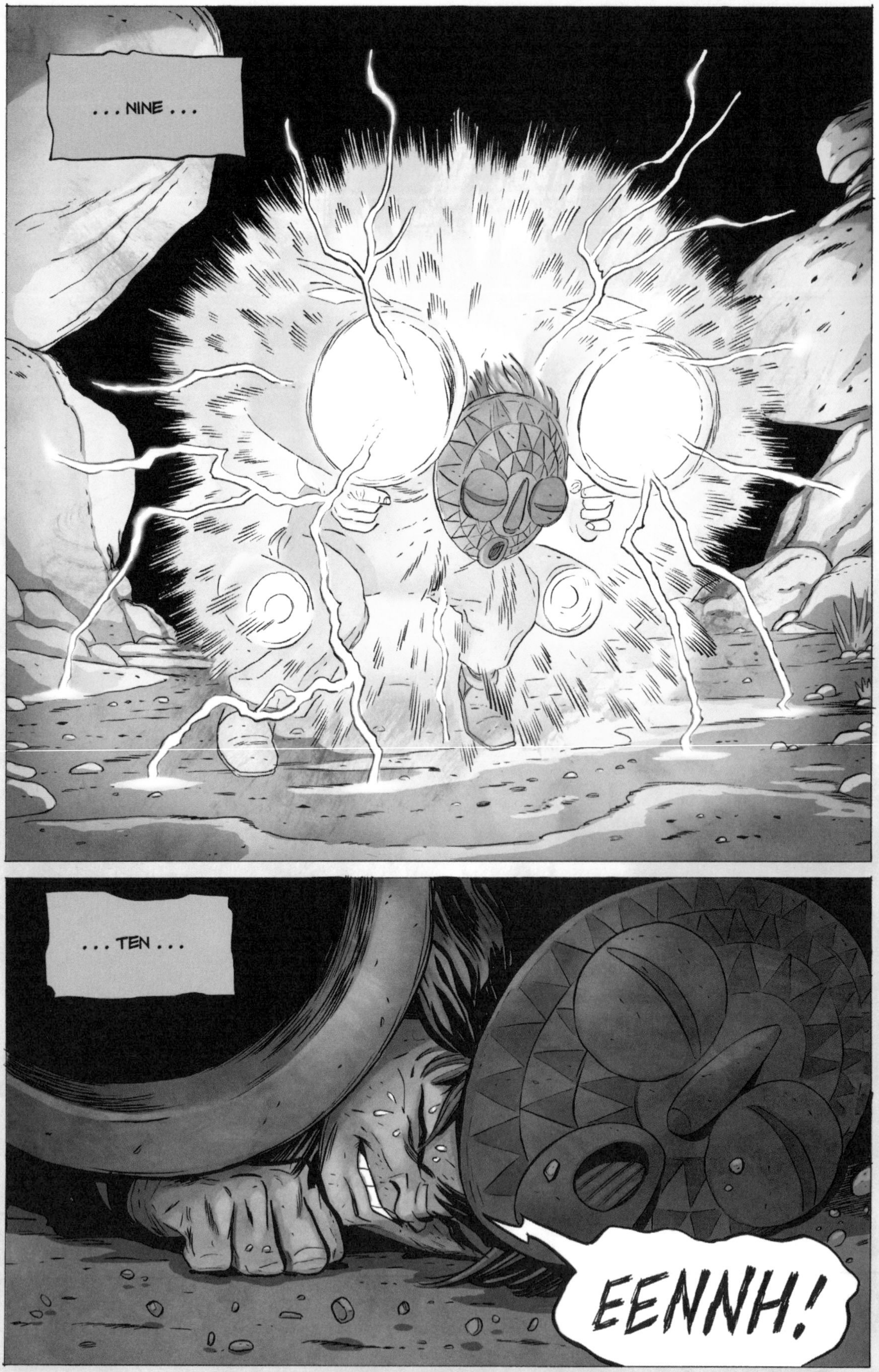
. . . NINE . . .
. . . TEN . . .
EENNH!

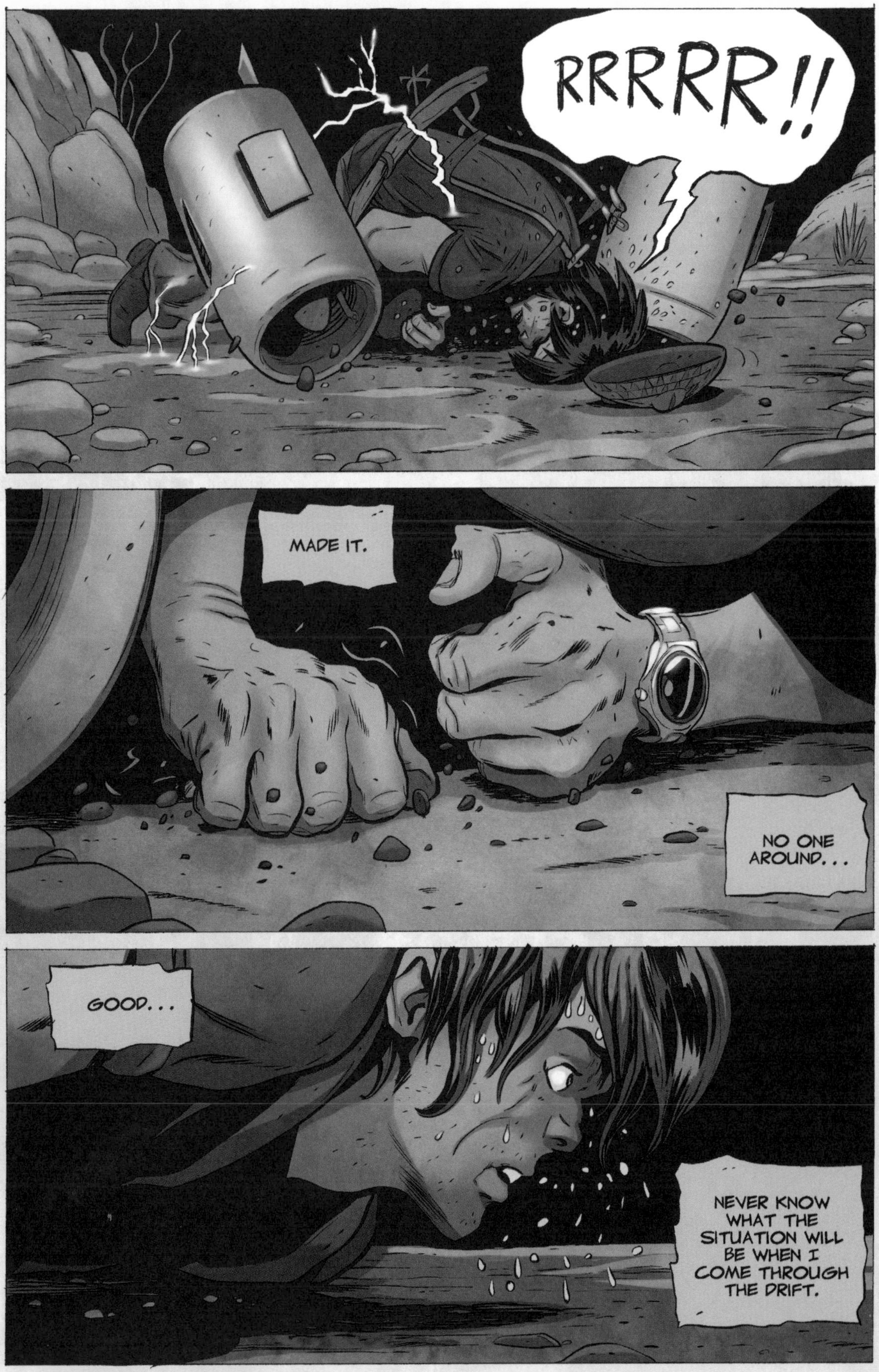
RRRRR!!
MADE IT.
NO ONE AROUND...
GOOD...
NEVER KNOW WHAT THE SITUATION WILL BE WHEN I COME THROUGH THE DRIFT.

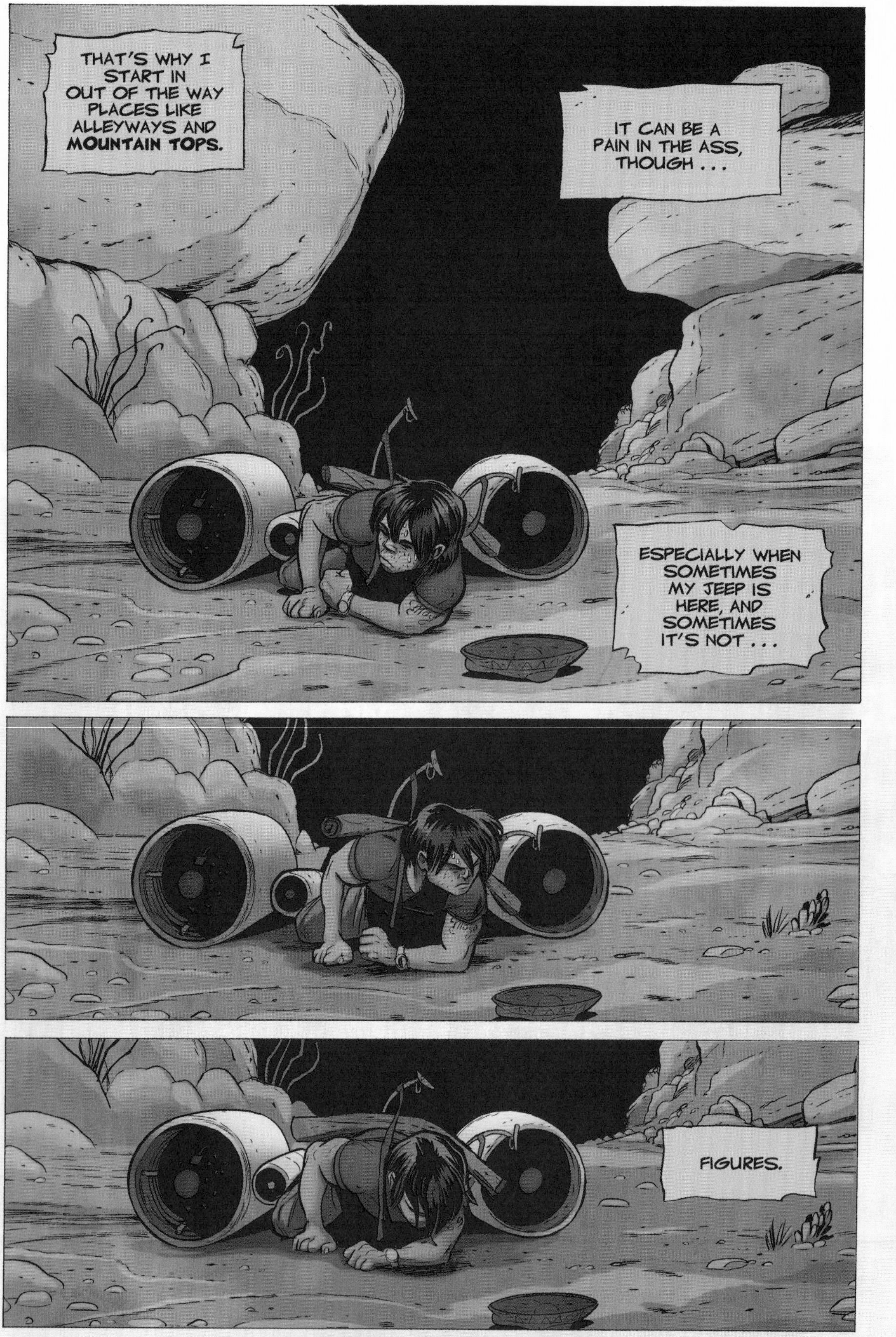
THAT'S WHY I START IN OUT OF THE WAY PLACES LIKE ALLEYWAYS AND **MOUNTAIN TOPS.**
IT CAN BE A PAIN IN THE ASS, THOUGH . . .
ESPECIALLY WHEN SOMETIMES MY JEEP IS HERE, AND SOMETIMES IT'S NOT . . .
FIGURES.

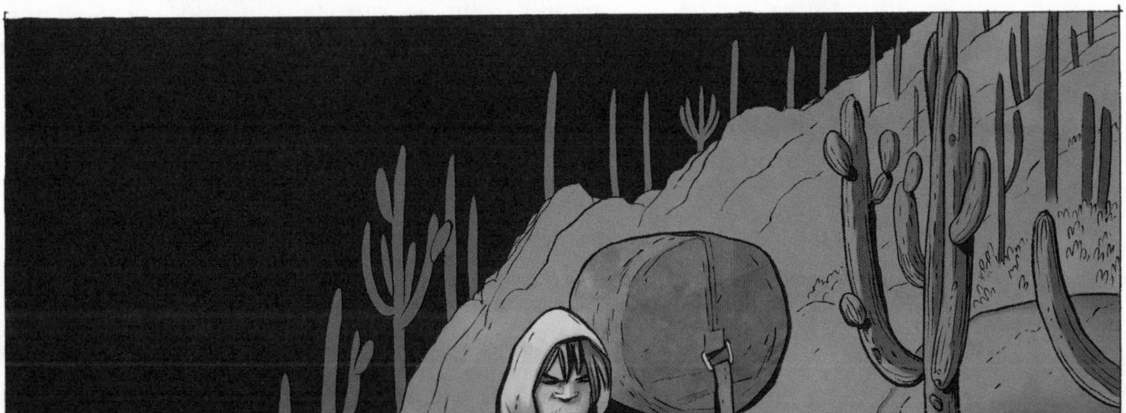
ANNIE'S KILLER COULD BE ANYWHERE . . .
BUT THIS IS THE PARALLEL WORLD WHERE HE FIRST ATTACKED ME,
WHY HERE?

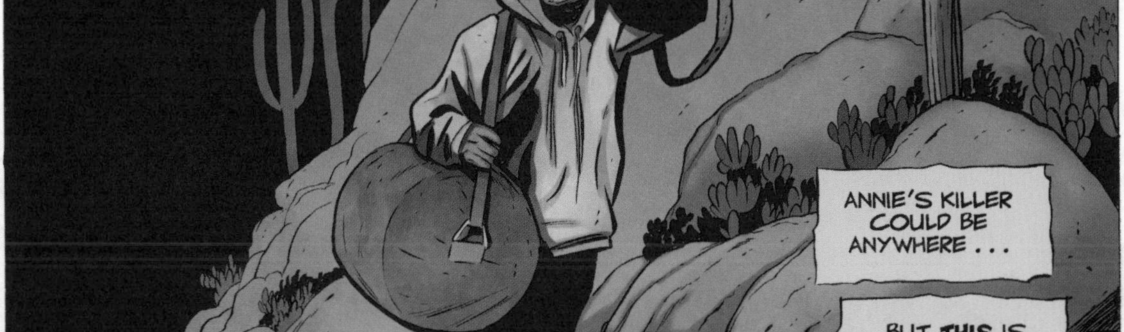
MAYBE IT WAS RANDOM.
I'VE DRIFTED DOZENS OF TIMES AND I STILL DON'T KNOW ALL THE RULES . . .

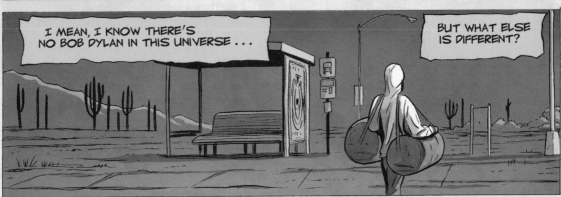

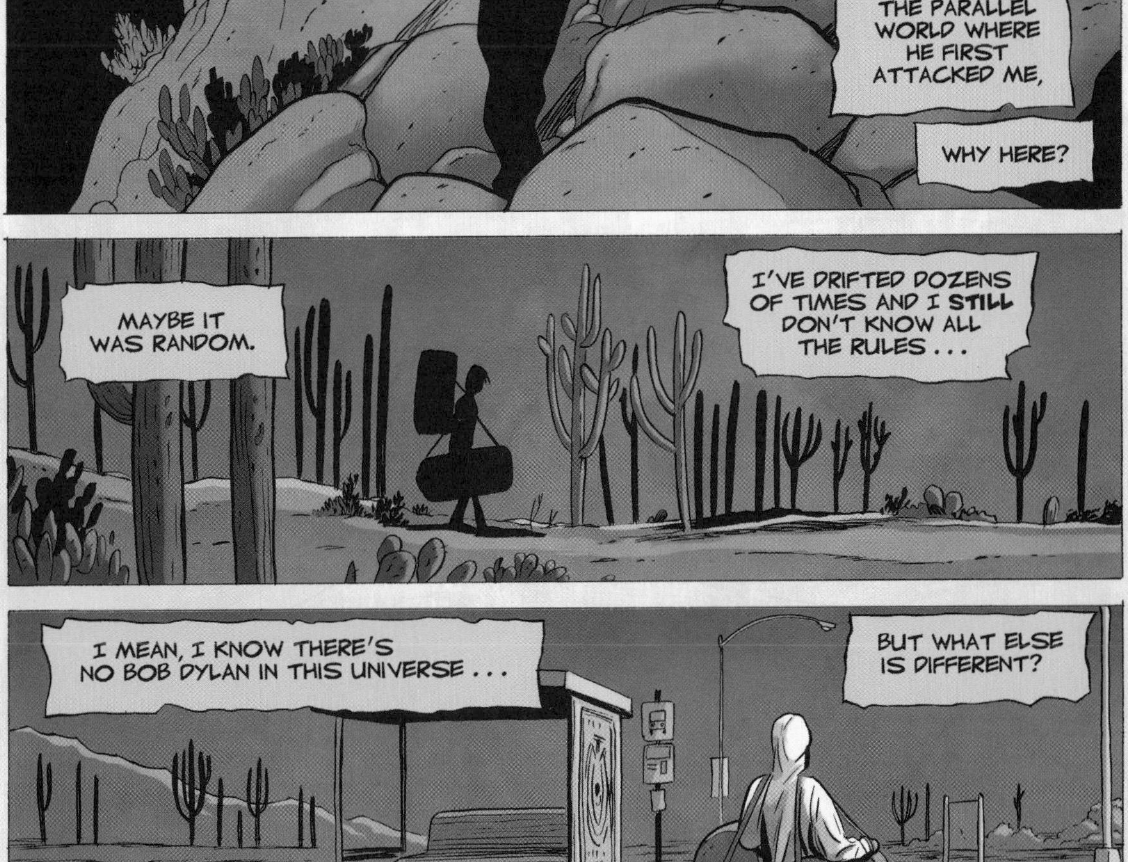
I MEAN, I KNOW THERE'S NO BOB DYLAN IN THIS UNIVERSE . . .
BUT WHAT ELSE IS DIFFERENT?

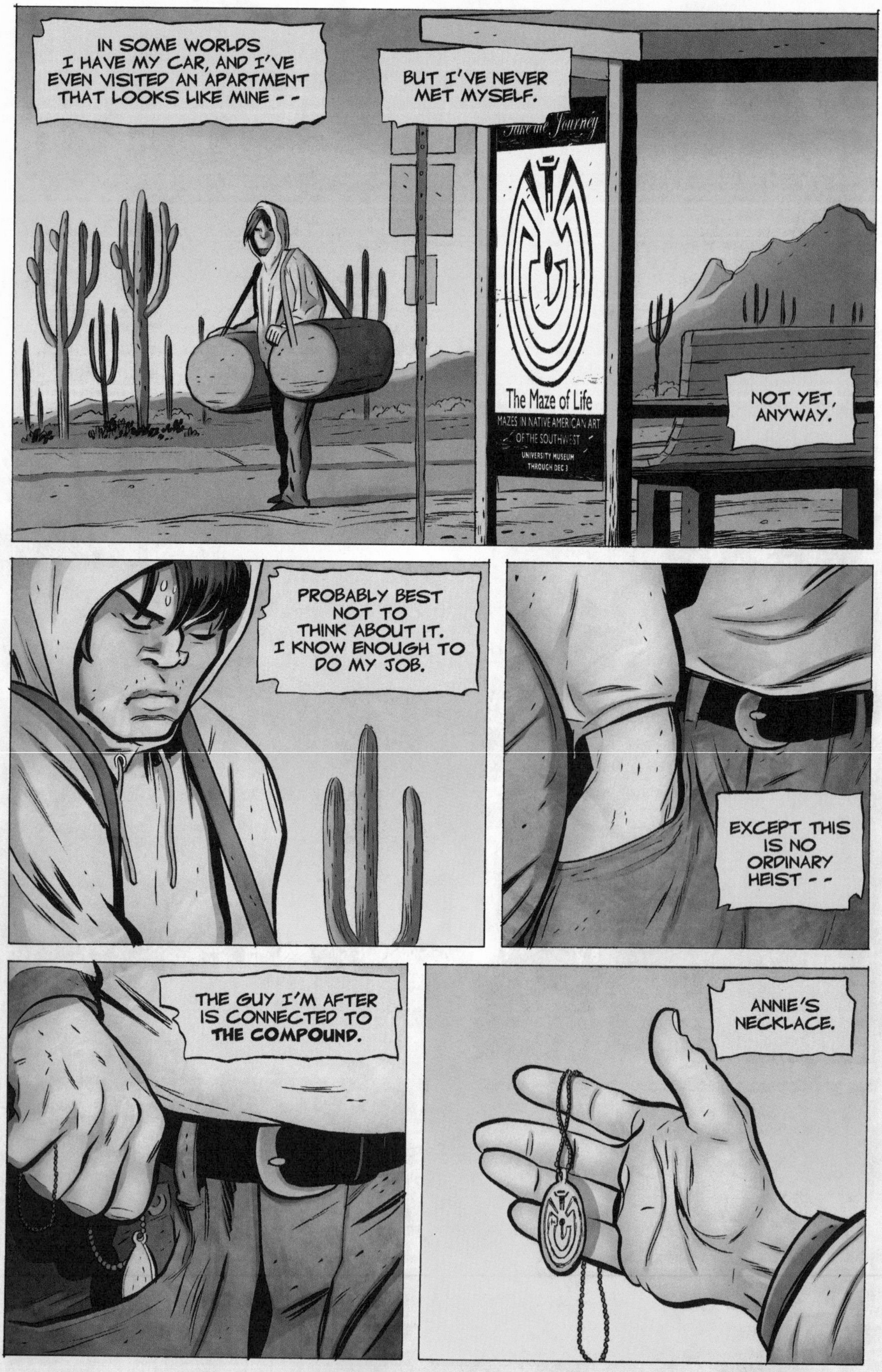
IN SOME WORLDS I HAVE MY CAR, AND I'VE EVEN VISITED AN APARTMENT THAT LOOKS LIKE MINE - -
BUT I'VE NEVER MET MYSELF.
The Maze of Life
MAZES IN NATIVE AMERICAN ART OF THE SOUTHWEST
UNIVERSITY MUSEUM
THROUGH DEC 3
NOT YET, ANYWAY.
PROBABLY BEST NOT TO THINK ABOUT IT. I KNOW ENOUGH TO DO MY JOB.
EXCEPT THIS IS NO ORDINARY HEIST - -
THE GUY I'M AFTER IS CONNECTED TO THE COMPOUND.
ANNIE'S NECKLACE.

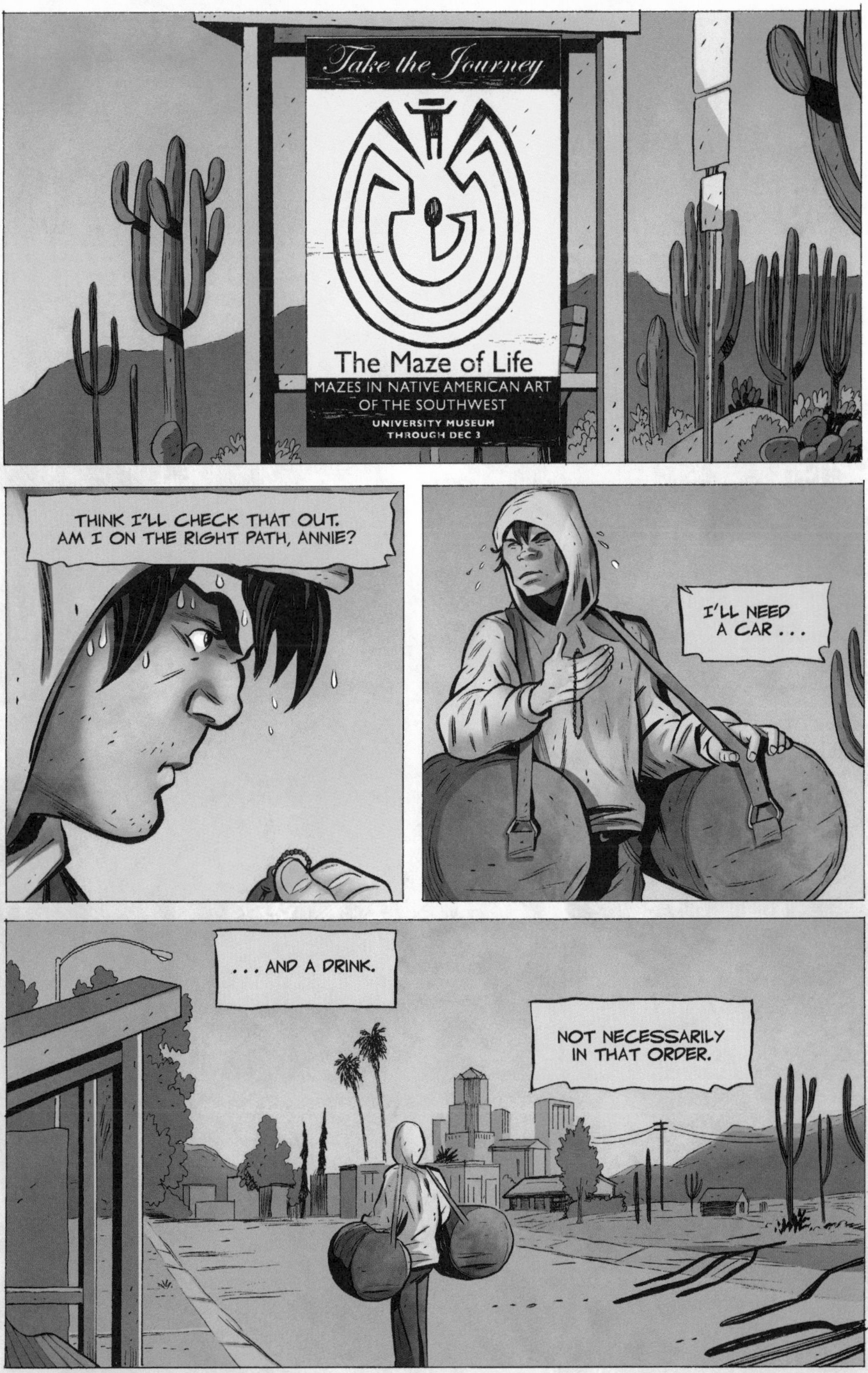
Take the Journey
The Maze of Life
MAZES IN NATIVE AMERICAN ART
OF THE SOUTHWEST
UNIVERSITY MUSEUM
THROUGH DEC 3
THINK I'LL CHECK THAT OUT.
AM I ON THE RIGHT PATH, ANNIE?
I'LL NEED
A CAR . . .
. . . AND A DRINK.
NOT NECESSARILY
IN THAT ORDER.

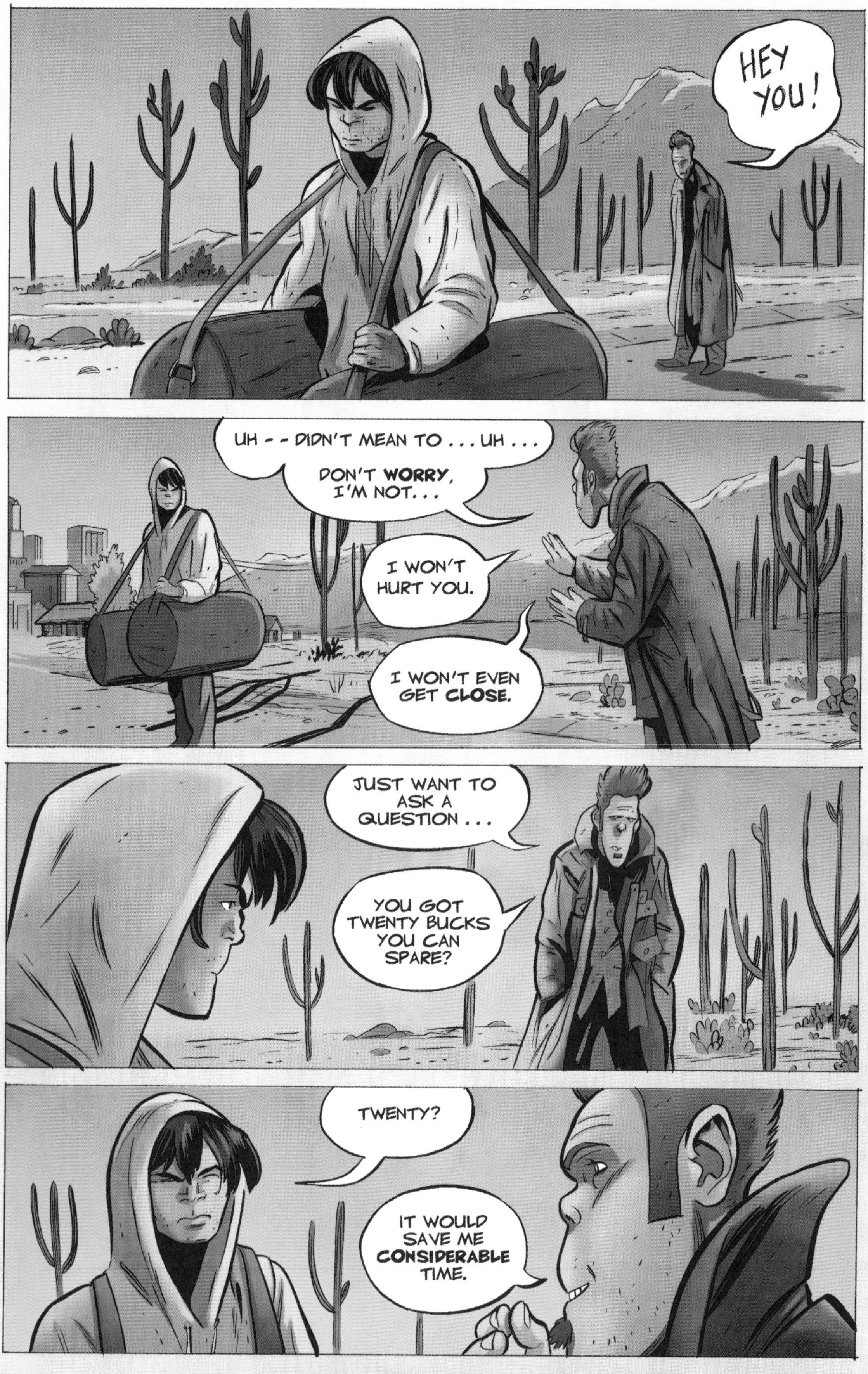
HEY YOU!
UH - - DIDN'T MEAN TO . . . UH . . .
DON'T WORRY, I'M NOT. . .
I WON'T HURT YOU.
I WON'T EVEN GET CLOSE.
JUST WANT TO ASK A QUESTION . . .
YOU GOT TWENTY BUCKS YOU CAN SPARE?
TWENTY?
IT WOULD SAVE ME CONSIDERABLE TIME.

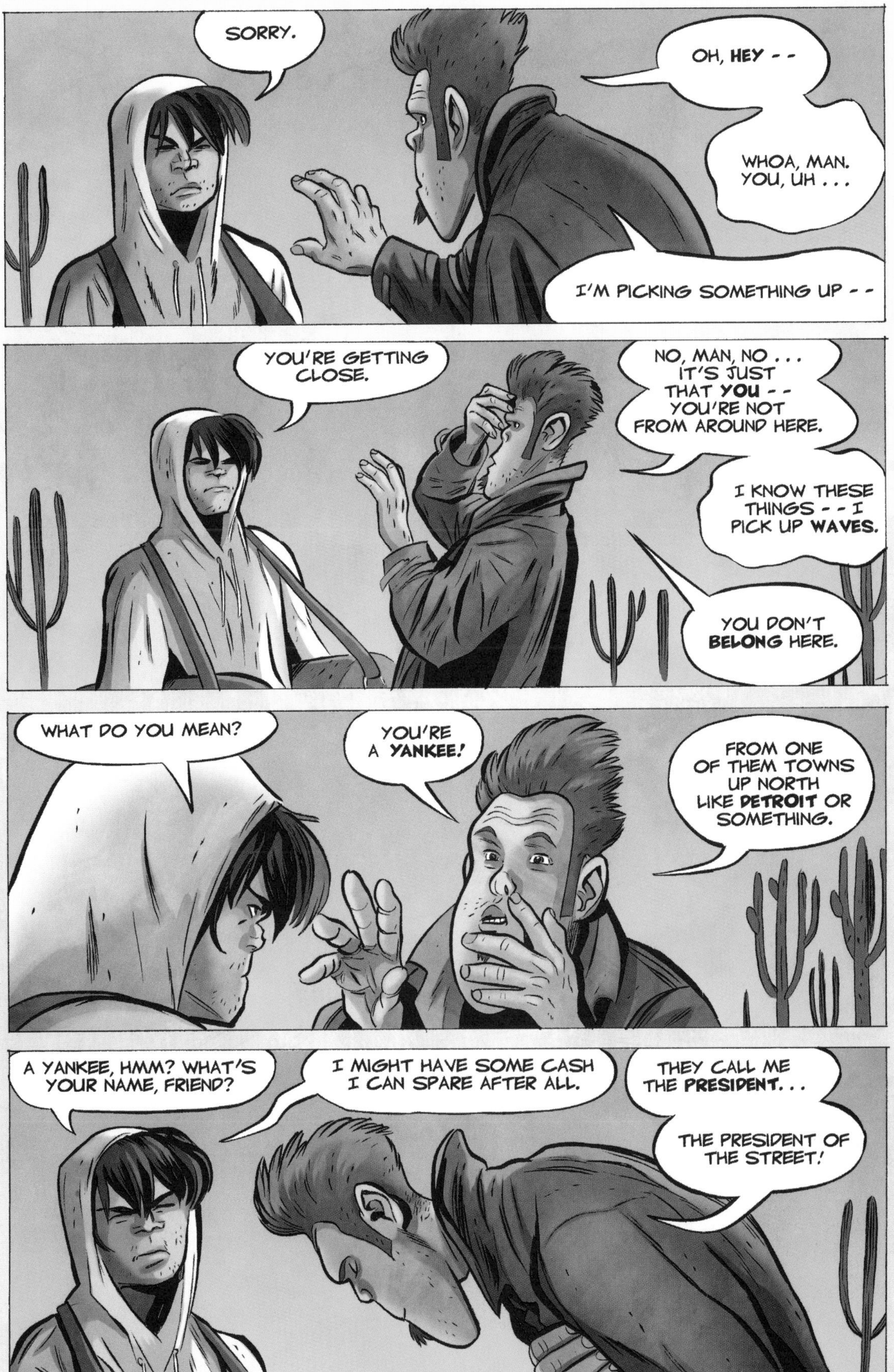
SORRY.
OH, HEY - -
WHOA, MAN. YOU, UH . . .
I'M PICKING SOMETHING UP - -
YOU'RE GETTING CLOSE.
NO, MAN, NO . . . IT'S JUST THAT YOU - - YOU'RE NOT FROM AROUND HERE.
I KNOW THESE THINGS - - I PICK UP WAVES.
YOU DON'T BELONG HERE.
WHAT DO YOU MEAN?
YOU'RE A YANKEE!
FROM ONE OF THEM TOWNS UP NORTH LIKE DETROIT OR SOMETHING.
A YANKEE, HMM? WHAT'S YOUR NAME, FRIEND?
I MIGHT HAVE SOME CASH I CAN SPARE AFTER ALL.
THEY CALL ME THE PRESIDENT. . .
THE PRESIDENT OF THE STREET!

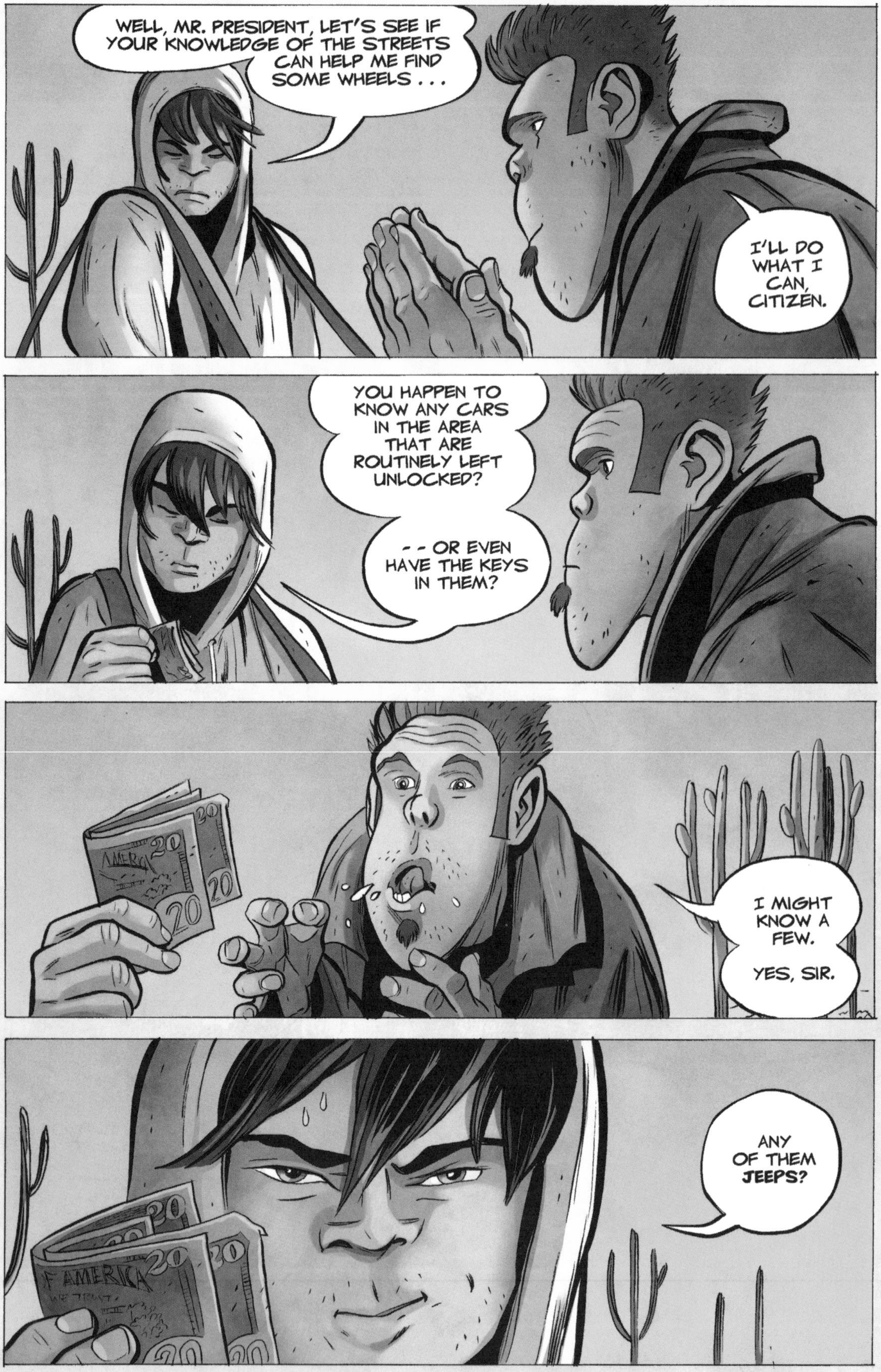
WELL, MR. PRESIDENT, LET'S SEE IF YOUR KNOWLEDGE OF THE STREETS CAN HELP ME FIND SOME WHEELS . . .
I'LL DO WHAT I CAN, CITIZEN.
YOU HAPPEN TO KNOW ANY CARS IN THE AREA THAT ARE ROUTINELY LEFT UNLOCKED?
- - OR EVEN HAVE THE KEYS IN THEM?
I MIGHT KNOW A FEW.
YES, SIR.
ANY OF THEM JEEPS?

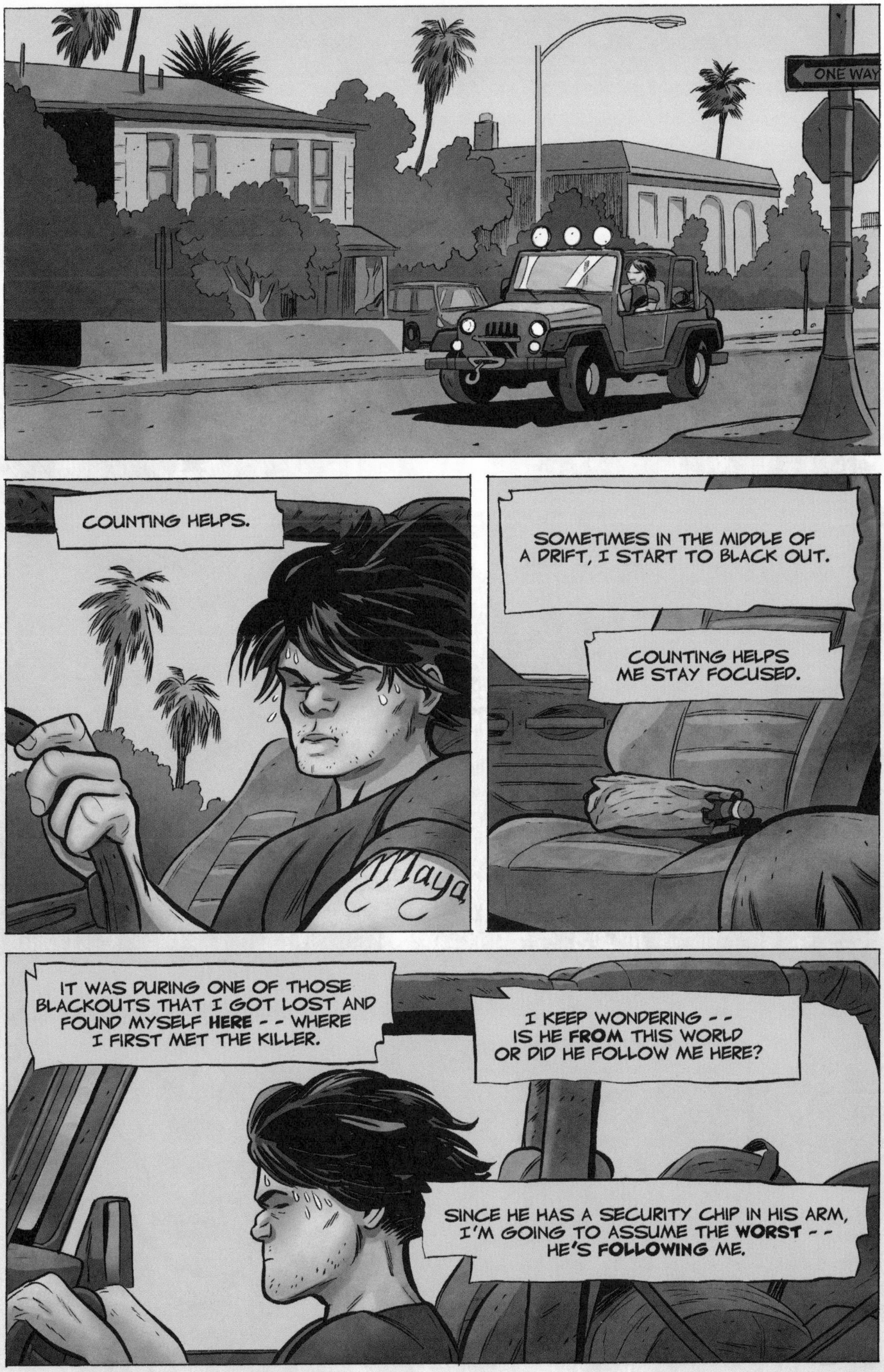
ONE WAY
COUNTING HELPS.
SOMETIMES IN THE MIDDLE OF A DRIFT, I START TO BLACK OUT.
COUNTING HELPS ME STAY FOCUSED.
Maya
IT WAS DURING ONE OF THOSE BLACKOUTS THAT I GOT LOST AND FOUND MYSELF HERE - - WHERE I FIRST MET THE KILLER.
I KEEP WONDERING - - IS HE FROM THIS WORLD OR DID HE FOLLOW ME HERE?
SINCE HE HAS A SECURITY CHIP IN HIS ARM, I'M GOING TO ASSUME THE WORST - - HE'S FOLLOWING ME.

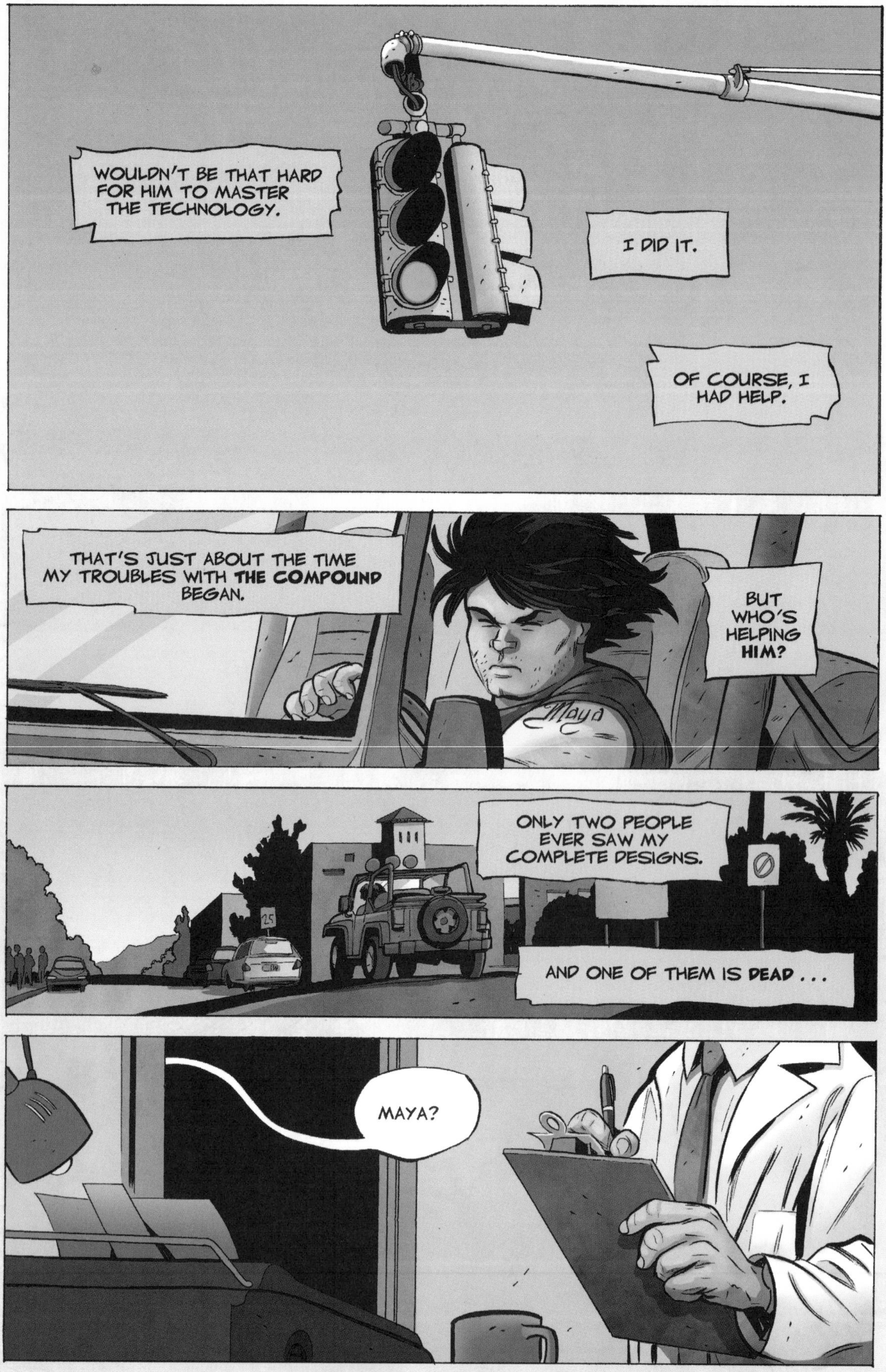
WOULDN'T BE THAT HARD FOR HIM TO MASTER THE TECHNOLOGY.
I DID IT.
OF COURSE, I HAD HELP.
THAT'S JUST ABOUT THE TIME MY TROUBLES WITH **THE COMPOUND** BEGAN.
BUT WHO'S HELPING **HIM?**
Maya
ONLY TWO PEOPLE EVER SAW MY COMPLETE DESIGNS.
25
AND ONE OF THEM IS **DEAD . . .**
MAYA?

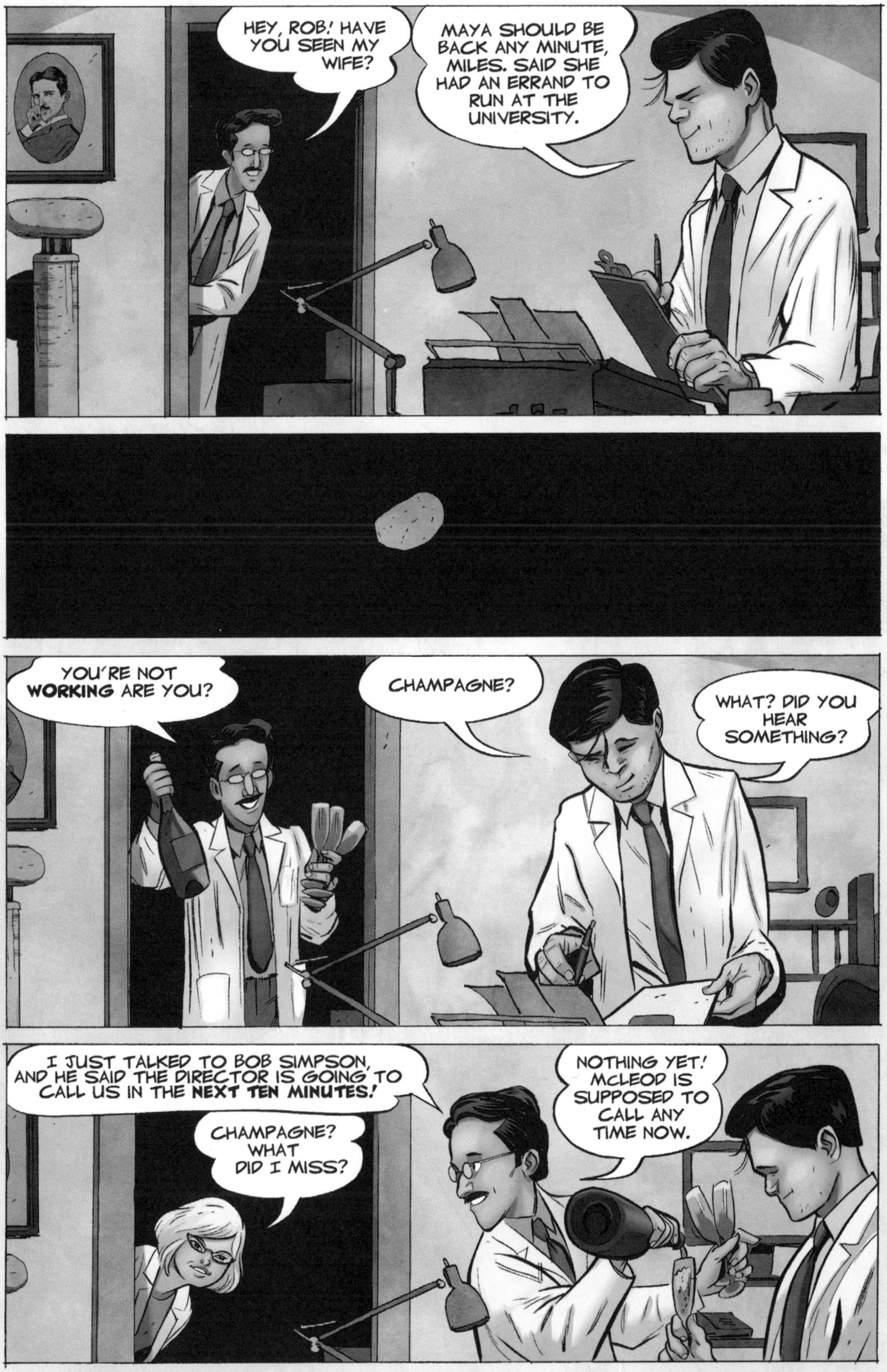
HEY, ROB! HAVE YOU SEEN MY WIFE?
MAYA SHOULD BE BACK ANY MINUTE, MILES. SAID SHE HAD AN ERRAND TO RUN AT THE UNIVERSITY.
YOU'RE NOT WORKING ARE YOU?
CHAMPAGNE?
WHAT? DID YOU HEAR SOMETHING?
I JUST TALKED TO BOB SIMPSON, AND HE SAID THE DIRECTOR IS GOING TO CALL US IN THE NEXT TEN MINUTES!
CHAMPAGNE? WHAT DID I MISS?
NOTHING YET! McLEOD IS SUPPOSED TO CALL ANY TIME NOW.

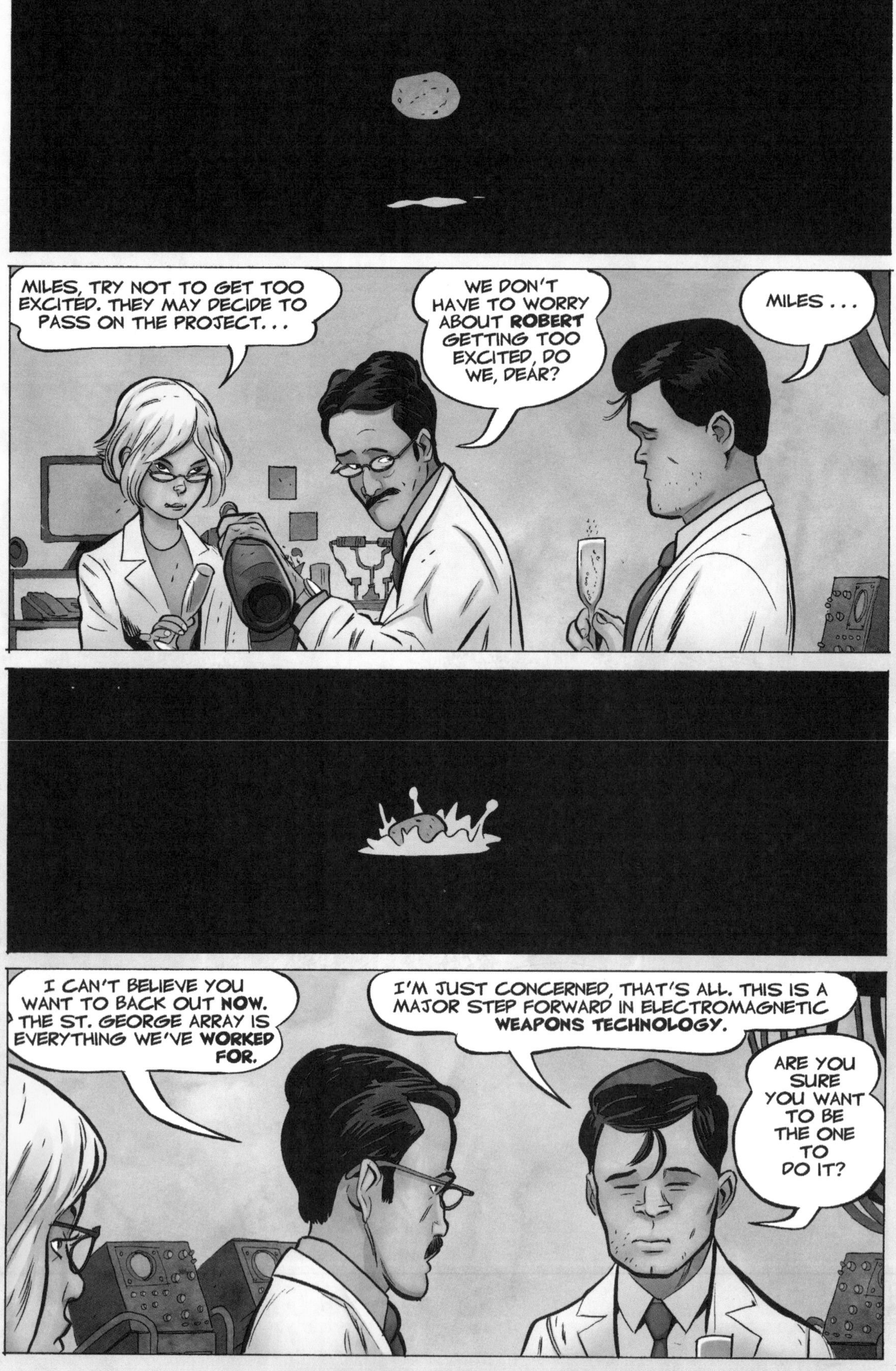
MILES, TRY NOT TO GET TOO EXCITED. THEY MAY DECIDE TO PASS ON THE PROJECT...
WE DON'T HAVE TO WORRY ABOUT **ROBERT** GETTING TOO EXCITED, DO WE, DEAR?
MILES...
I CAN'T BELIEVE YOU WANT TO BACK OUT **NOW**. THE ST. GEORGE ARRAY IS EVERYTHING WE'VE **WORKED FOR.**
I'M JUST CONCERNED, THAT'S ALL. THIS IS A MAJOR STEP FORWARD IN ELECTROMAGNETIC **WEAPONS TECHNOLOGY.**
ARE YOU SURE YOU WANT TO BE THE ONE TO DO IT?

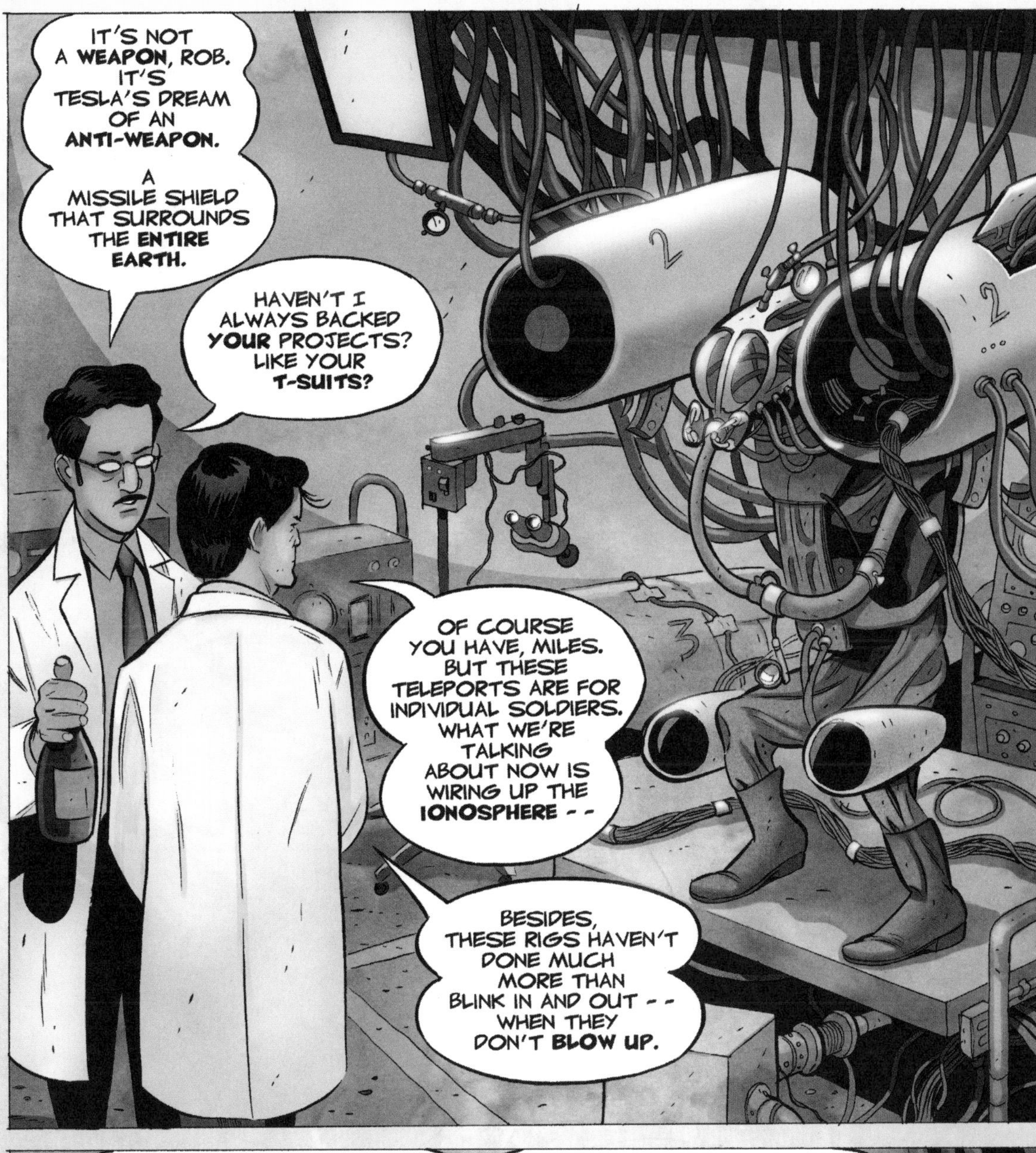
IT'S NOT A WEAPON, ROB. IT'S TESLA'S DREAM OF AN ANTI-WEAPON.
A MISSILE SHIELD THAT SURROUNDS THE ENTIRE EARTH.
HAVEN'T I ALWAYS BACKED YOUR PROJECTS? LIKE YOUR T-SUITS?
OF COURSE YOU HAVE, MILES. BUT THESE TELEPORTS ARE FOR INDIVIDUAL SOLDIERS. WHAT WE'RE TALKING ABOUT NOW IS WIRING UP THE IONOSPHERE - -
BESIDES, THESE RIGS HAVEN'T DONE MUCH MORE THAN BLINK IN AND OUT - - WHEN THEY DON'T BLOW UP.
2
2
3

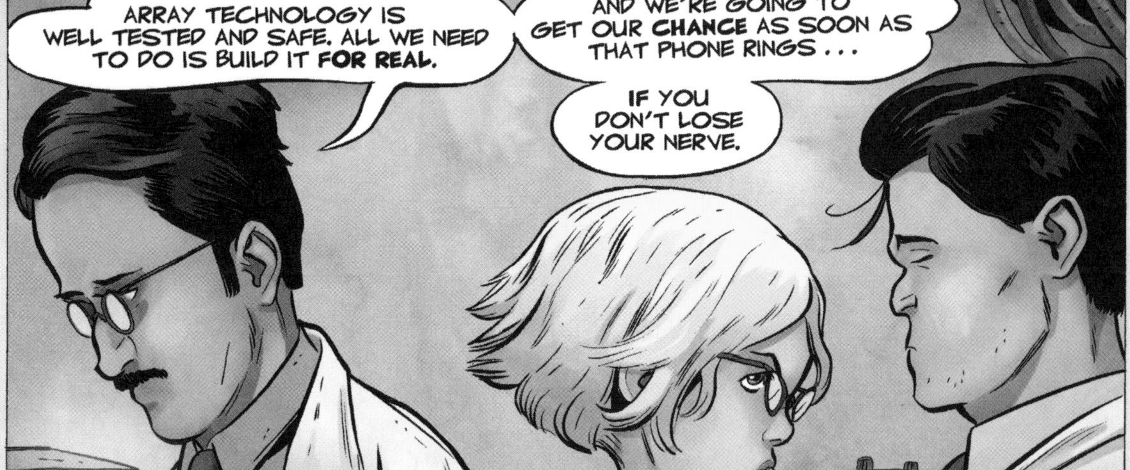
ARRAY TECHNOLOGY IS WELL TESTED AND SAFE. ALL WE NEED TO DO IS BUILD IT FOR REAL.
AND WE'RE GOING TO GET OUR CHANCE AS SOON AS THAT PHONE RINGS . . .
IF YOU DON'T LOSE YOUR NERVE.

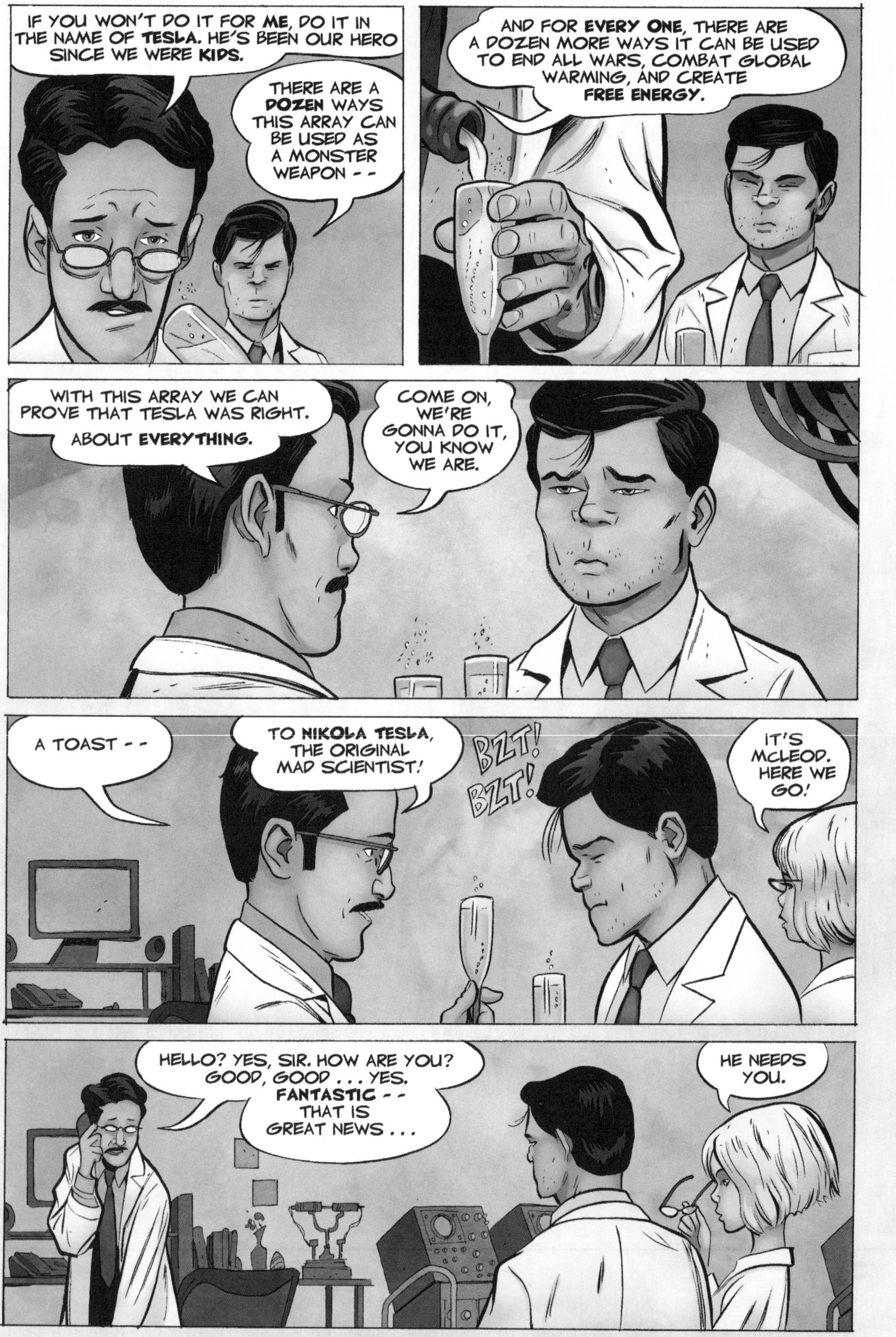
IF YOU WON'T DO IT FOR ME, DO IT IN THE NAME OF TESLA. HE'S BEEN OUR HERO SINCE WE WERE KIDS.
THERE ARE A DOZEN WAYS THIS ARRAY CAN BE USED AS A MONSTER WEAPON - -
AND FOR EVERY ONE, THERE ARE A DOZEN MORE WAYS IT CAN BE USED TO END ALL WARS, COMBAT GLOBAL WARMING, AND CREATE FREE ENERGY.
WITH THIS ARRAY WE CAN PROVE THAT TESLA WAS RIGHT. ABOUT EVERYTHING.
COME ON, WE'RE GONNA DO IT, YOU KNOW WE ARE.
A TOAST - -
TO NIKOLA TESLA, THE ORIGINAL MAD SCIENTIST!
BZT! BZT!
IT'S MCLEOD. HERE WE GO!
HELLO? YES, SIR. HOW ARE YOU? GOOD, GOOD . . . YES. FANTASTIC - - THAT IS GREAT NEWS . . .
HE NEEDS YOU.

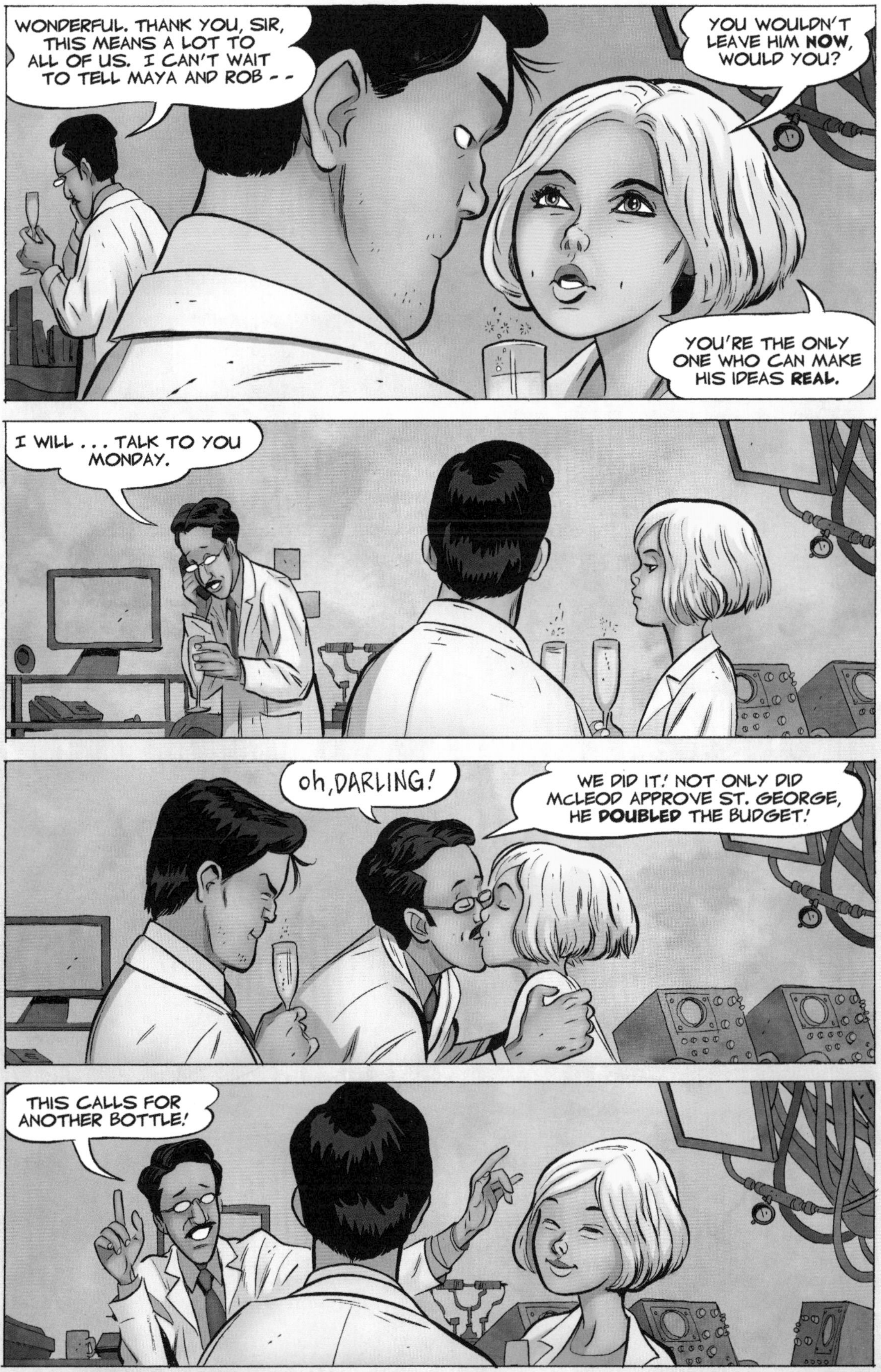
WONDERFUL. THANK YOU, SIR, THIS MEANS A LOT TO ALL OF US. I CAN'T WAIT TO TELL MAYA AND ROB - -
YOU WOULDN'T LEAVE HIM NOW, WOULD YOU?
YOU'RE THE ONLY ONE WHO CAN MAKE HIS IDEAS REAL.
I WILL . . . TALK TO YOU MONDAY.
oh, DARLING!
WE DID IT! NOT ONLY DID McLEOD APPROVE ST. GEORGE, HE DOUBLED THE BUDGET!
THIS CALLS FOR ANOTHER BOTTLE!

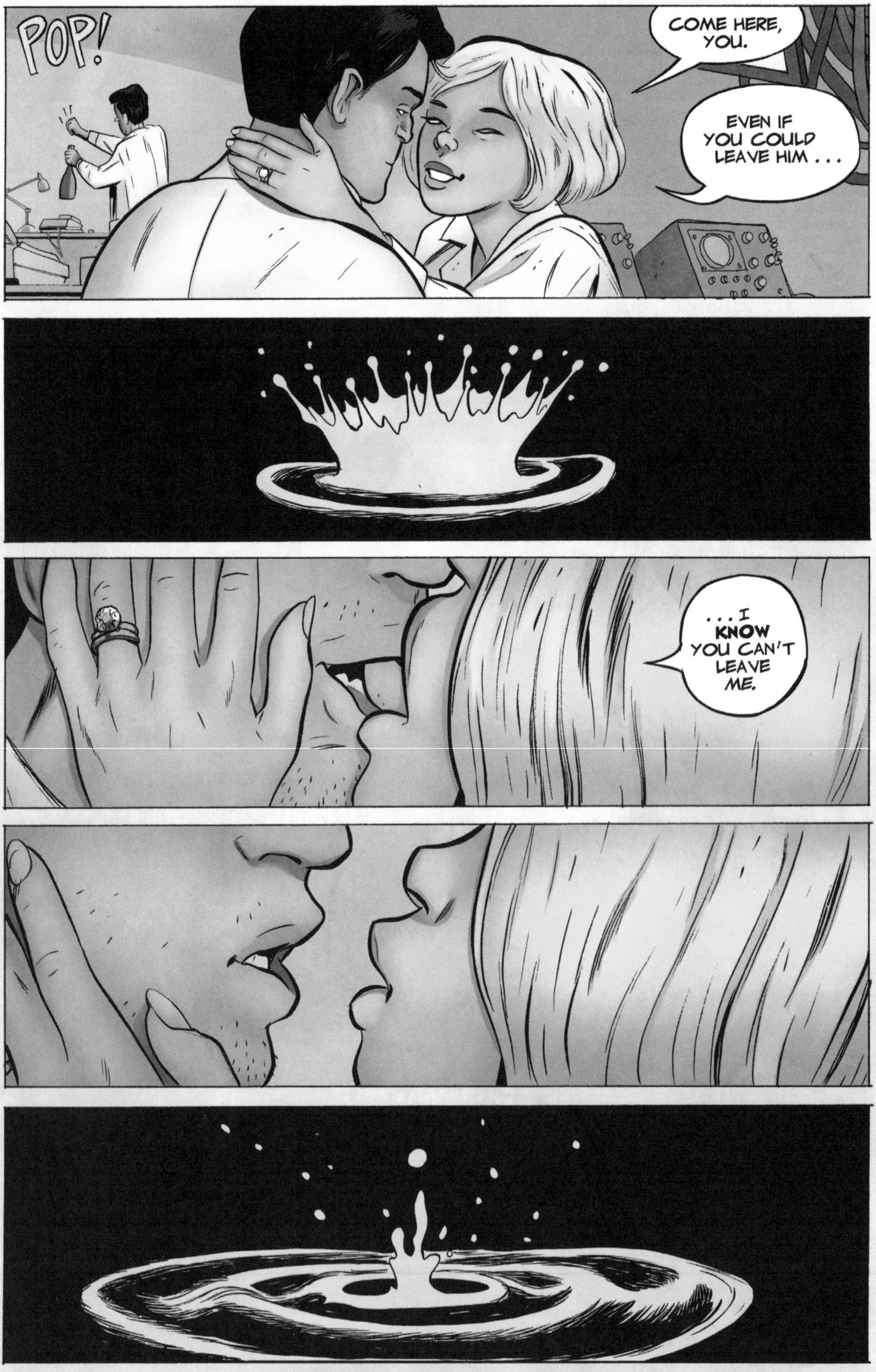
POP!
COME HERE, YOU.
EVEN IF YOU COULD LEAVE HIM . . .
. . . I **KNOW** YOU CAN'T LEAVE ME.

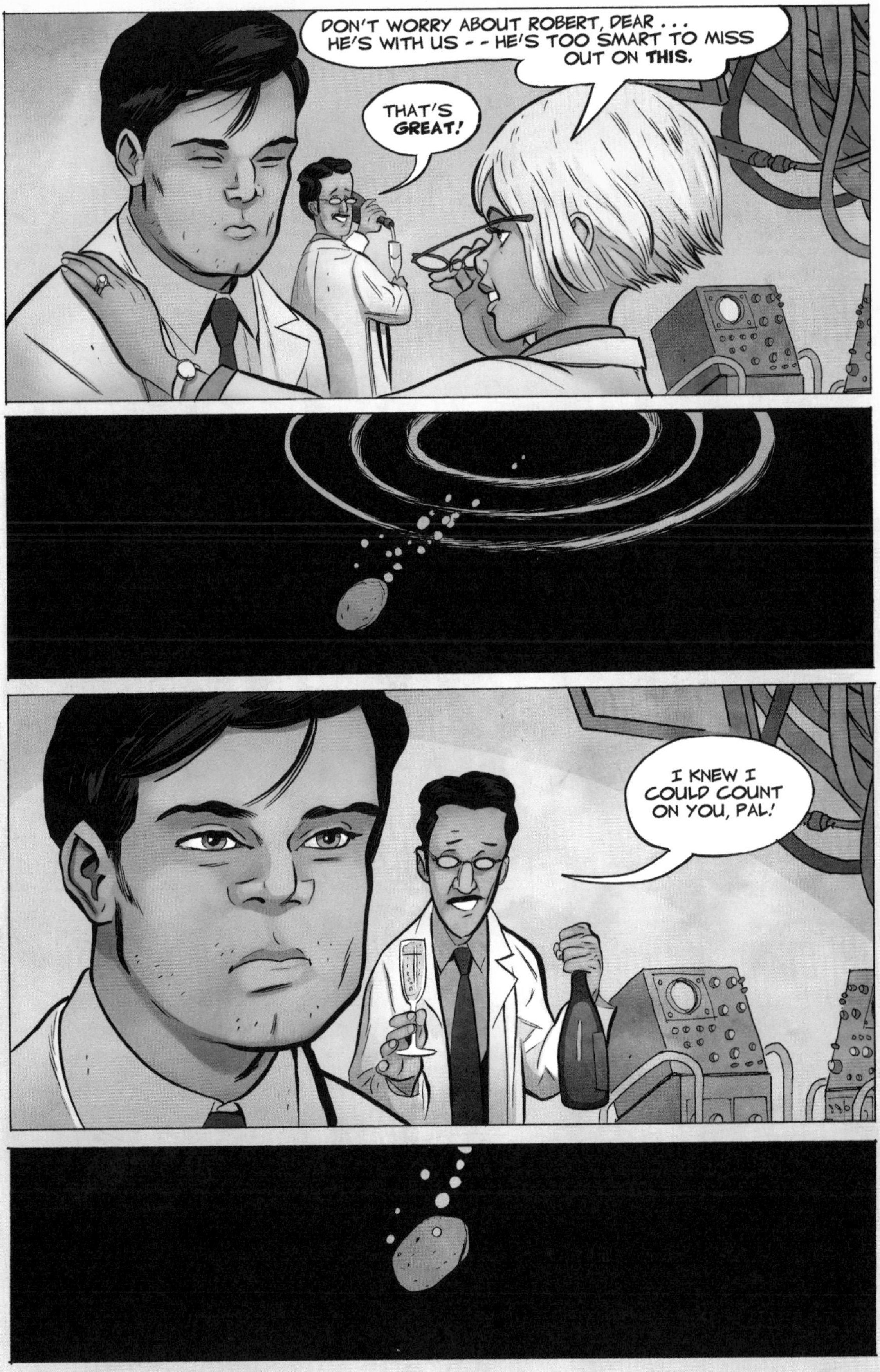
DON'T WORRY ABOUT ROBERT, DEAR . . . HE'S WITH US - - HE'S TOO SMART TO MISS OUT ON THIS.
THAT'S GREAT!
I KNEW I COULD COUNT ON YOU, PAL!

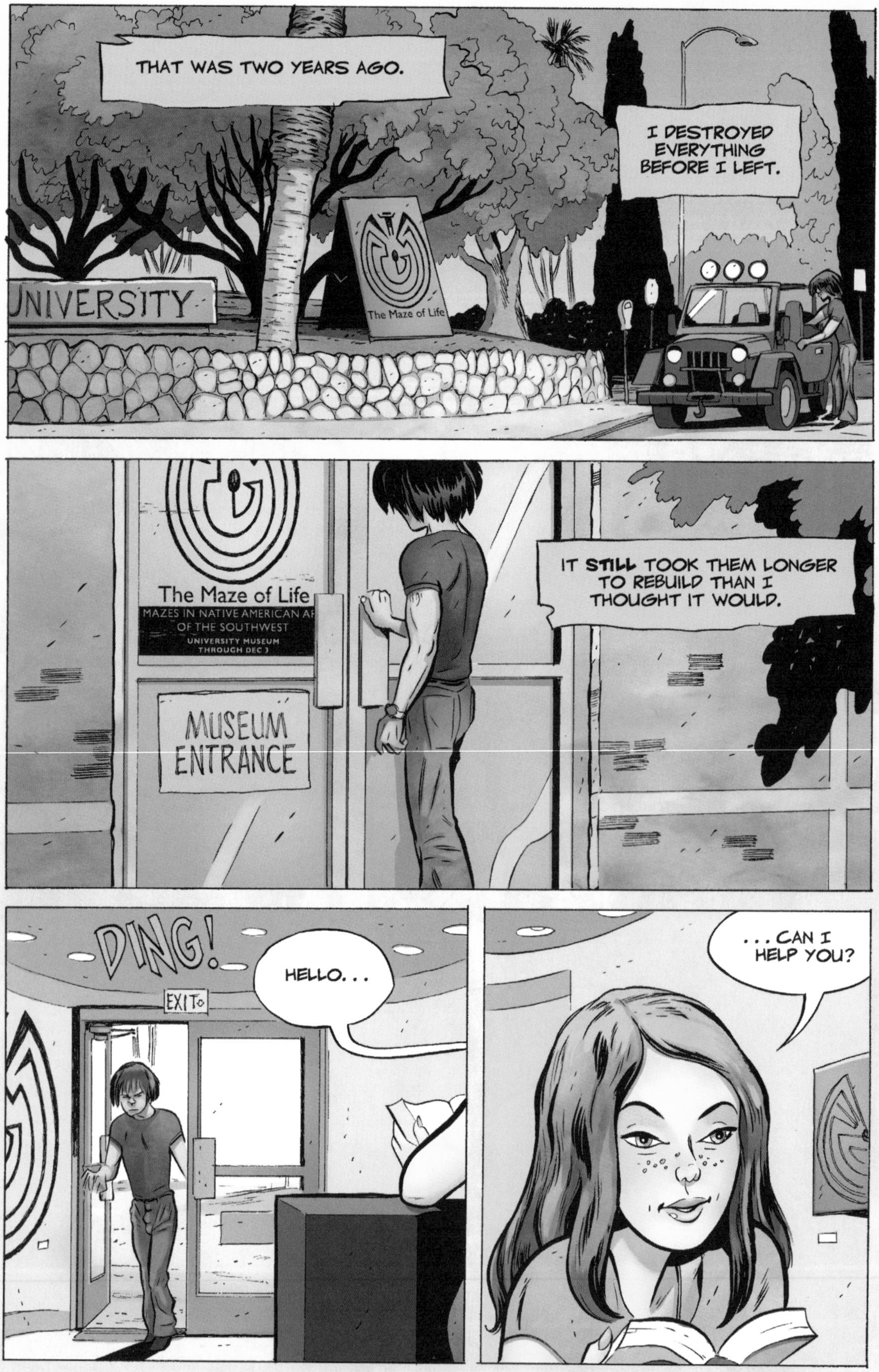
THAT WAS TWO YEARS AGO.
I DESTROYED EVERYTHING BEFORE I LEFT.
UNIVERSITY
The Maze of Life
The Maze of Life
MAZES IN NATIVE AMERICAN AR
OF THE SOUTHWEST
UNIVERSITY MUSEUM
THROUGH DEC 3
MUSEUM ENTRANCE
IT STILL TOOK THEM LONGER TO REBUILD THAN I THOUGHT IT WOULD.
DING!
EXIT
HELLO. . .
. . . CAN I HELP YOU?

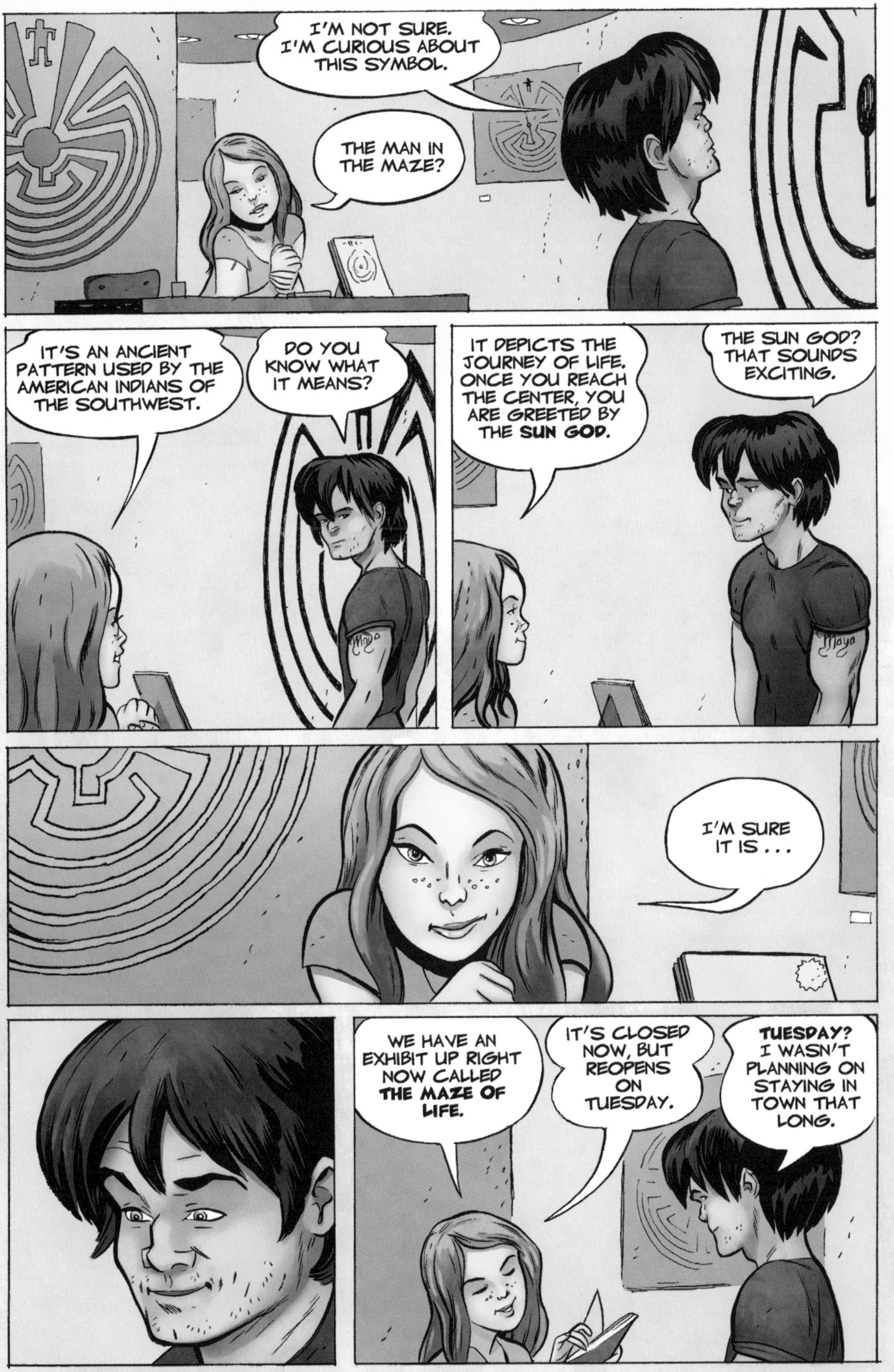
I'M NOT SURE. I'M CURIOUS ABOUT THIS SYMBOL.
THE MAN IN THE MAZE?
IT'S AN ANCIENT PATTERN USED BY THE AMERICAN INDIANS OF THE SOUTHWEST.
DO YOU KNOW WHAT IT MEANS?
IT DEPICTS THE JOURNEY OF LIFE. ONCE YOU REACH THE CENTER, YOU ARE GREETED BY THE **SUN GOD**.
THE SUN GOD? THAT SOUNDS EXCITING.
I'M SURE IT IS . . .
WE HAVE AN EXHIBIT UP RIGHT NOW CALLED **THE MAZE OF LIFE.**
IT'S CLOSED NOW, BUT REOPENS ON TUESDAY.
TUESDAY? I WASN'T PLANNING ON STAYING IN TOWN THAT LONG.

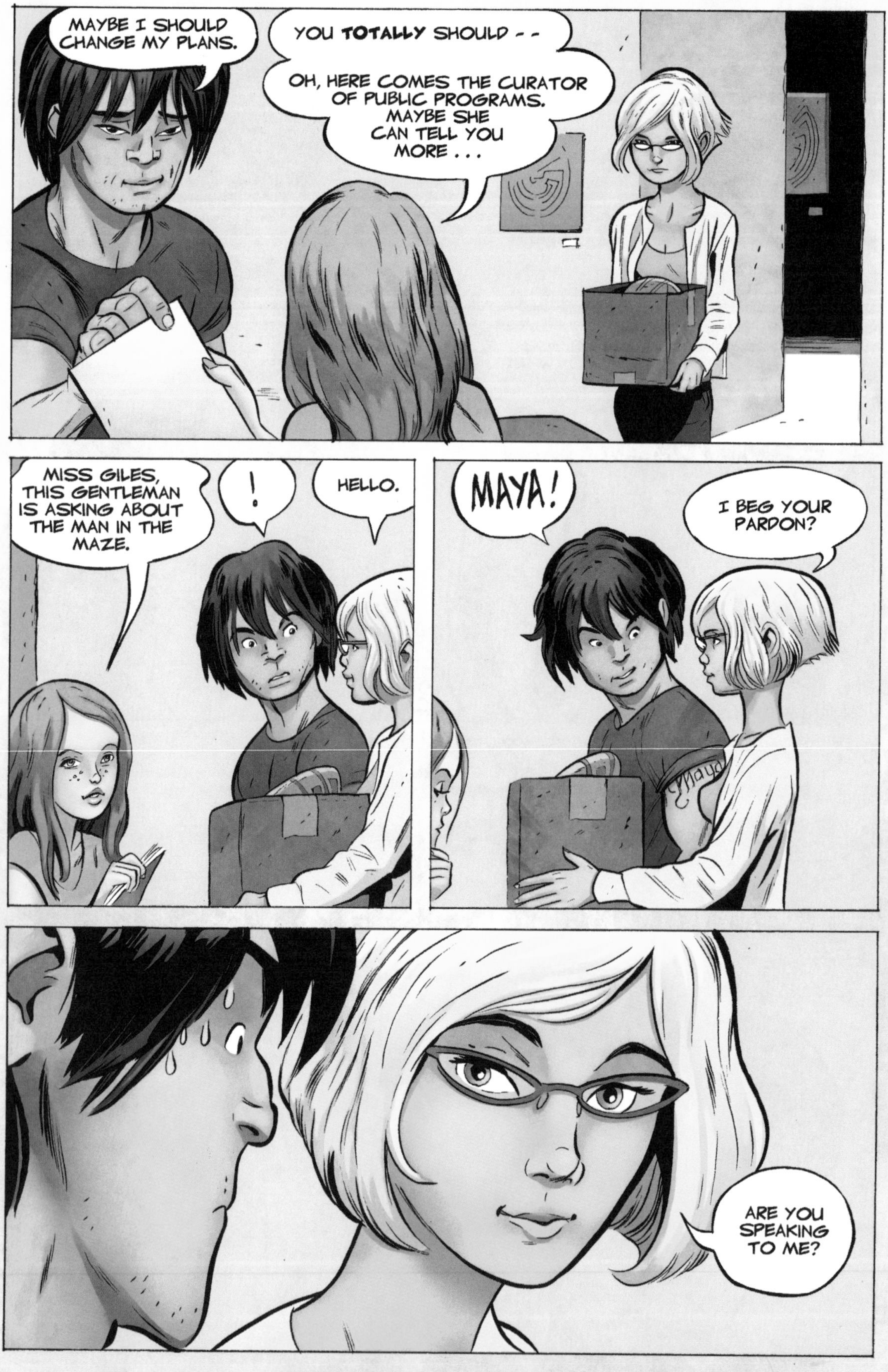
MAYBE I SHOULD CHANGE MY PLANS.
YOU **TOTALLY** SHOULD - -
OH, HERE COMES THE CURATOR OF PUBLIC PROGRAMS. MAYBE SHE CAN TELL YOU MORE . . .
MISS GILES, THIS GENTLEMAN IS ASKING ABOUT THE MAN IN THE MAZE.
!
HELLO.
MAYA!
I BEG YOUR PARDON?
Maya
ARE YOU SPEAKING TO ME?

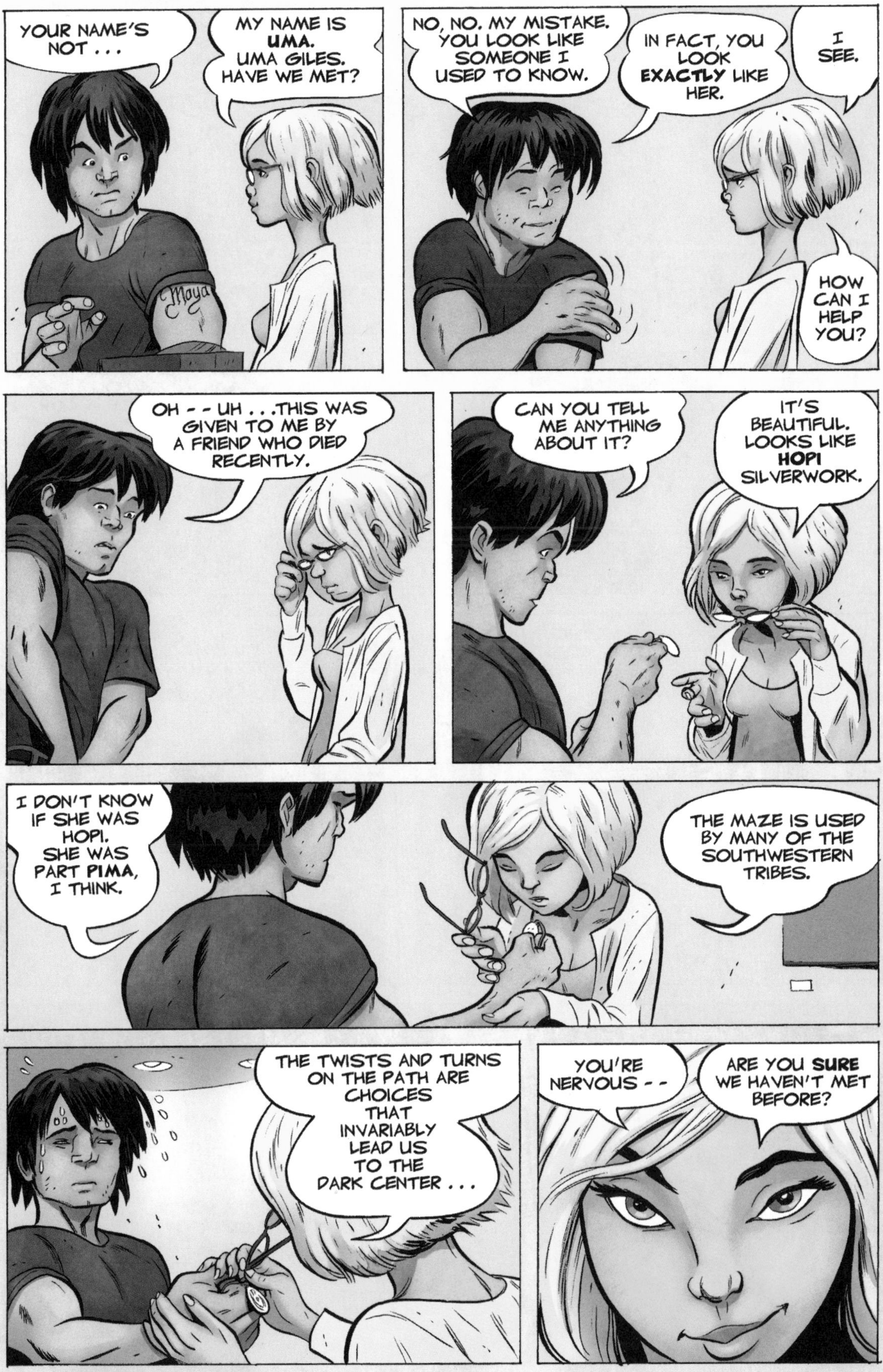
YOUR NAME'S NOT . . .
MY NAME IS UMA. UMA GILES. HAVE WE MET?
Maya
NO, NO. MY MISTAKE. YOU LOOK LIKE SOMEONE I USED TO KNOW.
IN FACT, YOU LOOK EXACTLY LIKE HER.
I SEE.
HOW CAN I HELP YOU?
OH - - UH . . .THIS WAS GIVEN TO ME BY A FRIEND WHO DIED RECENTLY.
CAN YOU TELL ME ANYTHING ABOUT IT?
IT'S BEAUTIFUL. LOOKS LIKE HOPI SILVERWORK.
I DON'T KNOW IF SHE WAS HOPI. SHE WAS PART PIMA, I THINK.
THE MAZE IS USED BY MANY OF THE SOUTHWESTERN TRIBES.
THE TWISTS AND TURNS ON THE PATH ARE CHOICES THAT INVARIABLY LEAD US TO THE DARK CENTER . . .
YOU'RE NERVOUS - -
ARE YOU SURE WE HAVEN'T MET BEFORE?

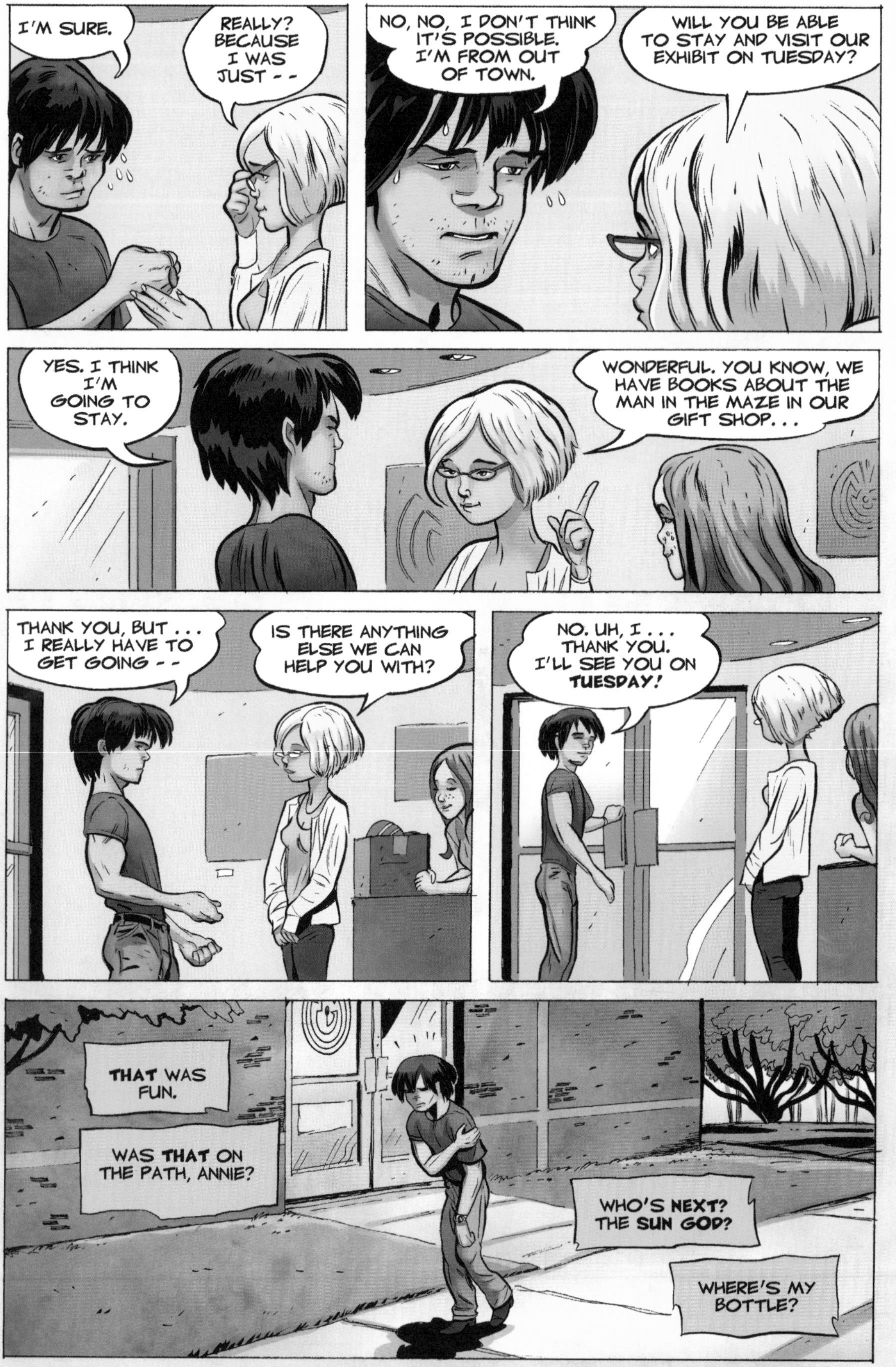
I'M SURE.
REALLY? BECAUSE I WAS JUST - -
NO, NO, I DON'T THINK IT'S POSSIBLE. I'M FROM OUT OF TOWN.
WILL YOU BE ABLE TO STAY AND VISIT OUR EXHIBIT ON TUESDAY?
YES. I THINK I'M GOING TO STAY.
WONDERFUL. YOU KNOW, WE HAVE BOOKS ABOUT THE MAN IN THE MAZE IN OUR GIFT SHOP. . .
THANK YOU, BUT . . . I REALLY HAVE TO GET GOING - -
IS THERE ANYTHING ELSE WE CAN HELP YOU WITH?
NO. UH, I . . . THANK YOU. I'LL SEE YOU ON TUESDAY!
THAT WAS FUN.
WAS THAT ON THE PATH, ANNIE?
WHO'S NEXT? THE SUN GOD?
WHERE'S MY BOTTLE?

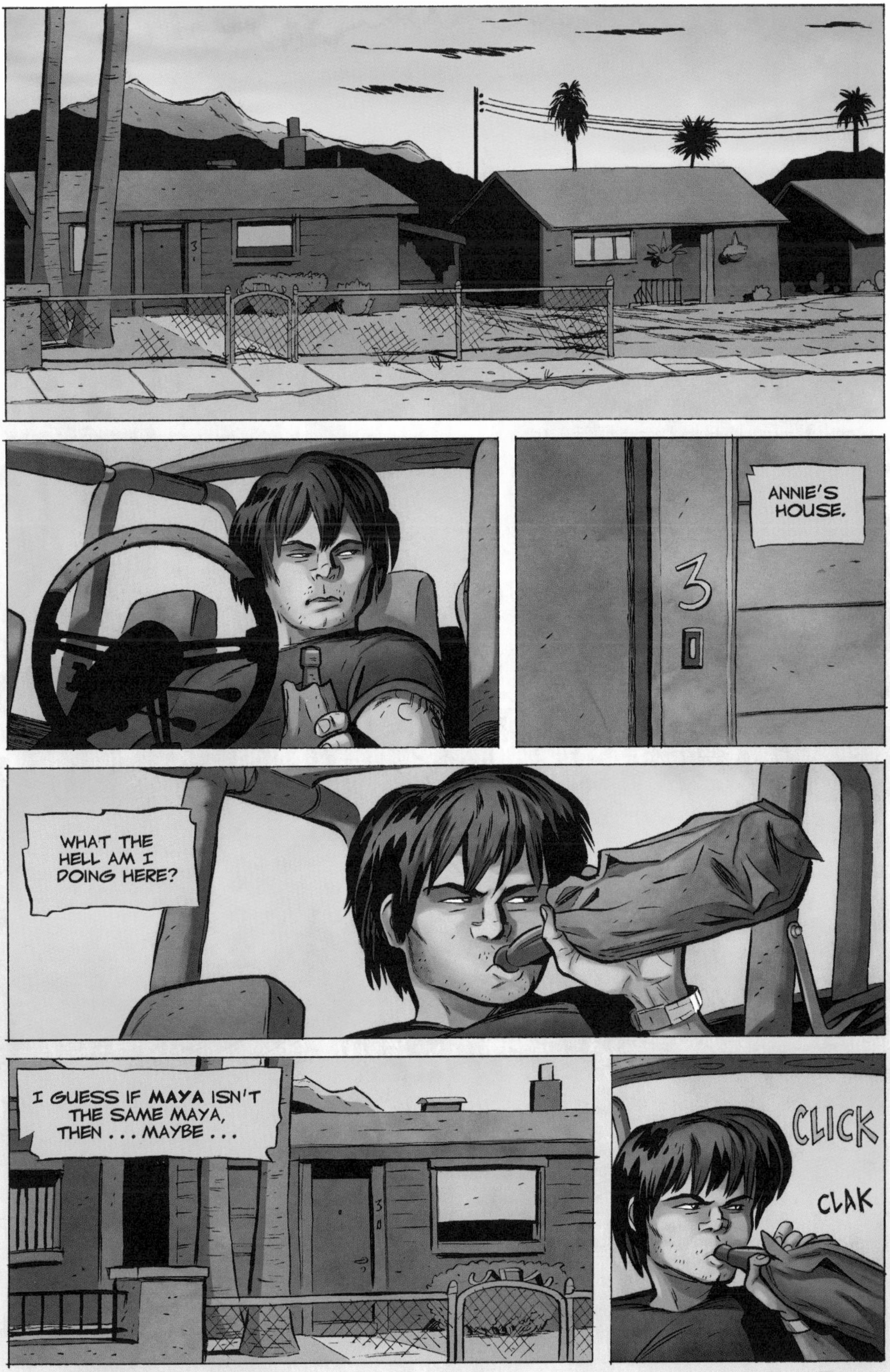

ANNIE'S HOUSE.
WHAT THE HELL AM I DOING HERE?
I GUESS IF **MAYA** ISN'T THE SAME MAYA, THEN . . . MAYBE . . .
CLICK
CLAK

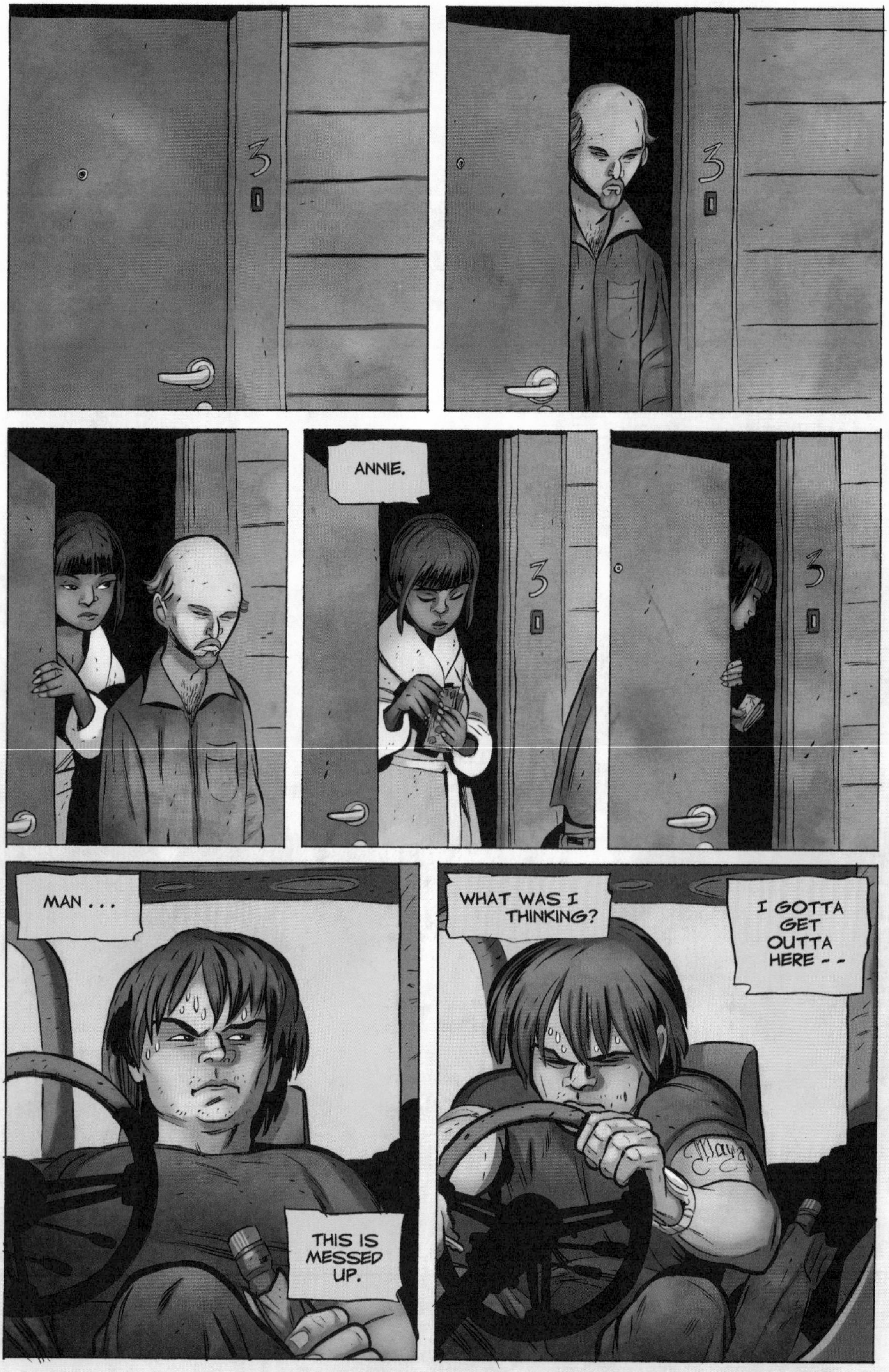
ANNIE.
MAN . . .
THIS IS MESSED UP.
WHAT WAS I THINKING?
I GOTTA GET OUTTA HERE - -

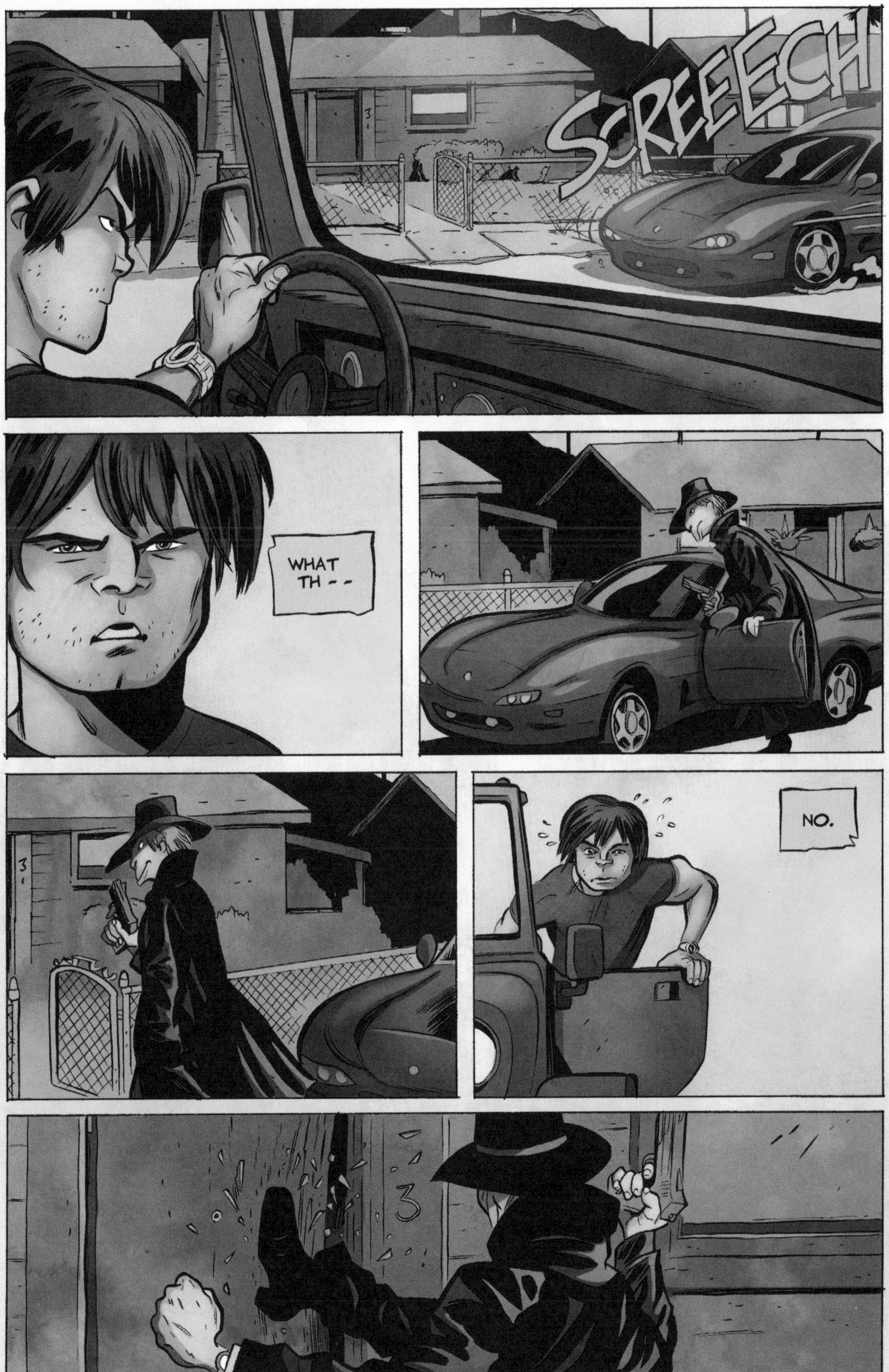
SCREEECH
WHAT TH --
NO.

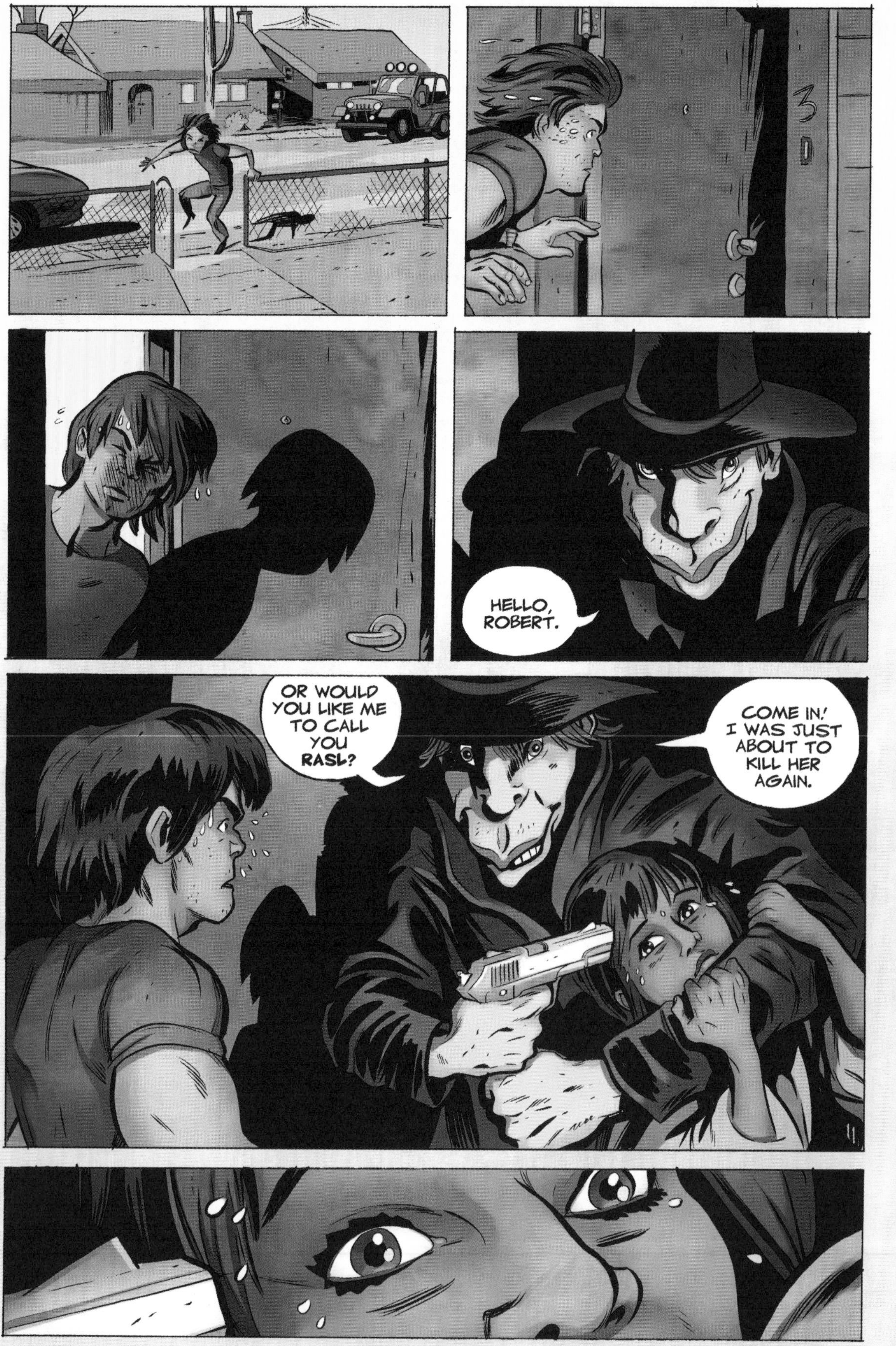
HELLO, ROBERT.
OR WOULD YOU LIKE ME TO CALL YOU RASL?
COME IN! I WAS JUST ABOUT TO KILL HER AGAIN.

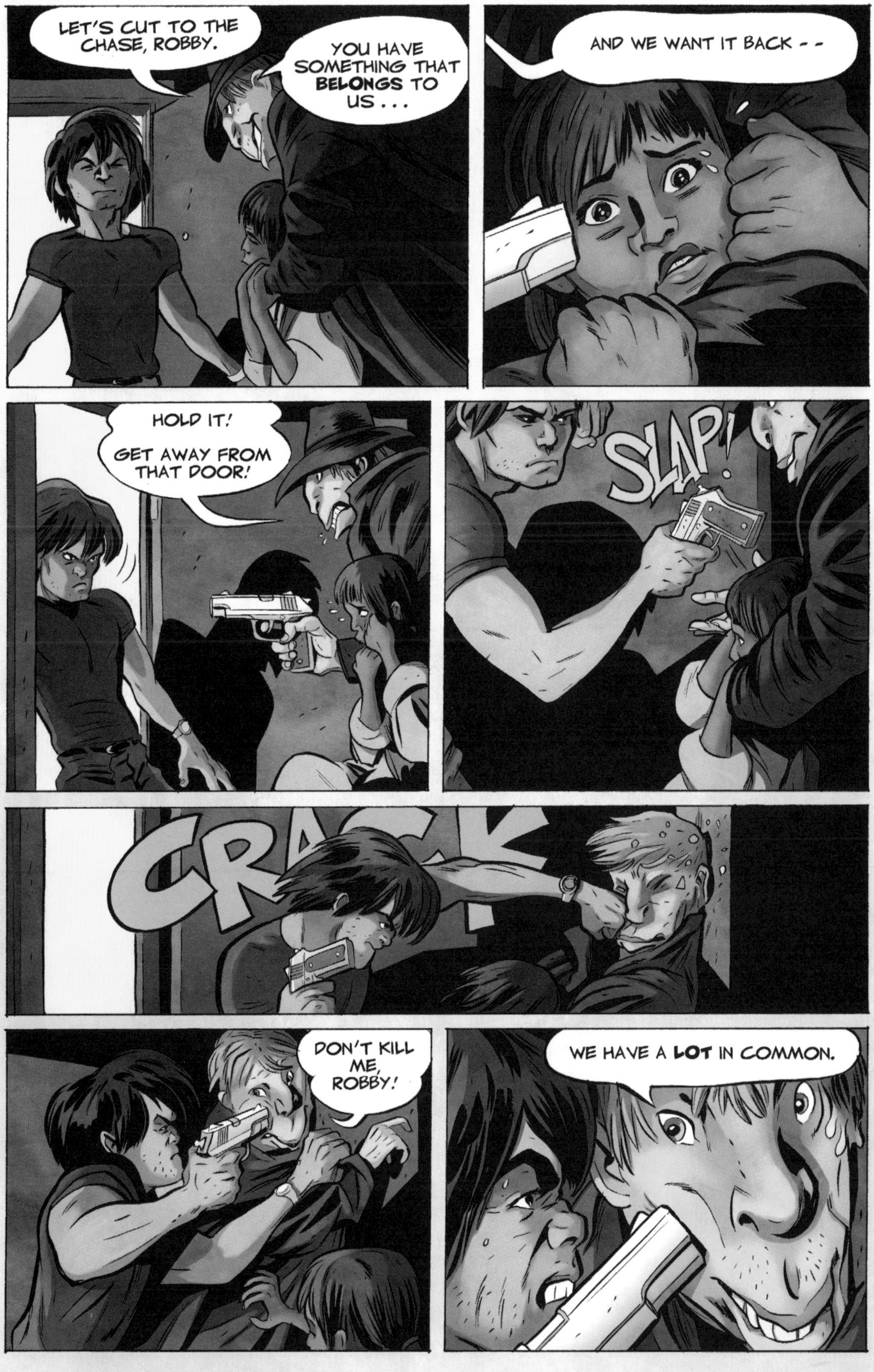
LET'S CUT TO THE CHASE, ROBBY.
YOU HAVE SOMETHING THAT **BELONGS** TO US...
AND WE WANT IT BACK - -
HOLD IT!
GET AWAY FROM THAT DOOR!
SLAP!
CRACK
DON'T KILL ME, ROBBY!
WE HAVE A **LOT** IN COMMON.

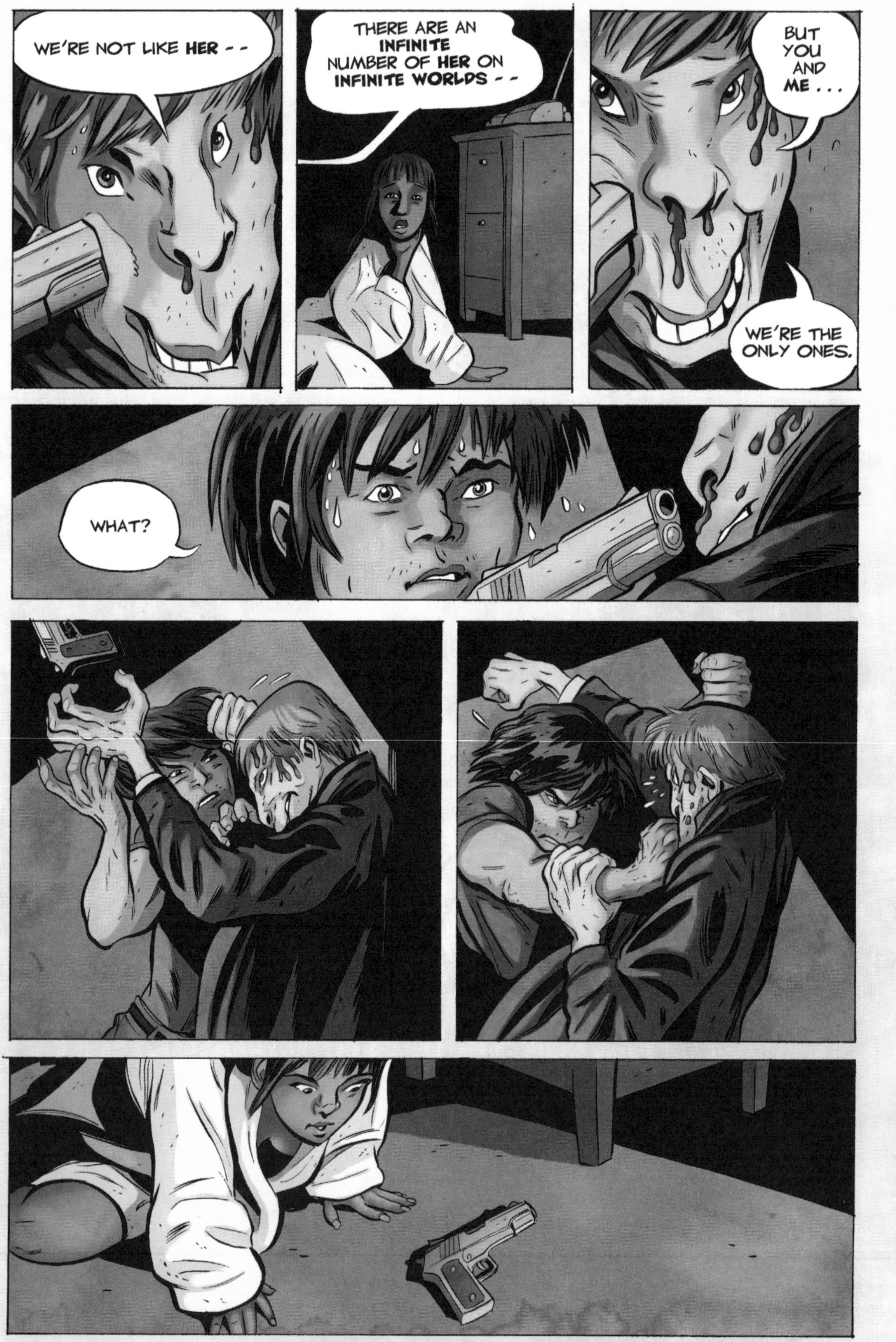
WE'RE NOT LIKE HER - -
THERE ARE AN INFINITE NUMBER OF HER ON INFINITE WORLDS - -
BUT YOU AND ME . . .
WE'RE THE ONLY ONES.
WHAT?

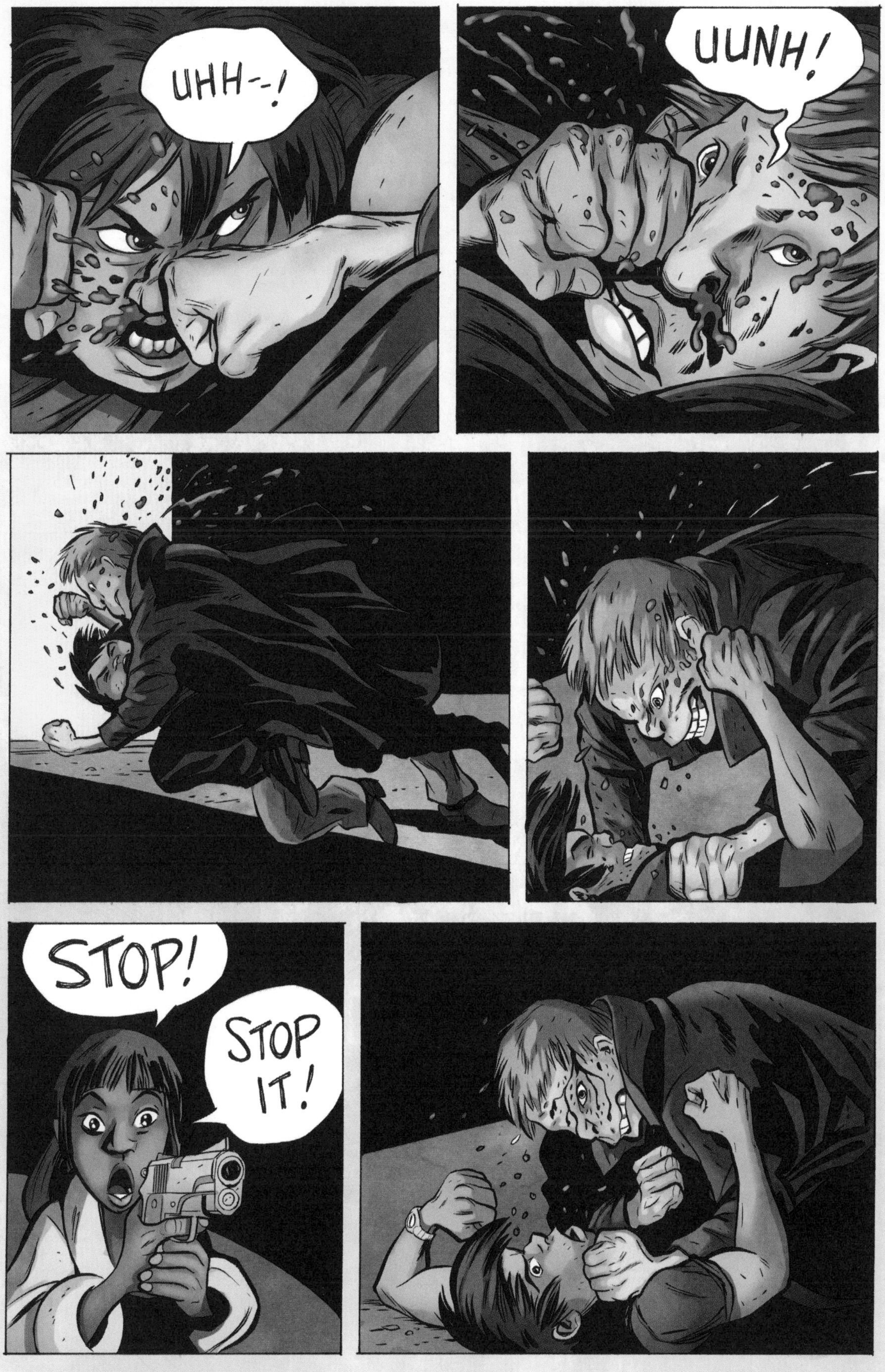
UHH--!
UUNH!
STOP!
STOP IT!

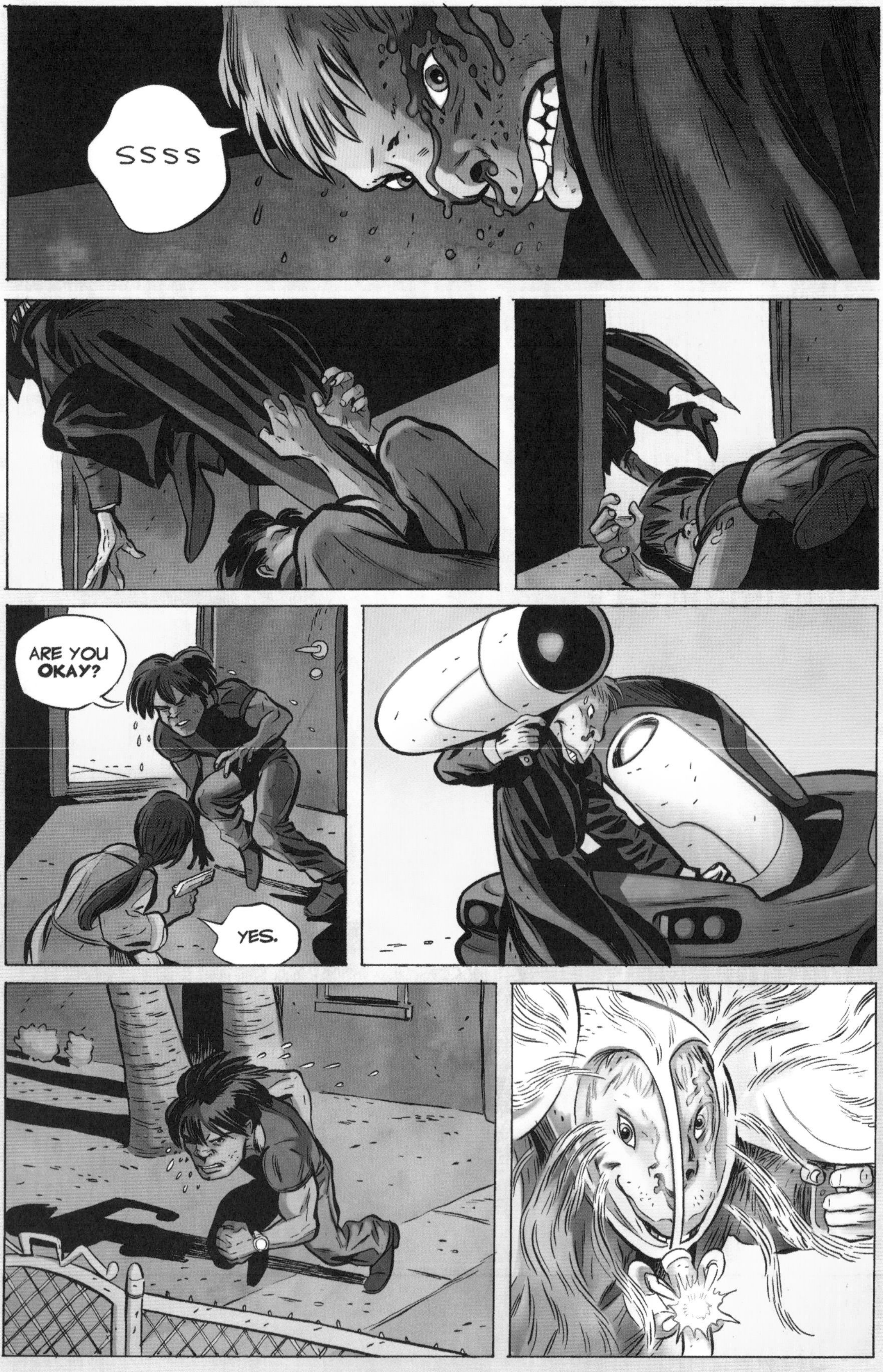
SSSS
ARE YOU OKAY?
YES.

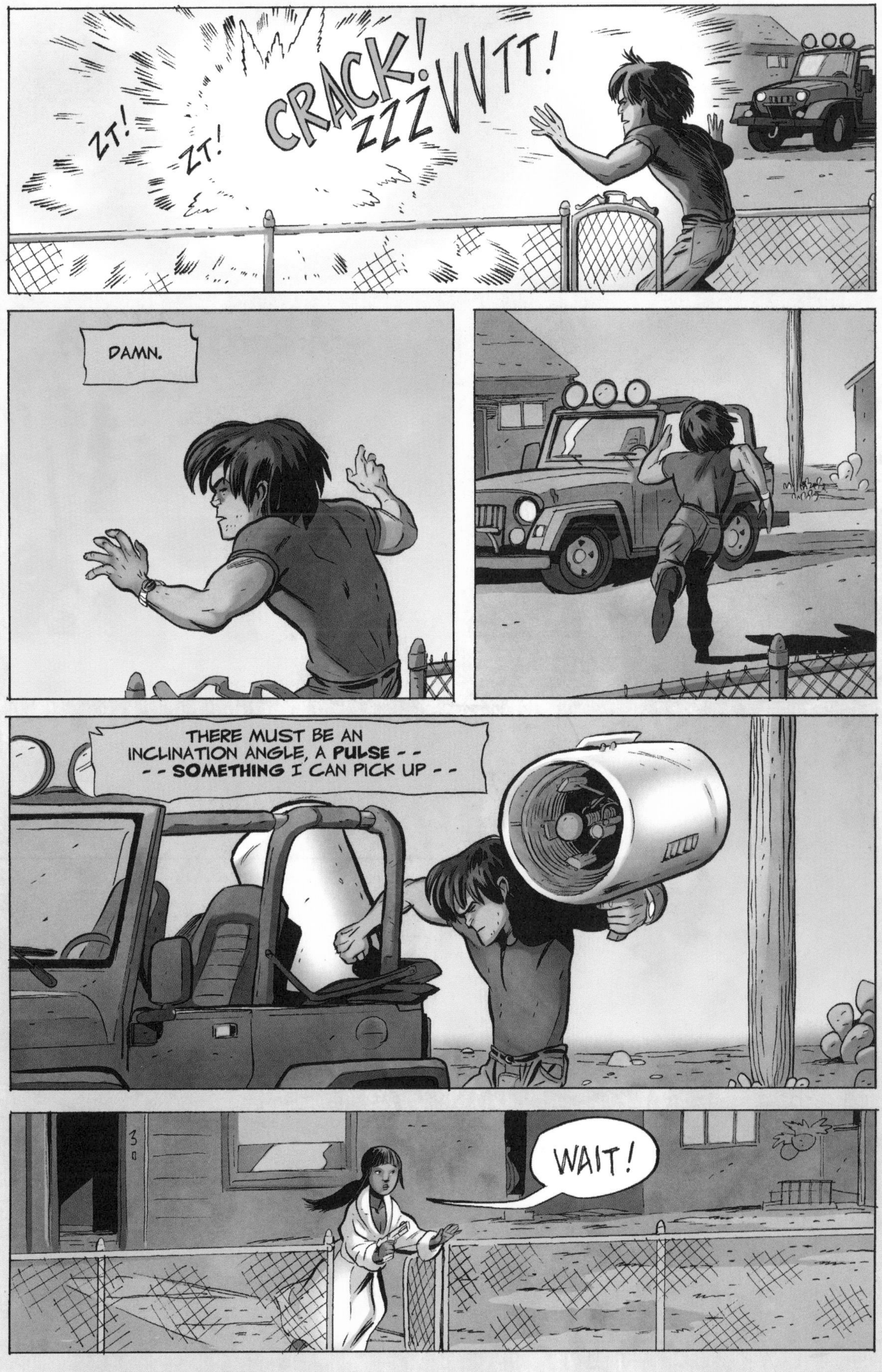
ZT!
ZT!
CRACK!
ZZZVVVTT!
DAMN.
THERE MUST BE AN INCLINATION ANGLE, A **PULSE** - - - - **SOMETHING** I CAN PICK UP - -
WAIT!

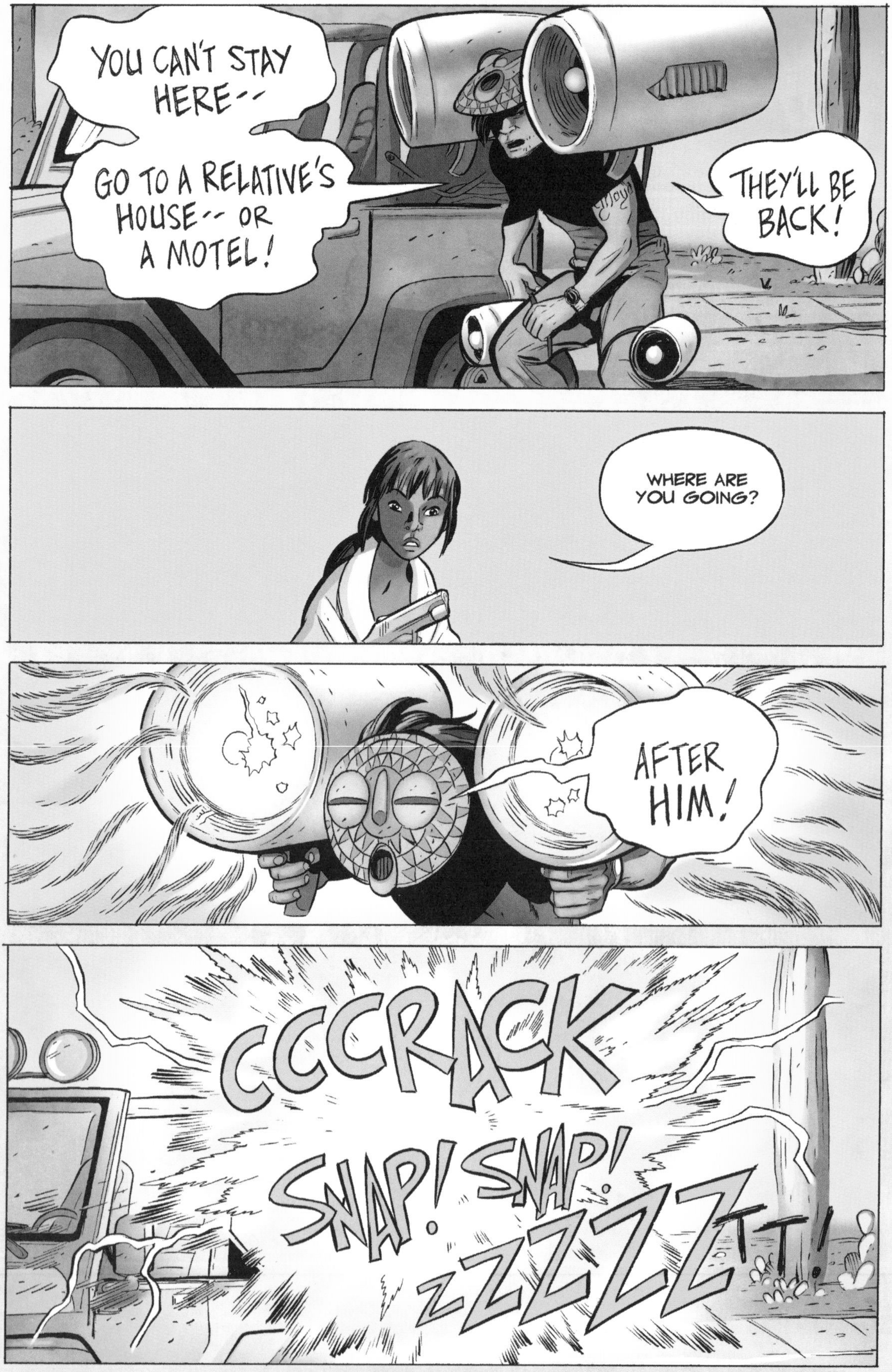
YOU CAN'T STAY HERE--
GO TO A RELATIVE'S HOUSE-- OR A MOTEL!
THEY'LL BE BACK!
WHERE ARE YOU GOING?
AFTER HIM!
CCCRACK
SNAP! SNAP!
zZZZZTT!

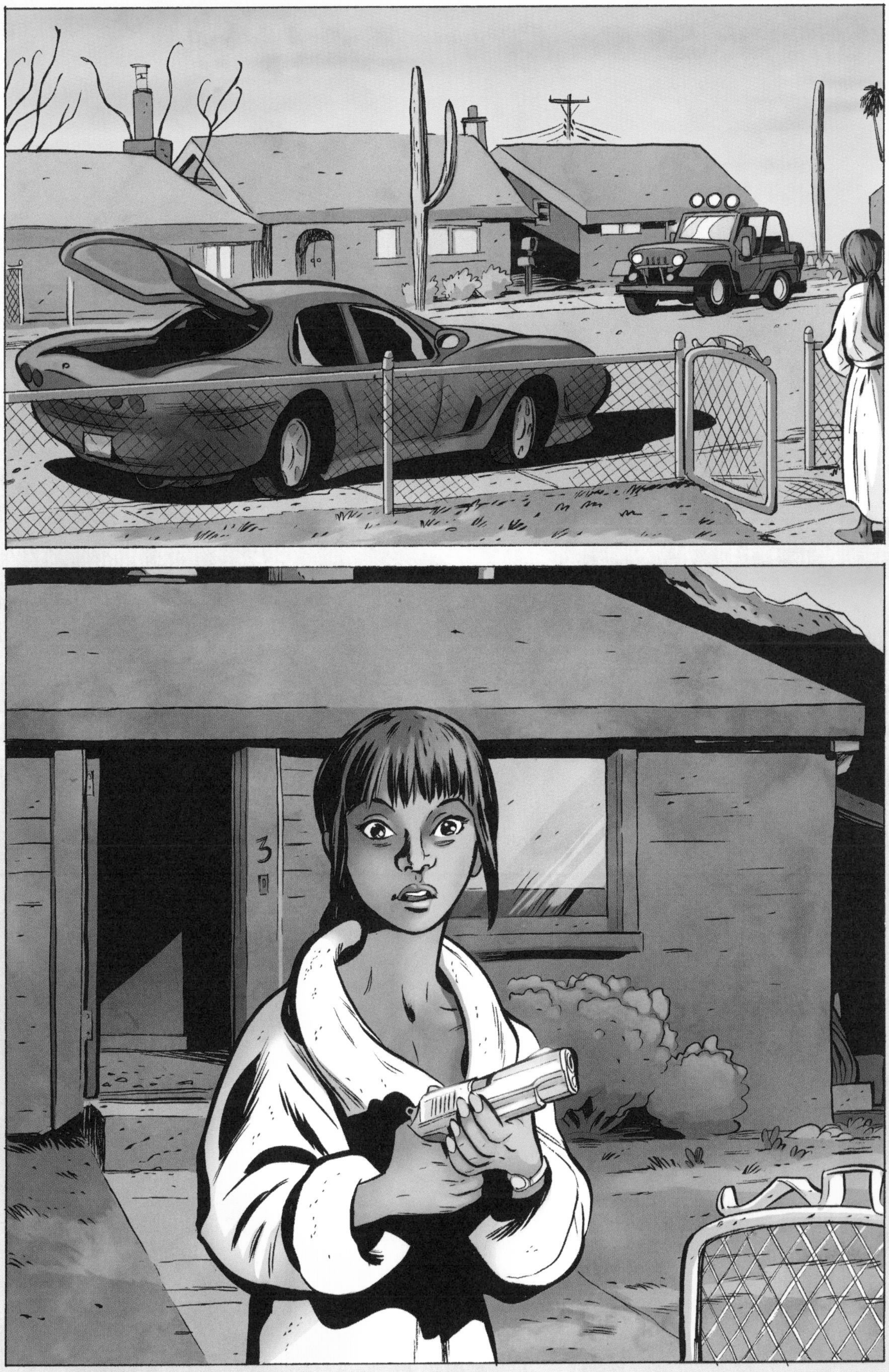
3

ACT TWO

THE FIRE OF ST. GEORGE

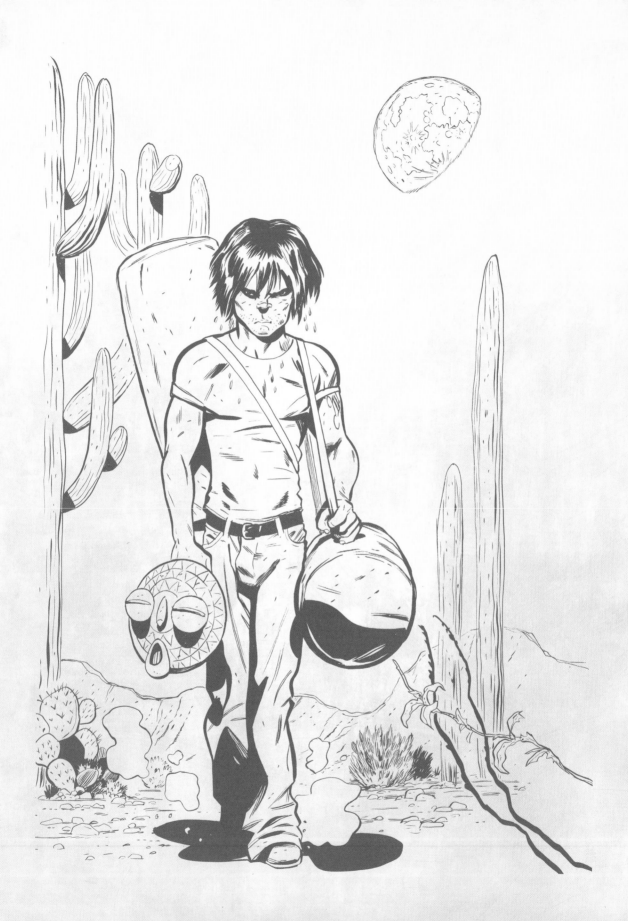

""The spread of civilization may be likened to a fire---
first a feeble spark, next a flickering flame, then a mighty blaze,
ever increasing in speed and power."

-Nikola Tesla

IV
OPENING DOORS

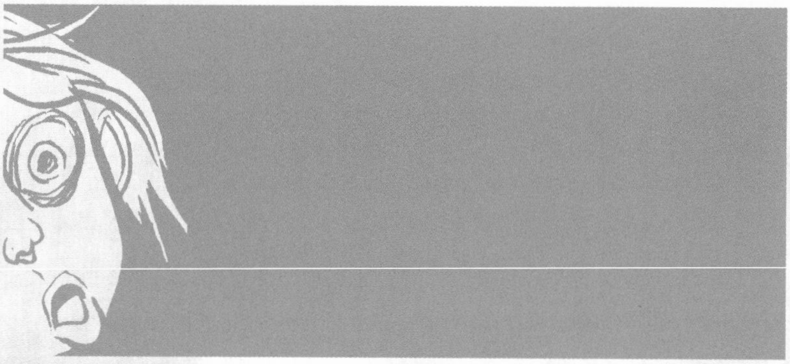

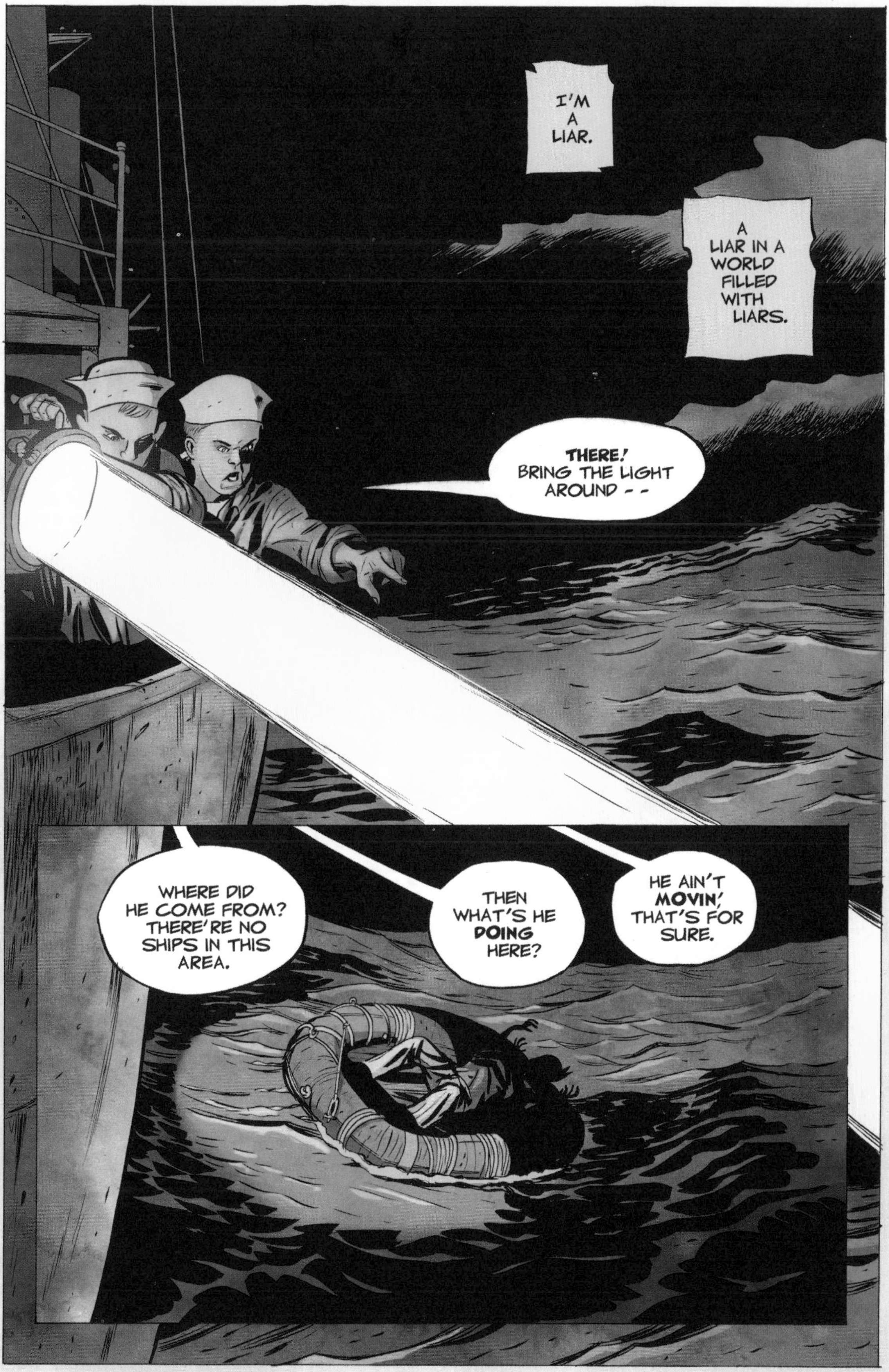
I'M A LIAR.
A LIAR IN A WORLD FILLED WITH LIARS.
THERE! BRING THE LIGHT AROUND - -
WHERE DID HE COME FROM? THERE'RE NO SHIPS IN THIS AREA.
THEN WHAT'S HE DOING HERE?
HE AIN'T MOVIN', THAT'S FOR SURE.

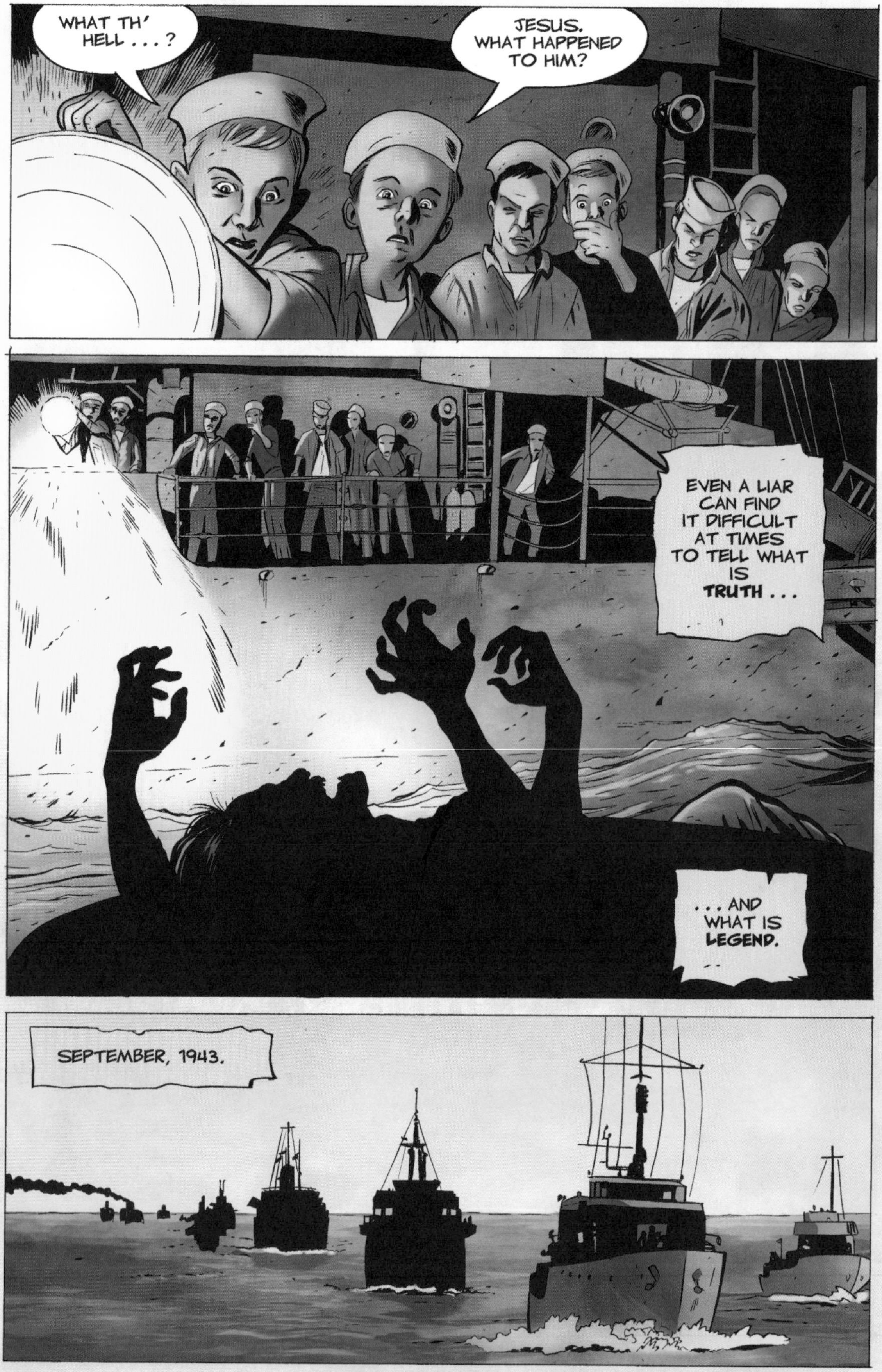

WHAT TH' HELL . . . ?
JESUS. WHAT HAPPENED TO HIM?
EVEN A LIAR CAN FIND IT DIFFICULT AT TIMES TO TELL WHAT IS **TRUTH** . . .
. . . AND WHAT IS **LEGEND.**
SEPTEMBER, 1943.

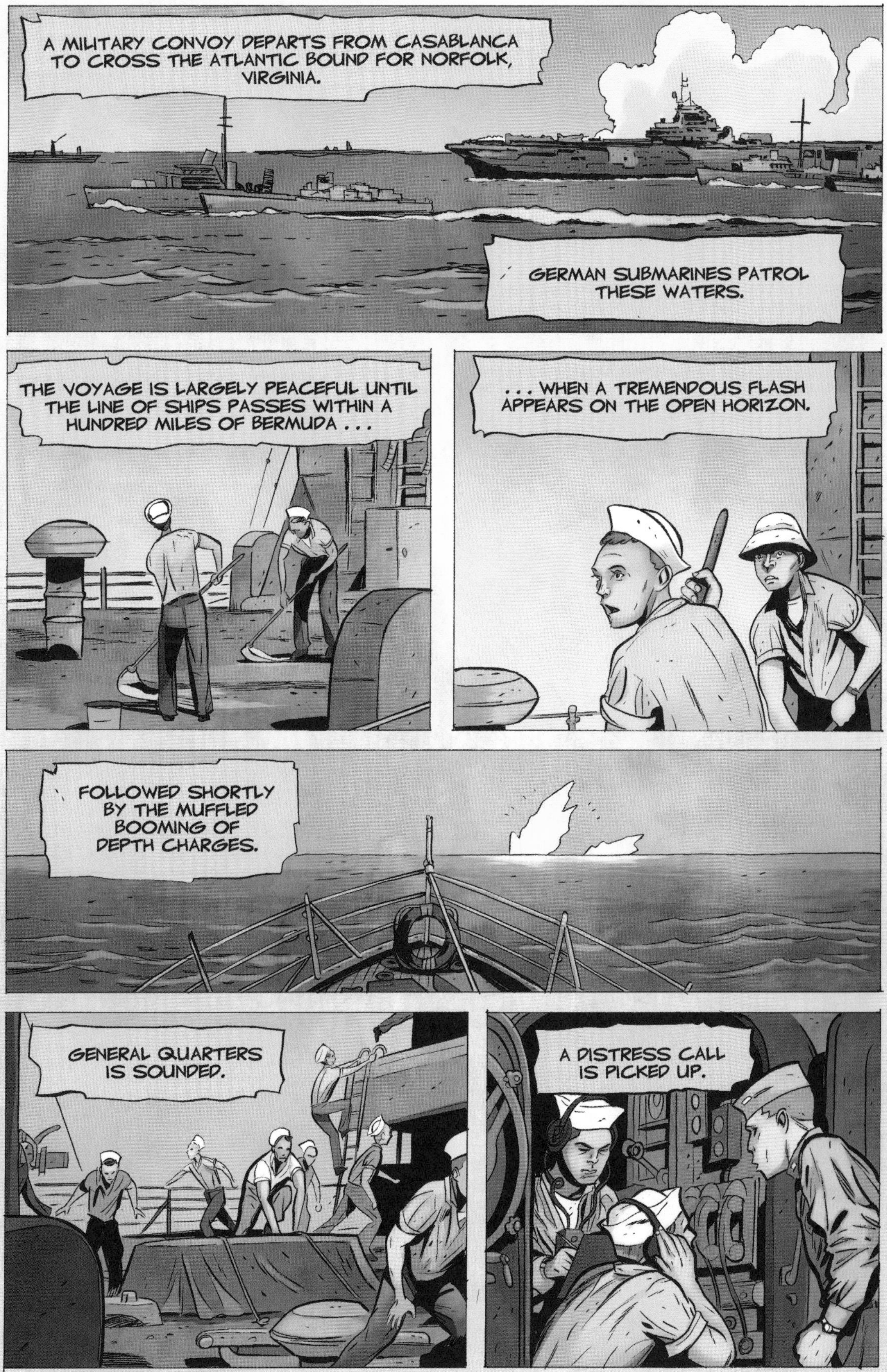
A MILITARY CONVOY DEPARTS FROM CASABLANCA TO CROSS THE ATLANTIC BOUND FOR NORFOLK, VIRGINIA.
GERMAN SUBMARINES PATROL THESE WATERS.
THE VOYAGE IS LARGELY PEACEFUL UNTIL THE LINE OF SHIPS PASSES WITHIN A HUNDRED MILES OF BERMUDA . . .
. . . WHEN A TREMENDOUS FLASH APPEARS ON THE OPEN HORIZON.
FOLLOWED SHORTLY BY THE MUFFLED BOOMING OF DEPTH CHARGES.
GENERAL QUARTERS IS SOUNDED.
A DISTRESS CALL IS PICKED UP.

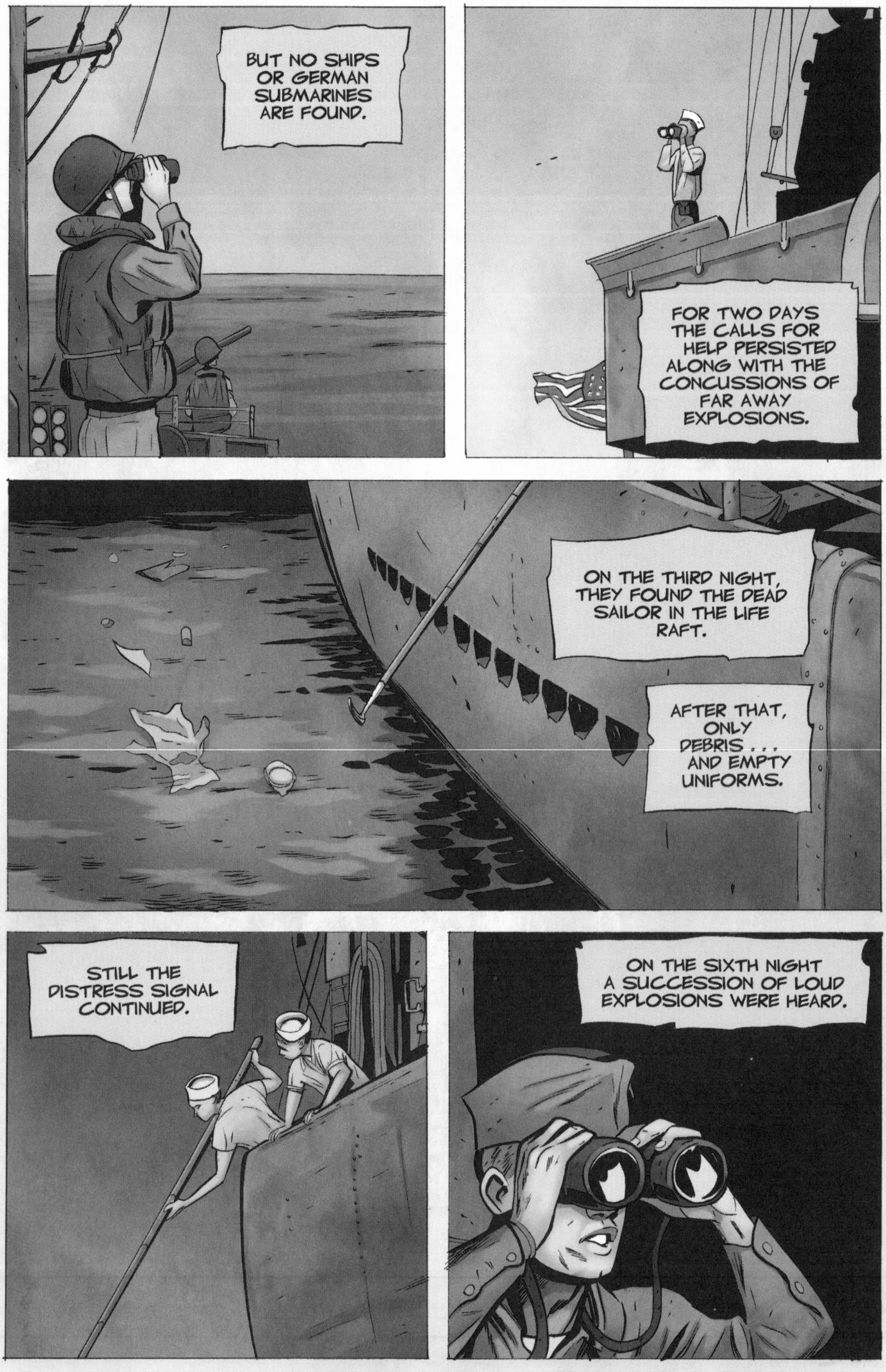
BUT NO SHIPS OR GERMAN SUBMARINES ARE FOUND.
FOR TWO DAYS THE CALLS FOR HELP PERSISTED ALONG WITH THE CONCUSSIONS OF FAR AWAY EXPLOSIONS.
ON THE THIRD NIGHT, THEY FOUND THE DEAD SAILOR IN THE LIFE RAFT.
AFTER THAT, ONLY DEBRIS . . . AND EMPTY UNIFORMS.
STILL THE DISTRESS SIGNAL CONTINUED.
ON THE SIXTH NIGHT A SUCCESSION OF LOUD EXPLOSIONS WERE HEARD.

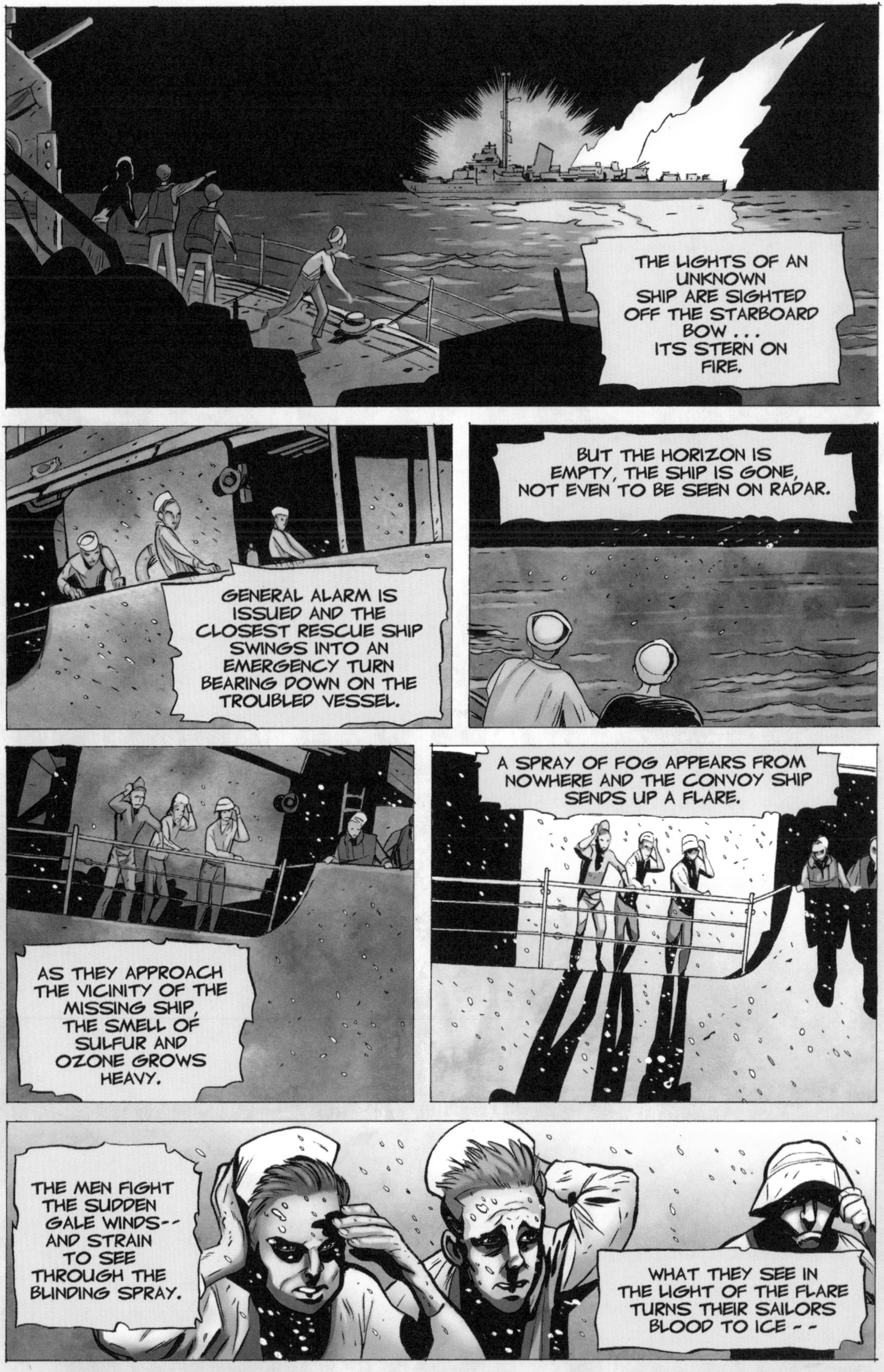
THE LIGHTS OF AN UNKNOWN SHIP ARE SIGHTED OFF THE STARBOARD BOW . . . ITS STERN ON FIRE.
GENERAL ALARM IS ISSUED AND THE CLOSEST RESCUE SHIP SWINGS INTO AN EMERGENCY TURN BEARING DOWN ON THE TROUBLED VESSEL.
BUT THE HORIZON IS EMPTY, THE SHIP IS GONE, NOT EVEN TO BE SEEN ON RADAR.
AS THEY APPROACH THE VICINITY OF THE MISSING SHIP, THE SMELL OF SULFUR AND OZONE GROWS HEAVY.
A SPRAY OF FOG APPEARS FROM NOWHERE AND THE CONVOY SHIP SENDS UP A FLARE.
THE MEN FIGHT THE SUDDEN GALE WINDS-- AND STRAIN TO SEE THROUGH THE BLINDING SPRAY.
WHAT THEY SEE IN THE LIGHT OF THE FLARE TURNS THEIR SAILORS BLOOD TO ICE --

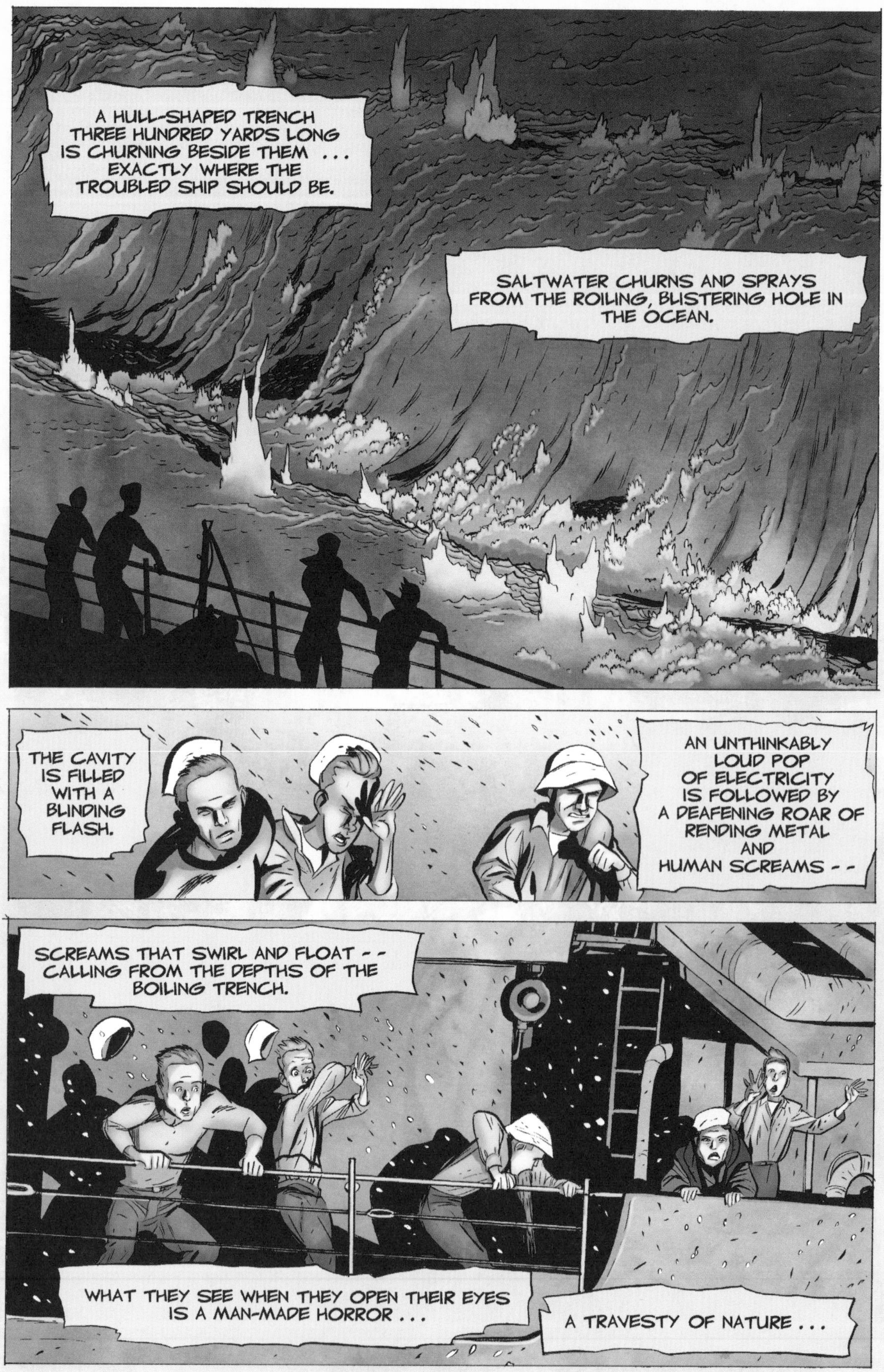
A HULL-SHAPED TRENCH THREE HUNDRED YARDS LONG IS CHURNING BESIDE THEM . . . EXACTLY WHERE THE TROUBLED SHIP SHOULD BE.
SALTWATER CHURNS AND SPRAYS FROM THE ROILING, BLISTERING HOLE IN THE OCEAN.
THE CAVITY IS FILLED WITH A BLINDING FLASH.
AN UNTHINKABLY LOUD POP OF ELECTRICITY IS FOLLOWED BY A DEAFENING ROAR OF RENDING METAL AND HUMAN SCREAMS - -
SCREAMS THAT SWIRL AND FLOAT - - CALLING FROM THE DEPTHS OF THE BOILING TRENCH.
WHAT THEY SEE WHEN THEY OPEN THEIR EYES IS A MAN-MADE HORROR . . .
A TRAVESTY OF NATURE . . .

THAT WAS
THE BEGINNING.

THE BEGINNING OF THE LIES.

THE BEGINNING OF
EVERYTHING
THAT LED ME HERE . . .

. . .TO THIS QUIET
LITTLE BACKSTREET
IN A TUCSON BARRIO.

ZT ZT!

ZZ

CRACK!

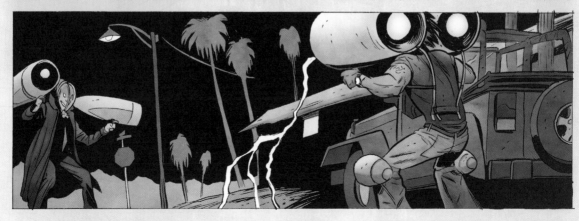

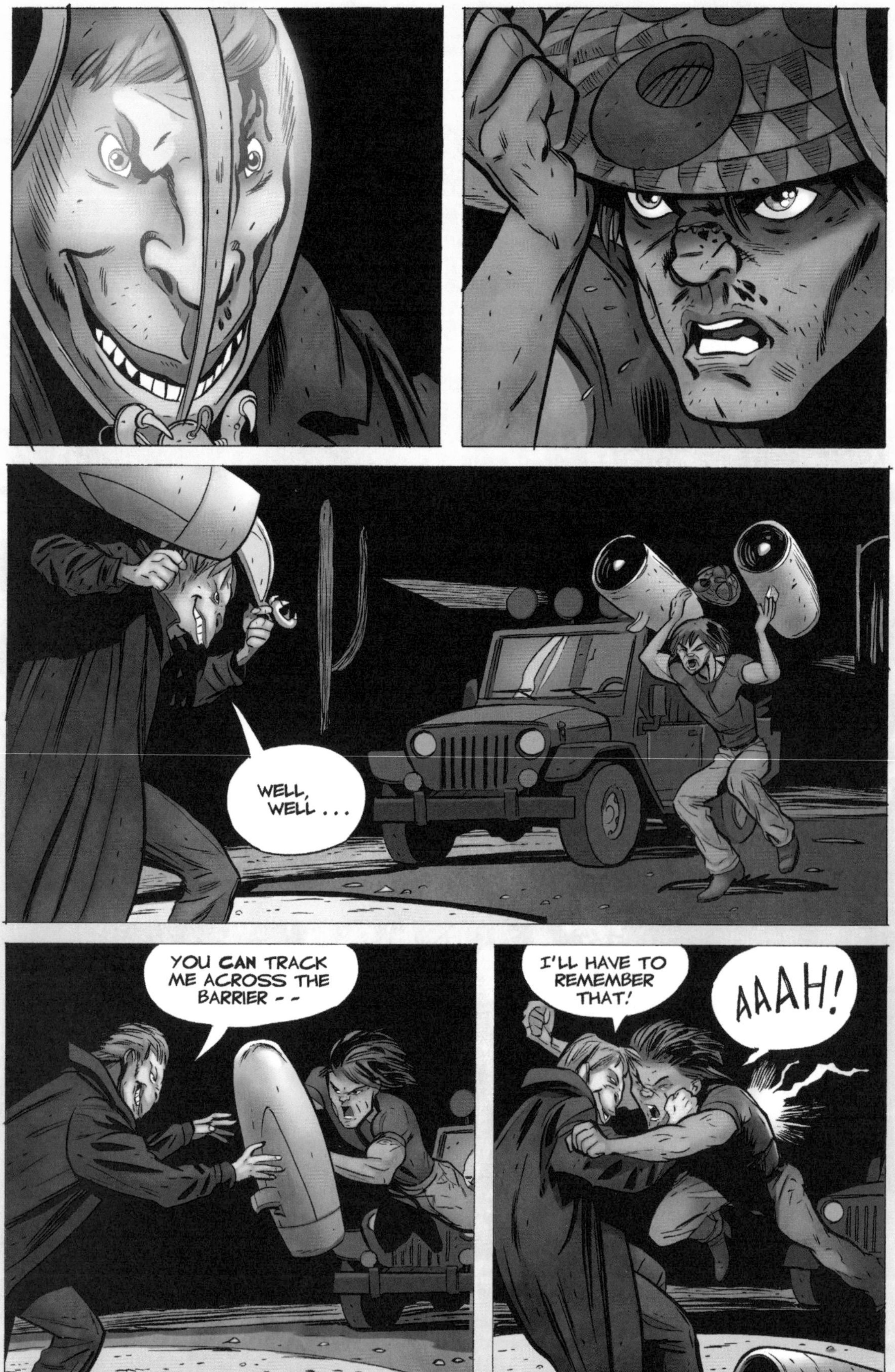
WELL, WELL . . .
YOU CAN TRACK ME ACROSS THE BARRIER - -
I'LL HAVE TO REMEMBER THAT!
AAAH!

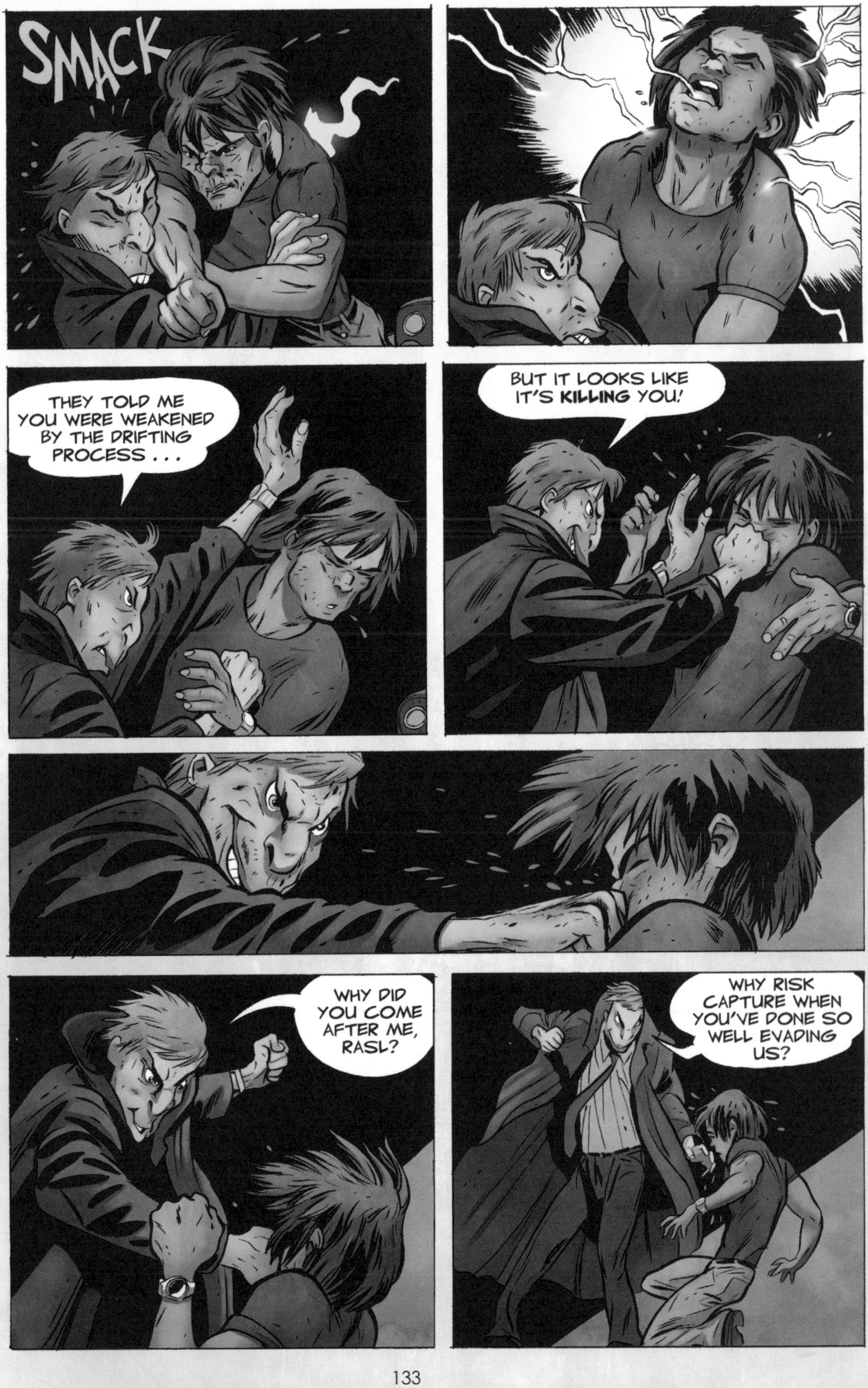
SMACK
THEY TOLD ME YOU WERE WEAKENED BY THE DRIFTING PROCESS . . .
BUT IT LOOKS LIKE IT'S **KILLING** YOU!
WHY DID YOU COME AFTER ME, RASL?
WHY RISK CAPTURE WHEN YOU'VE DONE SO WELL EVADING US?

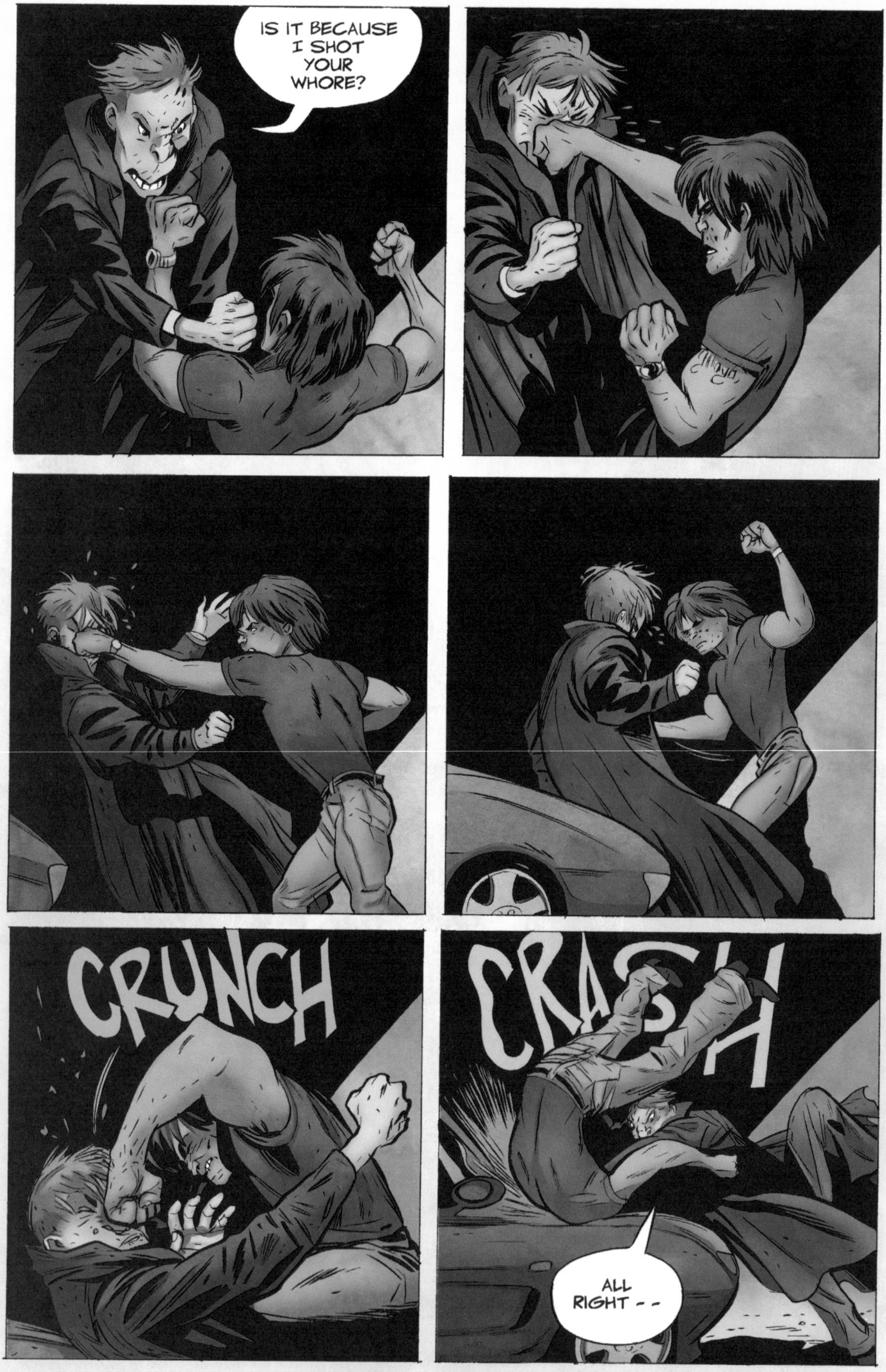
IS IT BECAUSE I SHOT YOUR WHORE?
CRUNCH
CRASH
ALL RIGHT - -

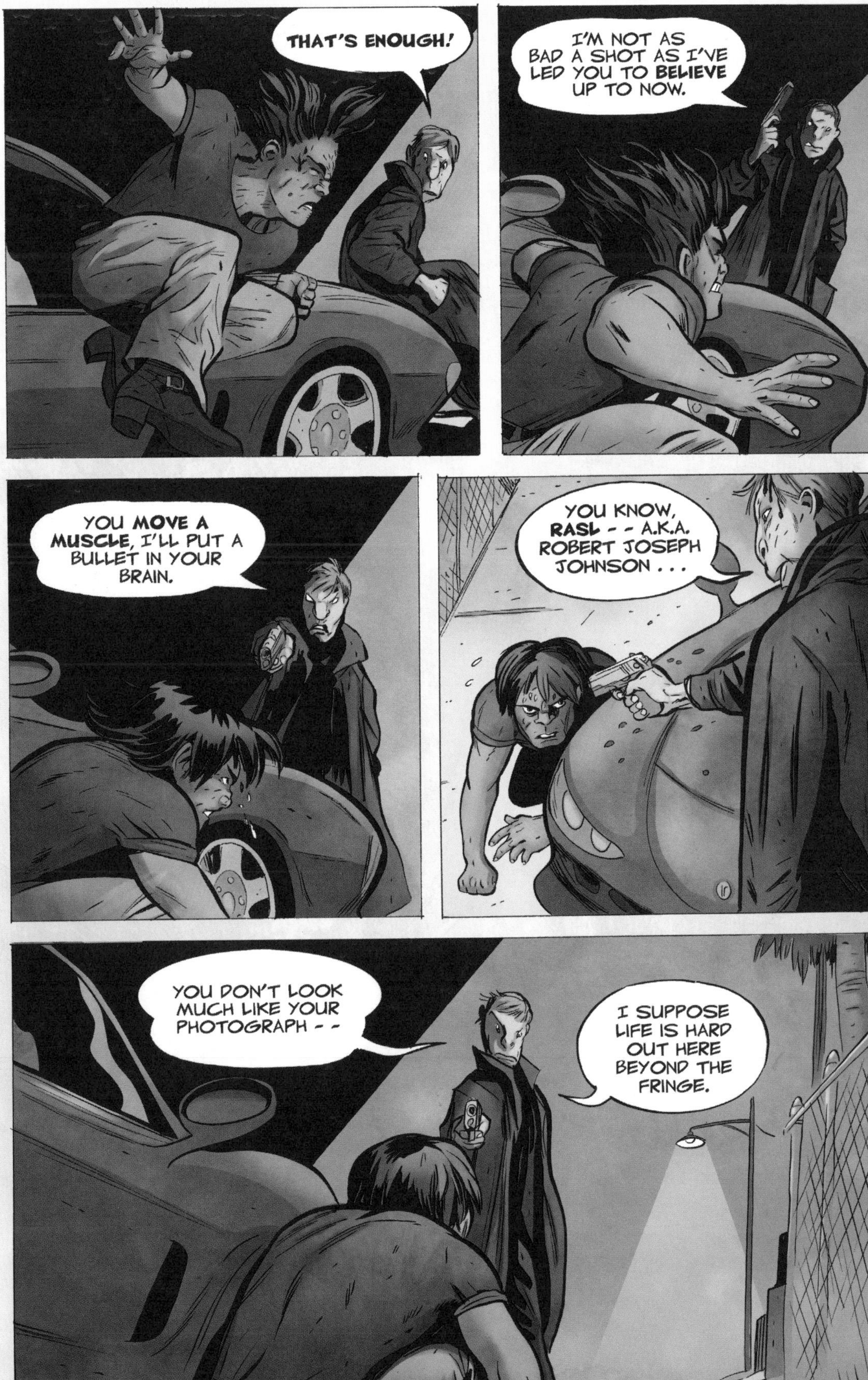

THAT'S ENOUGH!
I'M NOT AS BAD A SHOT AS I'VE LED YOU TO BELIEVE UP TO NOW.
YOU MOVE A MUSCLE, I'LL PUT A BULLET IN YOUR BRAIN.
YOU KNOW, RASL - - A.K.A. ROBERT JOSEPH JOHNSON . . .
YOU DON'T LOOK MUCH LIKE YOUR PHOTOGRAPH - -
I SUPPOSE LIFE IS HARD OUT HERE BEYOND THE FRINGE.

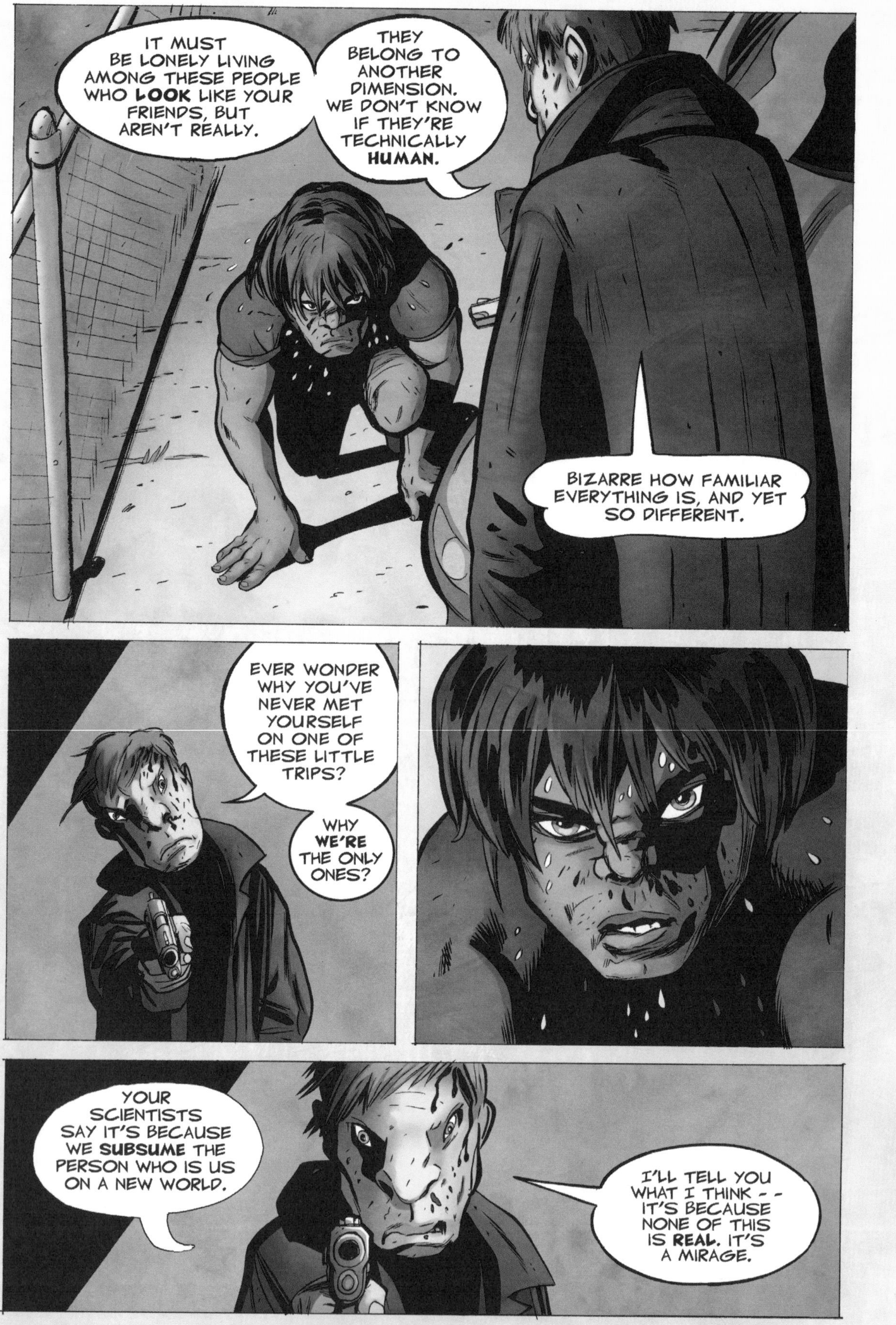
IT MUST BE LONELY LIVING AMONG THESE PEOPLE WHO **LOOK** LIKE YOUR FRIENDS, BUT AREN'T REALLY.
THEY BELONG TO ANOTHER DIMENSION. WE DON'T KNOW IF THEY'RE TECHNICALLY **HUMAN.**
BIZARRE HOW FAMILIAR EVERYTHING IS, AND YET SO DIFFERENT.
EVER WONDER WHY YOU'VE NEVER MET YOURSELF ON ONE OF THESE LITTLE TRIPS?
WHY **WE'RE** THE ONLY ONES?
YOUR SCIENTISTS SAY IT'S BECAUSE WE **SUBSUME** THE PERSON WHO IS US ON A NEW WORLD.
I'LL TELL YOU WHAT I THINK - - IT'S BECAUSE NONE OF THIS IS **REAL.** IT'S A MIRAGE.

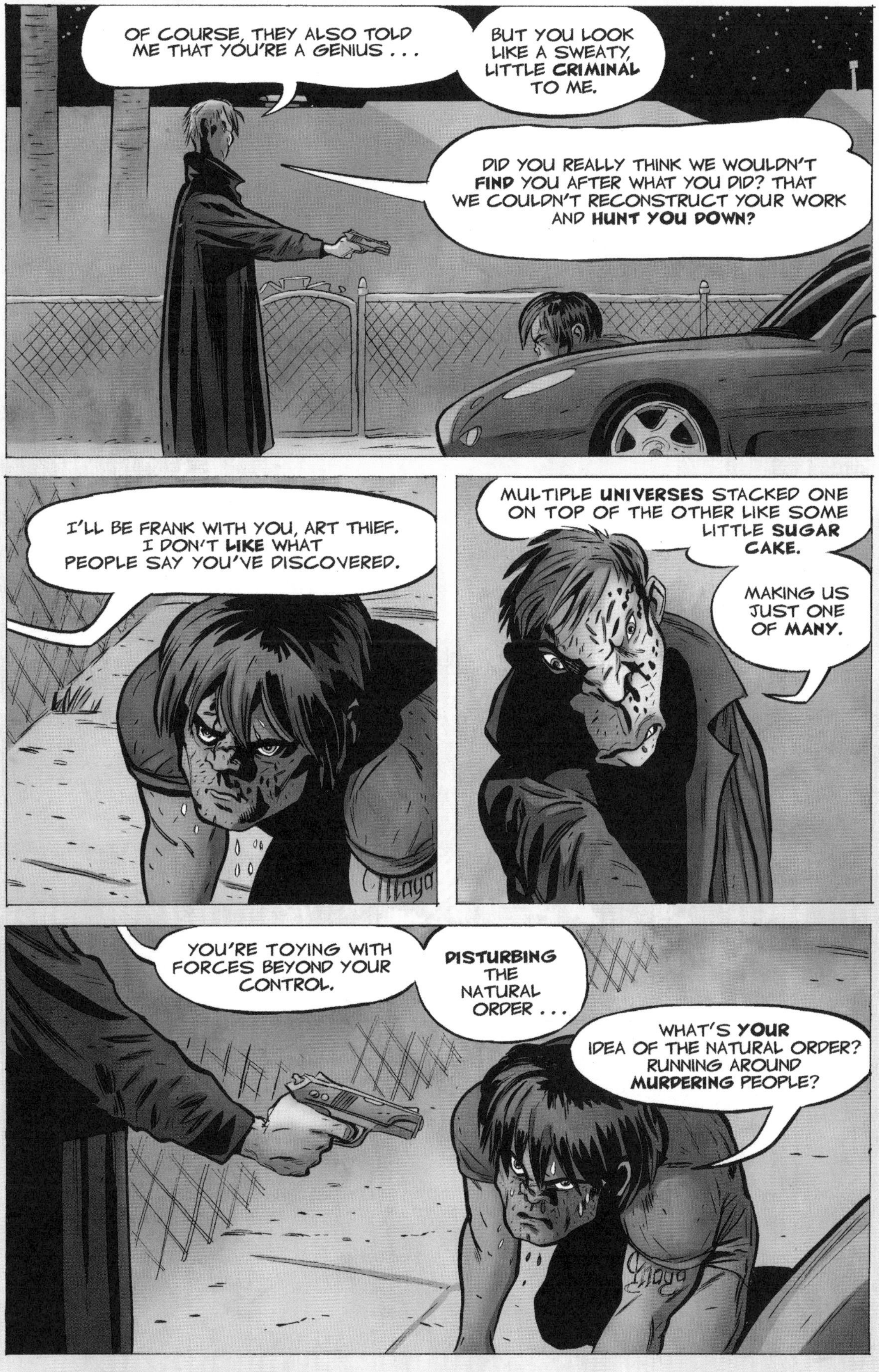
OF COURSE, THEY ALSO TOLD ME THAT YOU'RE A GENIUS . . .
BUT YOU LOOK LIKE A SWEATY, LITTLE CRIMINAL TO ME.
DID YOU REALLY THINK WE WOULDN'T FIND YOU AFTER WHAT YOU DID? THAT WE COULDN'T RECONSTRUCT YOUR WORK AND HUNT YOU DOWN?
I'LL BE FRANK WITH YOU, ART THIEF. I DON'T LIKE WHAT PEOPLE SAY YOU'VE DISCOVERED.
MULTIPLE UNIVERSES STACKED ONE ON TOP OF THE OTHER LIKE SOME LITTLE SUGAR CAKE.
MAKING US JUST ONE OF MANY.
YOU'RE TOYING WITH FORCES BEYOND YOUR CONTROL.
DISTURBING THE NATURAL ORDER . . .
WHAT'S YOUR IDEA OF THE NATURAL ORDER? RUNNING AROUND MURDERING PEOPLE?

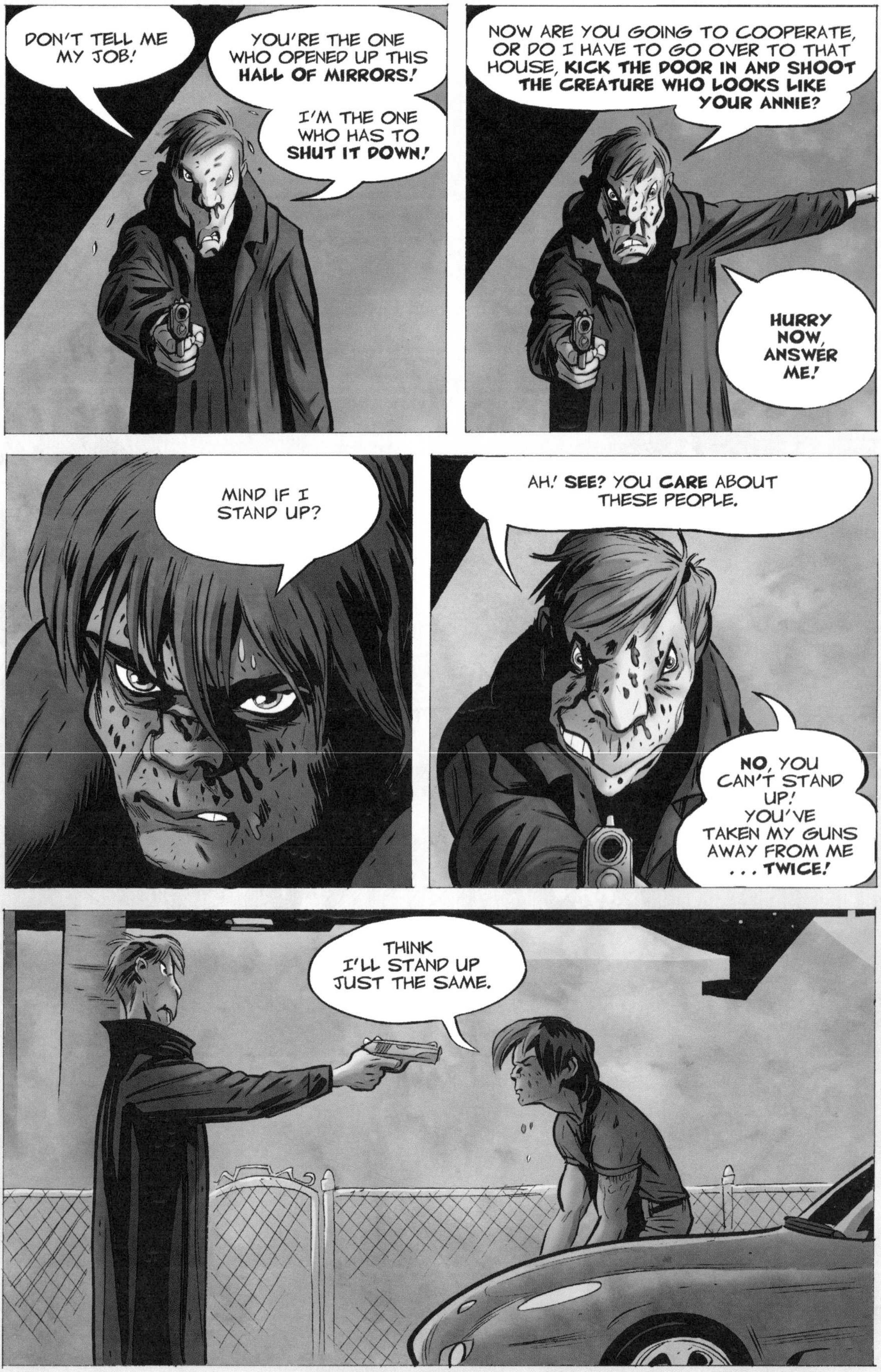
DON'T TELL ME MY JOB!
YOU'RE THE ONE WHO OPENED UP THIS HALL OF MIRRORS!
I'M THE ONE WHO HAS TO SHUT IT DOWN!
NOW ARE YOU GOING TO COOPERATE, OR DO I HAVE TO GO OVER TO THAT HOUSE, KICK THE DOOR IN AND SHOOT THE CREATURE WHO LOOKS LIKE YOUR ANNIE?
HURRY NOW, ANSWER ME!
MIND IF I STAND UP?
AH! SEE? YOU CARE ABOUT THESE PEOPLE.
NO, YOU CAN'T STAND UP! YOU'VE TAKEN MY GUNS AWAY FROM ME . . . TWICE!
THINK I'LL STAND UP JUST THE SAME.

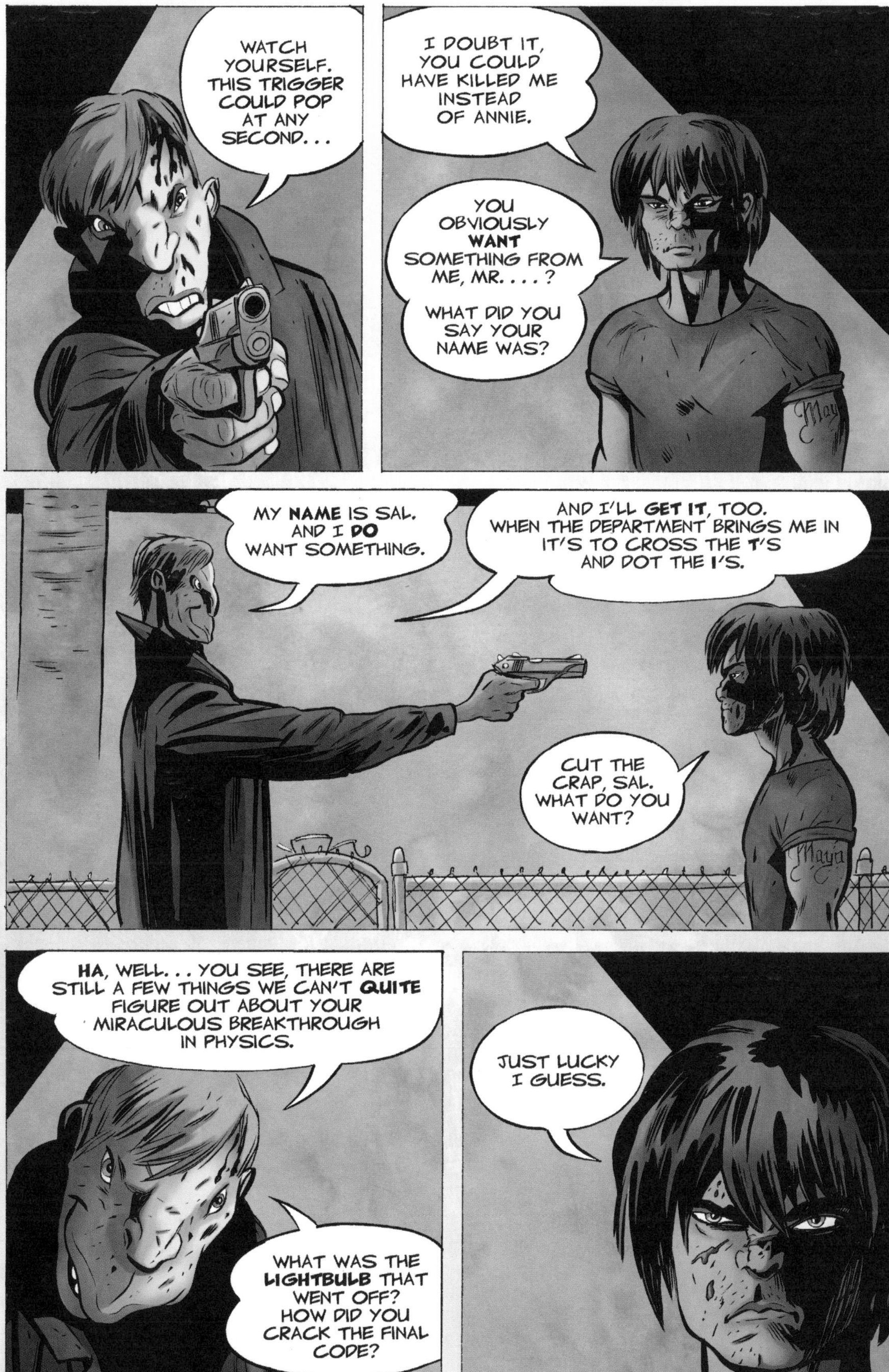
WATCH YOURSELF. THIS TRIGGER COULD POP AT ANY SECOND...
I DOUBT IT, YOU COULD HAVE KILLED ME INSTEAD OF ANNIE.
YOU OBVIOUSLY WANT SOMETHING FROM ME, MR....?
WHAT DID YOU SAY YOUR NAME WAS?
Maya
MY NAME IS SAL. AND I DO WANT SOMETHING.
AND I'LL GET IT, TOO. WHEN THE DEPARTMENT BRINGS ME IN IT'S TO CROSS THE T'S AND DOT THE I'S.
CUT THE CRAP, SAL. WHAT DO YOU WANT?
Maya
HA, WELL... YOU SEE, THERE ARE STILL A FEW THINGS WE CAN'T QUITE FIGURE OUT ABOUT YOUR MIRACULOUS BREAKTHROUGH IN PHYSICS.
WHAT WAS THE LIGHTBULB THAT WENT OFF? HOW DID YOU CRACK THE FINAL CODE?
JUST LUCKY I GUESS.

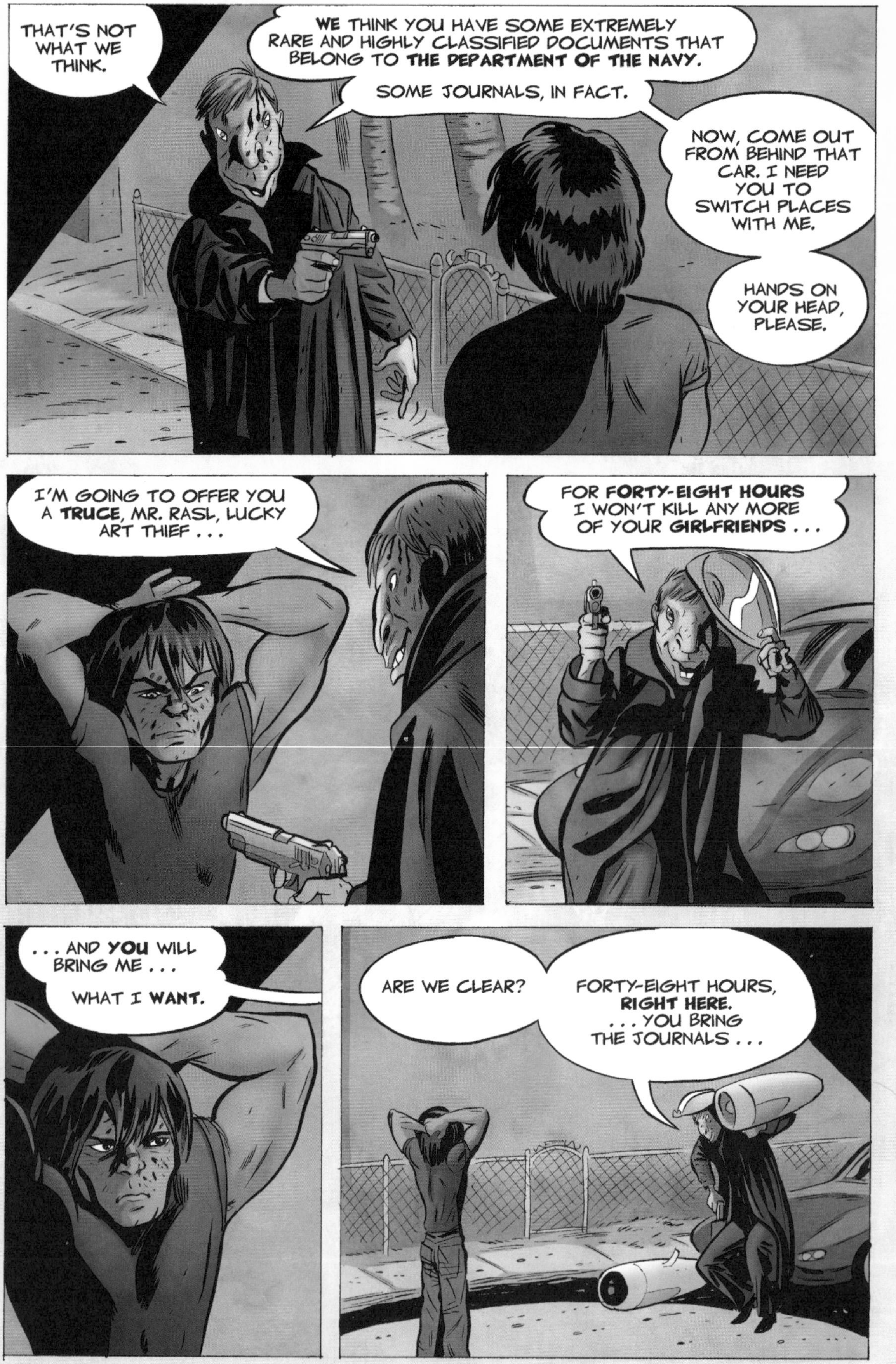
THAT'S NOT WHAT WE THINK.
WE THINK YOU HAVE SOME EXTREMELY RARE AND HIGHLY CLASSIFIED DOCUMENTS THAT BELONG TO THE DEPARTMENT OF THE NAVY.
SOME JOURNALS, IN FACT.
NOW, COME OUT FROM BEHIND THAT CAR. I NEED YOU TO SWITCH PLACES WITH ME.
HANDS ON YOUR HEAD, PLEASE.
I'M GOING TO OFFER YOU A TRUCE, MR. RASL, LUCKY ART THIEF . . .
FOR FORTY-EIGHT HOURS I WON'T KILL ANY MORE OF YOUR GIRLFRIENDS . . .
. . . AND YOU WILL BRING ME . . .
WHAT I WANT.
ARE WE CLEAR?
FORTY-EIGHT HOURS, RIGHT HERE. . . . YOU BRING THE JOURNALS . . .

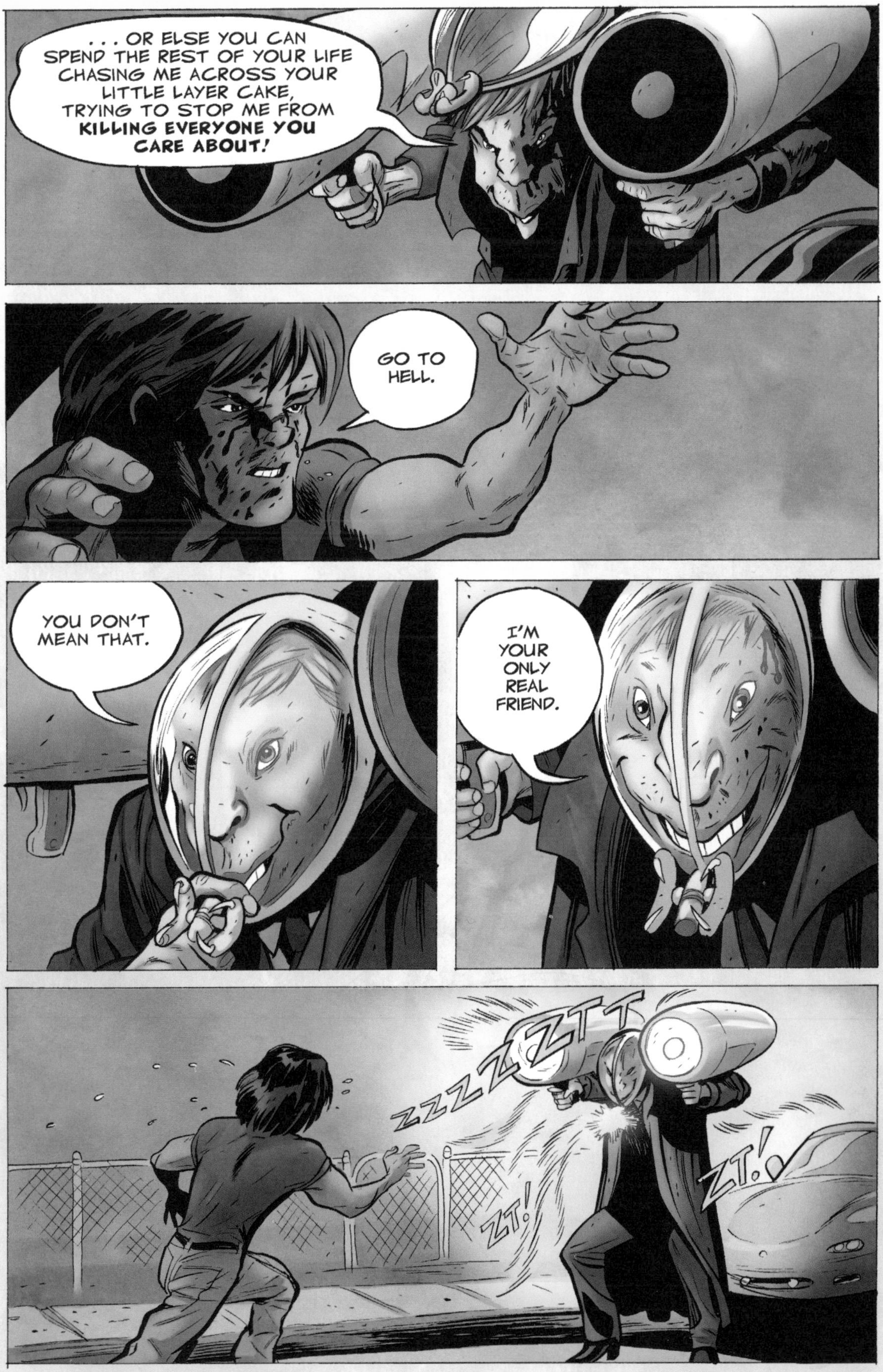
. . . OR ELSE YOU CAN SPEND THE REST OF YOUR LIFE CHASING ME ACROSS YOUR LITTLE LAYER CAKE, TRYING TO STOP ME FROM **KILLING EVERYONE YOU CARE ABOUT!**
GO TO HELL.
YOU DON'T MEAN THAT.
I'M YOUR ONLY REAL FRIEND.
ZZZZZZTTT
ZT!
ZT!

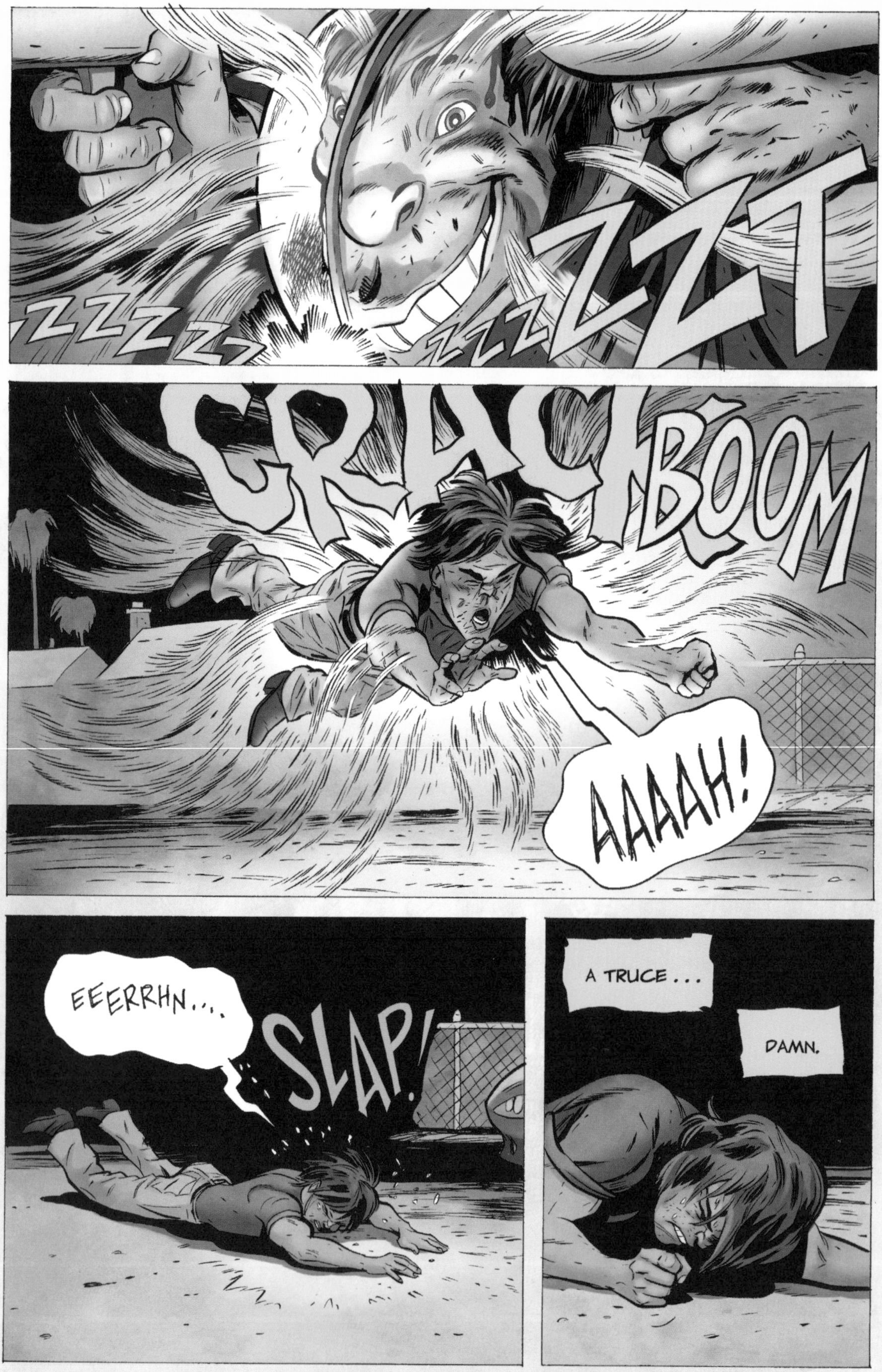

ZZZZZZ
ZZZZZZT
CRACK
BOOM
AAAAH!
EEERRHN....
SLAP!
A TRUCE...
DAMN.

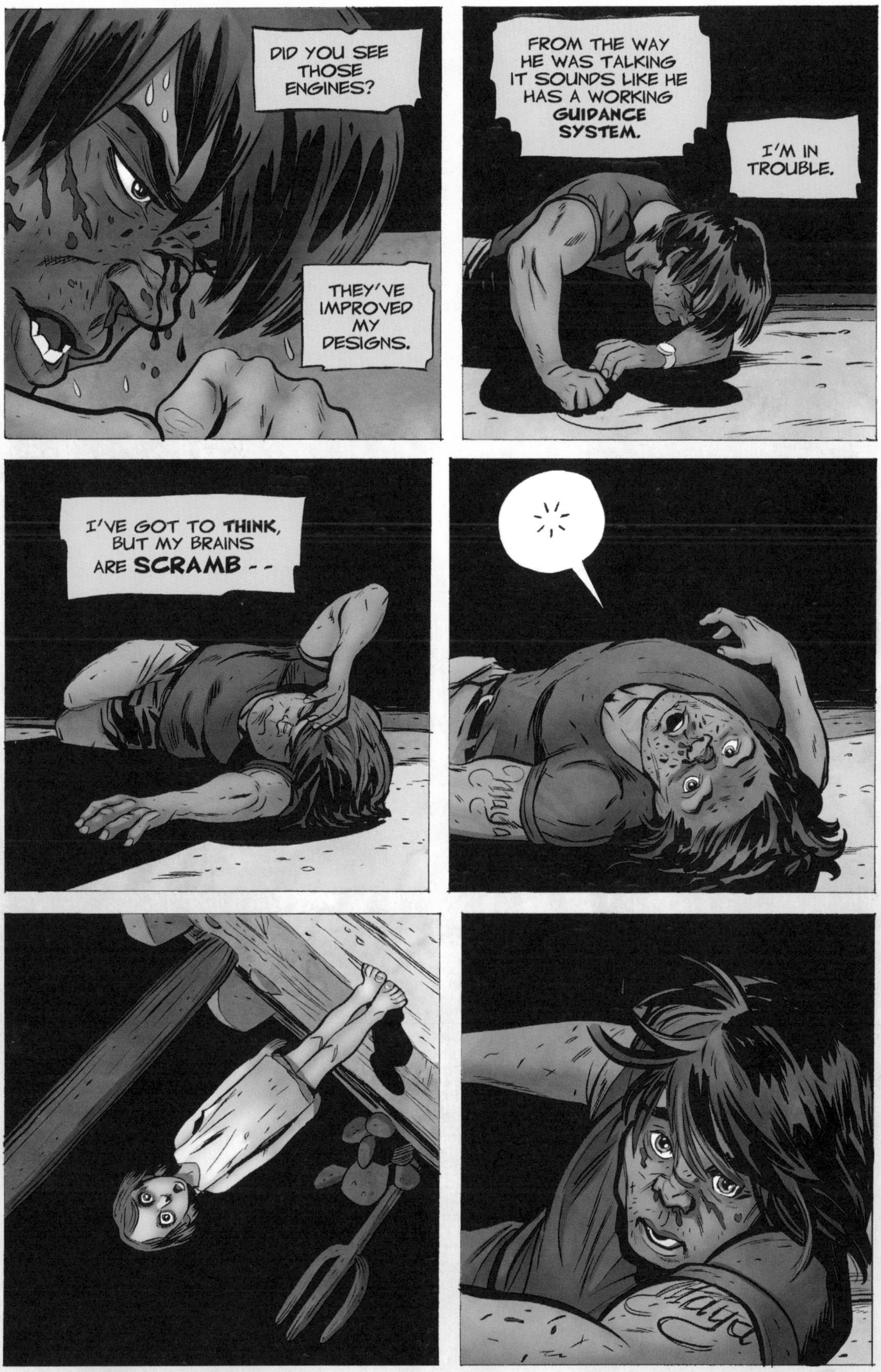
DID YOU SEE THOSE ENGINES?
THEY'VE IMPROVED MY DESIGNS.
FROM THE WAY HE WAS TALKING IT SOUNDS LIKE HE HAS A WORKING GUIDANCE SYSTEM.
I'M IN TROUBLE.
I'VE GOT TO THINK, BUT MY BRAINS ARE SCRAMB - -

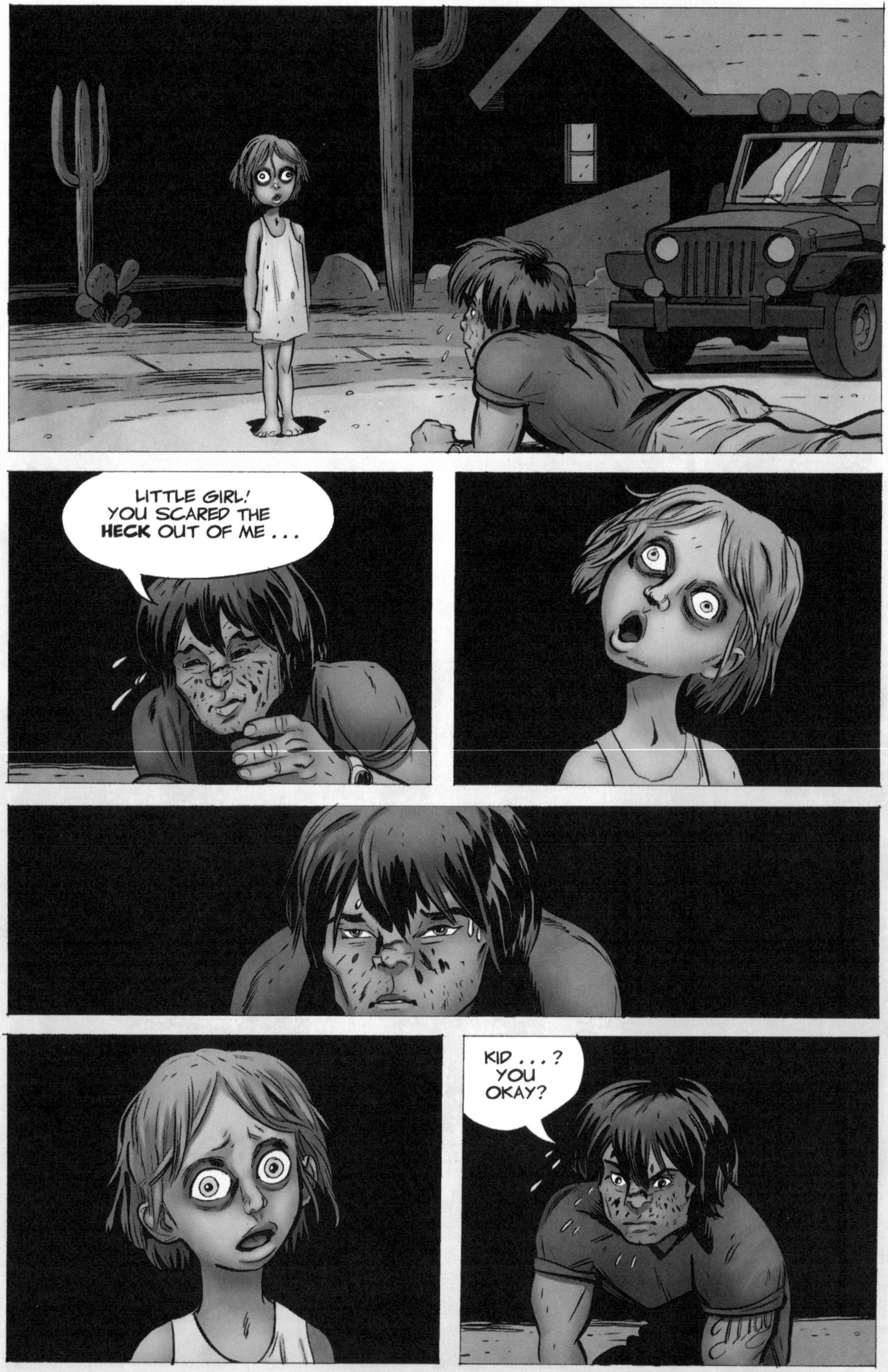
LITTLE GIRL! YOU SCARED THE HECK OUT OF ME . . .
KID . . . ? YOU OKAY?

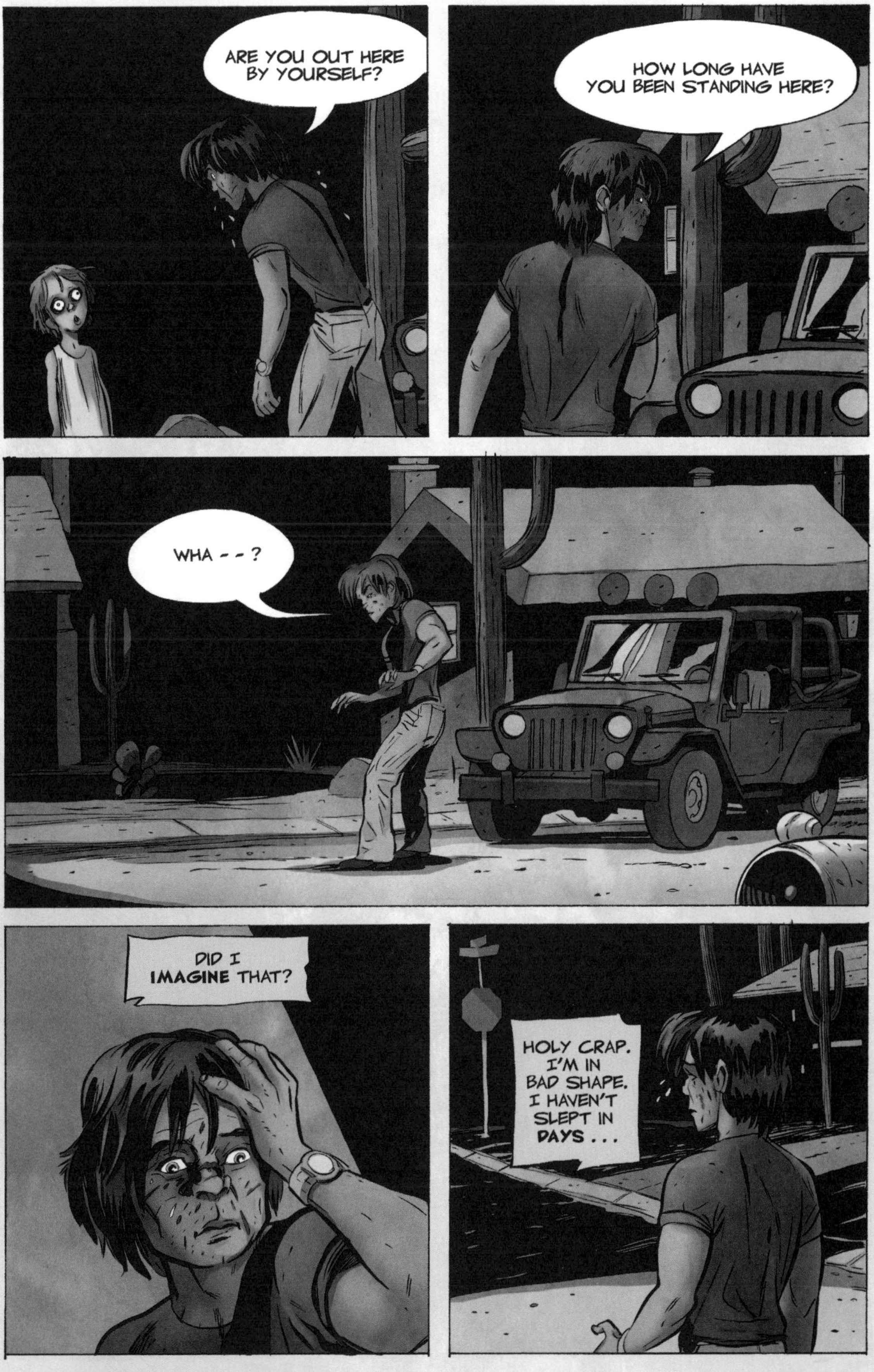
ARE YOU OUT HERE BY YOURSELF?
HOW LONG HAVE YOU BEEN STANDING HERE?
WHA - - ?
DID I IMAGINE THAT?
HOLY CRAP. I'M IN BAD SHAPE. I HAVEN'T SLEPT IN DAYS . . .

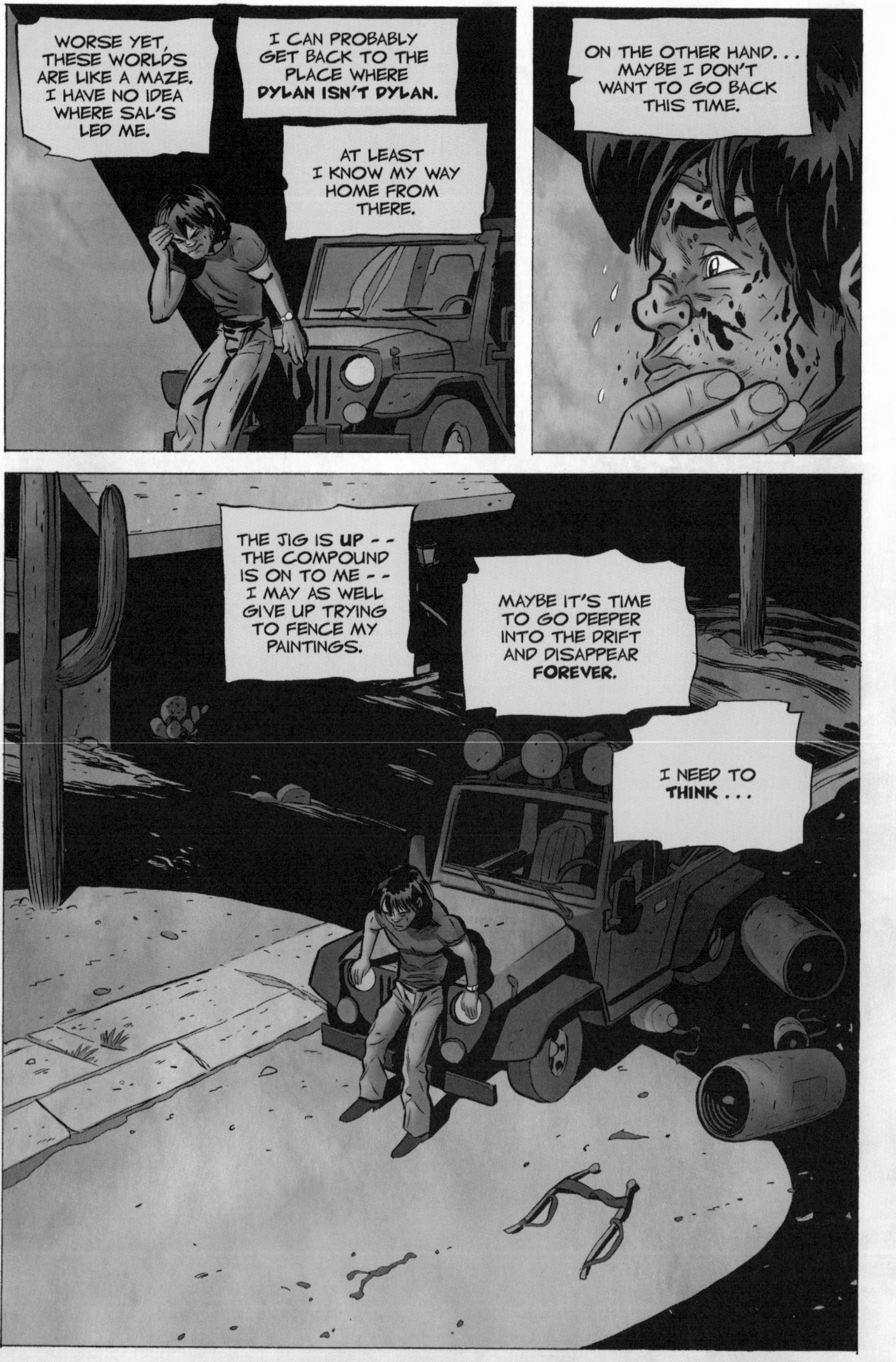
WORSE YET, THESE WORLDS ARE LIKE A MAZE. I HAVE NO IDEA WHERE SAL'S LED ME.
I CAN PROBABLY GET BACK TO THE PLACE WHERE **DYLAN ISN'T DYLAN.**
AT LEAST I KNOW MY WAY HOME FROM THERE.
ON THE OTHER HAND... MAYBE I DON'T WANT TO GO BACK THIS TIME.
THE JIG IS **UP** -- THE COMPOUND IS ON TO ME -- I MAY AS WELL GIVE UP TRYING TO FENCE MY PAINTINGS.
MAYBE IT'S TIME TO GO DEEPER INTO THE DRIFT AND DISAPPEAR **FOREVER.**
I NEED TO **THINK...**

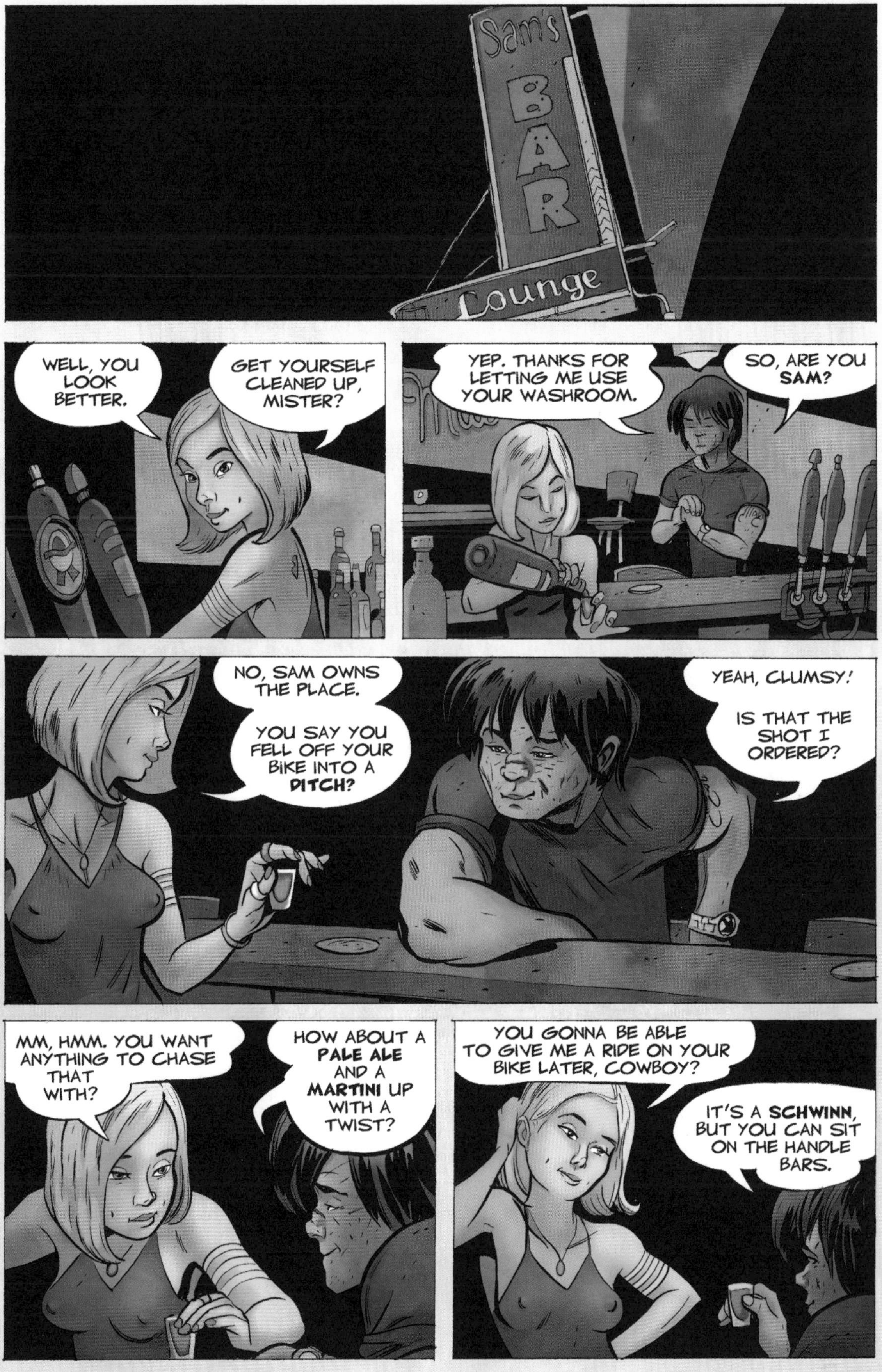
Sam's
BAR
Lounge
WELL, YOU LOOK BETTER.
GET YOURSELF CLEANED UP, MISTER?
YEP. THANKS FOR LETTING ME USE YOUR WASHROOM.
SO, ARE YOU **SAM?**
NO, SAM OWNS THE PLACE.
YOU SAY YOU FELL OFF YOUR BIKE INTO A **DITCH?**
YEAH, CLUMSY!
IS THAT THE SHOT I ORDERED?
MM, HMM. YOU WANT ANYTHING TO CHASE THAT WITH?
HOW ABOUT A **PALE ALE** AND A **MARTINI** UP WITH A TWIST?
YOU GONNA BE ABLE TO GIVE ME A RIDE ON YOUR BIKE LATER, COWBOY?
IT'S A **SCHWINN**, BUT YOU CAN SIT ON THE HANDLE BARS.

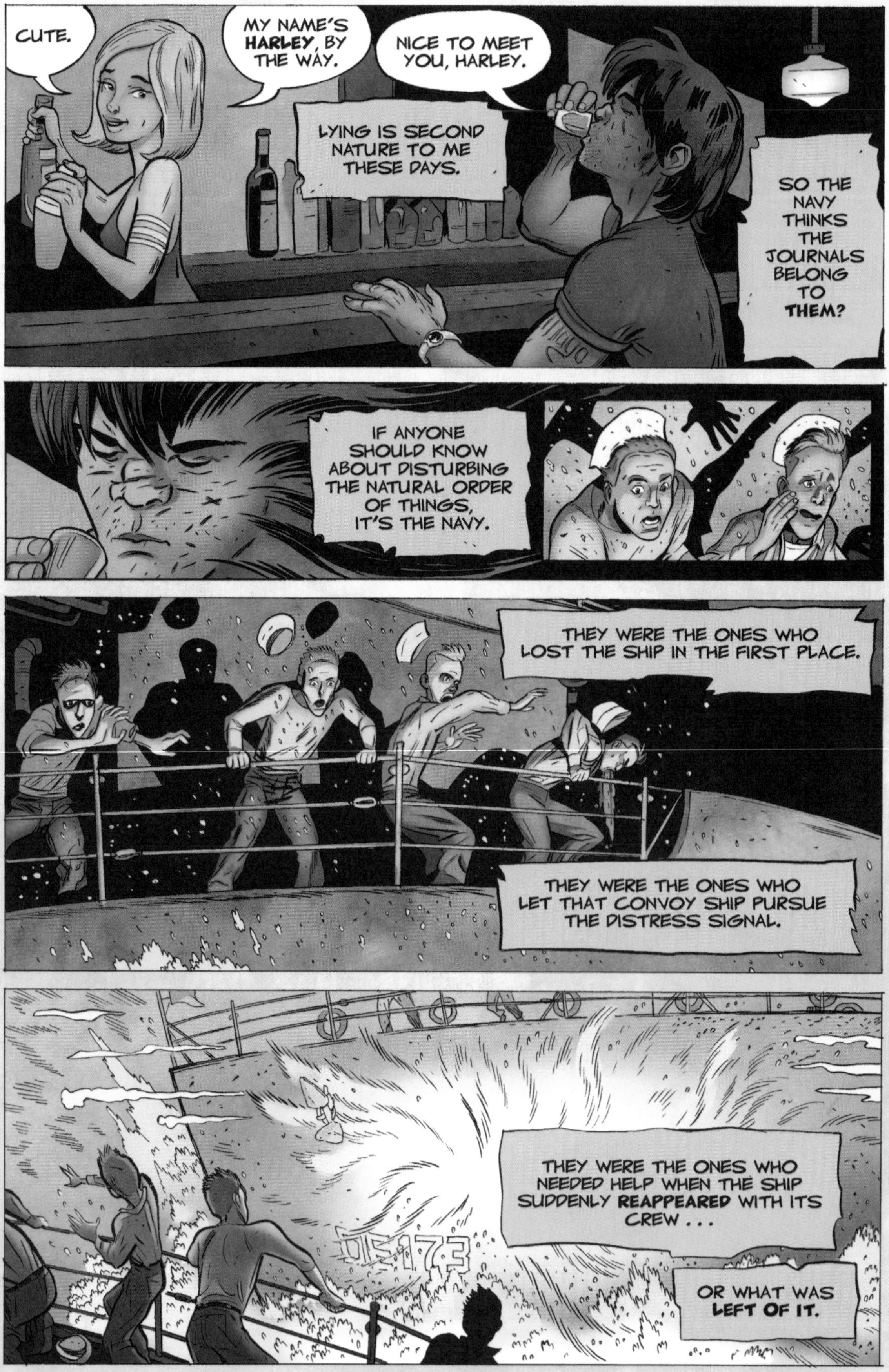

CUTE.
MY NAME'S HARLEY, BY THE WAY.
NICE TO MEET YOU, HARLEY.
LYING IS SECOND NATURE TO ME THESE DAYS.
SO THE NAVY THINKS THE JOURNALS BELONG TO THEM?
IF ANYONE SHOULD KNOW ABOUT DISTURBING THE NATURAL ORDER OF THINGS, IT'S THE NAVY.
THEY WERE THE ONES WHO LOST THE SHIP IN THE FIRST PLACE.
THEY WERE THE ONES WHO LET THAT CONVOY SHIP PURSUE THE DISTRESS SIGNAL.
THEY WERE THE ONES WHO NEEDED HELP WHEN THE SHIP SUDDENLY REAPPEARED WITH ITS CREW . . .
DE173
OR WHAT WAS LEFT OF IT.

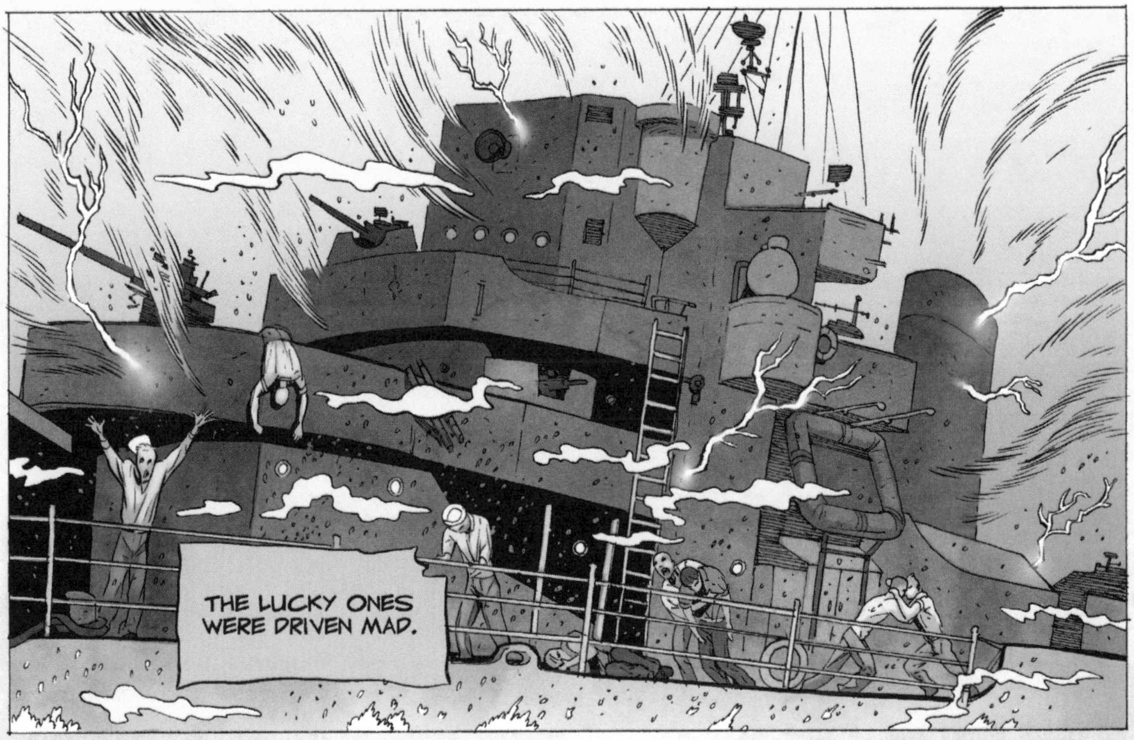
THE LUCKY ONES WERE DRIVEN MAD.

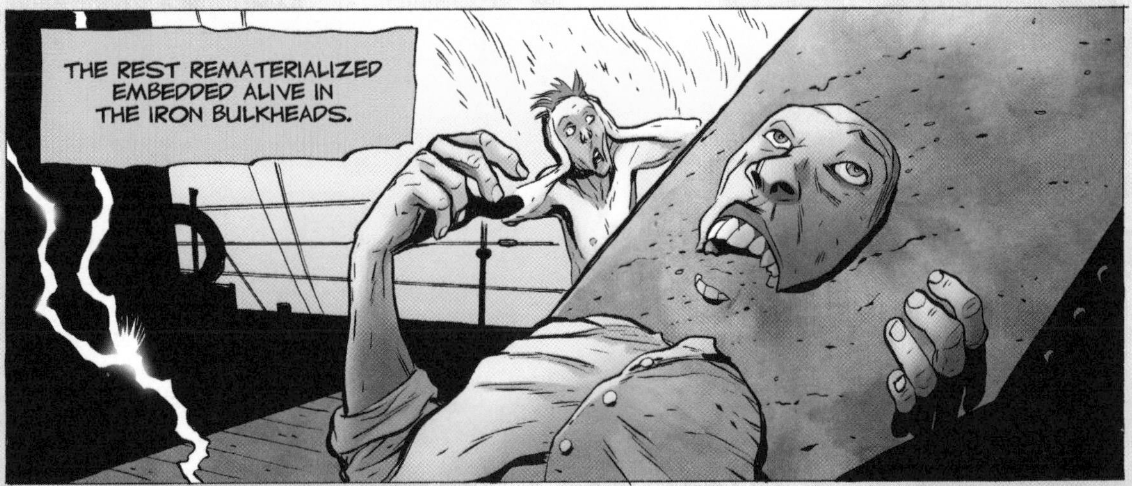
THE REST REMATERIALIZED EMBEDDED ALIVE IN THE IRON BULKHEADS.

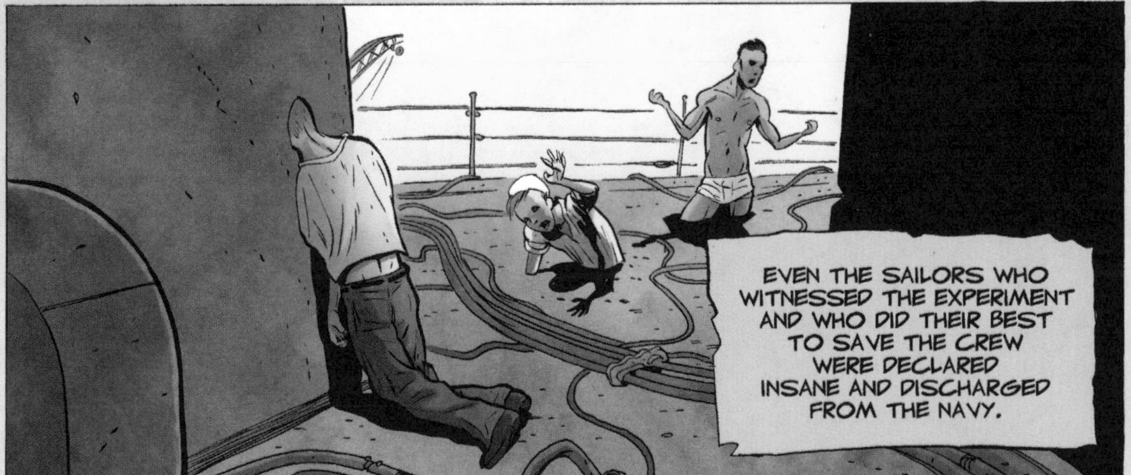
EVEN THE SAILORS WHO WITNESSED THE EXPERIMENT AND WHO DID THEIR BEST TO SAVE THE CREW WERE DECLARED INSANE AND DISCHARGED FROM THE NAVY.

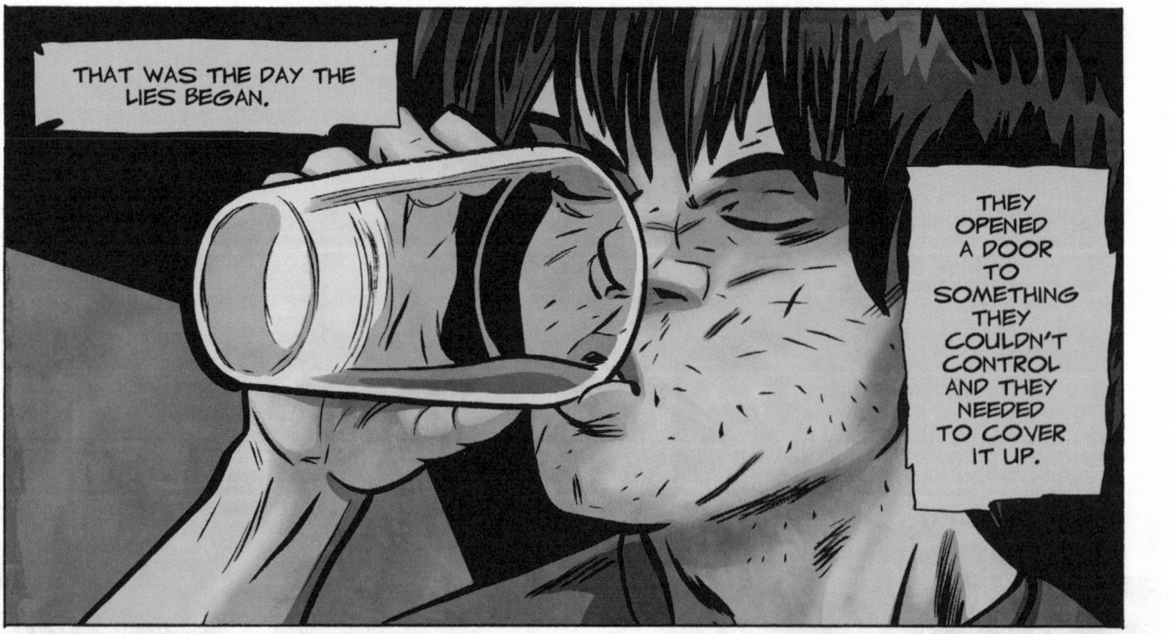
THAT WAS THE DAY THE LIES BEGAN.
THEY OPENED A DOOR TO SOMETHING THEY COULDN'T CONTROL AND THEY NEEDED TO COVER IT UP.

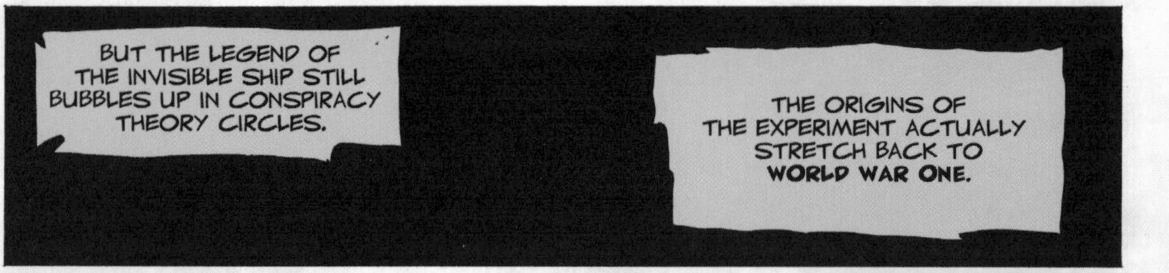
BUT THE LEGEND OF THE INVISIBLE SHIP STILL BUBBLES UP IN CONSPIRACY THEORY CIRCLES.
THE ORIGINS OF THE EXPERIMENT ACTUALLY STRETCH BACK TO WORLD WAR ONE.

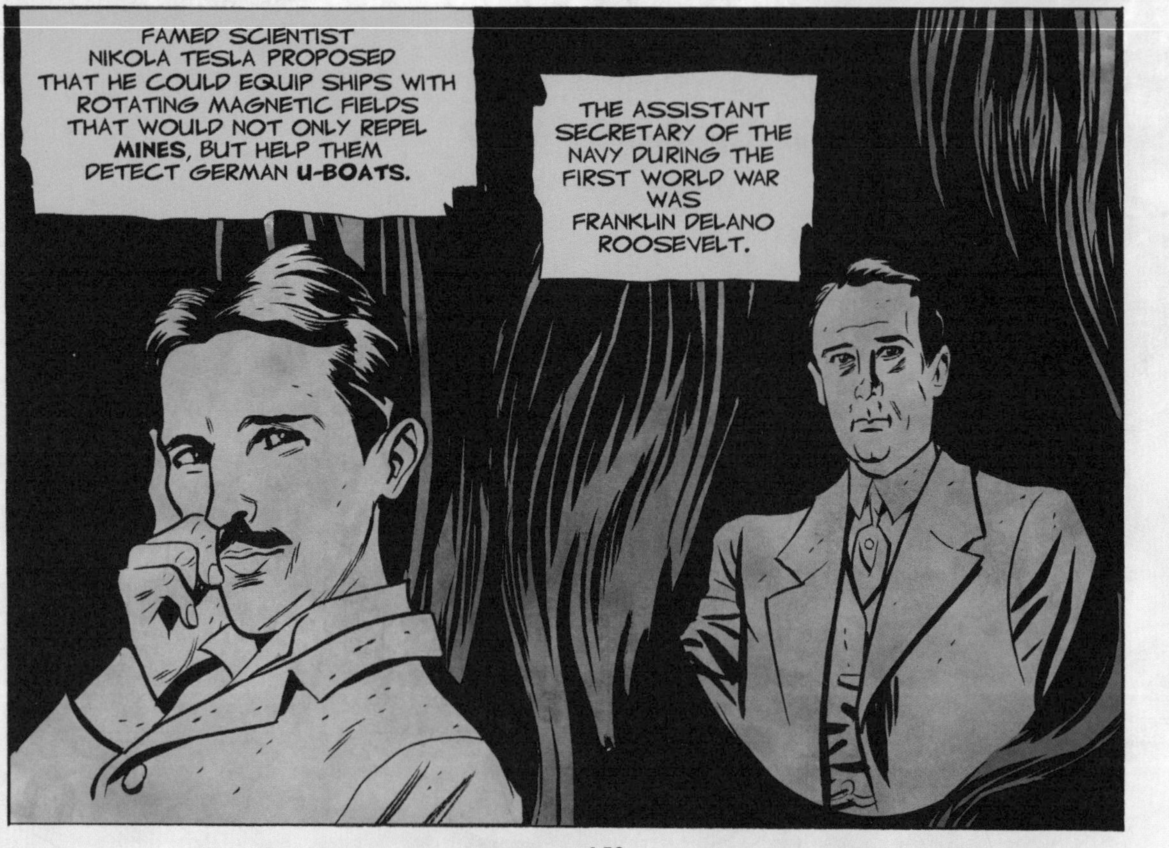
FAMED SCIENTIST NIKOLA TESLA PROPOSED THAT HE COULD EQUIP SHIPS WITH ROTATING MAGNETIC FIELDS THAT WOULD NOT ONLY REPEL MINES, BUT HELP THEM DETECT GERMAN U-BOATS.
THE ASSISTANT SECRETARY OF THE NAVY DURING THE FIRST WORLD WAR WAS FRANKLIN DELANO ROOSEVELT.

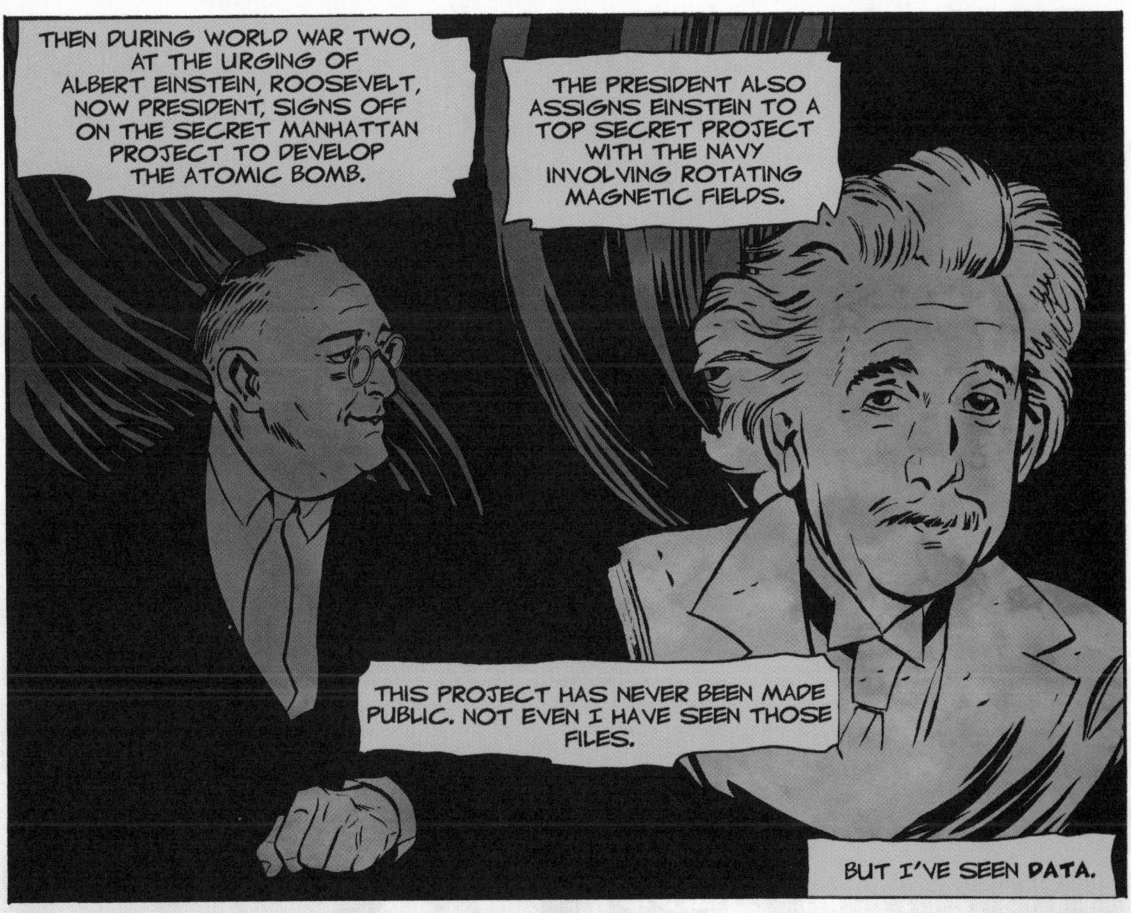
THEN DURING WORLD WAR TWO, AT THE URGING OF ALBERT EINSTEIN, ROOSEVELT, NOW PRESIDENT, SIGNS OFF ON THE SECRET MANHATTAN PROJECT TO DEVELOP THE ATOMIC BOMB.
THE PRESIDENT ALSO ASSIGNS EINSTEIN TO A TOP SECRET PROJECT WITH THE NAVY INVOLVING ROTATING MAGNETIC FIELDS.
THIS PROJECT HAS NEVER BEEN MADE PUBLIC. NOT EVEN I HAVE SEEN THOSE FILES.
BUT I'VE SEEN **DATA.**

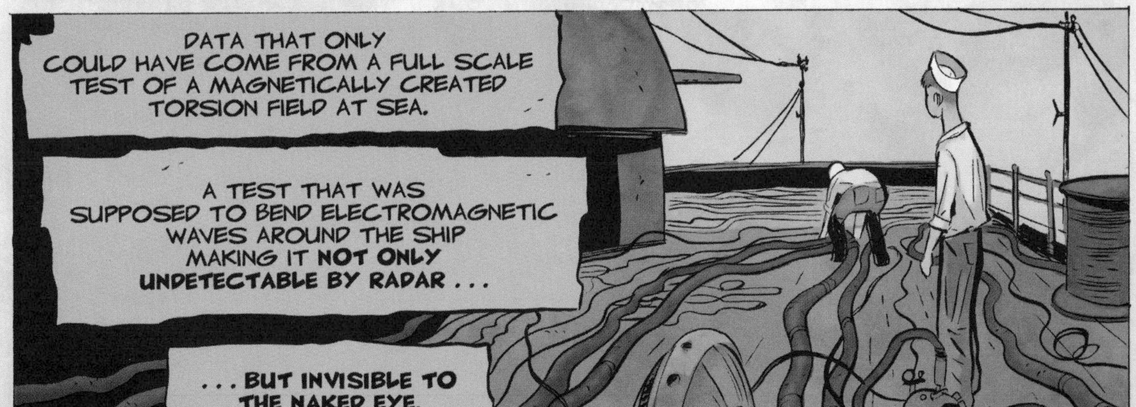
DATA THAT ONLY COULD HAVE COME FROM A FULL SCALE TEST OF A MAGNETICALLY CREATED TORSION FIELD AT SEA.
A TEST THAT WAS SUPPOSED TO BEND ELECTROMAGNETIC WAVES AROUND THE SHIP MAKING IT **NOT ONLY UNDETECTABLE BY RADAR . . .**
. . . BUT INVISIBLE TO THE NAKED EYE.

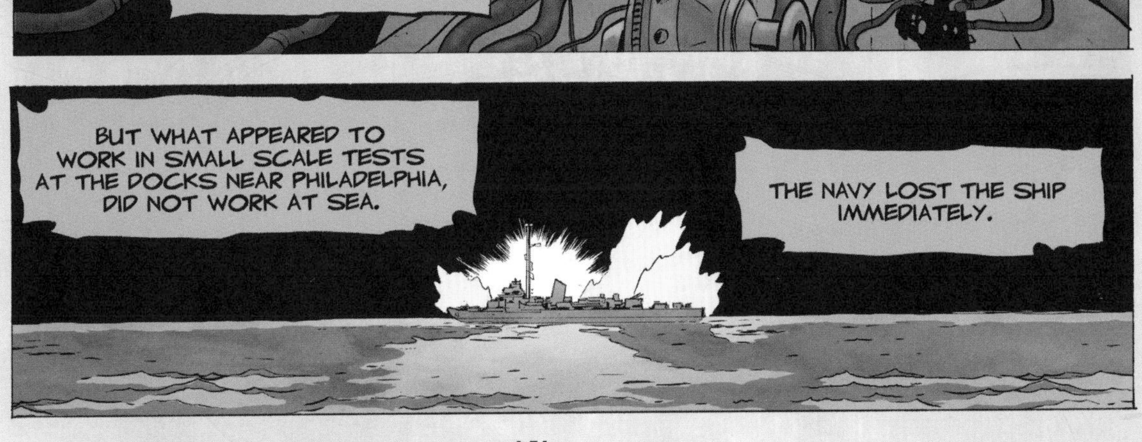
BUT WHAT APPEARED TO WORK IN SMALL SCALE TESTS AT THE DOCKS NEAR PHILADELPHIA, DID NOT WORK AT SEA.
THE NAVY LOST THE SHIP IMMEDIATELY.

THE DATA I'VE SEEN WOULD INDICATE THAT THE ENTIRE SHIP AND ITS CREW WOULD VANISH FROM SIGHT AND REAPPEAR MYSTERIOUSLY HUNDREDS OF MILES AWAY . . .

. . . OVER AND OVER AGAIN FOR SIX DAYS.

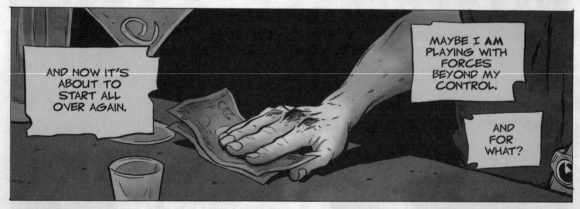

AND NOW IT'S ABOUT TO START ALL OVER AGAIN.

MAYBE I AM PLAYING WITH FORCES BEYOND MY CONTROL.

AND FOR WHAT?

WHY SHOULD I RISK MY NECK AGAINST THESE KILLERS?

THE REAL ANNIE IS DEAD. I HAVE NO REASON TO GO BACK.

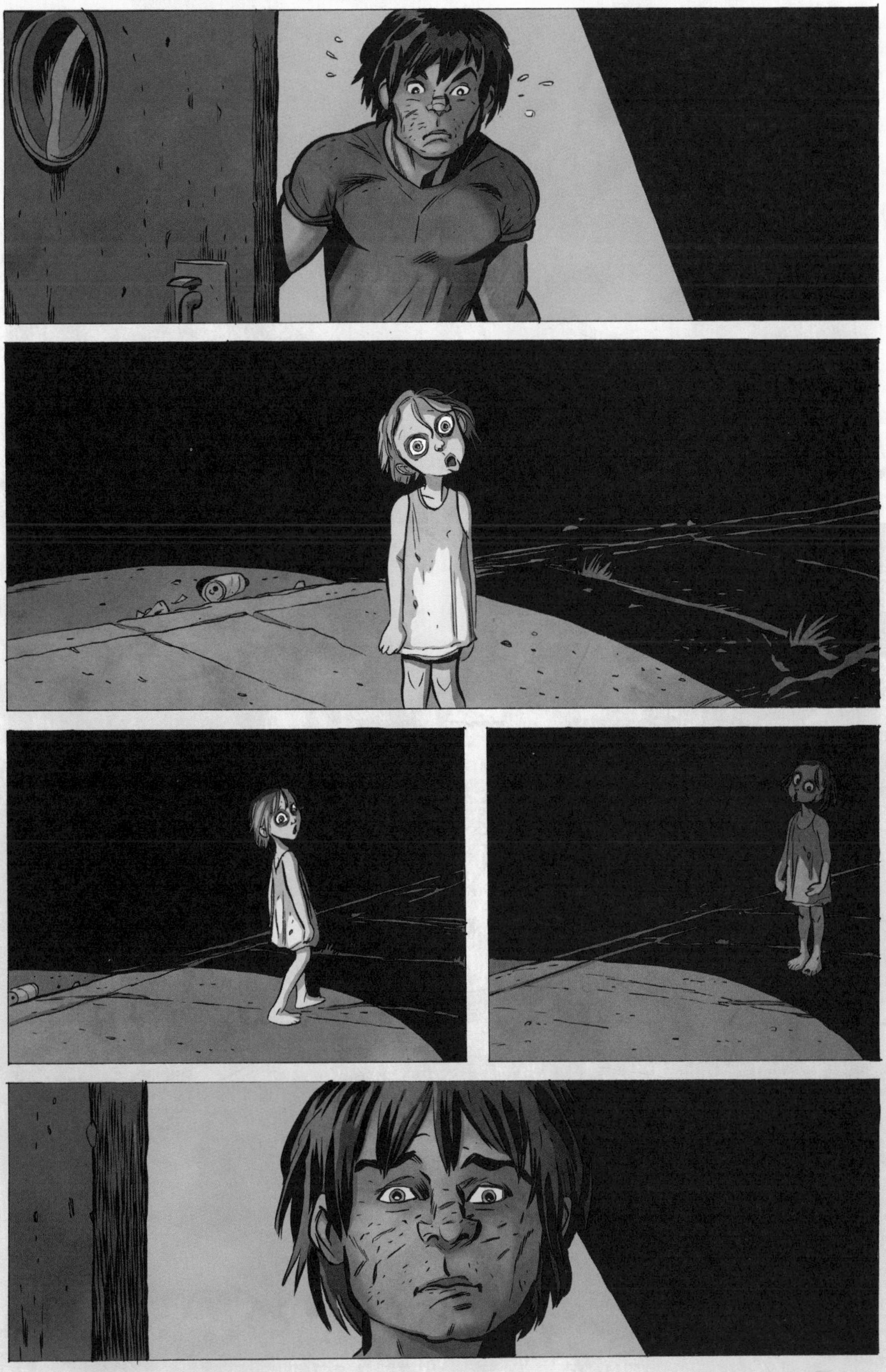

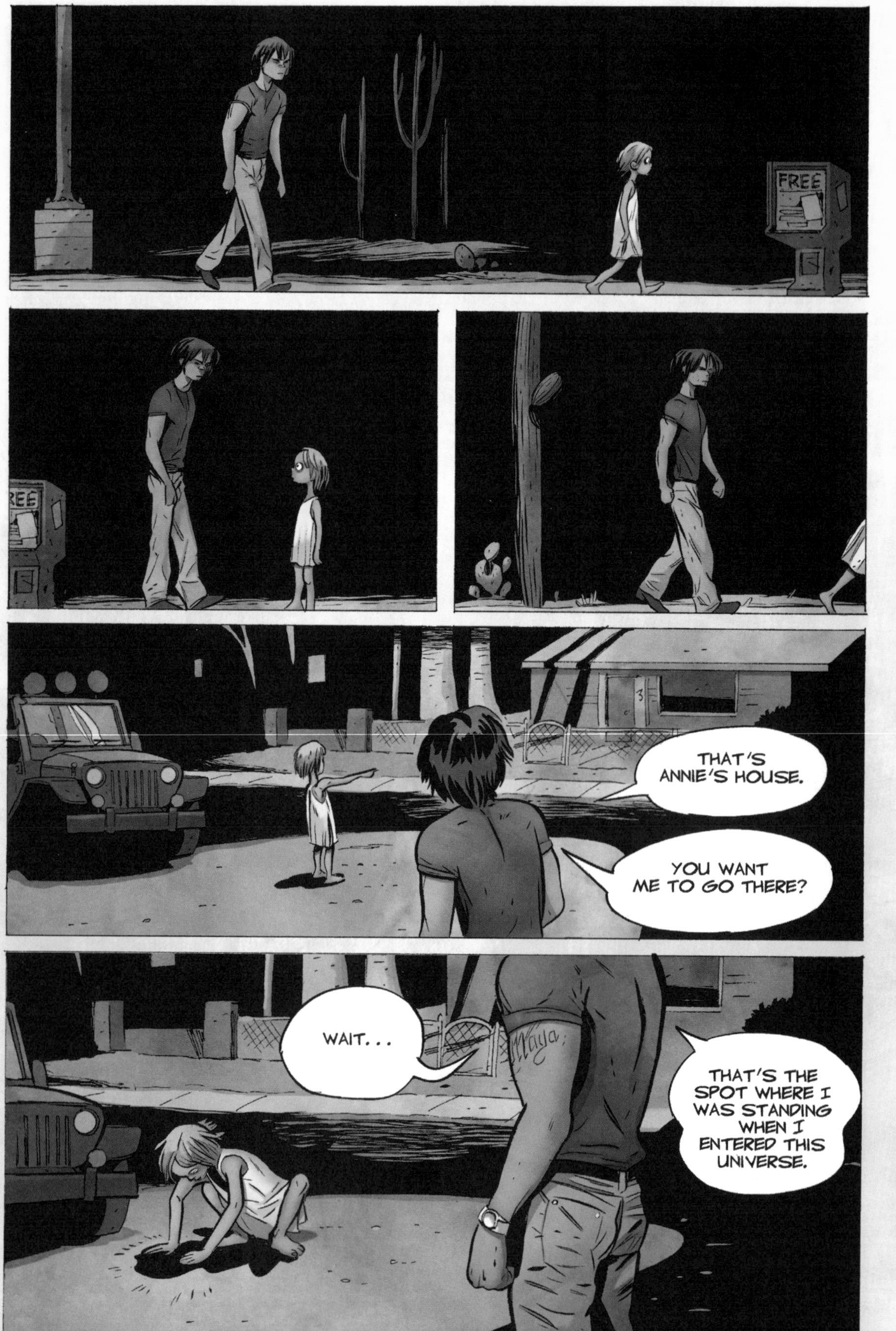
FREE
THAT'S ANNIE'S HOUSE.
YOU WANT ME TO GO THERE?
WAIT. . .
THAT'S THE SPOT WHERE I WAS STANDING WHEN I ENTERED THIS UNIVERSE.

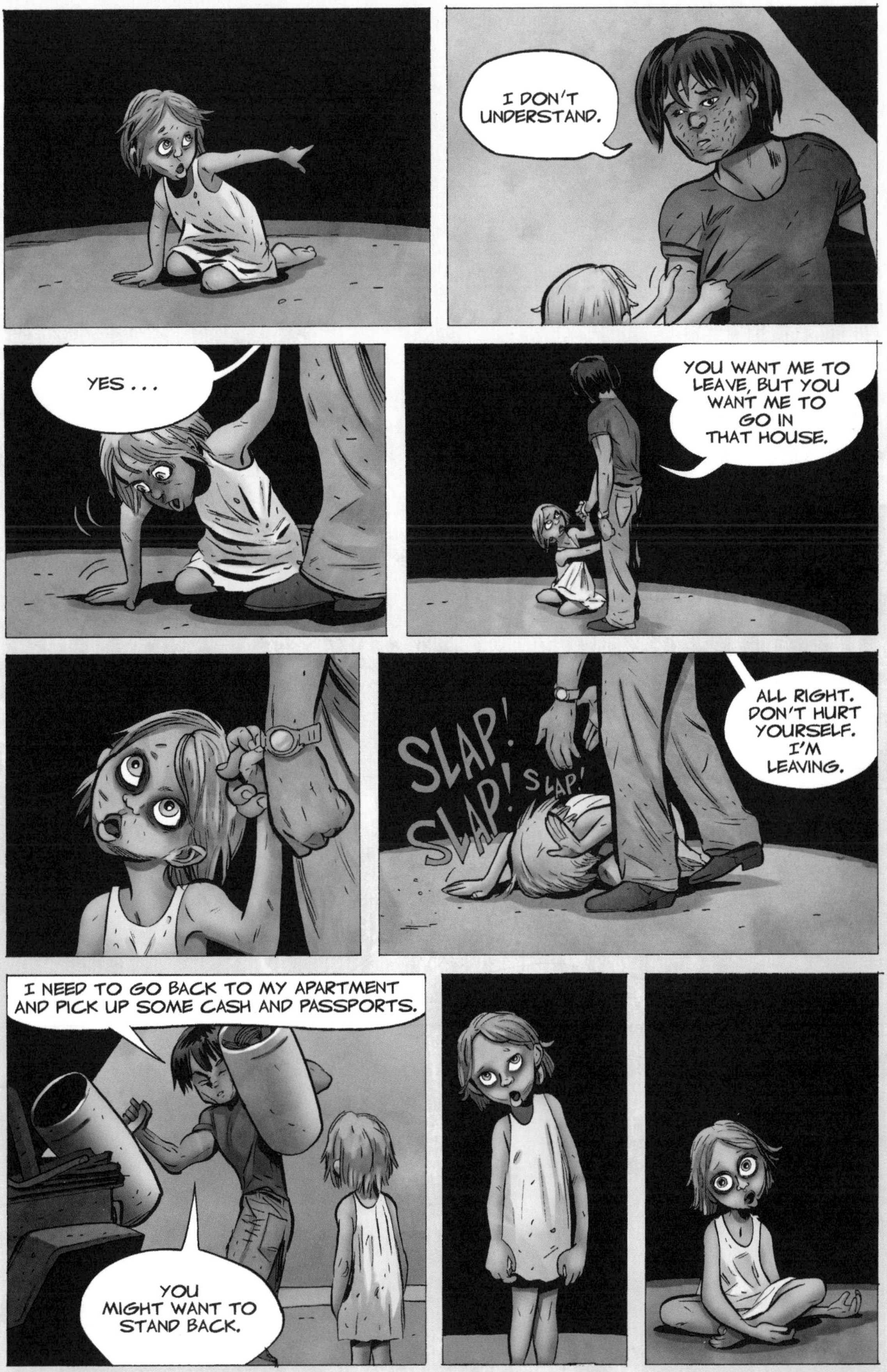
I DON'T UNDERSTAND.
YES . . .
YOU WANT ME TO LEAVE, BUT YOU WANT ME TO GO IN THAT HOUSE.
SLAP! SLAP! SLAP!
ALL RIGHT. DON'T HURT YOURSELF. I'M LEAVING.
I NEED TO GO BACK TO MY APARTMENT AND PICK UP SOME CASH AND PASSPORTS.
YOU MIGHT WANT TO STAND BACK.

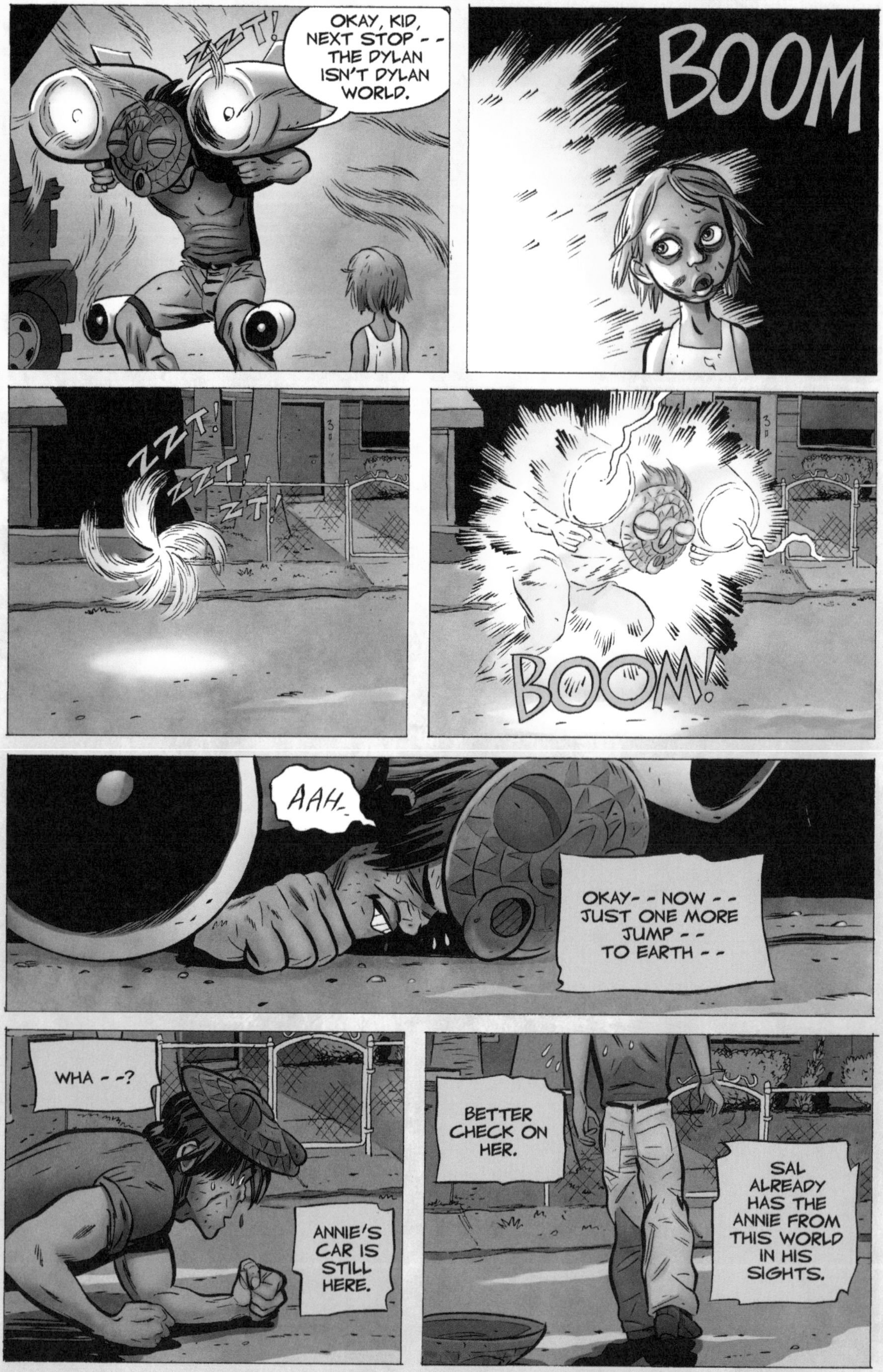
ZZZT!
OKAY, KID, NEXT STOP - - THE DYLAN ISN'T DYLAN WORLD.
BOOM
ZZZT!
ZZZT!
ZZT!
BOOM!
AAH
OKAY- - NOW - - JUST ONE MORE JUMP - - TO EARTH - -
WHA - -?
ANNIE'S CAR IS STILL HERE.
BETTER CHECK ON HER.
SAL ALREADY HAS THE ANNIE FROM THIS WORLD IN HIS SIGHTS.

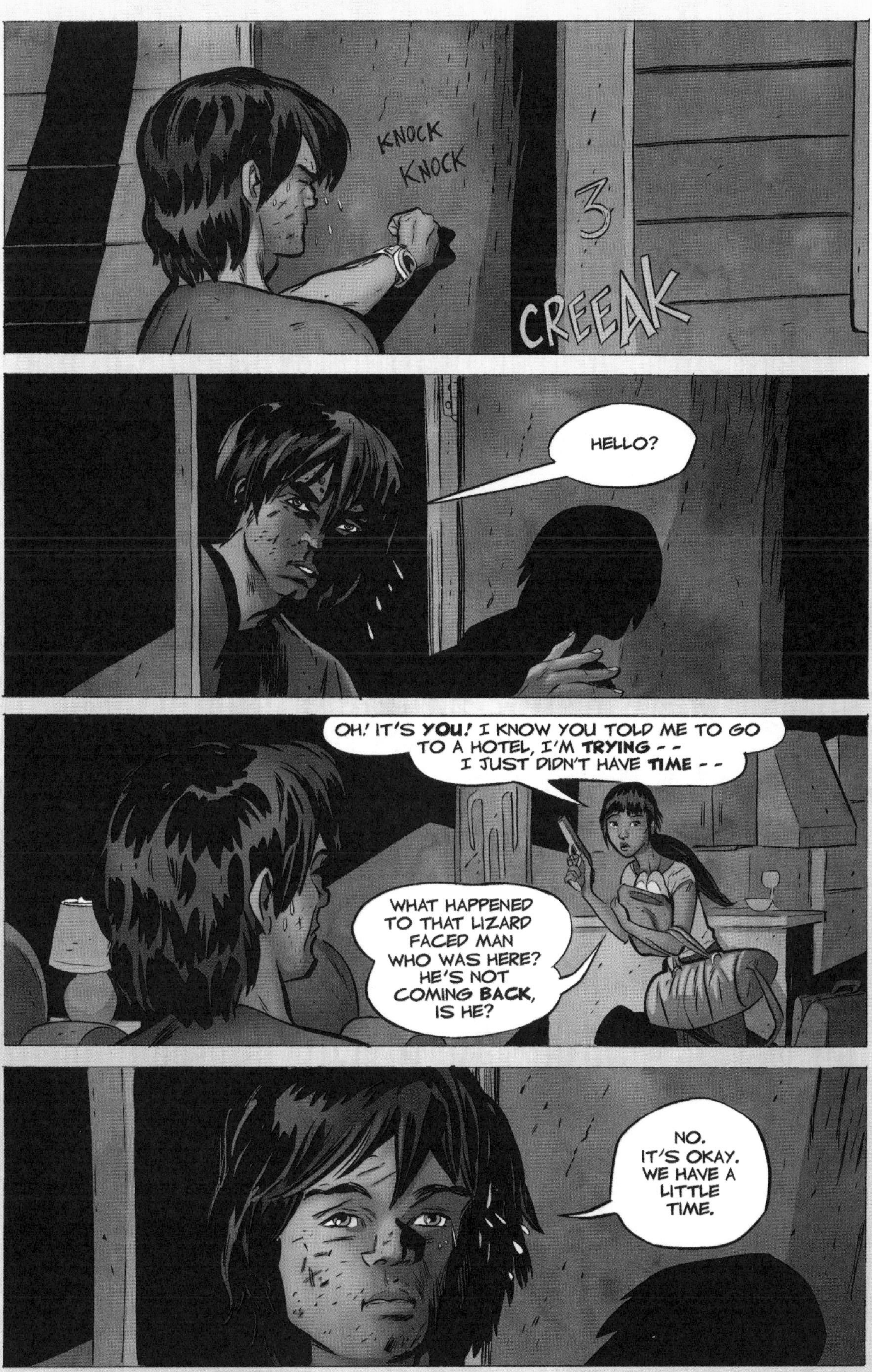
KNOCK
KNOCK
3
CREEAK
HELLO?
OH! IT'S YOU! I KNOW YOU TOLD ME TO GO TO A HOTEL, I'M TRYING - - I JUST DIDN'T HAVE TIME - -
WHAT HAPPENED TO THAT LIZARD FACED MAN WHO WAS HERE? HE'S NOT COMING BACK, IS HE?
NO. IT'S OKAY. WE HAVE A LITTLE TIME.

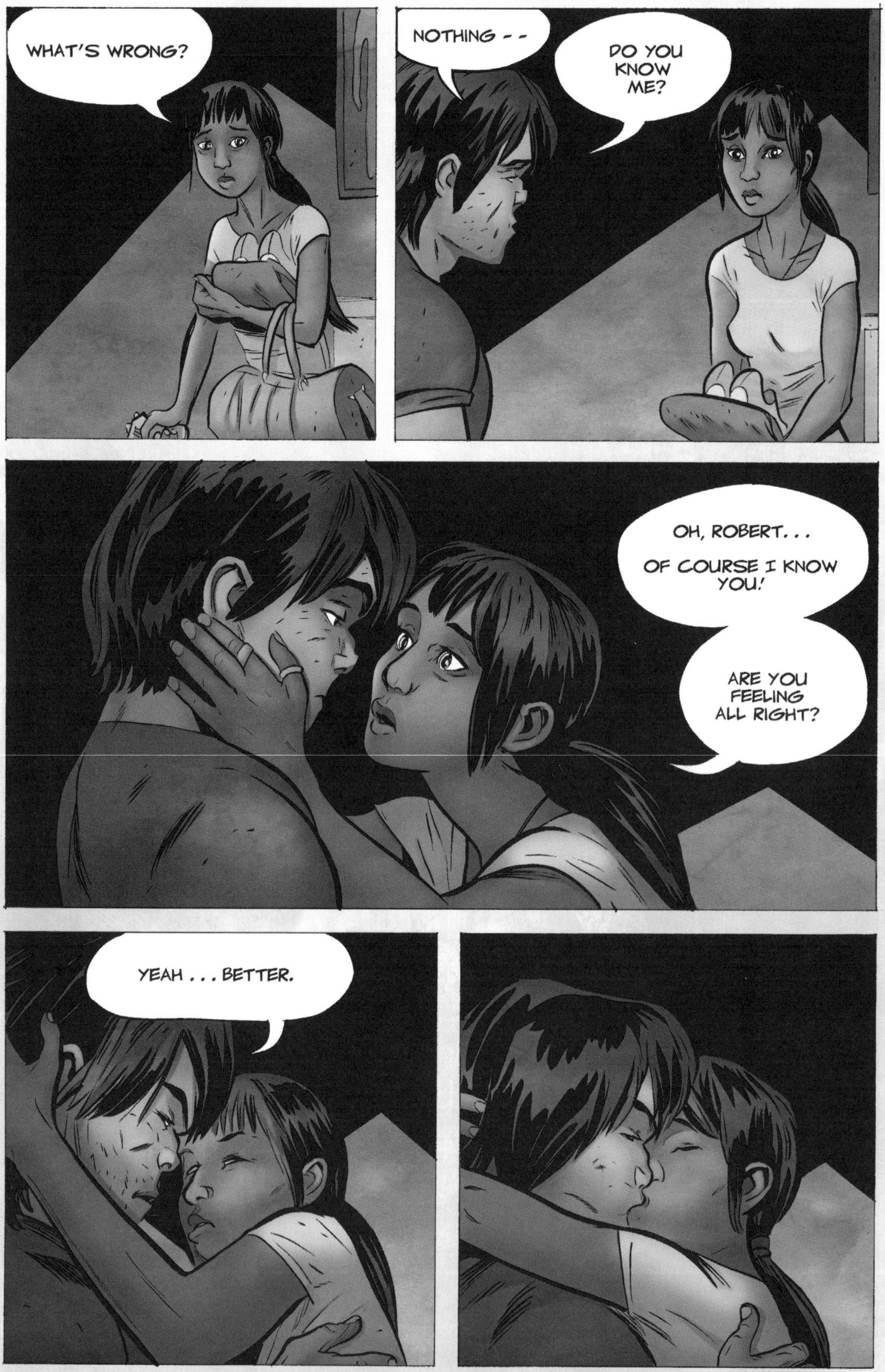
WHAT'S WRONG?
NOTHING - -
DO YOU KNOW ME?
OH, ROBERT. . .
OF COURSE I KNOW YOU!
ARE YOU FEELING ALL RIGHT?
YEAH . . . BETTER.

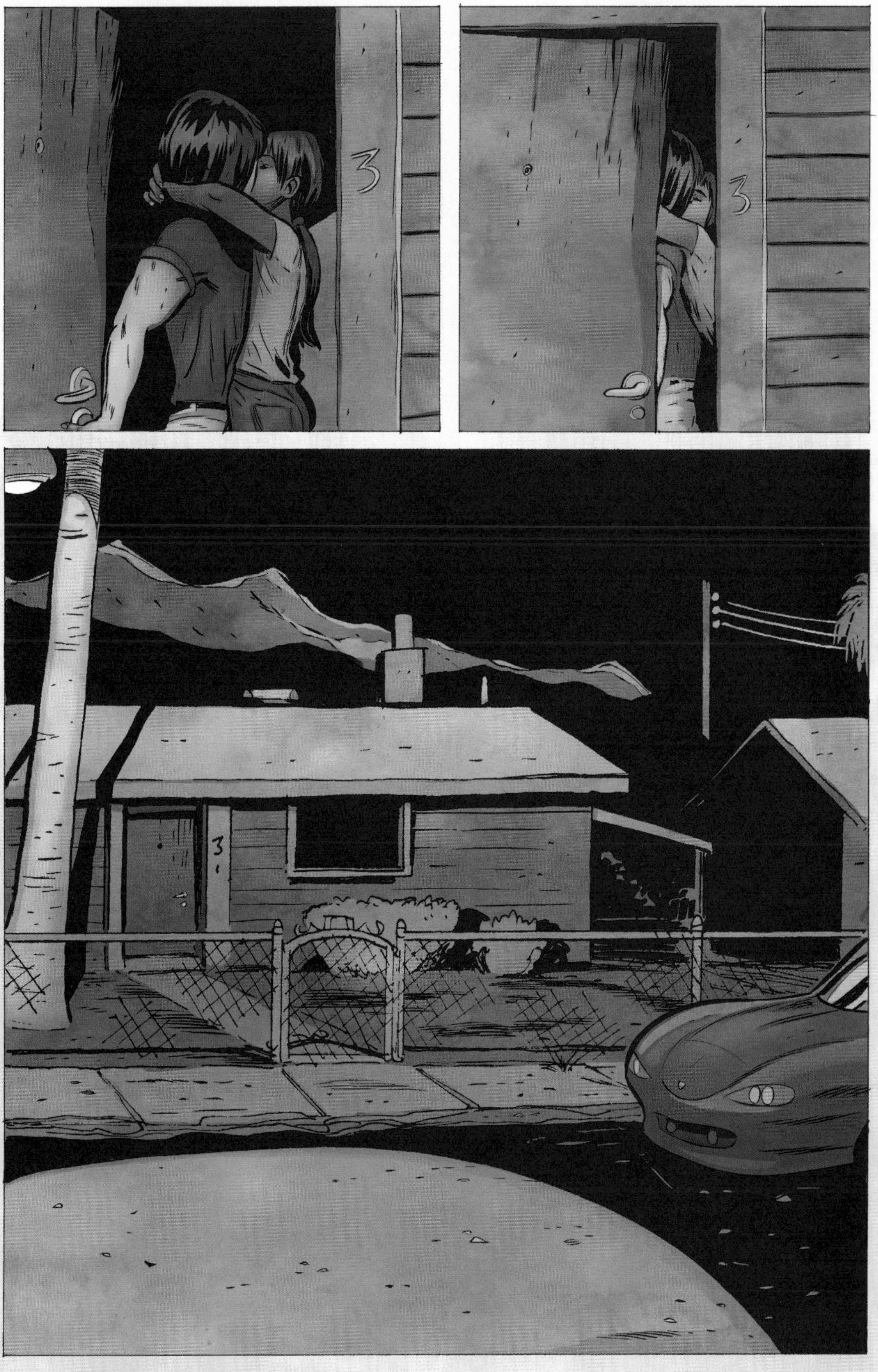

V

UMA

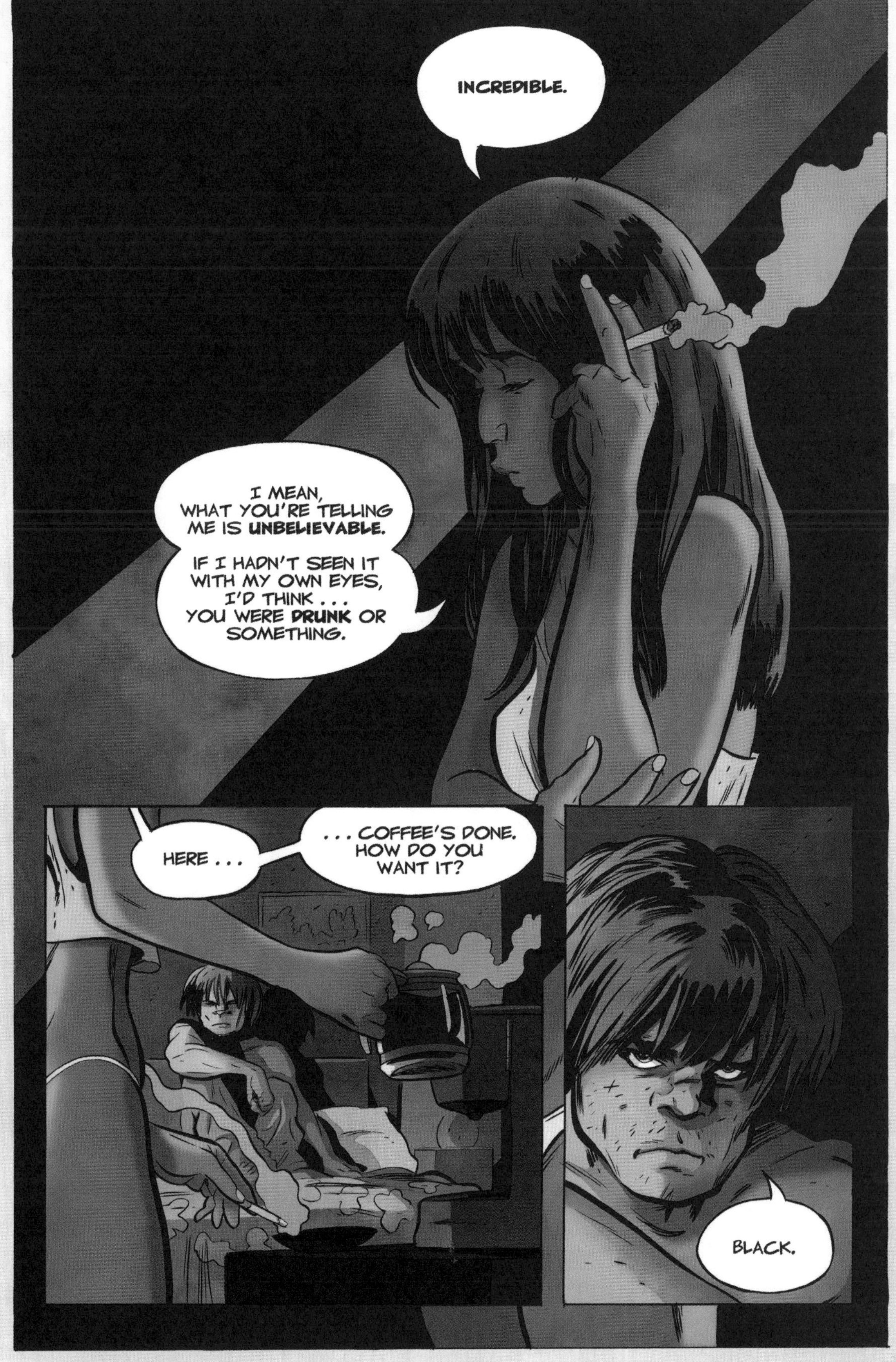
INCREDIBLE.
I MEAN, WHAT YOU'RE TELLING ME IS UNBELIEVABLE.
IF I HADN'T SEEN IT WITH MY OWN EYES, I'D THINK . . . YOU WERE DRUNK OR SOMETHING.
HERE . . .
. . . COFFEE'S DONE. HOW DO YOU WANT IT?
BLACK.

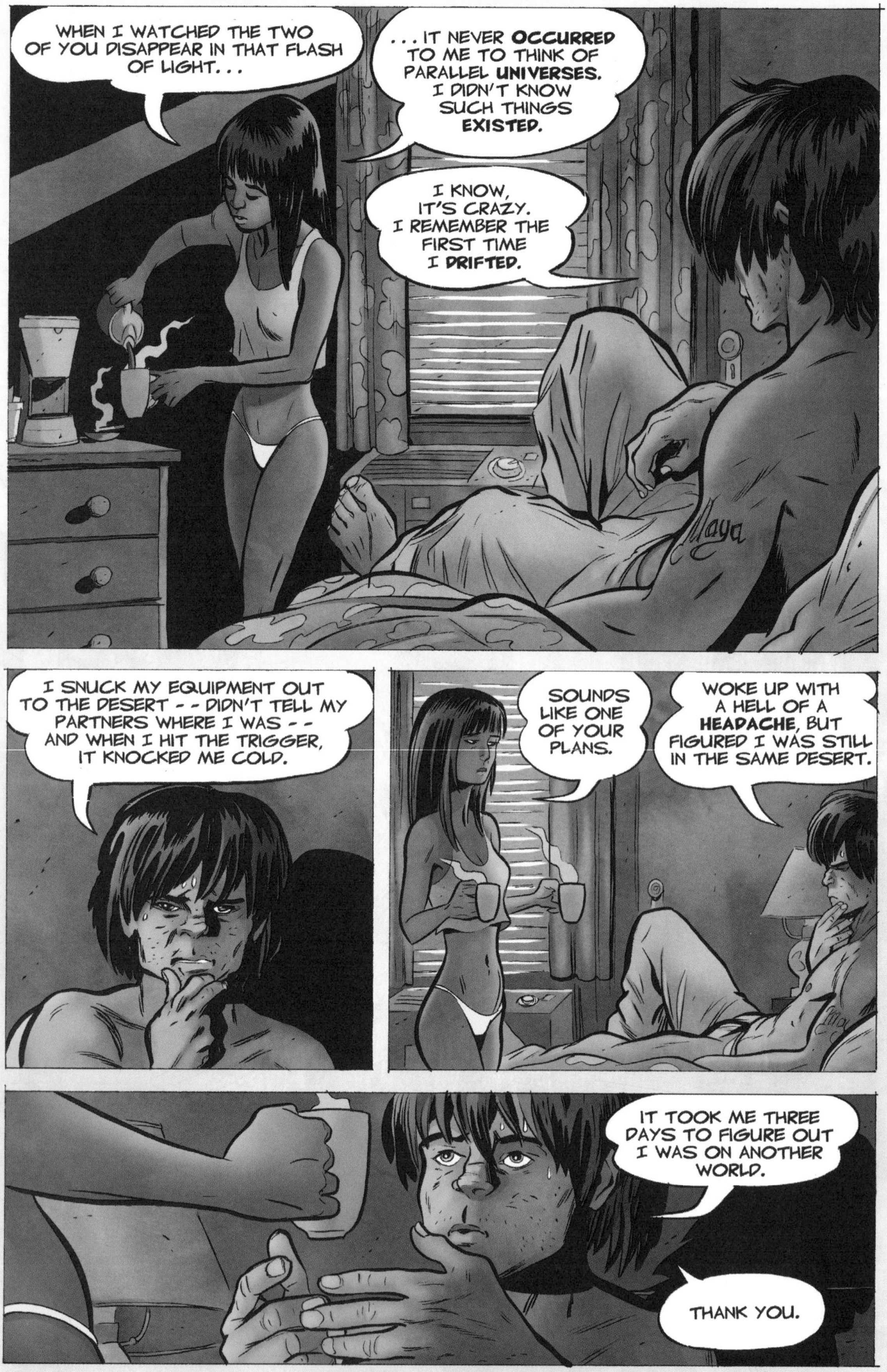
WHEN I WATCHED THE TWO OF YOU DISAPPEAR IN THAT FLASH OF LIGHT. . .
. . . IT NEVER OCCURRED TO ME TO THINK OF PARALLEL UNIVERSES. I DIDN'T KNOW SUCH THINGS EXISTED.
I KNOW, IT'S CRAZY. I REMEMBER THE FIRST TIME I DRIFTED.
Maya
I SNUCK MY EQUIPMENT OUT TO THE DESERT - - DIDN'T TELL MY PARTNERS WHERE I WAS - - AND WHEN I HIT THE TRIGGER, IT KNOCKED ME COLD.
SOUNDS LIKE ONE OF YOUR PLANS.
WOKE UP WITH A HELL OF A HEADACHE, BUT FIGURED I WAS STILL IN THE SAME DESERT.
IT TOOK ME THREE DAYS TO FIGURE OUT I WAS ON ANOTHER WORLD.
THANK YOU.

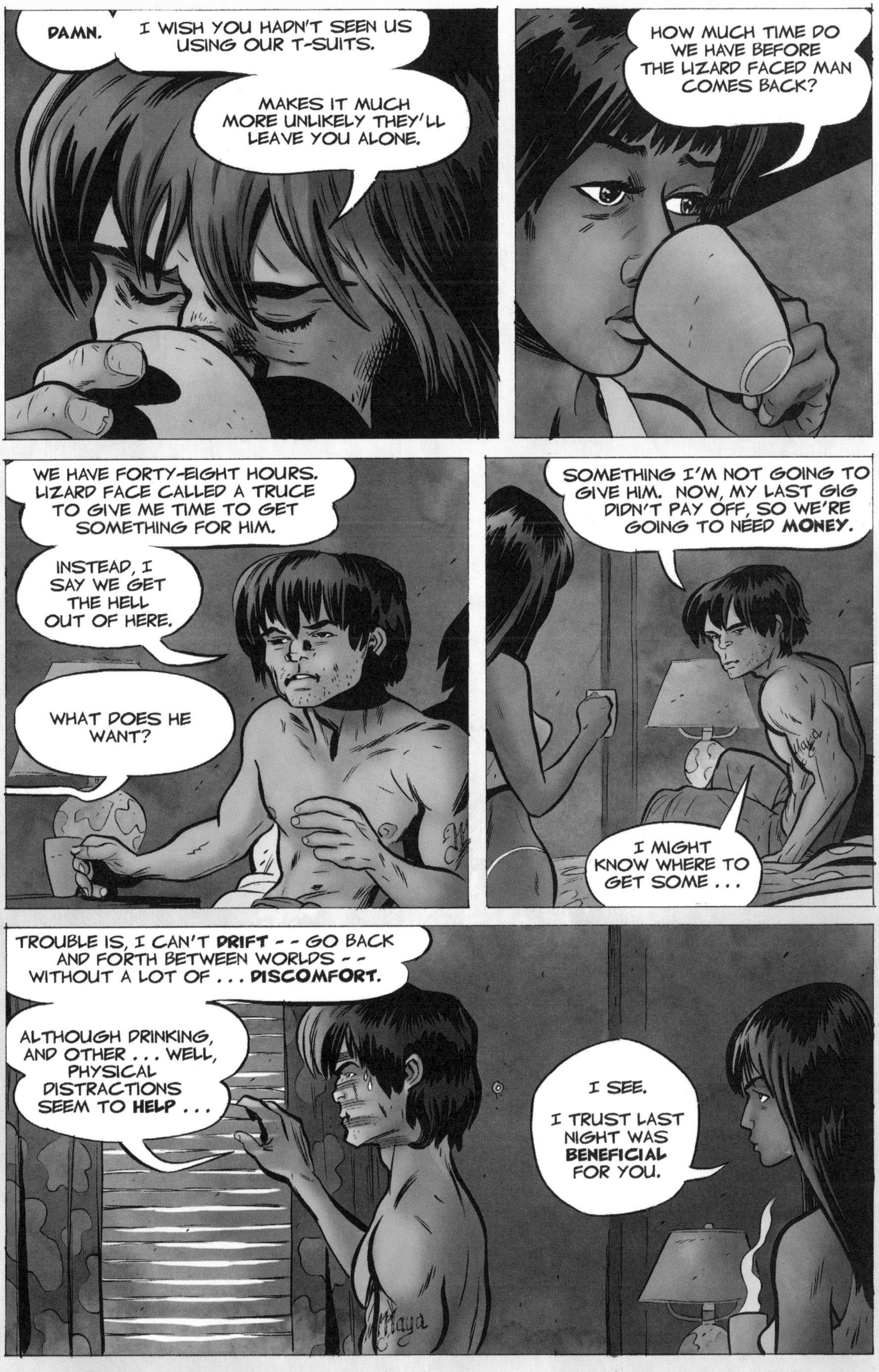
DAMN.
I WISH YOU HADN'T SEEN US USING OUR T-SUITS.
MAKES IT MUCH MORE UNLIKELY THEY'LL LEAVE YOU ALONE.
HOW MUCH TIME DO WE HAVE BEFORE THE LIZARD FACED MAN COMES BACK?
WE HAVE FORTY-EIGHT HOURS. LIZARD FACE CALLED A TRUCE TO GIVE ME TIME TO GET SOMETHING FOR HIM.
INSTEAD, I SAY WE GET THE HELL OUT OF HERE.
WHAT DOES HE WANT?
SOMETHING I'M NOT GOING TO GIVE HIM. NOW, MY LAST GIG DIDN'T PAY OFF, SO WE'RE GOING TO NEED MONEY.
I MIGHT KNOW WHERE TO GET SOME . . .
TROUBLE IS, I CAN'T DRIFT - - GO BACK AND FORTH BETWEEN WORLDS - - WITHOUT A LOT OF . . . DISCOMFORT.
ALTHOUGH DRINKING, AND OTHER . . . WELL, PHYSICAL DISTRACTIONS SEEM TO HELP . . .
I SEE.
I TRUST LAST NIGHT WAS BENEFICIAL FOR YOU.
Maya

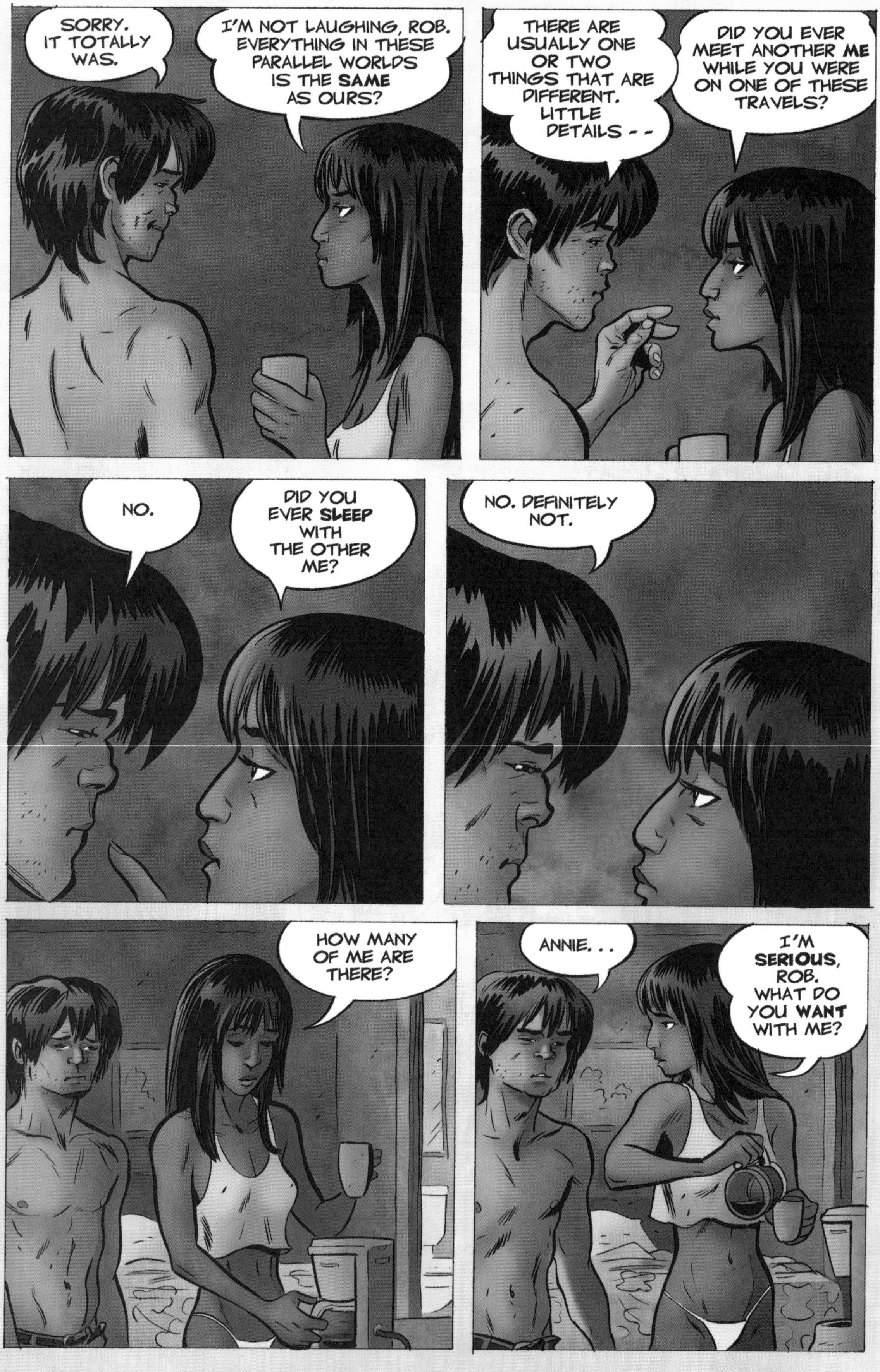
SORRY. IT TOTALLY WAS.
I'M NOT LAUGHING, ROB. EVERYTHING IN THESE PARALLEL WORLDS IS THE **SAME** AS OURS?
THERE ARE USUALLY ONE OR TWO THINGS THAT ARE DIFFERENT. LITTLE DETAILS - -
DID YOU EVER MEET ANOTHER **ME** WHILE YOU WERE ON ONE OF THESE TRAVELS?
NO.
DID YOU EVER **SLEEP** WITH THE OTHER ME?
NO. DEFINITELY NOT.
HOW MANY OF ME ARE THERE?
ANNIE. . .
I'M **SERIOUS**, ROB. WHAT DO YOU **WANT** WITH ME?

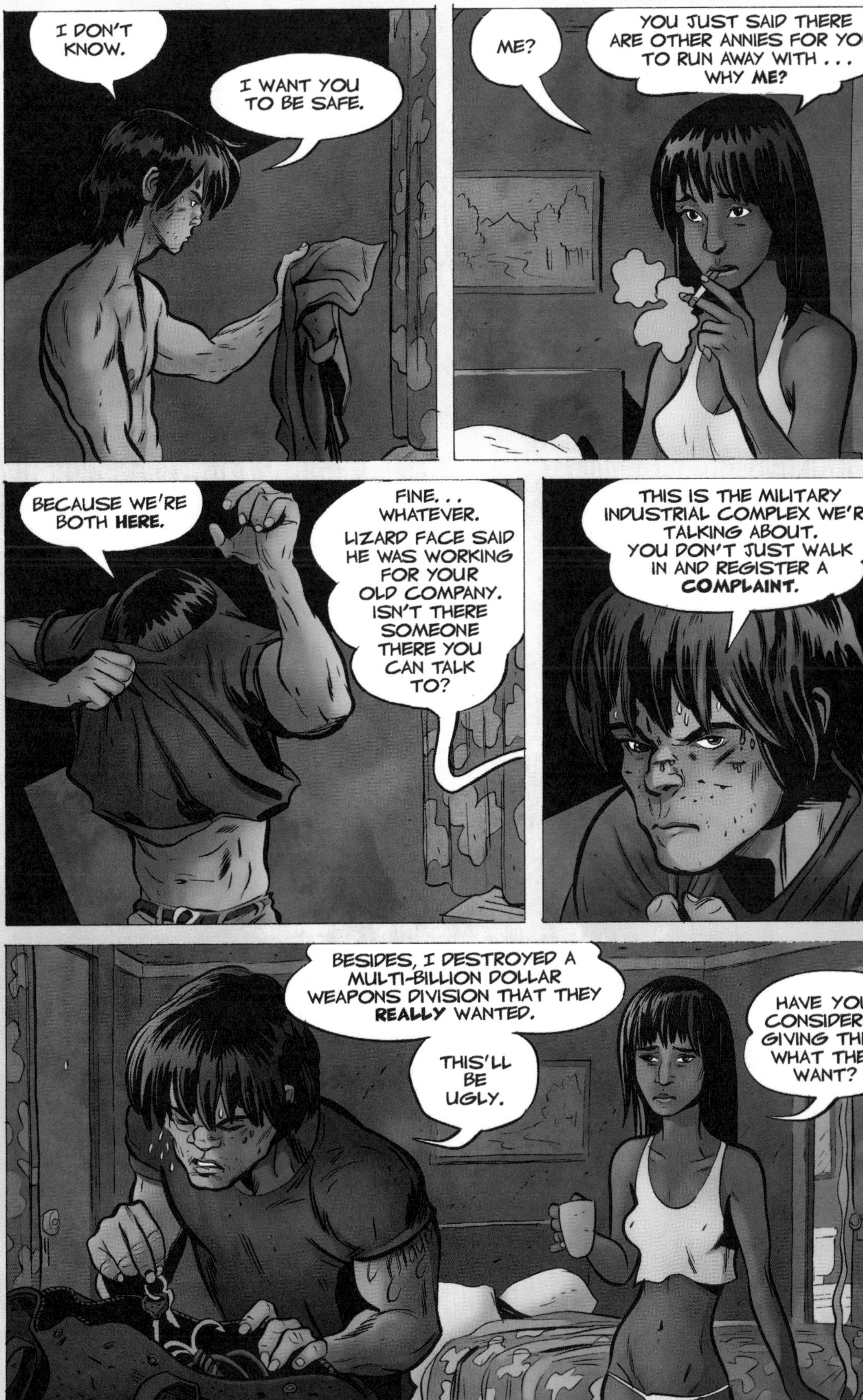
I DON'T KNOW.
I WANT YOU TO BE SAFE.
ME?
YOU JUST SAID THERE ARE OTHER ANNIES FOR YOU TO RUN AWAY WITH . . . WHY ME?
BECAUSE WE'RE BOTH HERE.
FINE. . . WHATEVER.
LIZARD FACE SAID HE WAS WORKING FOR YOUR OLD COMPANY. ISN'T THERE SOMEONE THERE YOU CAN TALK TO?
THIS IS THE MILITARY INDUSTRIAL COMPLEX WE'RE TALKING ABOUT. YOU DON'T JUST WALK IN AND REGISTER A COMPLAINT.
BESIDES, I DESTROYED A MULTI-BILLION DOLLAR WEAPONS DIVISION THAT THEY REALLY WANTED.
THIS'LL BE UGLY.
HAVE YOU CONSIDERED GIVING THEM WHAT THEY WANT?

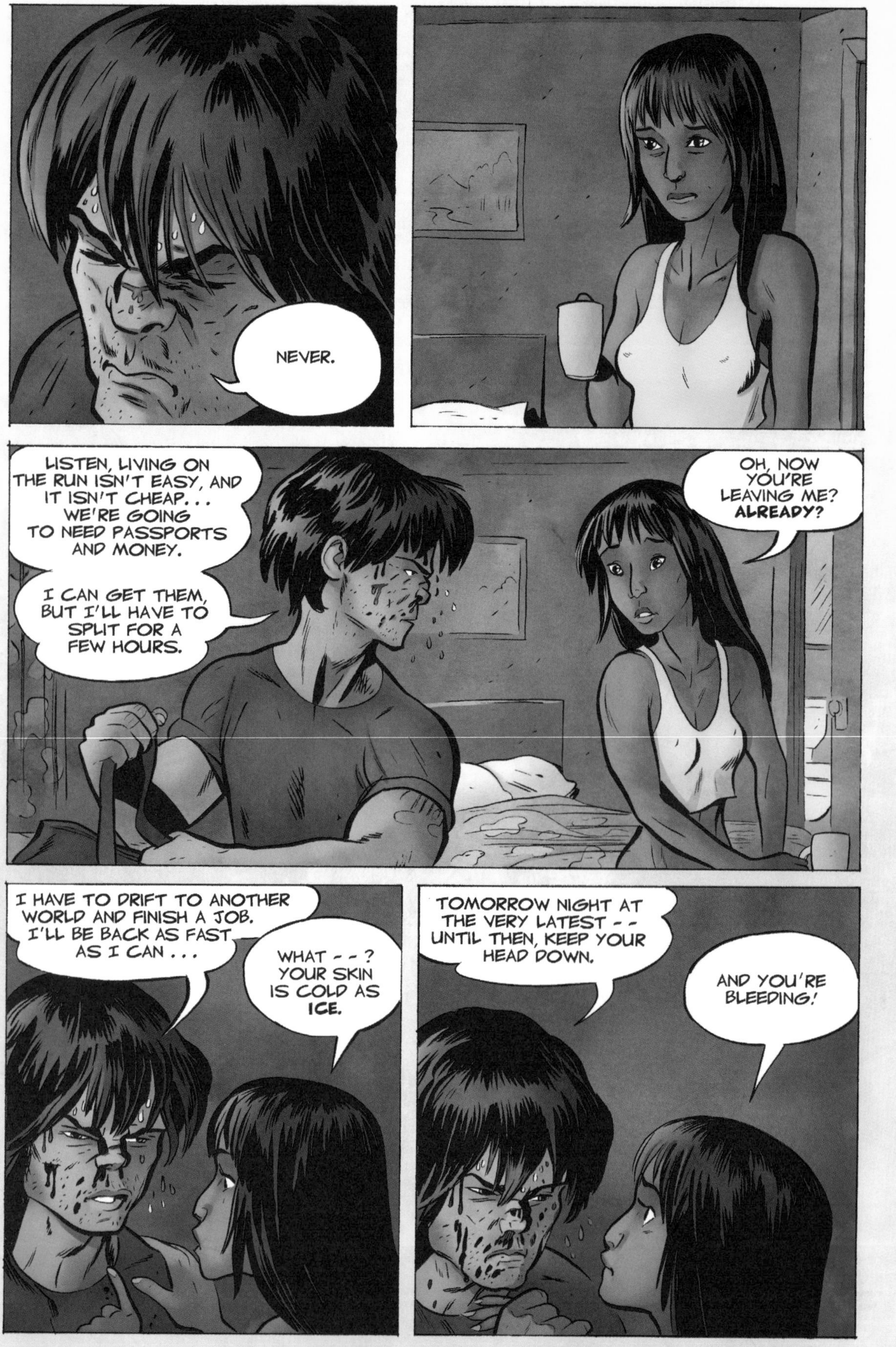
NEVER.
LISTEN, LIVING ON THE RUN ISN'T EASY, AND IT ISN'T CHEAP... WE'RE GOING TO NEED PASSPORTS AND MONEY.
I CAN GET THEM, BUT I'LL HAVE TO SPLIT FOR A FEW HOURS.
OH, NOW YOU'RE LEAVING ME? ALREADY?
I HAVE TO DRIFT TO ANOTHER WORLD AND FINISH A JOB. I'LL BE BACK AS FAST AS I CAN...
WHAT - - ? YOUR SKIN IS COLD AS ICE.
TOMORROW NIGHT AT THE VERY LATEST - - UNTIL THEN, KEEP YOUR HEAD DOWN.
AND YOU'RE BLEEDING!

IT'S NOTHING.

IF FOR SOME REASON I **DON'T** SHOW UP BY NIGHTFALL, YOU HAVE TO GET OUT OF HERE . . .

THERE'S A LITTLE BIT OF MONEY IN THE DRESSER.

YOU CAN GO ANYWHERE YOU WANT, JUST DON'T GO BACK TO YOUR HOUSE.

UNDERSTAND?

GOOD.

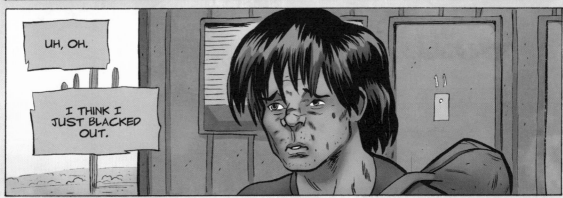

UH, OH.

I THINK I JUST BLACKED OUT.

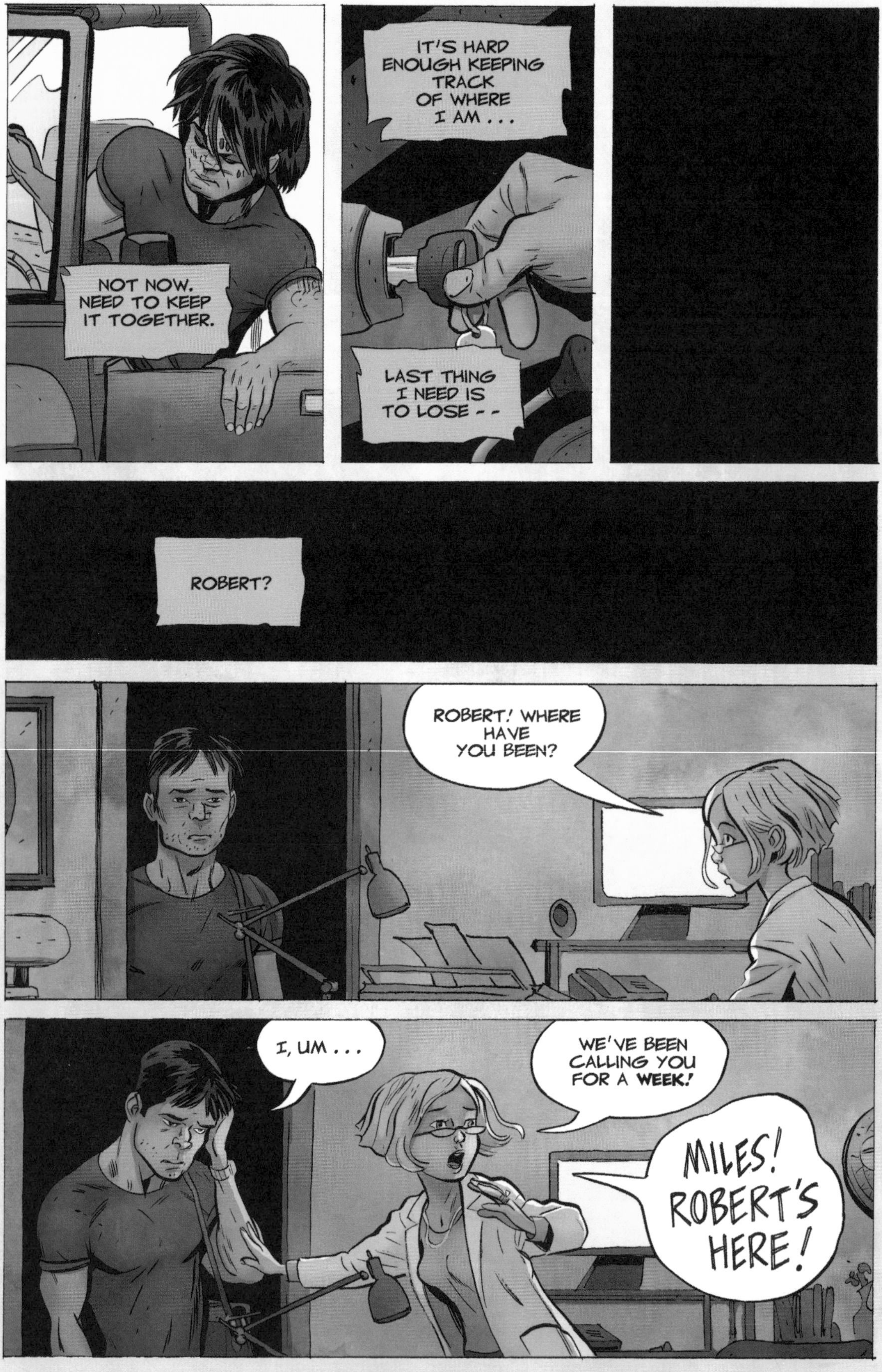
NOT NOW. NEED TO KEEP IT TOGETHER.
IT'S HARD ENOUGH KEEPING TRACK OF WHERE I AM . . .
LAST THING I NEED IS TO LOSE - -
ROBERT?
ROBERT! WHERE HAVE YOU BEEN?
I, UM . . .
WE'VE BEEN CALLING YOU FOR A **WEEK!**
MILES! ROBERT'S HERE!

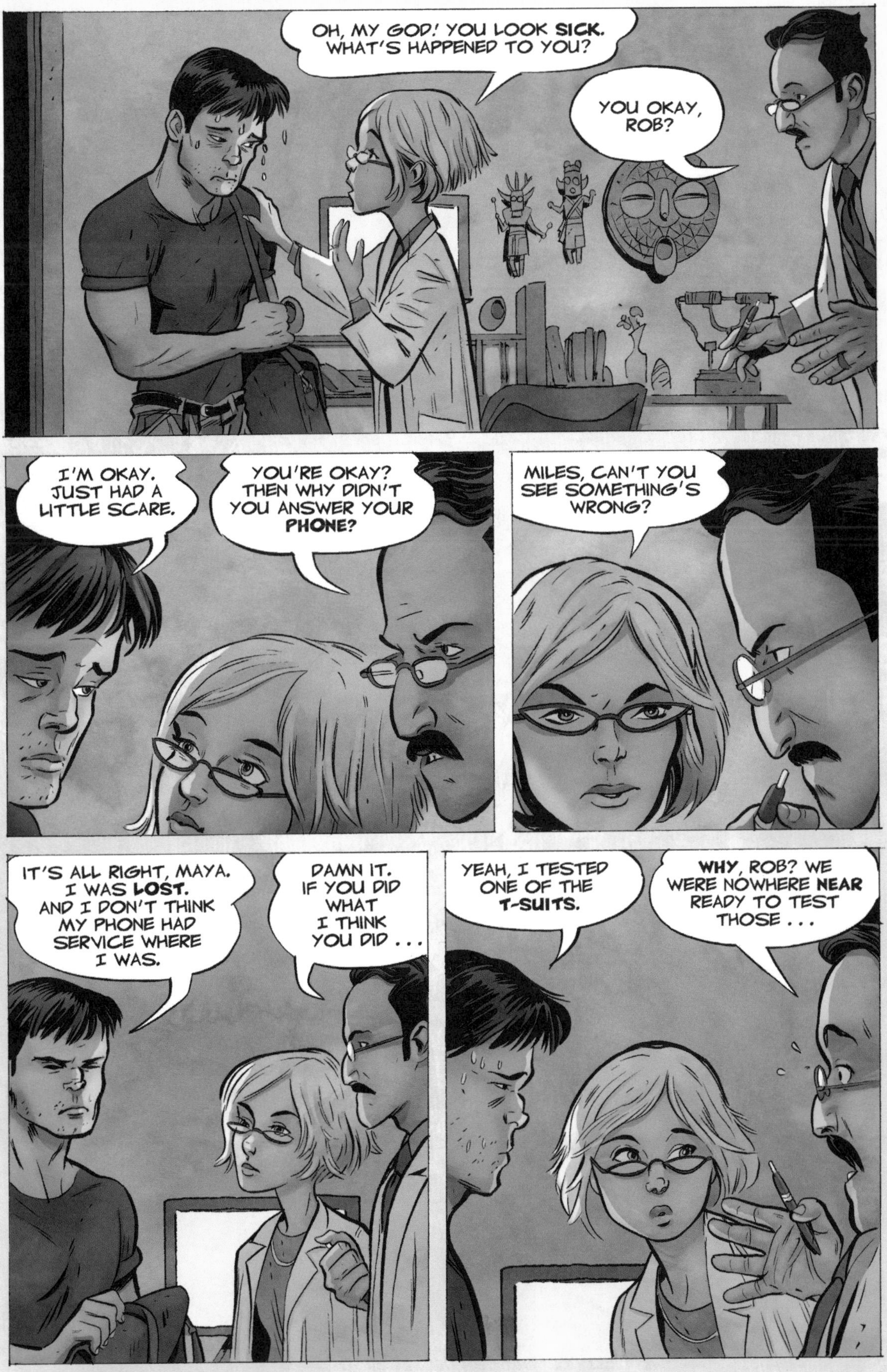
OH, MY GOD! YOU LOOK SICK. WHAT'S HAPPENED TO YOU?
YOU OKAY, ROB?
I'M OKAY. JUST HAD A LITTLE SCARE.
YOU'RE OKAY? THEN WHY DIDN'T YOU ANSWER YOUR PHONE?
MILES, CAN'T YOU SEE SOMETHING'S WRONG?
IT'S ALL RIGHT, MAYA. I WAS LOST. AND I DON'T THINK MY PHONE HAD SERVICE WHERE I WAS.
DAMN IT. IF YOU DID WHAT I THINK YOU DID . . .
YEAH, I TESTED ONE OF THE T-SUITS.
WHY, ROB? WE WERE NOWHERE NEAR READY TO TEST THOSE . . .

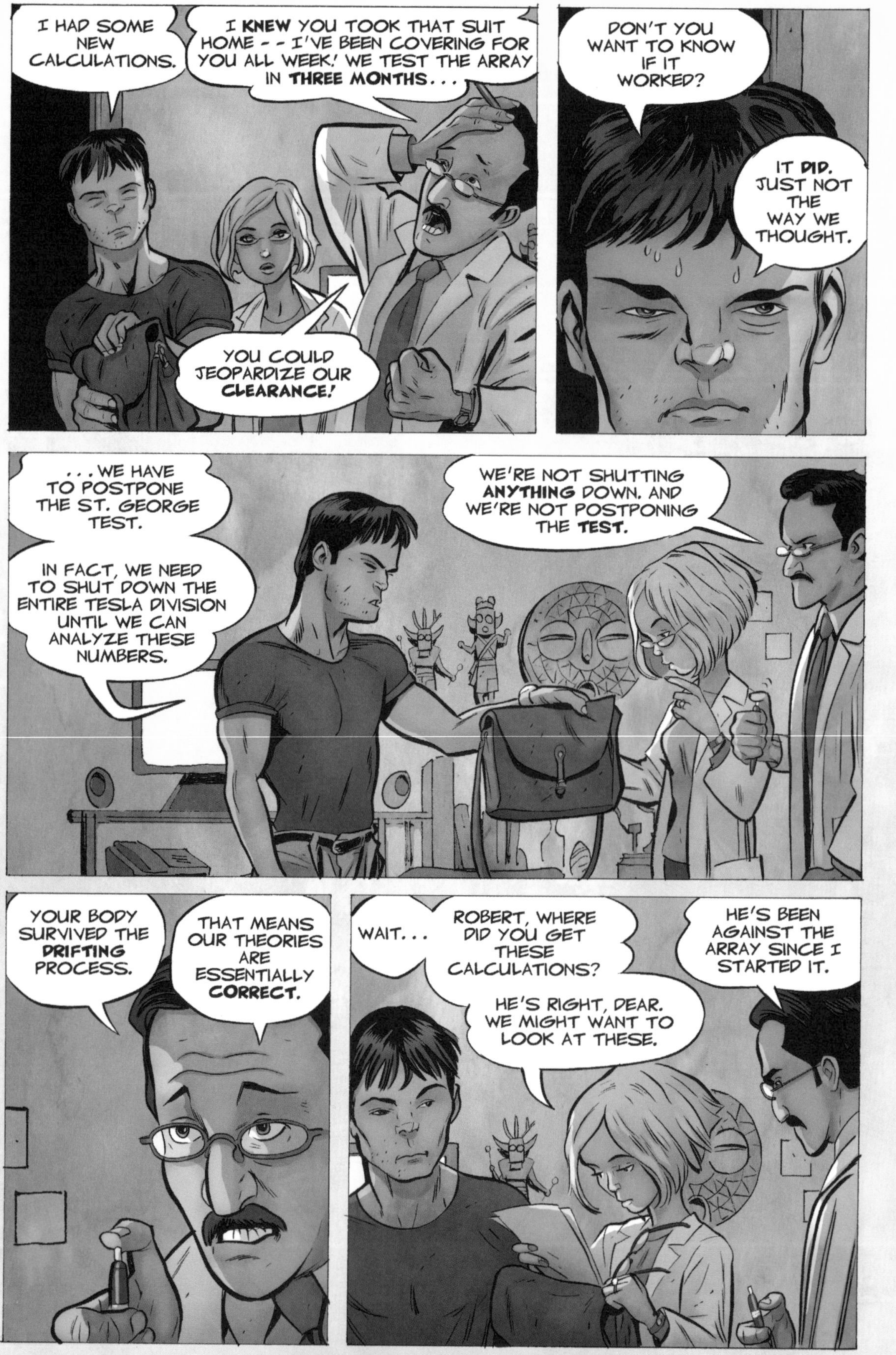
I HAD SOME NEW CALCULATIONS.
I KNEW YOU TOOK THAT SUIT HOME - - I'VE BEEN COVERING FOR YOU ALL WEEK! WE TEST THE ARRAY IN THREE MONTHS . . .
YOU COULD JEOPARDIZE OUR CLEARANCE!
DON'T YOU WANT TO KNOW IF IT WORKED?
IT DID. JUST NOT THE WAY WE THOUGHT.
. . . WE HAVE TO POSTPONE THE ST. GEORGE TEST.
IN FACT, WE NEED TO SHUT DOWN THE ENTIRE TESLA DIVISION UNTIL WE CAN ANALYZE THESE NUMBERS.
WE'RE NOT SHUTTING ANYTHING DOWN. AND WE'RE NOT POSTPONING THE TEST.
YOUR BODY SURVIVED THE DRIFTING PROCESS.
THAT MEANS OUR THEORIES ARE ESSENTIALLY CORRECT.
WAIT. . .
ROBERT, WHERE DID YOU GET THESE CALCULATIONS?
HE'S BEEN AGAINST THE ARRAY SINCE I STARTED IT.
HE'S RIGHT, DEAR. WE MIGHT WANT TO LOOK AT THESE.

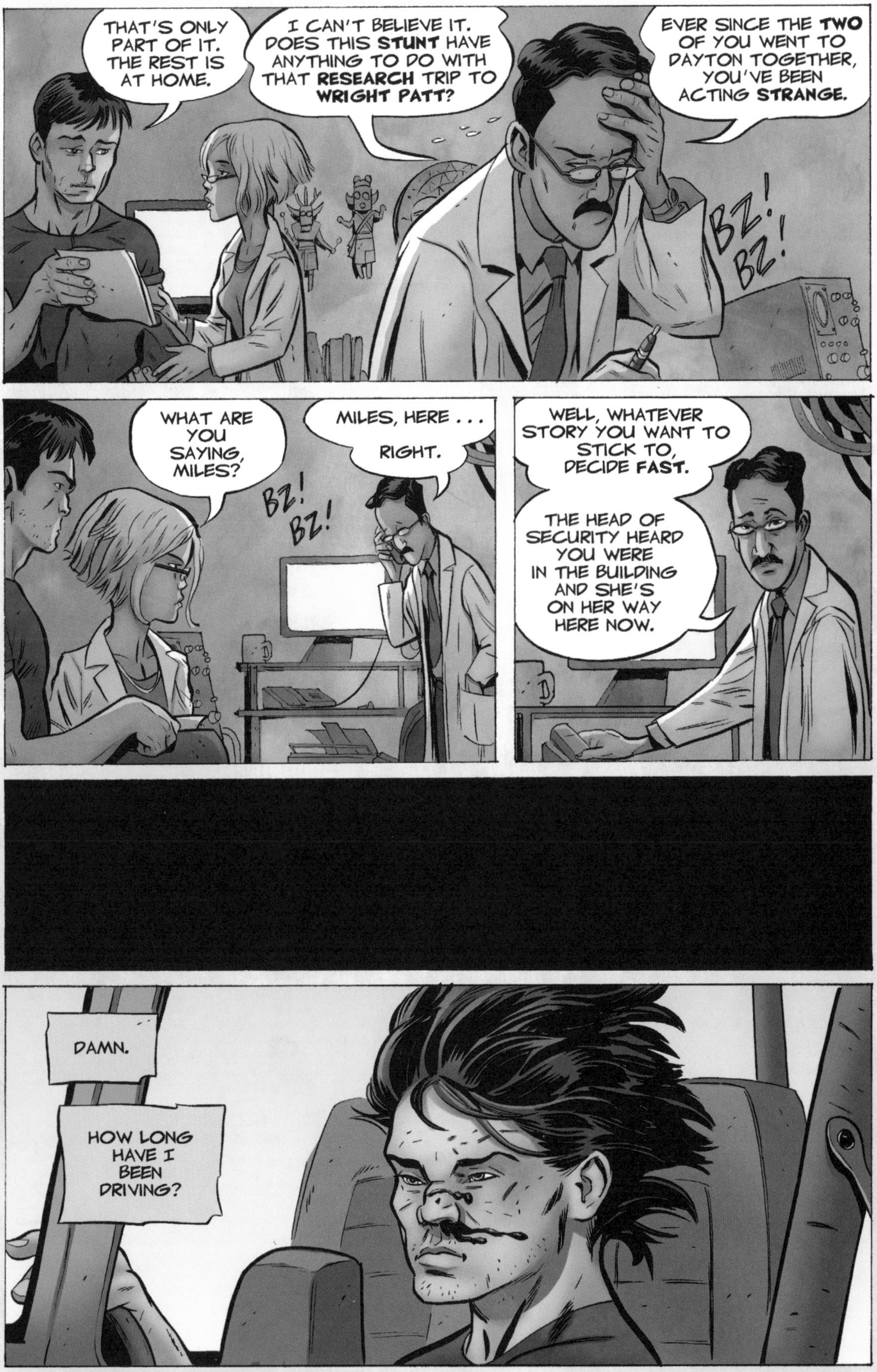
THAT'S ONLY PART OF IT. THE REST IS AT HOME.
I CAN'T BELIEVE IT. DOES THIS STUNT HAVE ANYTHING TO DO WITH THAT RESEARCH TRIP TO WRIGHT PATT?
EVER SINCE THE TWO OF YOU WENT TO DAYTON TOGETHER, YOU'VE BEEN ACTING STRANGE.
BZ! BZ!
WHAT ARE YOU SAYING, MILES?
MILES, HERE . . .
RIGHT.
BZ! BZ!
WELL, WHATEVER STORY YOU WANT TO STICK TO, DECIDE FAST.
THE HEAD OF SECURITY HEARD YOU WERE IN THE BUILDING AND SHE'S ON HER WAY HERE NOW.
DAMN.
HOW LONG HAVE I BEEN DRIVING?

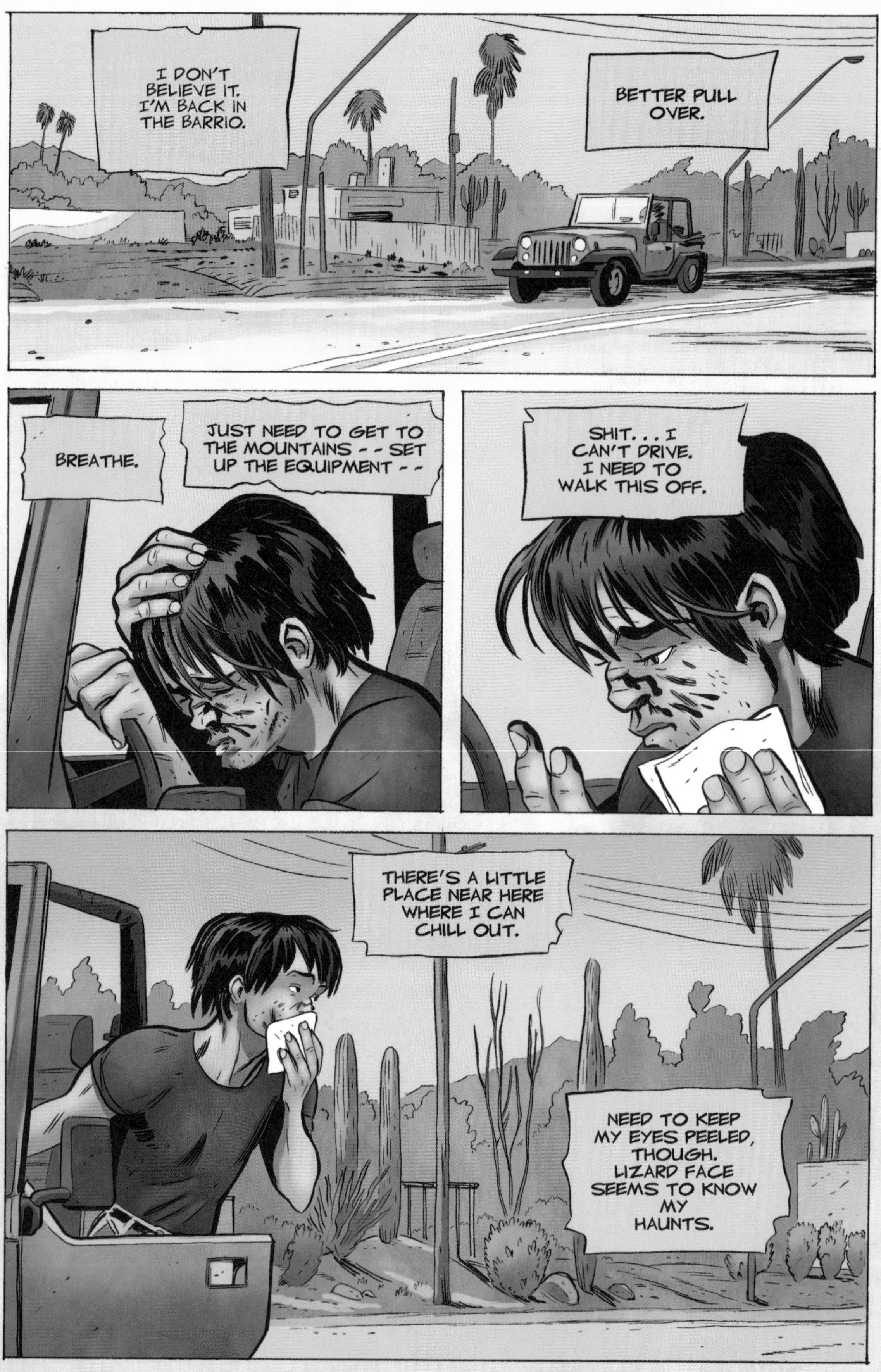
I DON'T BELIEVE IT. I'M BACK IN THE BARRIO.
BETTER PULL OVER.
BREATHE.
JUST NEED TO GET TO THE MOUNTAINS - - SET UP THE EQUIPMENT - -
SHIT. . . I CAN'T DRIVE. I NEED TO WALK THIS OFF.
THERE'S A LITTLE PLACE NEAR HERE WHERE I CAN CHILL OUT.
NEED TO KEEP MY EYES PEELED, THOUGH. LIZARD FACE SEEMS TO KNOW MY HAUNTS.

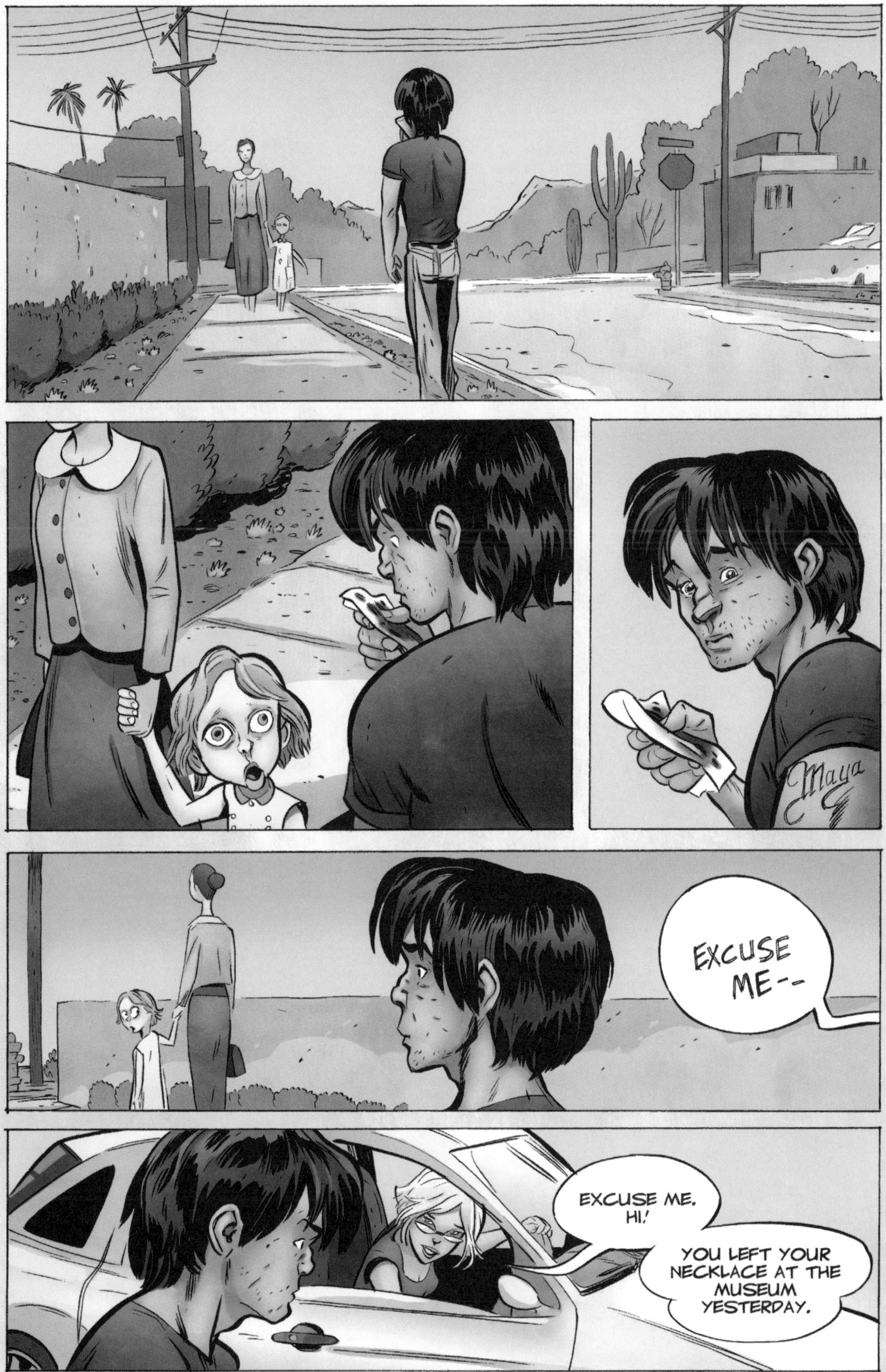
Maya
EXCUSE ME--
EXCUSE ME. HI!
YOU LEFT YOUR NECKLACE AT THE MUSEUM YESTERDAY.

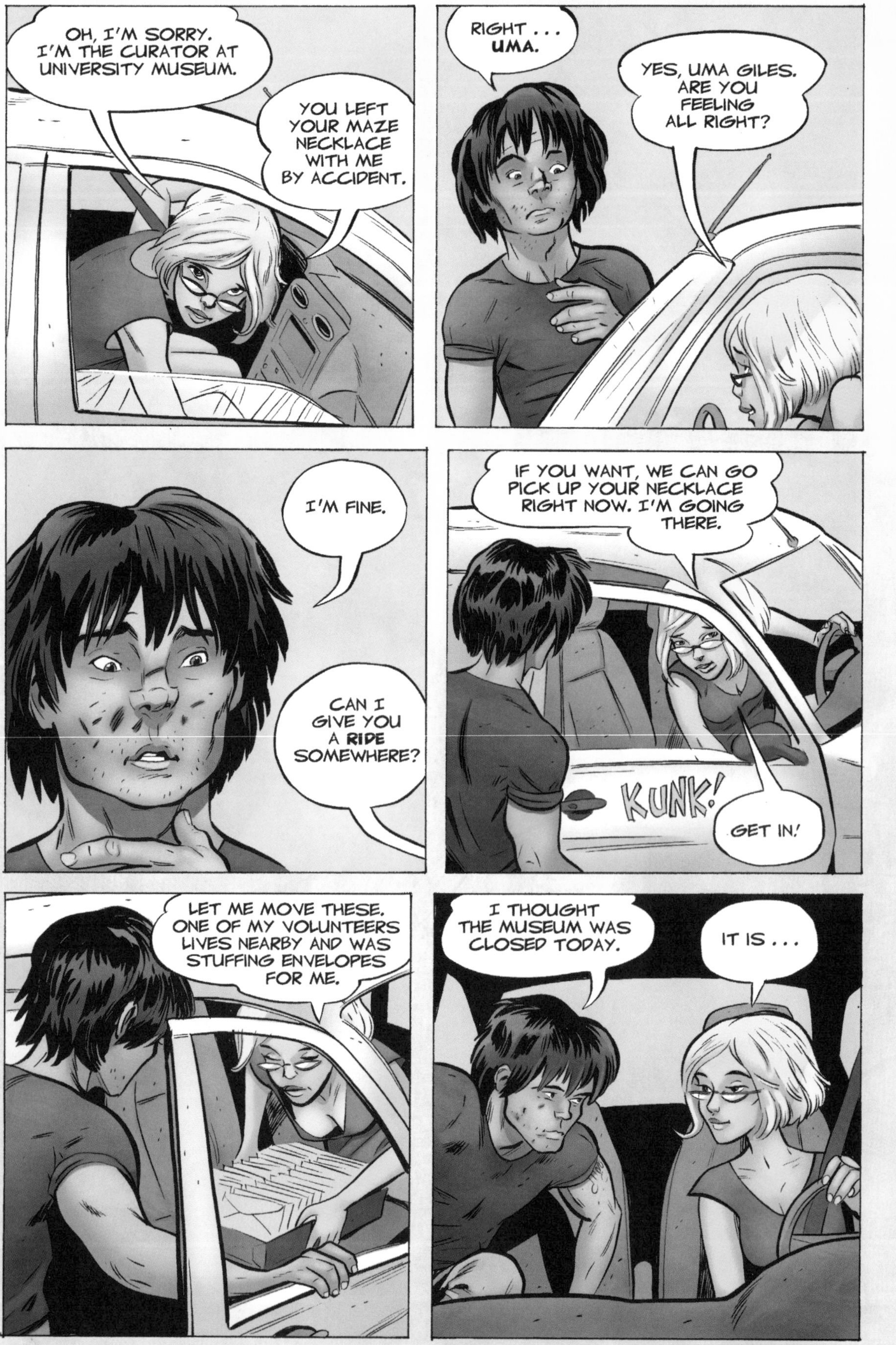
OH, I'M SORRY. I'M THE CURATOR AT UNIVERSITY MUSEUM.
YOU LEFT YOUR MAZE NECKLACE WITH ME BY ACCIDENT.
RIGHT . . . UMA.
YES, UMA GILES. ARE YOU FEELING ALL RIGHT?
I'M FINE.
CAN I GIVE YOU A RIDE SOMEWHERE?
IF YOU WANT, WE CAN GO PICK UP YOUR NECKLACE RIGHT NOW. I'M GOING THERE.
KUNK!
GET IN!
LET ME MOVE THESE. ONE OF MY VOLUNTEERS LIVES NEARBY AND WAS STUFFING ENVELOPES FOR ME.
I THOUGHT THE MUSEUM WAS CLOSED TODAY.
IT IS . . .

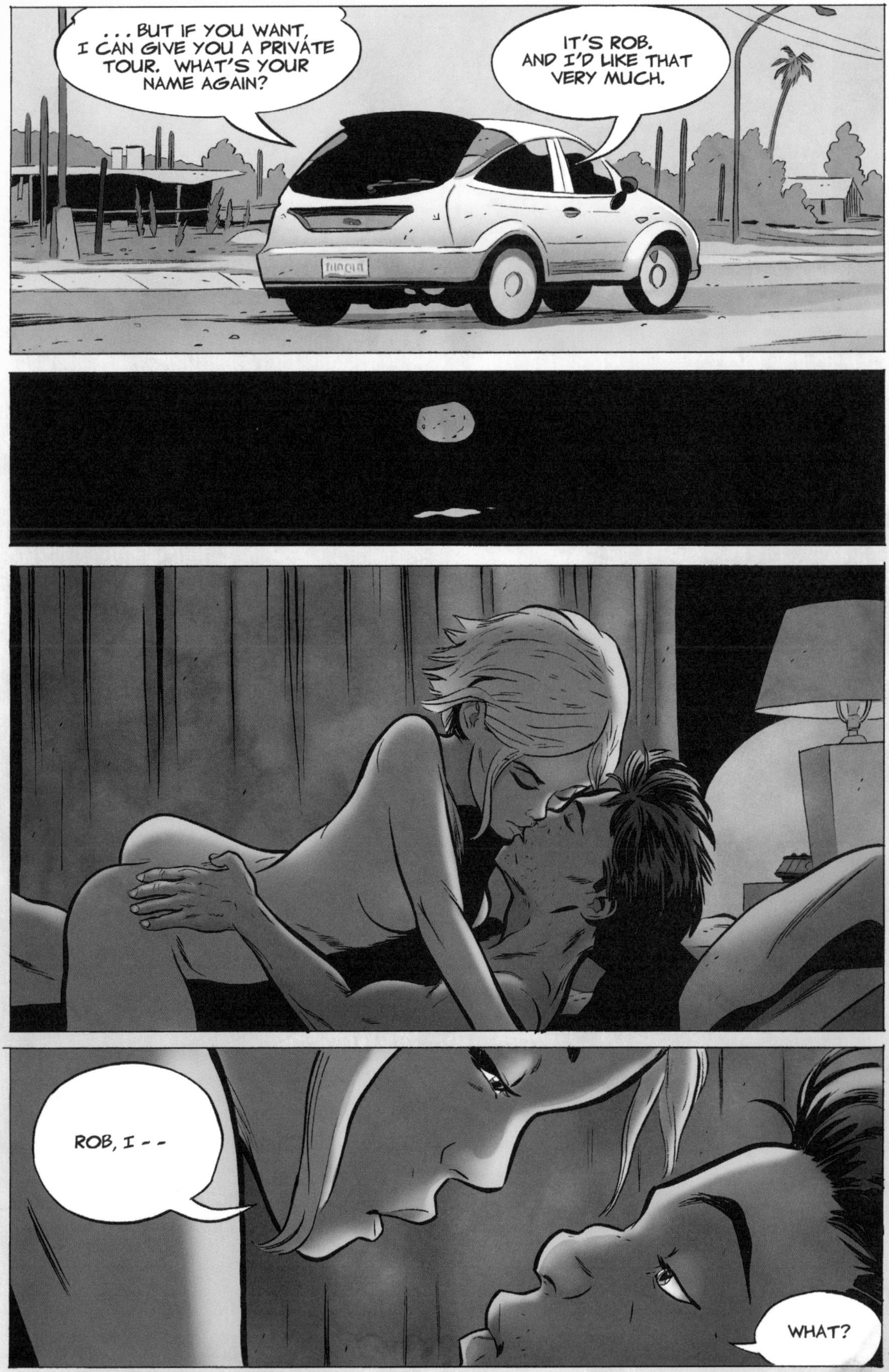
. . . BUT IF YOU WANT, I CAN GIVE YOU A PRIVATE TOUR. WHAT'S YOUR NAME AGAIN?
IT'S ROB. AND I'D LIKE THAT VERY MUCH.
ROB, I - -
WHAT?

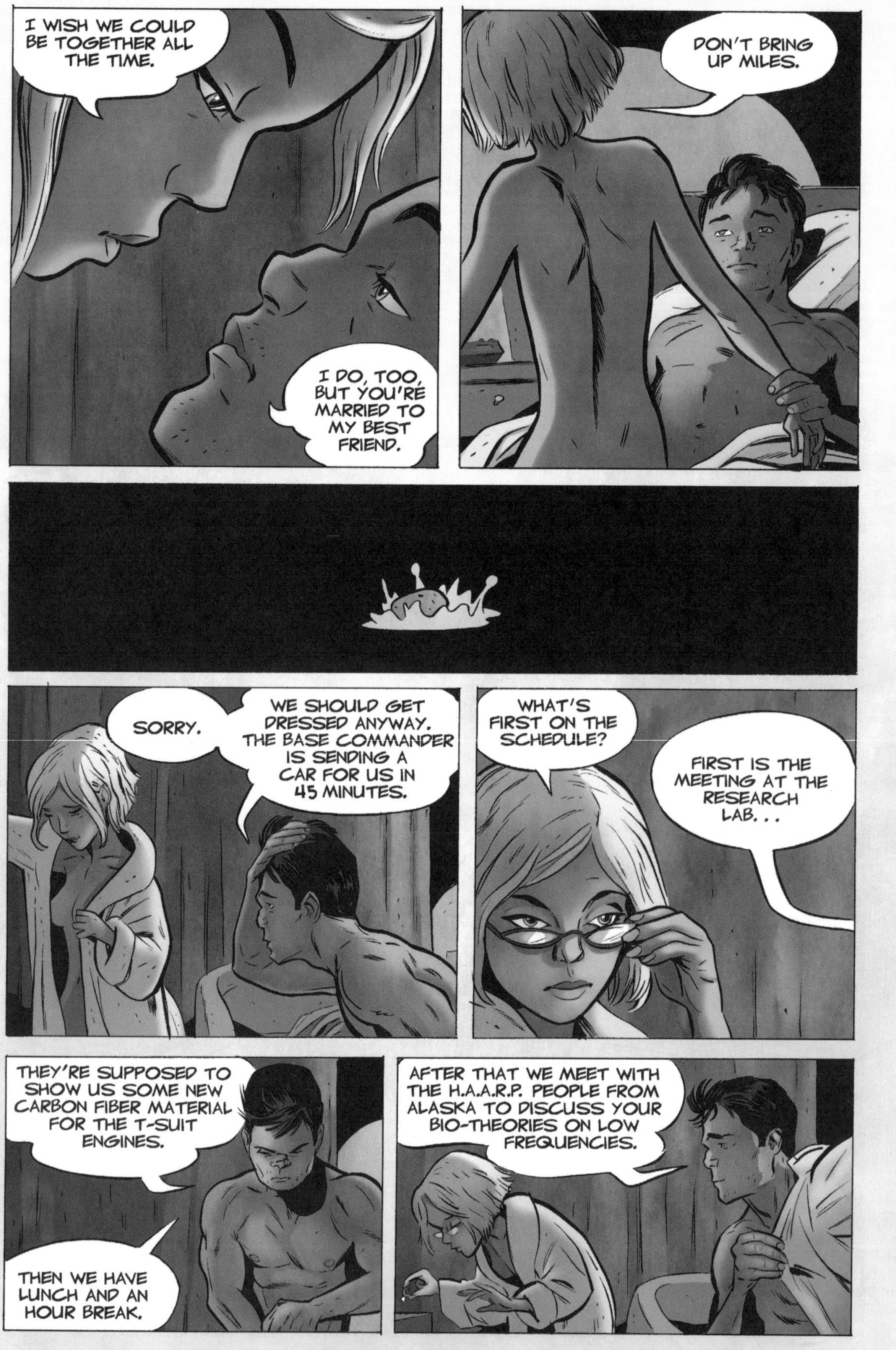
I WISH WE COULD BE TOGETHER ALL THE TIME.
I DO, TOO, BUT YOU'RE MARRIED TO MY BEST FRIEND.
DON'T BRING UP MILES.
SORRY.
WE SHOULD GET DRESSED ANYWAY. THE BASE COMMANDER IS SENDING A CAR FOR US IN 45 MINUTES.
WHAT'S FIRST ON THE SCHEDULE?
FIRST IS THE MEETING AT THE RESEARCH LAB. . .
THEY'RE SUPPOSED TO SHOW US SOME NEW CARBON FIBER MATERIAL FOR THE T-SUIT ENGINES.
THEN WE HAVE LUNCH AND AN HOUR BREAK.
AFTER THAT WE MEET WITH THE H.A.A.R.P. PEOPLE FROM ALASKA TO DISCUSS YOUR BIO-THEORIES ON LOW FREQUENCIES.

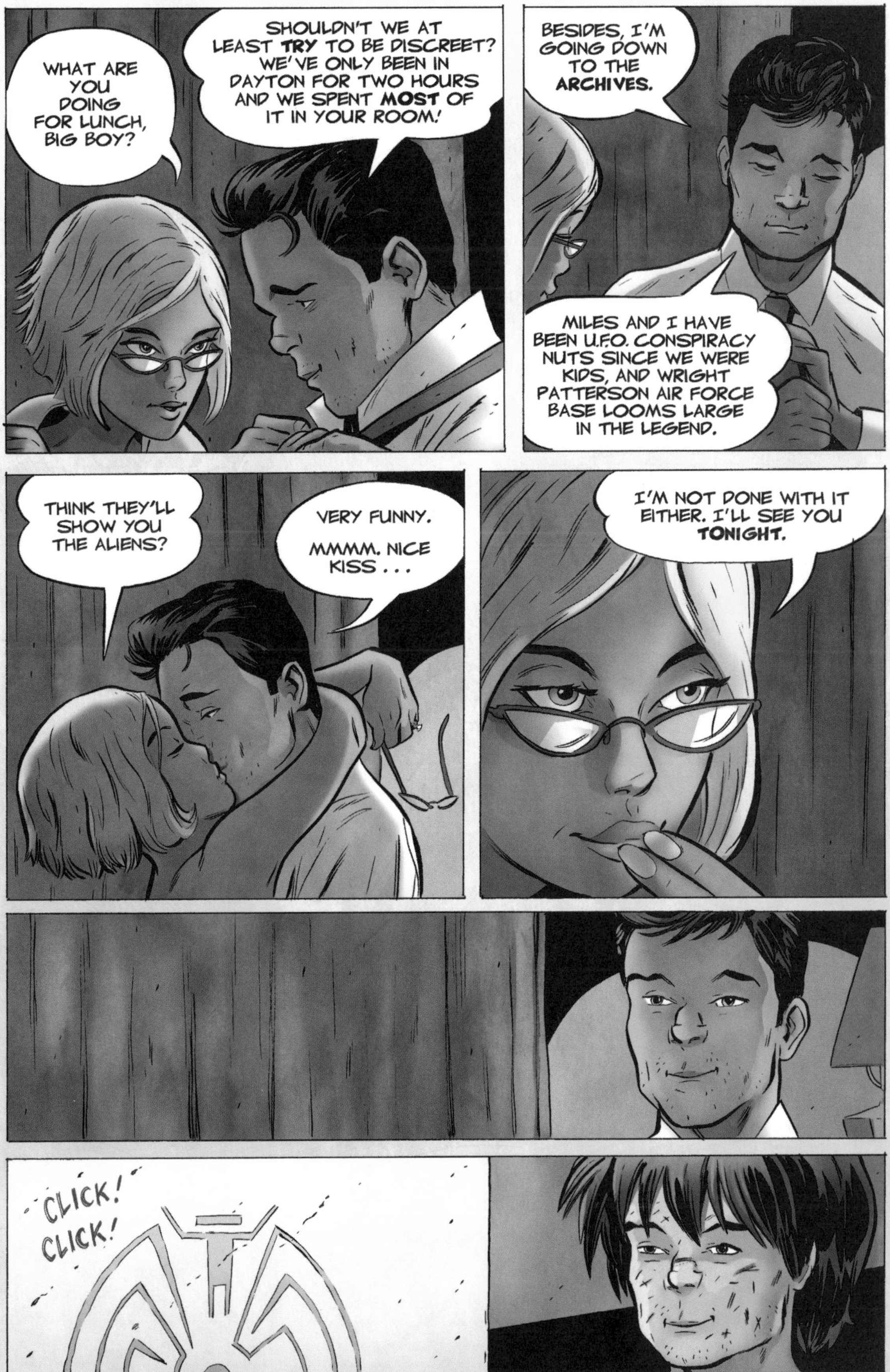
WHAT ARE YOU DOING FOR LUNCH, BIG BOY?
SHOULDN'T WE AT LEAST TRY TO BE DISCREET? WE'VE ONLY BEEN IN DAYTON FOR TWO HOURS AND WE SPENT MOST OF IT IN YOUR ROOM!
BESIDES, I'M GOING DOWN TO THE ARCHIVES.
MILES AND I HAVE BEEN U.F.O. CONSPIRACY NUTS SINCE WE WERE KIDS, AND WRIGHT PATTERSON AIR FORCE BASE LOOMS LARGE IN THE LEGEND.
THINK THEY'LL SHOW YOU THE ALIENS?
VERY FUNNY.
MMMM. NICE KISS . . .
I'M NOT DONE WITH IT EITHER. I'LL SEE YOU TONIGHT.
CLICK!
CLICK!

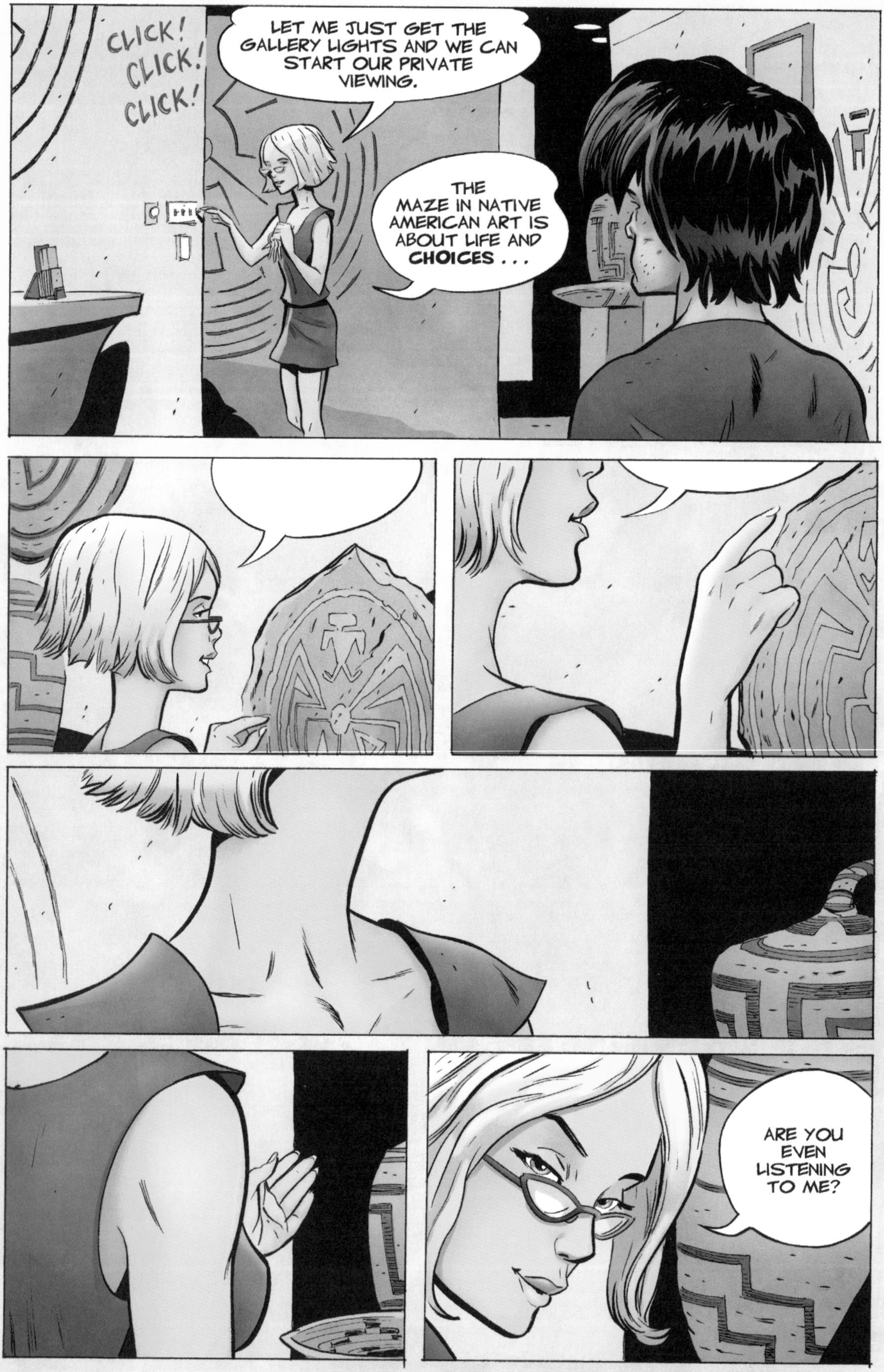
CLICK! CLICK! CLICK!
LET ME JUST GET THE GALLERY LIGHTS AND WE CAN START OUR PRIVATE VIEWING.
THE MAZE IN NATIVE AMERICAN ART IS ABOUT LIFE AND CHOICES . . .
ARE YOU EVEN LISTENING TO ME?

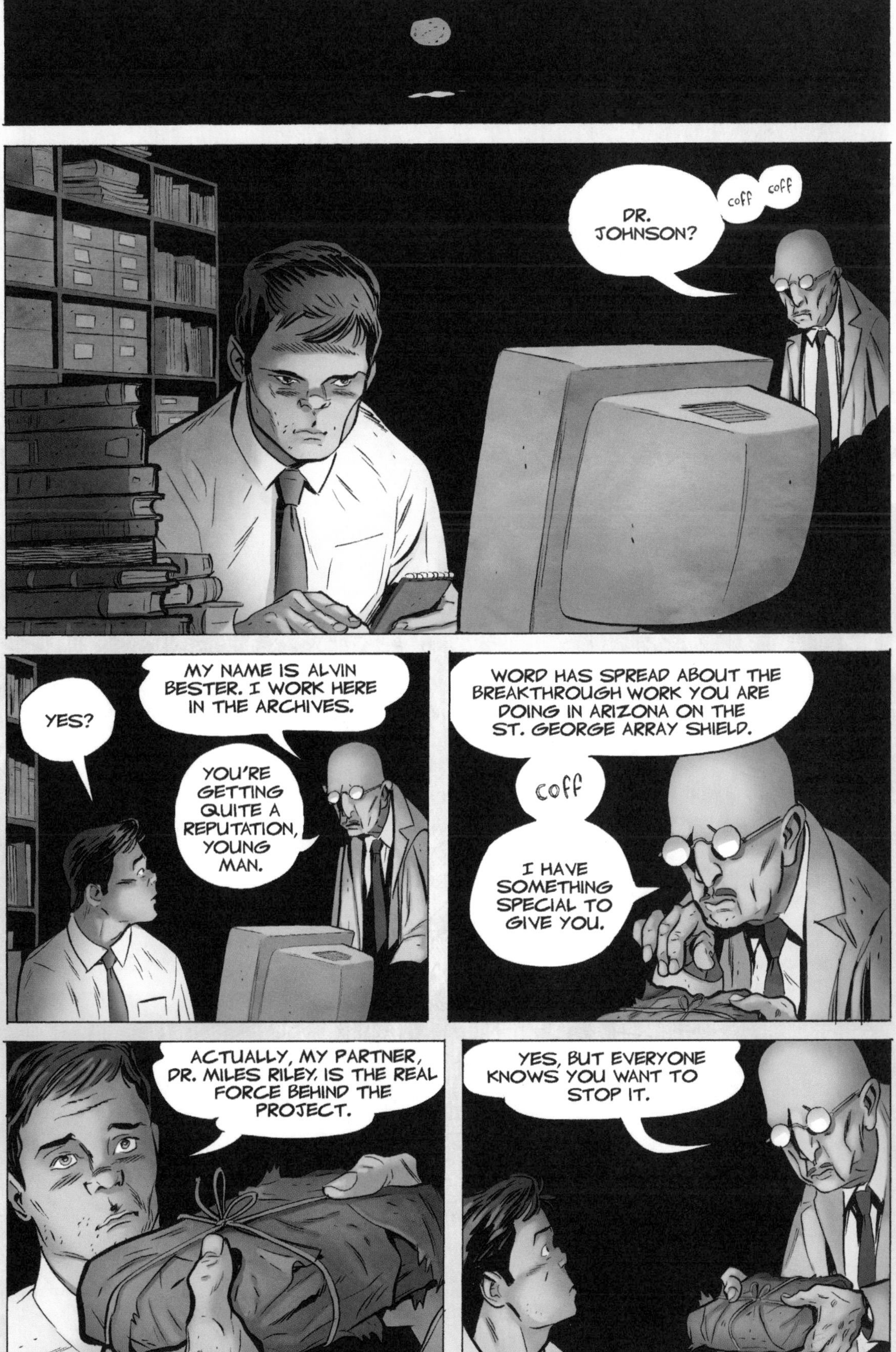
DR. JOHNSON?
coff coff
YES?
MY NAME IS ALVIN BESTER. I WORK HERE IN THE ARCHIVES.
YOU'RE GETTING QUITE A REPUTATION, YOUNG MAN.
WORD HAS SPREAD ABOUT THE BREAKTHROUGH WORK YOU ARE DOING IN ARIZONA ON THE ST. GEORGE ARRAY SHIELD.
coff
I HAVE SOMETHING SPECIAL TO GIVE YOU.
ACTUALLY, MY PARTNER, DR. MILES RILEY, IS THE REAL FORCE BEHIND THE PROJECT.
YES, BUT EVERYONE KNOWS YOU WANT TO STOP IT.

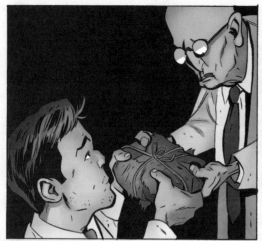

LOG BOOKS?

THEY BELONGED TO **HIM**.

I WAS HERE IN 1943 WHEN THEY CONFISCATED HIS PAPERS AND BROUGHT THEM TO DAYTON.

WHO?

TESLA.

NIKOLA TESLA? THESE ARE TESLA'S MISSING JOURNALS?

NO, NO, NO . . .

IT CAN'T BE.

THESE . . .

HEY!

WHERE - - ?

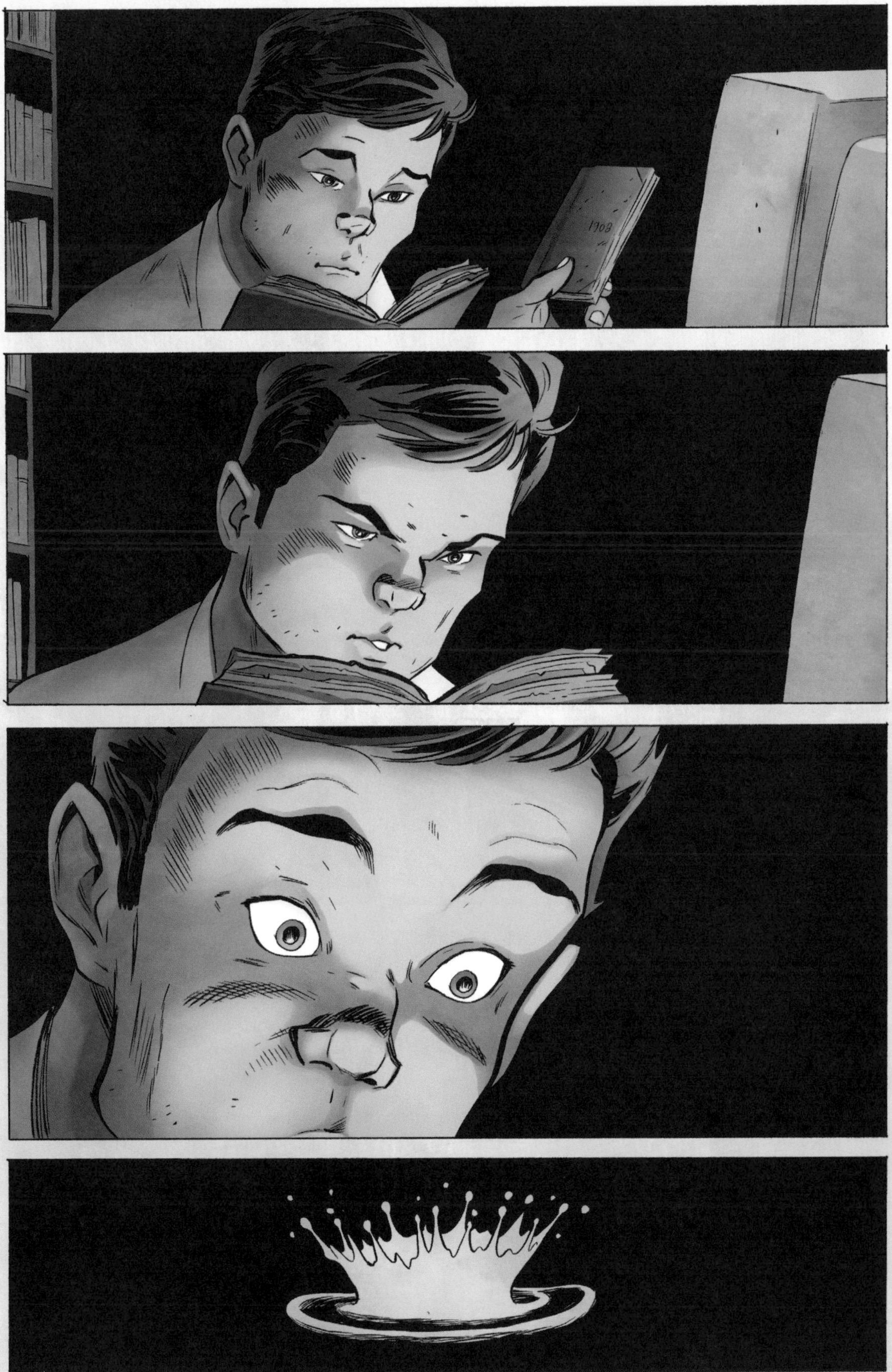
1908

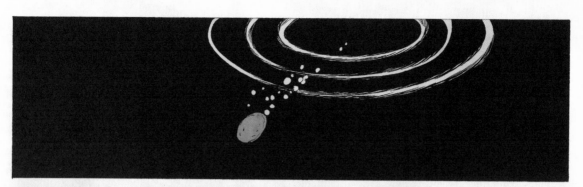

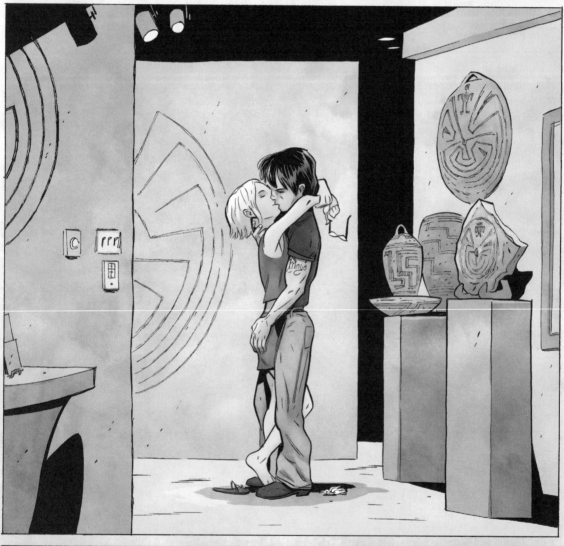

VI

THE MAD SCIENTIST

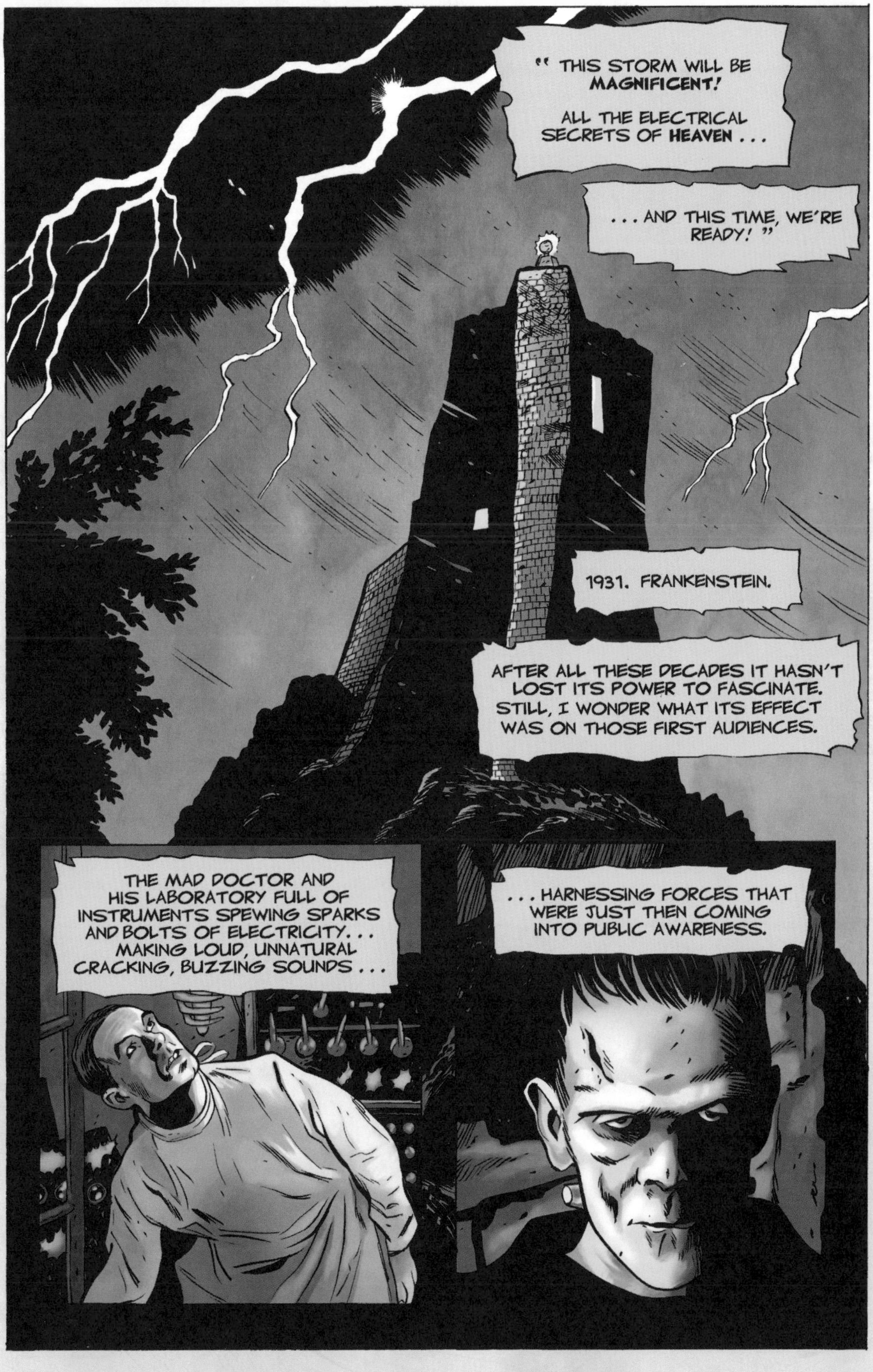
" THIS STORM WILL BE MAGNIFICENT! ALL THE ELECTRICAL SECRETS OF HEAVEN . . .
. . . AND THIS TIME, WE'RE READY! "
1931. FRANKENSTEIN.
AFTER ALL THESE DECADES IT HASN'T LOST ITS POWER TO FASCINATE. STILL, I WONDER WHAT ITS EFFECT WAS ON THOSE FIRST AUDIENCES.
THE MAD DOCTOR AND HIS LABORATORY FULL OF INSTRUMENTS SPEWING SPARKS AND BOLTS OF ELECTRICITY. . . MAKING LOUD, UNNATURAL CRACKING, BUZZING SOUNDS . . .
. . . HARNESSING FORCES THAT WERE JUST THEN COMING INTO PUBLIC AWARENESS.

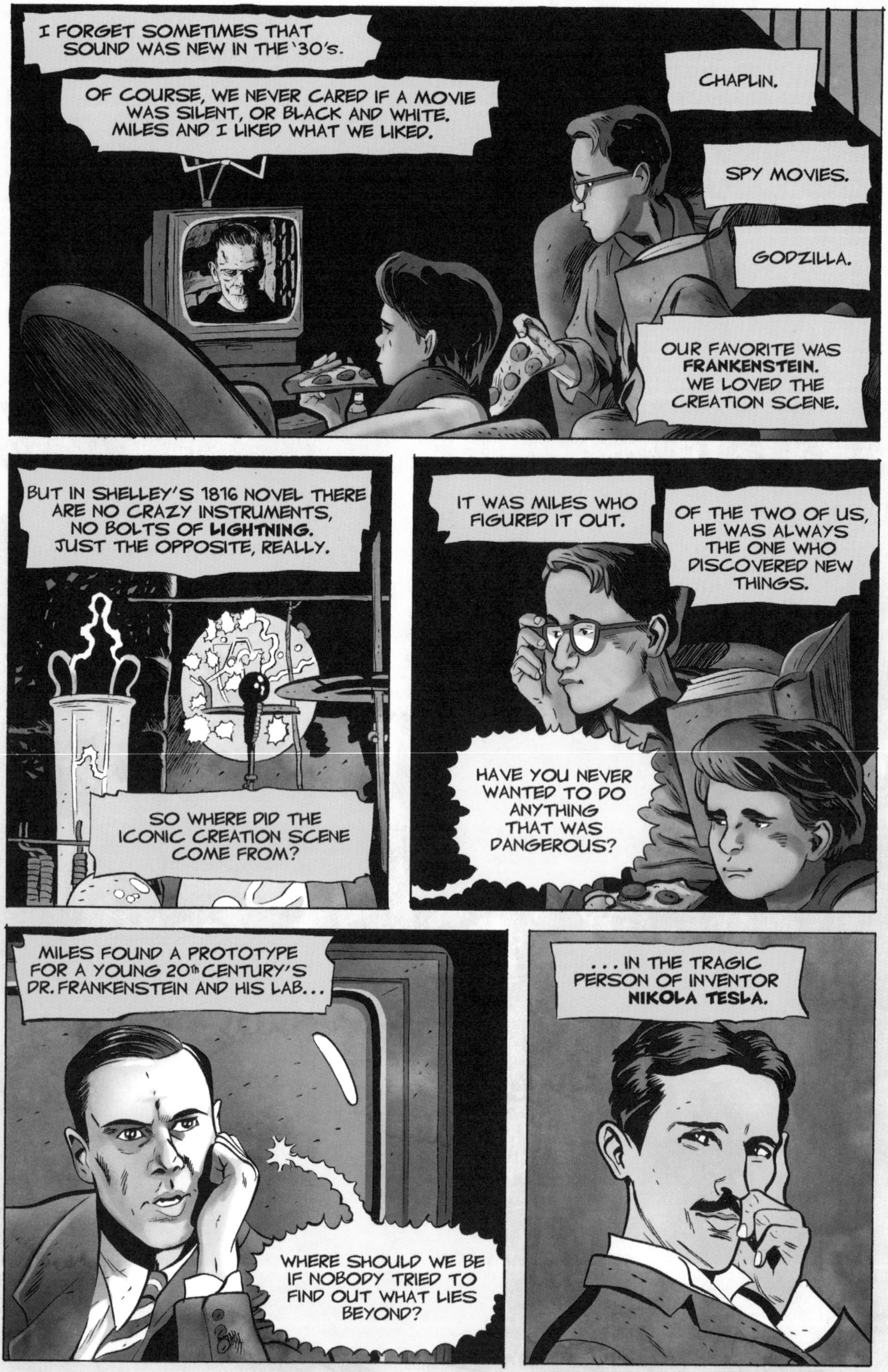
I FORGET SOMETIMES THAT SOUND WAS NEW IN THE '30's.
OF COURSE, WE NEVER CARED IF A MOVIE WAS SILENT, OR BLACK AND WHITE. MILES AND I LIKED WHAT WE LIKED.
CHAPLIN.
SPY MOVIES.
GODZILLA.
OUR FAVORITE WAS **FRANKENSTEIN.** WE LOVED THE CREATION SCENE.
BUT IN SHELLEY'S 1816 NOVEL THERE ARE NO CRAZY INSTRUMENTS, NO BOLTS OF **LIGHTNING.** JUST THE OPPOSITE, REALLY.
SO WHERE DID THE ICONIC CREATION SCENE COME FROM?
IT WAS MILES WHO FIGURED IT OUT.
OF THE TWO OF US, HE WAS ALWAYS THE ONE WHO DISCOVERED NEW THINGS.
HAVE YOU NEVER WANTED TO DO ANYTHING THAT WAS DANGEROUS?
MILES FOUND A PROTOTYPE FOR A YOUNG 20th CENTURY'S DR. FRANKENSTEIN AND HIS LAB...
WHERE SHOULD WE BE IF NOBODY TRIED TO FIND OUT WHAT LIES BEYOND?
... IN THE TRAGIC PERSON OF INVENTOR **NIKOLA TESLA.**

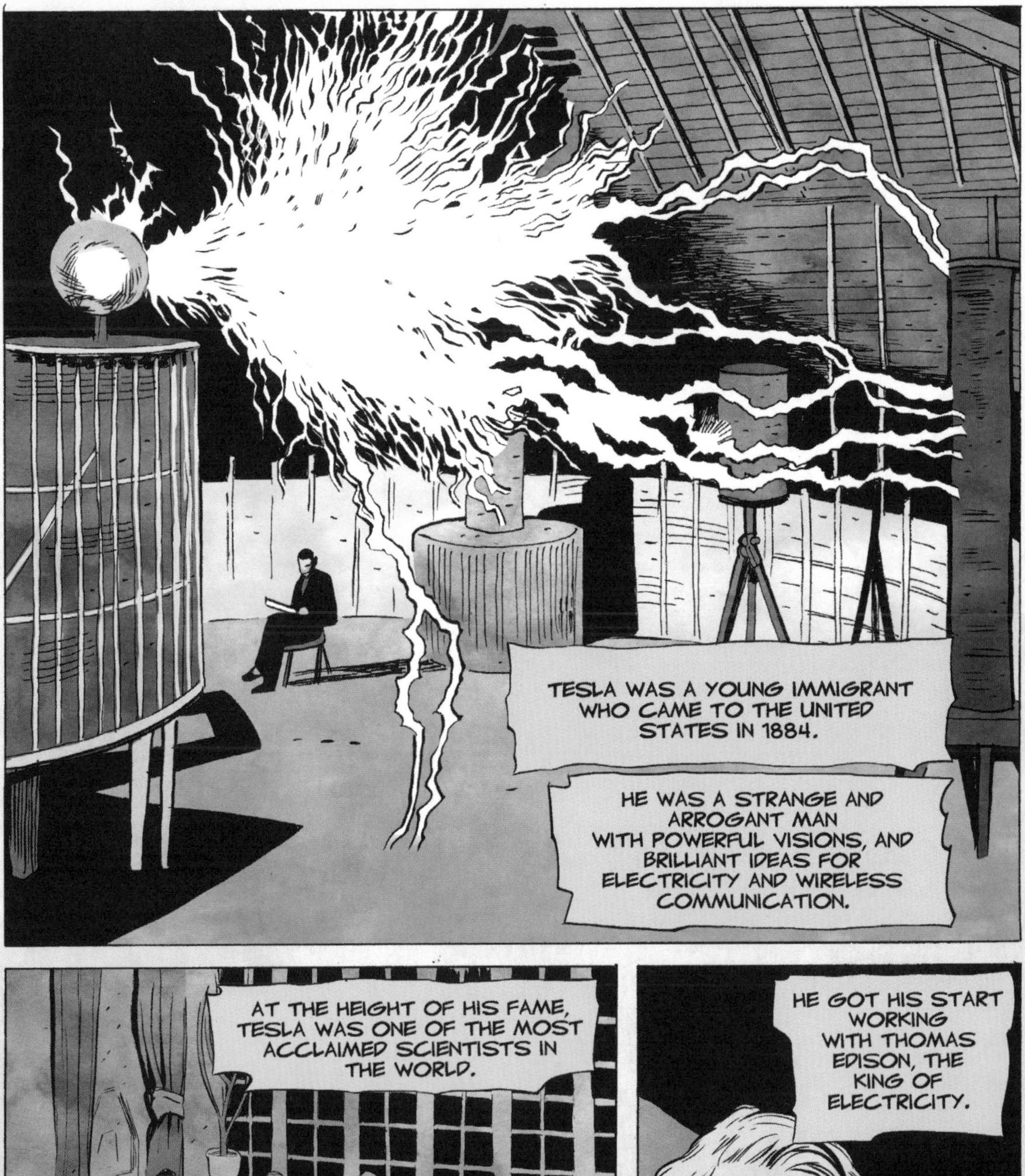
TESLA WAS A YOUNG IMMIGRANT WHO CAME TO THE UNITED STATES IN 1884.
HE WAS A STRANGE AND ARROGANT MAN WITH POWERFUL VISIONS, AND BRILLIANT IDEAS FOR ELECTRICITY AND WIRELESS COMMUNICATION.

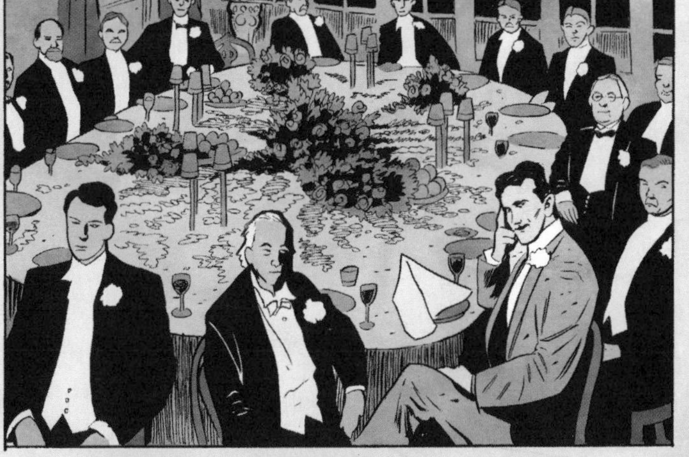
AT THE HEIGHT OF HIS FAME, TESLA WAS ONE OF THE MOST ACCLAIMED SCIENTISTS IN THE WORLD.

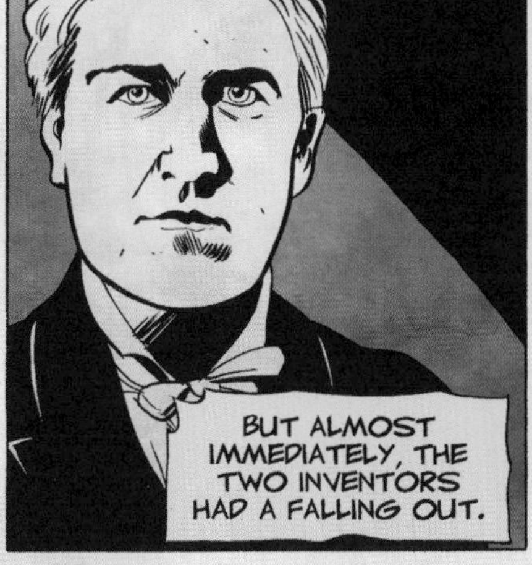
HE GOT HIS START WORKING WITH THOMAS EDISON, THE KING OF ELECTRICITY.
BUT ALMOST IMMEDIATELY, THE TWO INVENTORS HAD A FALLING OUT.

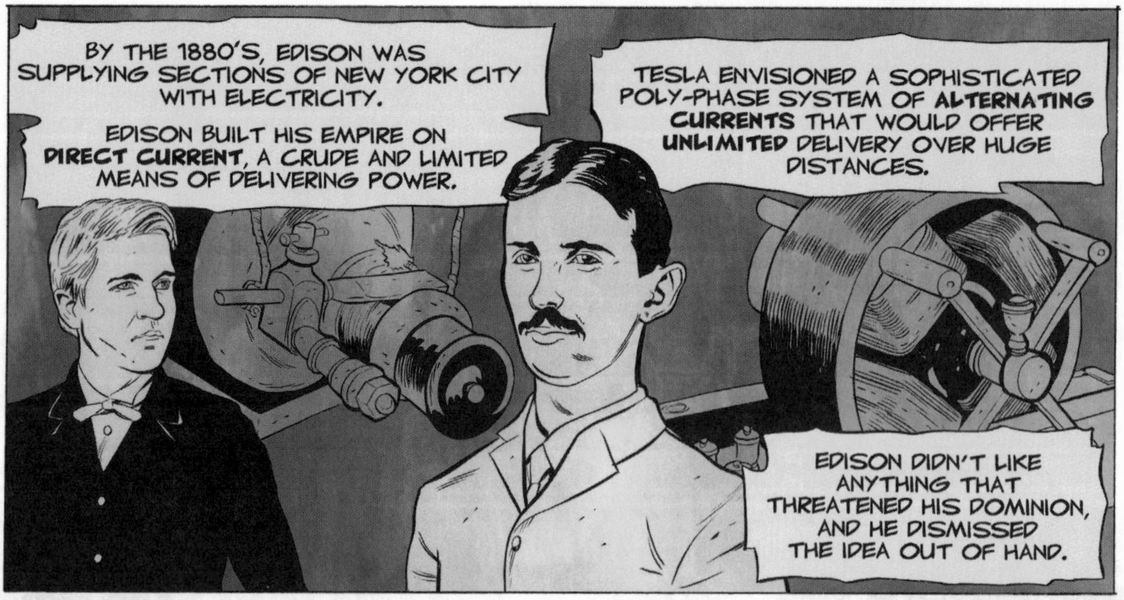
BY THE 1880'S, EDISON WAS SUPPLYING SECTIONS OF NEW YORK CITY WITH ELECTRICITY.
EDISON BUILT HIS EMPIRE ON DIRECT CURRENT, A CRUDE AND LIMITED MEANS OF DELIVERING POWER.
TESLA ENVISIONED A SOPHISTICATED POLY-PHASE SYSTEM OF ALTERNATING CURRENTS THAT WOULD OFFER UNLIMITED DELIVERY OVER HUGE DISTANCES.
EDISON DIDN'T LIKE ANYTHING THAT THREATENED HIS DOMINION, AND HE DISMISSED THE IDEA OUT OF HAND.

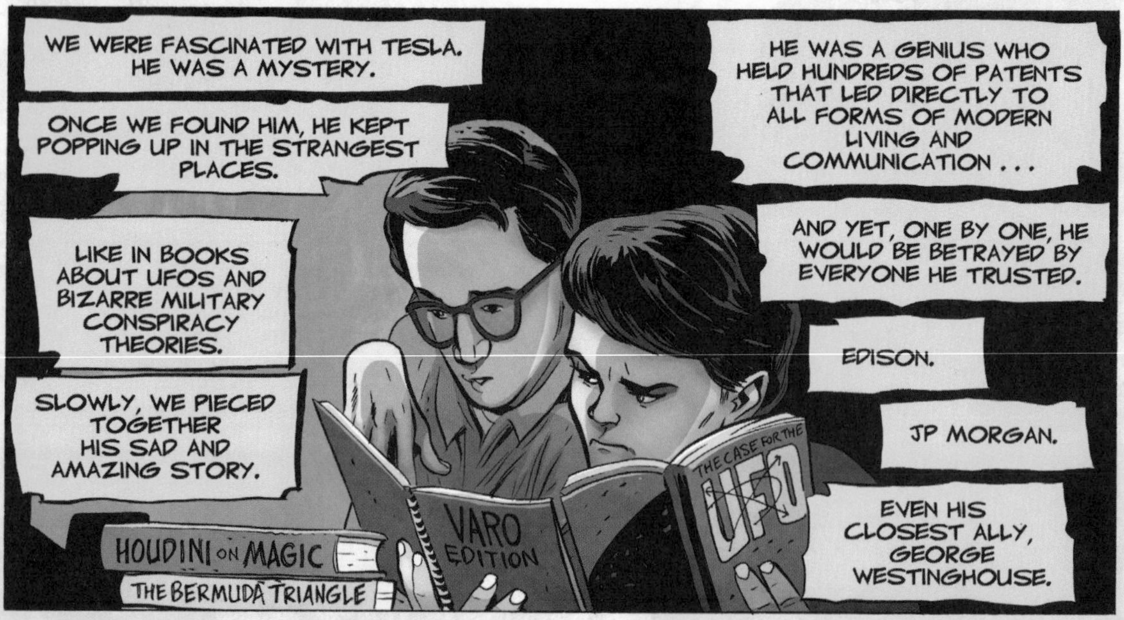
WE WERE FASCINATED WITH TESLA. HE WAS A MYSTERY.
ONCE WE FOUND HIM, HE KEPT POPPING UP IN THE STRANGEST PLACES.
LIKE IN BOOKS ABOUT UFOS AND BIZARRE MILITARY CONSPIRACY THEORIES.
SLOWLY, WE PIECED TOGETHER HIS SAD AND AMAZING STORY.
HOUDINI ON MAGIC
THE BERMUDA TRIANGLE
VARO EDITION
THE CASE FOR THE UFO
HE WAS A GENIUS WHO HELD HUNDREDS OF PATENTS THAT LED DIRECTLY TO ALL FORMS OF MODERN LIVING AND COMMUNICATION . . .
AND YET, ONE BY ONE, HE WOULD BE BETRAYED BY EVERYONE HE TRUSTED.
EDISON.
JP MORGAN.
EVEN HIS CLOSEST ALLY, GEORGE WESTINGHOUSE.

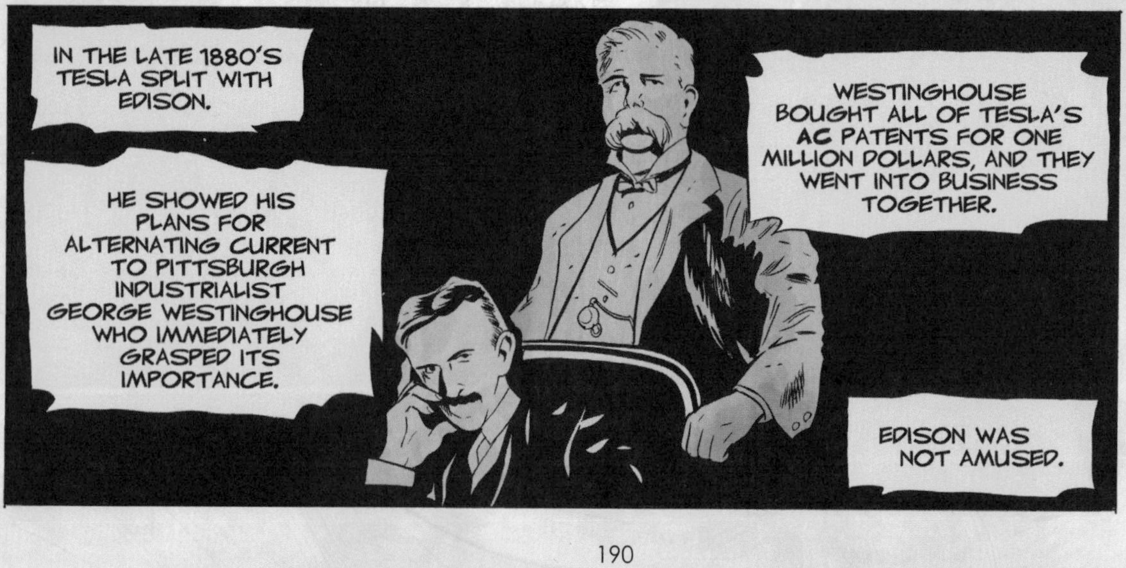
IN THE LATE 1880'S TESLA SPLIT WITH EDISON.
HE SHOWED HIS PLANS FOR ALTERNATING CURRENT TO PITTSBURGH INDUSTRIALIST GEORGE WESTINGHOUSE WHO IMMEDIATELY GRASPED ITS IMPORTANCE.
WESTINGHOUSE BOUGHT ALL OF TESLA'S AC PATENTS FOR ONE MILLION DOLLARS, AND THEY WENT INTO BUSINESS TOGETHER.
EDISON WAS NOT AMUSED.

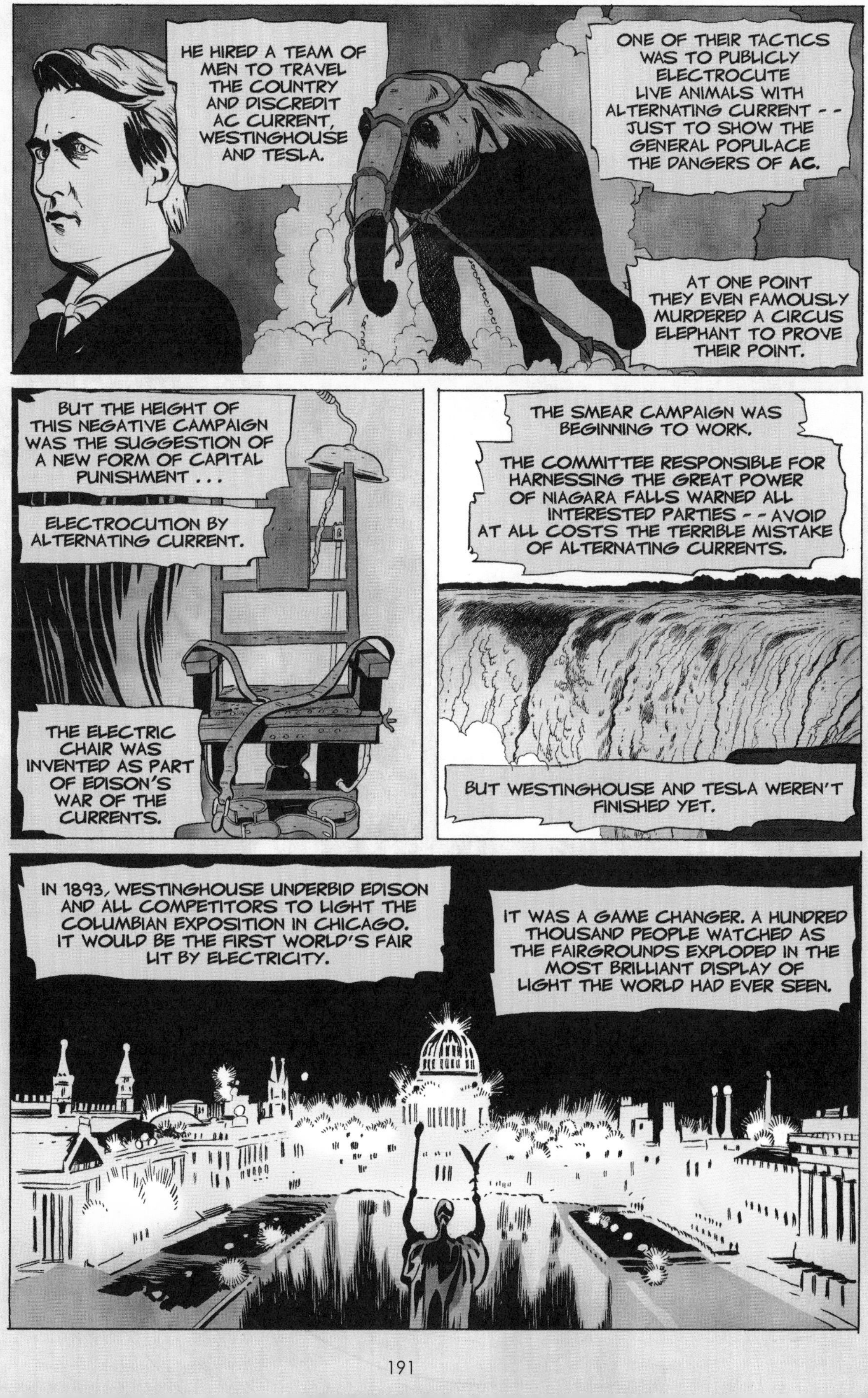
HE HIRED A TEAM OF MEN TO TRAVEL THE COUNTRY AND DISCREDIT AC CURRENT, WESTINGHOUSE AND TESLA.
ONE OF THEIR TACTICS WAS TO PUBLICLY ELECTROCUTE LIVE ANIMALS WITH ALTERNATING CURRENT - - JUST TO SHOW THE GENERAL POPULACE THE DANGERS OF AC.
AT ONE POINT THEY EVEN FAMOUSLY MURDERED A CIRCUS ELEPHANT TO PROVE THEIR POINT.
BUT THE HEIGHT OF THIS NEGATIVE CAMPAIGN WAS THE SUGGESTION OF A NEW FORM OF CAPITAL PUNISHMENT . . .
ELECTROCUTION BY ALTERNATING CURRENT.
THE ELECTRIC CHAIR WAS INVENTED AS PART OF EDISON'S WAR OF THE CURRENTS.
THE SMEAR CAMPAIGN WAS BEGINNING TO WORK.
THE COMMITTEE RESPONSIBLE FOR HARNESSING THE GREAT POWER OF NIAGARA FALLS WARNED ALL INTERESTED PARTIES - - AVOID AT ALL COSTS THE TERRIBLE MISTAKE OF ALTERNATING CURRENTS.
BUT WESTINGHOUSE AND TESLA WEREN'T FINISHED YET.
IN 1893, WESTINGHOUSE UNDERBID EDISON AND ALL COMPETITORS TO LIGHT THE COLUMBIAN EXPOSITION IN CHICAGO. IT WOULD BE THE FIRST WORLD'S FAIR LIT BY ELECTRICITY.
IT WAS A GAME CHANGER. A HUNDRED THOUSAND PEOPLE WATCHED AS THE FAIRGROUNDS EXPLODED IN THE MOST BRILLIANT DISPLAY OF LIGHT THE WORLD HAD EVER SEEN.

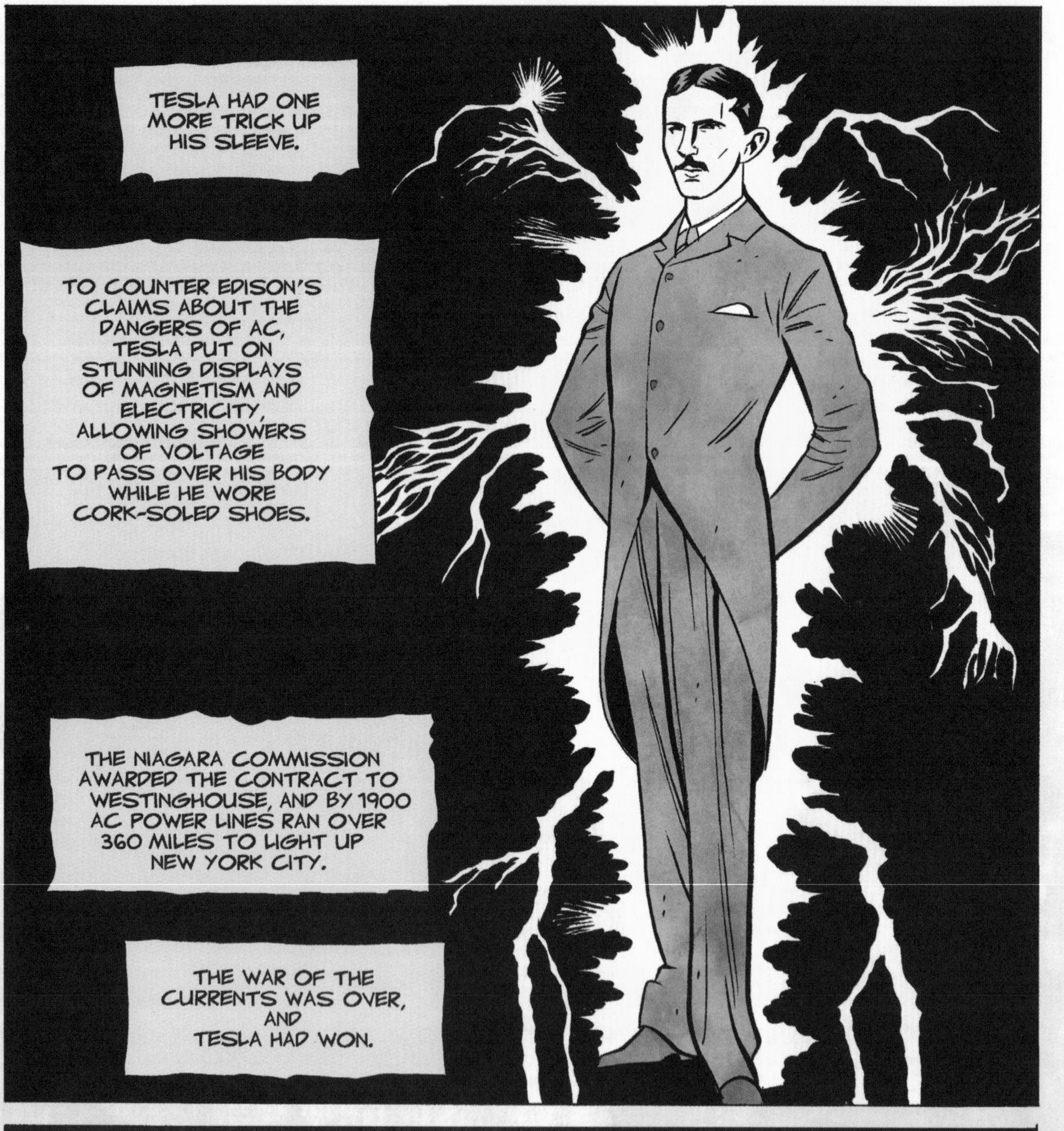
TESLA HAD ONE MORE TRICK UP HIS SLEEVE.
TO COUNTER EDISON'S CLAIMS ABOUT THE DANGERS OF AC, TESLA PUT ON STUNNING DISPLAYS OF MAGNETISM AND ELECTRICITY, ALLOWING SHOWERS OF VOLTAGE TO PASS OVER HIS BODY WHILE HE WORE CORK-SOLED SHOES.
THE NIAGARA COMMISSION AWARDED THE CONTRACT TO WESTINGHOUSE, AND BY 1900 AC POWER LINES RAN OVER 360 MILES TO LIGHT UP NEW YORK CITY.
THE WAR OF THE CURRENTS WAS OVER, AND TESLA HAD WON.

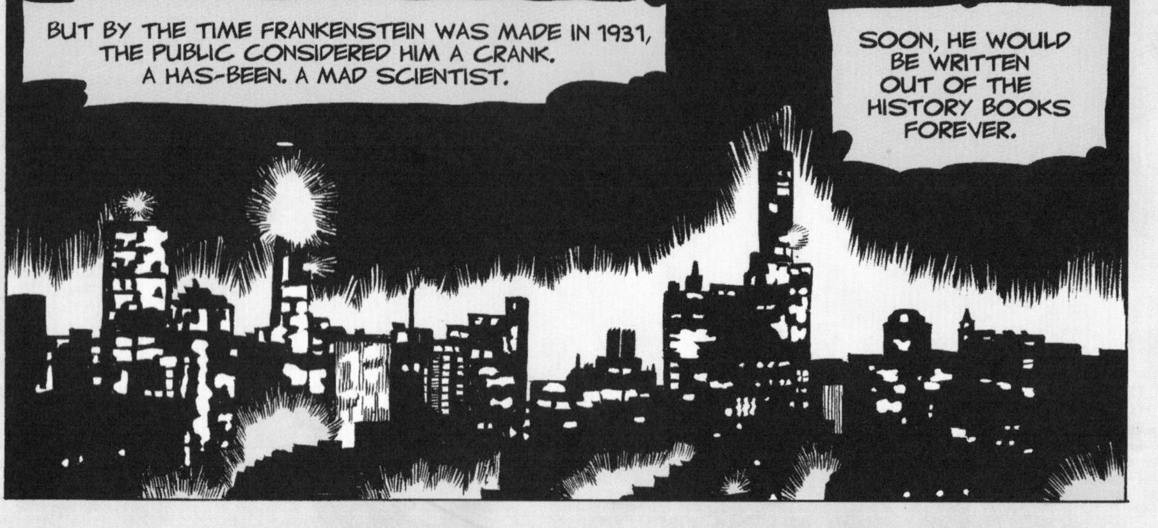
BUT BY THE TIME FRANKENSTEIN WAS MADE IN 1931, THE PUBLIC CONSIDERED HIM A CRANK. A HAS-BEEN. A MAD SCIENTIST.
SOON, HE WOULD BE WRITTEN OUT OF THE HISTORY BOOKS FOREVER.

IT WASN'T NIKOLA TESLA'S RISE TO POWER THAT FASCINATED US AS MUCH AS HIS FALL FROM GRACE.

I REMEMBER THAT LAST SUMMER BEFORE HIGH SCHOOL, MILES AND I RIDING OUR BIKES ALL OVER TOWN LOOKING FOR BOOKSTORES THAT SPECIALIZED IN UNEXPLAINED PHENOMENON AND NAZI CULTS. FUN STUFF.

THOSE WERE PLEASANT DAYS.

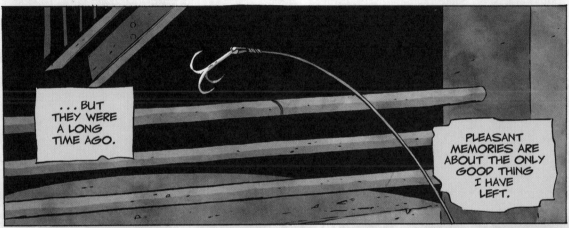

. . . BUT THEY WERE A LONG TIME AGO.

PLEASANT MEMORIES ARE ABOUT THE ONLY GOOD THING I HAVE LEFT.

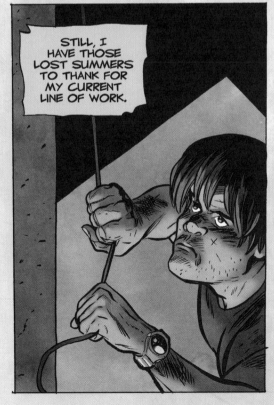

STILL, I HAVE THOSE LOST SUMMERS TO THANK FOR MY CURRENT LINE OF WORK.

193

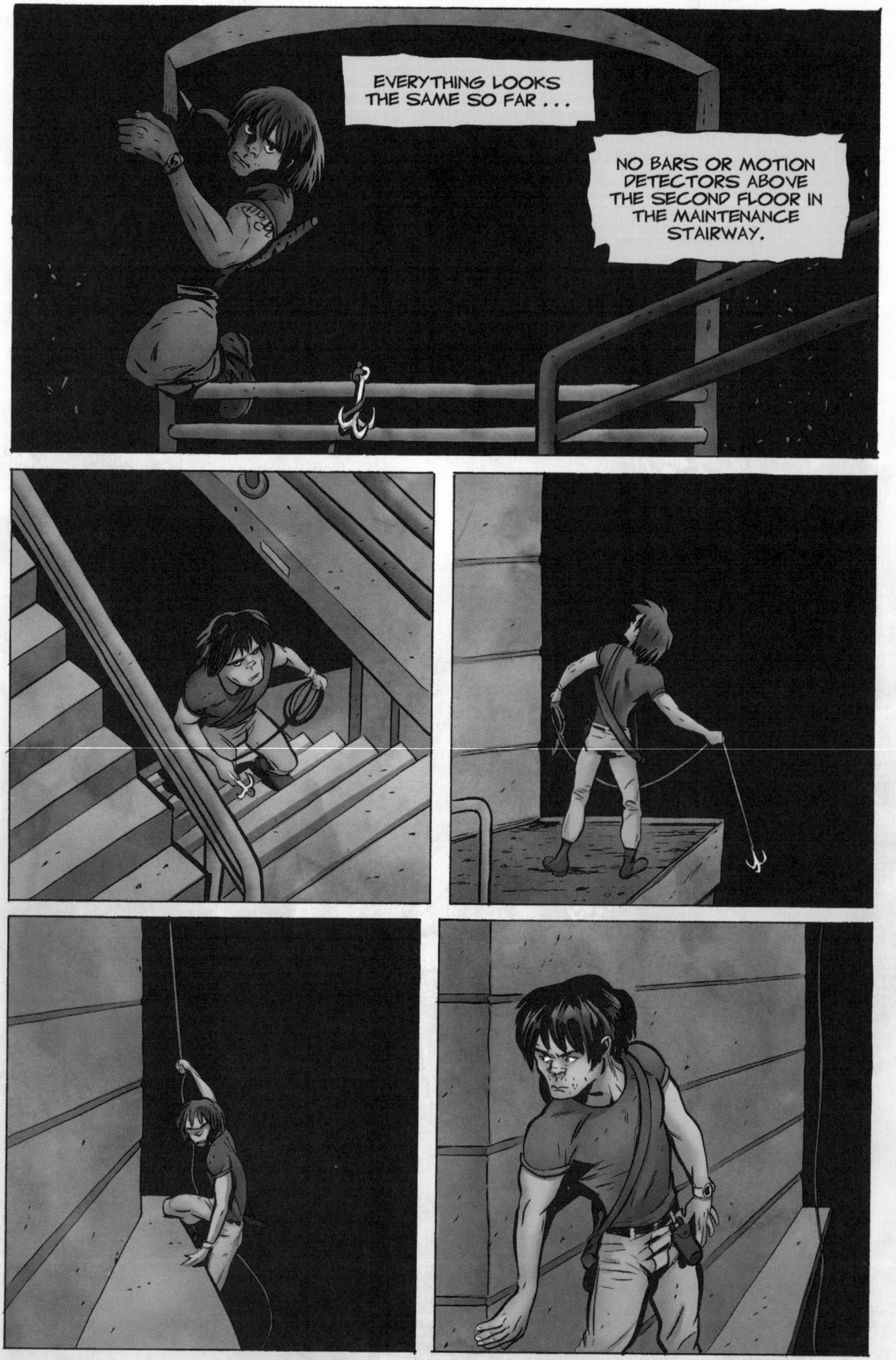
EVERYTHING LOOKS THE SAME SO FAR . . .
NO BARS OR MOTION DETECTORS ABOVE THE SECOND FLOOR IN THE MAINTENANCE STAIRWAY.

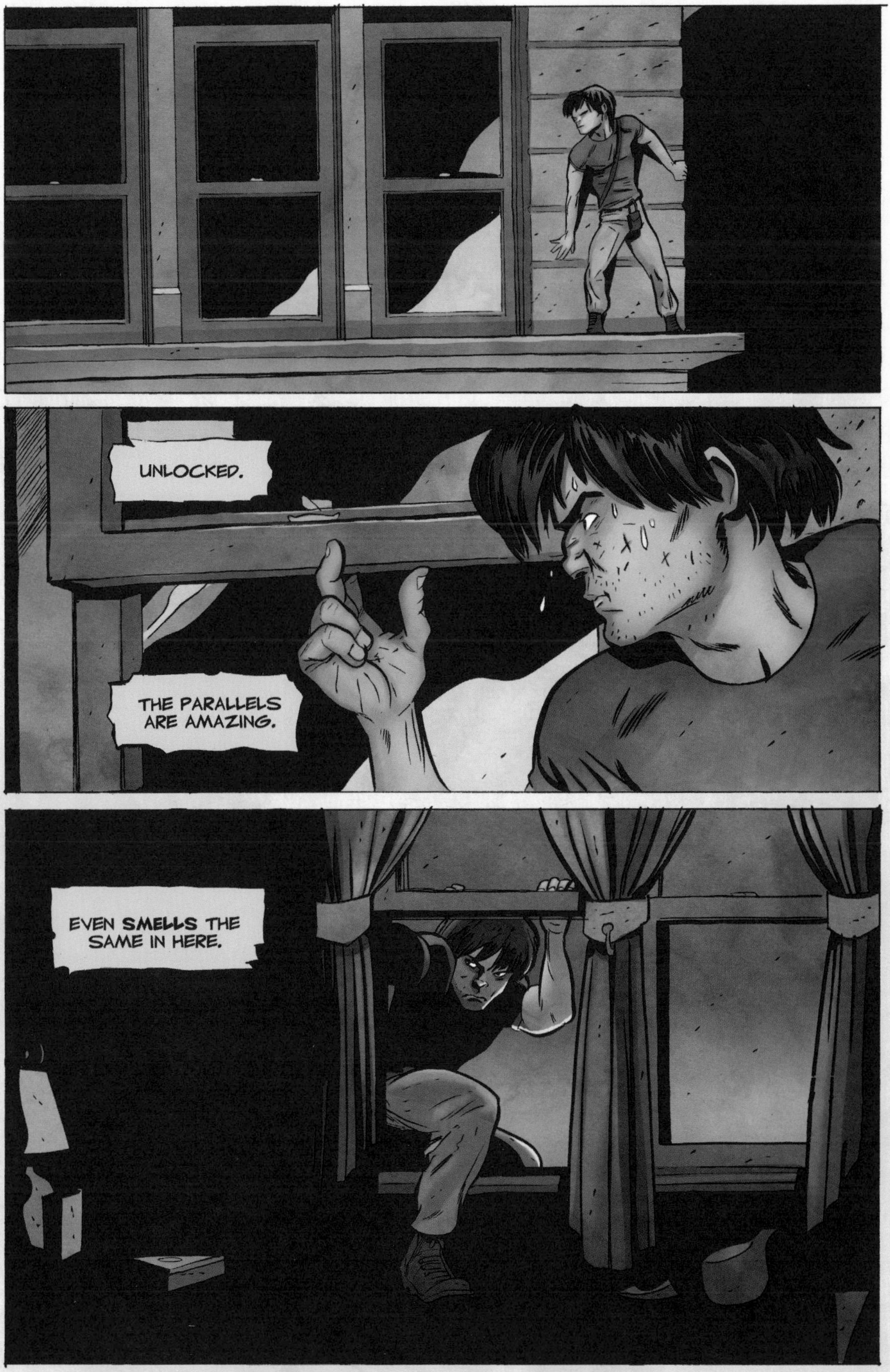
UNLOCKED.
THE PARALLELS ARE AMAZING.
EVEN SMELLS THE SAME IN HERE.

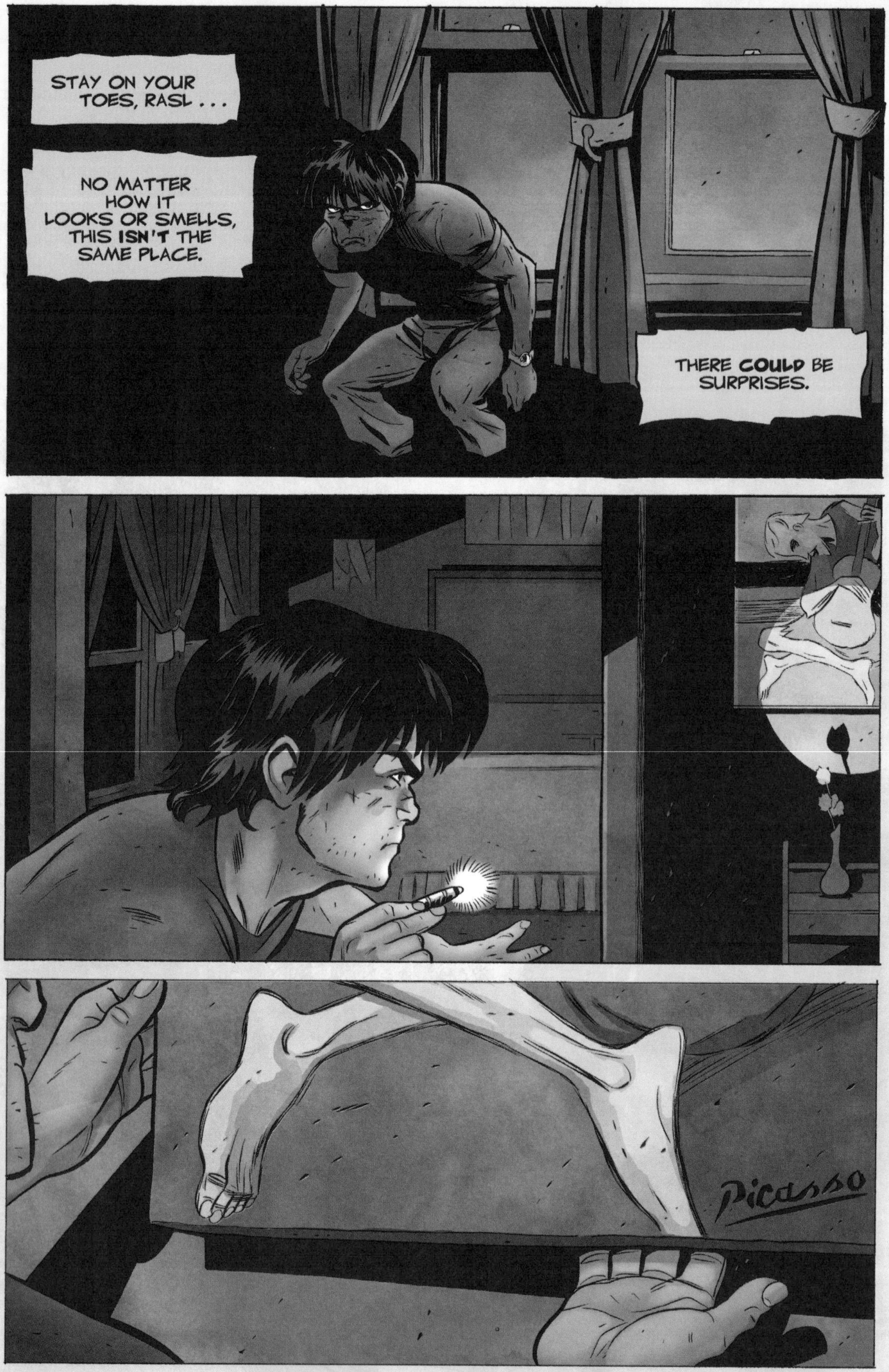
STAY ON YOUR TOES, RASL . . .
NO MATTER HOW IT LOOKS OR SMELLS, THIS **ISN'T** THE SAME PLACE.
THERE **COULD** BE SURPRISES.
Picasso

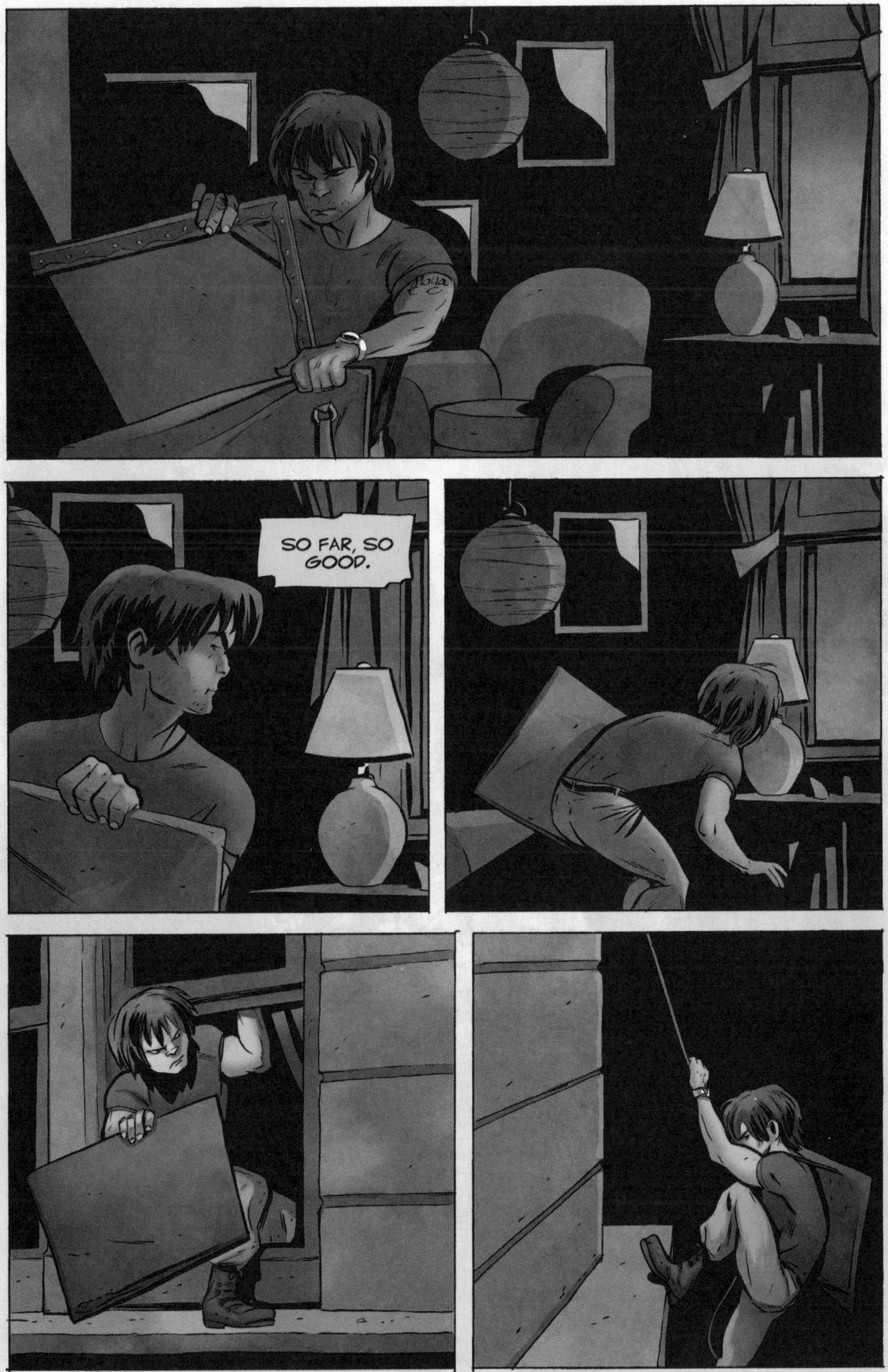
SO FAR, SO GOOD.

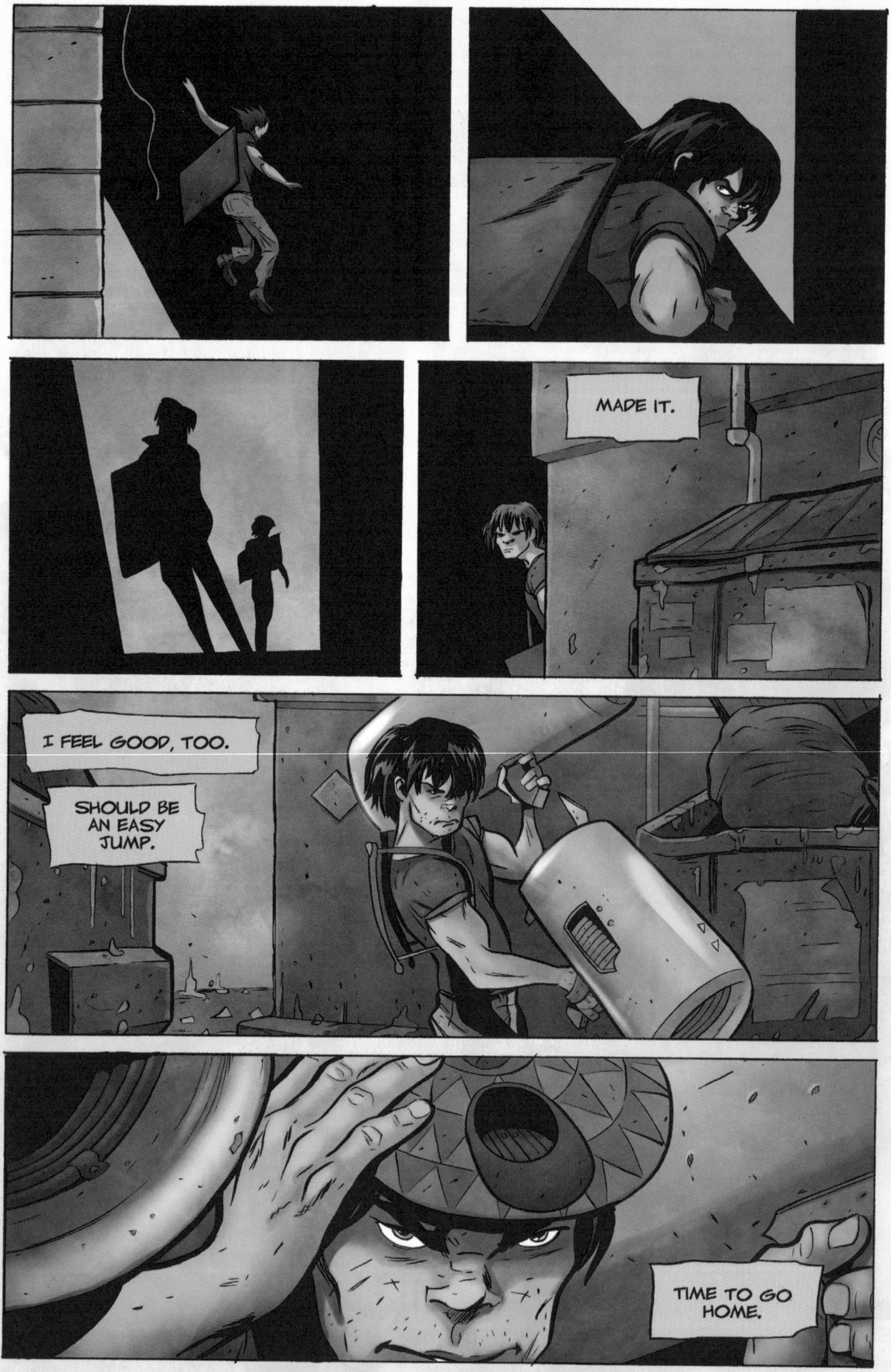
MADE IT.
I FEEL GOOD, TOO.
SHOULD BE AN EASY JUMP.
TIME TO GO HOME.

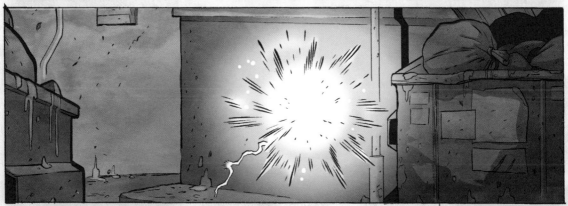

ONCE THE WAR OF THE CURRENTS WAS OVER, NIKOLA TESLA TURNED HIS MIND TO HIS REAL INTEREST . . .

. . . THE **NATURE** AND **MEANING** OF ELECTRICITY.

HE BELIEVED THAT ELECTRICITY WAS A FLUID THAT FLOWED THROUGH US. THAT WE ARE ALL RESONATING BODIES OF MATTER.

TESLA BELIEVED THAT ELECTRICITY WAS **LIFE FORCE** ITSELF.

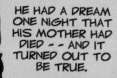HE HAD A DREAM ONE NIGHT THAT HIS MOTHER HAD DIED -- AND IT TURNED OUT TO BE TRUE.

HE WONDERED HOW THIS CONNECTION BETWEEN TWO PEOPLE WAS POSSIBLE.

AND THEN NIKOLA HAD A TRULY ASTONISHING THOUGHT.

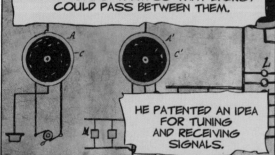IF TWO RESONATING BODIES WERE SENDING OUT VIBRATIONS INTO SPACE, IT WAS ONLY A MATTER OF FINDING THE PROPER FREQUENCY AND ATTUNING THEM SO THAT ENERGY COULD PASS BETWEEN THEM.

HE PATENTED AN IDEA FOR TUNING AND RECEIVING SIGNALS.

HIS NEW PLAN WAS TO TRANSMIT ENERGY -- WITHOUT WIRES -- THROUGH THE UPPER ATMOSPHERE.

HE BUILT A LABORATORY IN THE COLORADO ROCKIES WHERE HE COULD WORK IN SECRET, GATHERING DATA FOR HIS BIG IDEA --

THE **SMALLEST** PART OF WHICH WOULD BE SENDING A SIGNAL FROM **PIKES PEAK** TO **PARIS**.

CIGAR?

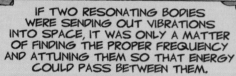

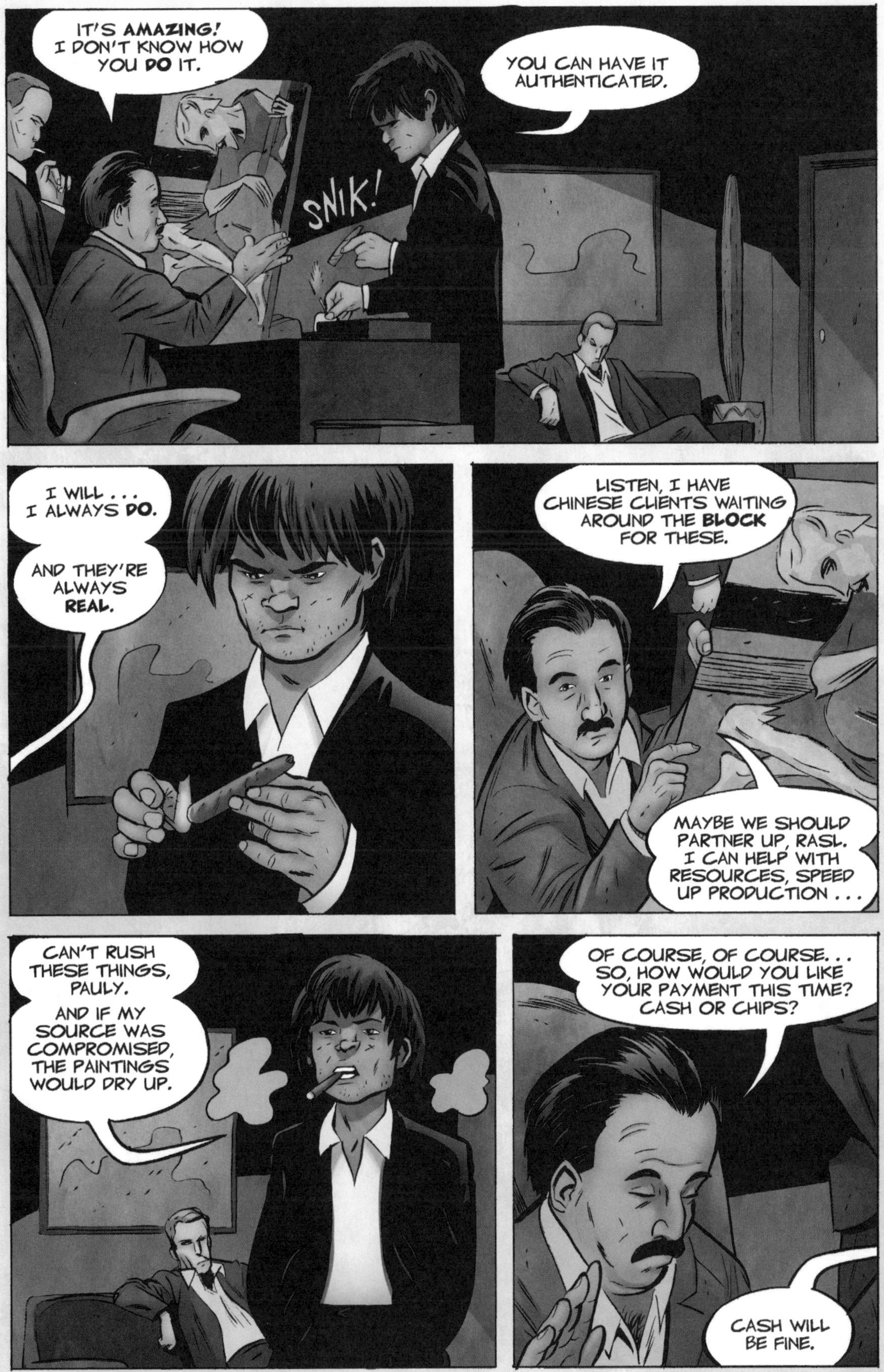
IT'S AMAZING! I DON'T KNOW HOW YOU DO IT.
YOU CAN HAVE IT AUTHENTICATED.
SNIK!
I WILL . . . I ALWAYS DO.
AND THEY'RE ALWAYS REAL.
LISTEN, I HAVE CHINESE CLIENTS WAITING AROUND THE BLOCK FOR THESE.
MAYBE WE SHOULD PARTNER UP, RASL. I CAN HELP WITH RESOURCES, SPEED UP PRODUCTION . . .
CAN'T RUSH THESE THINGS, PAULY.
AND IF MY SOURCE WAS COMPROMISED, THE PAINTINGS WOULD DRY UP.
OF COURSE, OF COURSE. . . SO, HOW WOULD YOU LIKE YOUR PAYMENT THIS TIME? CASH OR CHIPS?
CASH WILL BE FINE.

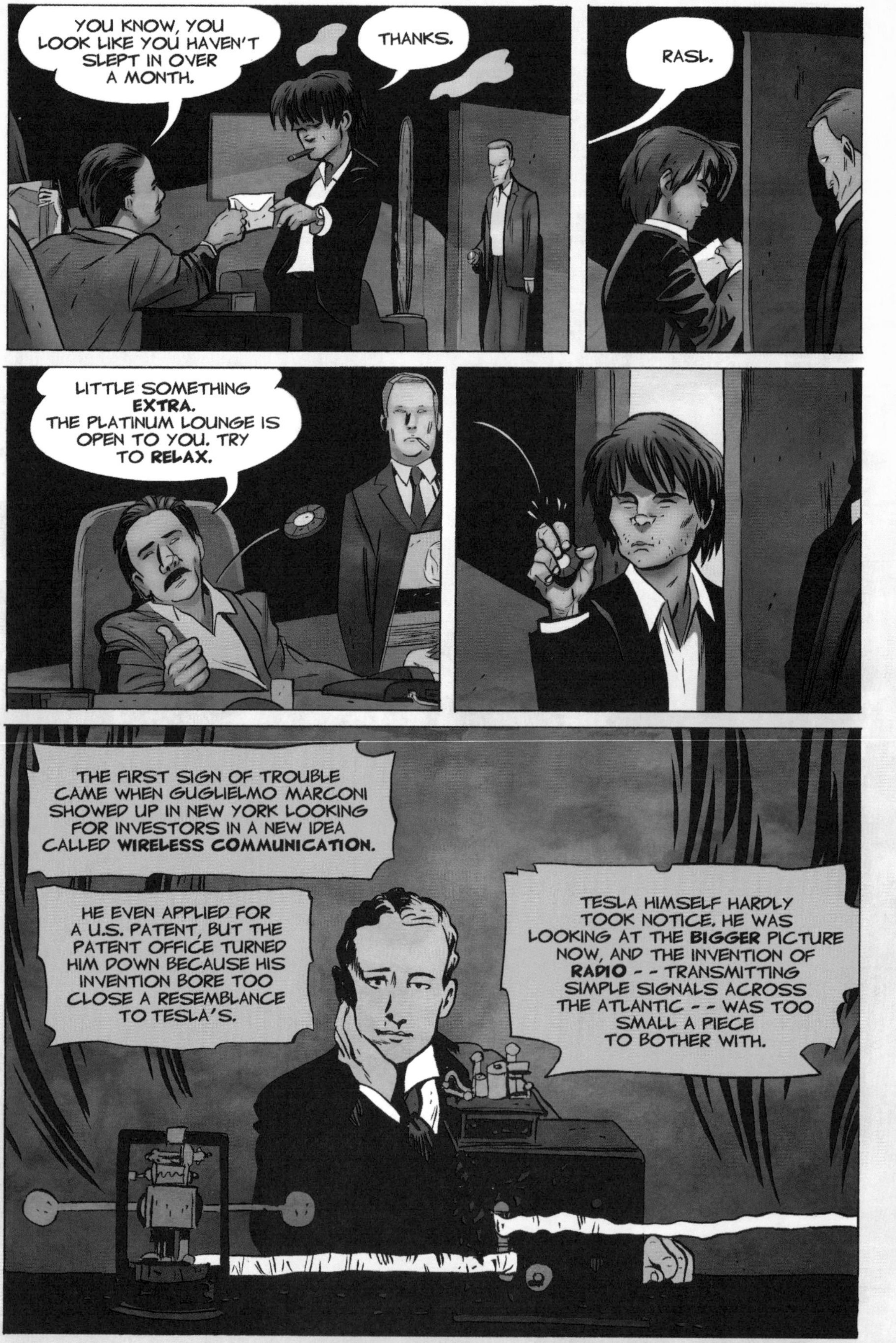
YOU KNOW, YOU LOOK LIKE YOU HAVEN'T SLEPT IN OVER A MONTH.
THANKS.
RASL.
LITTLE SOMETHING **EXTRA**. THE PLATINUM LOUNGE IS OPEN TO YOU. TRY TO **RELAX**.
THE FIRST SIGN OF TROUBLE CAME WHEN GUGLIELMO MARCONI SHOWED UP IN NEW YORK LOOKING FOR INVESTORS IN A NEW IDEA CALLED **WIRELESS COMMUNICATION**.
HE EVEN APPLIED FOR A U.S. PATENT, BUT THE PATENT OFFICE TURNED HIM DOWN BECAUSE HIS INVENTION BORE TOO CLOSE A RESEMBLANCE TO TESLA'S.
TESLA HIMSELF HARDLY TOOK NOTICE. HE WAS LOOKING AT THE **BIGGER** PICTURE NOW, AND THE INVENTION OF **RADIO** - - TRANSMITTING SIMPLE SIGNALS ACROSS THE ATLANTIC - - WAS TOO SMALL A PIECE TO BOTHER WITH.

NEXT CAME BAD NEWS FROM HIS GREAT FRIEND AND PATRON GEORGE WESTINGHOUSE.

IN A GESTURE OF EXTREME LOYALTY, TESLA TORE UP HIS CONTRACT THAT GUARANTEED HIM A ROYALTY ON EVERY HORSEPOWER THAT WAS GENERATED. THE COMPANY WAS **SAVED**.

THE WAR OF THE CURRENTS HAD OVER EXTENDED HIS COMPANY AND WESTINGHOUSE WAS IN FINANCIAL TROUBLE.

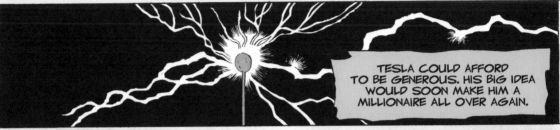

TESLA COULD AFFORD TO BE GENEROUS. HIS BIG IDEA WOULD SOON MAKE HIM A MILLIONAIRE ALL OVER AGAIN.

HOWEVER, AFTER MONTHS OF ALARMING THE LOCAL TOWNSFOLK WITH THUNDER THAT COULD BE HEARD TWENTY MILES AWAY, AND BOLTS OF MAN-MADE LIGHTNING OVER A HUNDRED FEET LONG, THE PEOPLE OF COLORADO SPRINGS HAD HAD ENOUGH.

THEY DIDN'T RUN HIM OFF WITH TORCHES AND PITCH FORKS, BUT IT WAS TIME FOR THE MAD SCIENTIST TO GO.

NO PROBLEM. TESLA HAD WHAT HE WANTED -- KNOWLEDGE THAT WOULD SOON GIVE MANKIND THE POWER OF THE UNIVERSE.

HE HEADED BACK EAST AND SET UP A MEETING WITH THE MOST POWERFUL FINANCIER IN THE WORLD . . .

J. PIERPONT MORGAN.

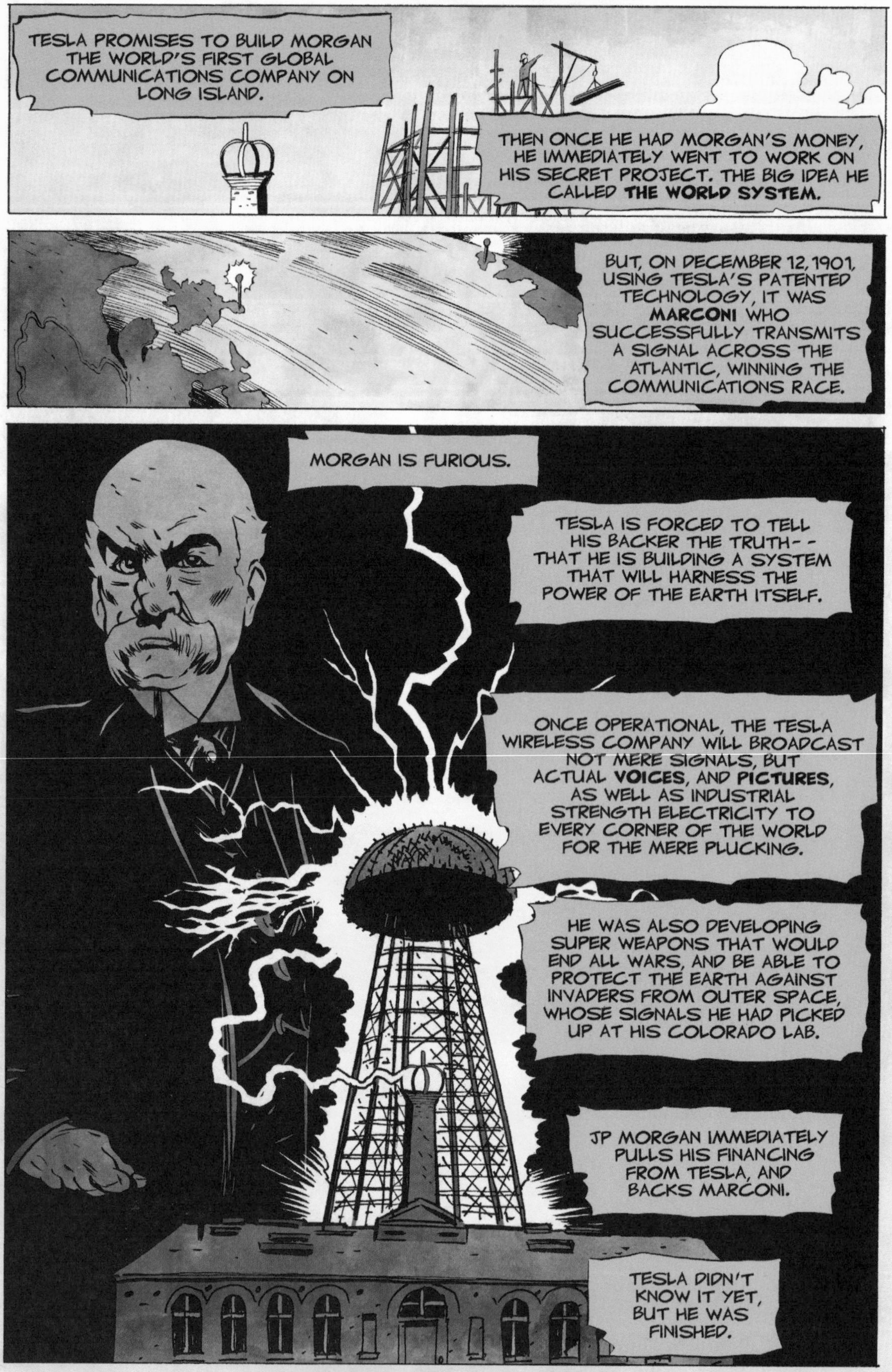
TESLA PROMISES TO BUILD MORGAN THE WORLD'S FIRST GLOBAL COMMUNICATIONS COMPANY ON LONG ISLAND.
THEN ONCE HE HAD MORGAN'S MONEY, HE IMMEDIATELY WENT TO WORK ON HIS SECRET PROJECT. THE BIG IDEA HE CALLED **THE WORLD SYSTEM.**
BUT, ON DECEMBER 12, 1901, USING TESLA'S PATENTED TECHNOLOGY, IT WAS **MARCONI** WHO SUCCESSFULLY TRANSMITS A SIGNAL ACROSS THE ATLANTIC, WINNING THE COMMUNICATIONS RACE.
MORGAN IS FURIOUS.
TESLA IS FORCED TO TELL HIS BACKER THE TRUTH-- THAT HE IS BUILDING A SYSTEM THAT WILL HARNESS THE POWER OF THE EARTH ITSELF.
ONCE OPERATIONAL, THE TESLA WIRELESS COMPANY WILL BROADCAST NOT MERE SIGNALS, BUT ACTUAL **VOICES**, AND **PICTURES**, AS WELL AS INDUSTRIAL STRENGTH ELECTRICITY TO EVERY CORNER OF THE WORLD FOR THE MERE PLUCKING.
HE WAS ALSO DEVELOPING SUPER WEAPONS THAT WOULD END ALL WARS, AND BE ABLE TO PROTECT THE EARTH AGAINST INVADERS FROM OUTER SPACE, WHOSE SIGNALS HE HAD PICKED UP AT HIS COLORADO LAB.
JP MORGAN IMMEDIATELY PULLS HIS FINANCING FROM TESLA, AND BACKS MARCONI.
TESLA DIDN'T KNOW IT YET, BUT HE WAS FINISHED.

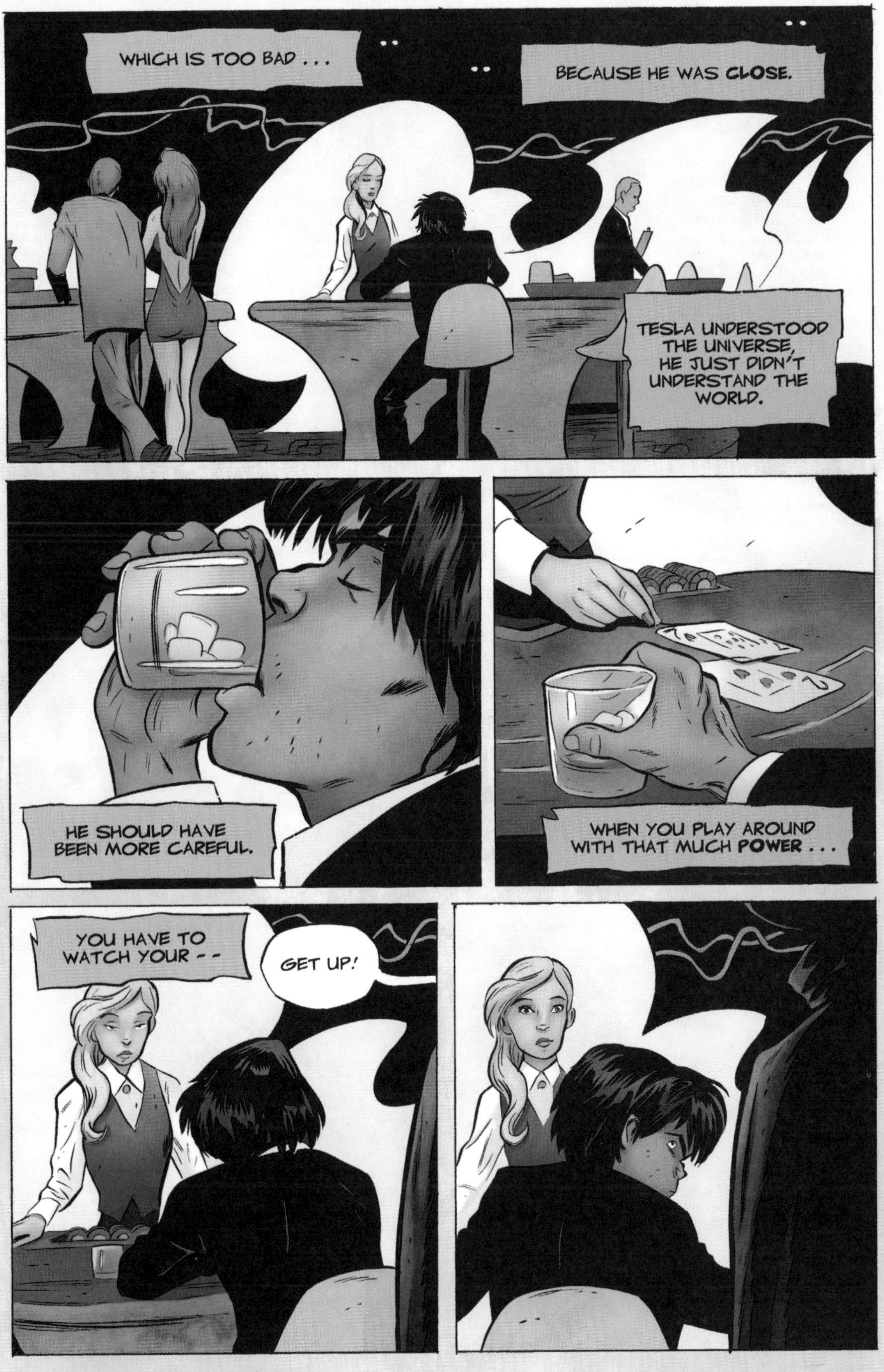
WHICH IS TOO BAD . . .
BECAUSE HE WAS CLOSE.
TESLA UNDERSTOOD THE UNIVERSE, HE JUST DIDN'T UNDERSTAND THE WORLD.
HE SHOULD HAVE BEEN MORE CAREFUL.
WHEN YOU PLAY AROUND WITH THAT MUCH POWER . . .
YOU HAVE TO WATCH YOUR - -
GET UP!

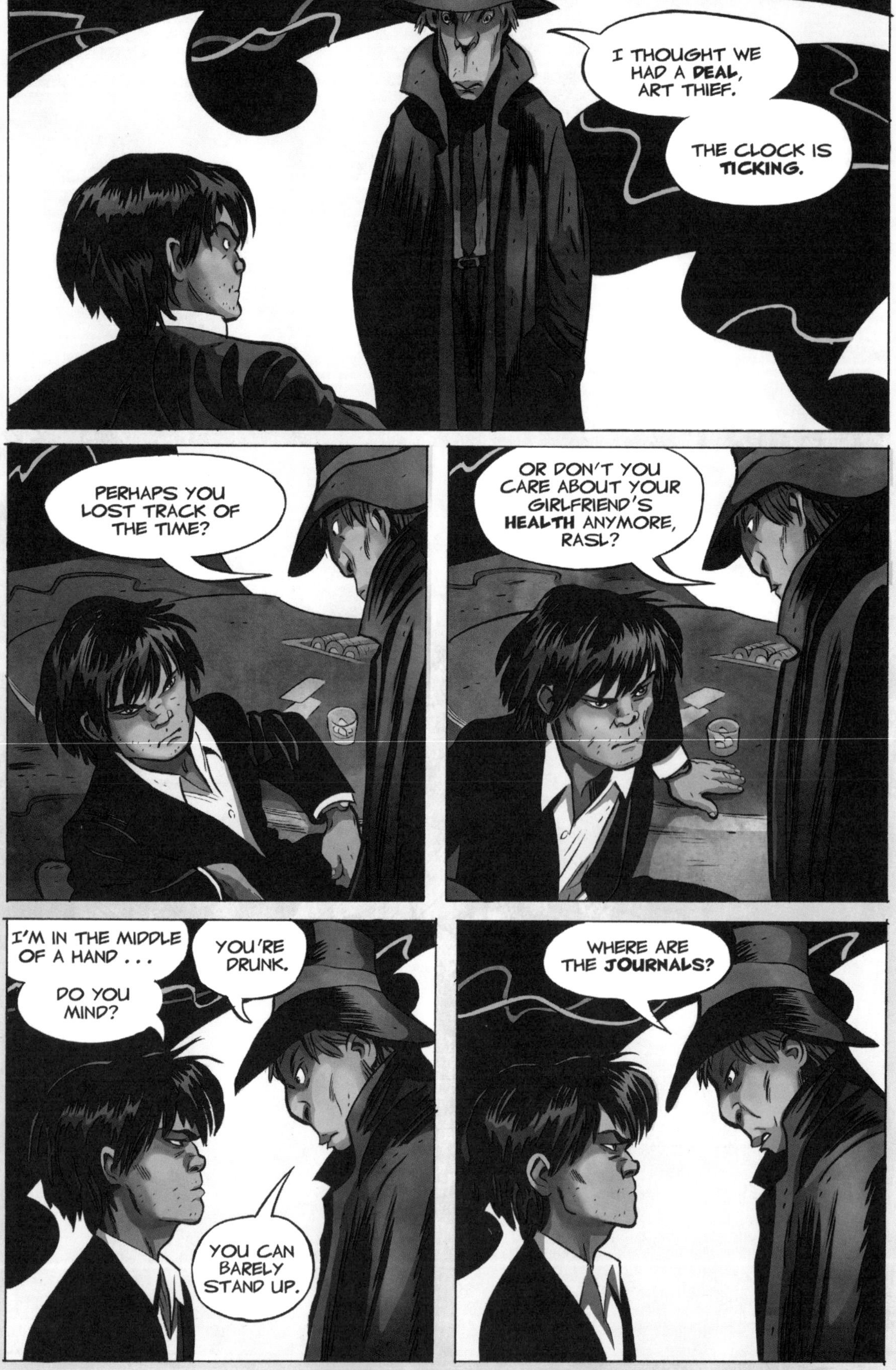
I THOUGHT WE HAD A **DEAL**, ART THIEF.
THE CLOCK IS **TICKING**.
PERHAPS YOU LOST TRACK OF THE TIME?
OR DON'T YOU CARE ABOUT YOUR GIRLFRIEND'S **HEALTH** ANYMORE, RASL?
I'M IN THE MIDDLE OF A HAND . . .
DO YOU MIND?
YOU'RE DRUNK.
YOU CAN BARELY STAND UP.
WHERE ARE THE **JOURNALS**?

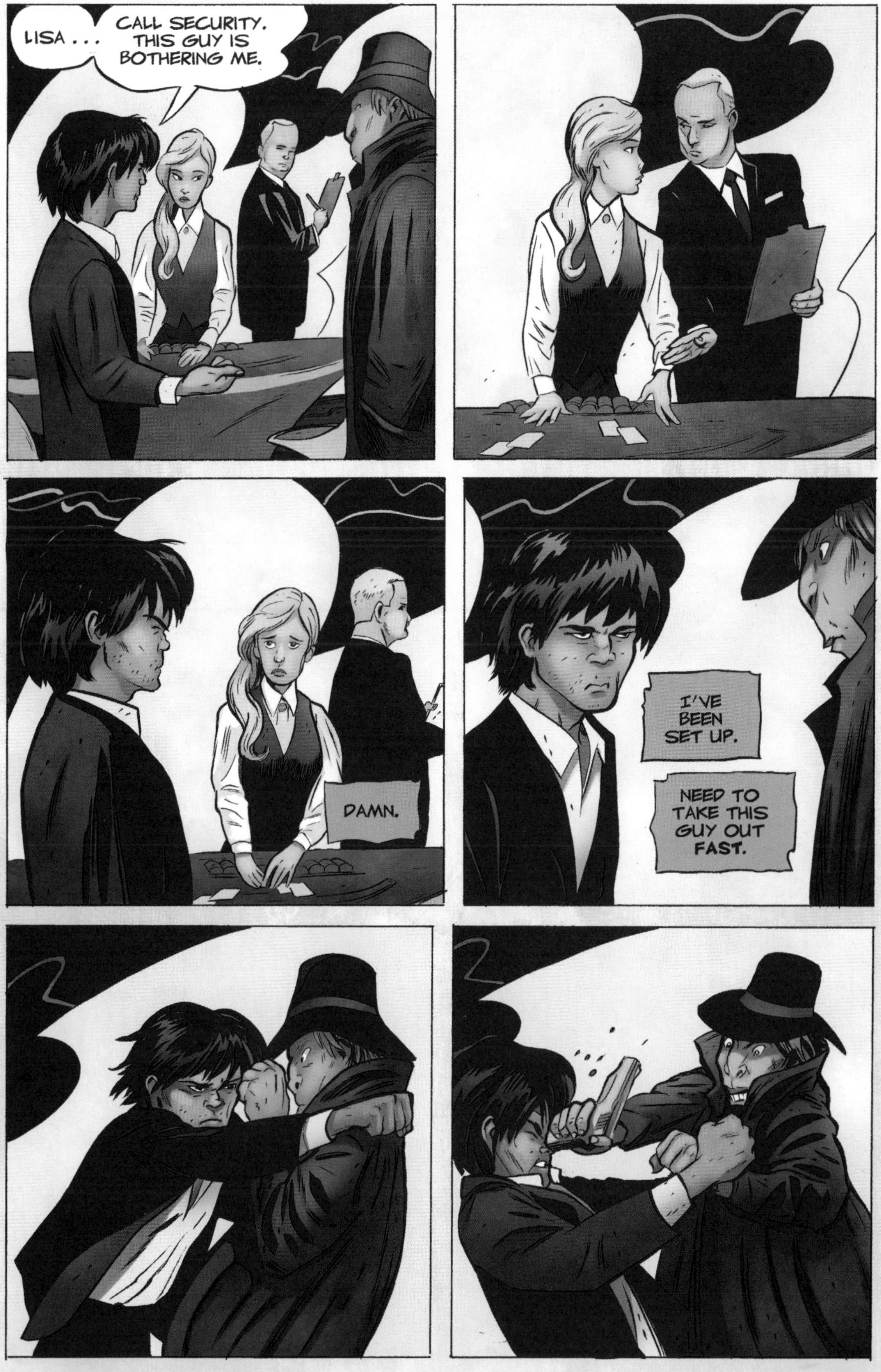
LISA . . .
CALL SECURITY. THIS GUY IS BOTHERING ME.
DAMN.
I'VE BEEN SET UP.
NEED TO TAKE THIS GUY OUT FAST.

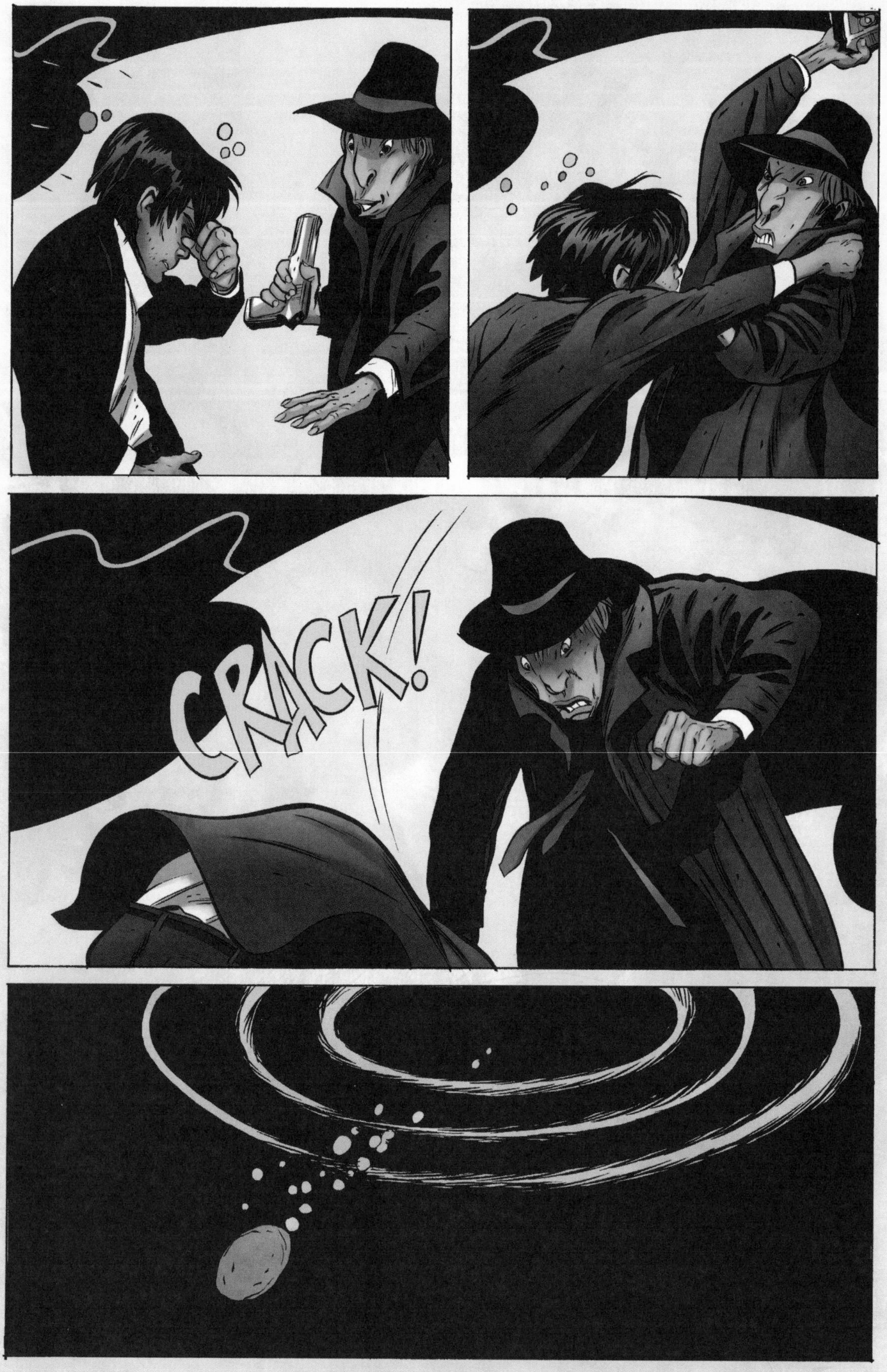
CRACK!

VII
BRIGHTER THAN THE SUN

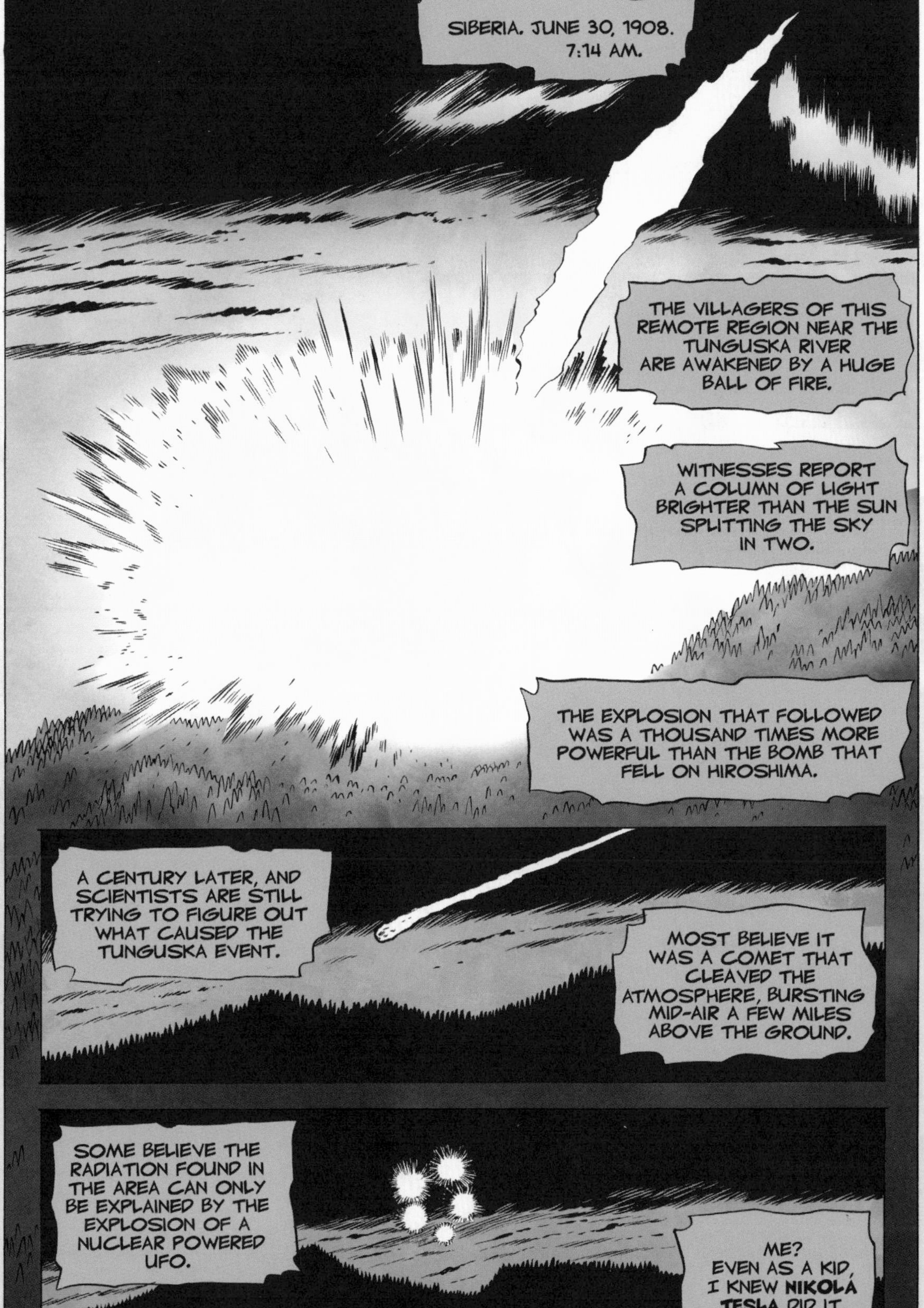
SIBERIA. JUNE 30, 1908. 7:14 AM.
THE VILLAGERS OF THIS REMOTE REGION NEAR THE TUNGUSKA RIVER ARE AWAKENED BY A HUGE BALL OF FIRE.
WITNESSES REPORT A COLUMN OF LIGHT BRIGHTER THAN THE SUN SPLITTING THE SKY IN TWO.
THE EXPLOSION THAT FOLLOWED WAS A THOUSAND TIMES MORE POWERFUL THAN THE BOMB THAT FELL ON HIROSHIMA.
A CENTURY LATER, AND SCIENTISTS ARE STILL TRYING TO FIGURE OUT WHAT CAUSED THE TUNGUSKA EVENT.
MOST BELIEVE IT WAS A COMET THAT CLEAVED THE ATMOSPHERE, BURSTING MID-AIR A FEW MILES ABOVE THE GROUND.
SOME BELIEVE THE RADIATION FOUND IN THE AREA CAN ONLY BE EXPLAINED BY THE EXPLOSION OF A NUCLEAR POWERED UFO.
ME? EVEN AS A KID, I KNEW **NIKOLA TESLA** DID IT.

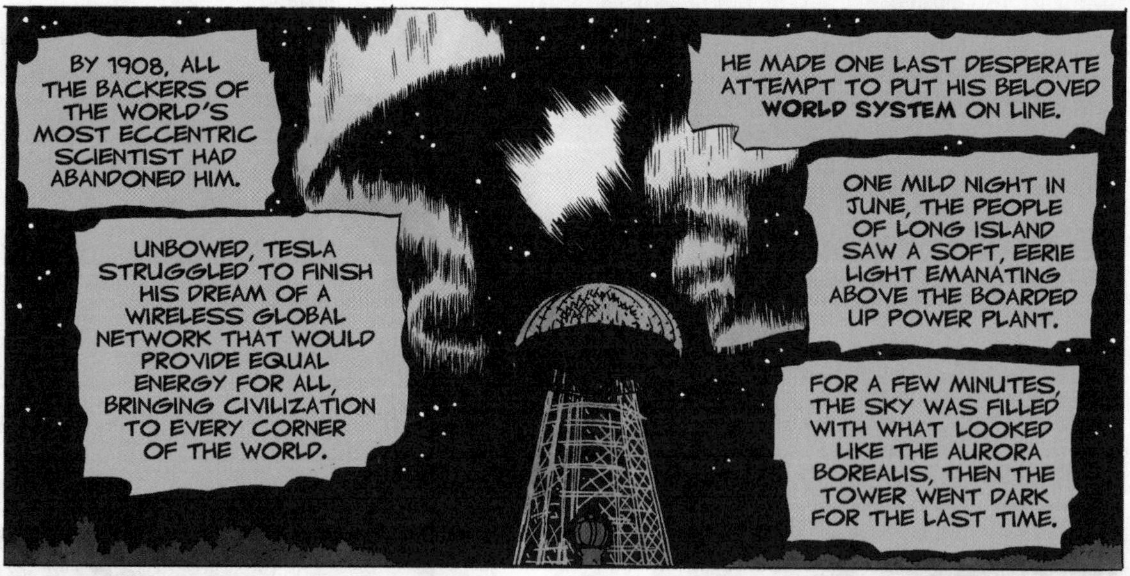
BY 1908, ALL THE BACKERS OF THE WORLD'S MOST ECCENTRIC SCIENTIST HAD ABANDONED HIM.
UNBOWED, TESLA STRUGGLED TO FINISH HIS DREAM OF A WIRELESS GLOBAL NETWORK THAT WOULD PROVIDE EQUAL ENERGY FOR ALL, BRINGING CIVILIZATION TO EVERY CORNER OF THE WORLD.
HE MADE ONE LAST DESPERATE ATTEMPT TO PUT HIS BELOVED **WORLD SYSTEM** ON LINE.
ONE MILD NIGHT IN JUNE, THE PEOPLE OF LONG ISLAND SAW A SOFT, EERIE LIGHT EMANATING ABOVE THE BOARDED UP POWER PLANT.
FOR A FEW MINUTES, THE SKY WAS FILLED WITH WHAT LOOKED LIKE THE AURORA BOREALIS, THEN THE TOWER WENT DARK FOR THE LAST TIME.

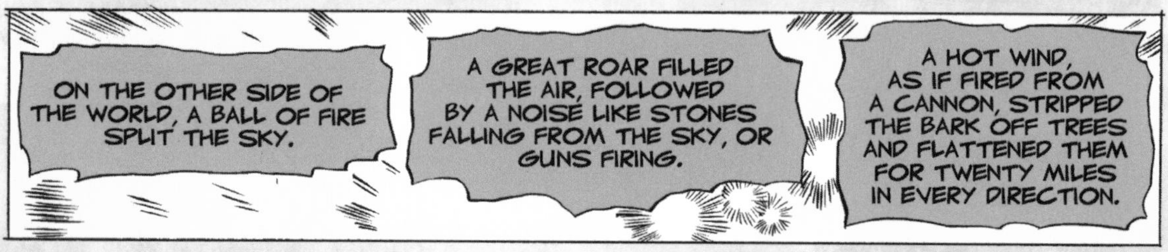
ON THE OTHER SIDE OF THE WORLD, A BALL OF FIRE SPLIT THE SKY.
A GREAT ROAR FILLED THE AIR, FOLLOWED BY A NOISE LIKE STONES FALLING FROM THE SKY, OR GUNS FIRING.
A HOT WIND, AS IF FIRED FROM A CANNON, STRIPPED THE BARK OFF TREES AND FLATTENED THEM FOR TWENTY MILES IN EVERY DIRECTION.

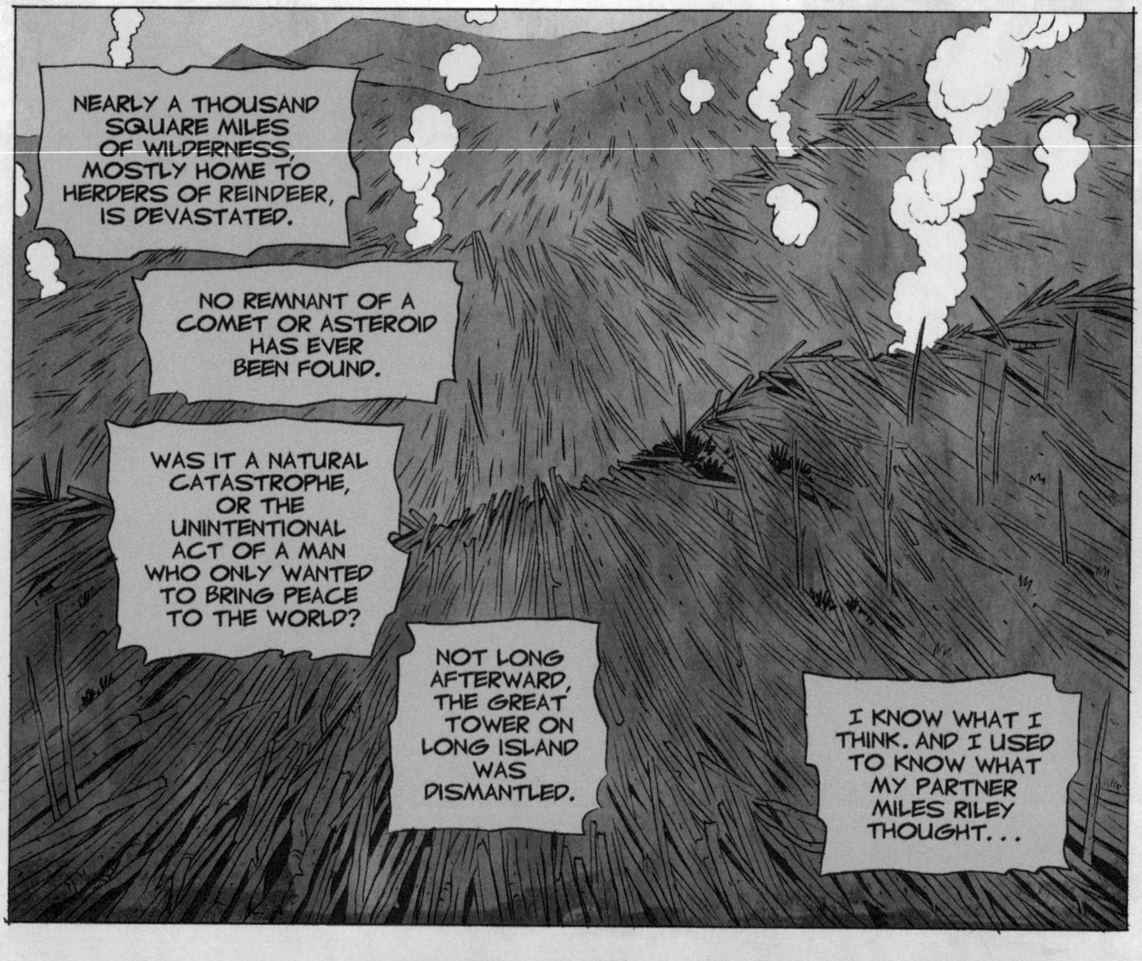
NEARLY A THOUSAND SQUARE MILES OF WILDERNESS, MOSTLY HOME TO HERDERS OF REINDEER, IS DEVASTATED.
NO REMNANT OF A COMET OR ASTEROID HAS EVER BEEN FOUND.
WAS IT A NATURAL CATASTROPHE, OR THE UNINTENTIONAL ACT OF A MAN WHO ONLY WANTED TO BRING PEACE TO THE WORLD?
NOT LONG AFTERWARD, THE GREAT TOWER ON LONG ISLAND WAS DISMANTLED.
I KNOW WHAT I THINK. AND I USED TO KNOW WHAT MY PARTNER MILES RILEY THOUGHT. . .

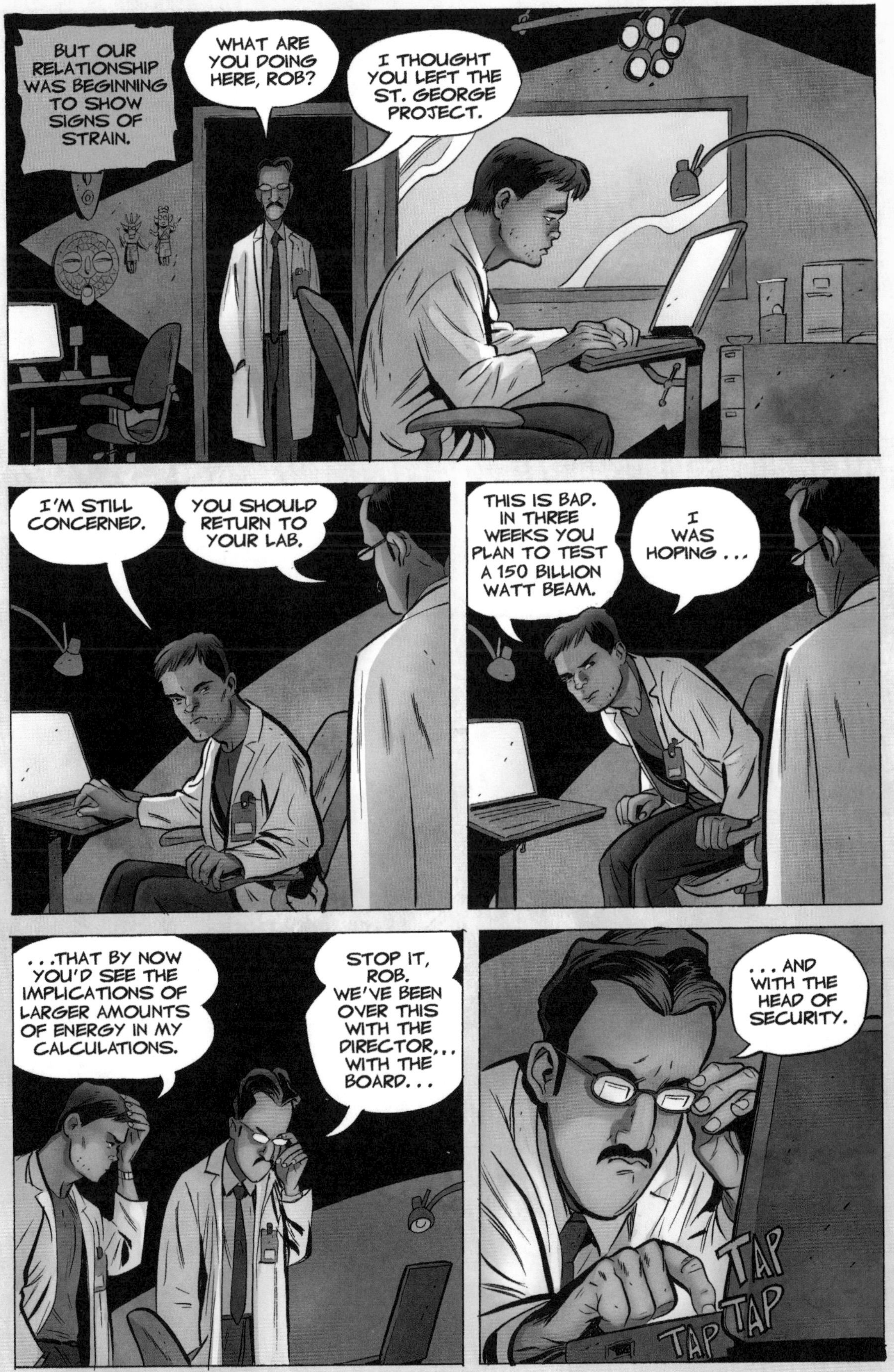
BUT OUR RELATIONSHIP WAS BEGINNING TO SHOW SIGNS OF STRAIN.
WHAT ARE YOU DOING HERE, ROB?
I THOUGHT YOU LEFT THE ST. GEORGE PROJECT.
I'M STILL CONCERNED.
YOU SHOULD RETURN TO YOUR LAB.
THIS IS BAD. IN THREE WEEKS YOU PLAN TO TEST A 150 BILLION WATT BEAM.
I WAS HOPING . . .
. . .THAT BY NOW YOU'D SEE THE IMPLICATIONS OF LARGER AMOUNTS OF ENERGY IN MY CALCULATIONS.
STOP IT, ROB. WE'VE BEEN OVER THIS WITH THE DIRECTOR,... WITH THE BOARD. . .
. . . AND WITH THE HEAD OF SECURITY.
TAP TAP TAP TAP

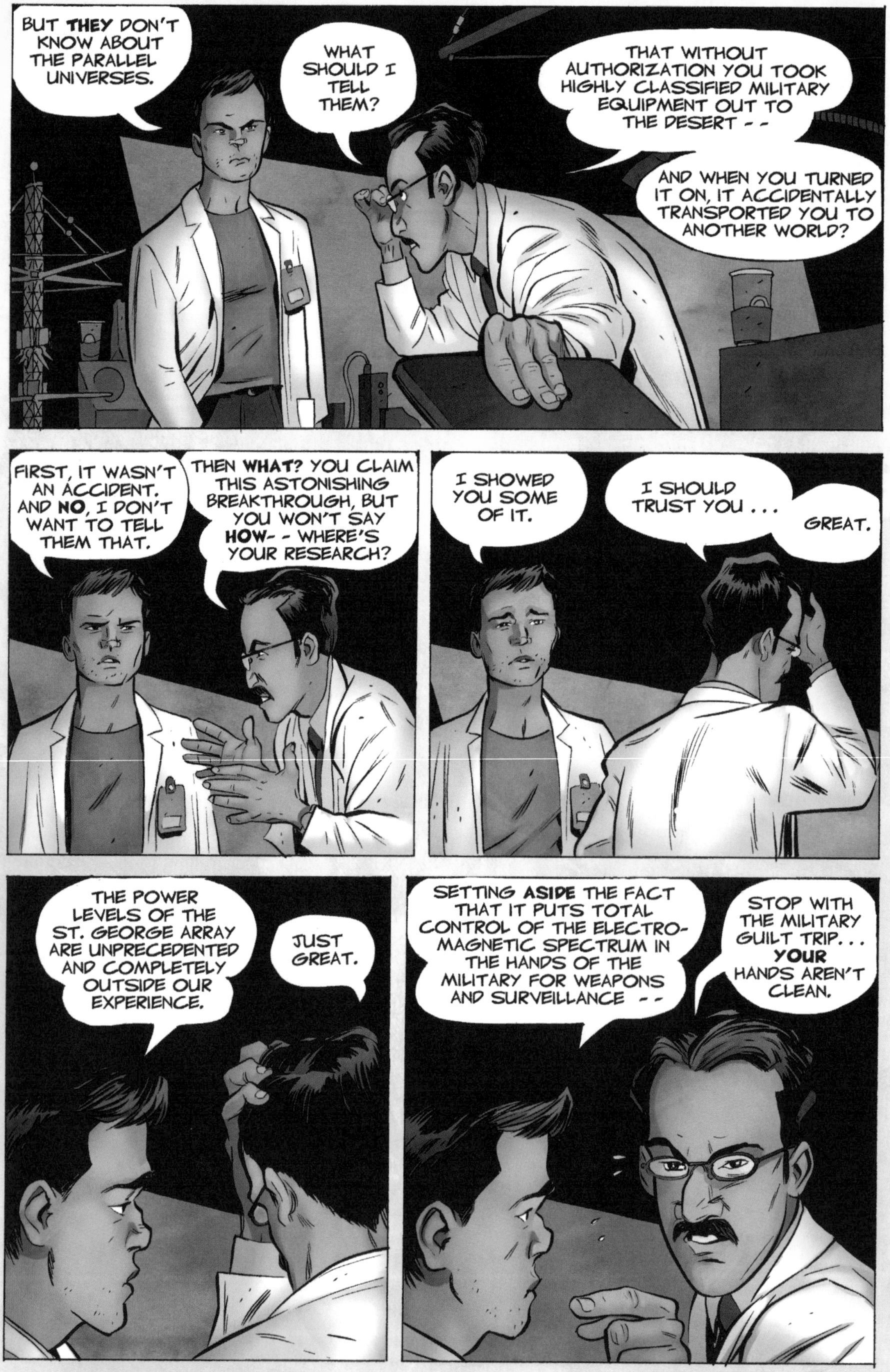
BUT THEY DON'T KNOW ABOUT THE PARALLEL UNIVERSES.
WHAT SHOULD I TELL THEM?
THAT WITHOUT AUTHORIZATION YOU TOOK HIGHLY CLASSIFIED MILITARY EQUIPMENT OUT TO THE DESERT - -
AND WHEN YOU TURNED IT ON, IT ACCIDENTALLY TRANSPORTED YOU TO ANOTHER WORLD?
FIRST, IT WASN'T AN ACCIDENT. AND NO, I DON'T WANT TO TELL THEM THAT.
THEN WHAT? YOU CLAIM THIS ASTONISHING BREAKTHROUGH, BUT YOU WON'T SAY HOW- - WHERE'S YOUR RESEARCH?
I SHOWED YOU SOME OF IT.
I SHOULD TRUST YOU . . .
GREAT.
THE POWER LEVELS OF THE ST. GEORGE ARRAY ARE UNPRECEDENTED AND COMPLETELY OUTSIDE OUR EXPERIENCE.
JUST GREAT.
SETTING ASIDE THE FACT THAT IT PUTS TOTAL CONTROL OF THE ELECTRO-MAGNETIC SPECTRUM IN THE HANDS OF THE MILITARY FOR WEAPONS AND SURVEILLANCE - -
STOP WITH THE MILITARY GUILT TRIP. . . YOUR HANDS AREN'T CLEAN.

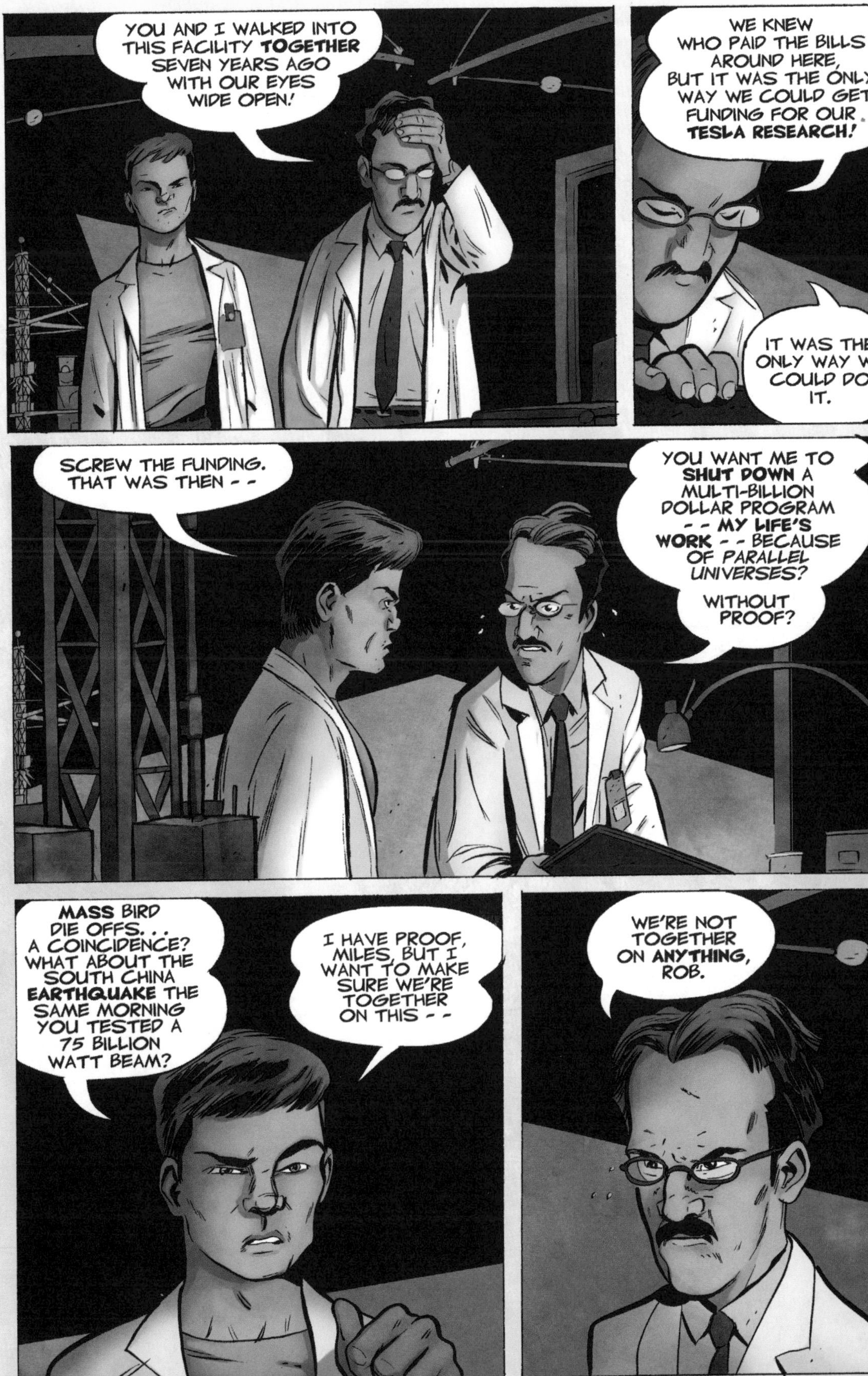
YOU AND I WALKED INTO THIS FACILITY TOGETHER SEVEN YEARS AGO WITH OUR EYES WIDE OPEN!
WE KNEW WHO PAID THE BILLS AROUND HERE, BUT IT WAS THE ONLY WAY WE COULD GET FUNDING FOR OUR TESLA RESEARCH!
IT WAS THE ONLY WAY WE COULD DO IT.
SCREW THE FUNDING. THAT WAS THEN - -
YOU WANT ME TO SHUT DOWN A MULTI-BILLION DOLLAR PROGRAM - - MY LIFE'S WORK - - BECAUSE OF PARALLEL UNIVERSES?
WITHOUT PROOF?
MASS BIRD DIE OFFS. . . A COINCIDENCE? WHAT ABOUT THE SOUTH CHINA EARTHQUAKE THE SAME MORNING YOU TESTED A 75 BILLION WATT BEAM?
I HAVE PROOF, MILES, BUT I WANT TO MAKE SURE WE'RE TOGETHER ON THIS - -
WE'RE NOT TOGETHER ON ANYTHING, ROB.

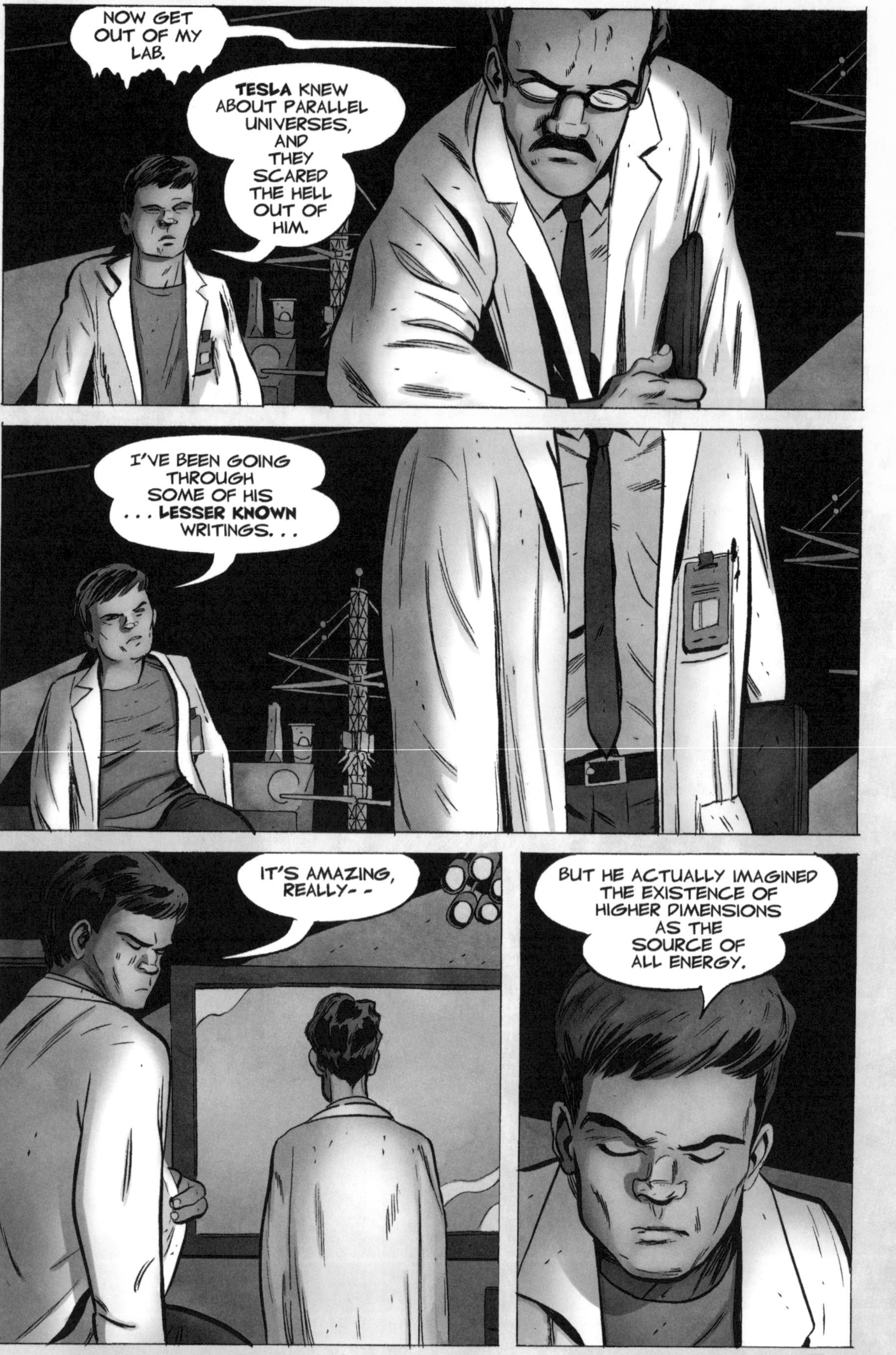
NOW GET OUT OF MY LAB.
TESLA KNEW ABOUT PARALLEL UNIVERSES, AND THEY SCARED THE HELL OUT OF HIM.
I'VE BEEN GOING THROUGH SOME OF HIS . . . LESSER KNOWN WRITINGS. . .
IT'S AMAZING, REALLY- -
BUT HE ACTUALLY IMAGINED THE EXISTENCE OF HIGHER DIMENSIONS AS THE SOURCE OF ALL ENERGY.

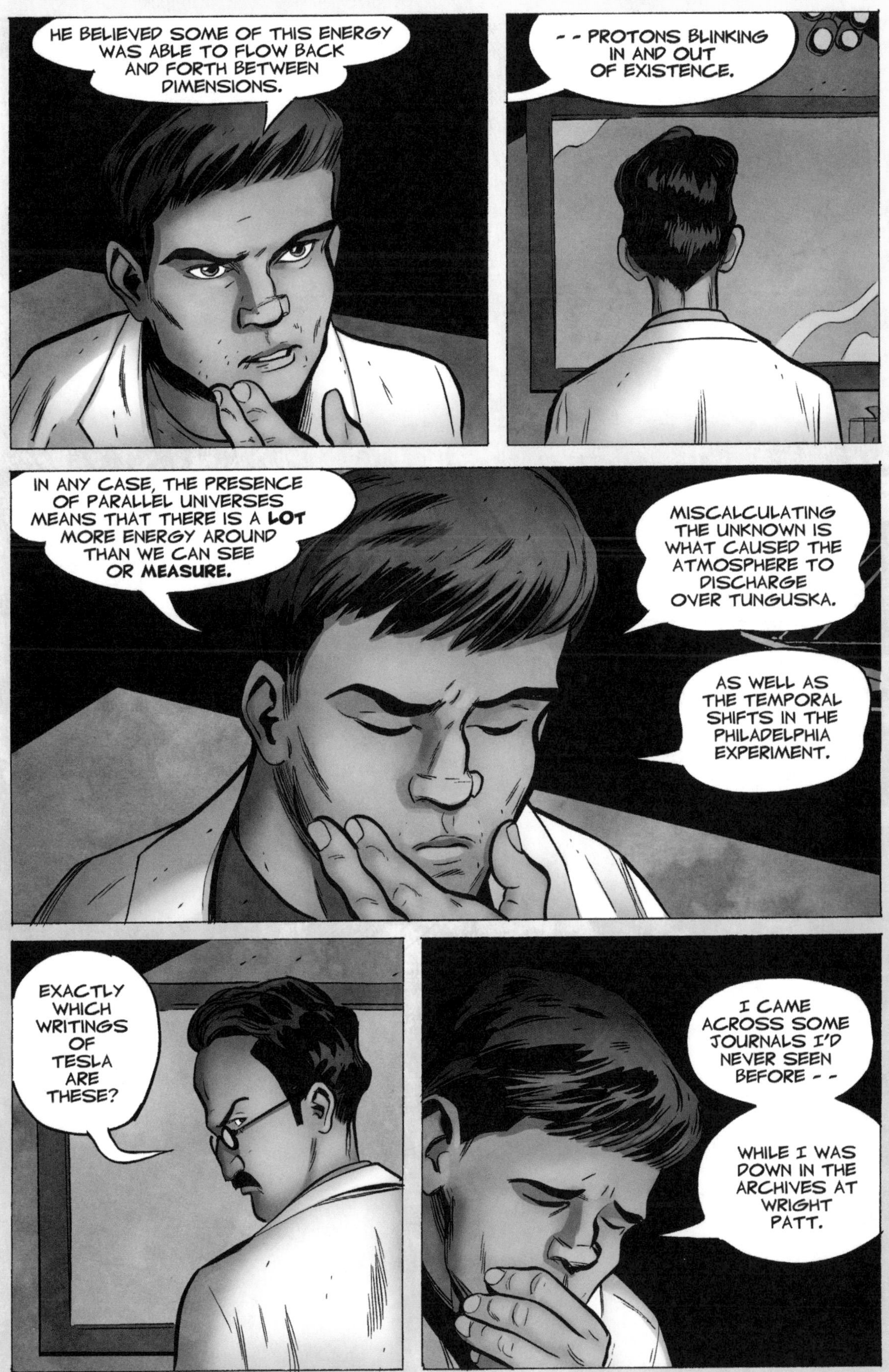
HE BELIEVED SOME OF THIS ENERGY WAS ABLE TO FLOW BACK AND FORTH BETWEEN DIMENSIONS.
- - PROTONS BLINKING IN AND OUT OF EXISTENCE.
IN ANY CASE, THE PRESENCE OF PARALLEL UNIVERSES MEANS THAT THERE IS A LOT MORE ENERGY AROUND THAN WE CAN SEE OR MEASURE.
MISCALCULATING THE UNKNOWN IS WHAT CAUSED THE ATMOSPHERE TO DISCHARGE OVER TUNGUSKA.
AS WELL AS THE TEMPORAL SHIFTS IN THE PHILADELPHIA EXPERIMENT.
EXACTLY WHICH WRITINGS OF TESLA ARE THESE?
I CAME ACROSS SOME JOURNALS I'D NEVER SEEN BEFORE - -
WHILE I WAS DOWN IN THE ARCHIVES AT WRIGHT PATT.

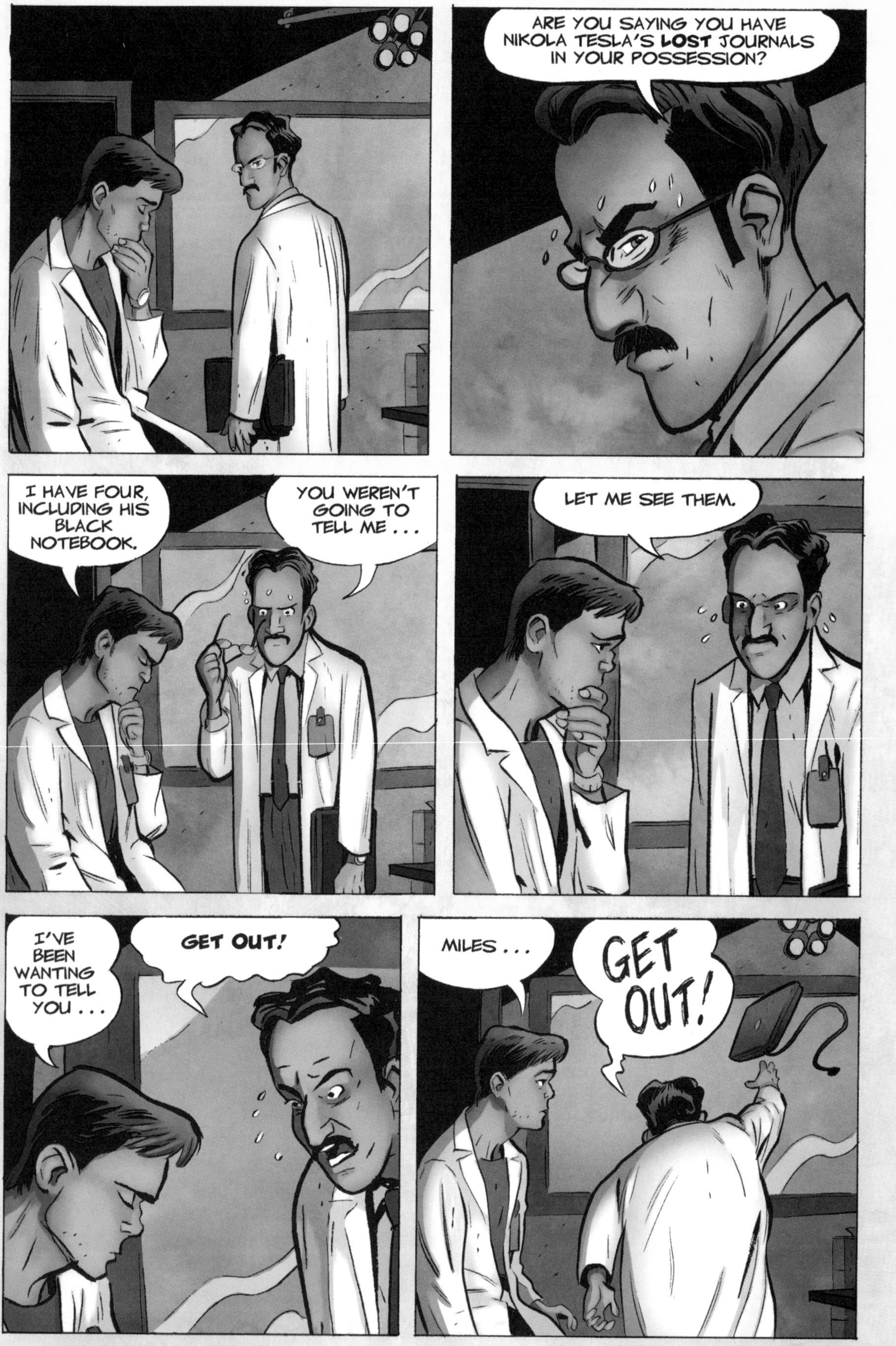
ARE YOU SAYING YOU HAVE NIKOLA TESLA'S **LOST** JOURNALS IN YOUR POSSESSION?
I HAVE FOUR, INCLUDING HIS BLACK NOTEBOOK.
YOU WEREN'T GOING TO TELL ME . . .
LET ME SEE THEM.
I'VE BEEN WANTING TO TELL YOU . . .
GET OUT!
MILES . . .
GET OUT!

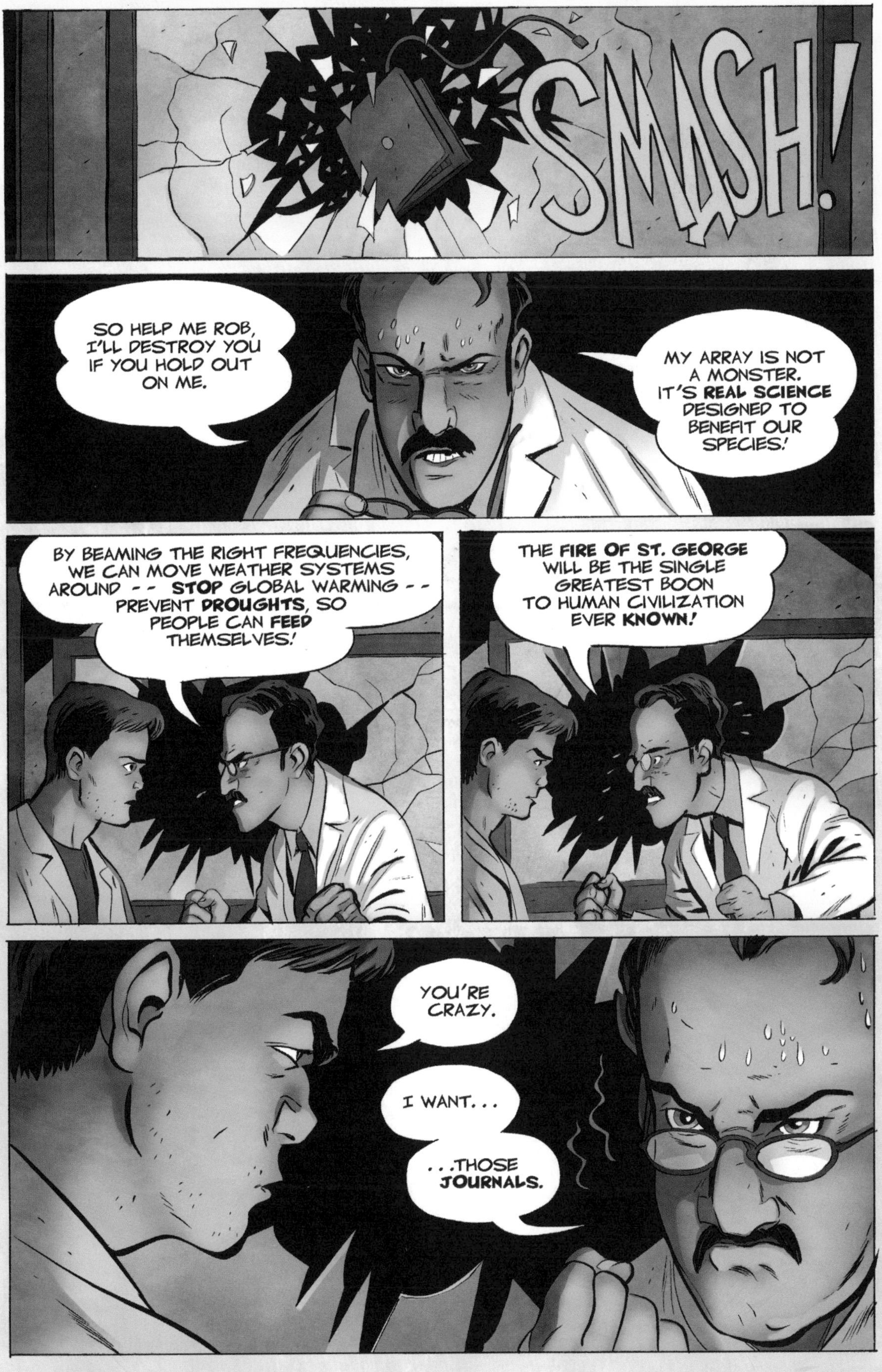
SMASH!
SO HELP ME ROB, I'LL DESTROY YOU IF YOU HOLD OUT ON ME.
MY ARRAY IS NOT A MONSTER. IT'S REAL SCIENCE DESIGNED TO BENEFIT OUR SPECIES!
BY BEAMING THE RIGHT FREQUENCIES, WE CAN MOVE WEATHER SYSTEMS AROUND -- STOP GLOBAL WARMING -- PREVENT DROUGHTS, SO PEOPLE CAN FEED THEMSELVES!
THE FIRE OF ST. GEORGE WILL BE THE SINGLE GREATEST BOON TO HUMAN CIVILIZATION EVER KNOWN!
YOU'RE CRAZY.
I WANT...
...THOSE JOURNALS.

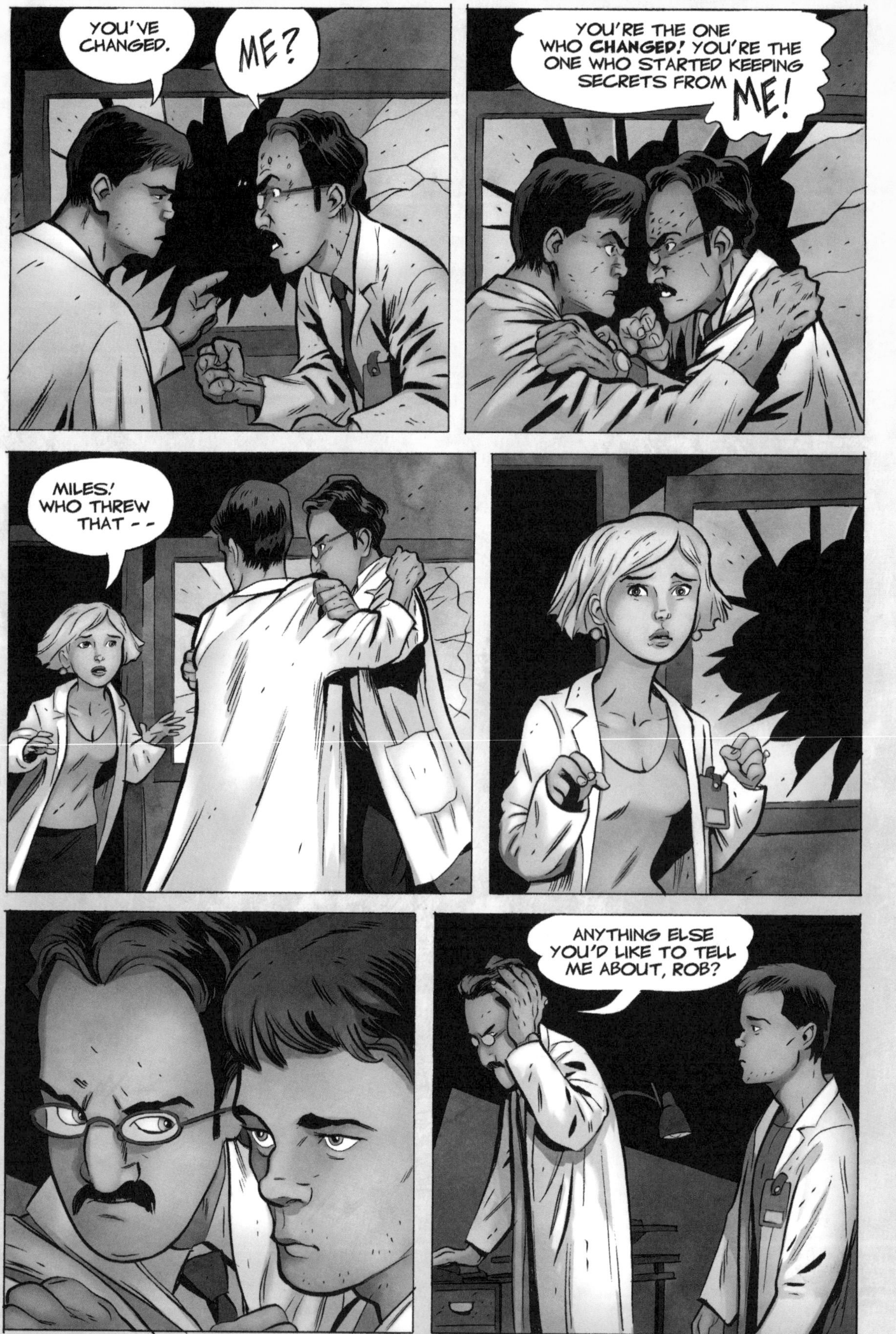
YOU'VE CHANGED.
ME?
YOU'RE THE ONE WHO **CHANGED!** YOU'RE THE ONE WHO STARTED KEEPING SECRETS FROM ME!
MILES! WHO THREW THAT - -
ANYTHING ELSE YOU'D LIKE TO TELL ME ABOUT, ROB?

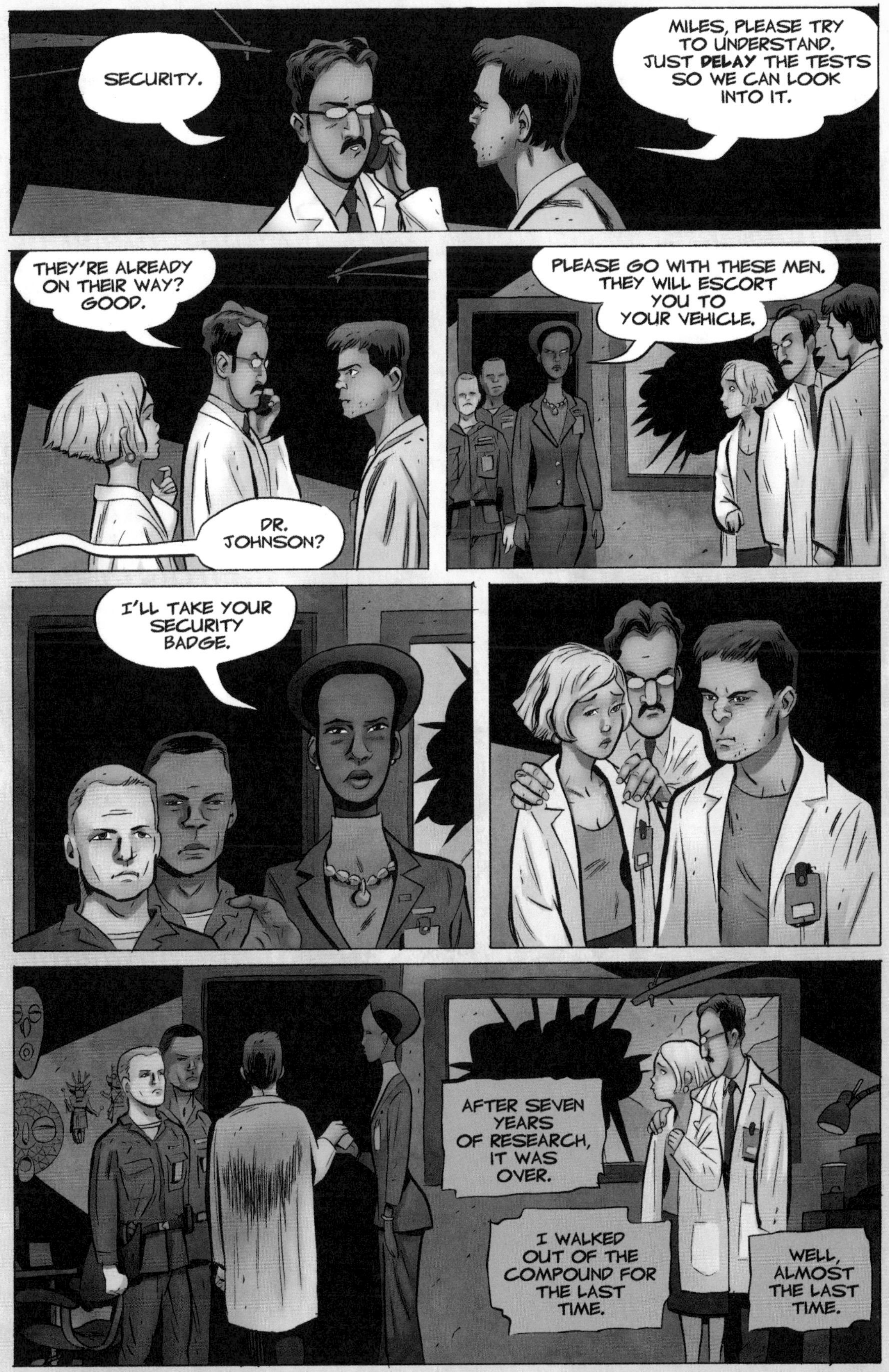
SECURITY.
MILES, PLEASE TRY TO UNDERSTAND. JUST DELAY THE TESTS SO WE CAN LOOK INTO IT.
THEY'RE ALREADY ON THEIR WAY? GOOD.
DR. JOHNSON?
PLEASE GO WITH THESE MEN. THEY WILL ESCORT YOU TO YOUR VEHICLE.
I'LL TAKE YOUR SECURITY BADGE.
AFTER SEVEN YEARS OF RESEARCH, IT WAS OVER.
I WALKED OUT OF THE COMPOUND FOR THE LAST TIME.
WELL, ALMOST THE LAST TIME.

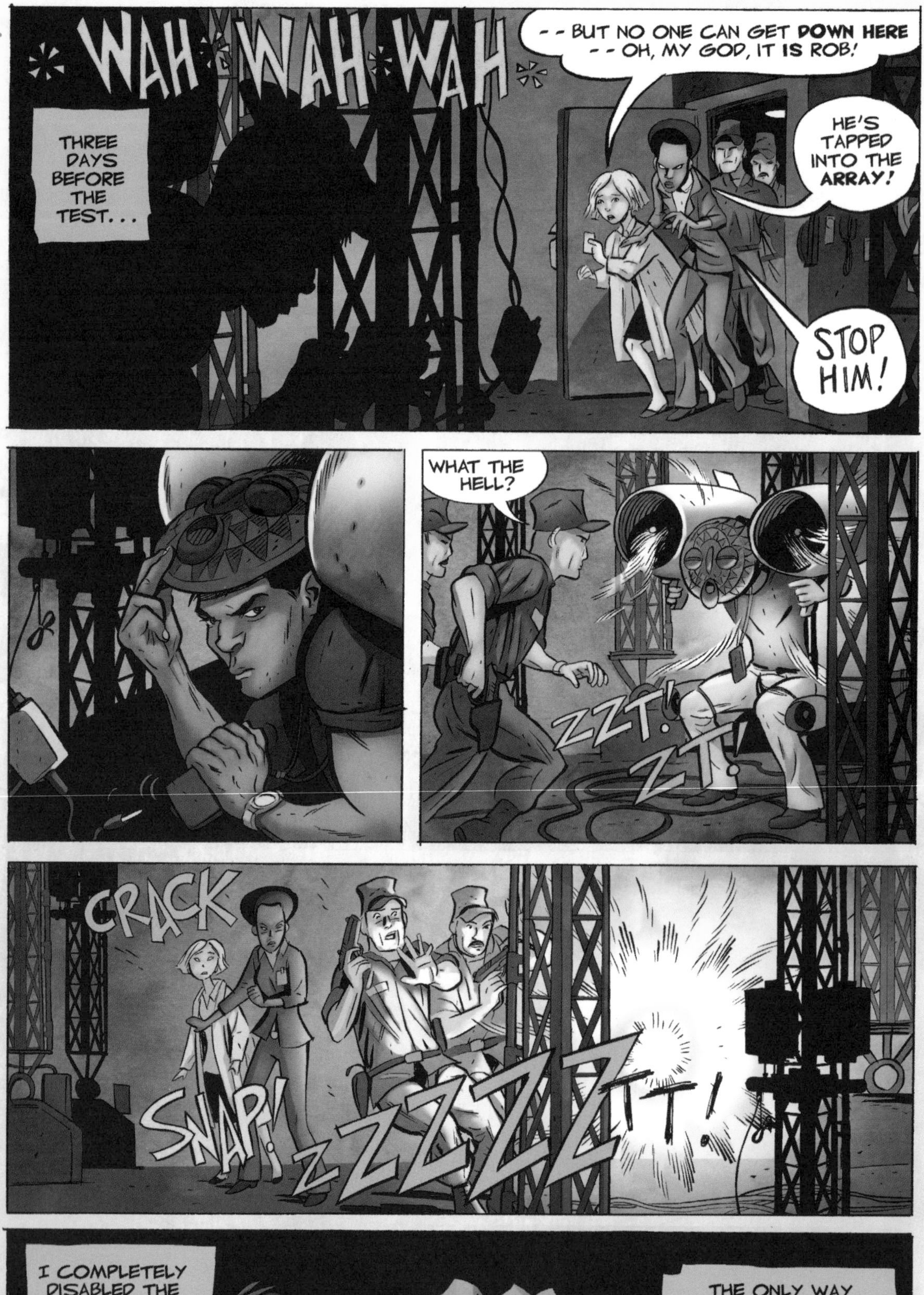
WAH WAH WAH
THREE DAYS BEFORE THE TEST...
-- BUT NO ONE CAN GET DOWN HERE -- OH, MY GOD, IT IS ROB!
HE'S TAPPED INTO THE ARRAY!
STOP HIM!
WHAT THE HELL?
ZZZT! ZT!
CRACK
SNAP! ZZZZZZTTT!
I COMPLETELY DISABLED THE ARRAY.
THE ONLY WAY THEY COULD FIRE IT NOW, WOULD BE TO SCRAP IT AND START FROM SCRATCH.

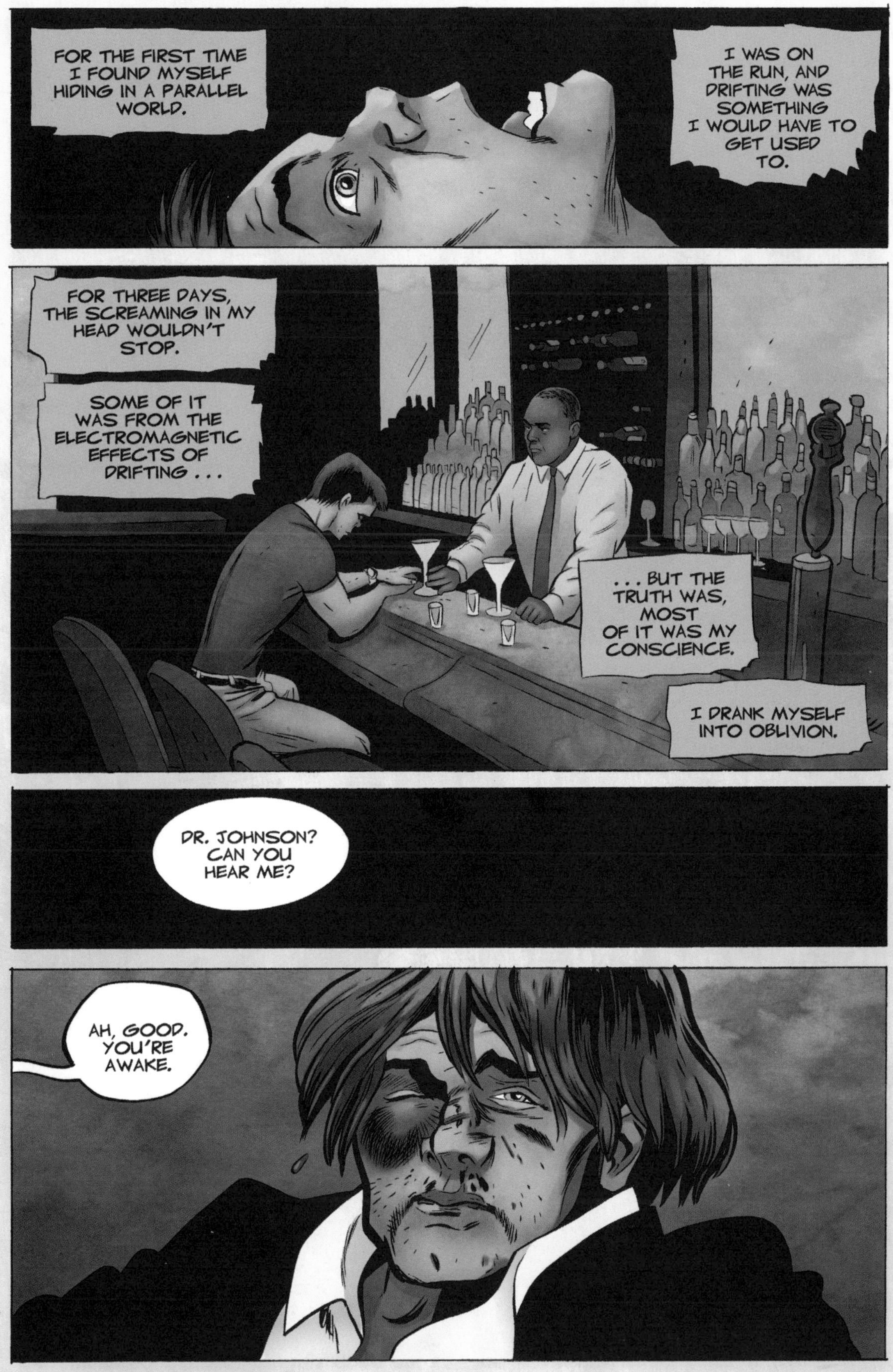
FOR THE FIRST TIME I FOUND MYSELF HIDING IN A PARALLEL WORLD.
I WAS ON THE RUN, AND DRIFTING WAS SOMETHING I WOULD HAVE TO GET USED TO.
FOR THREE DAYS, THE SCREAMING IN MY HEAD WOULDN'T STOP.
SOME OF IT WAS FROM THE ELECTROMAGNETIC EFFECTS OF DRIFTING . . .
. . . BUT THE TRUTH WAS, MOST OF IT WAS MY CONSCIENCE.
I DRANK MYSELF INTO OBLIVION.
DR. JOHNSON? CAN YOU HEAR ME?
AH, GOOD. YOU'RE AWAKE.

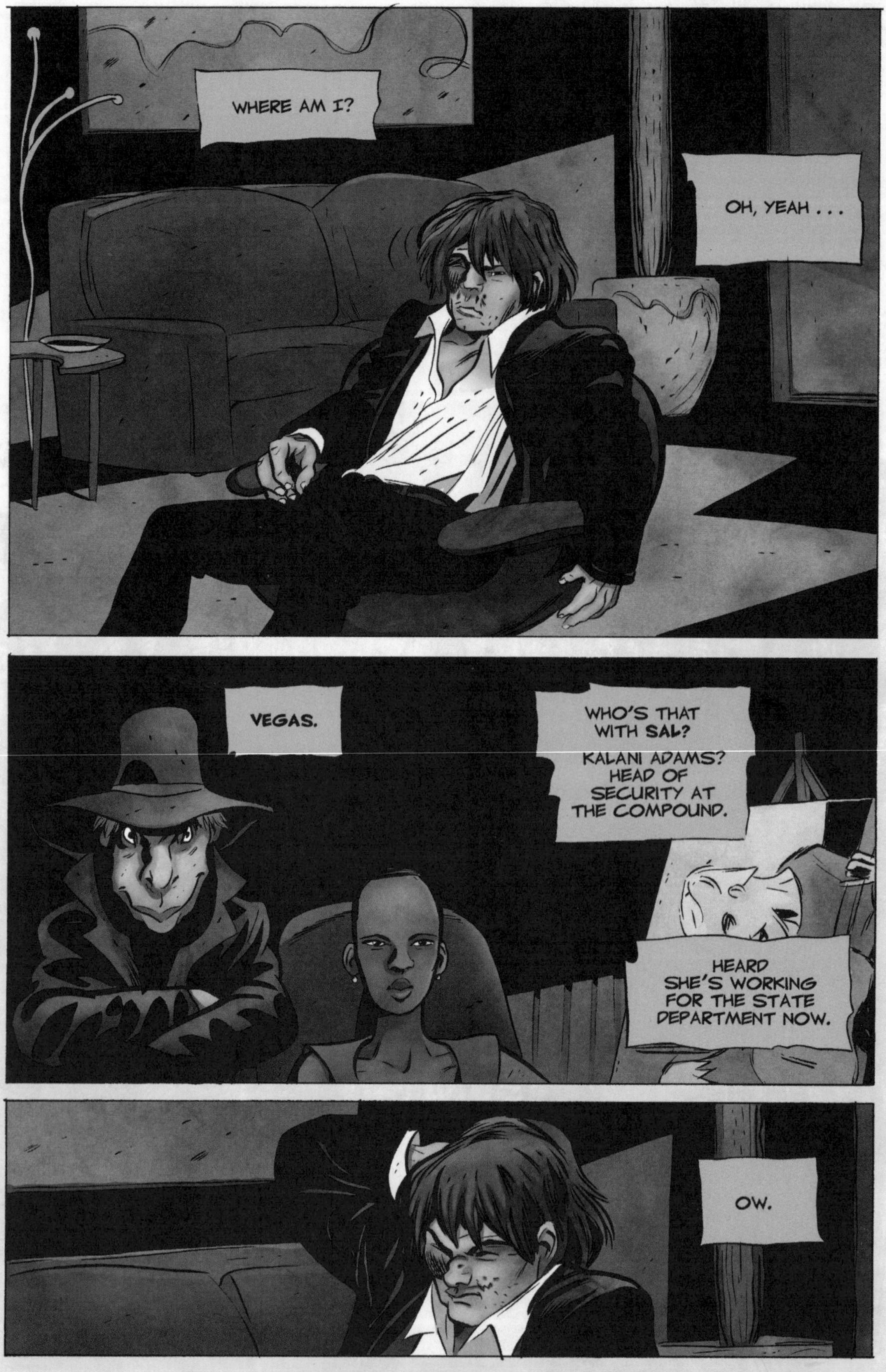
WHERE AM I?
OH, YEAH . . .
VEGAS.
WHO'S THAT WITH SAL?
KALANI ADAMS? HEAD OF SECURITY AT THE COMPOUND.
HEARD SHE'S WORKING FOR THE STATE DEPARTMENT NOW.
OW.

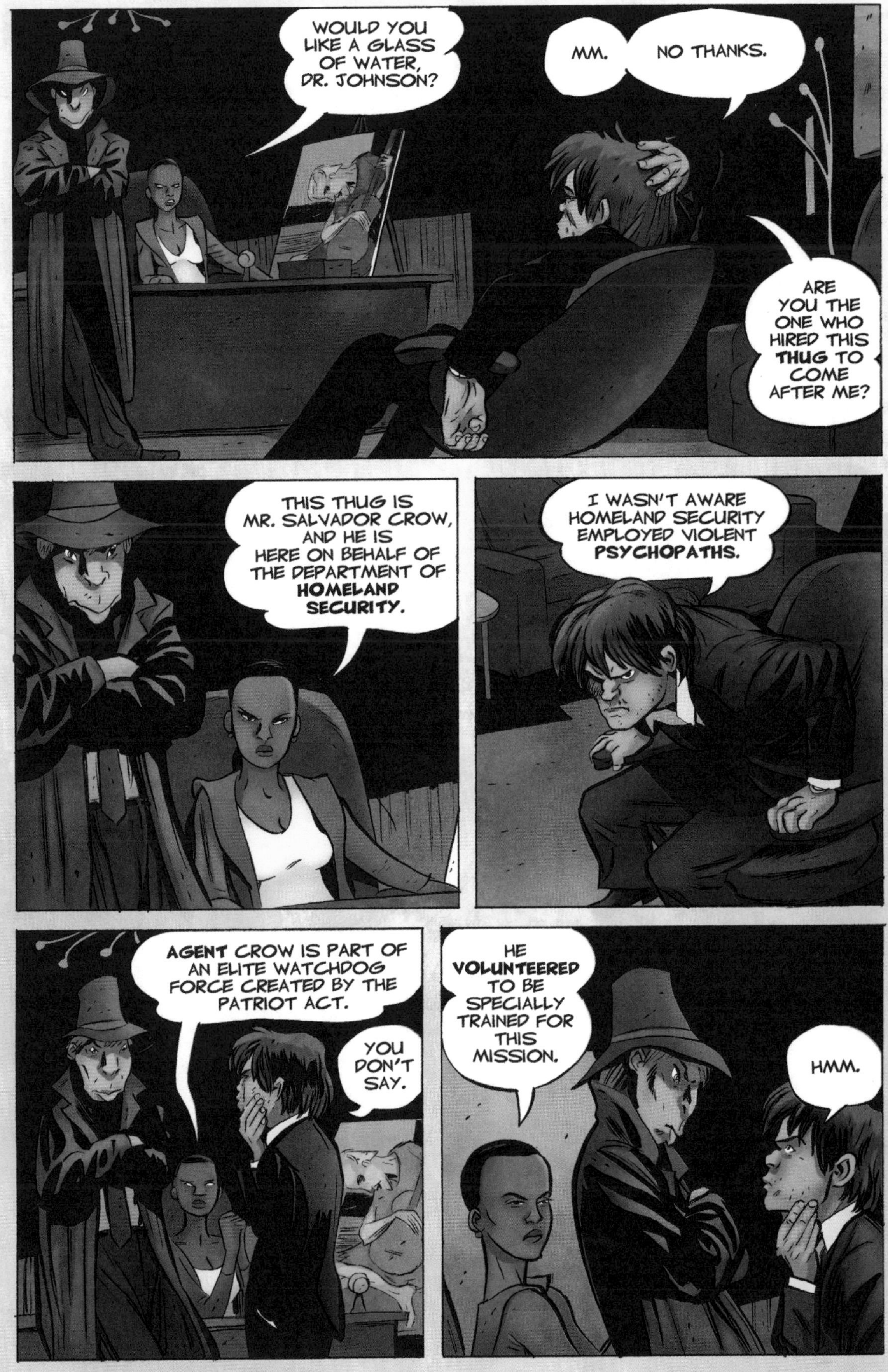
WOULD YOU LIKE A GLASS OF WATER, DR. JOHNSON?
MM.
NO THANKS.
ARE YOU THE ONE WHO HIRED THIS **THUG** TO COME AFTER ME?
THIS THUG IS MR. SALVADOR CROW, AND HE IS HERE ON BEHALF OF THE DEPARTMENT OF **HOMELAND SECURITY.**
I WASN'T AWARE HOMELAND SECURITY EMPLOYED VIOLENT **PSYCHOPATHS.**
AGENT CROW IS PART OF AN ELITE WATCHDOG FORCE CREATED BY THE PATRIOT ACT.
YOU DON'T SAY.
HE **VOLUNTEERED** TO BE SPECIALLY TRAINED FOR THIS MISSION.
HMM.

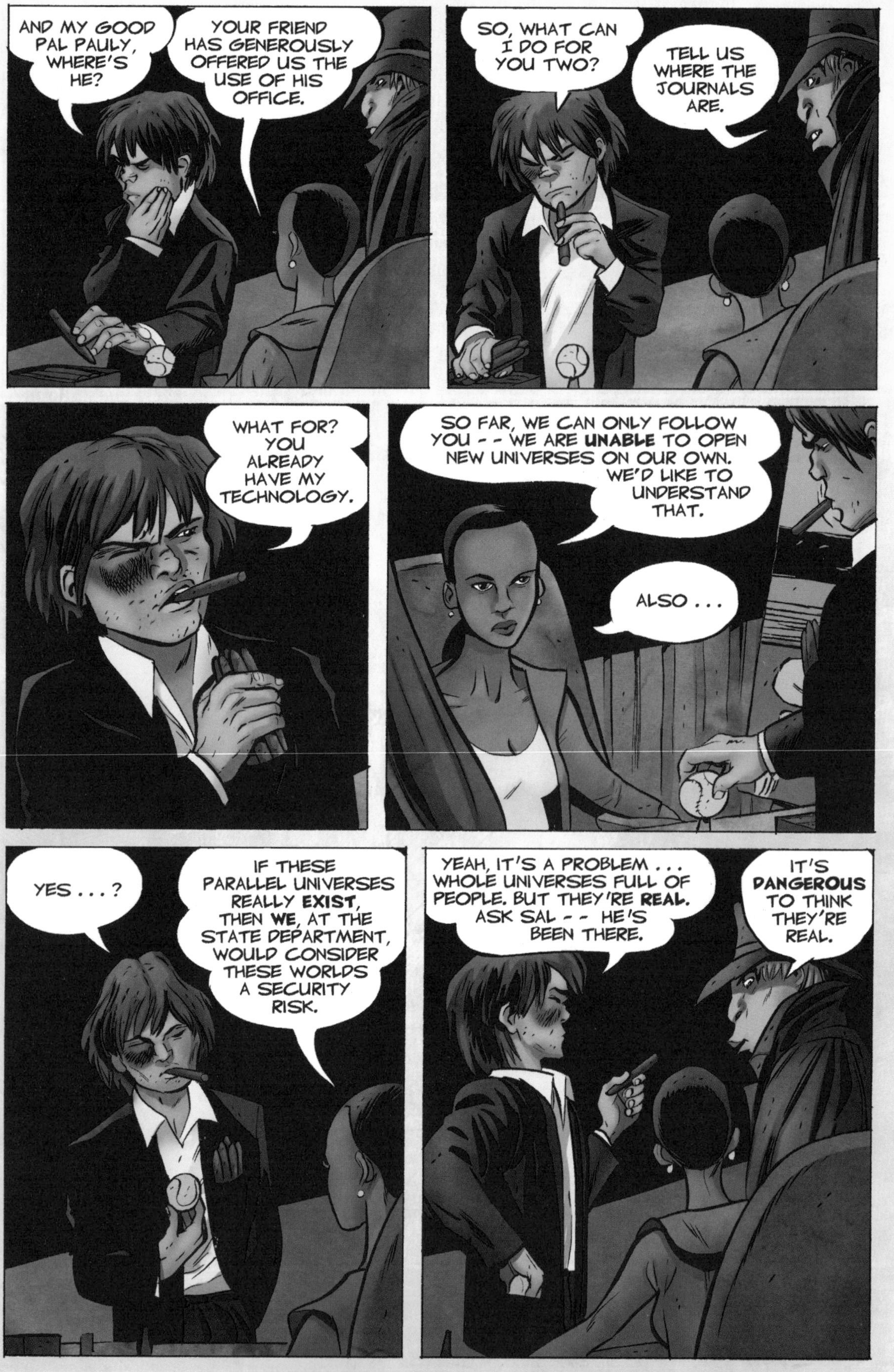
AND MY GOOD PAL PAULY, WHERE'S HE?
YOUR FRIEND HAS GENEROUSLY OFFERED US THE USE OF HIS OFFICE.
SO, WHAT CAN I DO FOR YOU TWO?
TELL US WHERE THE JOURNALS ARE.
WHAT FOR? YOU ALREADY HAVE MY TECHNOLOGY.
SO FAR, WE CAN ONLY FOLLOW YOU - - WE ARE UNABLE TO OPEN NEW UNIVERSES ON OUR OWN. WE'D LIKE TO UNDERSTAND THAT.
ALSO . . .
YES . . . ?
IF THESE PARALLEL UNIVERSES REALLY EXIST, THEN WE, AT THE STATE DEPARTMENT, WOULD CONSIDER THESE WORLDS A SECURITY RISK.
YEAH, IT'S A PROBLEM . . . WHOLE UNIVERSES FULL OF PEOPLE. BUT THEY'RE REAL. ASK SAL - - HE'S BEEN THERE.
IT'S DANGEROUS TO THINK THEY'RE REAL.

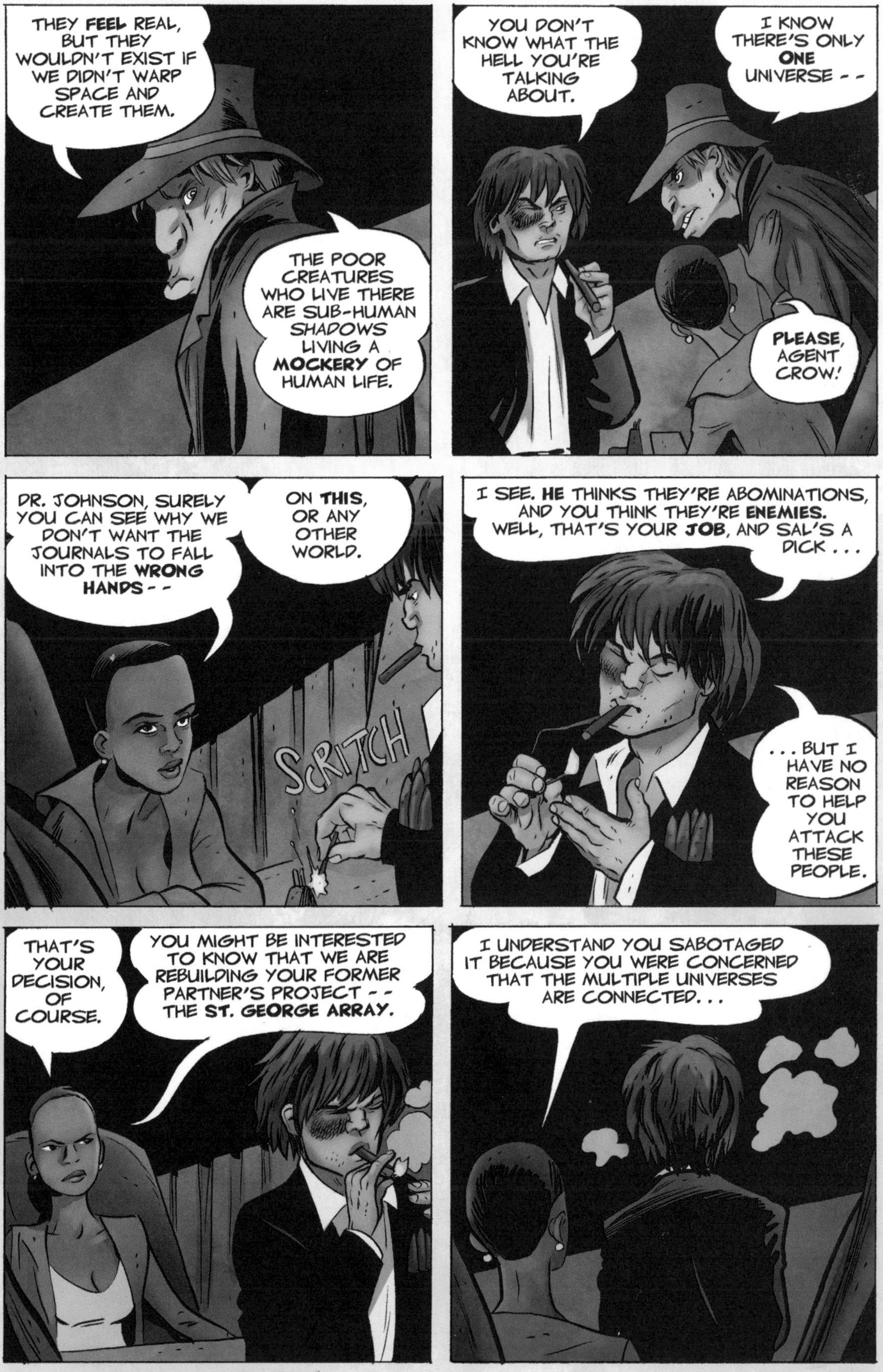
THEY FEEL REAL, BUT THEY WOULDN'T EXIST IF WE DIDN'T WARP SPACE AND CREATE THEM.
THE POOR CREATURES WHO LIVE THERE ARE SUB-HUMAN SHADOWS LIVING A MOCKERY OF HUMAN LIFE.
YOU DON'T KNOW WHAT THE HELL YOU'RE TALKING ABOUT.
I KNOW THERE'S ONLY ONE UNIVERSE - -
PLEASE, AGENT CROW!
DR. JOHNSON, SURELY YOU CAN SEE WHY WE DON'T WANT THE JOURNALS TO FALL INTO THE WRONG HANDS - -
ON THIS, OR ANY OTHER WORLD.
SCRITCH
I SEE. HE THINKS THEY'RE ABOMINATIONS, AND YOU THINK THEY'RE ENEMIES. WELL, THAT'S YOUR JOB, AND SAL'S A DICK . . .
. . . BUT I HAVE NO REASON TO HELP YOU ATTACK THESE PEOPLE.
THAT'S YOUR DECISION, OF COURSE.
YOU MIGHT BE INTERESTED TO KNOW THAT WE ARE REBUILDING YOUR FORMER PARTNER'S PROJECT - - THE ST. GEORGE ARRAY.
I UNDERSTAND YOU SABOTAGED IT BECAUSE YOU WERE CONCERNED THAT THE MULTIPLE UNIVERSES ARE CONNECTED. . .

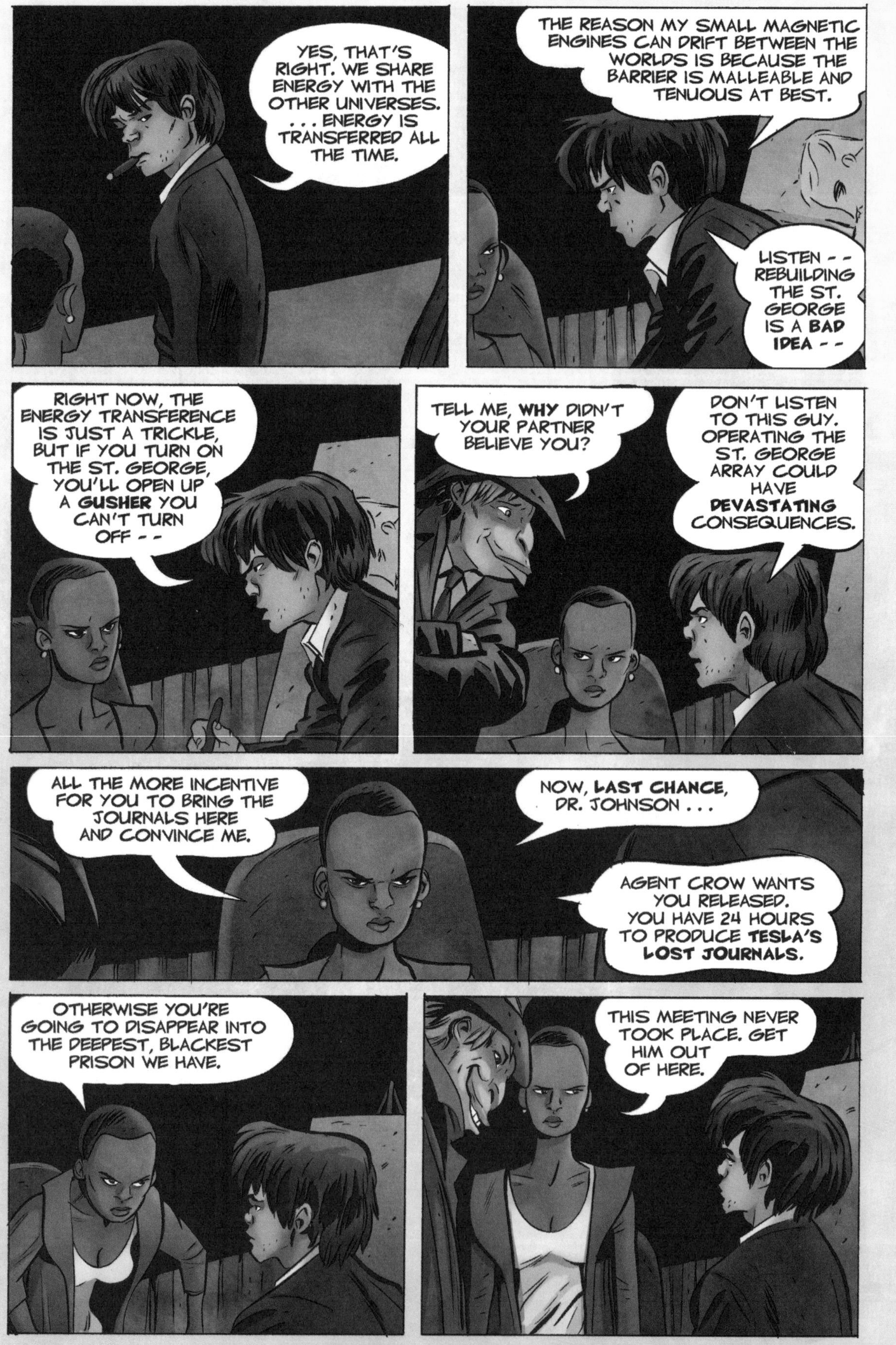
YES, THAT'S RIGHT. WE SHARE ENERGY WITH THE OTHER UNIVERSES. . . . ENERGY IS TRANSFERRED ALL THE TIME.
THE REASON MY SMALL MAGNETIC ENGINES CAN DRIFT BETWEEN THE WORLDS IS BECAUSE THE BARRIER IS MALLEABLE AND TENUOUS AT BEST.
LISTEN -- REBUILDING THE ST. GEORGE IS A BAD IDEA --
RIGHT NOW, THE ENERGY TRANSFERENCE IS JUST A TRICKLE, BUT IF YOU TURN ON THE ST. GEORGE, YOU'LL OPEN UP A GUSHER YOU CAN'T TURN OFF --
TELL ME, WHY DIDN'T YOUR PARTNER BELIEVE YOU?
DON'T LISTEN TO THIS GUY. OPERATING THE ST. GEORGE ARRAY COULD HAVE DEVASTATING CONSEQUENCES.
ALL THE MORE INCENTIVE FOR YOU TO BRING THE JOURNALS HERE AND CONVINCE ME.
NOW, LAST CHANCE, DR. JOHNSON . . .
AGENT CROW WANTS YOU RELEASED. YOU HAVE 24 HOURS TO PRODUCE TESLA'S LOST JOURNALS.
OTHERWISE YOU'RE GOING TO DISAPPEAR INTO THE DEEPEST, BLACKEST PRISON WE HAVE.
THIS MEETING NEVER TOOK PLACE. GET HIM OUT OF HERE.

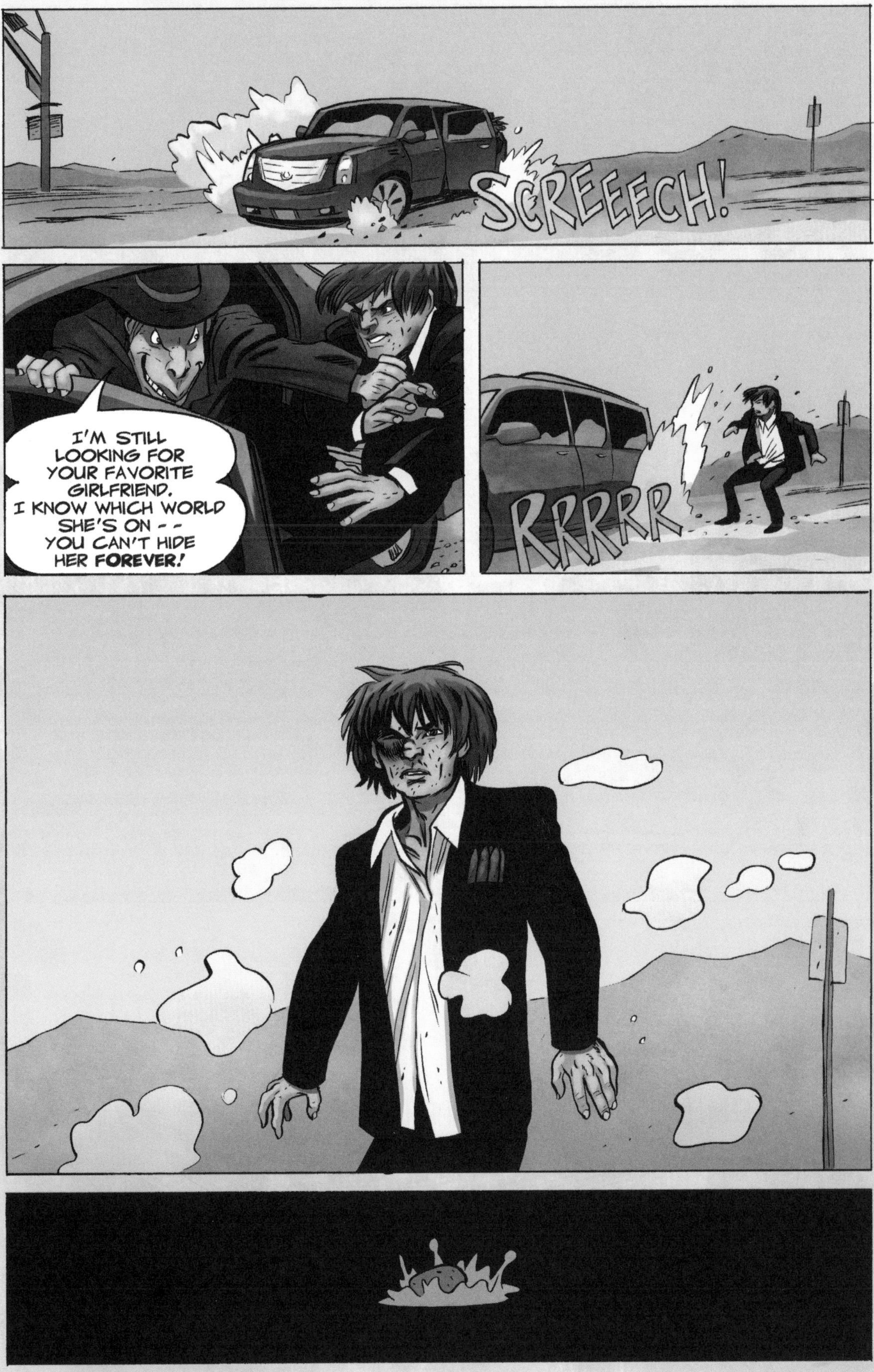
SCREEECH!
I'M STILL LOOKING FOR YOUR FAVORITE GIRLFRIEND. I KNOW WHICH WORLD SHE'S ON - - YOU CAN'T HIDE HER **FOREVER!**
RRRRR

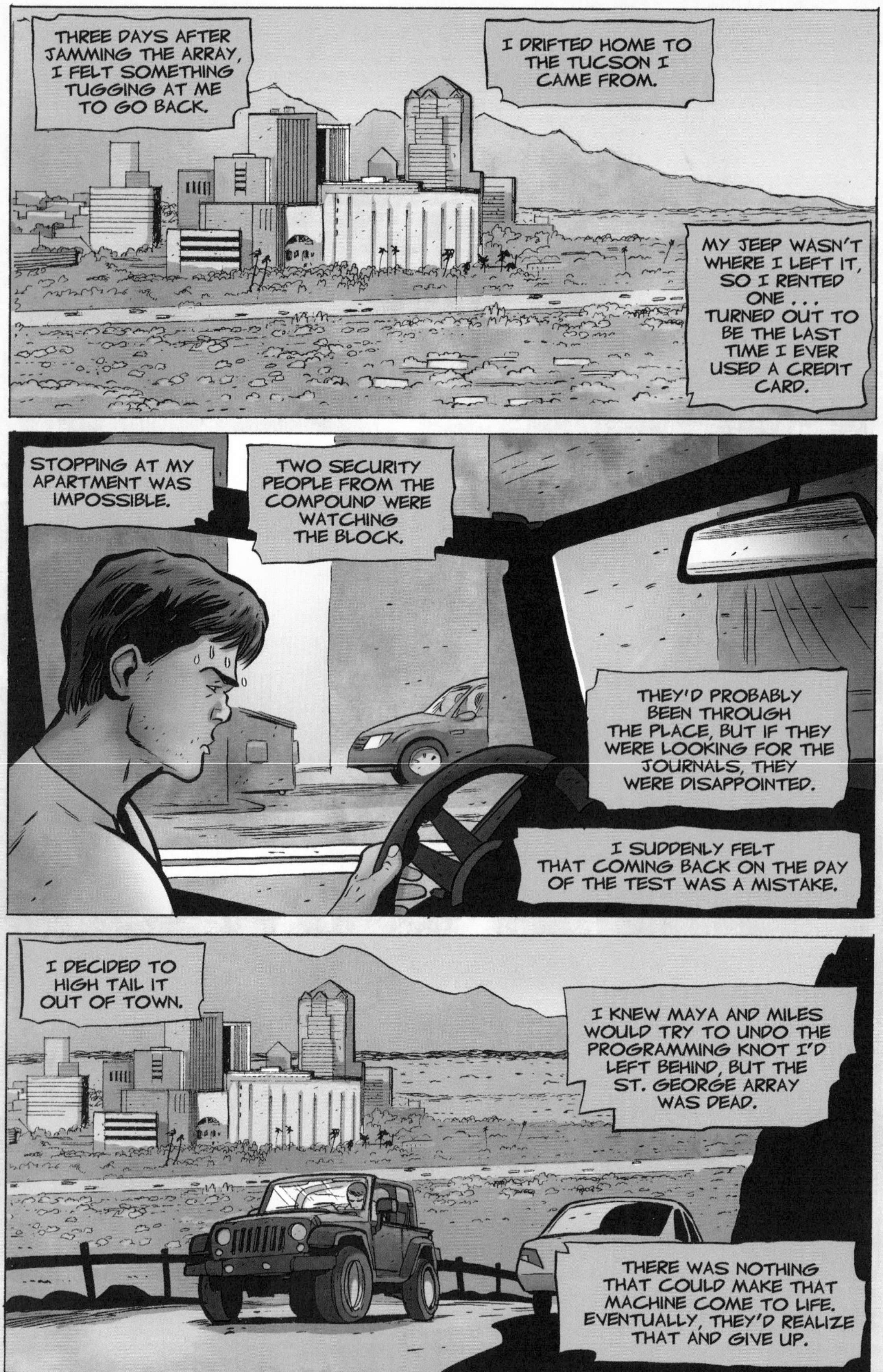
THREE DAYS AFTER JAMMING THE ARRAY, I FELT SOMETHING TUGGING AT ME TO GO BACK.
I DRIFTED HOME TO THE TUCSON I CAME FROM.
MY JEEP WASN'T WHERE I LEFT IT, SO I RENTED ONE . . . TURNED OUT TO BE THE LAST TIME I EVER USED A CREDIT CARD.
STOPPING AT MY APARTMENT WAS IMPOSSIBLE.
TWO SECURITY PEOPLE FROM THE COMPOUND WERE WATCHING THE BLOCK.
THEY'D PROBABLY BEEN THROUGH THE PLACE, BUT IF THEY WERE LOOKING FOR THE JOURNALS, THEY WERE DISAPPOINTED.
I SUDDENLY FELT THAT COMING BACK ON THE DAY OF THE TEST WAS A MISTAKE.
I DECIDED TO HIGH TAIL IT OUT OF TOWN.
I KNEW MAYA AND MILES WOULD TRY TO UNDO THE PROGRAMMING KNOT I'D LEFT BEHIND, BUT THE ST. GEORGE ARRAY WAS DEAD.
THERE WAS NOTHING THAT COULD MAKE THAT MACHINE COME TO LIFE. EVENTUALLY, THEY'D REALIZE THAT AND GIVE UP.

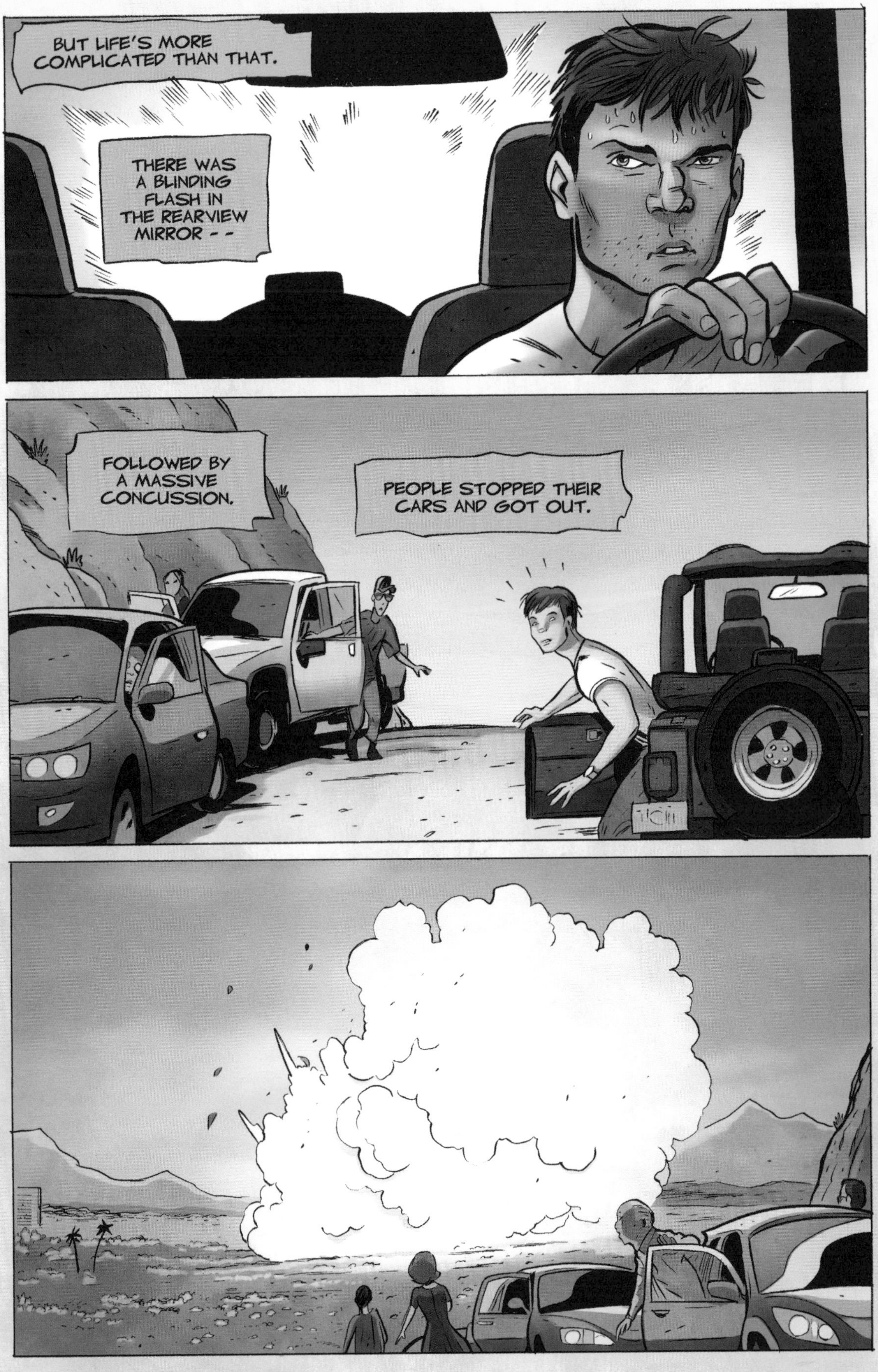
BUT LIFE'S MORE COMPLICATED THAN THAT.
THERE WAS A BLINDING FLASH IN THE REARVIEW MIRROR - -
FOLLOWED BY A MASSIVE CONCUSSION.
PEOPLE STOPPED THEIR CARS AND GOT OUT.

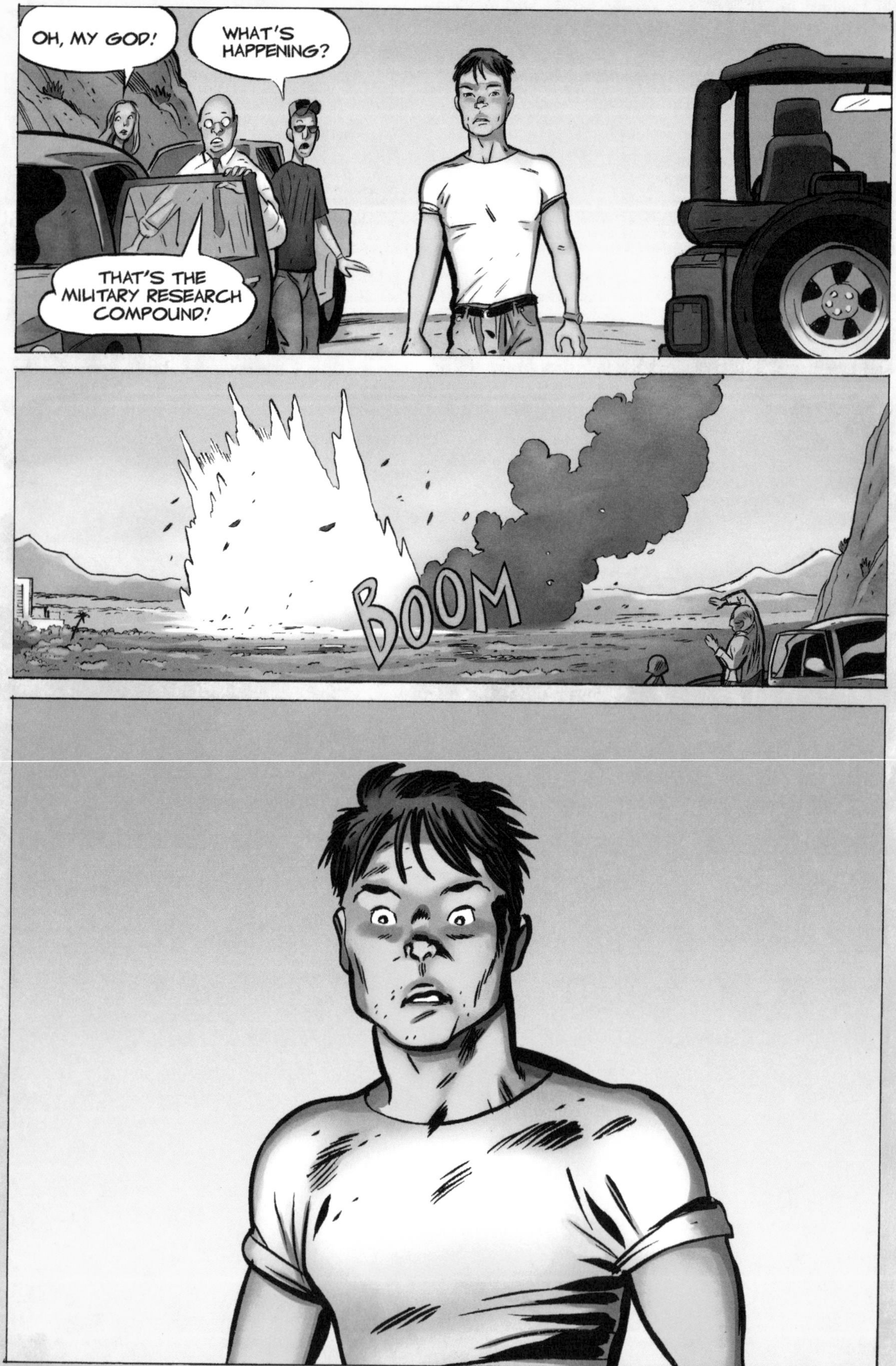
OH, MY GOD!
WHAT'S HAPPENING?
THAT'S THE MILITARY RESEARCH COMPOUND!
BOOM

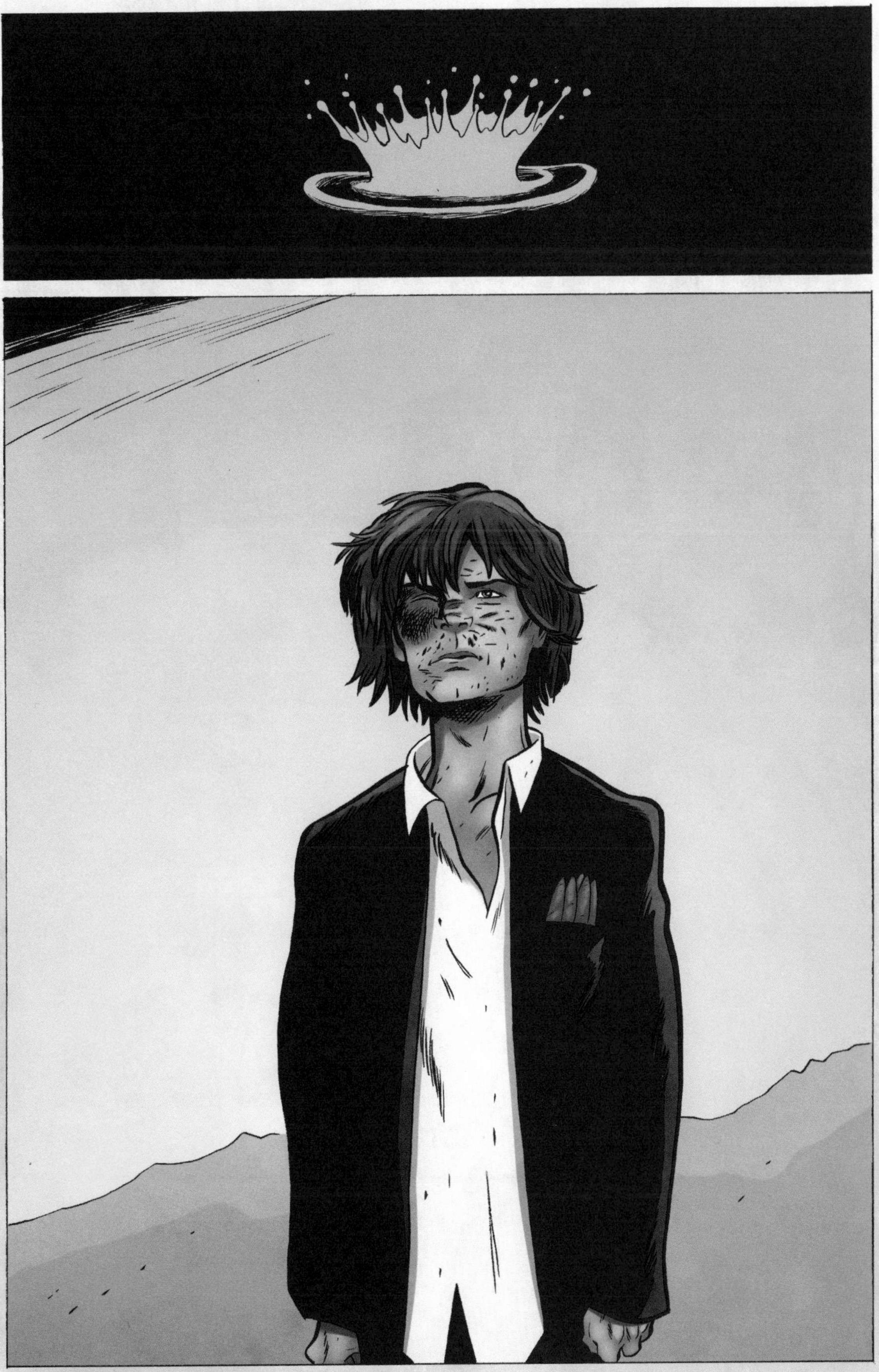

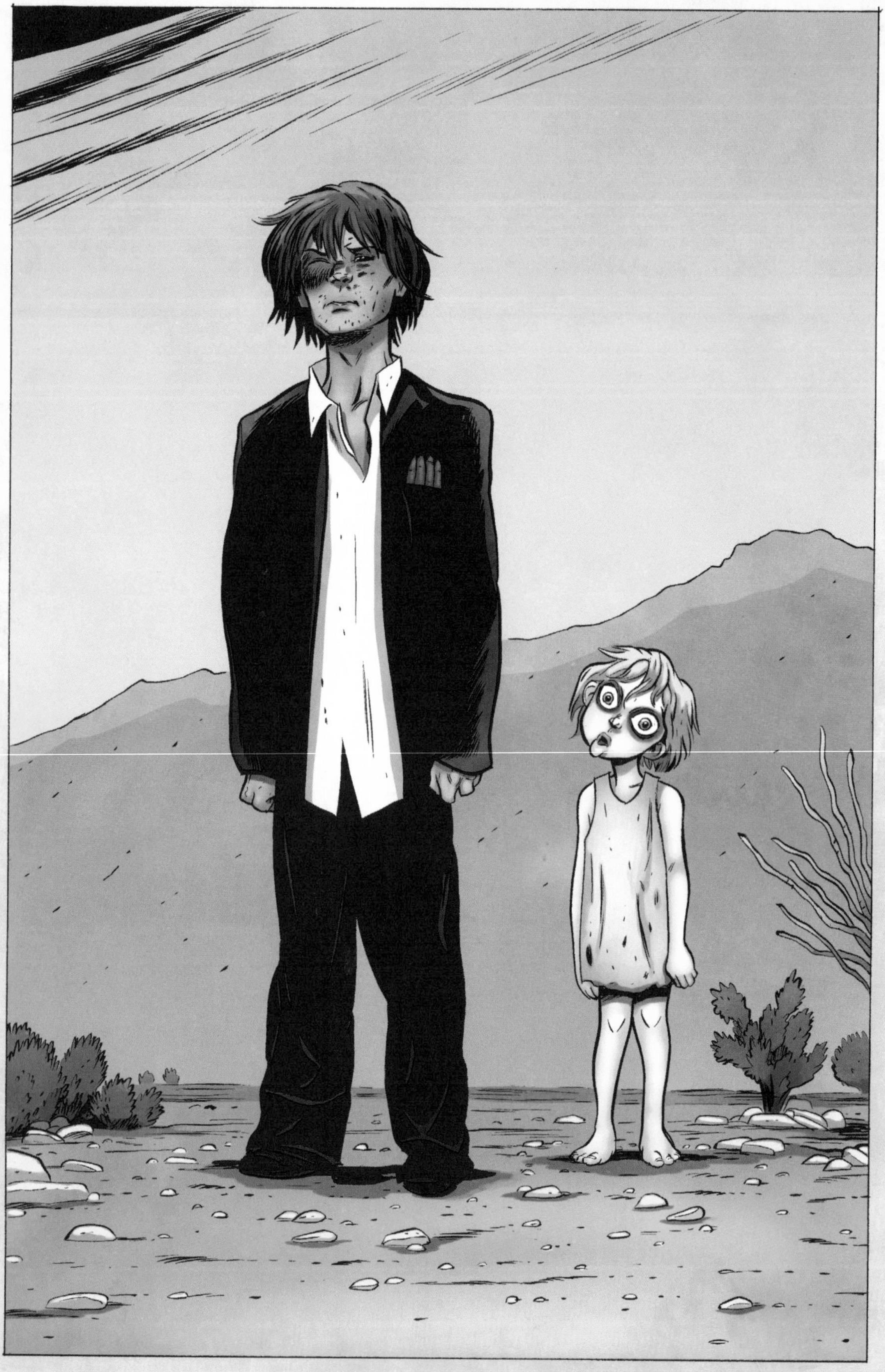

Act Three

Romance at the Speed of Light

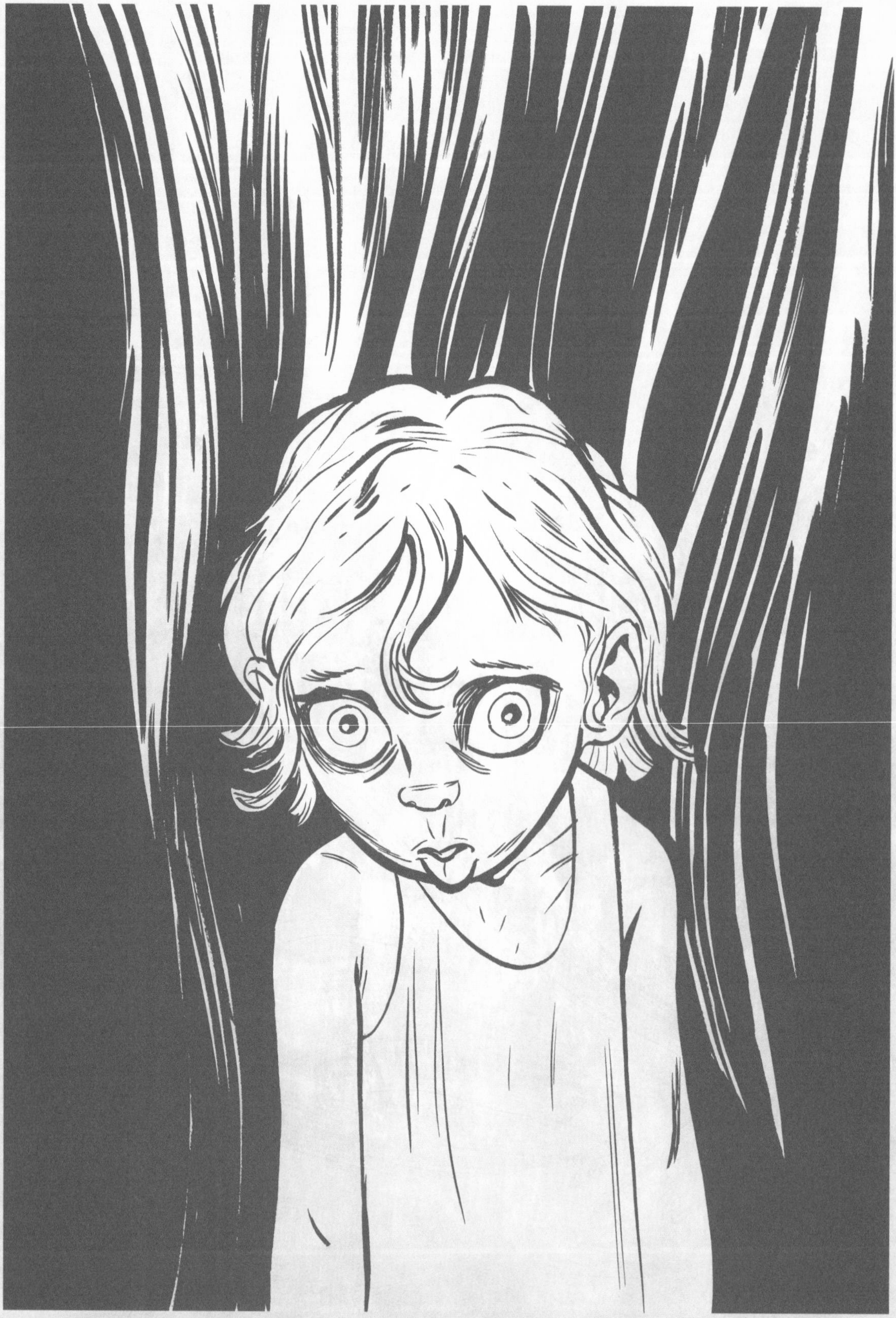

"Our virtues and our failures are inseparable, like force and matter. When they separate, man is no more."

-Nikola Tesla

VIII
ROMANCE AT THE SPEED OF LIGHT

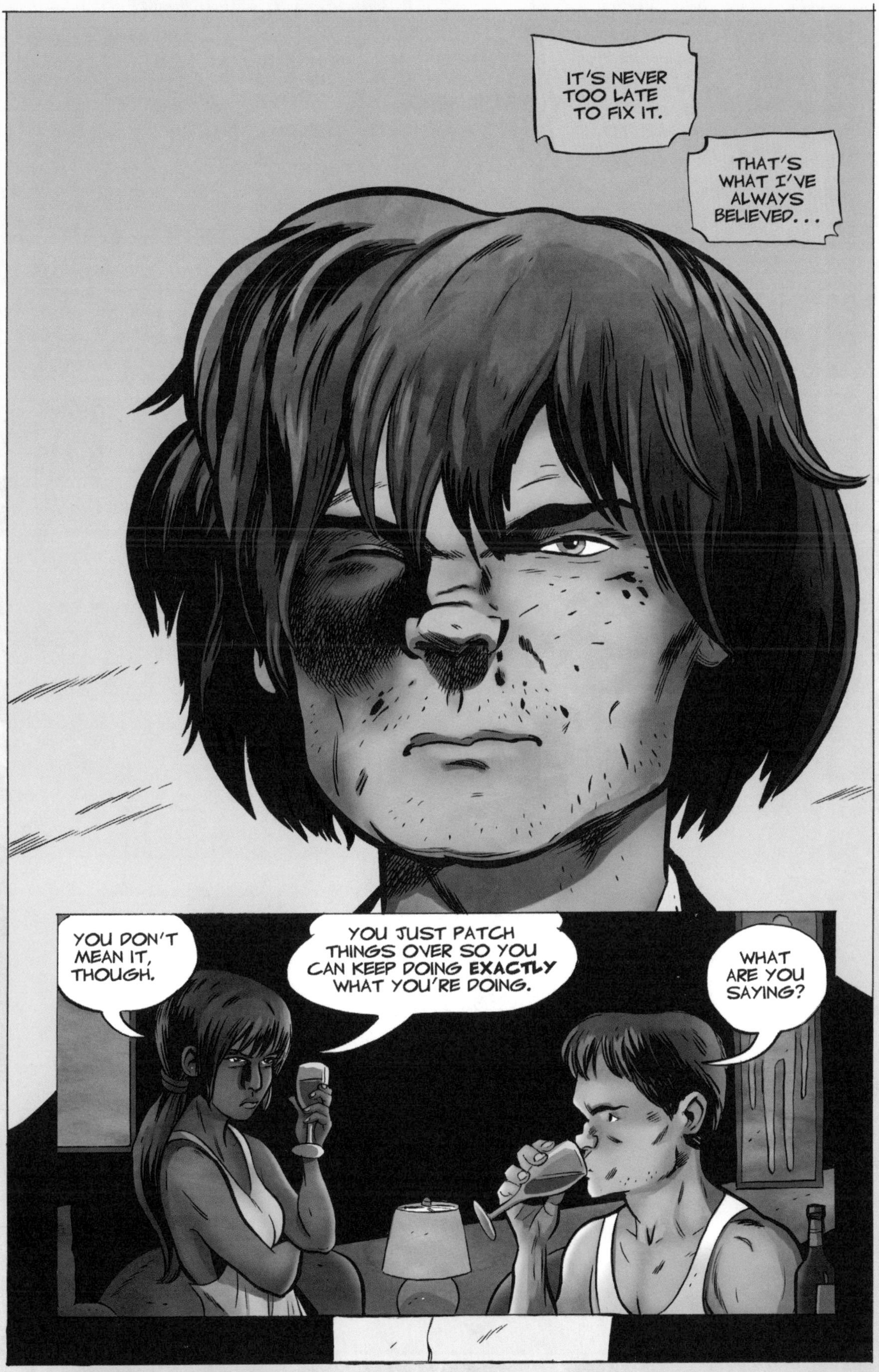

IT'S NEVER TOO LATE TO FIX IT.
THAT'S WHAT I'VE ALWAYS BELIEVED...
YOU DON'T MEAN IT, THOUGH.
YOU JUST PATCH THINGS OVER SO YOU CAN KEEP DOING **EXACTLY** WHAT YOU'RE DOING.
WHAT ARE YOU SAYING?

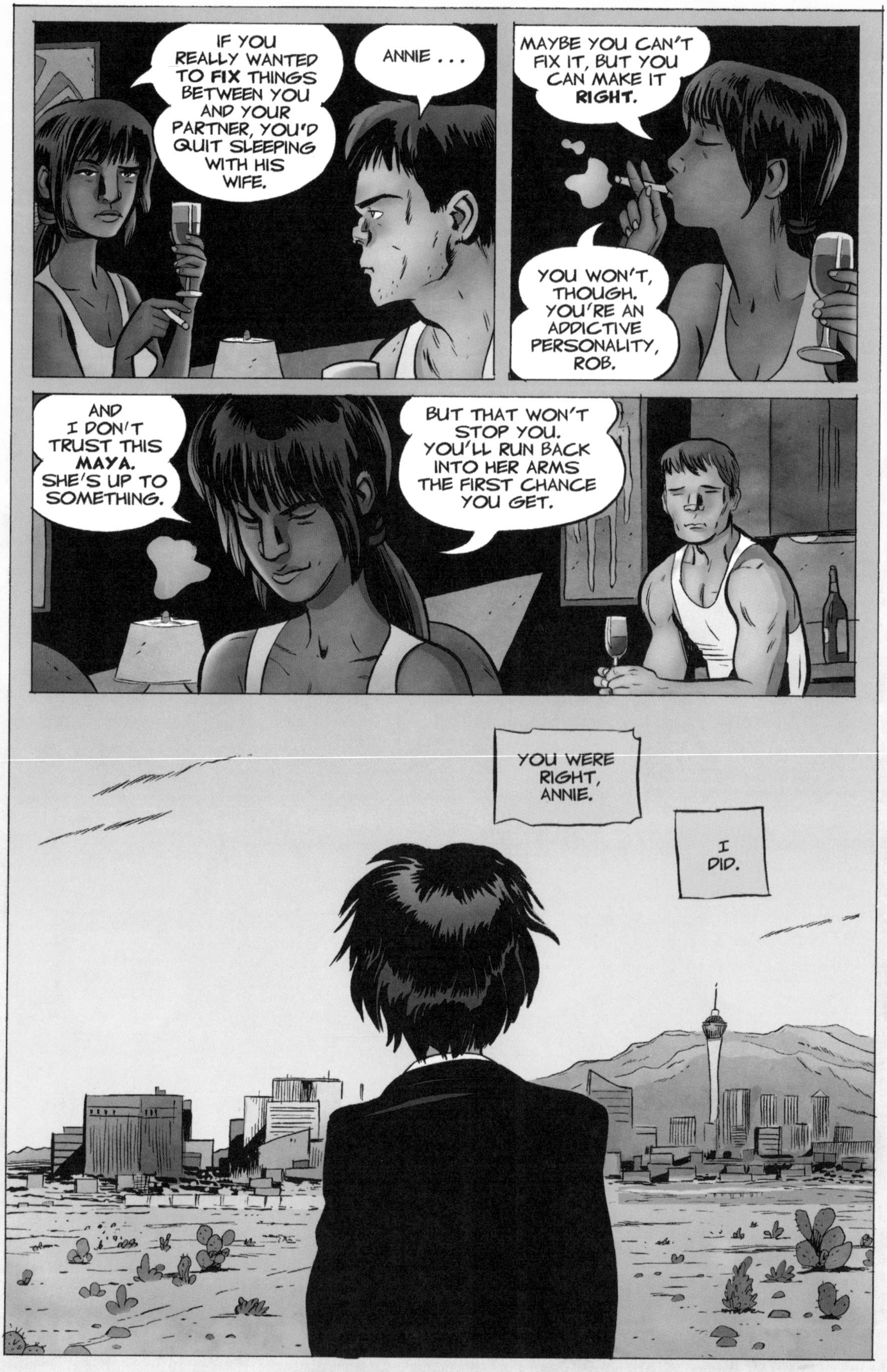
IF YOU REALLY WANTED TO FIX THINGS BETWEEN YOU AND YOUR PARTNER, YOU'D QUIT SLEEPING WITH HIS WIFE.
ANNIE . . .
MAYBE YOU CAN'T FIX IT, BUT YOU CAN MAKE IT RIGHT.
YOU WON'T, THOUGH. YOU'RE AN ADDICTIVE PERSONALITY, ROB.
AND I DON'T TRUST THIS MAYA. SHE'S UP TO SOMETHING.
BUT THAT WON'T STOP YOU. YOU'LL RUN BACK INTO HER ARMS THE FIRST CHANCE YOU GET.
YOU WERE RIGHT, ANNIE.
I DID.

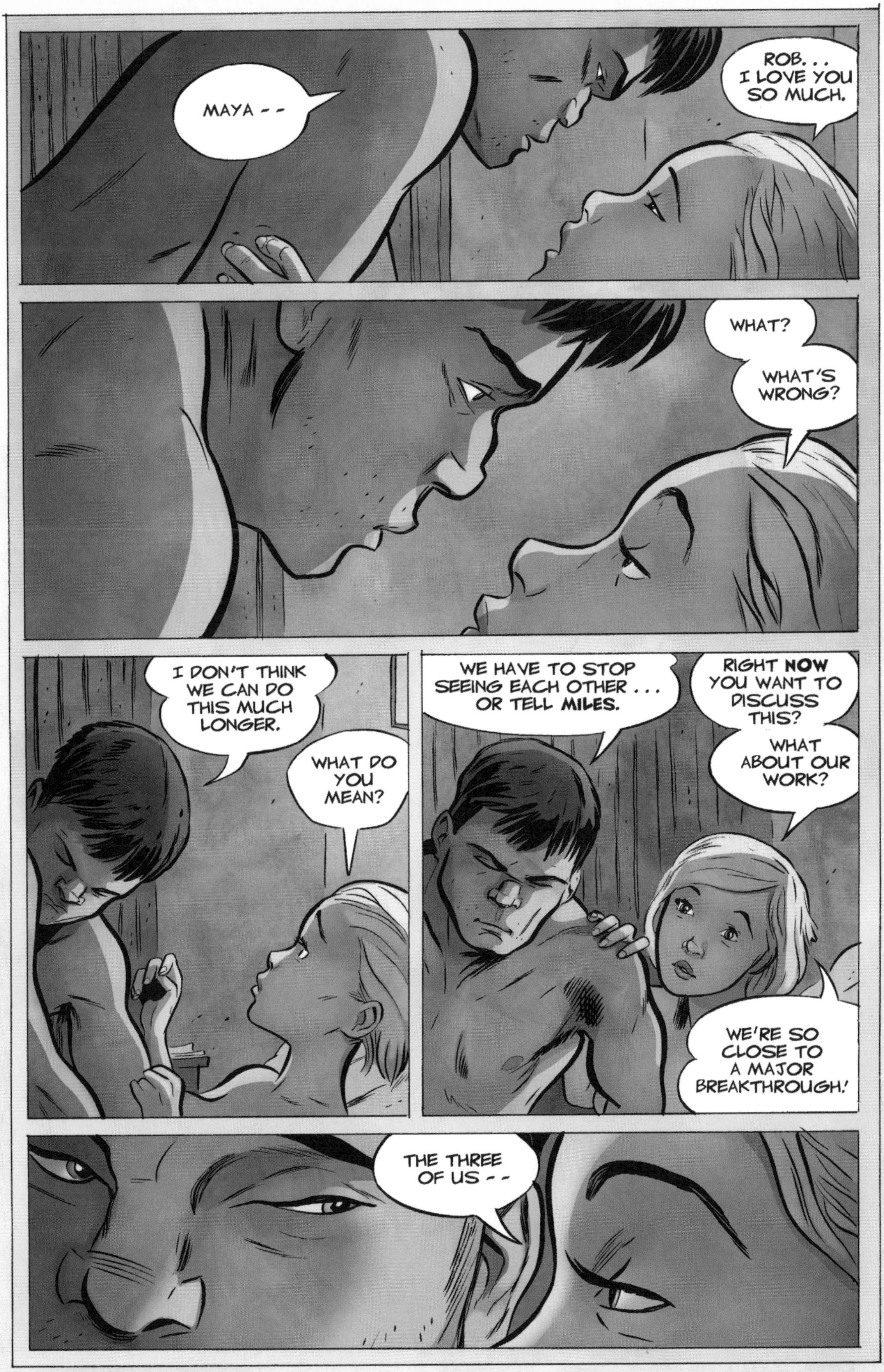

MAYA --
ROB... I LOVE YOU SO MUCH.
WHAT?
WHAT'S WRONG?
I DON'T THINK WE CAN DO THIS MUCH LONGER.
WHAT DO YOU MEAN?
WE HAVE TO STOP SEEING EACH OTHER... OR TELL **MILES**.
RIGHT **NOW** YOU WANT TO DISCUSS THIS?
WHAT ABOUT OUR WORK?
WE'RE SO CLOSE TO A MAJOR BREAKTHROUGH!
THE THREE OF US --

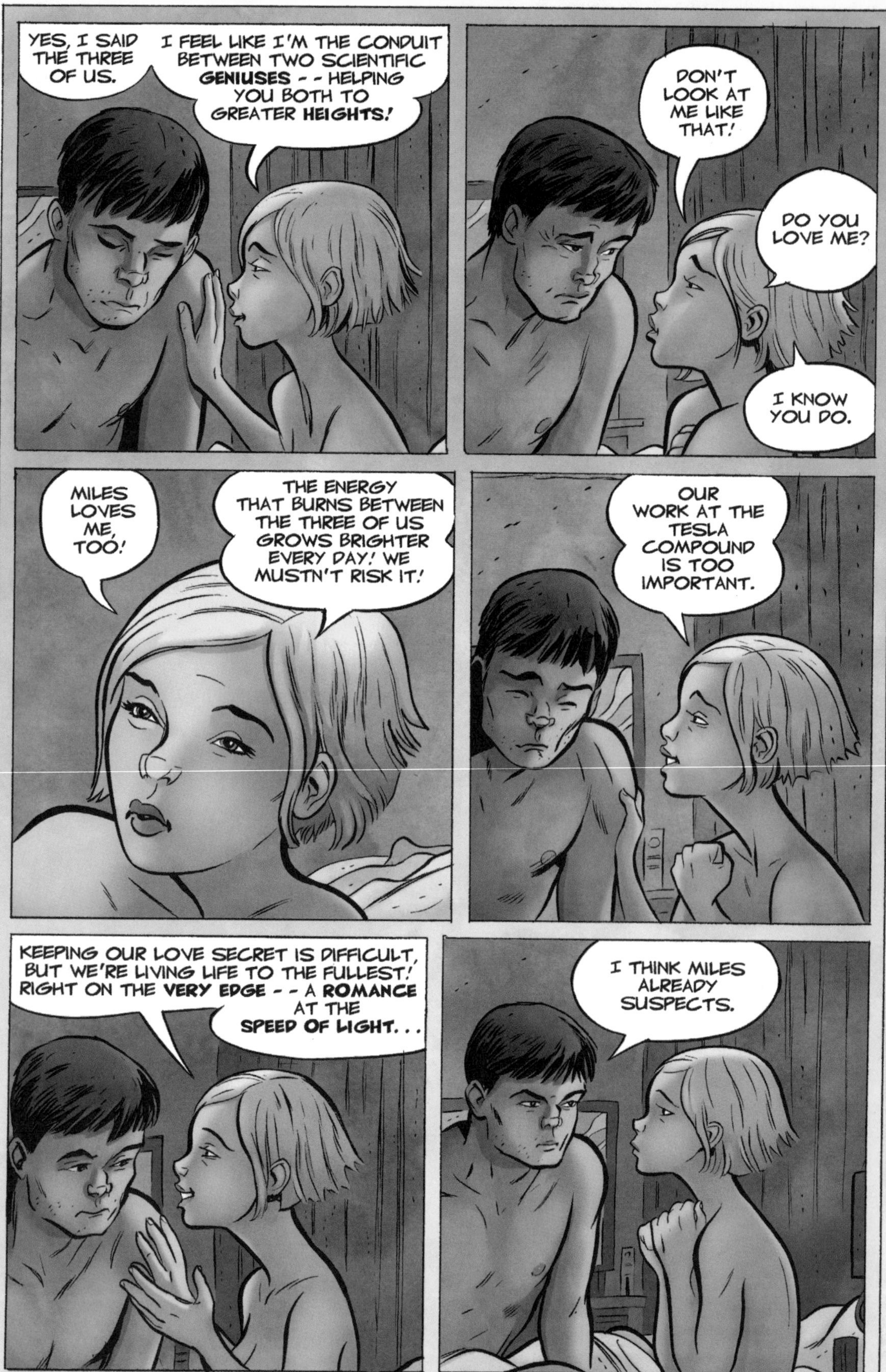
YES, I SAID THE THREE OF US.
I FEEL LIKE I'M THE CONDUIT BETWEEN TWO SCIENTIFIC GENIUSES - - HELPING YOU BOTH TO GREATER HEIGHTS!
DON'T LOOK AT ME LIKE THAT!
DO YOU LOVE ME?
I KNOW YOU DO.
MILES LOVES ME, TOO!
THE ENERGY THAT BURNS BETWEEN THE THREE OF US GROWS BRIGHTER EVERY DAY! WE MUSTN'T RISK IT!
OUR WORK AT THE TESLA COMPOUND IS TOO IMPORTANT.
KEEPING OUR LOVE SECRET IS DIFFICULT, BUT WE'RE LIVING LIFE TO THE FULLEST! RIGHT ON THE VERY EDGE - - A ROMANCE AT THE SPEED OF LIGHT. . .
I THINK MILES ALREADY SUSPECTS.

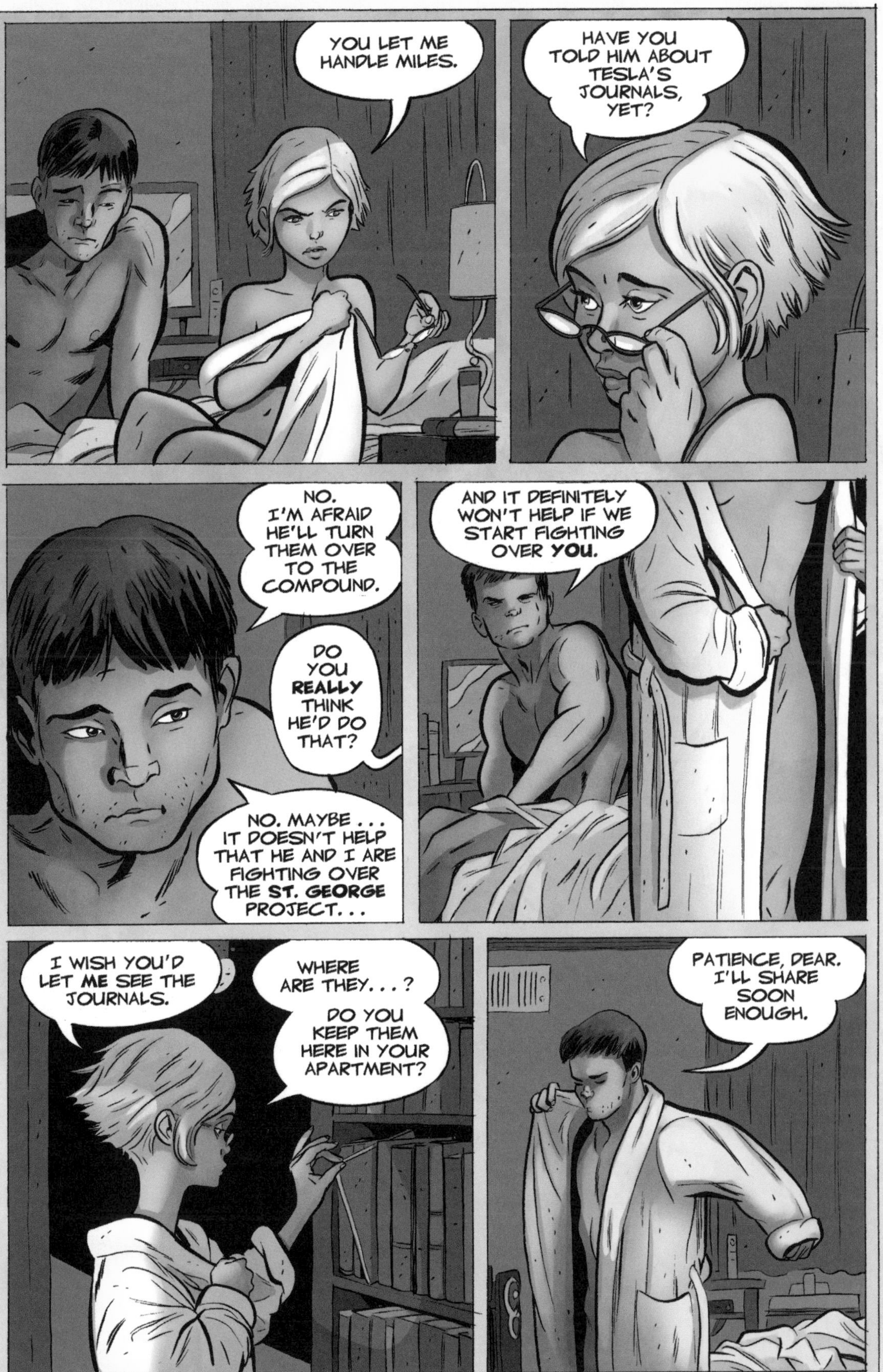
YOU LET ME HANDLE MILES.
HAVE YOU TOLD HIM ABOUT TESLA'S JOURNALS, YET?
NO. I'M AFRAID HE'LL TURN THEM OVER TO THE COMPOUND.
DO YOU REALLY THINK HE'D DO THAT?
NO. MAYBE . . . IT DOESN'T HELP THAT HE AND I ARE FIGHTING OVER THE ST. GEORGE PROJECT. . .
AND IT DEFINITELY WON'T HELP IF WE START FIGHTING OVER YOU.
I WISH YOU'D LET ME SEE THE JOURNALS.
WHERE ARE THEY. . . ?
DO YOU KEEP THEM HERE IN YOUR APARTMENT?
PATIENCE, DEAR. I'LL SHARE SOON ENOUGH.

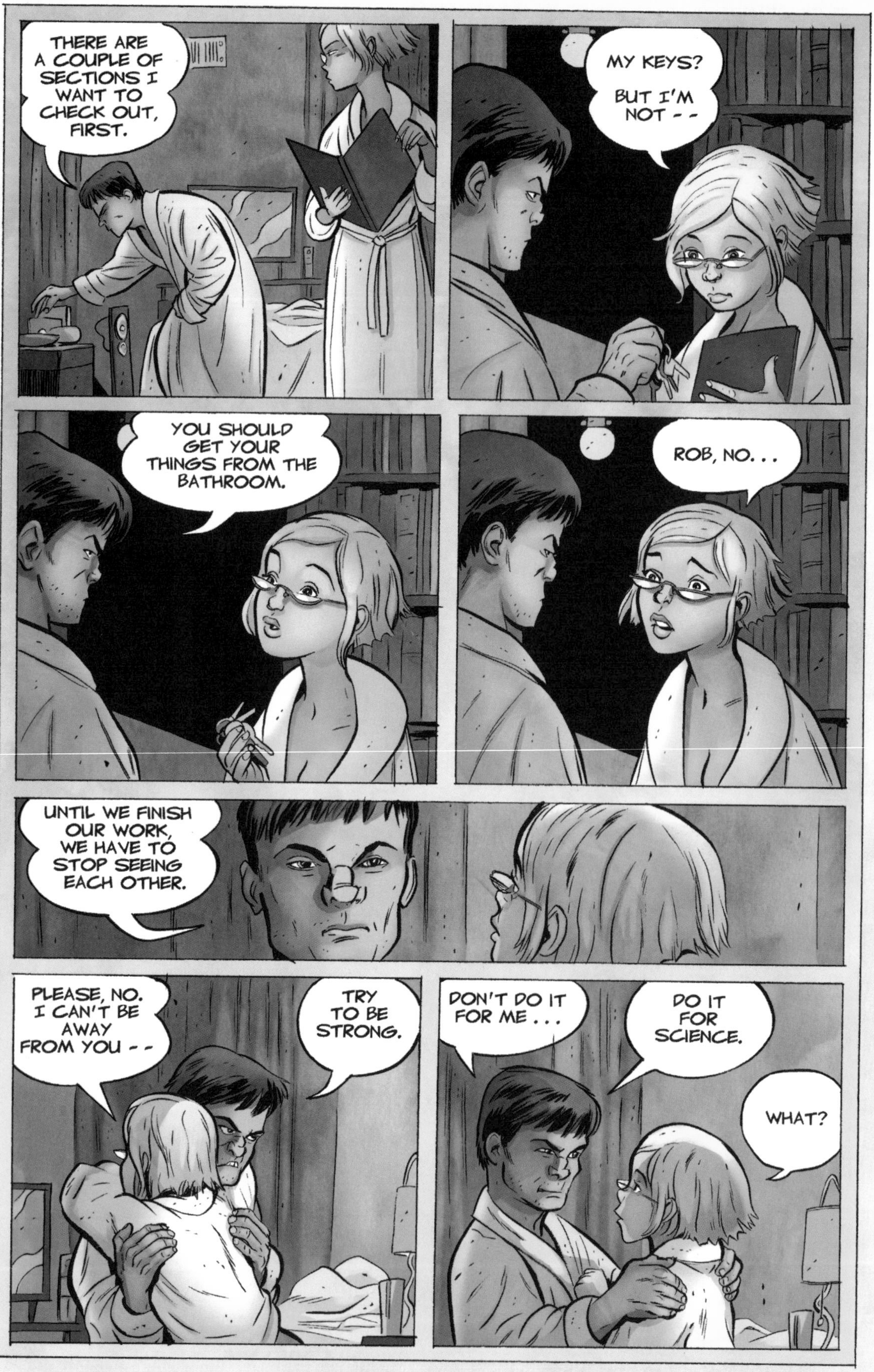
THERE ARE A COUPLE OF SECTIONS I WANT TO CHECK OUT, FIRST.
MY KEYS?
BUT I'M NOT - -
YOU SHOULD GET YOUR THINGS FROM THE BATHROOM.
ROB, NO...
UNTIL WE FINISH OUR WORK, WE HAVE TO STOP SEEING EACH OTHER.
PLEASE, NO. I CAN'T BE AWAY FROM YOU - -
TRY TO BE STRONG.
DON'T DO IT FOR ME...
DO IT FOR SCIENCE.
WHAT?

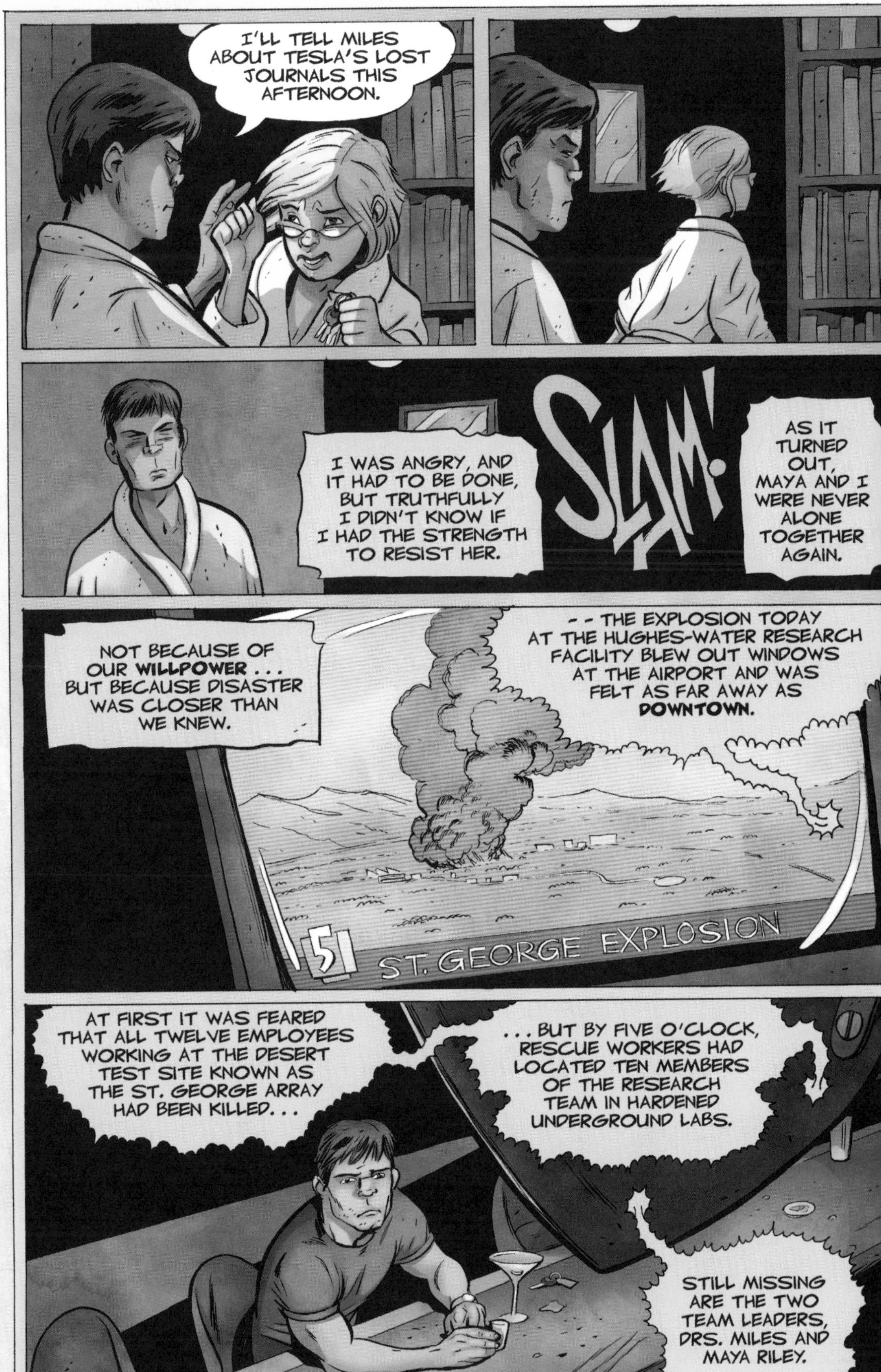
I'LL TELL MILES ABOUT TESLA'S LOST JOURNALS THIS AFTERNOON.
I WAS ANGRY, AND IT HAD TO BE DONE, BUT TRUTHFULLY I DIDN'T KNOW IF I HAD THE STRENGTH TO RESIST HER.
SLAM!
AS IT TURNED OUT, MAYA AND I WERE NEVER ALONE TOGETHER AGAIN.
NOT BECAUSE OF OUR WILLPOWER... BUT BECAUSE DISASTER WAS CLOSER THAN WE KNEW.
-- THE EXPLOSION TODAY AT THE HUGHES-WATER RESEARCH FACILITY BLEW OUT WINDOWS AT THE AIRPORT AND WAS FELT AS FAR AWAY AS DOWNTOWN.
5
ST. GEORGE EXPLOSION
AT FIRST IT WAS FEARED THAT ALL TWELVE EMPLOYEES WORKING AT THE DESERT TEST SITE KNOWN AS THE ST. GEORGE ARRAY HAD BEEN KILLED...
...BUT BY FIVE O'CLOCK, RESCUE WORKERS HAD LOCATED TEN MEMBERS OF THE RESEARCH TEAM IN HARDENED UNDERGROUND LABS.
STILL MISSING ARE THE TWO TEAM LEADERS, DRS. MILES AND MAYA RILEY.

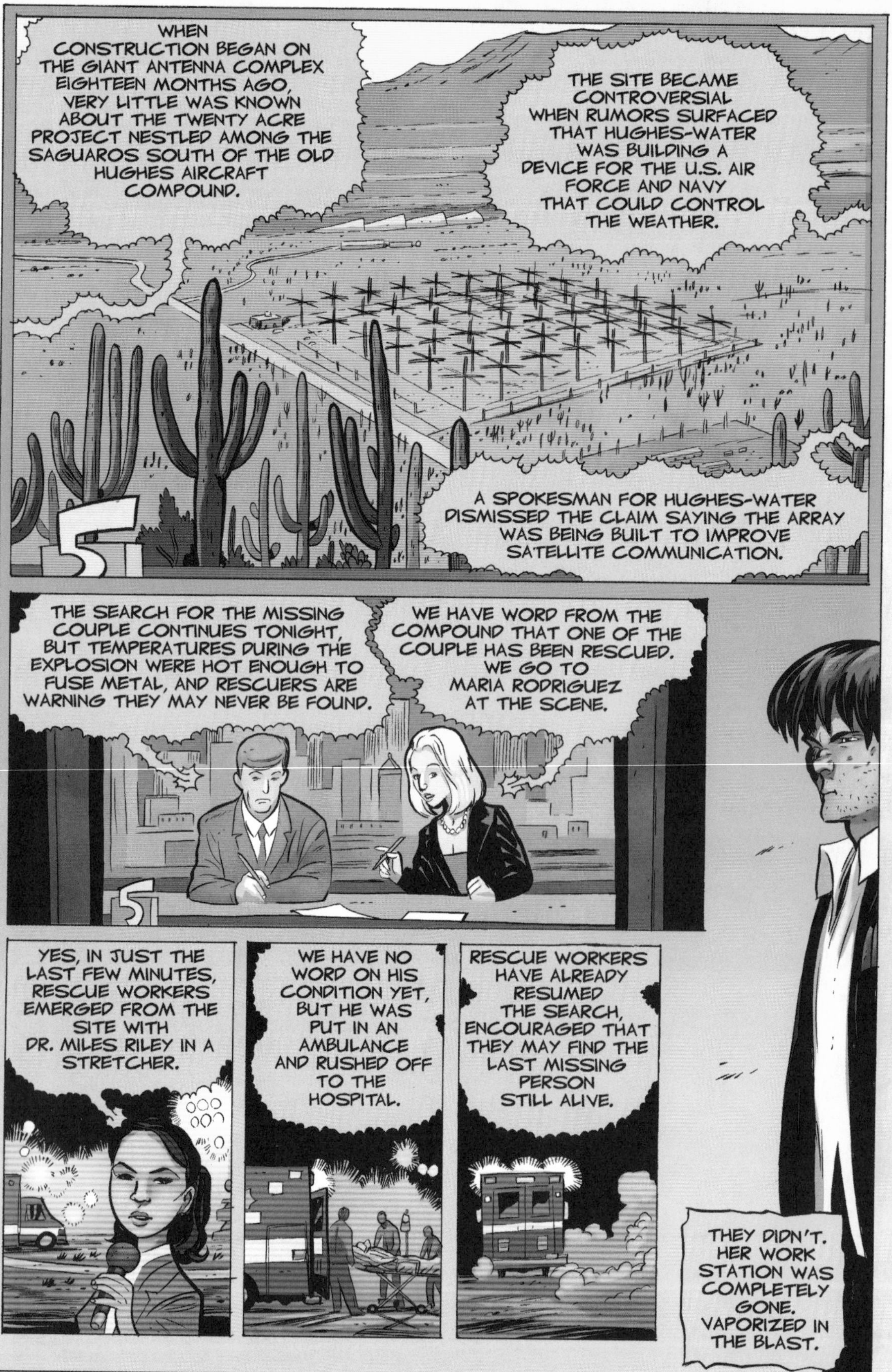
WHEN CONSTRUCTION BEGAN ON THE GIANT ANTENNA COMPLEX EIGHTEEN MONTHS AGO, VERY LITTLE WAS KNOWN ABOUT THE TWENTY ACRE PROJECT NESTLED AMONG THE SAGUAROS SOUTH OF THE OLD HUGHES AIRCRAFT COMPOUND.
THE SITE BECAME CONTROVERSIAL WHEN RUMORS SURFACED THAT HUGHES-WATER WAS BUILDING A DEVICE FOR THE U.S. AIR FORCE AND NAVY THAT COULD CONTROL THE WEATHER.
A SPOKESMAN FOR HUGHES-WATER DISMISSED THE CLAIM SAYING THE ARRAY WAS BEING BUILT TO IMPROVE SATELLITE COMMUNICATION.
THE SEARCH FOR THE MISSING COUPLE CONTINUES TONIGHT, BUT TEMPERATURES DURING THE EXPLOSION WERE HOT ENOUGH TO FUSE METAL, AND RESCUERS ARE WARNING THEY MAY NEVER BE FOUND.
WE HAVE WORD FROM THE COMPOUND THAT ONE OF THE COUPLE HAS BEEN RESCUED. WE GO TO MARIA RODRIGUEZ AT THE SCENE.
YES, IN JUST THE LAST FEW MINUTES, RESCUE WORKERS EMERGED FROM THE SITE WITH DR. MILES RILEY IN A STRETCHER.
WE HAVE NO WORD ON HIS CONDITION YET, BUT HE WAS PUT IN AN AMBULANCE AND RUSHED OFF TO THE HOSPITAL.
RESCUE WORKERS HAVE ALREADY RESUMED THE SEARCH, ENCOURAGED THAT THEY MAY FIND THE LAST MISSING PERSON STILL ALIVE.
THEY DIDN'T. HER WORK STATION WAS COMPLETELY GONE. VAPORIZED IN THE BLAST.

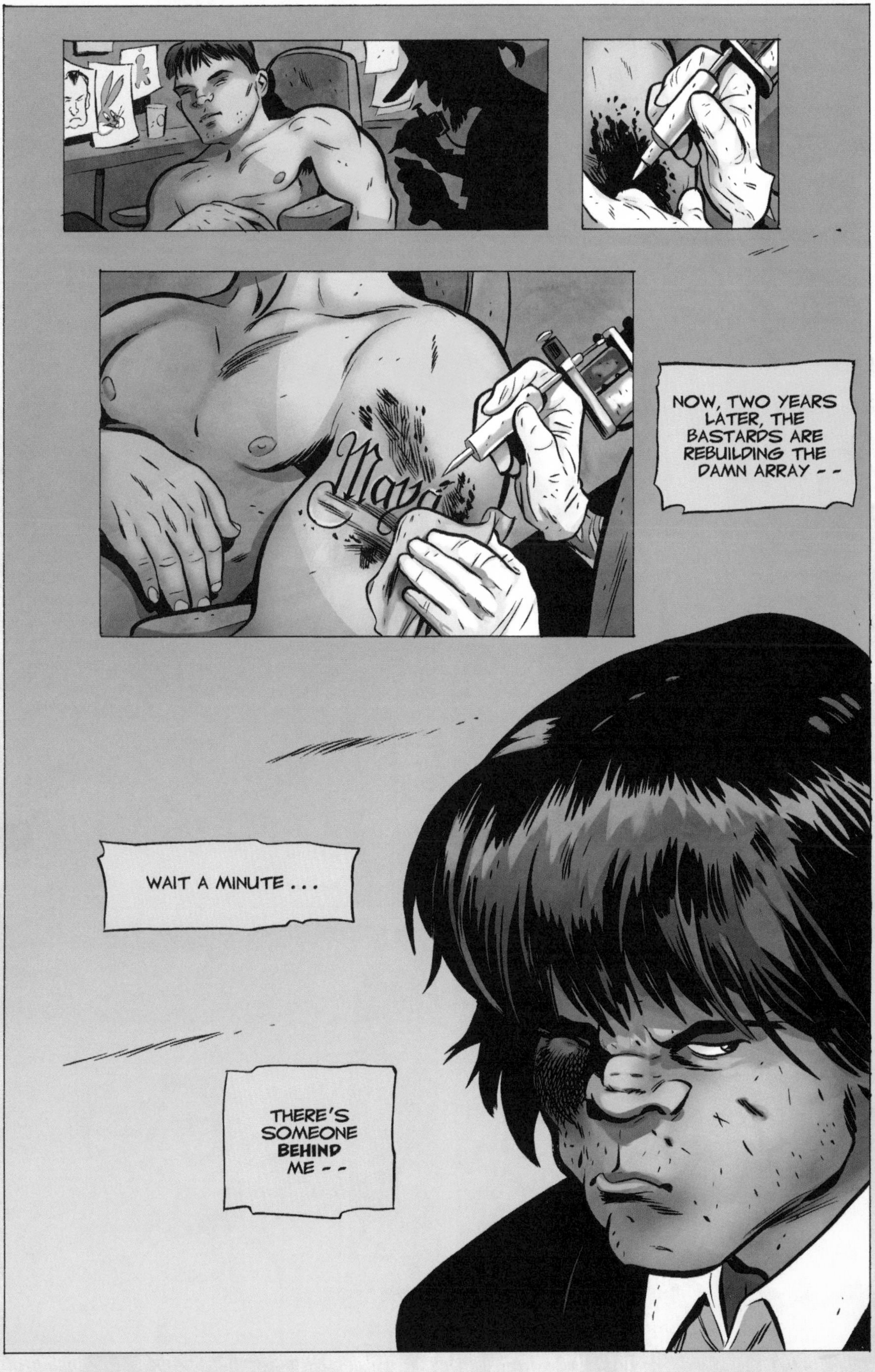
Maya
NOW, TWO YEARS LATER, THE BASTARDS ARE REBUILDING THE DAMN ARRAY - -
WAIT A MINUTE . . .
THERE'S SOMEONE BEHIND ME - -

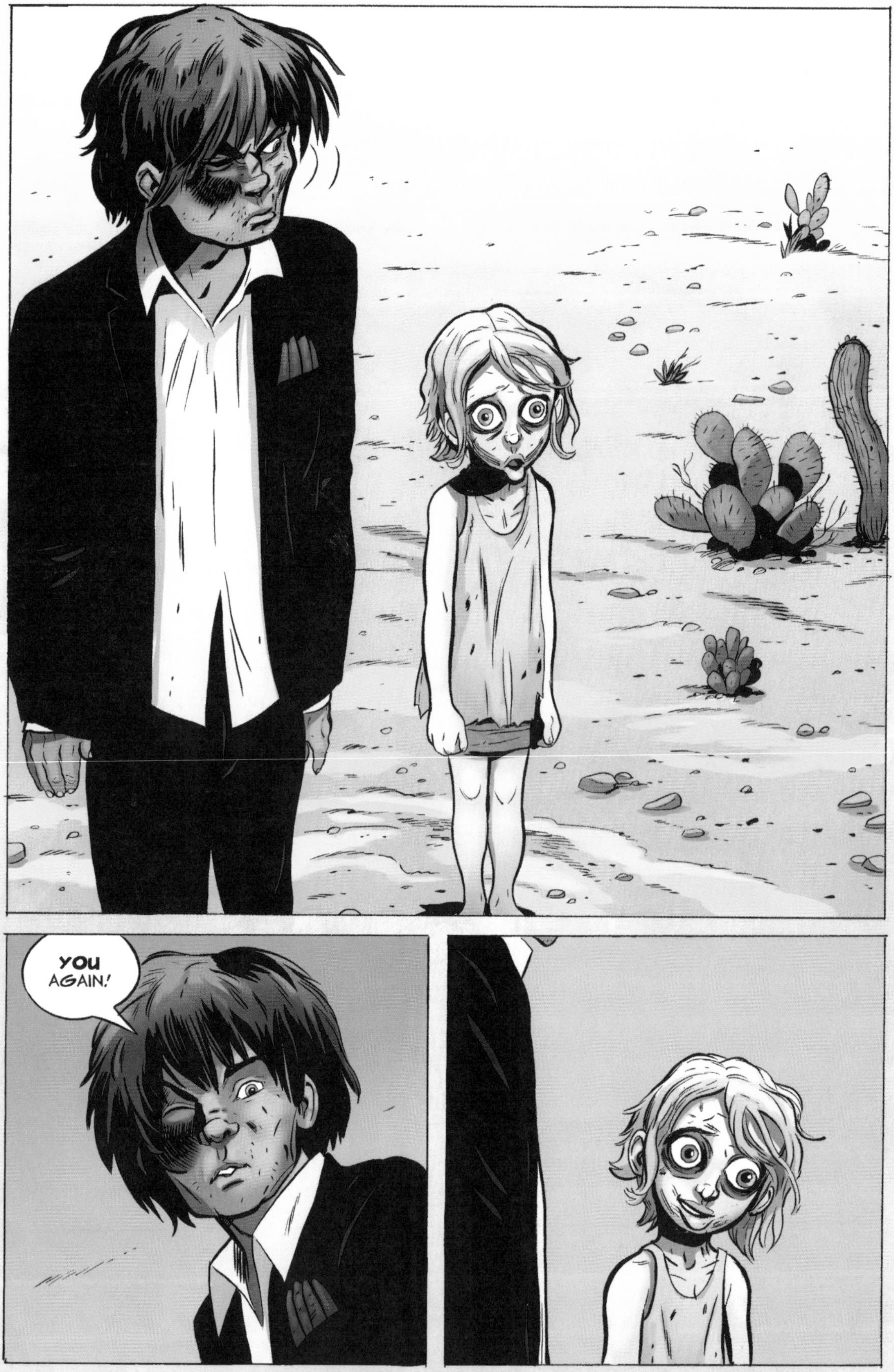
YOU AGAIN!

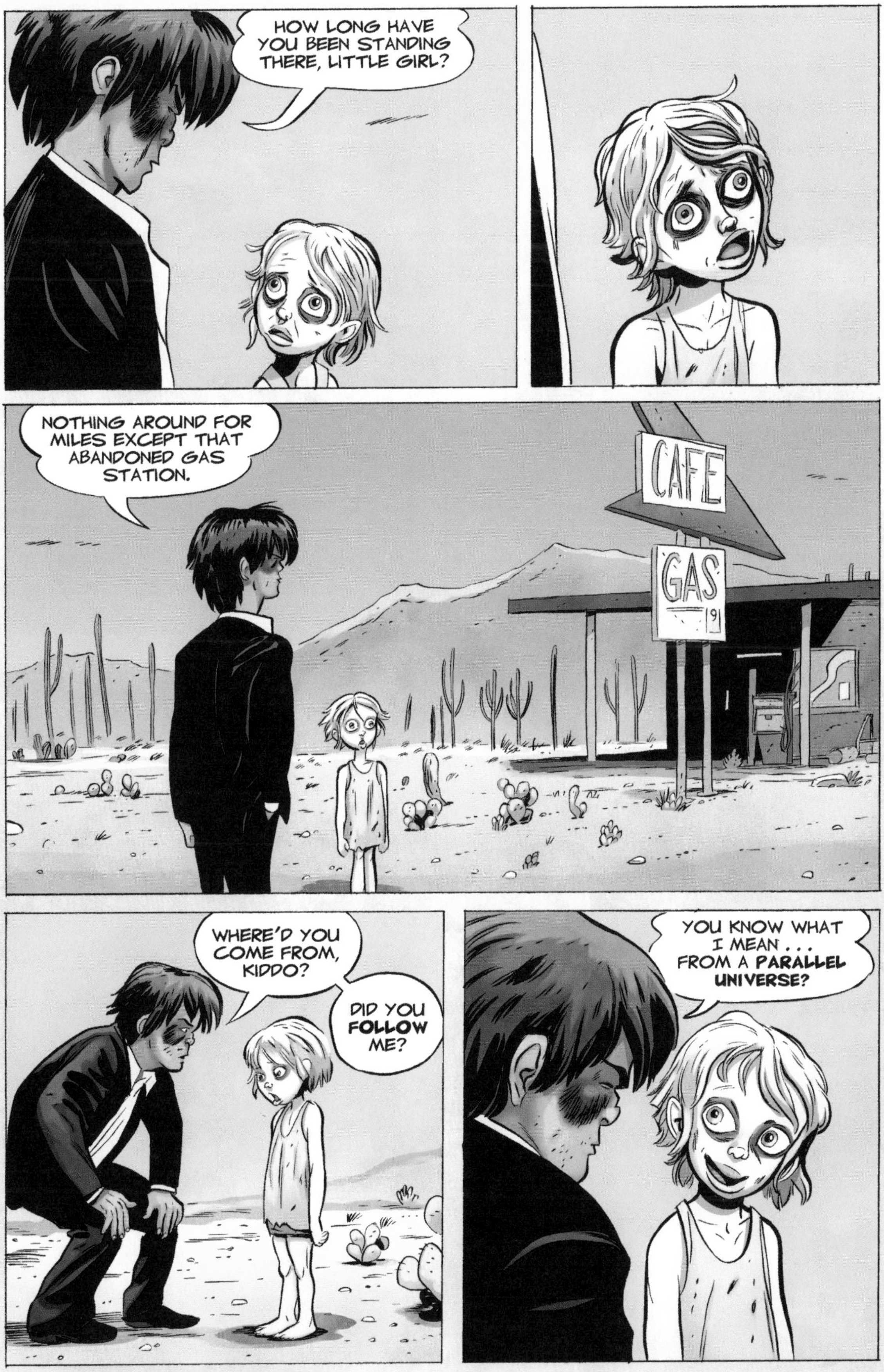
HOW LONG HAVE YOU BEEN STANDING THERE, LITTLE GIRL?
NOTHING AROUND FOR MILES EXCEPT THAT ABANDONED GAS STATION.
CAFE
GAS
19
WHERE'D YOU COME FROM, KIDDO?
DID YOU FOLLOW ME?
YOU KNOW WHAT I MEAN . . . FROM A PARALLEL UNIVERSE?

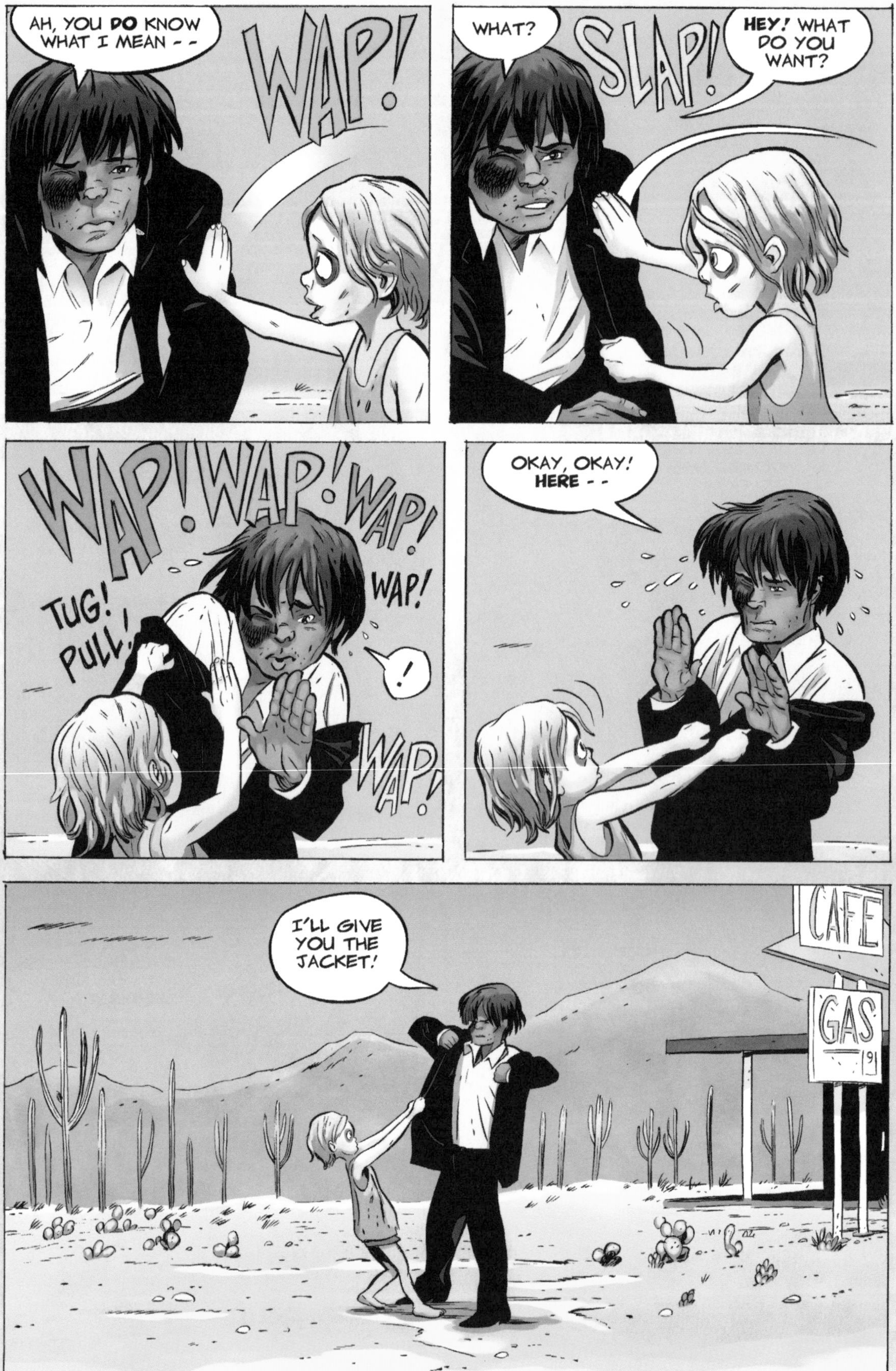
AH, YOU **DO** KNOW WHAT I MEAN - -
WAP!
WHAT?
SLAP!
HEY! WHAT DO YOU WANT?
WAP! WAP! WAP!
TUG! PULL!
WAP!
!
WAP!
OKAY, OKAY! **HERE** - -
I'LL GIVE YOU THE JACKET!
CAFE
GAS

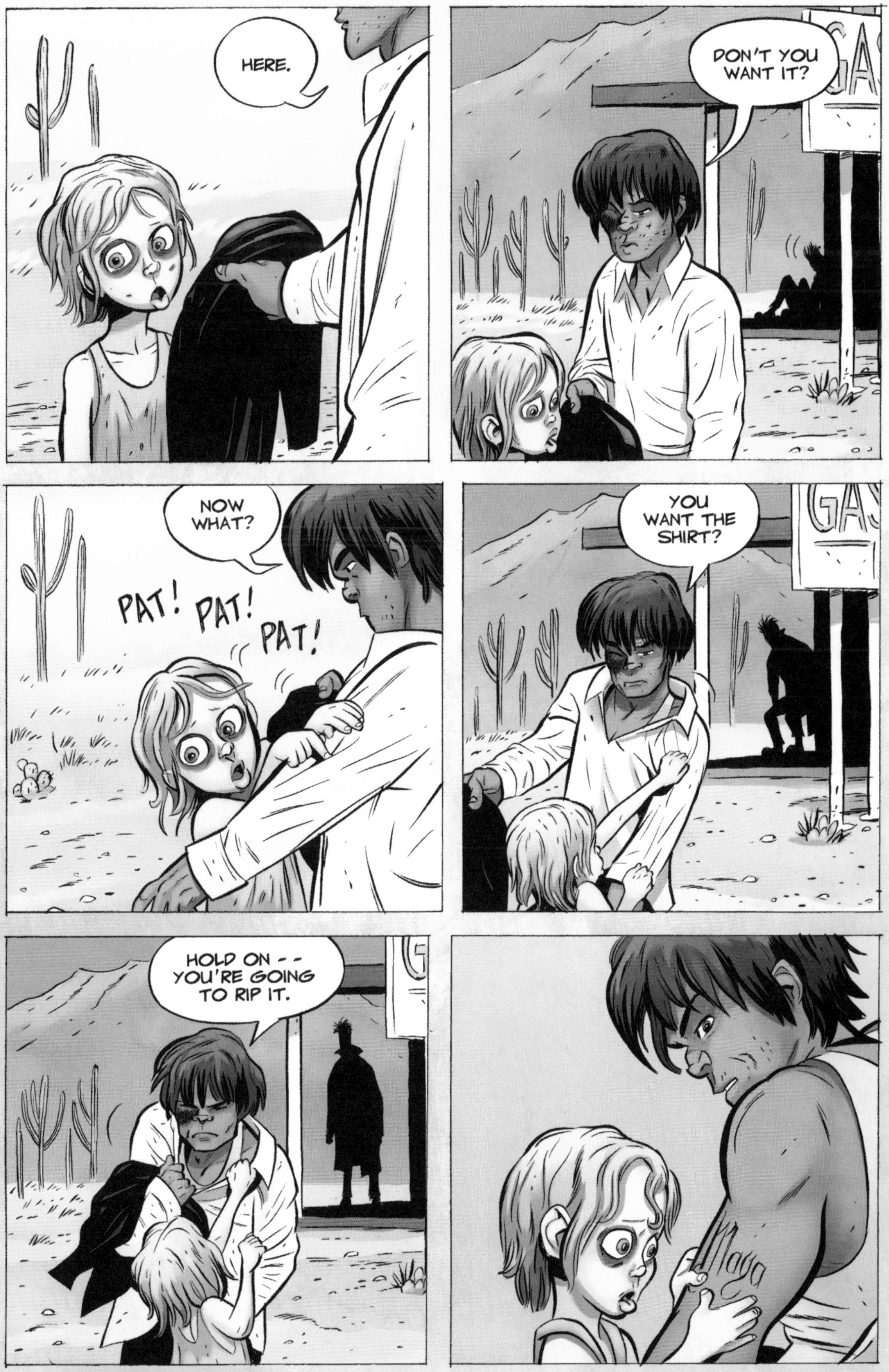
HERE.
DON'T YOU WANT IT?
NOW WHAT?
PAT! PAT! PAT!
YOU WANT THE SHIRT?
HOLD ON - - YOU'RE GOING TO RIP IT.
Maya

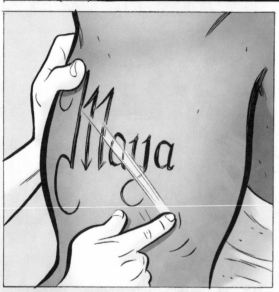

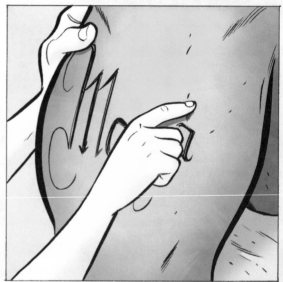

Maya
Maya
Maya
Maya
Maya
YOU CROSSED OUT MAYA'S NAME?
WHY? BECAUSE SHE'S DEAD?
Maya

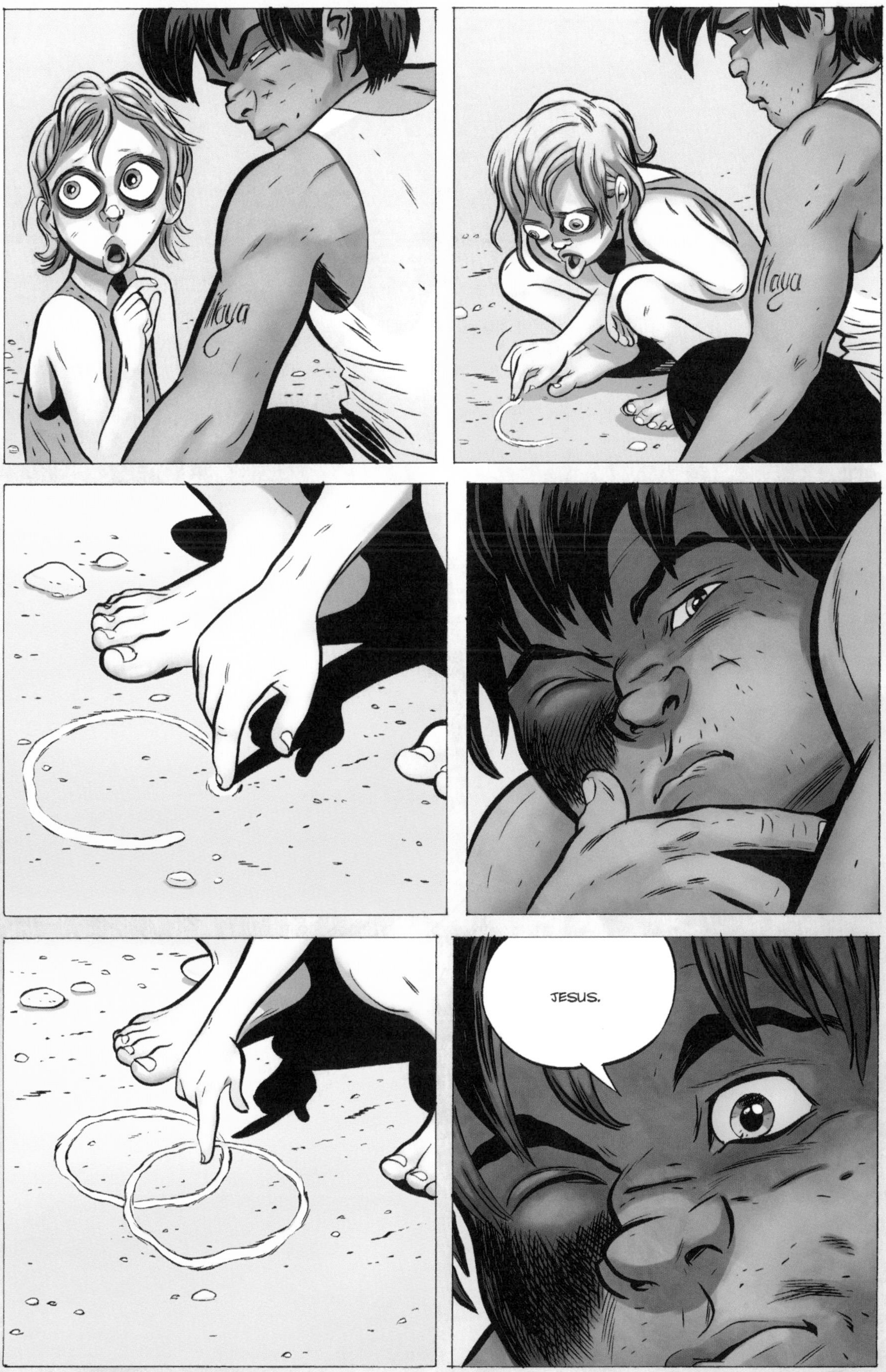
Maya
Maya
JESUS.

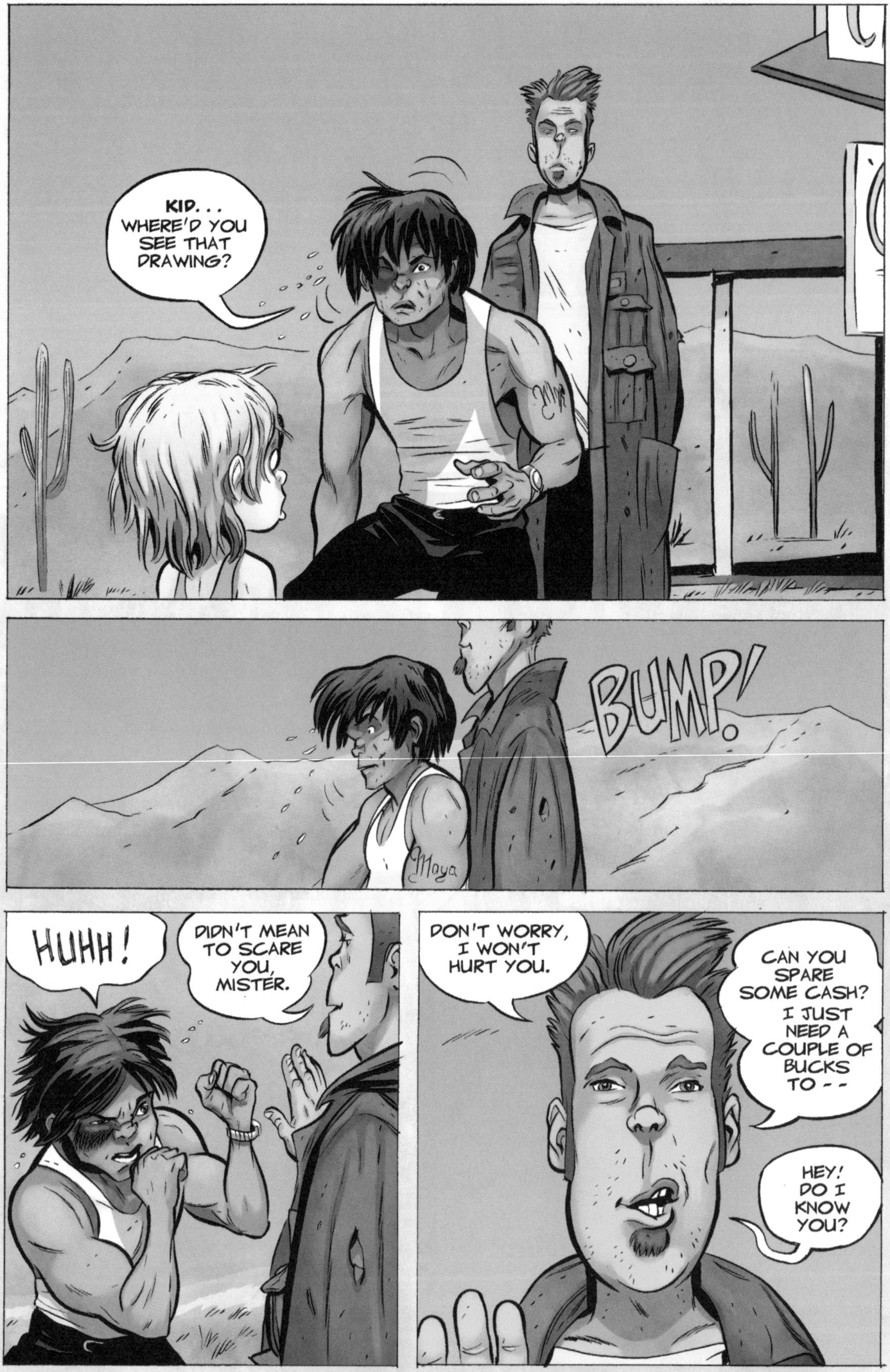
KID. . .
WHERE'D YOU SEE THAT DRAWING?
Maya
BUMP!
HUHH!
DIDN'T MEAN TO SCARE YOU, MISTER.
DON'T WORRY, I WON'T HURT YOU.
CAN YOU SPARE SOME CASH? I JUST NEED A COUPLE OF BUCKS TO - -
HEY! DO I KNOW YOU?

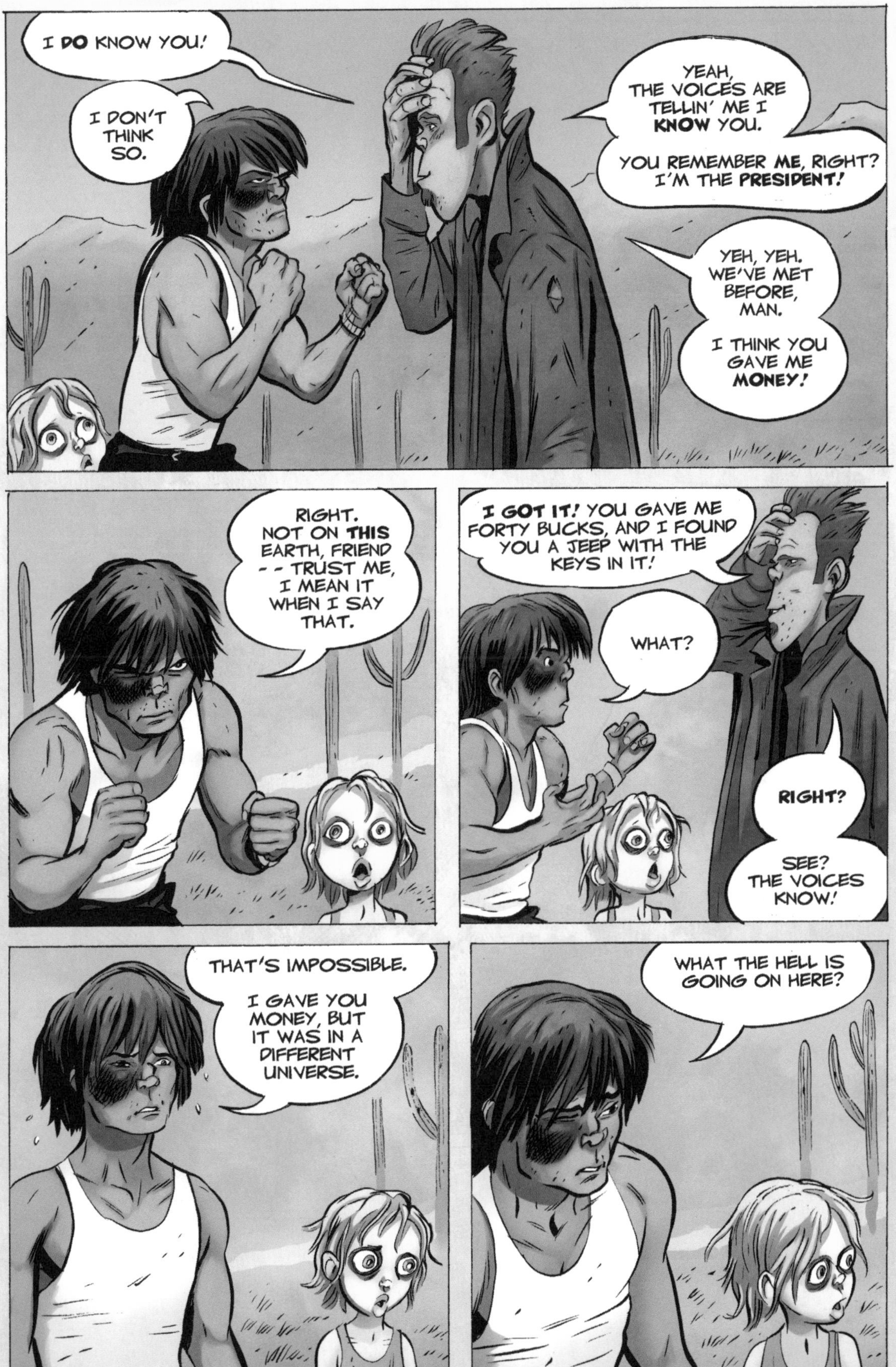
I DO KNOW YOU!
I DON'T THINK SO.
YEAH, THE VOICES ARE TELLIN' ME I KNOW YOU.
YOU REMEMBER ME, RIGHT? I'M THE PRESIDENT!
YEH, YEH. WE'VE MET BEFORE, MAN.
I THINK YOU GAVE ME MONEY!
RIGHT. NOT ON THIS EARTH, FRIEND -- TRUST ME, I MEAN IT WHEN I SAY THAT.
I GOT IT! YOU GAVE ME FORTY BUCKS, AND I FOUND YOU A JEEP WITH THE KEYS IN IT!
WHAT?
RIGHT?
SEE? THE VOICES KNOW!
THAT'S IMPOSSIBLE.
I GAVE YOU MONEY, BUT IT WAS IN A DIFFERENT UNIVERSE.
WHAT THE HELL IS GOING ON HERE?

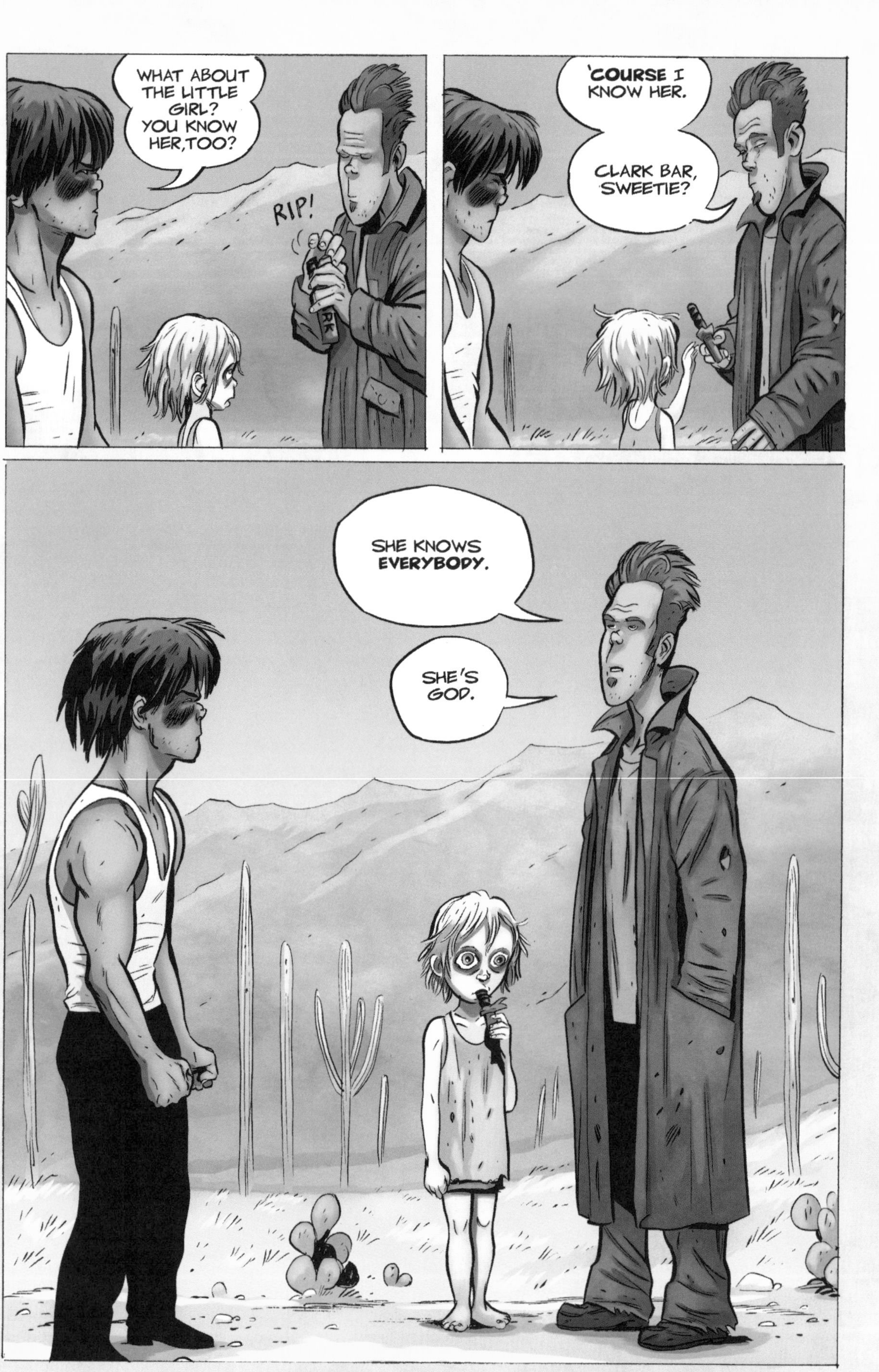
WHAT ABOUT THE LITTLE GIRL? YOU KNOW HER, TOO?
RIP!
'COURSE I KNOW HER.
CLARK BAR, SWEETIE?
SHE KNOWS EVERYBODY.
SHE'S GOD.

IX
THE WARNING

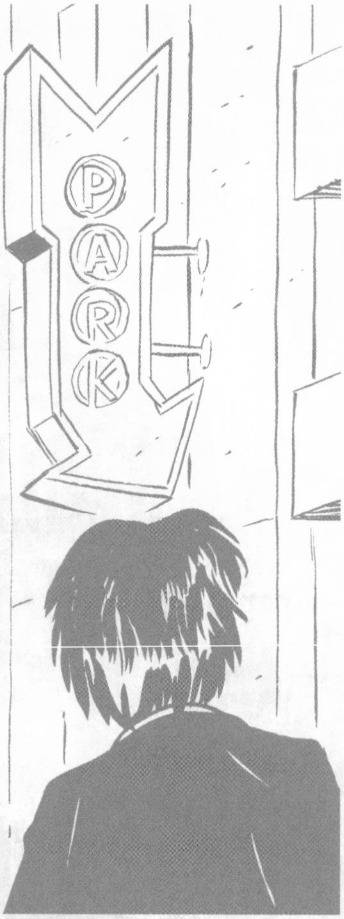
PARK

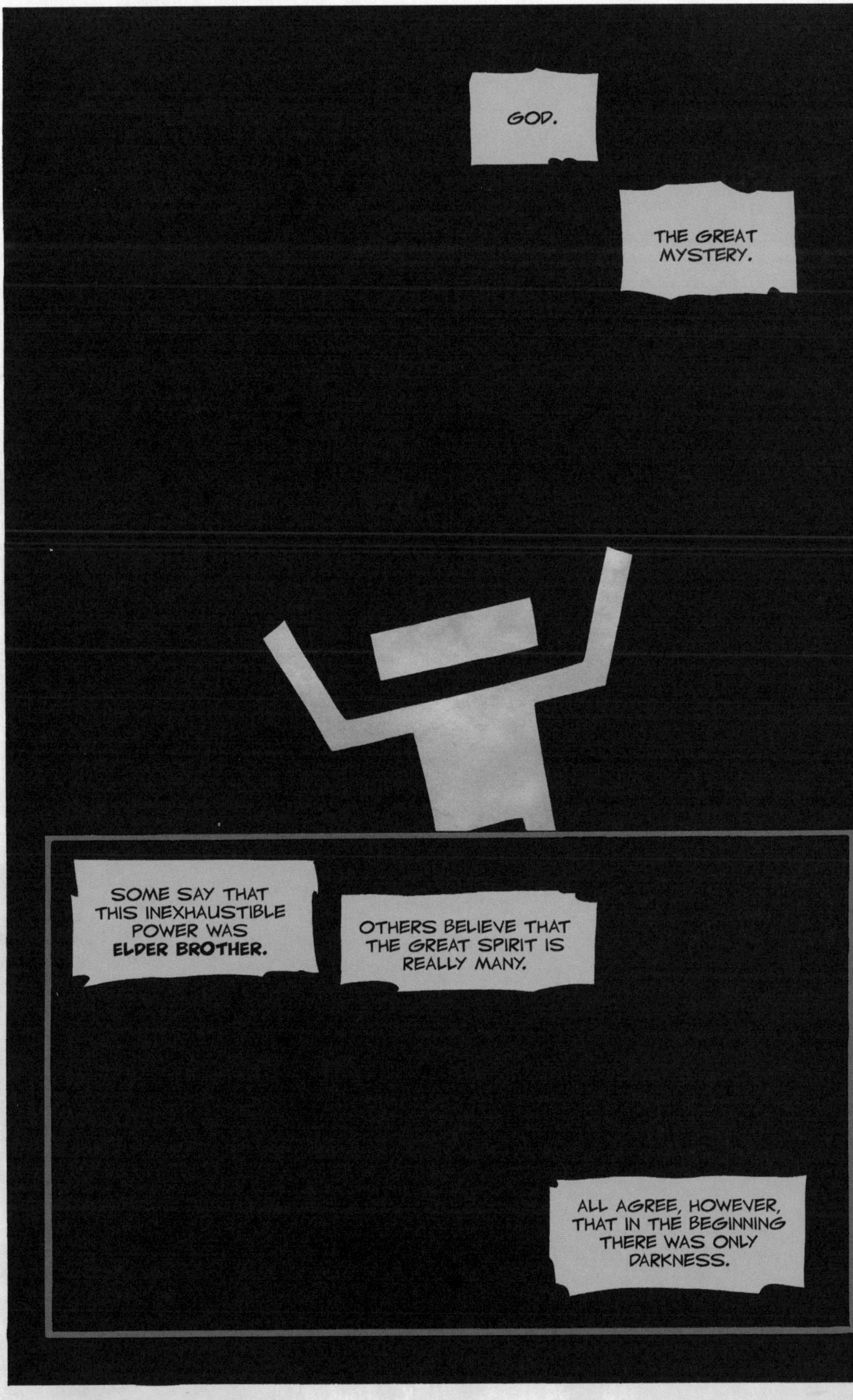
GOD.
THE GREAT MYSTERY.
SOME SAY THAT THIS INEXHAUSTIBLE POWER WAS ELDER BROTHER.
OTHERS BELIEVE THAT THE GREAT SPIRIT IS REALLY MANY.
ALL AGREE, HOWEVER, THAT IN THE BEGINNING THERE WAS ONLY DARKNESS.

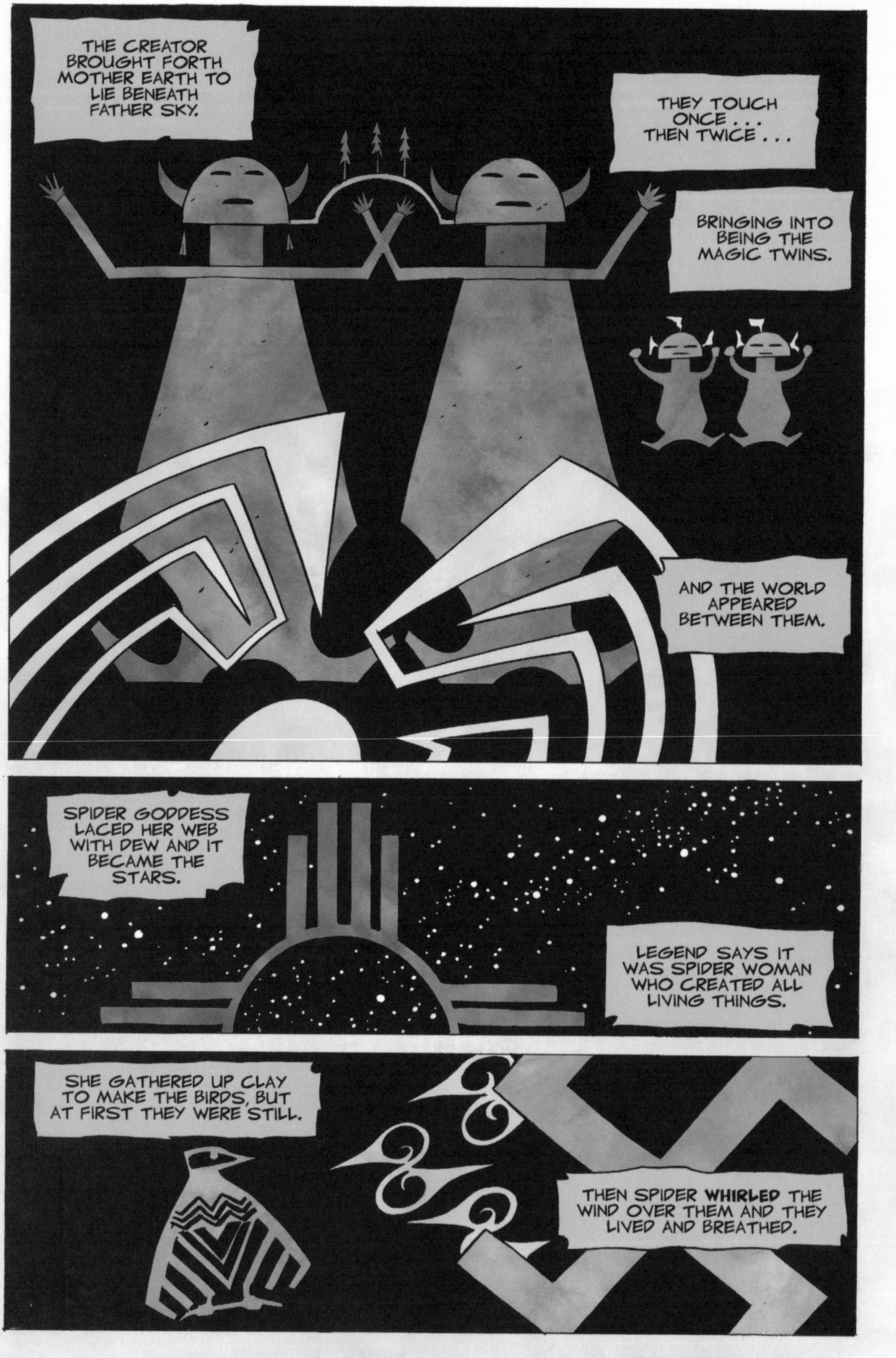
THE CREATOR BROUGHT FORTH MOTHER EARTH TO LIE BENEATH FATHER SKY.
THEY TOUCH ONCE . . . THEN TWICE . . .
BRINGING INTO BEING THE MAGIC TWINS.
AND THE WORLD APPEARED BETWEEN THEM.
SPIDER GODDESS LACED HER WEB WITH DEW AND IT BECAME THE STARS.
LEGEND SAYS IT WAS SPIDER WOMAN WHO CREATED ALL LIVING THINGS.
SHE GATHERED UP CLAY TO MAKE THE BIRDS, BUT AT FIRST THEY WERE STILL.
THEN SPIDER **WHIRLED** THE WIND OVER THEM AND THEY LIVED AND BREATHED.

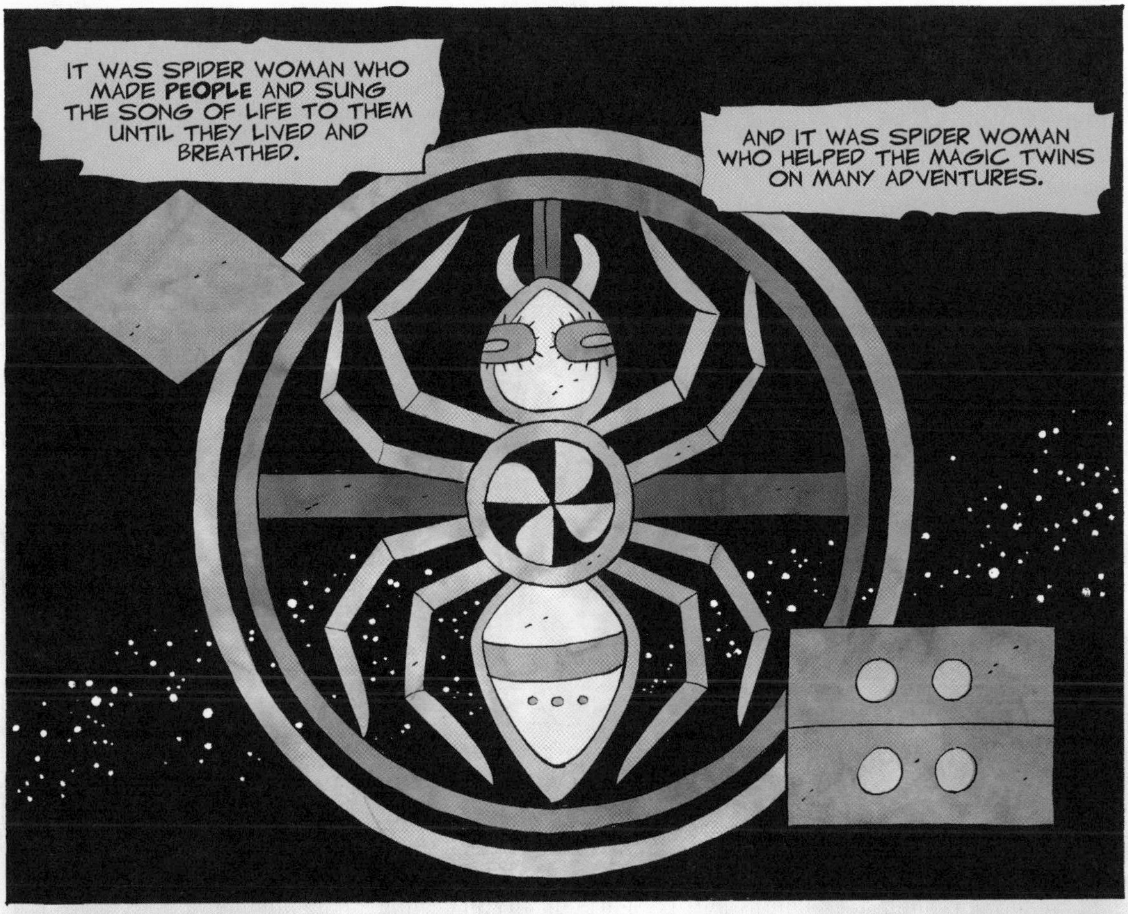
IT WAS SPIDER WOMAN WHO MADE **PEOPLE** AND SUNG THE SONG OF LIFE TO THEM UNTIL THEY LIVED AND BREATHED.
AND IT WAS SPIDER WOMAN WHO HELPED THE MAGIC TWINS ON MANY ADVENTURES.

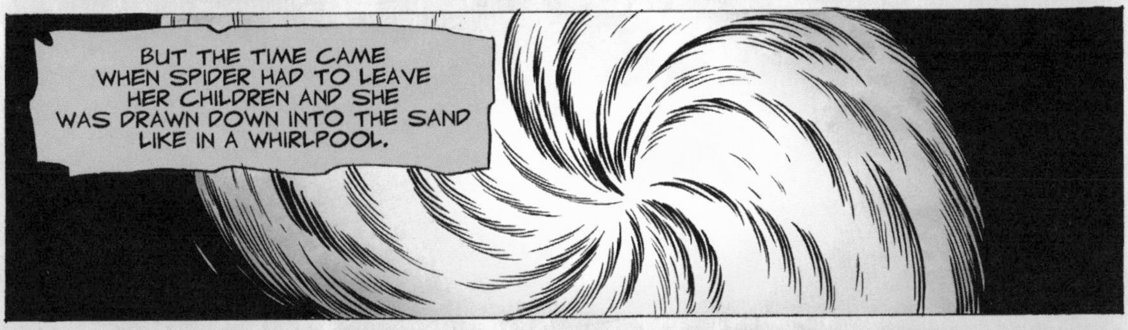
BUT THE TIME CAME WHEN SPIDER HAD TO LEAVE HER CHILDREN AND SHE WAS DRAWN DOWN INTO THE SAND LIKE IN A WHIRLPOOL.

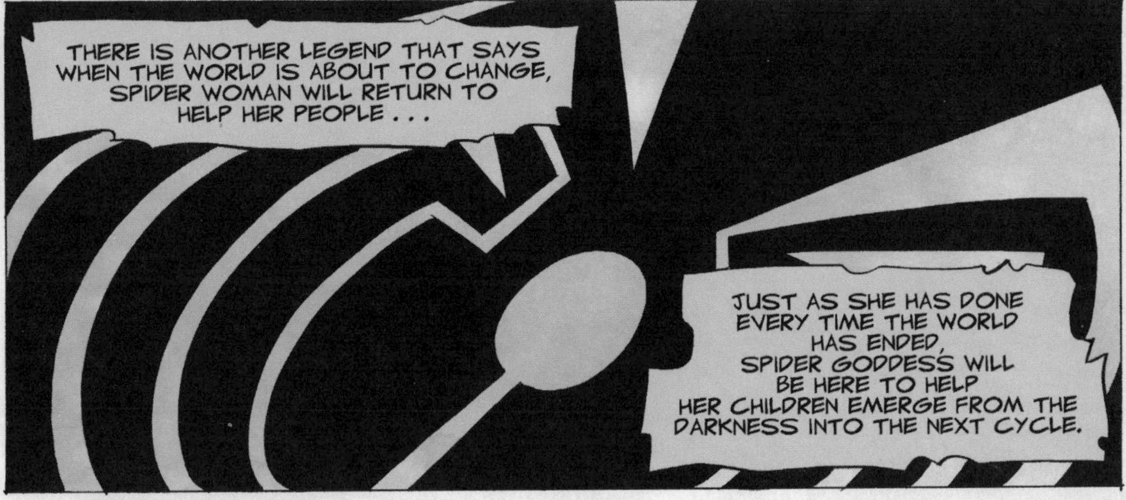
THERE IS ANOTHER LEGEND THAT SAYS WHEN THE WORLD IS ABOUT TO CHANGE, SPIDER WOMAN WILL RETURN TO HELP HER PEOPLE . . .
JUST AS SHE HAS DONE EVERY TIME THE WORLD HAS ENDED, SPIDER GODDESS WILL BE HERE TO HELP HER CHILDREN EMERGE FROM THE DARKNESS INTO THE NEXT CYCLE.

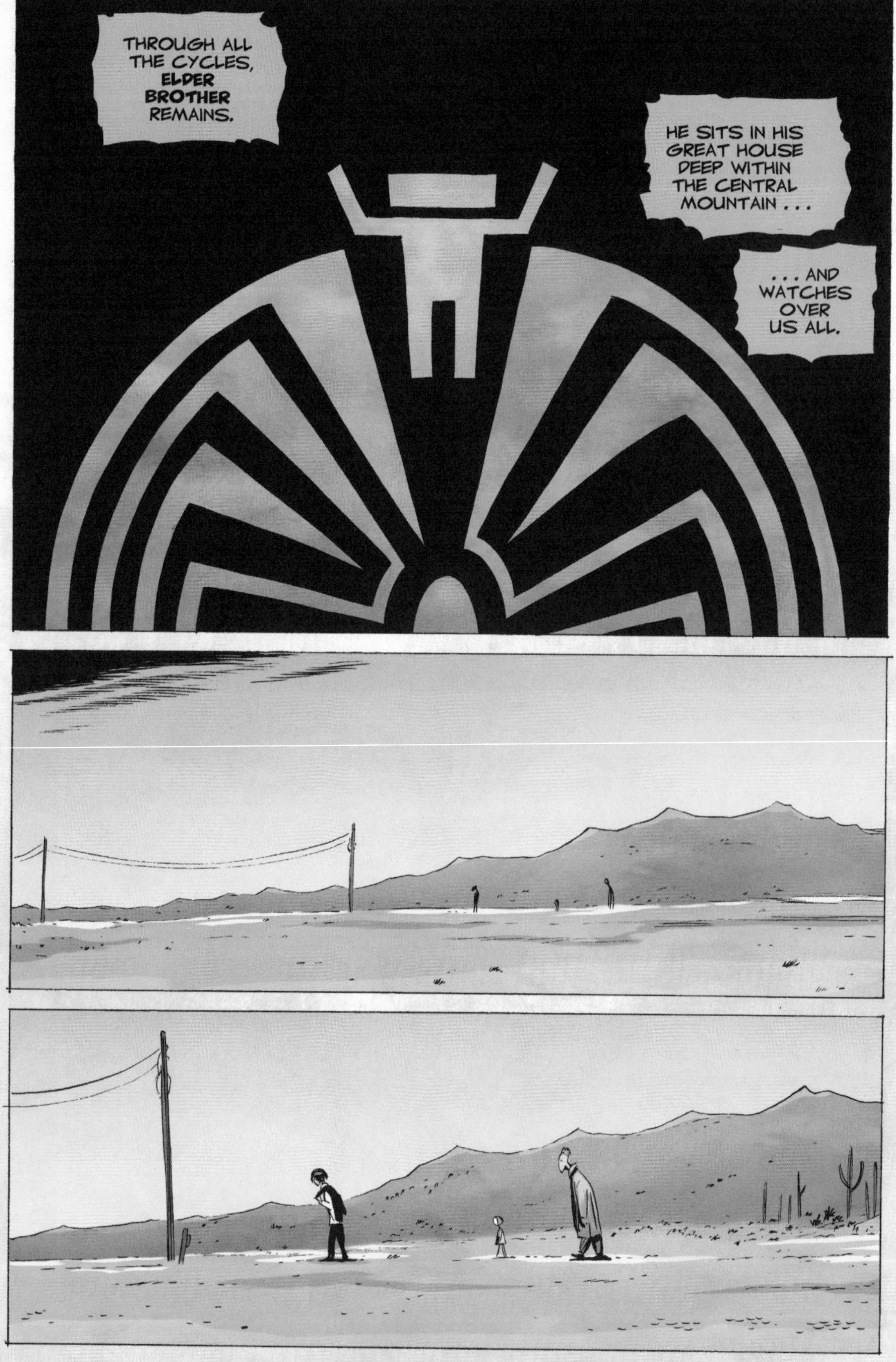
THROUGH ALL THE CYCLES, ELDER BROTHER REMAINS.
HE SITS IN HIS GREAT HOUSE DEEP WITHIN THE CENTRAL MOUNTAIN . . .
. . . AND WATCHES OVER US ALL.

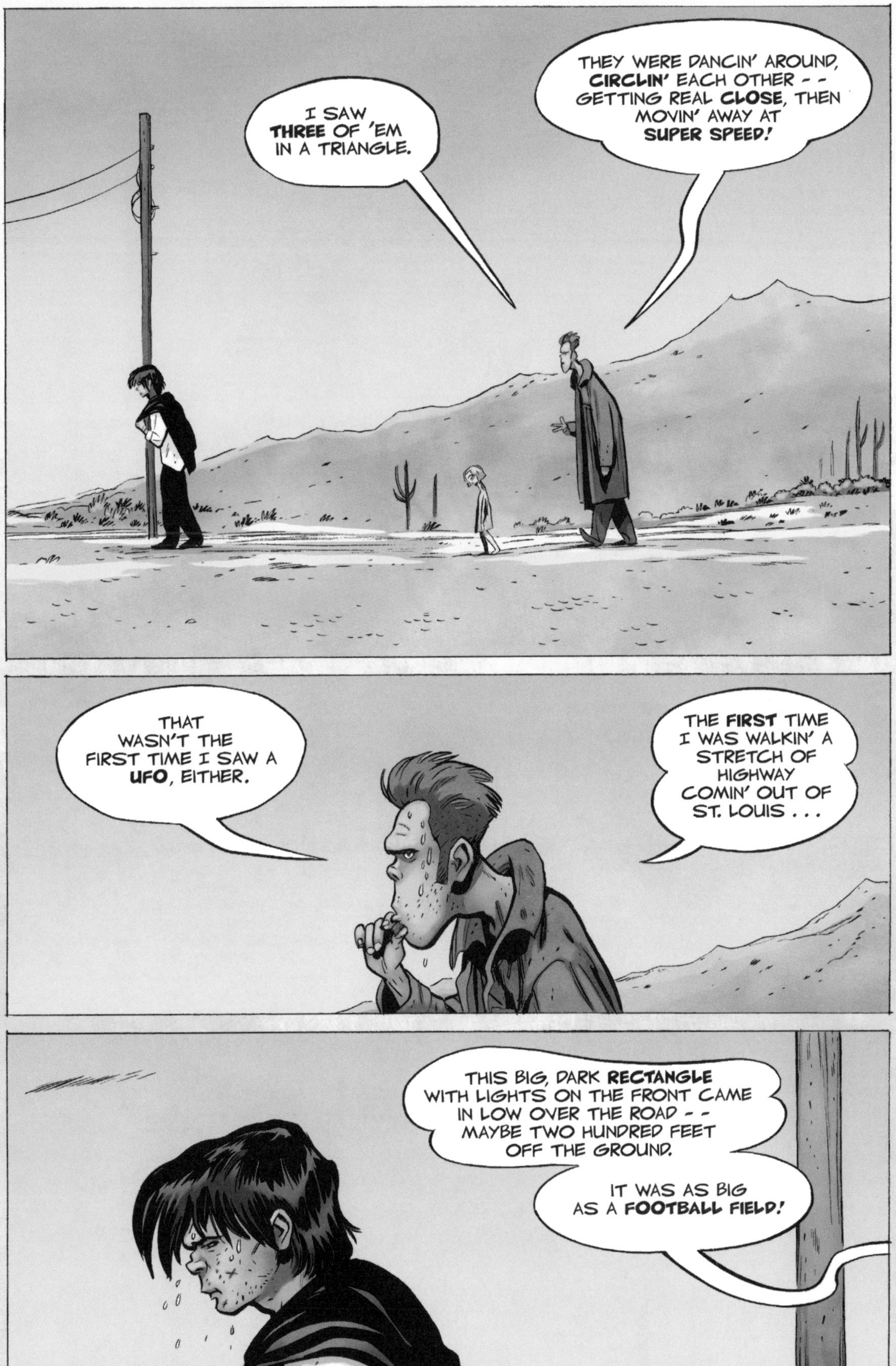
I SAW THREE OF 'EM IN A TRIANGLE.
THEY WERE DANCIN' AROUND, CIRCLIN' EACH OTHER - - GETTING REAL CLOSE, THEN MOVIN' AWAY AT SUPER SPEED!
THAT WASN'T THE FIRST TIME I SAW A UFO, EITHER.
THE FIRST TIME I WAS WALKIN' A STRETCH OF HIGHWAY COMIN' OUT OF ST. LOUIS . . .
THIS BIG, DARK RECTANGLE WITH LIGHTS ON THE FRONT CAME IN LOW OVER THE ROAD - - MAYBE TWO HUNDRED FEET OFF THE GROUND.
IT WAS AS BIG AS A FOOTBALL FIELD!

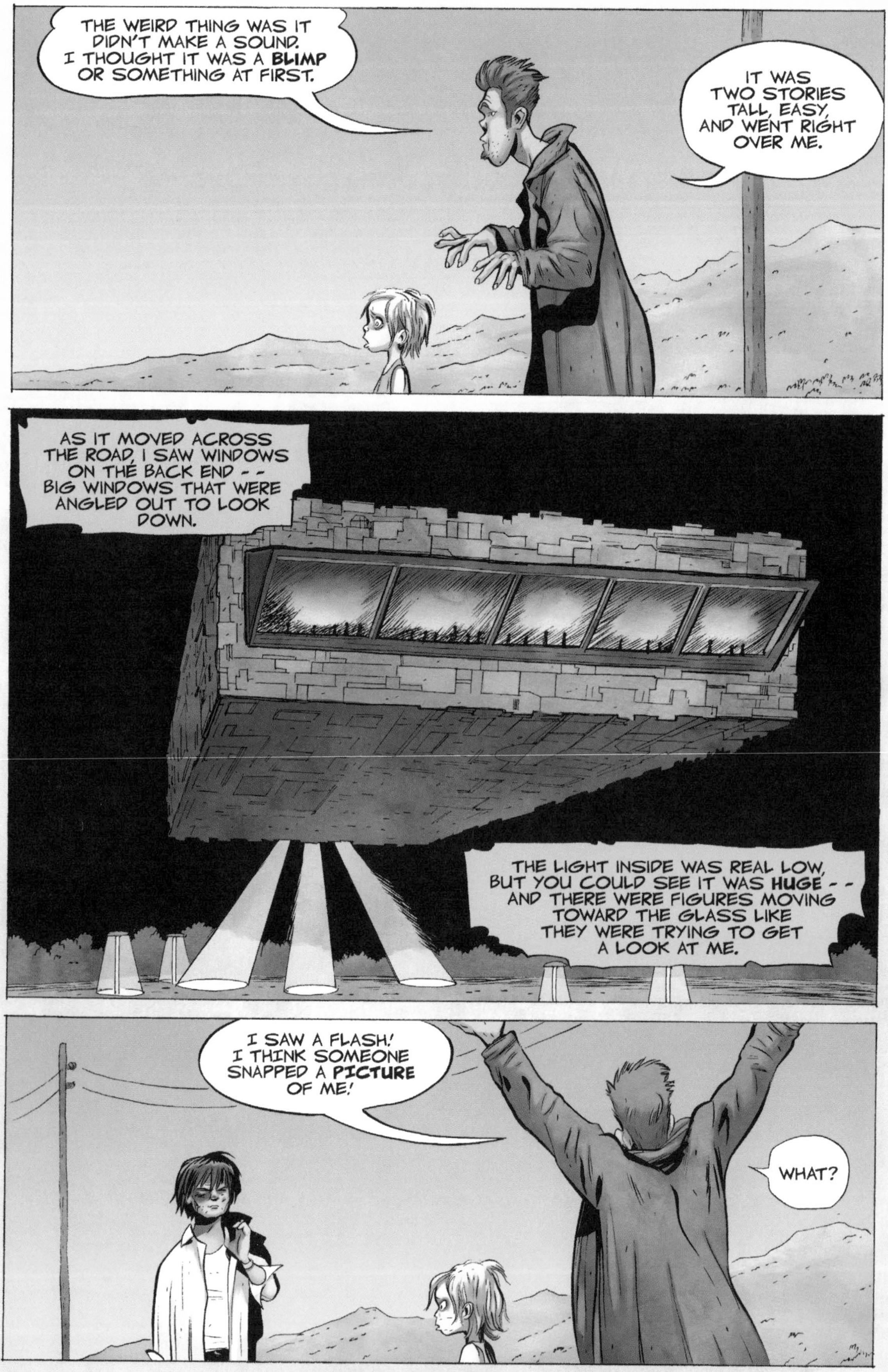
THE WEIRD THING WAS IT DIDN'T MAKE A SOUND. I THOUGHT IT WAS A BLIMP OR SOMETHING AT FIRST.
IT WAS TWO STORIES TALL, EASY, AND WENT RIGHT OVER ME.
AS IT MOVED ACROSS THE ROAD, I SAW WINDOWS ON THE BACK END - - BIG WINDOWS THAT WERE ANGLED OUT TO LOOK DOWN.
THE LIGHT INSIDE WAS REAL LOW, BUT YOU COULD SEE IT WAS HUGE - - AND THERE WERE FIGURES MOVING TOWARD THE GLASS LIKE THEY WERE TRYING TO GET A LOOK AT ME.
I SAW A FLASH! I THINK SOMEONE SNAPPED A PICTURE OF ME!
WHAT?

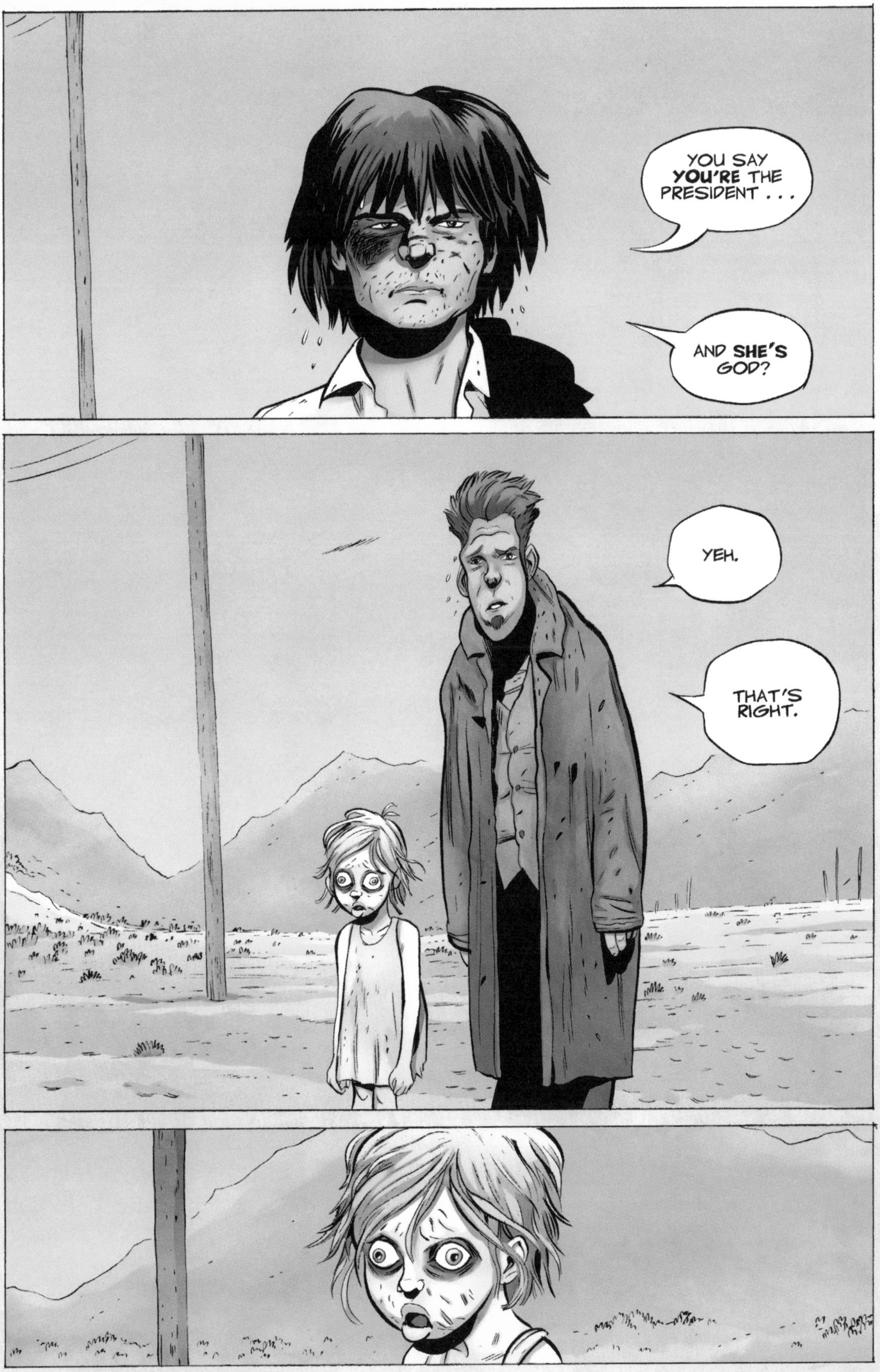
YOU SAY **YOU'RE** THE PRESIDENT . . .
AND **SHE'S** GOD?
YEH.
THAT'S RIGHT.

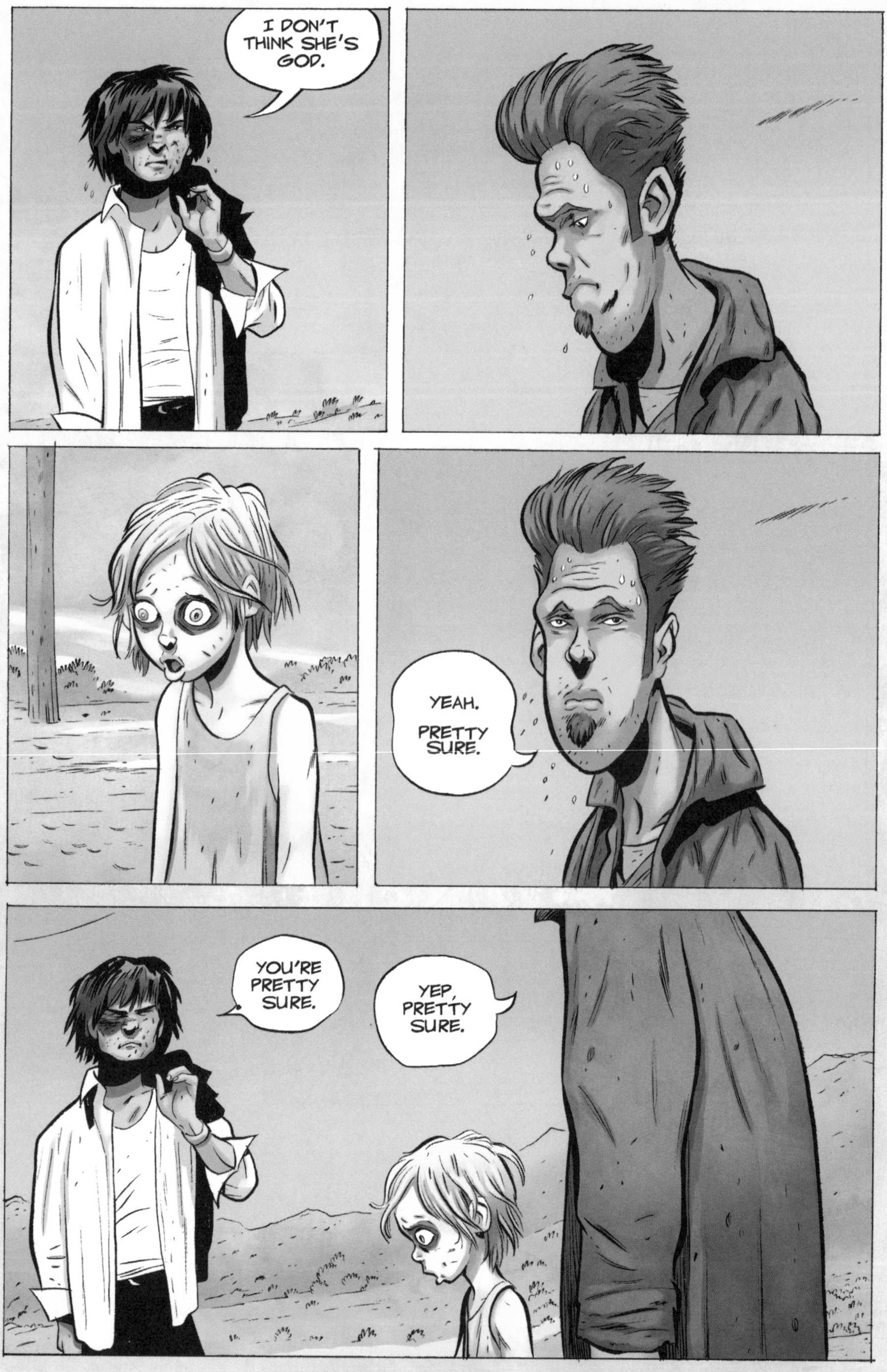
I DON'T THINK SHE'S GOD.
YEAH.
PRETTY SURE.
YOU'RE PRETTY SURE.
YEP, PRETTY SURE.

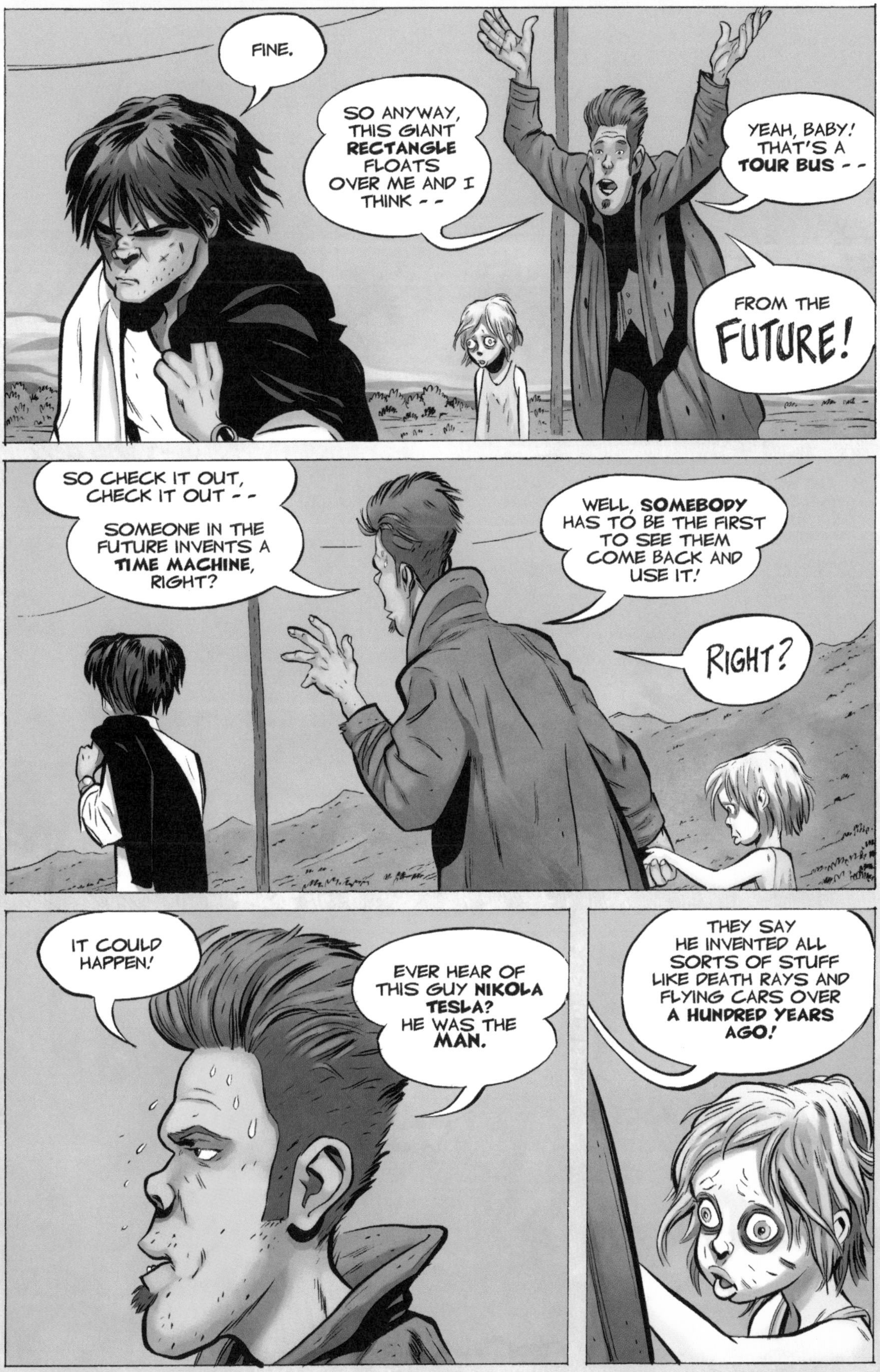
FINE.
SO ANYWAY, THIS GIANT RECTANGLE FLOATS OVER ME AND I THINK - -
YEAH, BABY! THAT'S A TOUR BUS - -
FROM THE FUTURE!
SO CHECK IT OUT, CHECK IT OUT - -
SOMEONE IN THE FUTURE INVENTS A TIME MACHINE, RIGHT?
WELL, SOMEBODY HAS TO BE THE FIRST TO SEE THEM COME BACK AND USE IT!
RIGHT?
IT COULD HAPPEN!
EVER HEAR OF THIS GUY NIKOLA TESLA? HE WAS THE MAN.
THEY SAY HE INVENTED ALL SORTS OF STUFF LIKE DEATH RAYS AND FLYING CARS OVER A HUNDRED YEARS AGO!

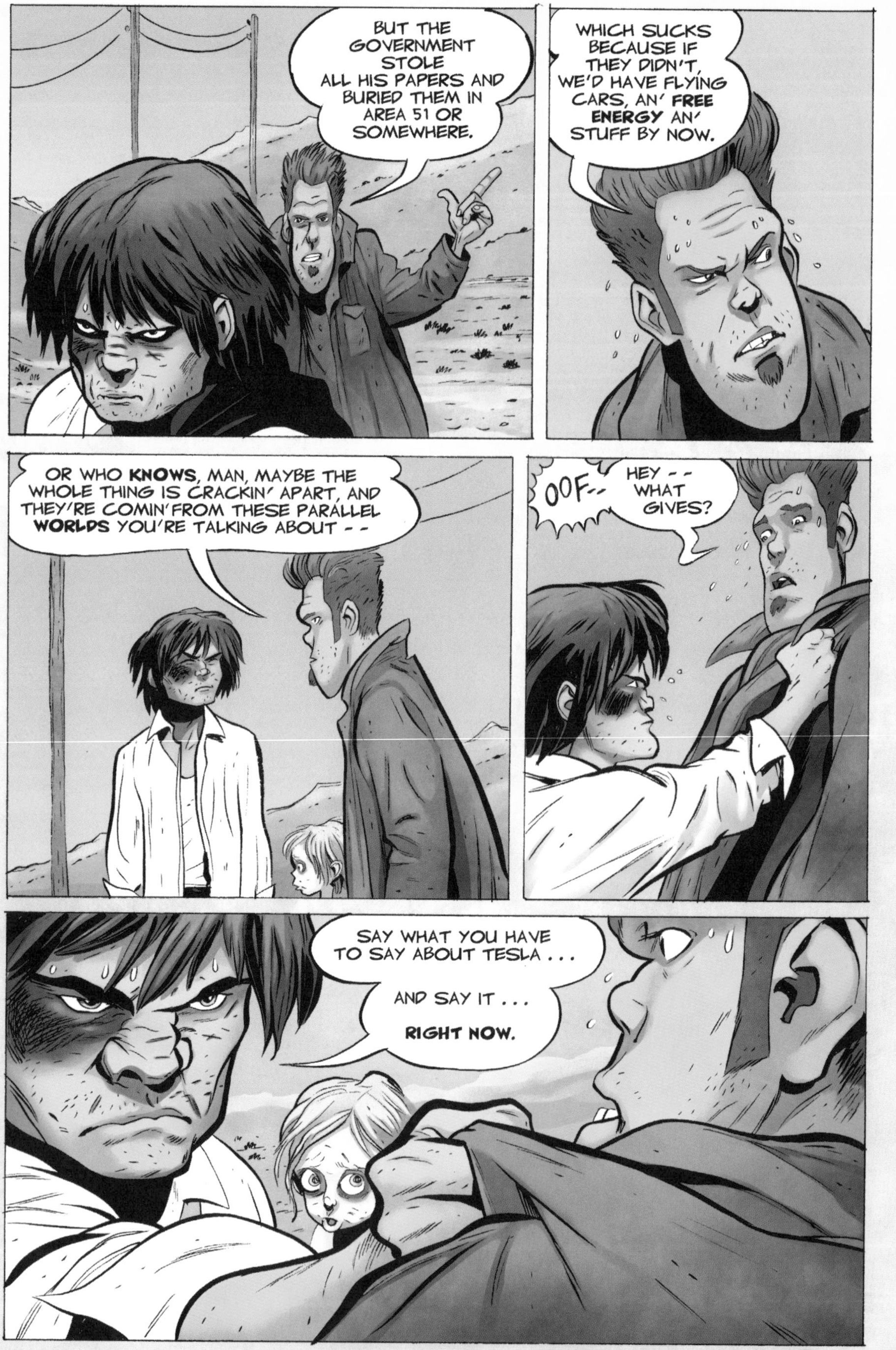
BUT THE GOVERNMENT STOLE ALL HIS PAPERS AND BURIED THEM IN AREA 51 OR SOMEWHERE.
WHICH SUCKS BECAUSE IF THEY DIDN'T, WE'D HAVE FLYING CARS, AN' FREE ENERGY AN' STUFF BY NOW.
OR WHO KNOWS, MAN, MAYBE THE WHOLE THING IS CRACKIN' APART, AND THEY'RE COMIN' FROM THESE PARALLEL WORLDS YOU'RE TALKING ABOUT --
OOF--
HEY -- WHAT GIVES?
SAY WHAT YOU HAVE TO SAY ABOUT TESLA . . .
AND SAY IT . . .
RIGHT NOW.

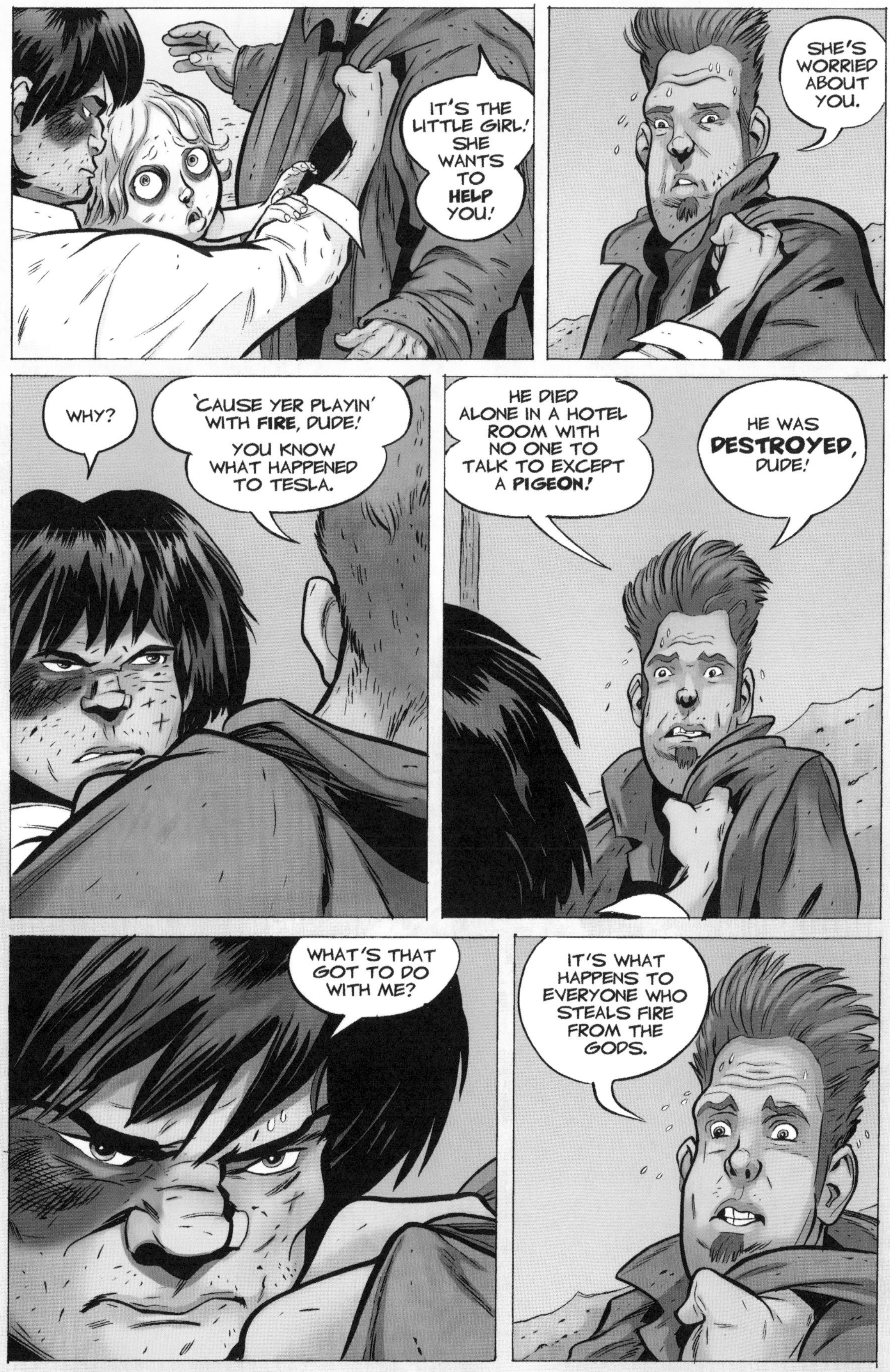
IT'S THE LITTLE GIRL! SHE WANTS TO HELP YOU!
SHE'S WORRIED ABOUT YOU.
WHY?
'CAUSE YER PLAYIN' WITH FIRE, DUDE!
YOU KNOW WHAT HAPPENED TO TESLA.
HE DIED ALONE IN A HOTEL ROOM WITH NO ONE TO TALK TO EXCEPT A PIGEON!
HE WAS DESTROYED, DUDE!
WHAT'S THAT GOT TO DO WITH ME?
IT'S WHAT HAPPENS TO EVERYONE WHO STEALS FIRE FROM THE GODS.

HMM.

THAT DRAWING YOU MADE IN THE SAND...

TWO INTERSECTING CIRCLES. I'VE SEEN IT BEFORE -- IN **TESLA'S** JOURNALS.

IT'S PART OF HIS UNIFIED FIELD THEORY.

THE OUTER AREAS REPRESENT TWO CLOUDS COMPOSED OF MANY DIMENSIONS.

IN THE MIDDLE LIES OUR UNIVERSE WITH ITS **THREE** DIMENSIONS.

THE 3-D WORLD IS CREATED AND POWERED BY THE INTERACTIONS OF THE HIGHER DIMENSIONAL CLOUDS --

HE WROTE BENEATH IT: "ALL ENERGY COMES FROM OUTER DIMENSIONS AND IS PERVASIVE THROUGHOUT."

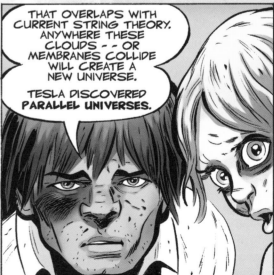

THAT OVERLAPS WITH CURRENT STRING THEORY. ANYWHERE THESE CLOUDS -- OR MEMBRANES COLLIDE WILL CREATE A NEW UNIVERSE.

TESLA DISCOVERED **PARALLEL UNIVERSES.**

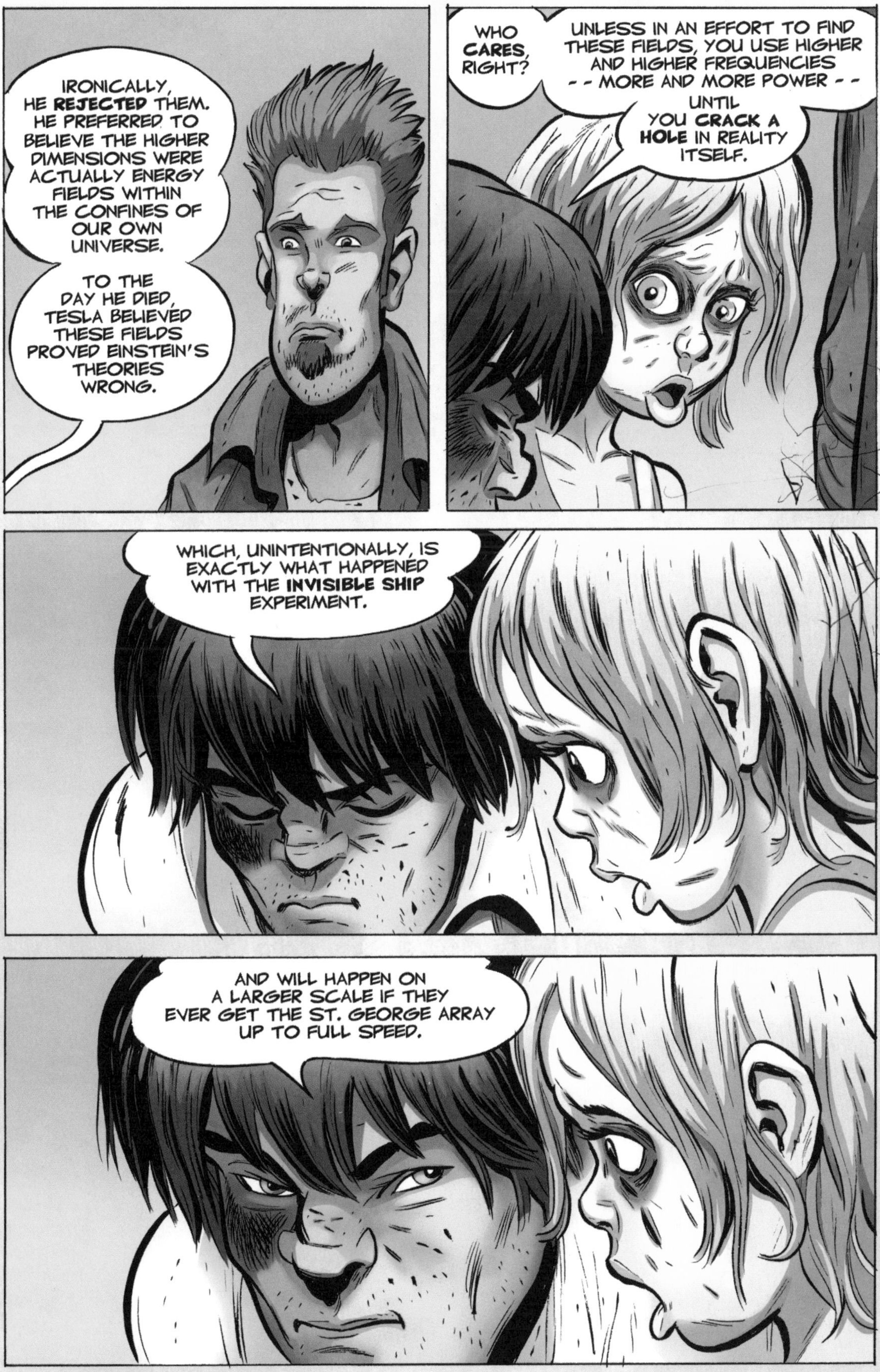
IRONICALLY, HE REJECTED THEM. HE PREFERRED TO BELIEVE THE HIGHER DIMENSIONS WERE ACTUALLY ENERGY FIELDS WITHIN THE CONFINES OF OUR OWN UNIVERSE.
TO THE DAY HE DIED, TESLA BELIEVED THESE FIELDS PROVED EINSTEIN'S THEORIES WRONG.
WHO CARES, RIGHT?
UNLESS IN AN EFFORT TO FIND THESE FIELDS, YOU USE HIGHER AND HIGHER FREQUENCIES - - MORE AND MORE POWER - -
UNTIL YOU CRACK A HOLE IN REALITY ITSELF.
WHICH, UNINTENTIONALLY, IS EXACTLY WHAT HAPPENED WITH THE INVISIBLE SHIP EXPERIMENT.
AND WILL HAPPEN ON A LARGER SCALE IF THEY EVER GET THE ST. GEORGE ARRAY UP TO FULL SPEED.

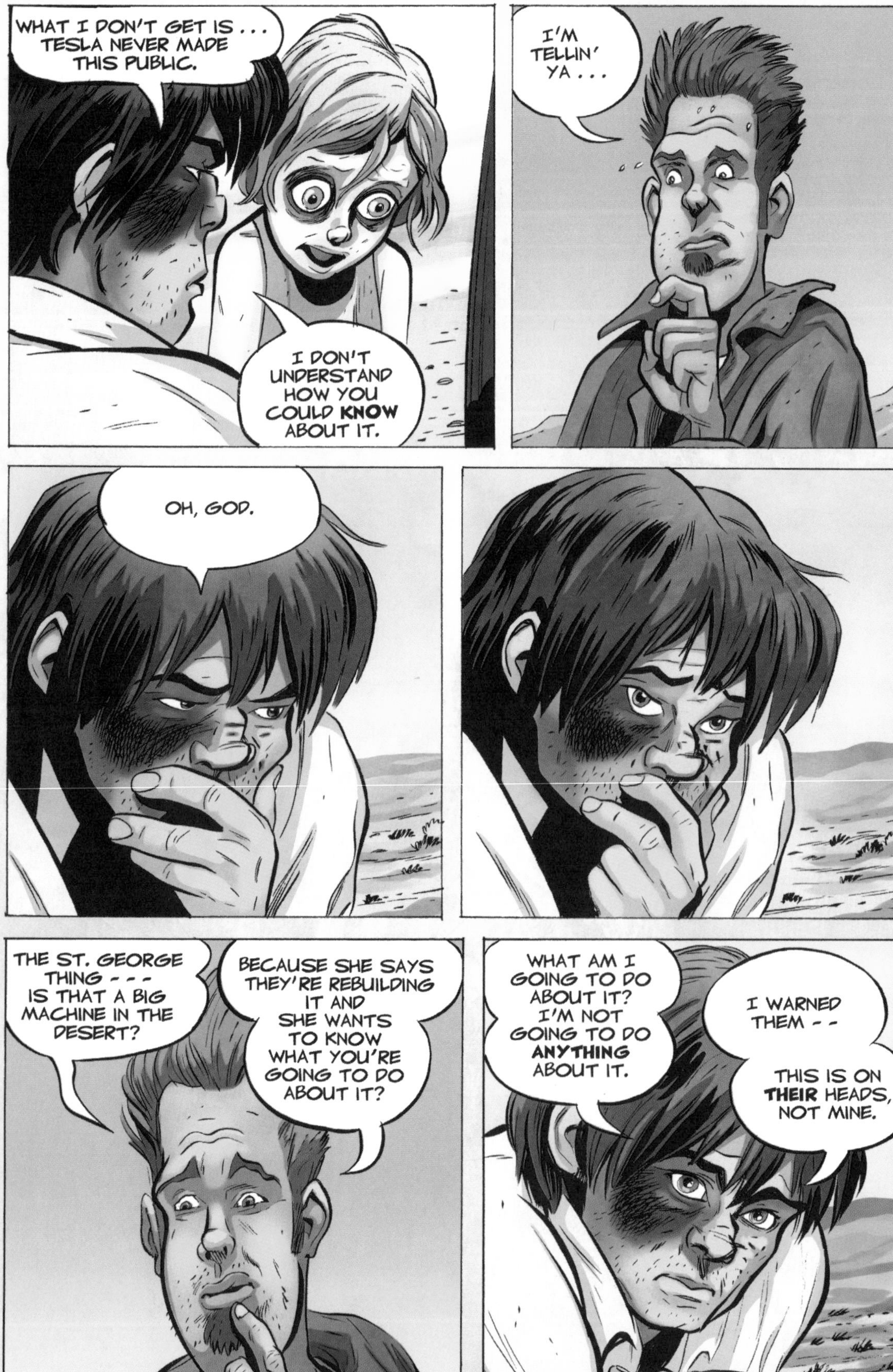
WHAT I DON'T GET IS . . . TESLA NEVER MADE THIS PUBLIC.
I DON'T UNDERSTAND HOW YOU COULD **KNOW** ABOUT IT.
I'M TELLIN' YA . . .
OH, GOD.
THE ST. GEORGE THING - - - IS THAT A BIG MACHINE IN THE DESERT?
BECAUSE SHE SAYS THEY'RE REBUILDING IT AND SHE WANTS TO KNOW WHAT YOU'RE GOING TO DO ABOUT IT?
WHAT AM I GOING TO DO ABOUT IT? I'M NOT GOING TO DO **ANYTHING** ABOUT IT.
I WARNED THEM - -
THIS IS ON **THEIR** HEADS, NOT MINE.

SO, WHAT ARE YOU GOING TO DO NOW?

WHAT I SHOULD'VE DONE THE MINUTE I GOT MY MONEY FROM PAULY.

GO STRAIGHT BACK TO THE WORLD ANNIE IS ON, INSTEAD OF GETTING DRUNK IN THE DAMN BAR.

ONCE I GET THERE, WE'RE GOING SO DEEP INTO THE DRIFT, NO ONE WILL EVER FIND US.

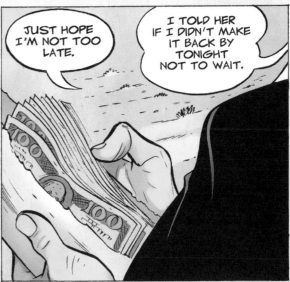

JUST HOPE I'M NOT TOO LATE.

I TOLD HER IF I DIDN'T MAKE IT BACK BY TONIGHT NOT TO WAIT.

I GAINED A FEW HOURS WHEN I DRIFTED HERE, BUT I COULD EASILY LOSE SOME WHEN I GO BACK. DAMN IT.

STUPID --

CARELESS --

I'M SORRY, ANNIE.

WAIT-- WHAT'S THE PLAN?

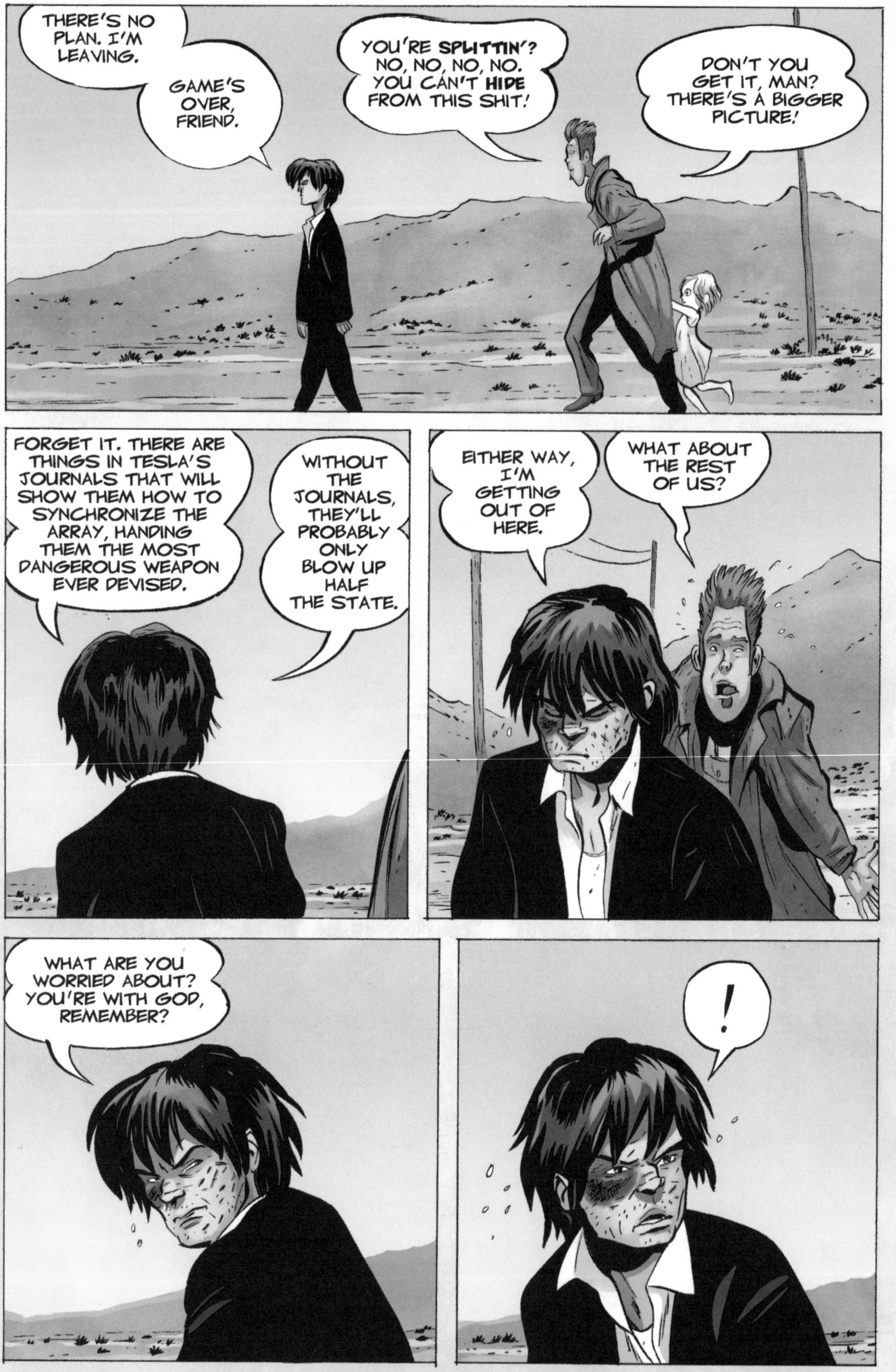
THERE'S NO PLAN. I'M LEAVING.
GAME'S OVER, FRIEND.
YOU'RE SPLITTIN'? NO, NO, NO, NO. YOU CAN'T HIDE FROM THIS SHIT!
DON'T YOU GET IT, MAN? THERE'S A BIGGER PICTURE!
FORGET IT. THERE ARE THINGS IN TESLA'S JOURNALS THAT WILL SHOW THEM HOW TO SYNCHRONIZE THE ARRAY, HANDING THEM THE MOST DANGEROUS WEAPON EVER DEVISED.
WITHOUT THE JOURNALS, THEY'LL PROBABLY ONLY BLOW UP HALF THE STATE.
EITHER WAY, I'M GETTING OUT OF HERE.
WHAT ABOUT THE REST OF US?
WHAT ARE YOU WORRIED ABOUT? YOU'RE WITH GOD, REMEMBER?
!

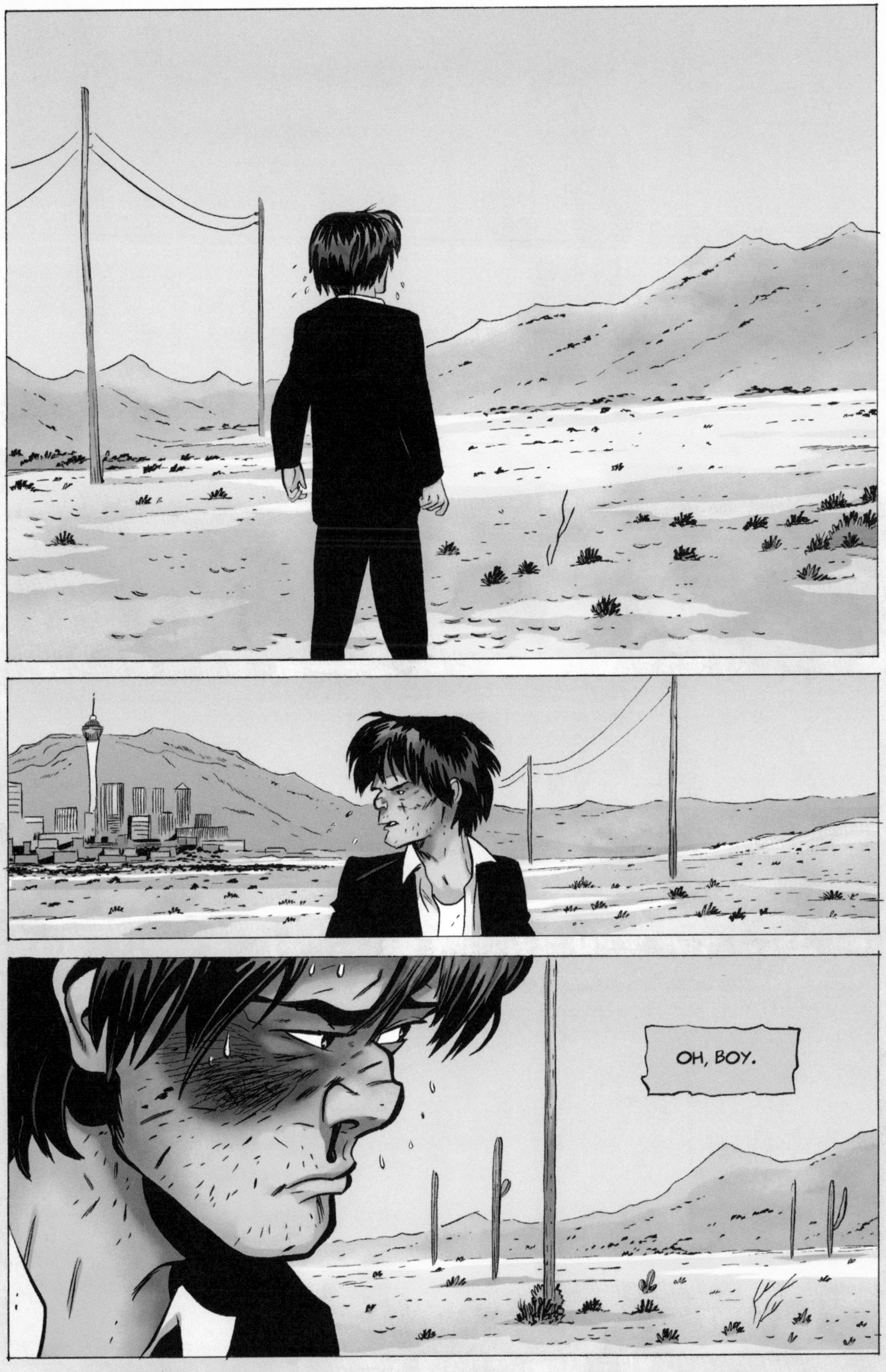
OH, BOY.

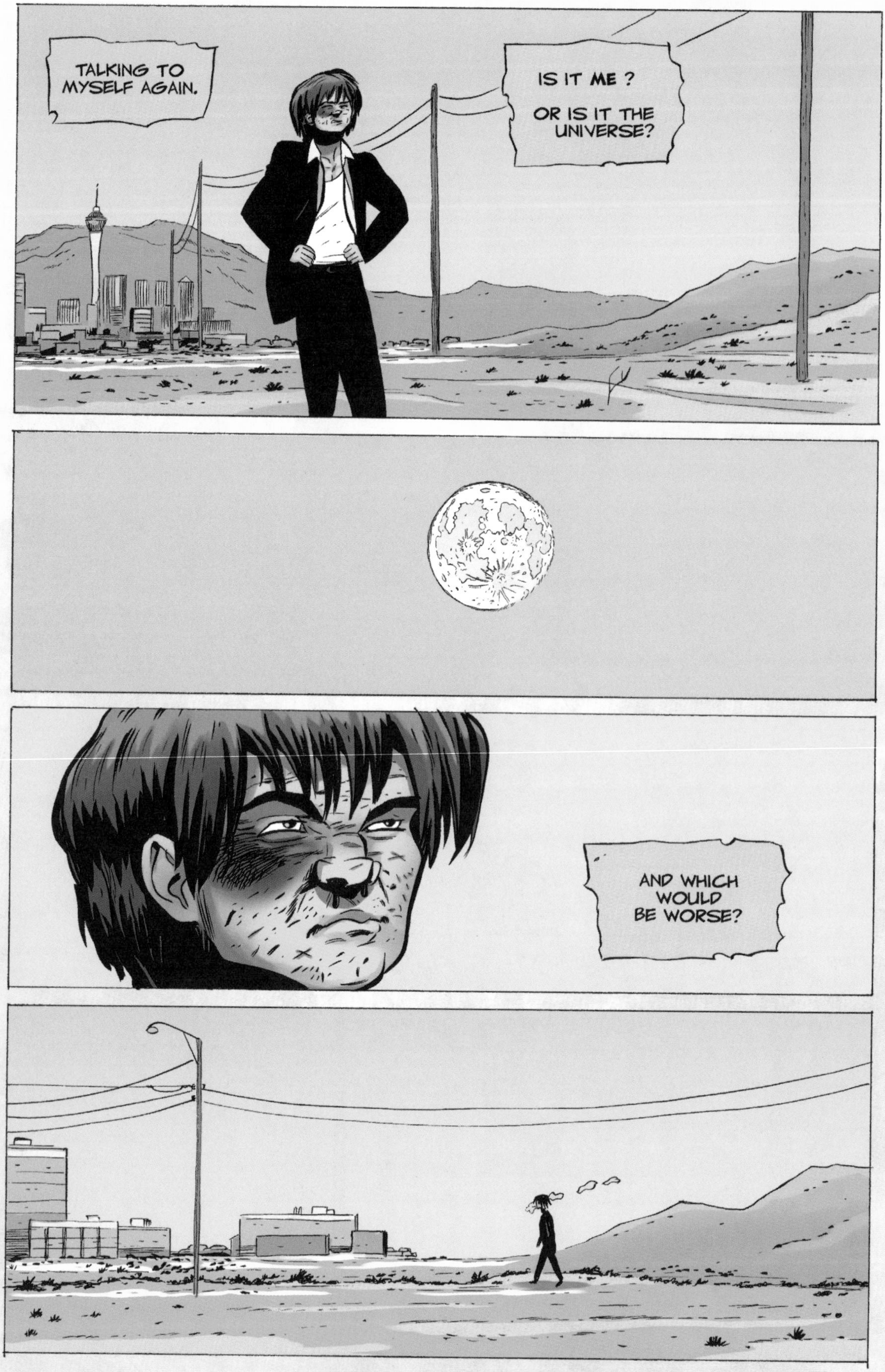
TALKING TO MYSELF AGAIN.
IS IT ME ?
OR IS IT THE UNIVERSE?
AND WHICH WOULD BE WORSE?

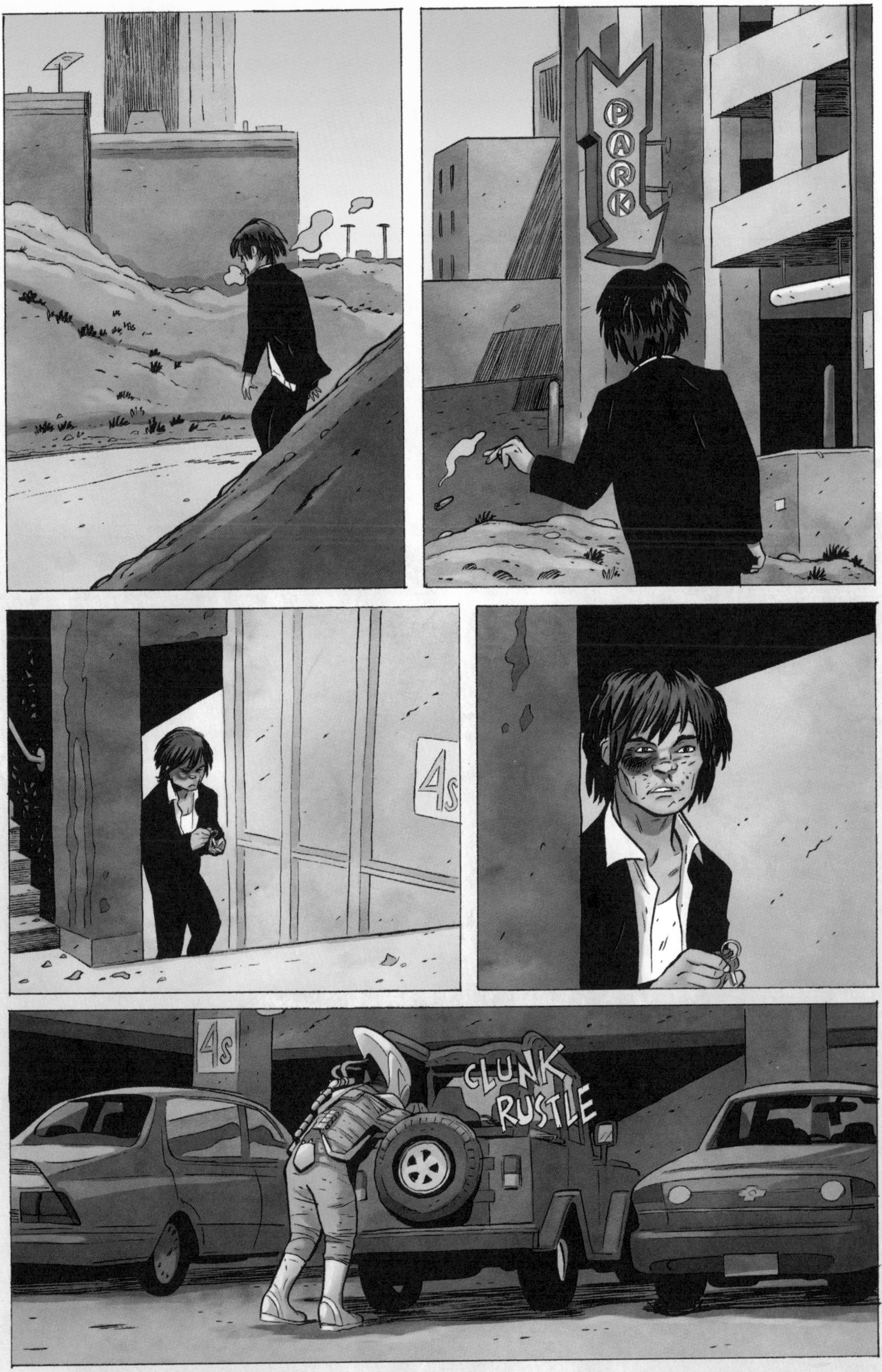
PARK
4s
4s
CLUNK
RUSTLE

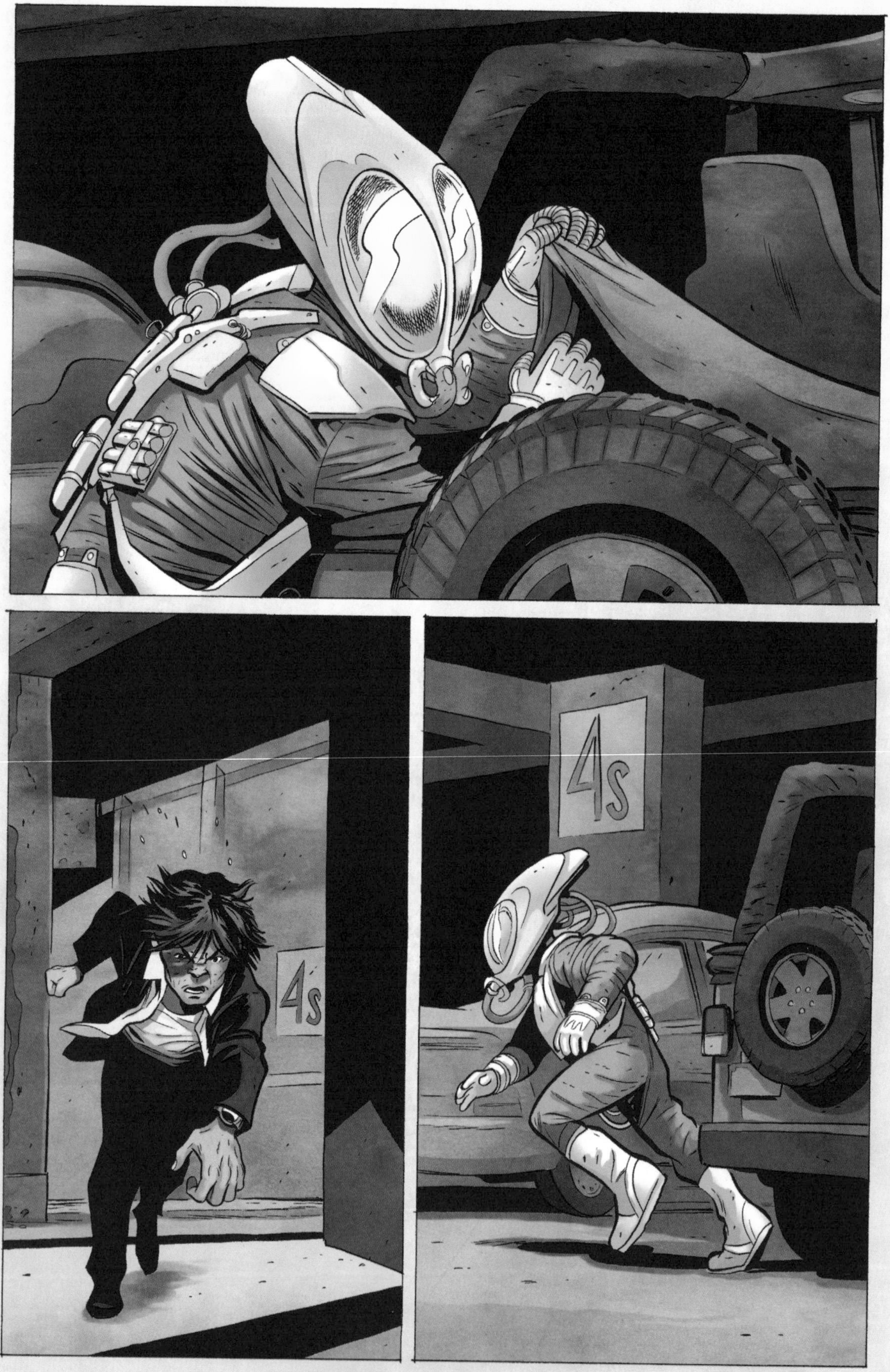
4s
4s

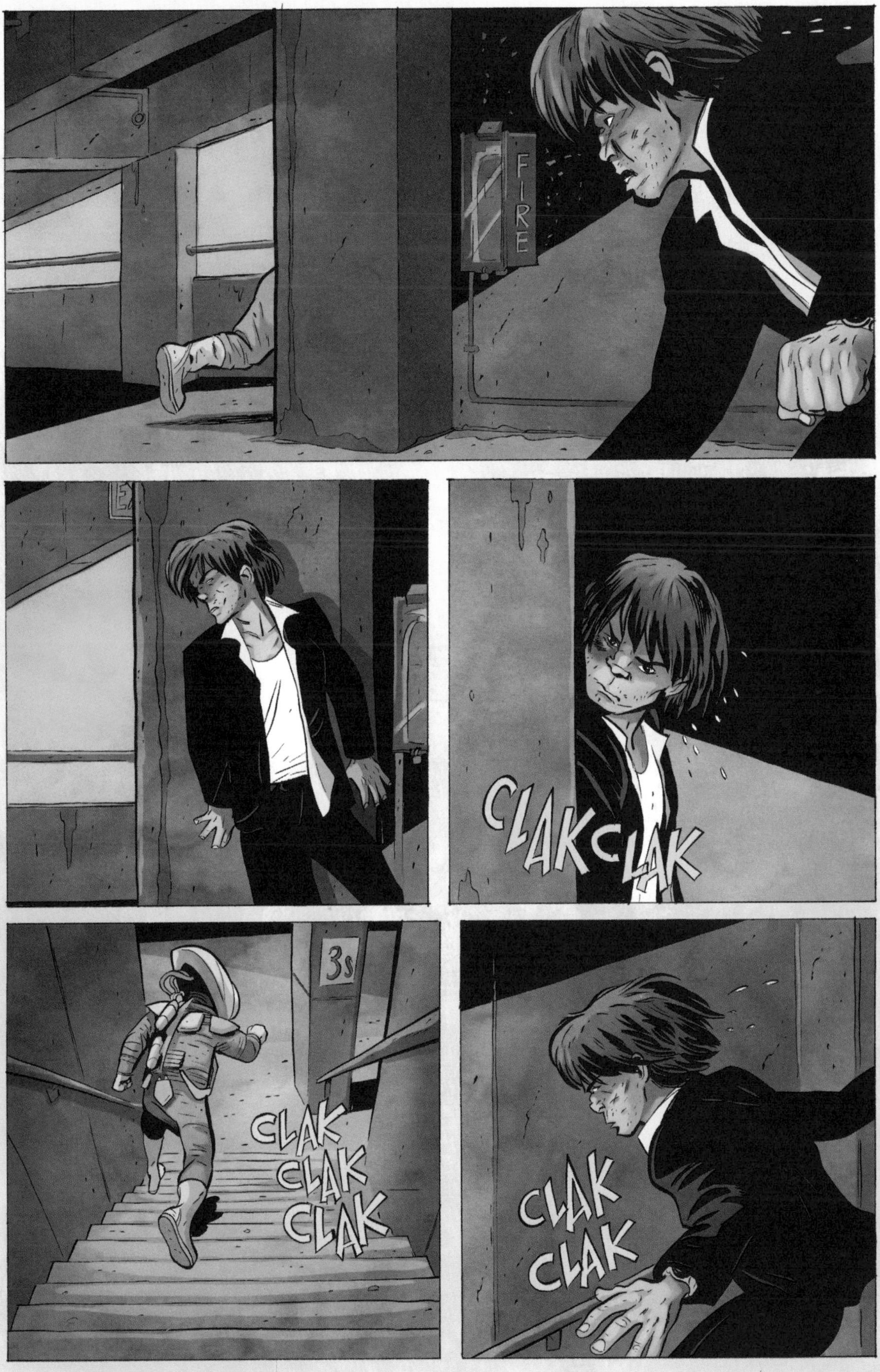
FIRE
CLAKCLAK
3s
CLAK
CLAK
CLAK
CLAK
CLAK

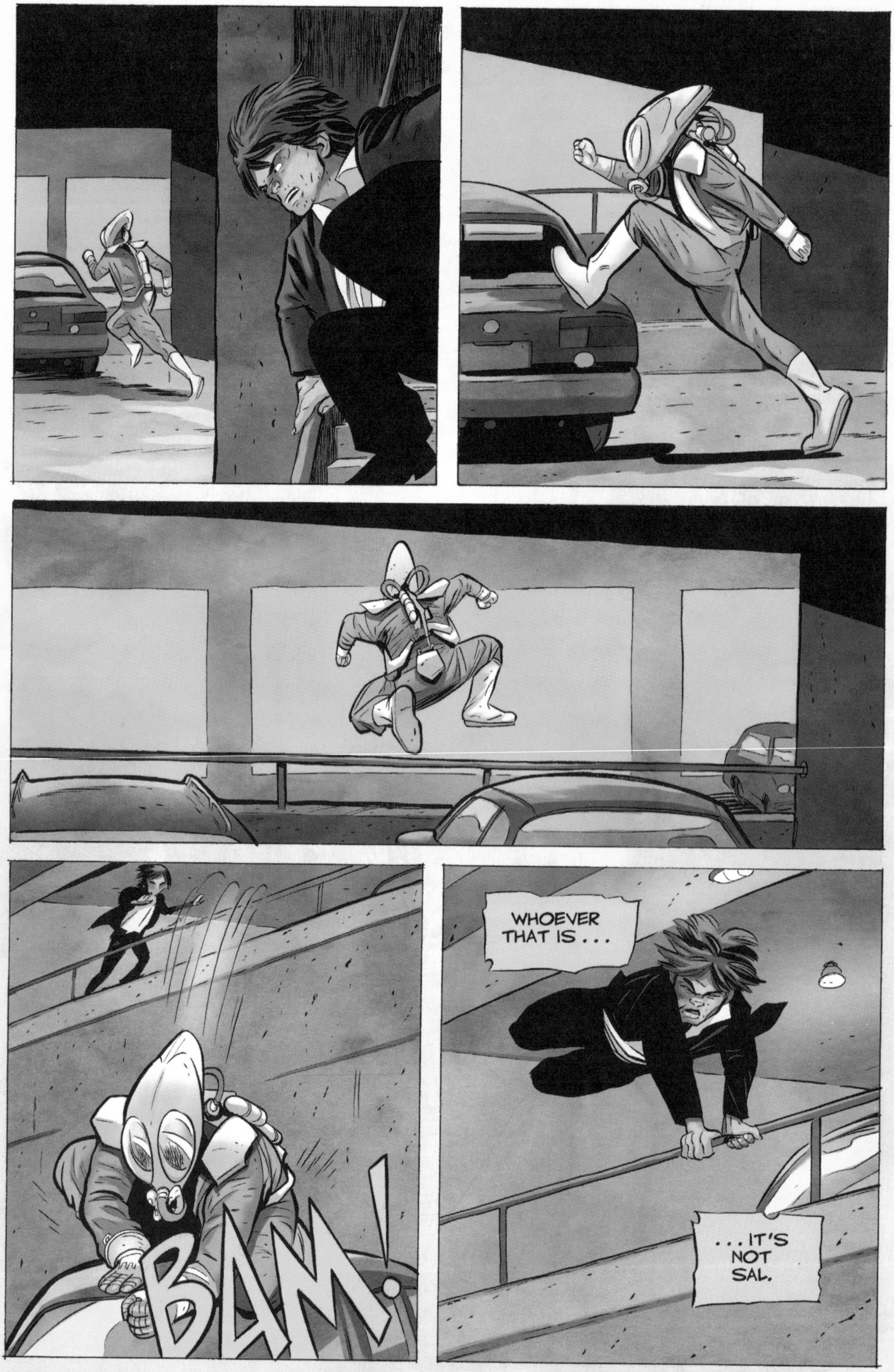
BAM!
WHOEVER THAT IS . . .
. . . IT'S NOT SAL.

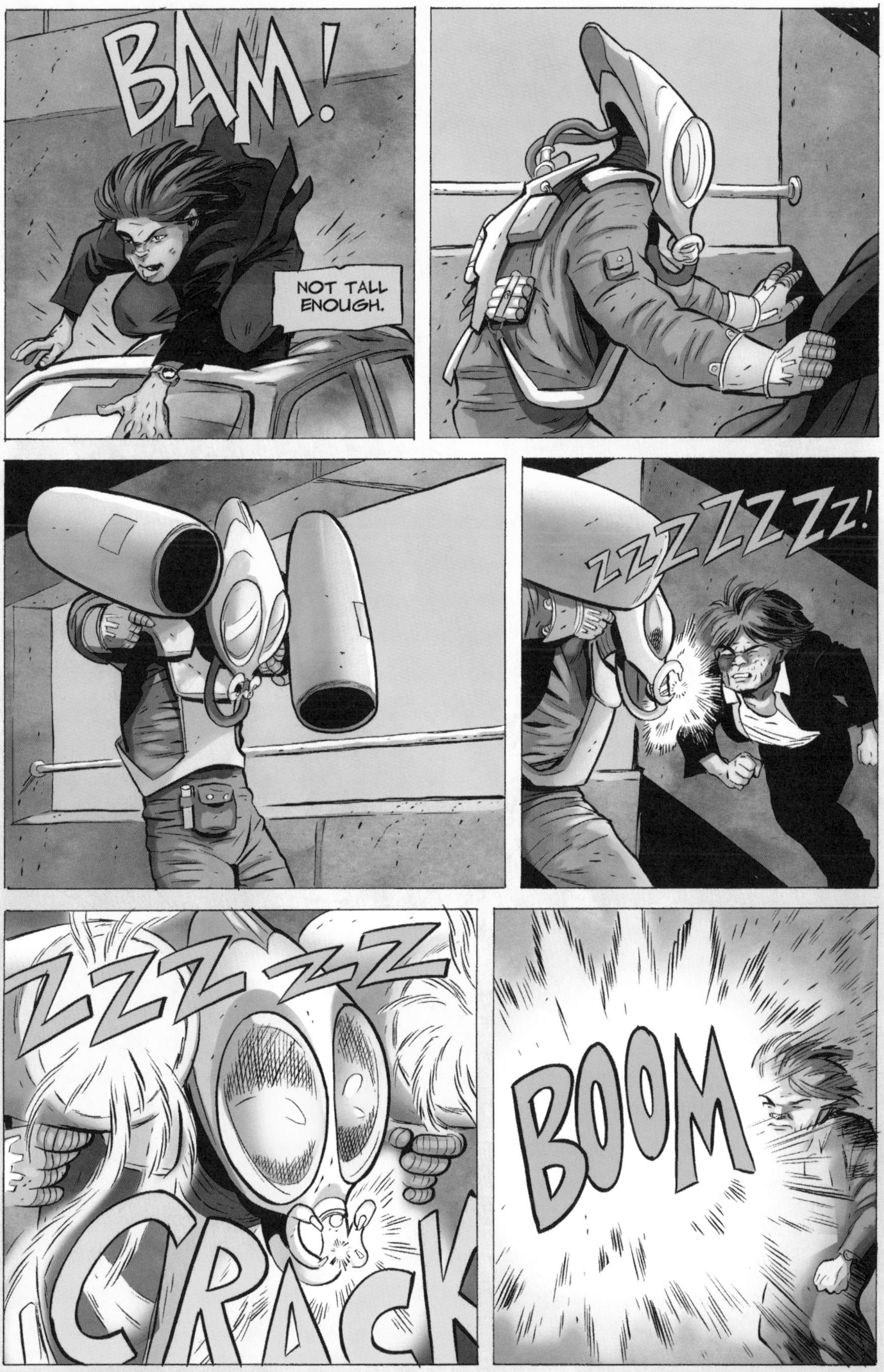
BAM!
NOT TALL ENOUGH.
ZZZZZZZZz!
ZZZZZZ
CRACK
BOOM

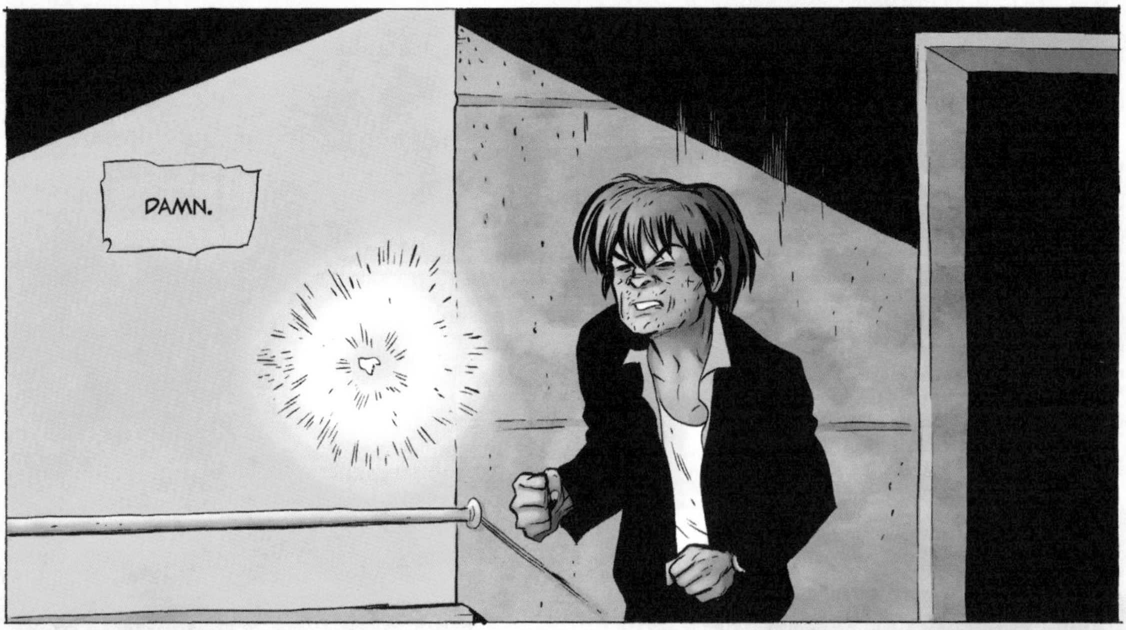
DAMN.

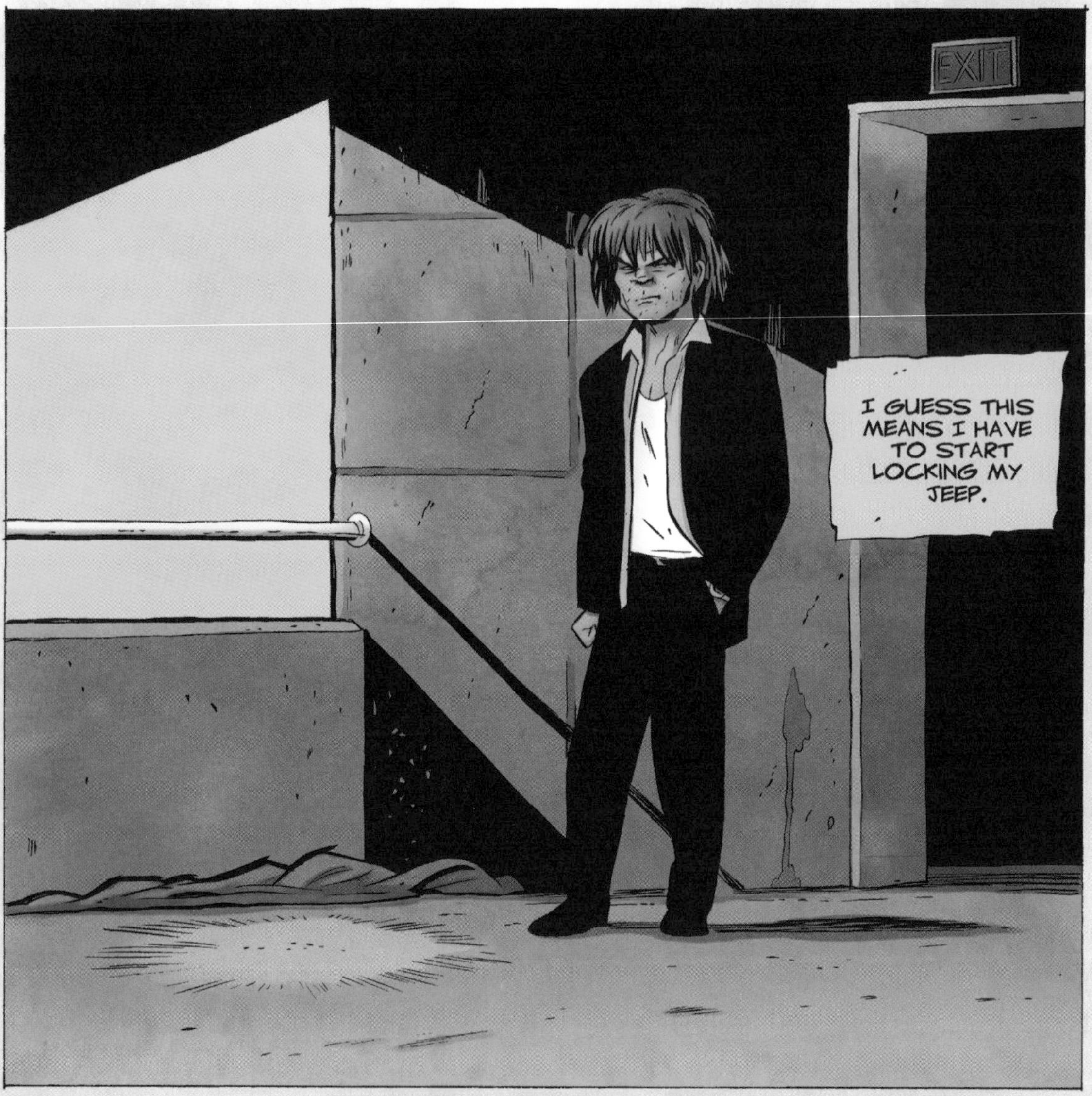
EXIT
I GUESS THIS MEANS I HAVE TO START LOCKING MY JEEP.

X

BEST LAID PLANS

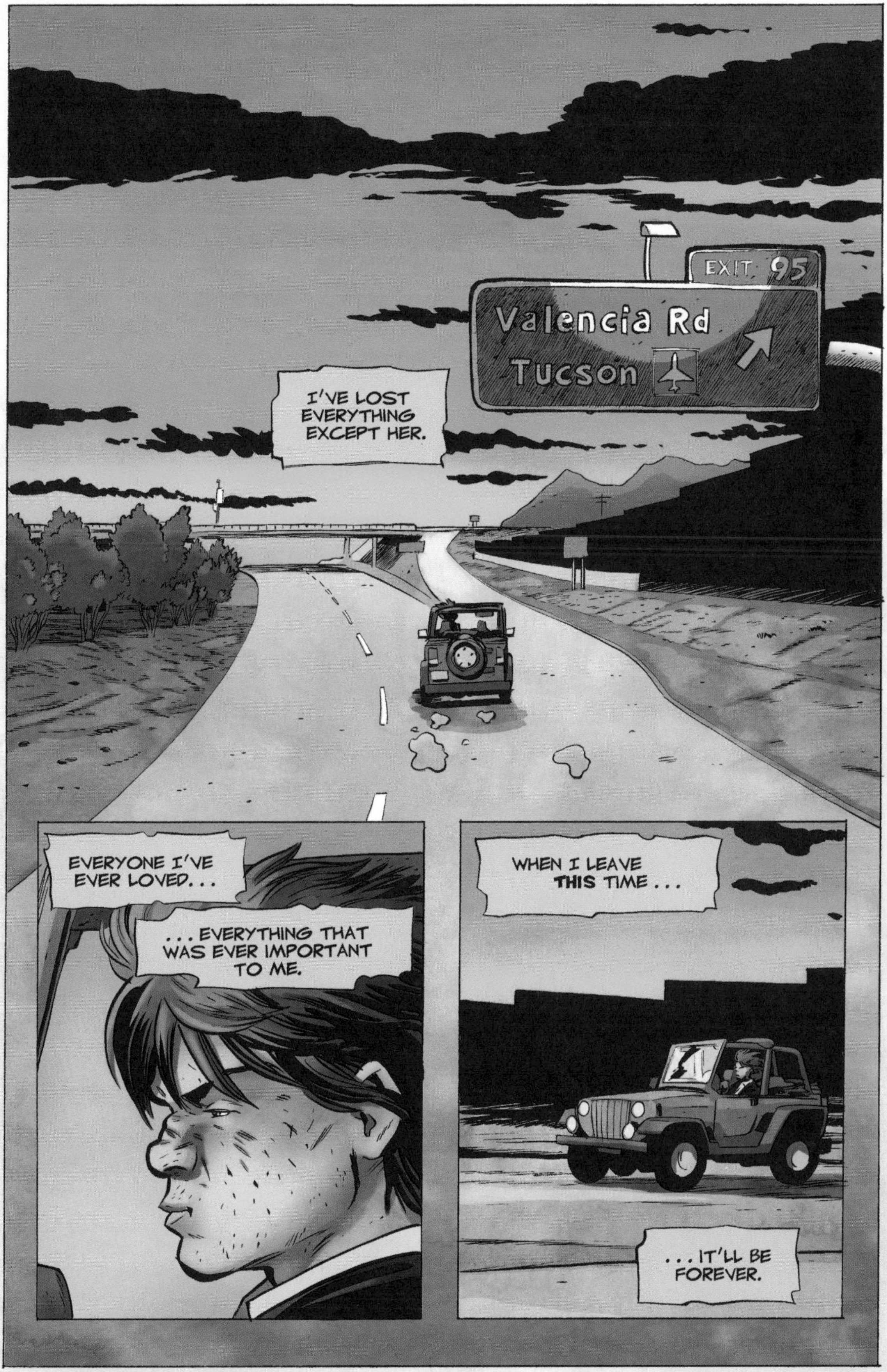
EXIT 95
Valencia Rd
Tucson
I'VE LOST EVERYTHING EXCEPT HER.
EVERYONE I'VE EVER LOVED...
...EVERYTHING THAT WAS EVER IMPORTANT TO ME.
WHEN I LEAVE **THIS** TIME...
...IT'LL BE FOREVER.

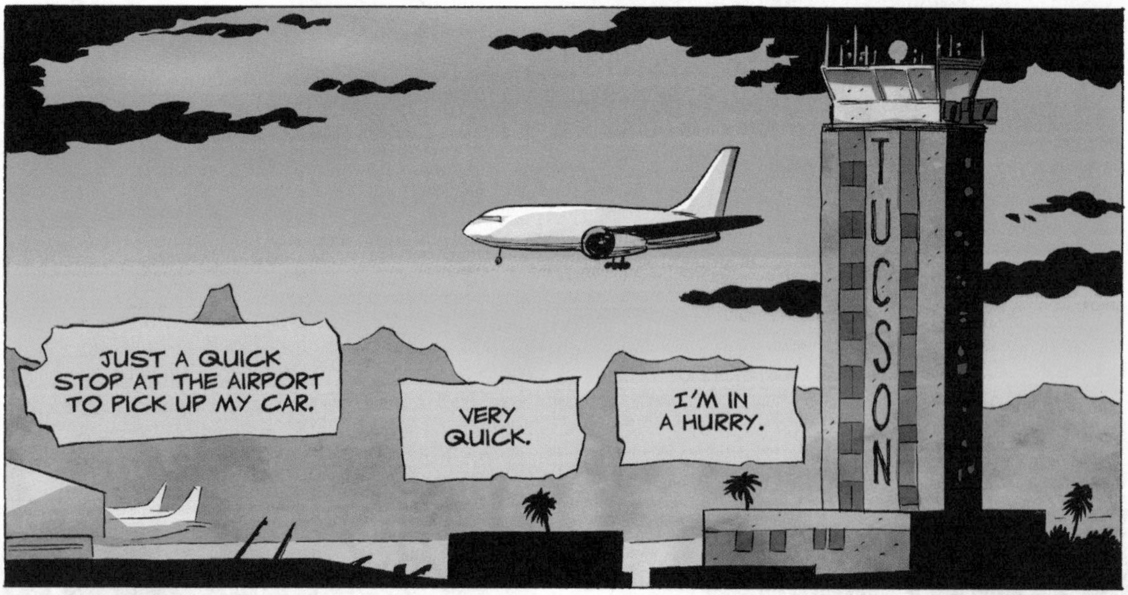
TUCSON
JUST A QUICK STOP AT THE AIRPORT TO PICK UP MY CAR.
VERY QUICK.
I'M IN A HURRY.

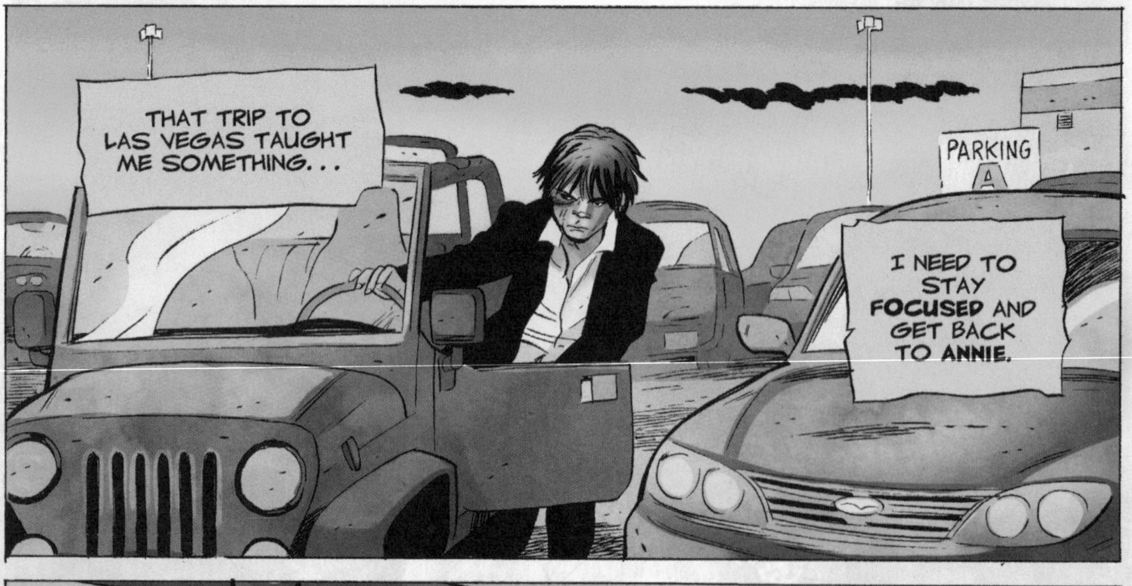
THAT TRIP TO LAS VEGAS TAUGHT ME SOMETHING. . .
PARKING A
I NEED TO STAY FOCUSED AND GET BACK TO ANNIE.

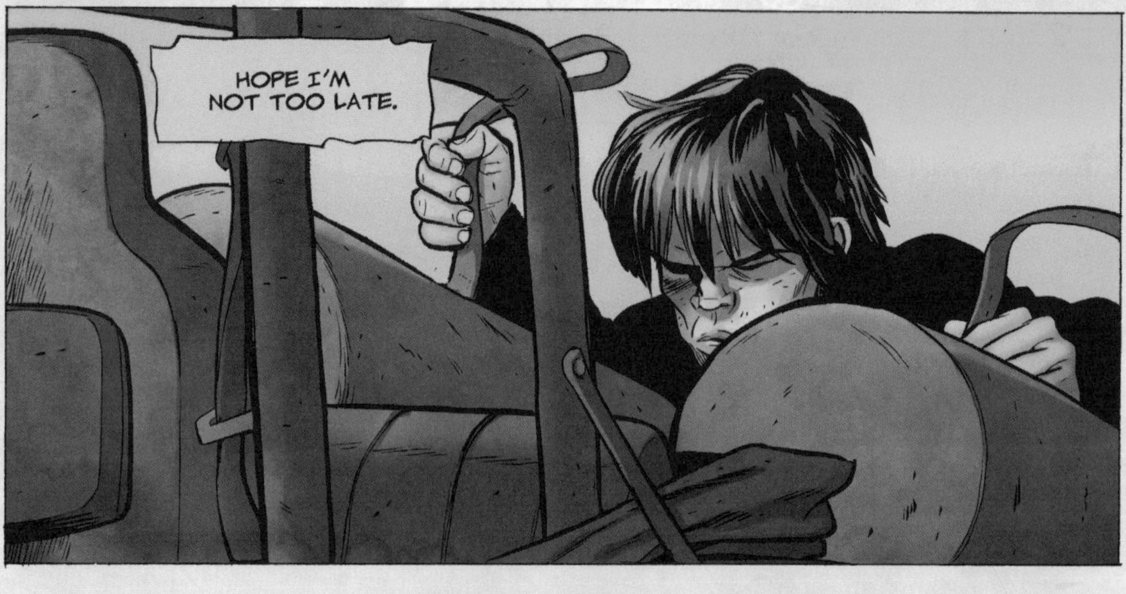
HOPE I'M NOT TOO LATE.

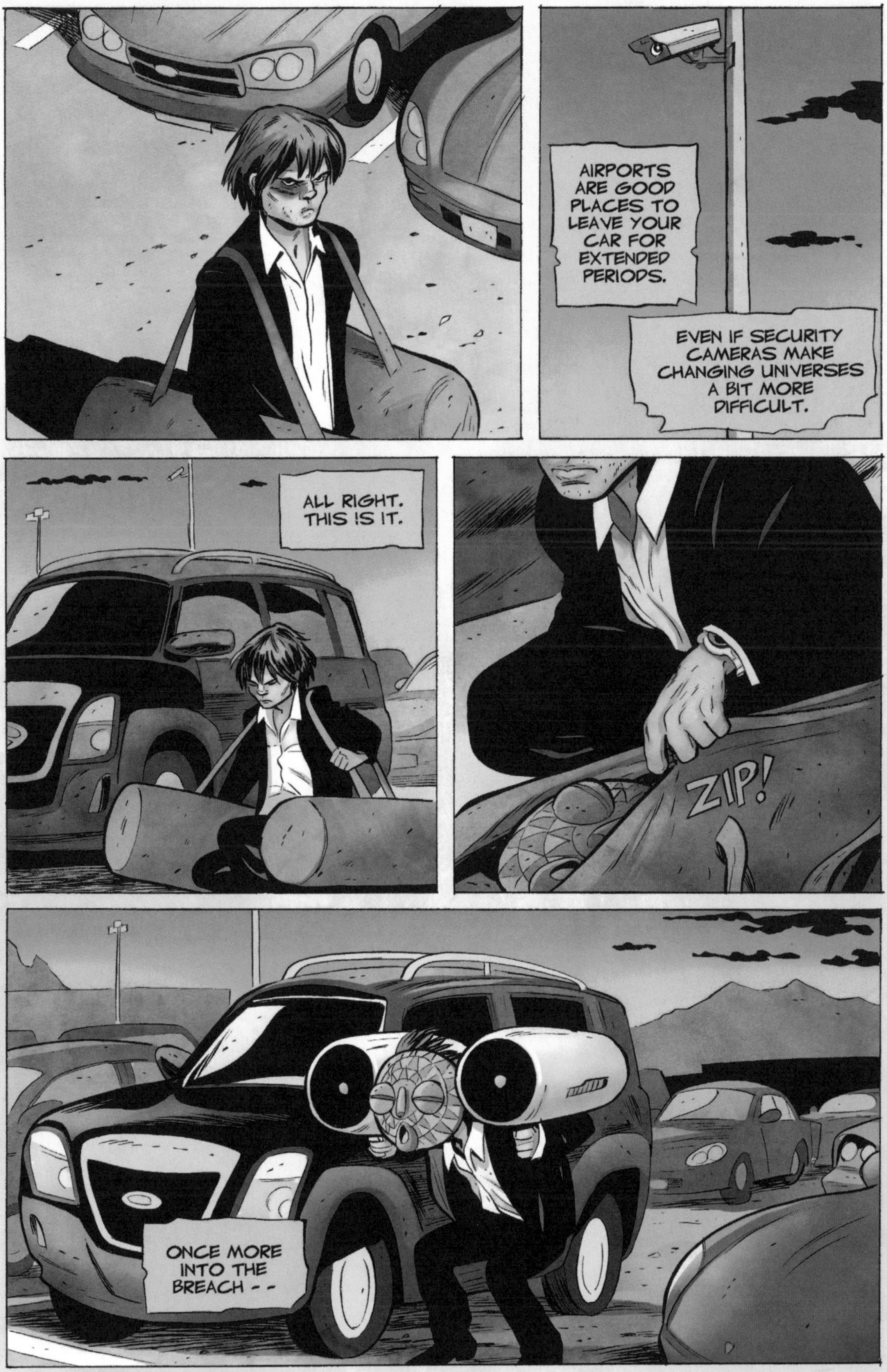
AIRPORTS ARE GOOD PLACES TO LEAVE YOUR CAR FOR EXTENDED PERIODS.
EVEN IF SECURITY CAMERAS MAKE CHANGING UNIVERSES A BIT MORE DIFFICULT.
ALL RIGHT. THIS IS IT.
ZIP!
ONCE MORE INTO THE BREACH --

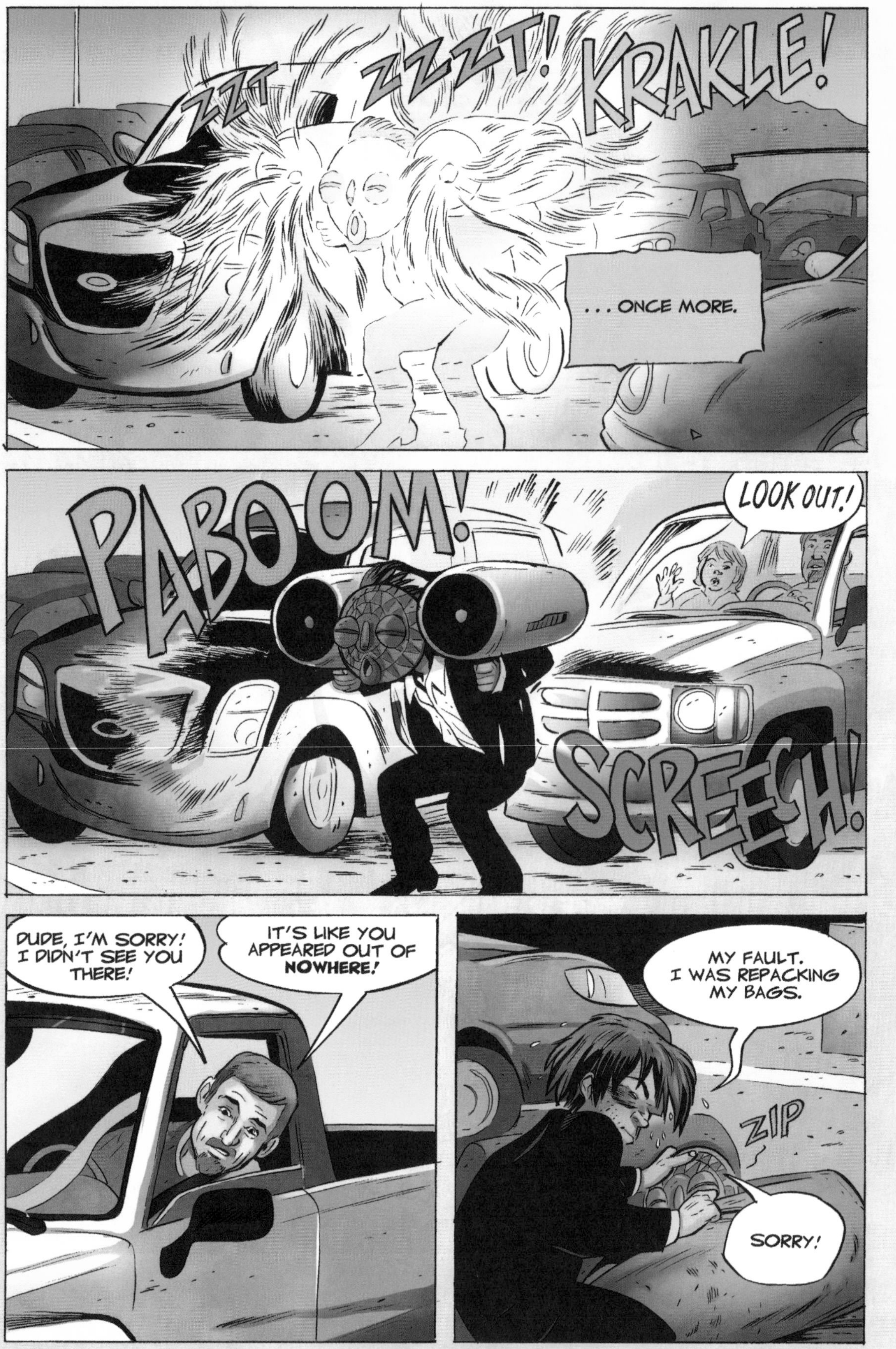
ZZZT
ZZZZT!
KRAKLE!
. . . ONCE MORE.
PABOOM!
LOOK OUT!
SCREECH!
DUDE, I'M SORRY! I DIDN'T SEE YOU THERE!
IT'S LIKE YOU APPEARED OUT OF **NOWHERE!**
MY FAULT. I WAS REPACKING MY BAGS.
ZIP
SORRY!

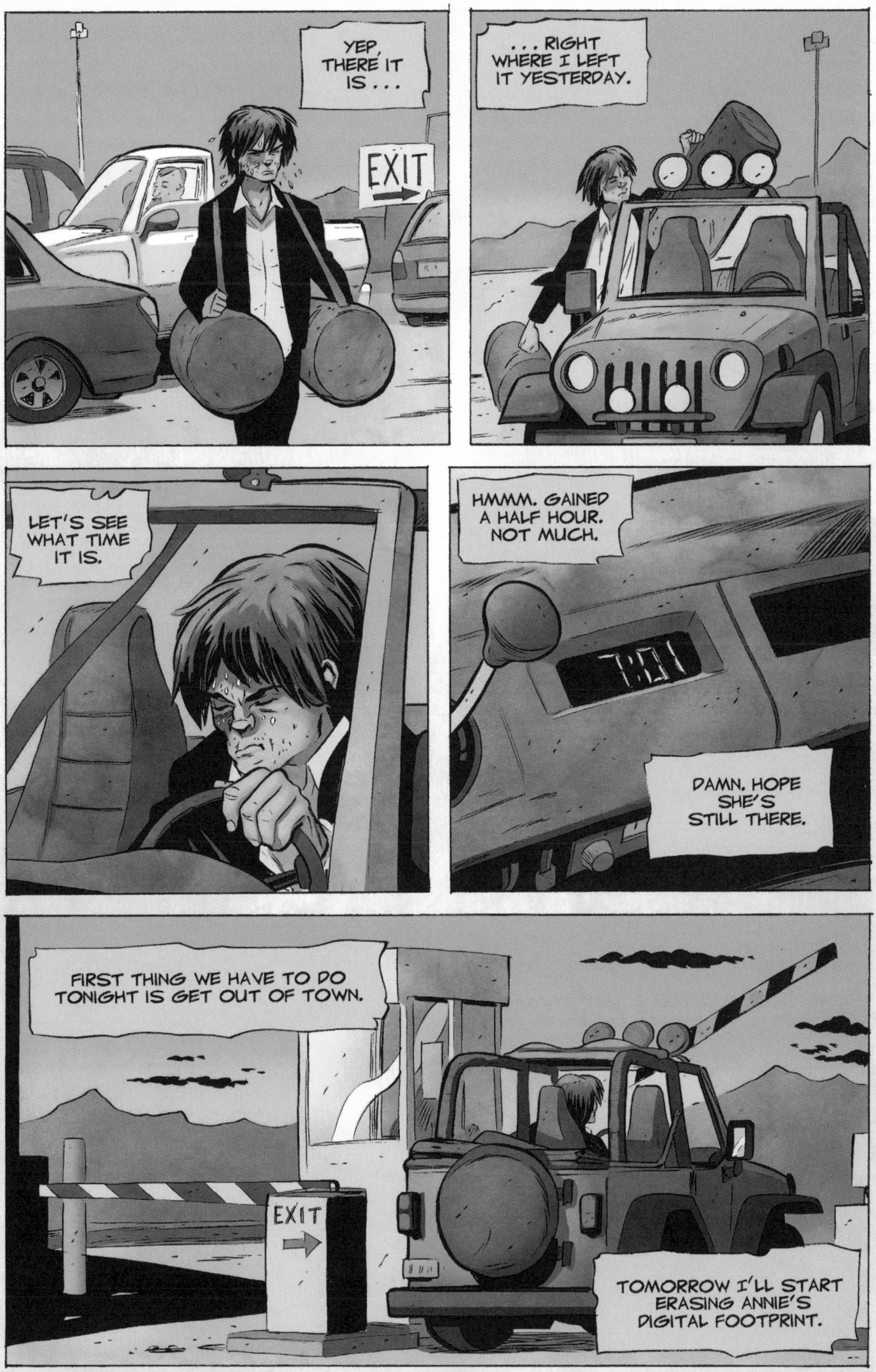
YEP, THERE IT IS . . .
EXIT
. . . RIGHT WHERE I LEFT IT YESTERDAY.
LET'S SEE WHAT TIME IT IS.
HMMM. GAINED A HALF HOUR. NOT MUCH.
7:31
DAMN. HOPE SHE'S STILL THERE.
FIRST THING WE HAVE TO DO TONIGHT IS GET OUT OF TOWN.
EXIT
TOMORROW I'LL START ERASING ANNIE'S DIGITAL FOOTPRINT.

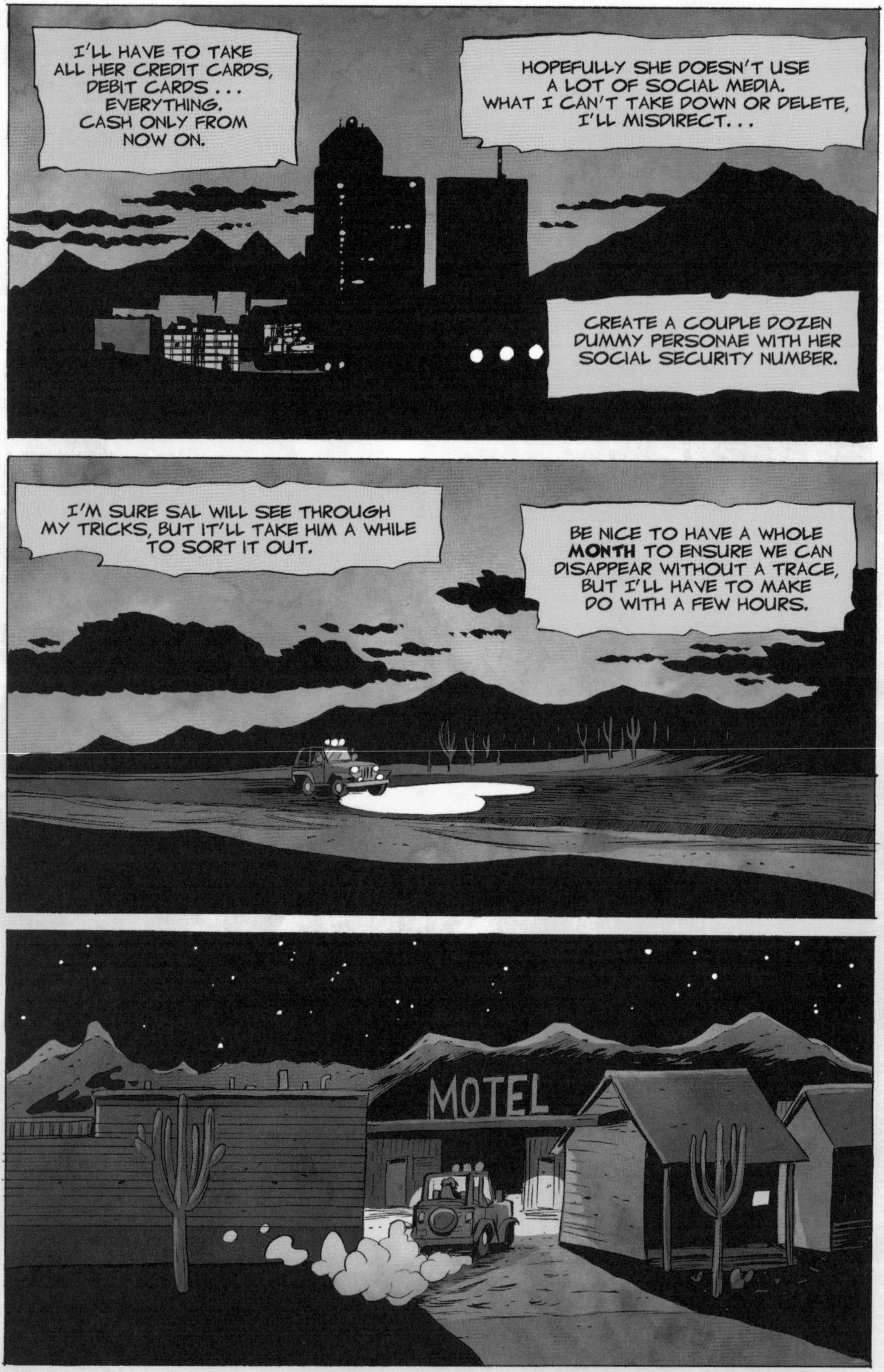
I'LL HAVE TO TAKE ALL HER CREDIT CARDS, DEBIT CARDS . . . EVERYTHING. CASH ONLY FROM NOW ON.
HOPEFULLY SHE DOESN'T USE A LOT OF SOCIAL MEDIA. WHAT I CAN'T TAKE DOWN OR DELETE, I'LL MISDIRECT . . .
CREATE A COUPLE DOZEN DUMMY PERSONAE WITH HER SOCIAL SECURITY NUMBER.
I'M SURE SAL WILL SEE THROUGH MY TRICKS, BUT IT'LL TAKE HIM A WHILE TO SORT IT OUT.
BE NICE TO HAVE A WHOLE **MONTH** TO ENSURE WE CAN DISAPPEAR WITHOUT A TRACE, BUT I'LL HAVE TO MAKE DO WITH A FEW HOURS.
MOTEL

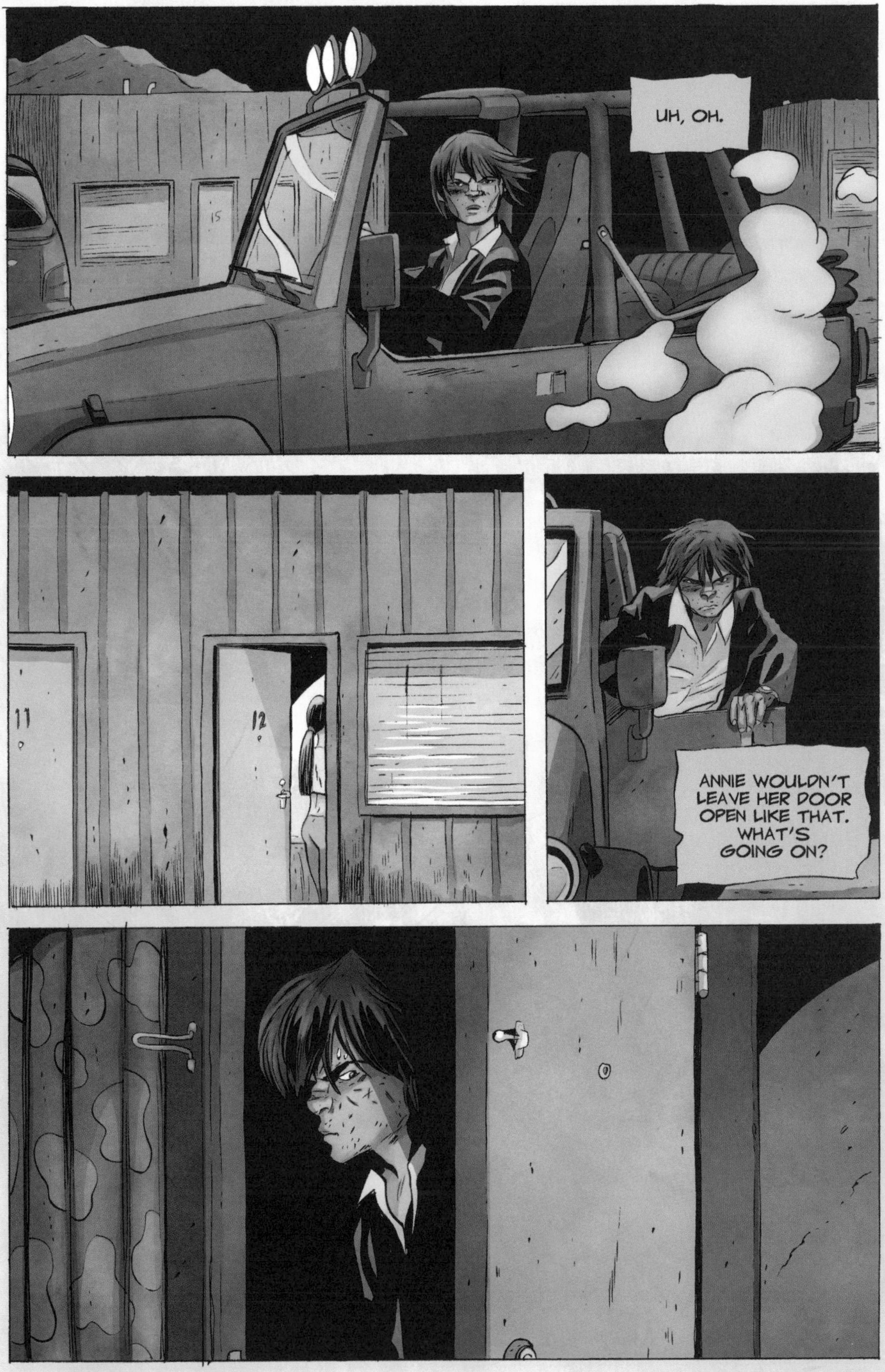
UH, OH.
ANNIE WOULDN'T LEAVE HER DOOR OPEN LIKE THAT. WHAT'S GOING ON?

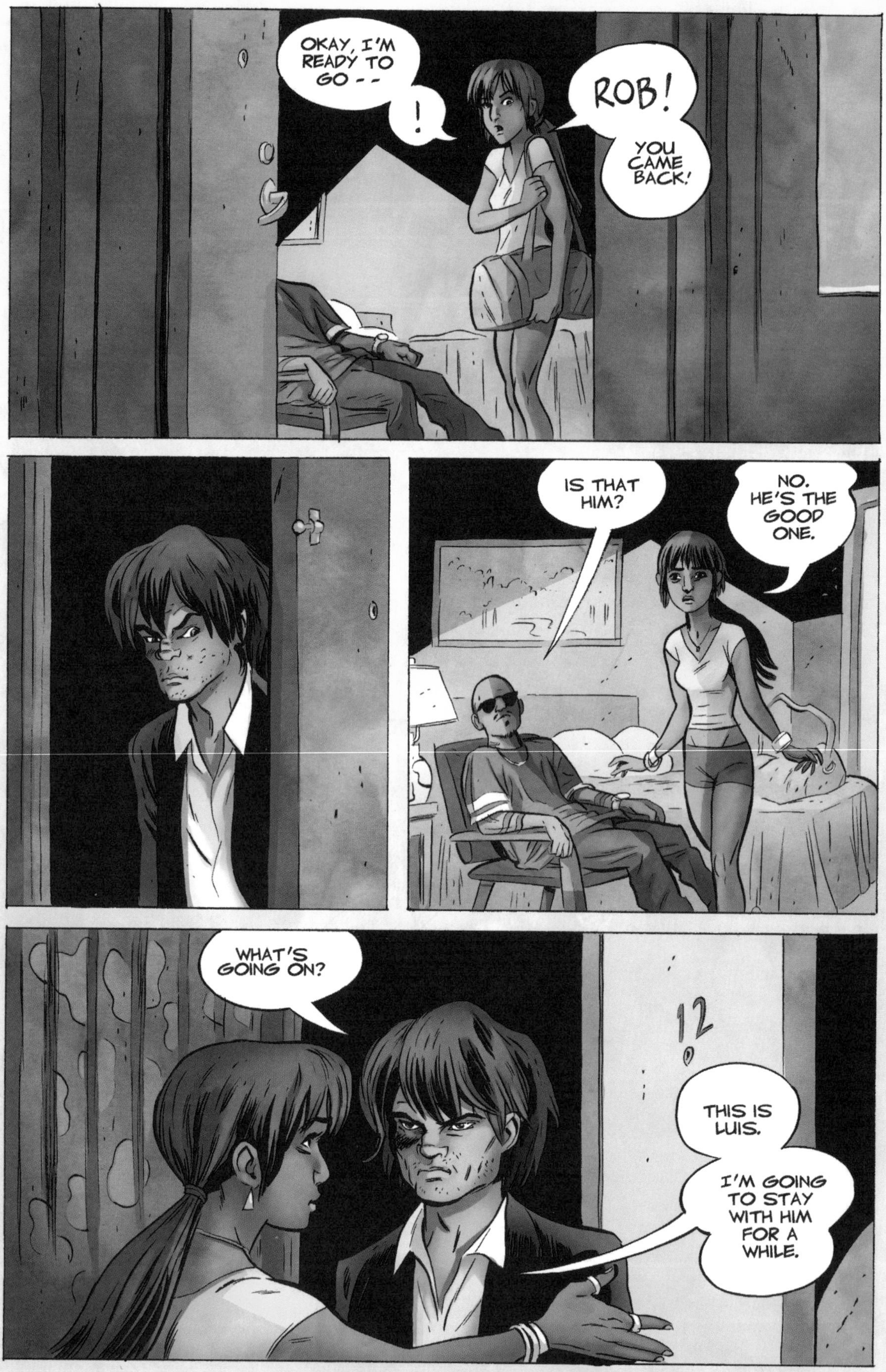
OKAY, I'M READY TO GO - -
!
ROB!
YOU CAME BACK!
IS THAT HIM?
NO. HE'S THE GOOD ONE.
WHAT'S GOING ON?
THIS IS LUIS.
I'M GOING TO STAY WITH HIM FOR A WHILE.

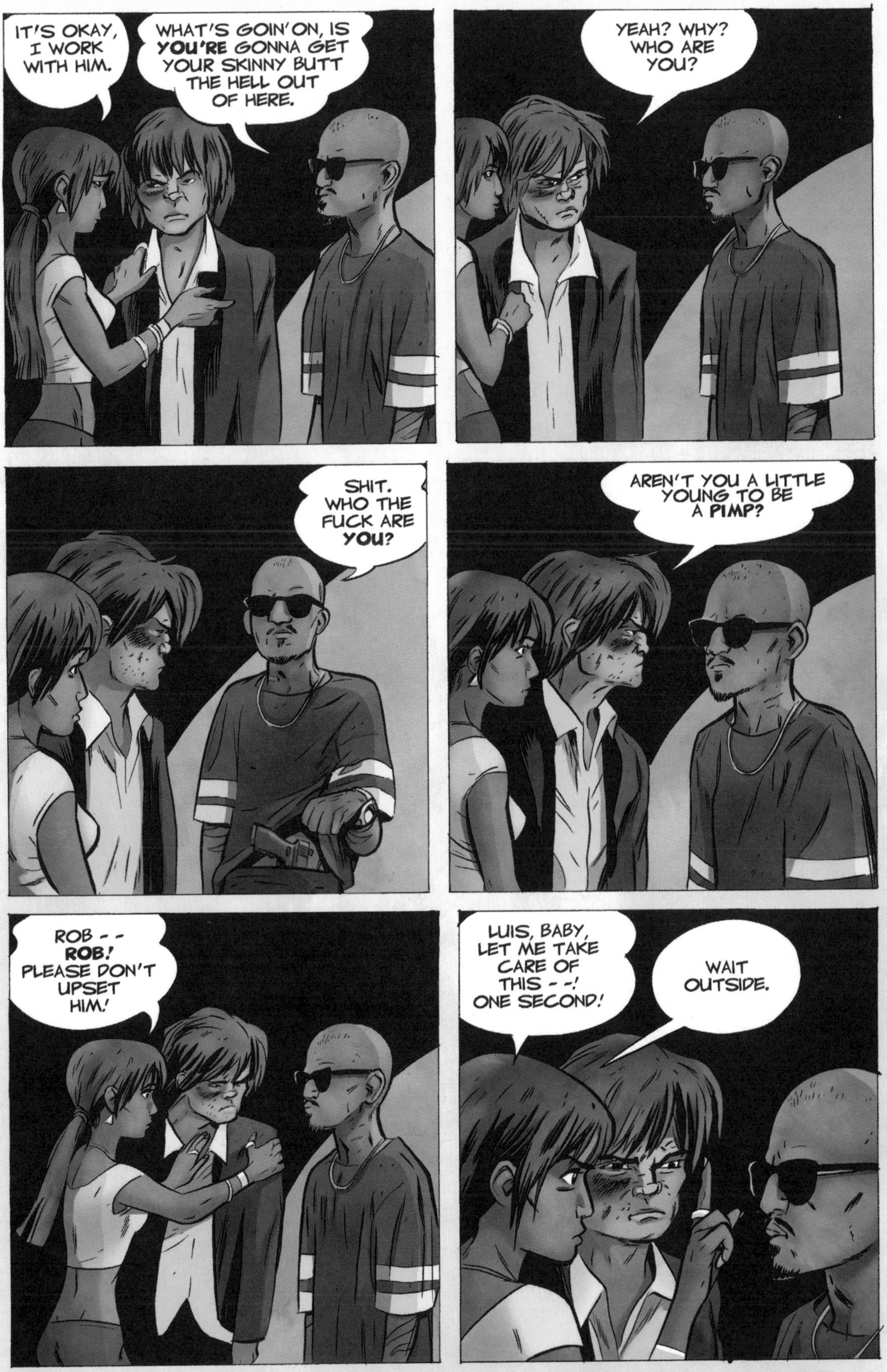
IT'S OKAY, I WORK WITH HIM.
WHAT'S GOIN' ON, IS YOU'RE GONNA GET YOUR SKINNY BUTT THE HELL OUT OF HERE.
YEAH? WHY? WHO ARE YOU?
SHIT. WHO THE FUCK ARE YOU?
AREN'T YOU A LITTLE YOUNG TO BE A PIMP?
ROB - - ROB! PLEASE DON'T UPSET HIM!
LUIS, BABY, LET ME TAKE CARE OF THIS - -! ONE SECOND!
WAIT OUTSIDE.

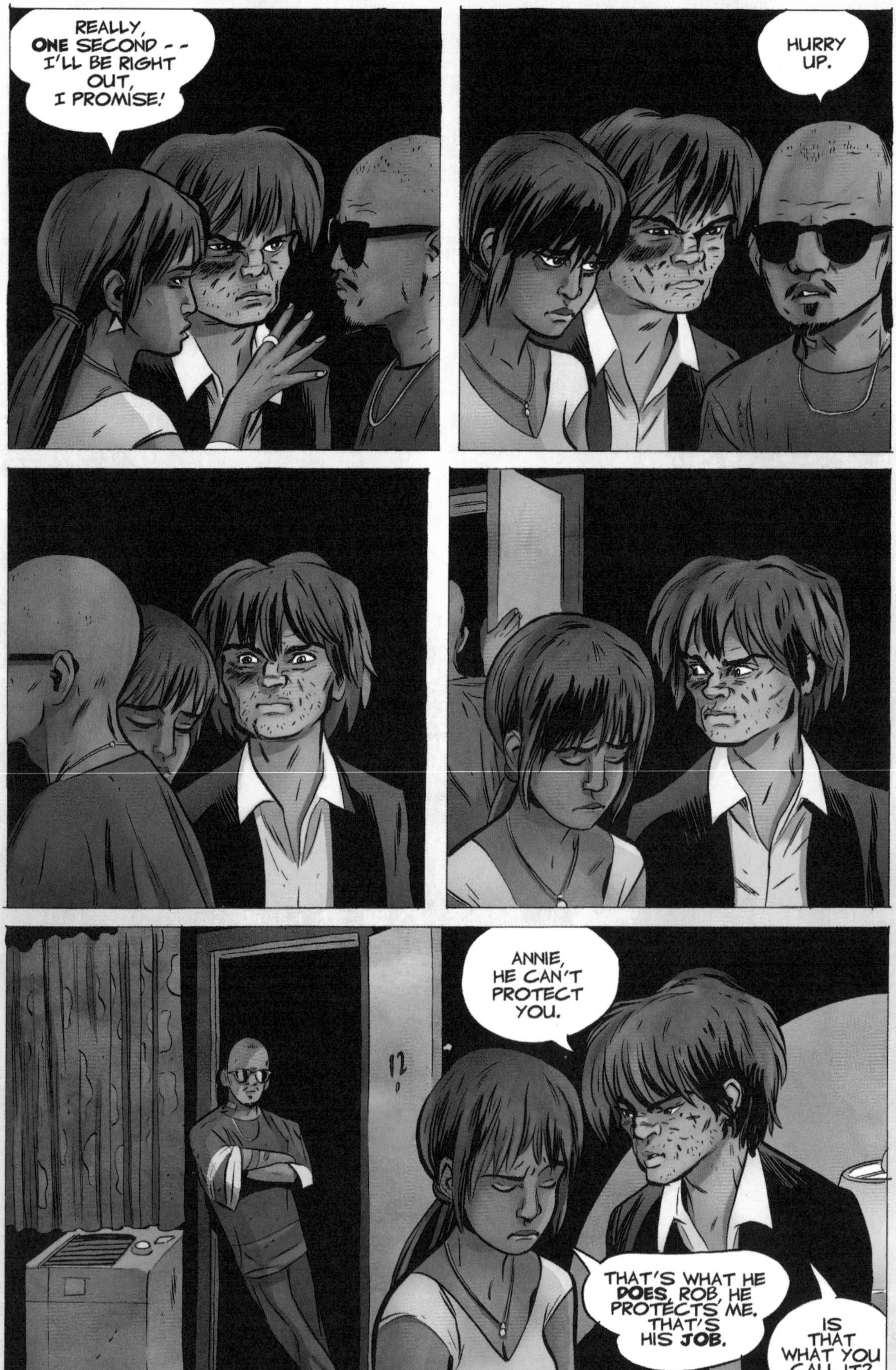
REALLY, ONE SECOND - - I'LL BE RIGHT OUT, I PROMISE!
HURRY UP.
ANNIE, HE CAN'T PROTECT YOU.
THAT'S WHAT HE DOES, ROB, HE PROTECTS ME. THAT'S HIS JOB.
IS THAT WHAT YOU CALL IT?

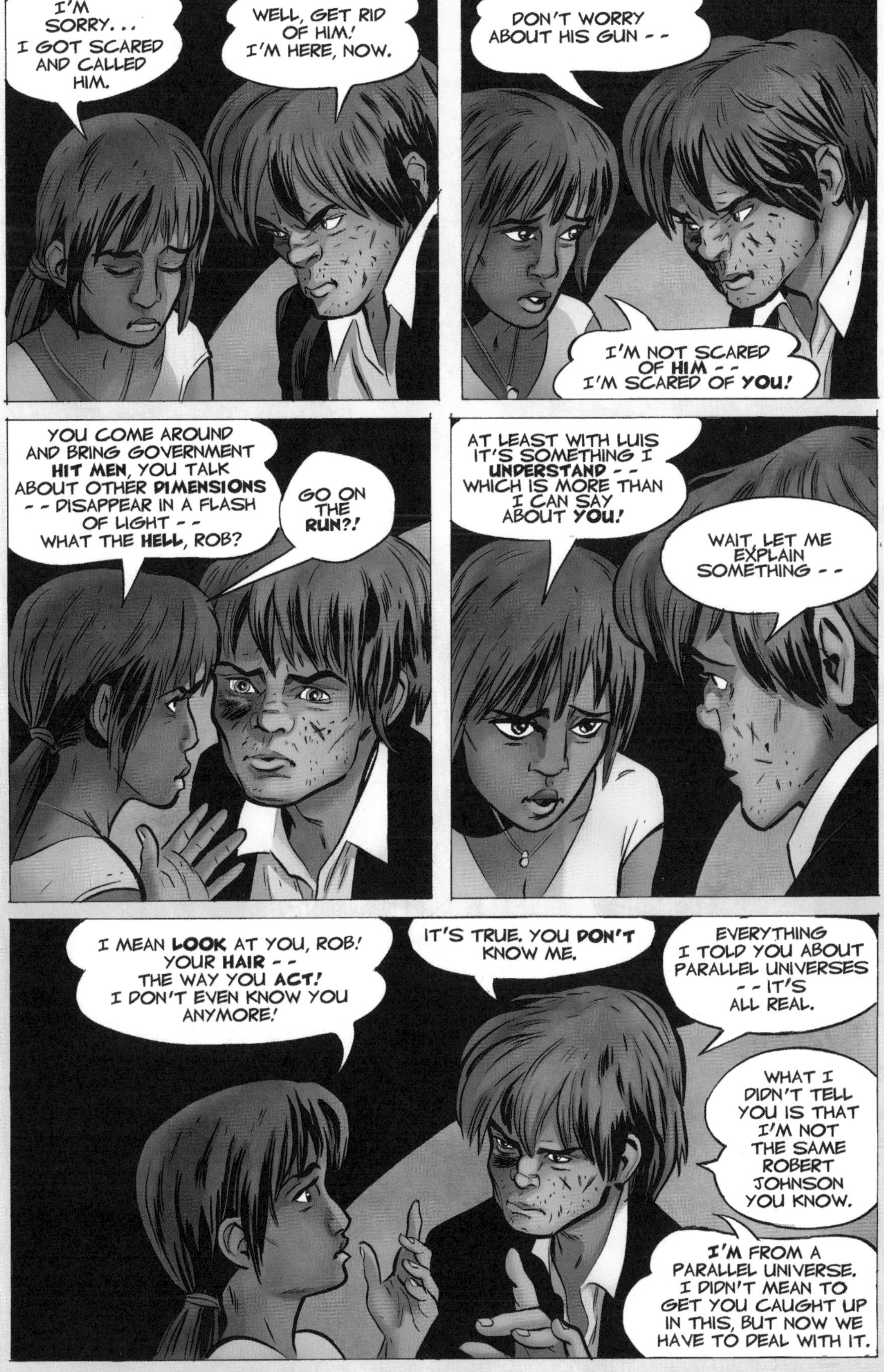
I'M SORRY... I GOT SCARED AND CALLED HIM.
WELL, GET RID OF HIM! I'M HERE, NOW.
DON'T WORRY ABOUT HIS GUN --
I'M NOT SCARED OF HIM -- I'M SCARED OF YOU!
YOU COME AROUND AND BRING GOVERNMENT HIT MEN, YOU TALK ABOUT OTHER DIMENSIONS -- DISAPPEAR IN A FLASH OF LIGHT -- WHAT THE HELL, ROB?
GO ON THE RUN?!
AT LEAST WITH LUIS IT'S SOMETHING I UNDERSTAND -- WHICH IS MORE THAN I CAN SAY ABOUT YOU!
WAIT, LET ME EXPLAIN SOMETHING --
I MEAN LOOK AT YOU, ROB! YOUR HAIR -- THE WAY YOU ACT! I DON'T EVEN KNOW YOU ANYMORE!
IT'S TRUE. YOU DON'T KNOW ME.
EVERYTHING I TOLD YOU ABOUT PARALLEL UNIVERSES -- IT'S ALL REAL.
WHAT I DIDN'T TELL YOU IS THAT I'M NOT THE SAME ROBERT JOHNSON YOU KNOW.
I'M FROM A PARALLEL UNIVERSE. I DIDN'T MEAN TO GET YOU CAUGHT UP IN THIS, BUT NOW WE HAVE TO DEAL WITH IT.

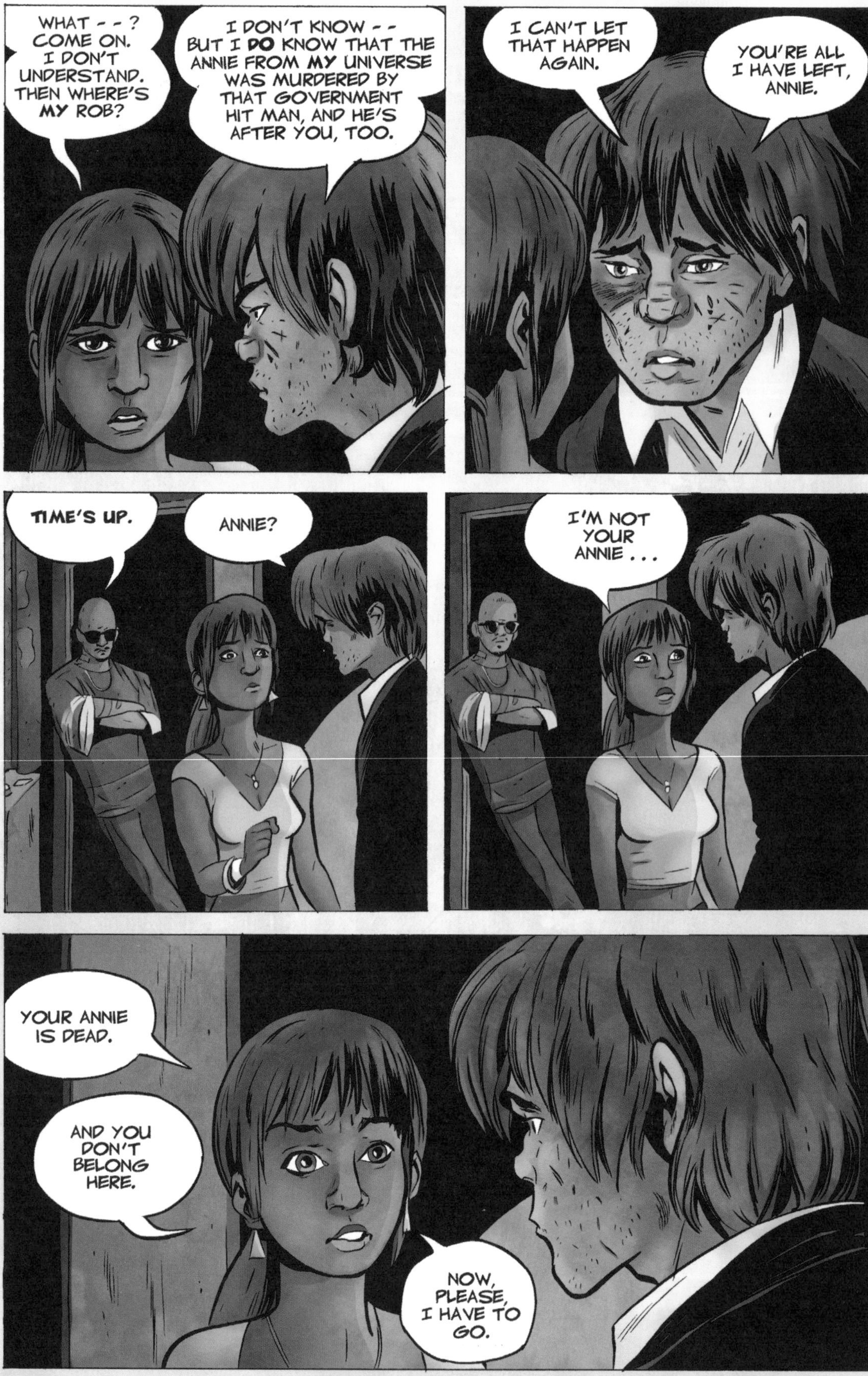
WHAT - - ? COME ON. I DON'T UNDERSTAND. THEN WHERE'S MY ROB?
I DON'T KNOW - - BUT I DO KNOW THAT THE ANNIE FROM MY UNIVERSE WAS MURDERED BY THAT GOVERNMENT HIT MAN, AND HE'S AFTER YOU, TOO.
I CAN'T LET THAT HAPPEN AGAIN.
YOU'RE ALL I HAVE LEFT, ANNIE.
TIME'S UP.
ANNIE?
I'M NOT YOUR ANNIE . . .
YOUR ANNIE IS DEAD.
AND YOU DON'T BELONG HERE.
NOW, PLEASE, I HAVE TO GO.

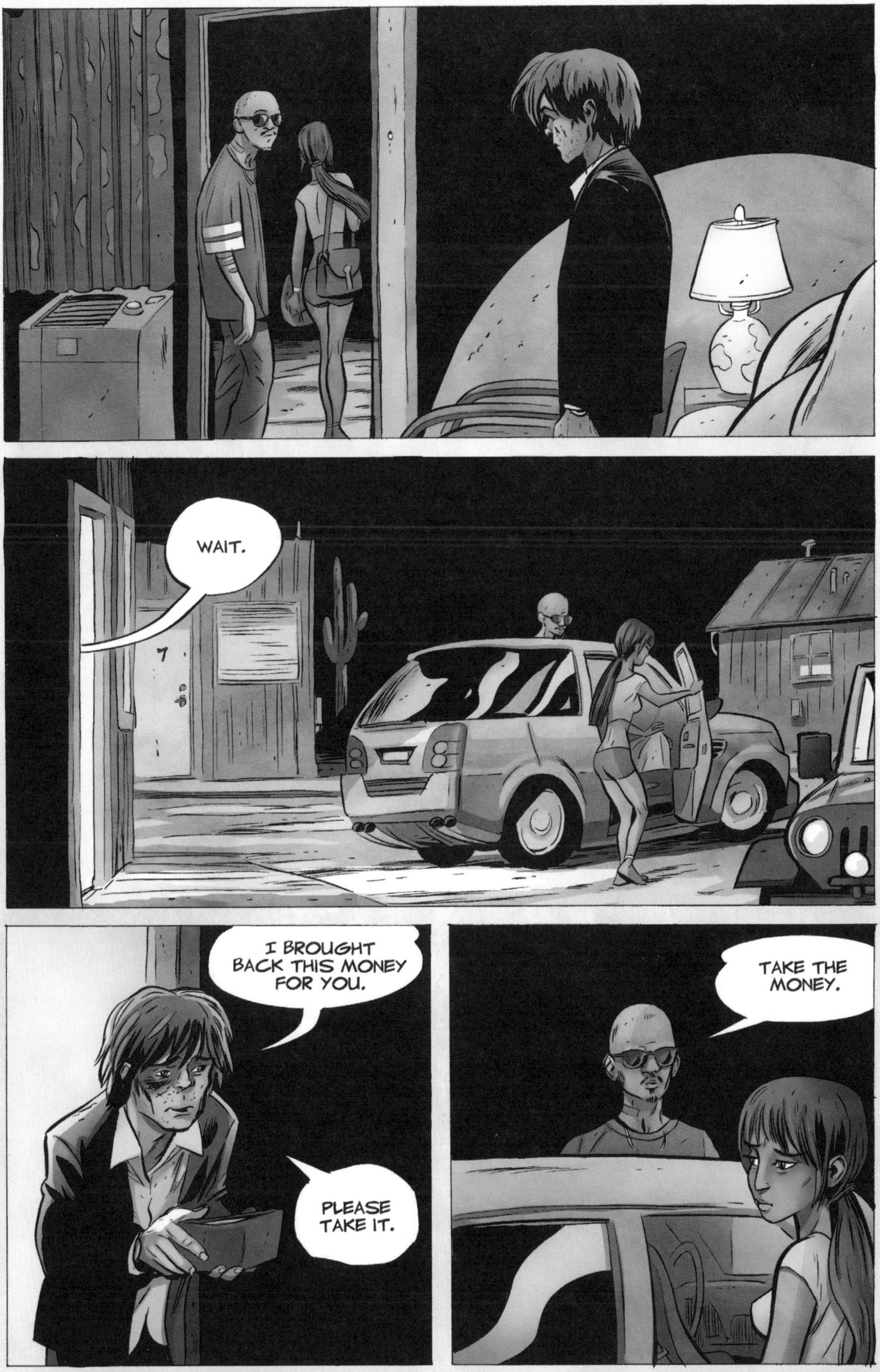
WAIT.
I BROUGHT BACK THIS MONEY FOR YOU.
PLEASE TAKE IT.
TAKE THE MONEY.

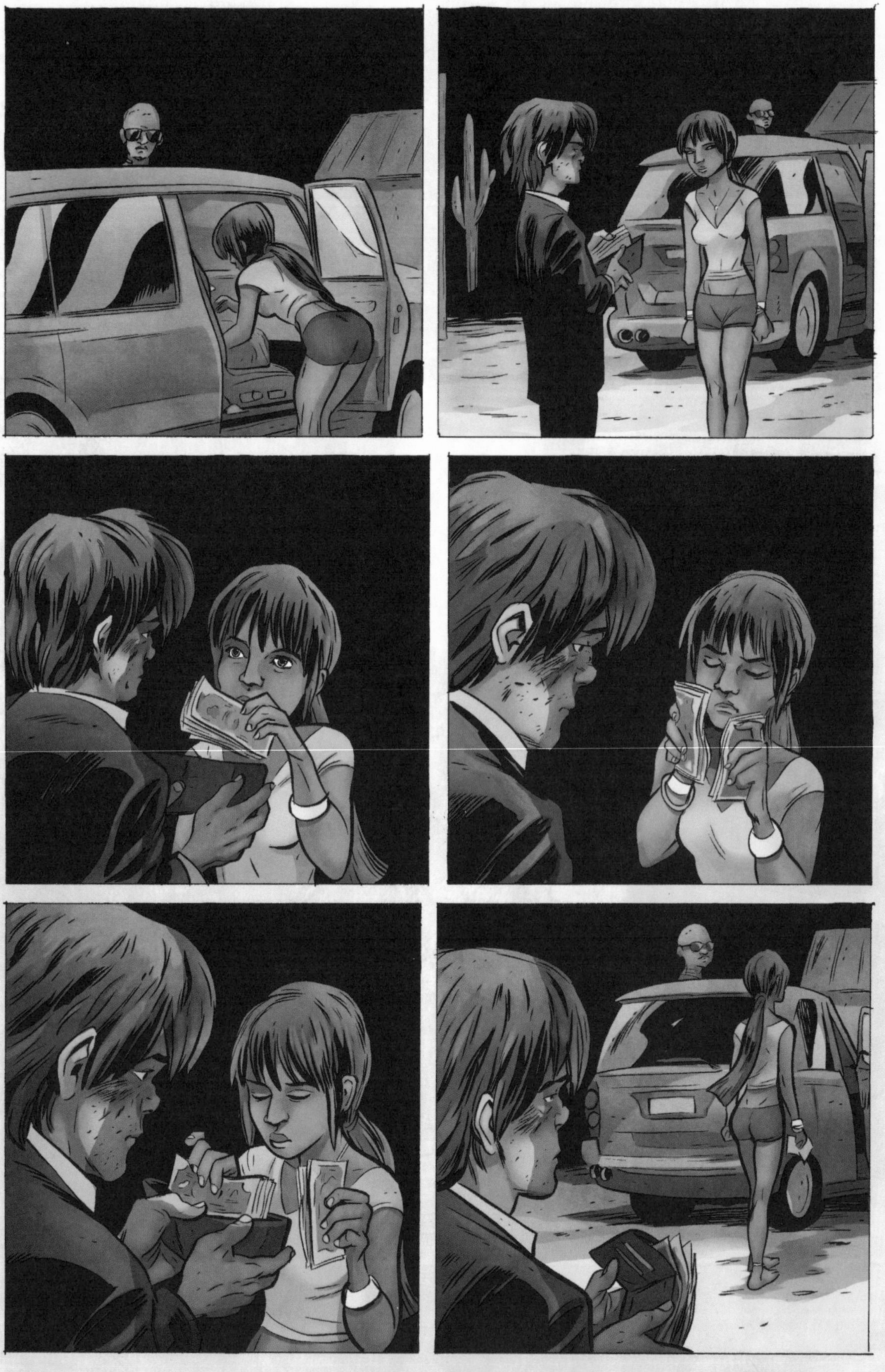

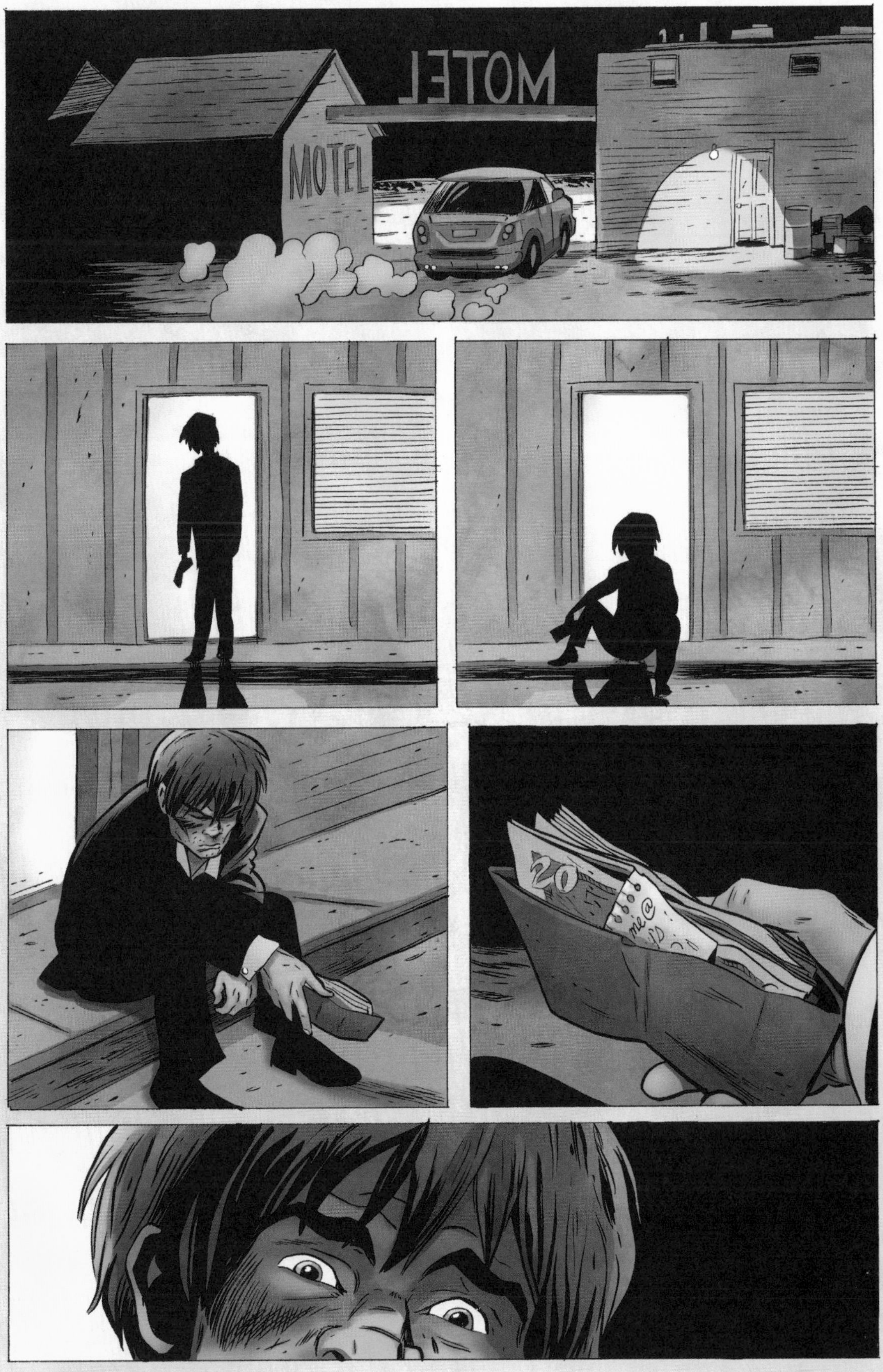
MOTEL

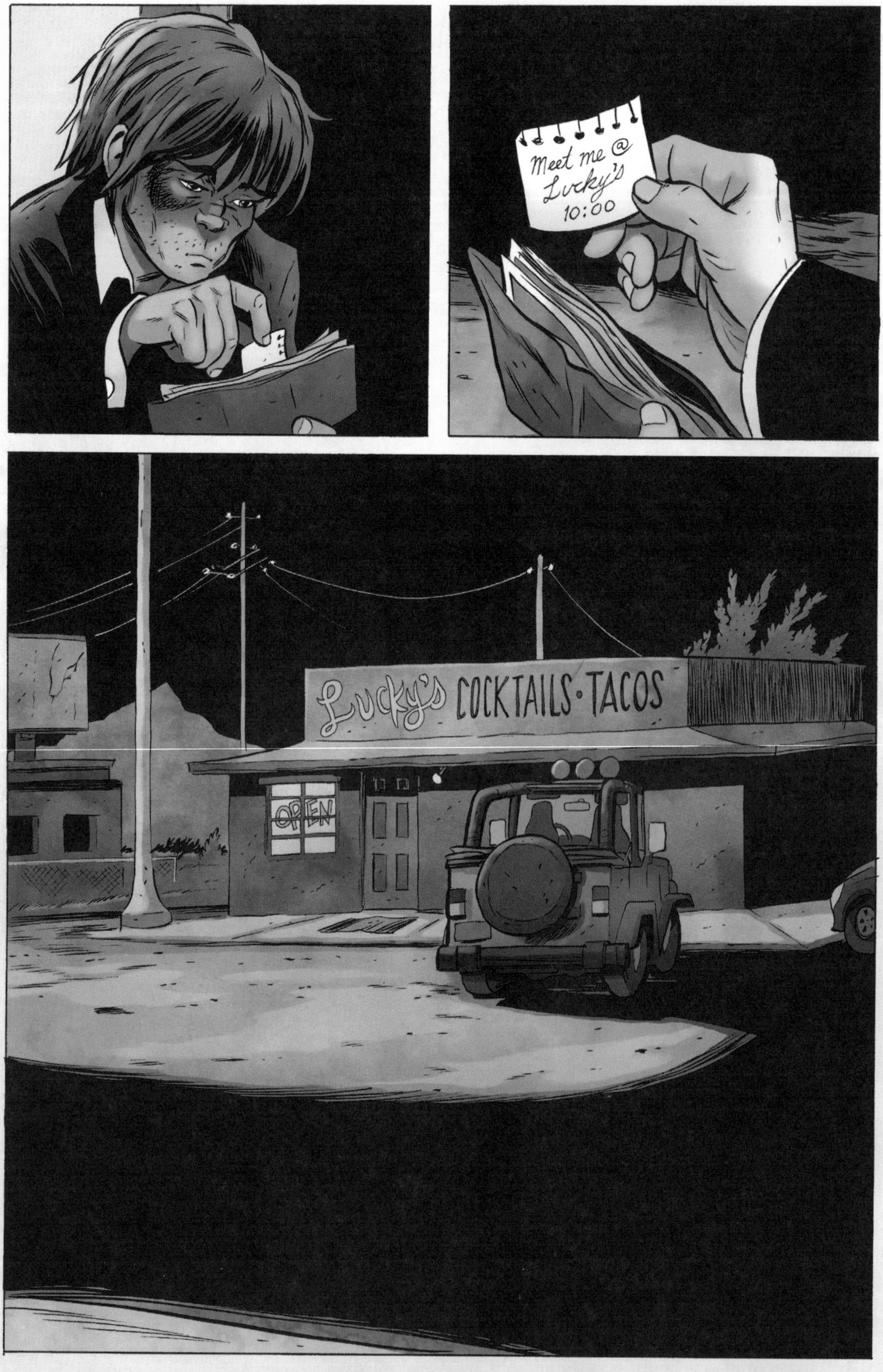

Meet me @ Lucky's 10:00
Lucky's COCKTAILS · TACOS
OPEN

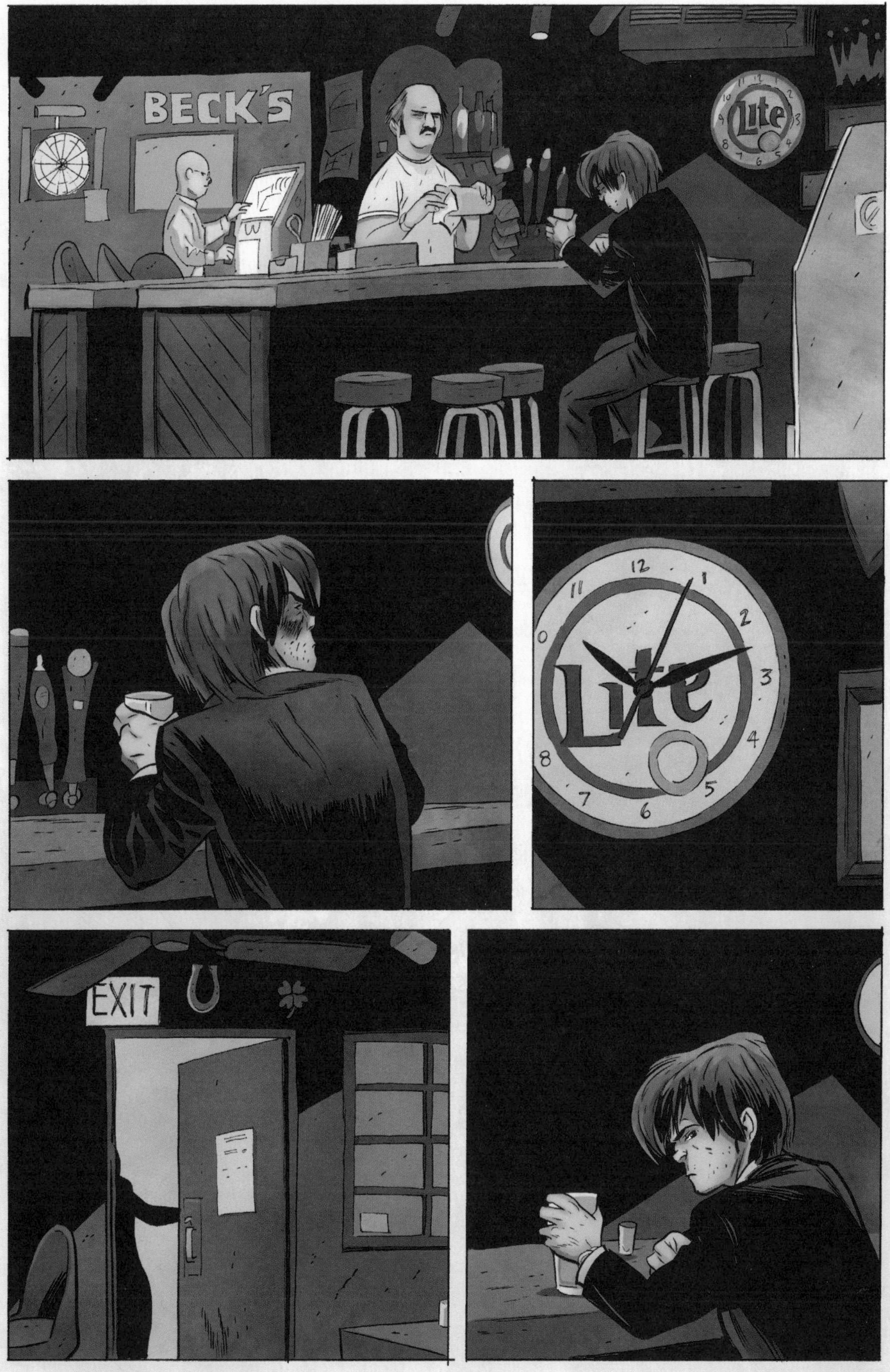
BECK'S
Lite
Lite
EXIT

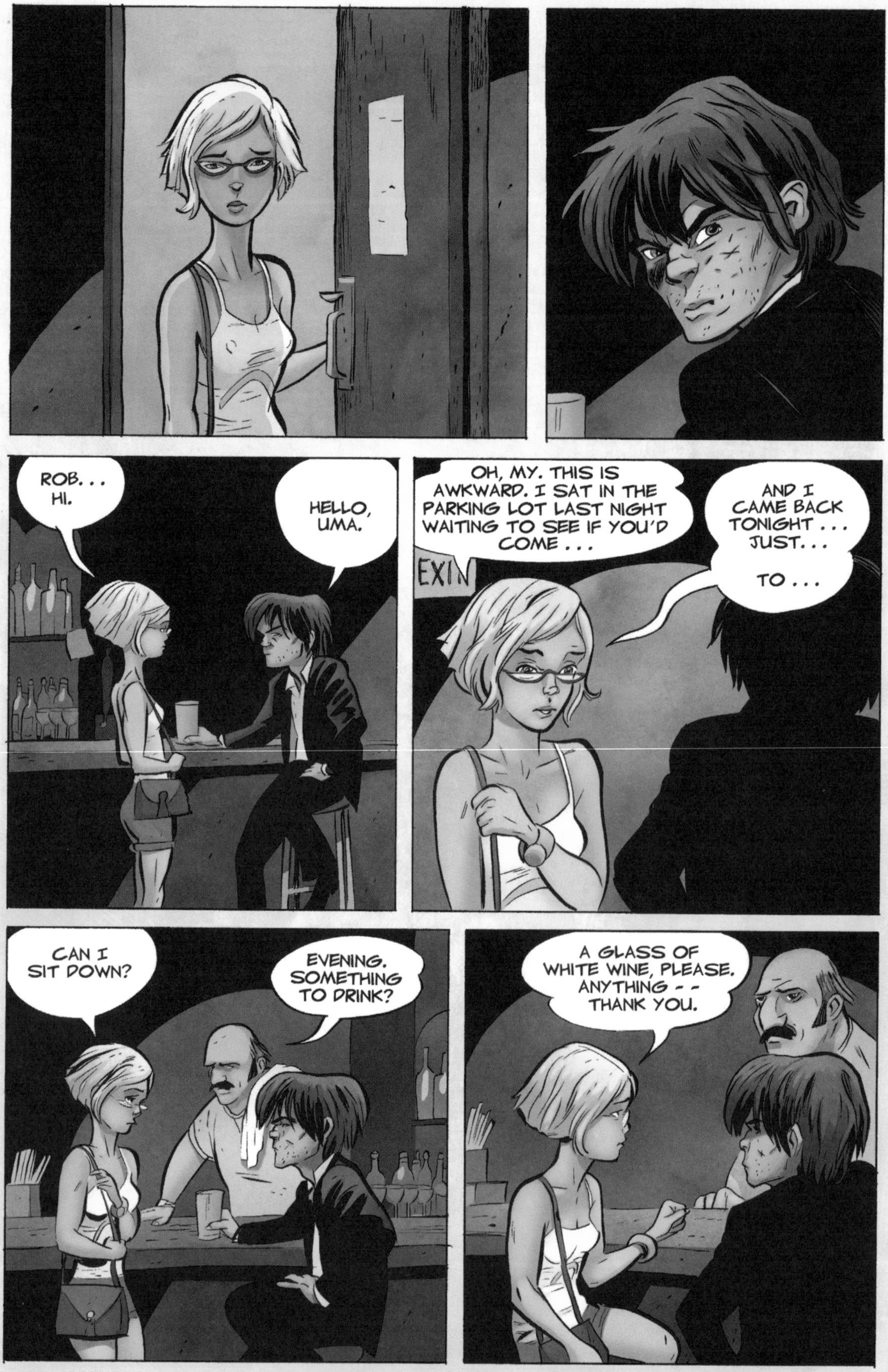
ROB... HI.
HELLO, UMA.
OH, MY. THIS IS AWKWARD. I SAT IN THE PARKING LOT LAST NIGHT WAITING TO SEE IF YOU'D COME...
AND I CAME BACK TONIGHT... JUST...
TO...
CAN I SIT DOWN?
EVENING. SOMETHING TO DRINK?
A GLASS OF WHITE WINE, PLEASE. ANYTHING -- THANK YOU.

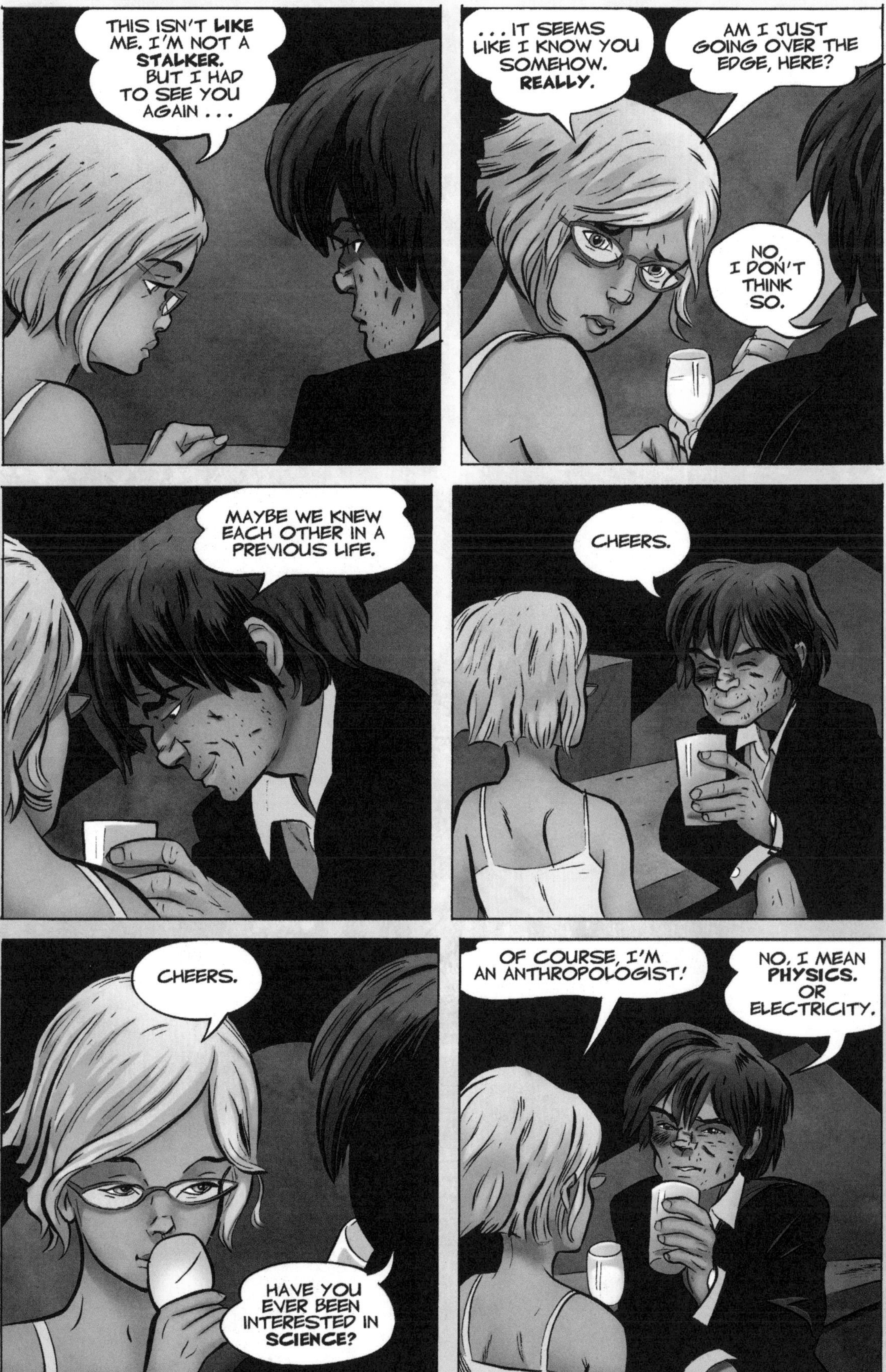
THIS ISN'T LIKE ME. I'M NOT A STALKER. BUT I HAD TO SEE YOU AGAIN . . .
. . . IT SEEMS LIKE I KNOW YOU SOMEHOW. REALLY.
AM I JUST GOING OVER THE EDGE, HERE?
NO, I DON'T THINK SO.
MAYBE WE KNEW EACH OTHER IN A PREVIOUS LIFE.
CHEERS.
CHEERS.
HAVE YOU EVER BEEN INTERESTED IN SCIENCE?
OF COURSE, I'M AN ANTHROPOLOGIST!
NO, I MEAN PHYSICS. OR ELECTRICITY.

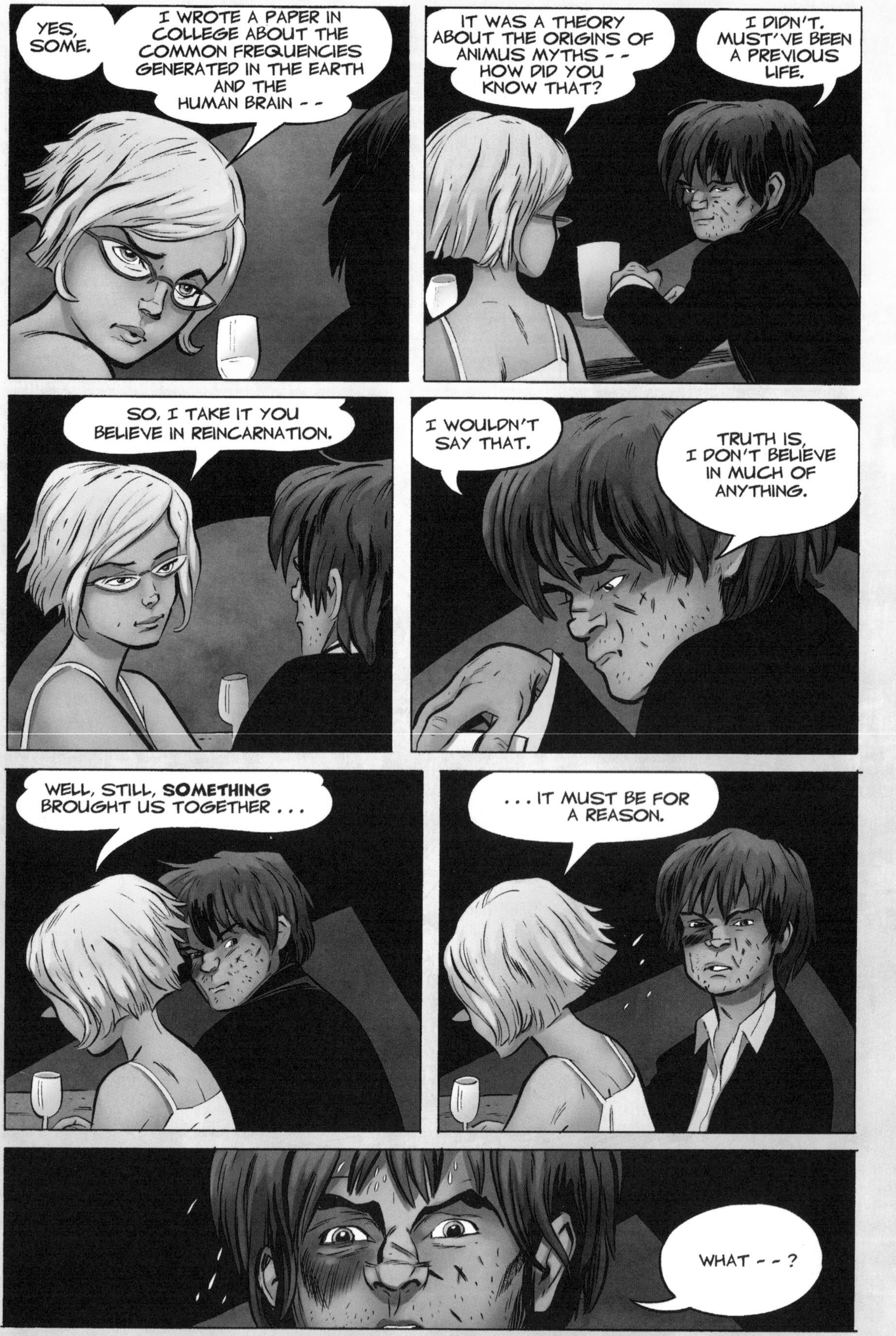
YES, SOME.
I WROTE A PAPER IN COLLEGE ABOUT THE COMMON FREQUENCIES GENERATED IN THE EARTH AND THE HUMAN BRAIN - -
IT WAS A THEORY ABOUT THE ORIGINS OF ANIMUS MYTHS - - HOW DID YOU KNOW THAT?
I DIDN'T. MUST'VE BEEN A PREVIOUS LIFE.
SO, I TAKE IT YOU BELIEVE IN REINCARNATION.
I WOULDN'T SAY THAT.
TRUTH IS, I DON'T BELIEVE IN MUCH OF ANYTHING.
WELL, STILL, SOMETHING BROUGHT US TOGETHER . . .
. . . IT MUST BE FOR A REASON.
WHAT - - ?

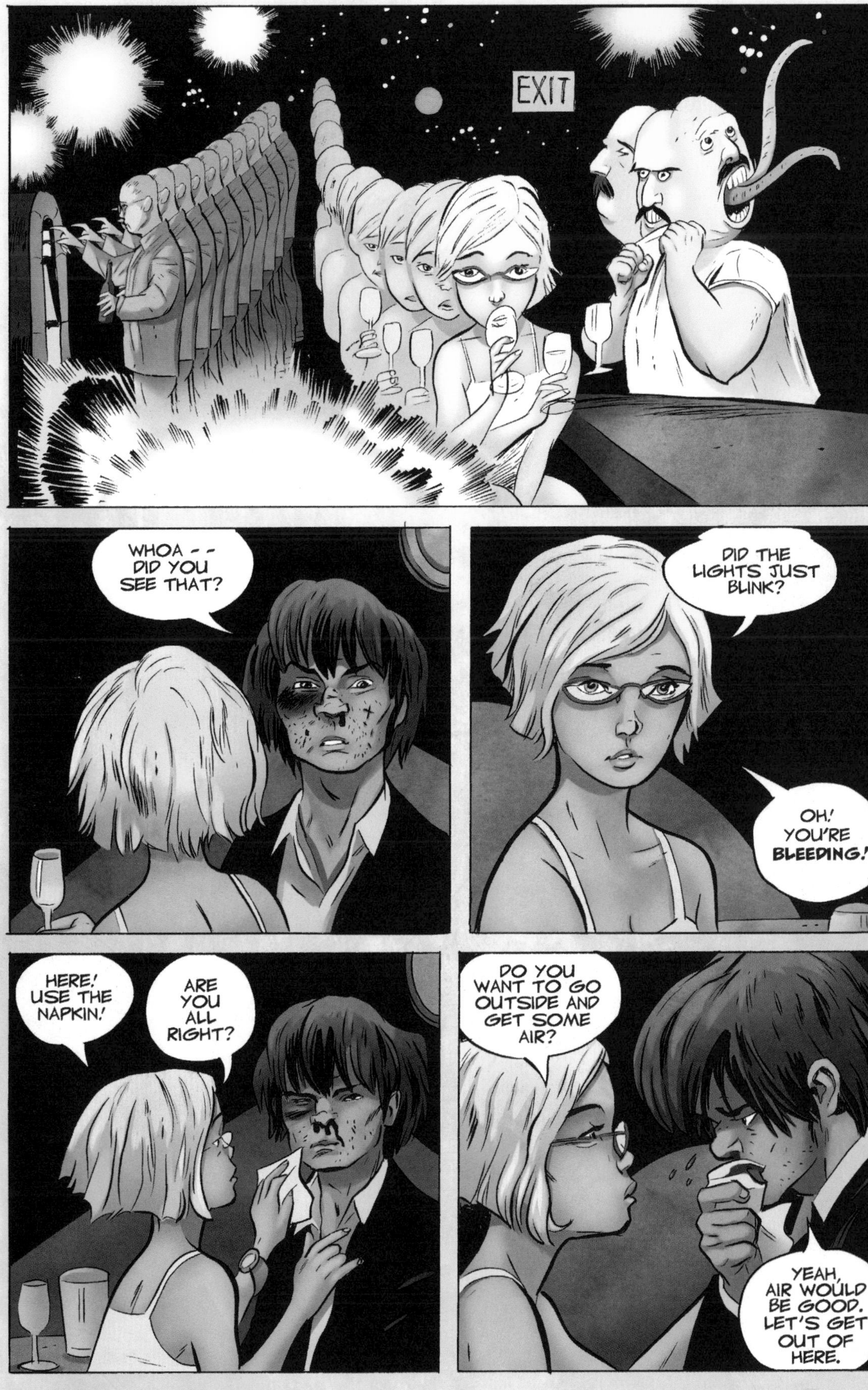
EXIT
WHOA -- DID YOU SEE THAT?
DID THE LIGHTS JUST BLINK?
OH! YOU'RE **BLEEDING!**
HERE! USE THE NAPKIN!
ARE YOU ALL RIGHT?
DO YOU WANT TO GO OUTSIDE AND GET SOME AIR?
YEAH, AIR WOULD BE GOOD. LET'S GET OUT OF HERE.

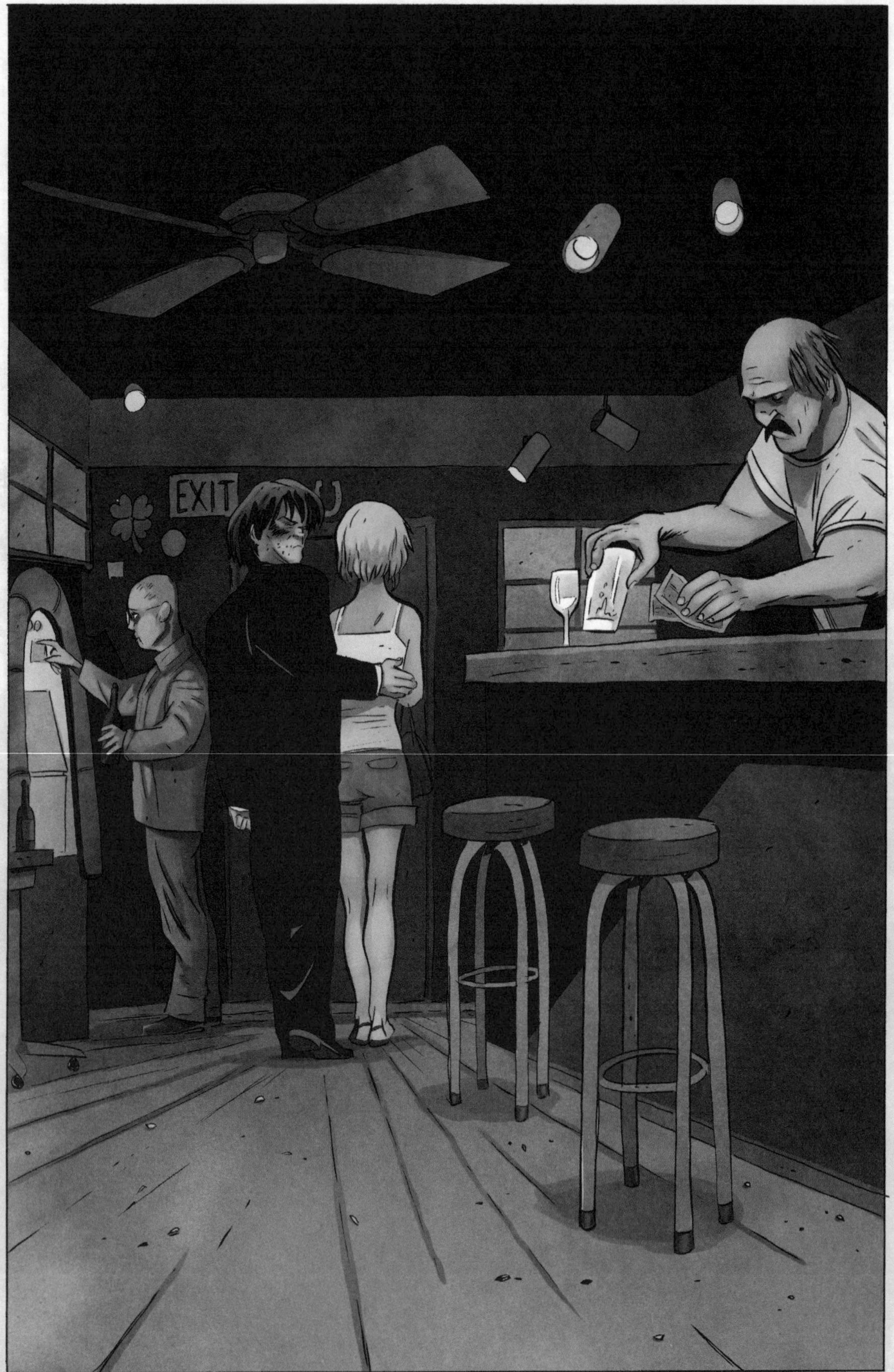
EXIT

XI
THE EVENT

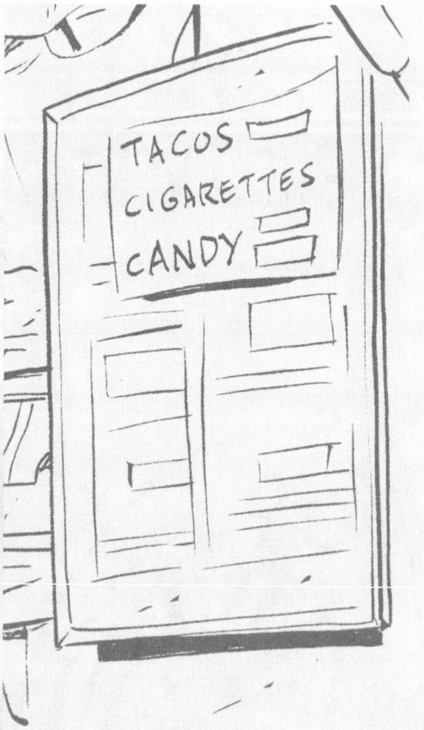
TACOS
CIGARETTES
CANDY

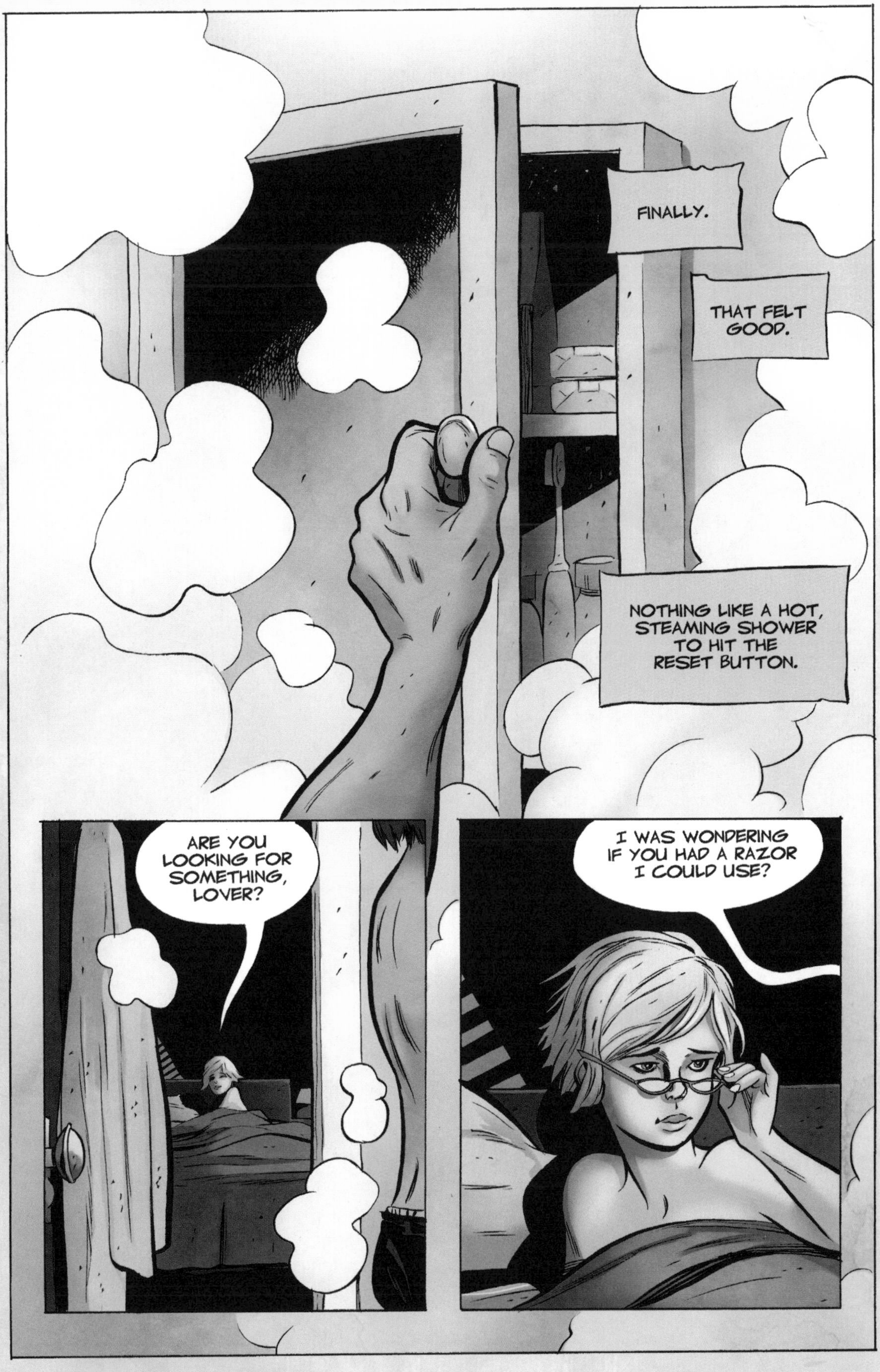
FINALLY.
THAT FELT GOOD.
NOTHING LIKE A HOT, STEAMING SHOWER TO HIT THE RESET BUTTON.
ARE YOU LOOKING FOR SOMETHING, LOVER?
I WAS WONDERING IF YOU HAD A RAZOR I COULD USE?

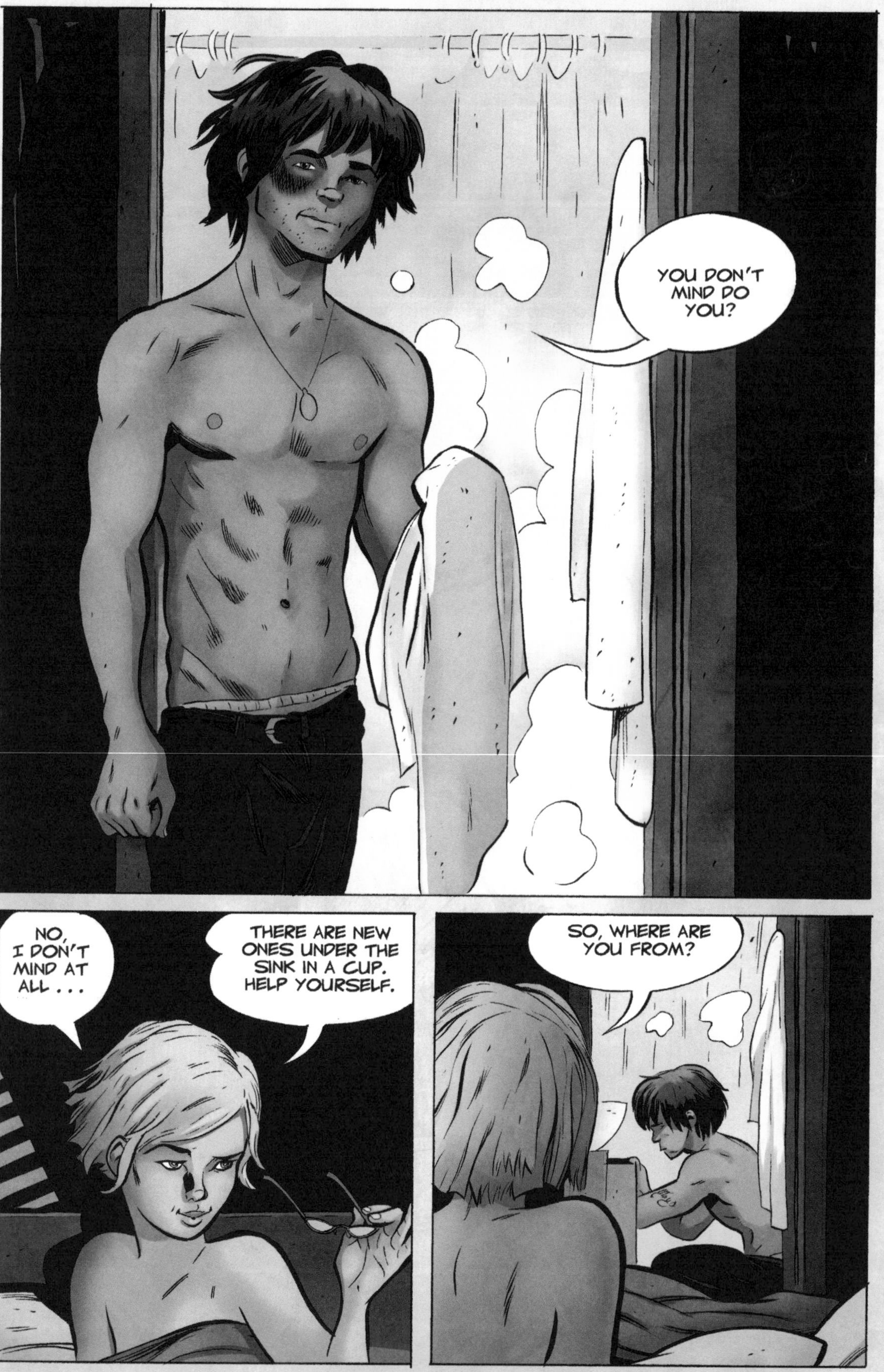
YOU DON'T MIND DO YOU?
NO, I DON'T MIND AT ALL . . .
THERE ARE NEW ONES UNDER THE SINK IN A CUP. HELP YOURSELF.
SO, WHERE ARE YOU FROM?

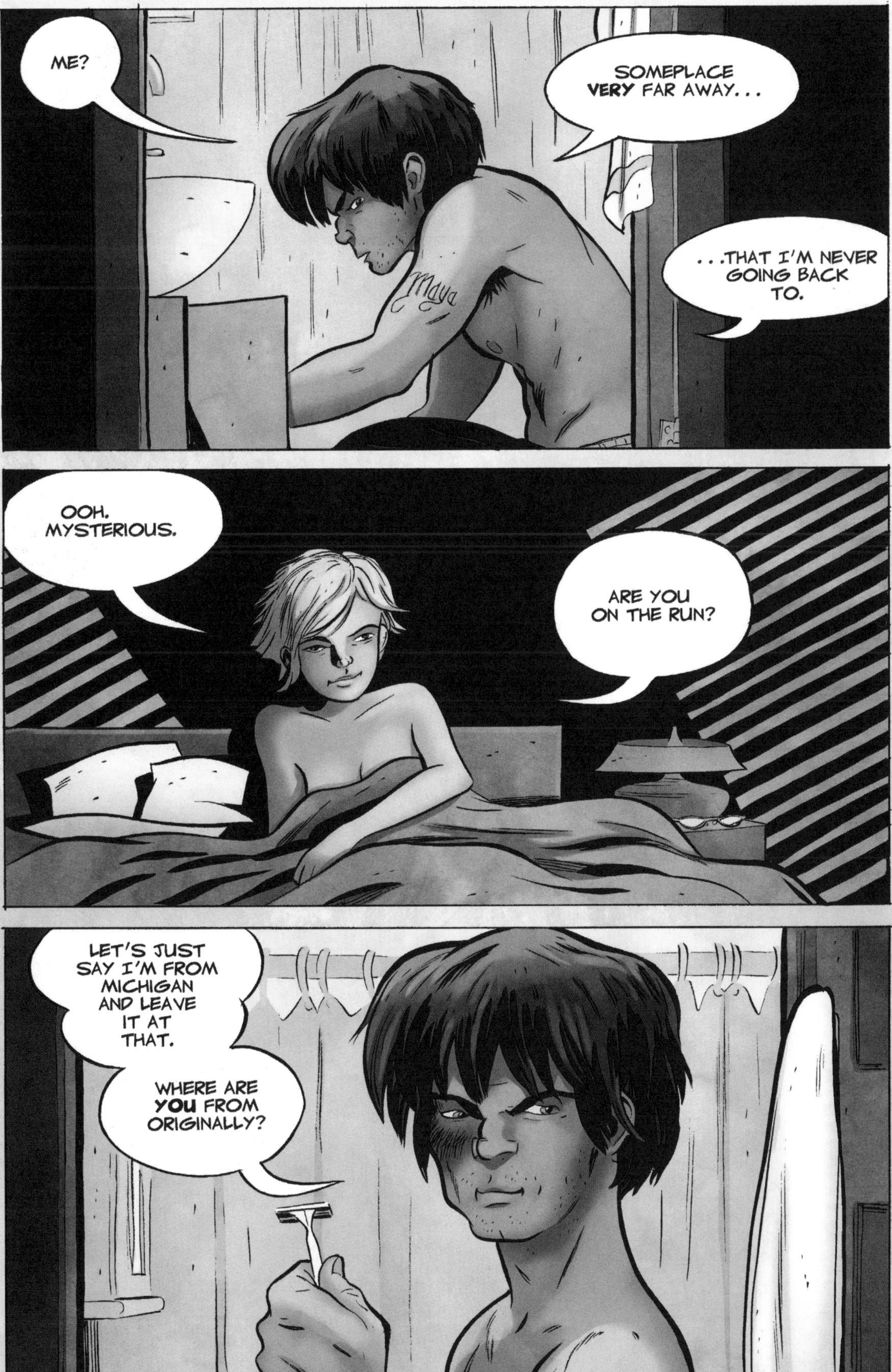
ME?
SOMEPLACE VERY FAR AWAY...
...THAT I'M NEVER GOING BACK TO.
OOH. MYSTERIOUS.
ARE YOU ON THE RUN?
LET'S JUST SAY I'M FROM MICHIGAN AND LEAVE IT AT THAT.
WHERE ARE YOU FROM ORIGINALLY?

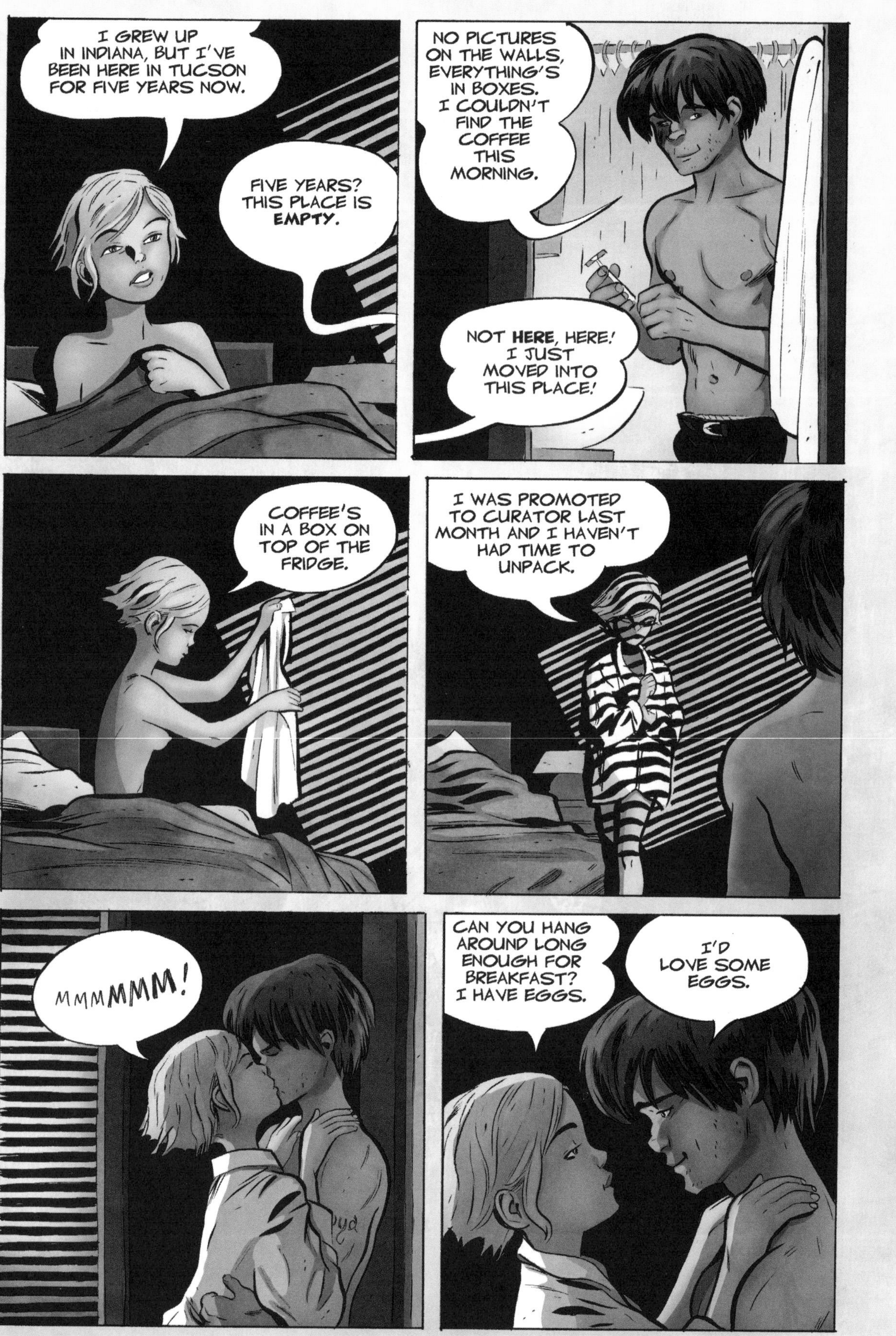
I GREW UP IN INDIANA, BUT I'VE BEEN HERE IN TUCSON FOR FIVE YEARS NOW.
FIVE YEARS? THIS PLACE IS **EMPTY**.
NO PICTURES ON THE WALLS, EVERYTHING'S IN BOXES. I COULDN'T FIND THE COFFEE THIS MORNING.
NOT **HERE**, HERE! I JUST MOVED INTO THIS PLACE!
COFFEE'S IN A BOX ON TOP OF THE FRIDGE.
I WAS PROMOTED TO CURATOR LAST MONTH AND I HAVEN'T HAD TIME TO UNPACK.
MMMMMM!
CAN YOU HANG AROUND LONG ENOUGH FOR BREAKFAST? I HAVE EGGS.
I'D LOVE SOME EGGS.

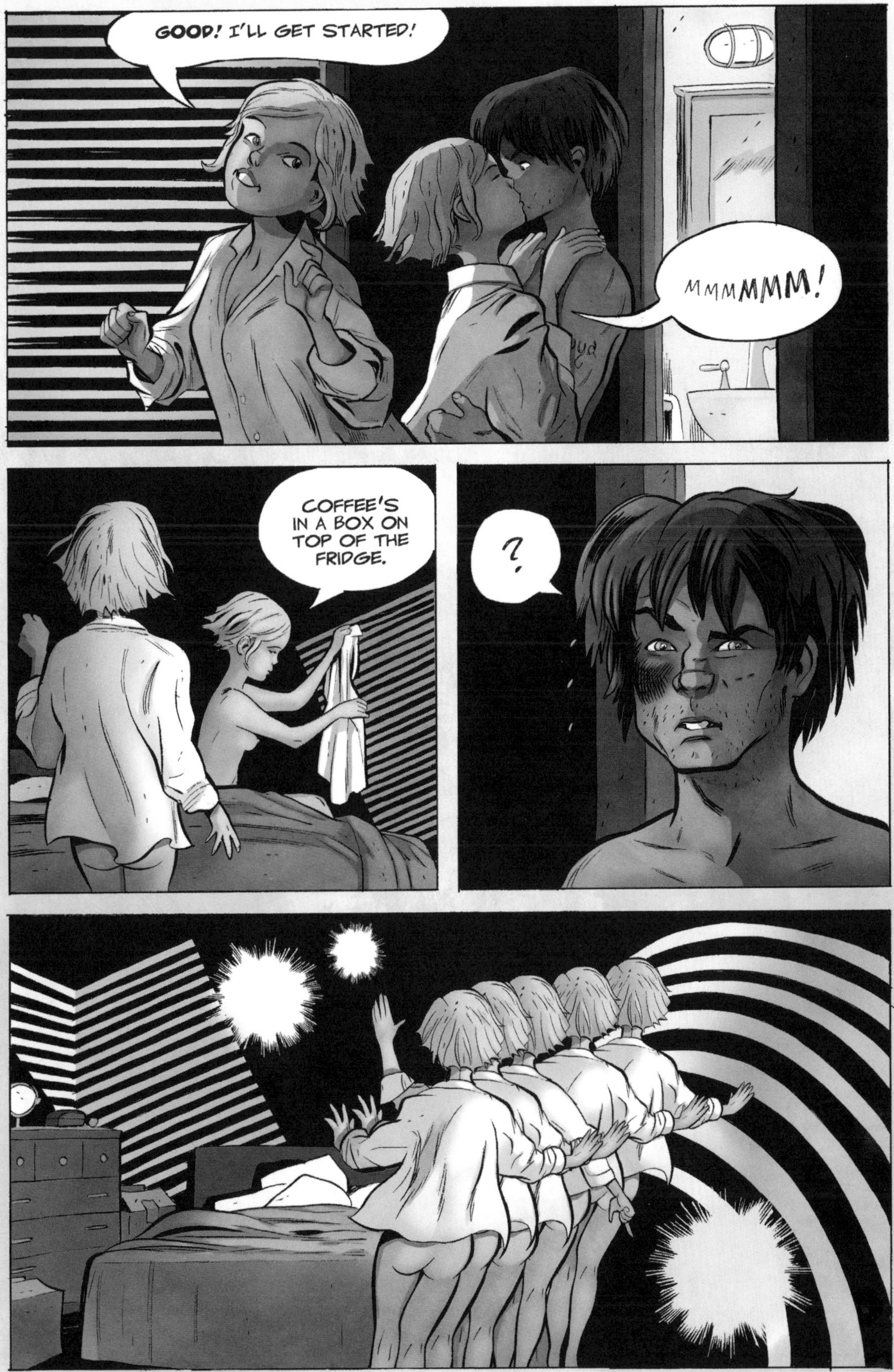
GOOD! I'LL GET STARTED!
MMMMMM!
COFFEE'S IN A BOX ON TOP OF THE FRIDGE.
?

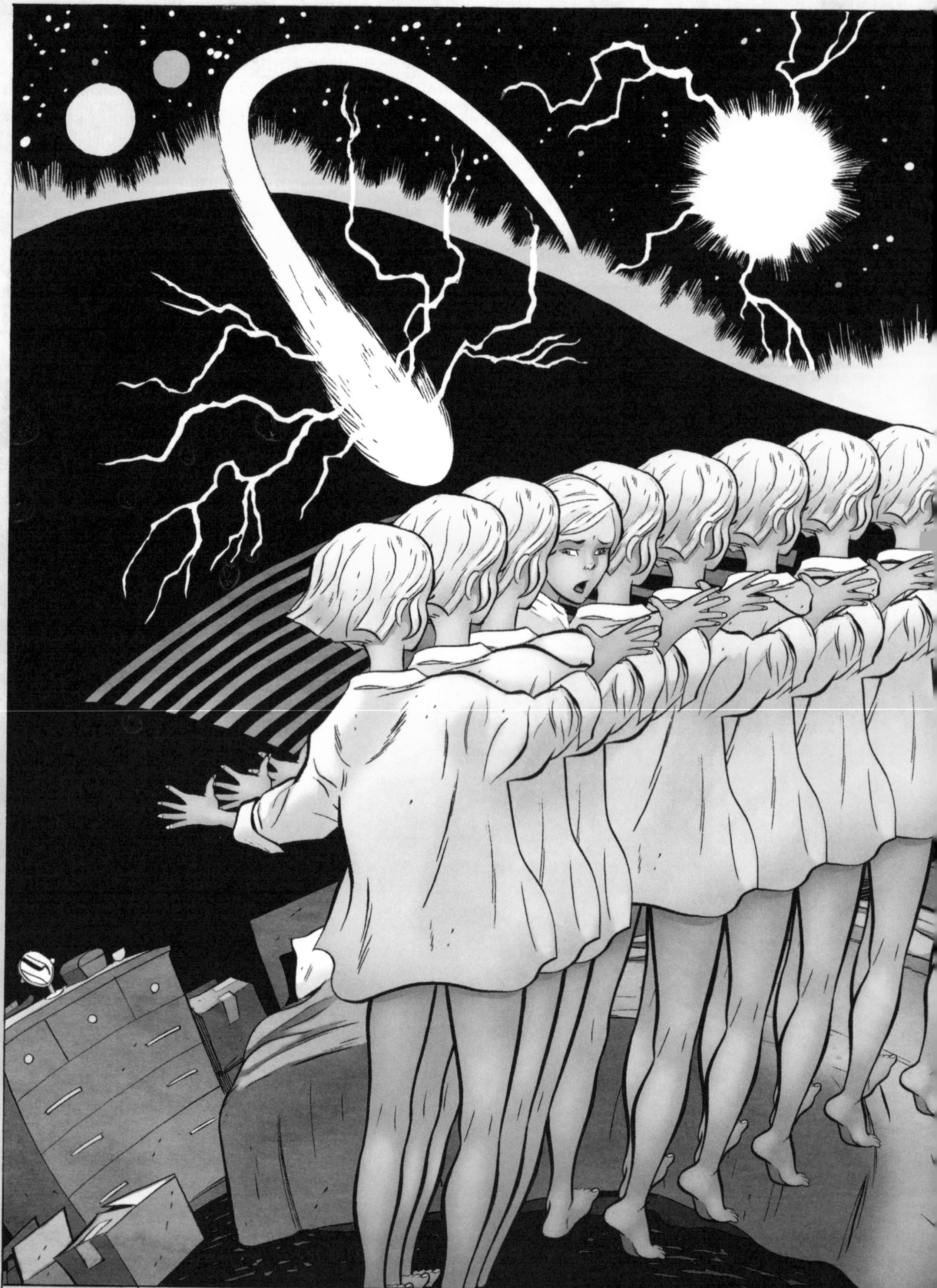

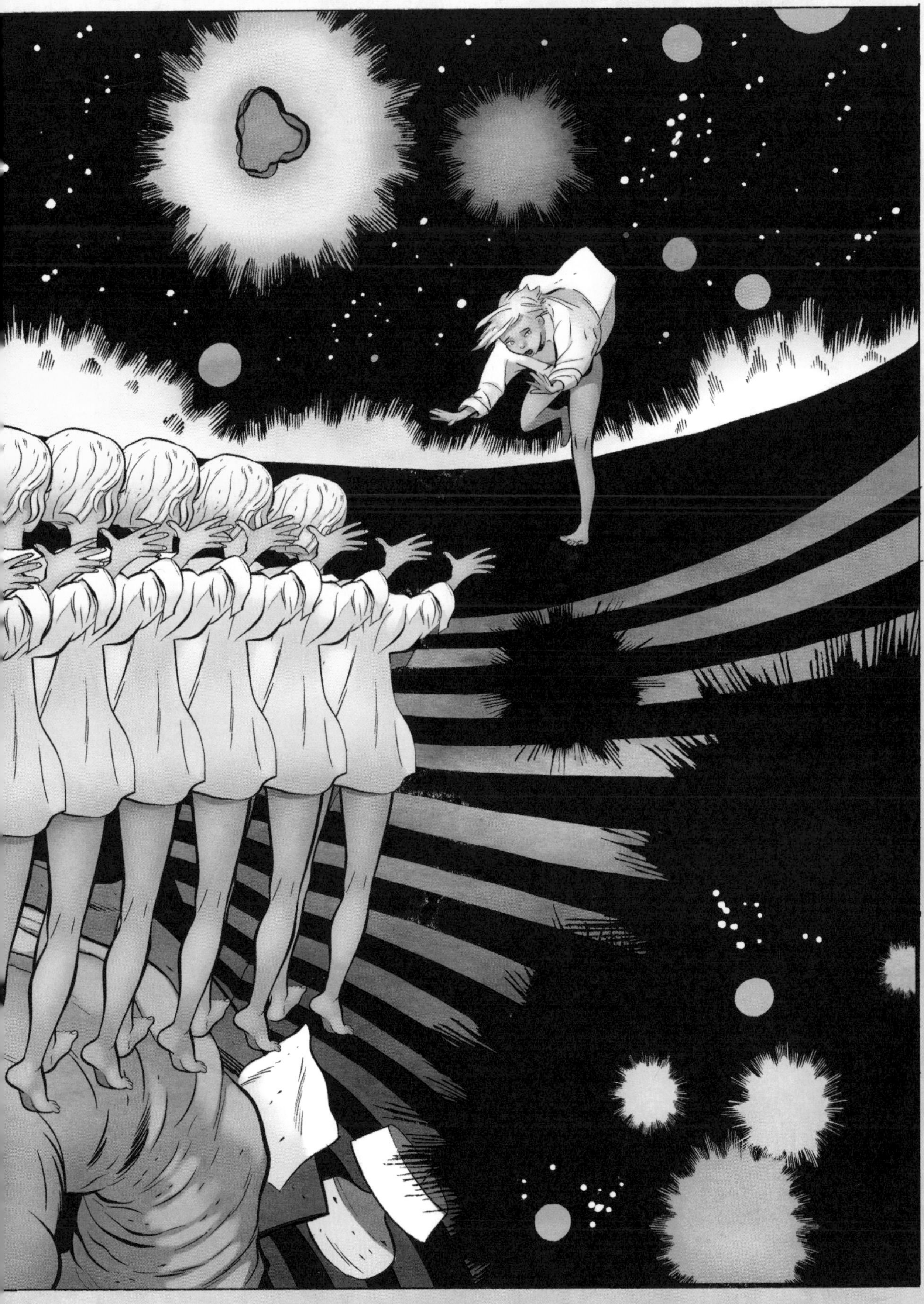

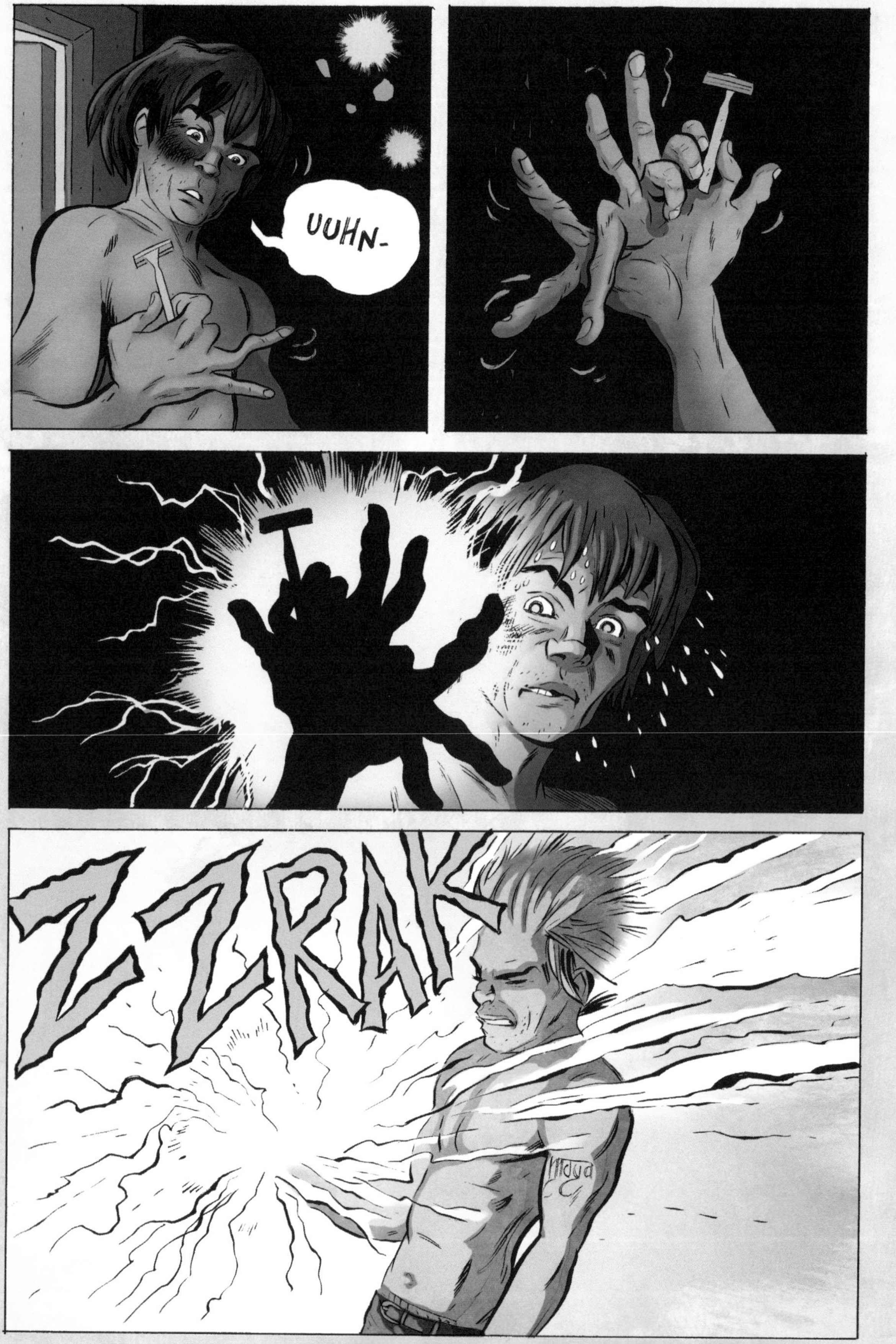
UUHN-
ZZRAK

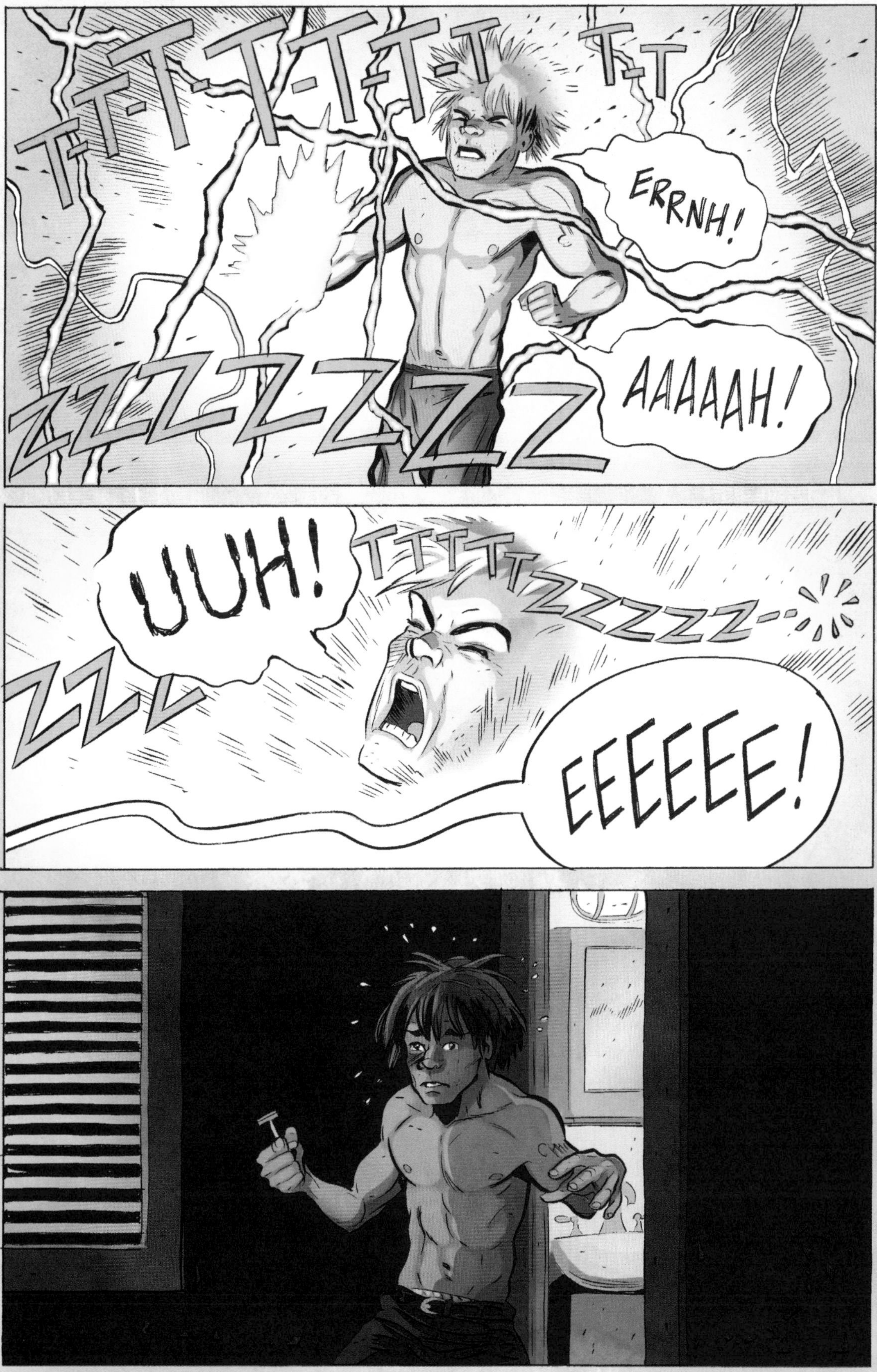
T-T-T-T-T-T-T-T T-T
ERRNH!
ZZZZZZZZ
AAAAAH!
UUH!
TTTTTZZZZZZ--
ZZZ
EEEEEE!

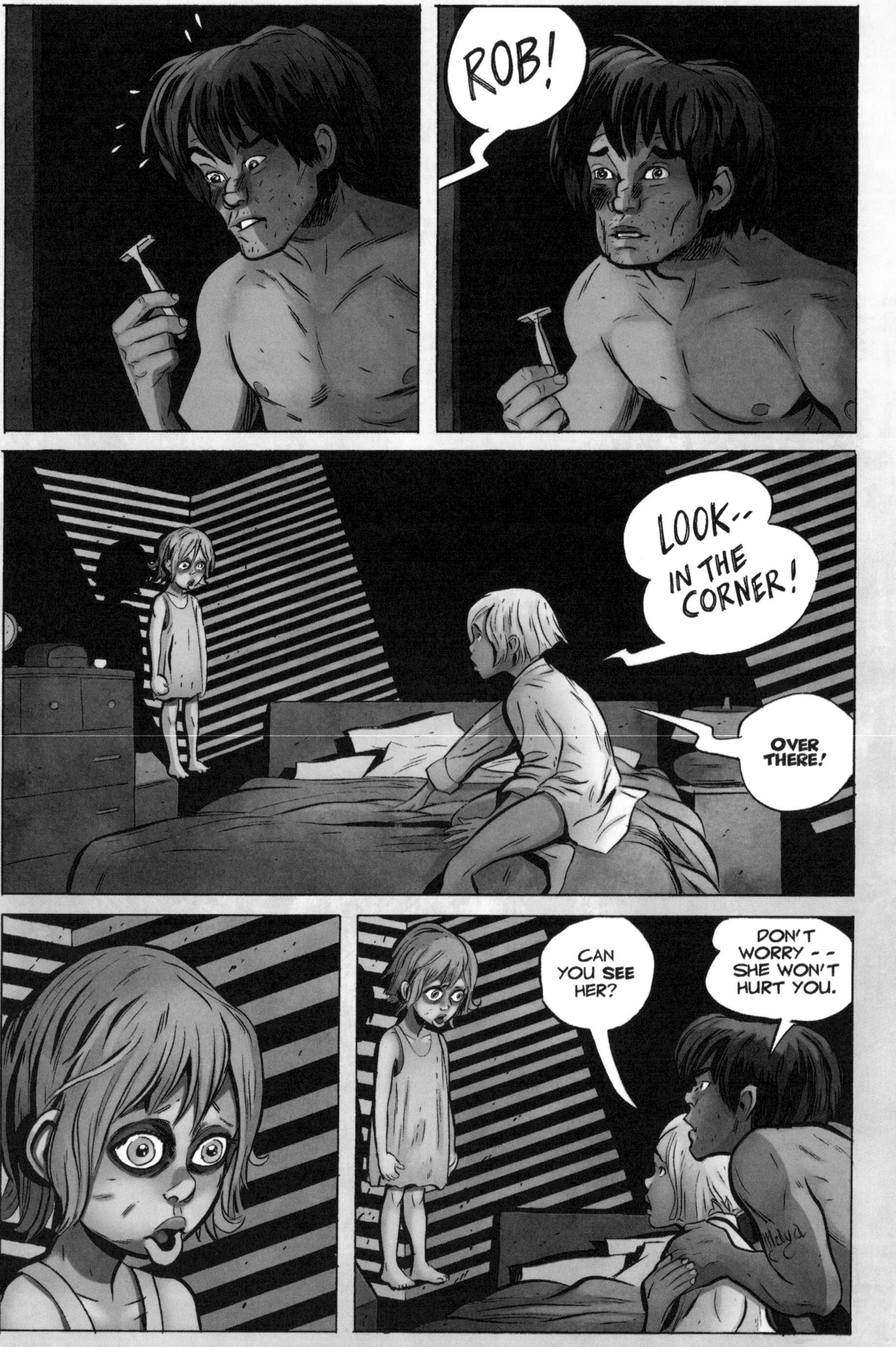
ROB!
LOOK-- IN THE CORNER!
OVER THERE!
CAN YOU SEE HER?
DON'T WORRY -- SHE WON'T HURT YOU.

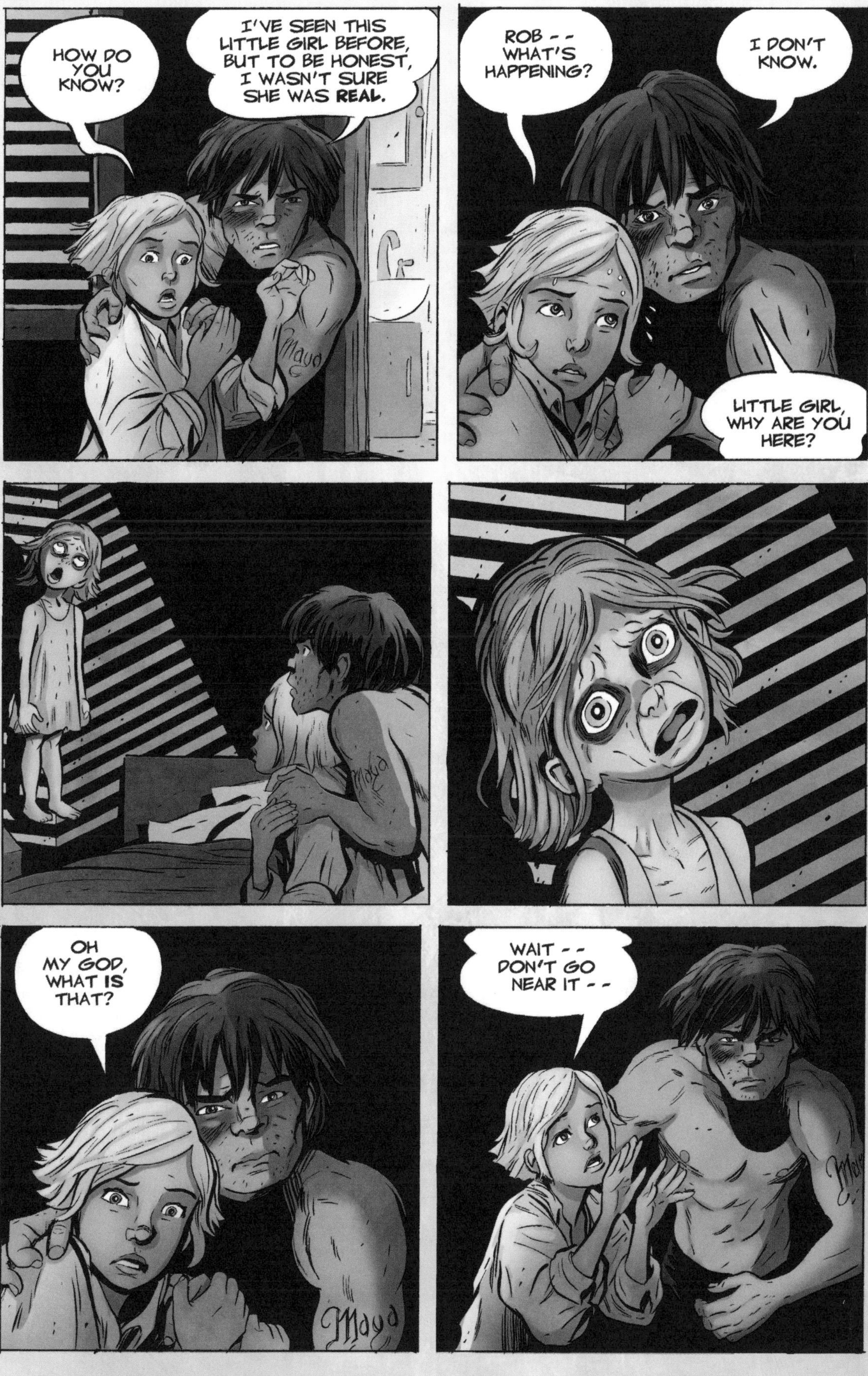
HOW DO YOU KNOW?
I'VE SEEN THIS LITTLE GIRL BEFORE, BUT TO BE HONEST, I WASN'T SURE SHE WAS **REAL.**
ROB - - WHAT'S HAPPENING?
I DON'T KNOW.
LITTLE GIRL, WHY ARE YOU HERE?
OH MY GOD, WHAT **IS** THAT?
WAIT - - DON'T GO NEAR IT - -

SHE'S FADING.

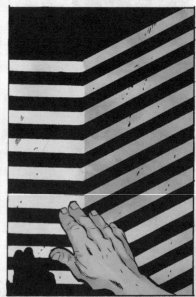

GONE.

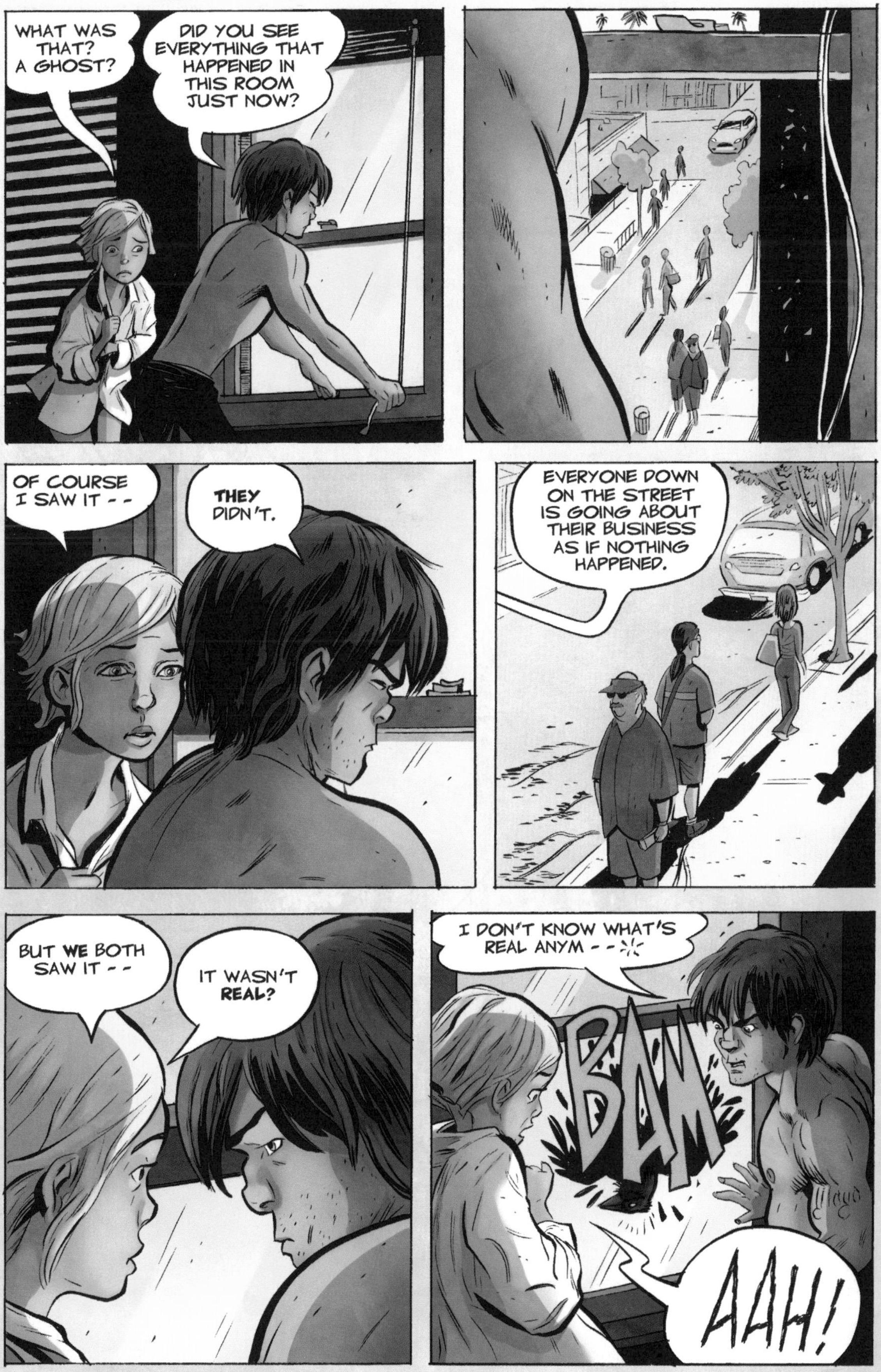
WHAT WAS THAT? A GHOST?
DID YOU SEE EVERYTHING THAT HAPPENED IN THIS ROOM JUST NOW?
OF COURSE I SAW IT - -
THEY DIDN'T.
EVERYONE DOWN ON THE STREET IS GOING ABOUT THEIR BUSINESS AS IF NOTHING HAPPENED.
BUT WE BOTH SAW IT - -
IT WASN'T REAL?
I DON'T KNOW WHAT'S REAL ANYM - -
BAM
AAH!

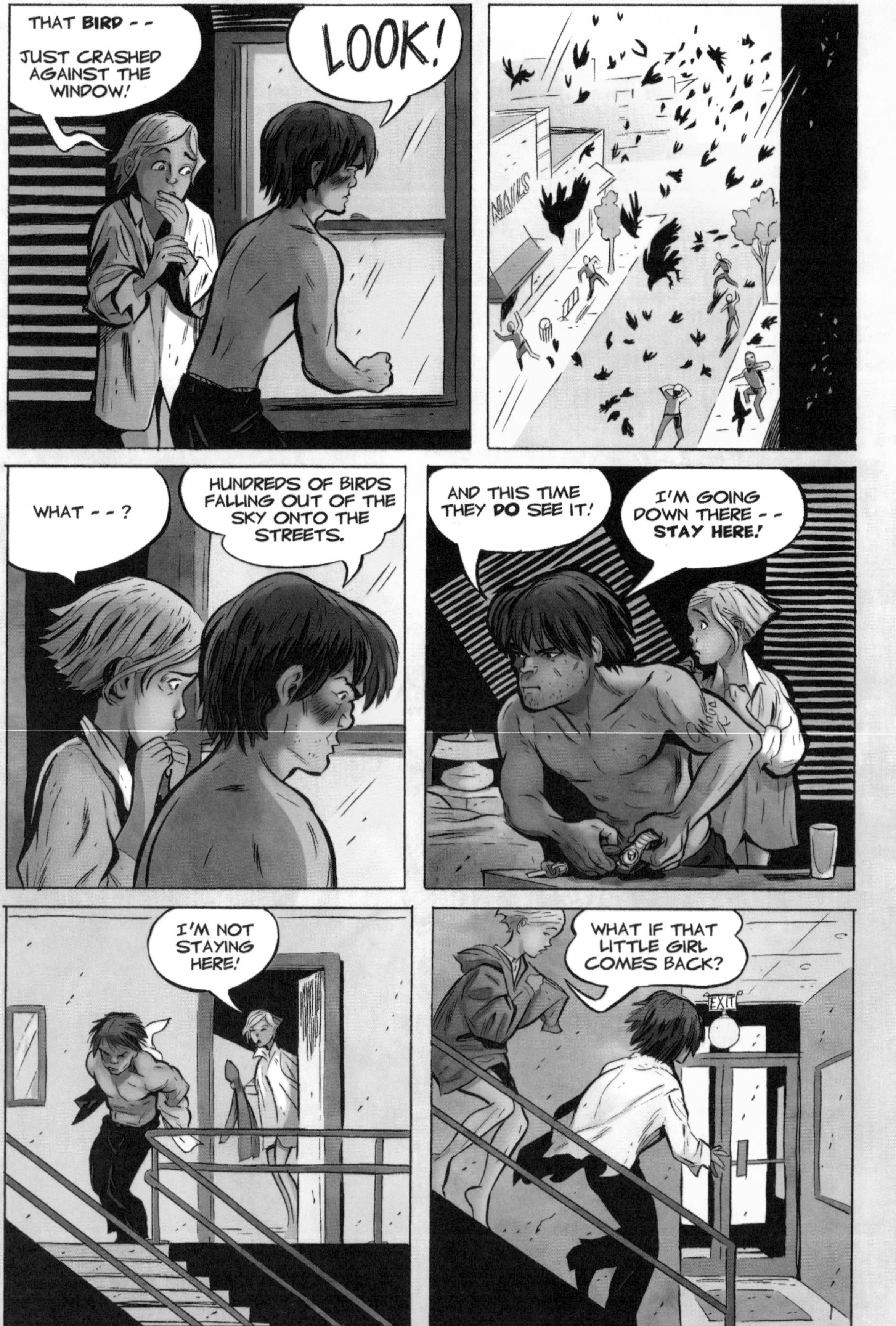
THAT BIRD - -
JUST CRASHED AGAINST THE WINDOW!
LOOK!
WHAT - - ?
HUNDREDS OF BIRDS FALLING OUT OF THE SKY ONTO THE STREETS.
AND THIS TIME THEY DO SEE IT!
I'M GOING DOWN THERE - - STAY HERE!
I'M NOT STAYING HERE!
WHAT IF THAT LITTLE GIRL COMES BACK?
EXIT

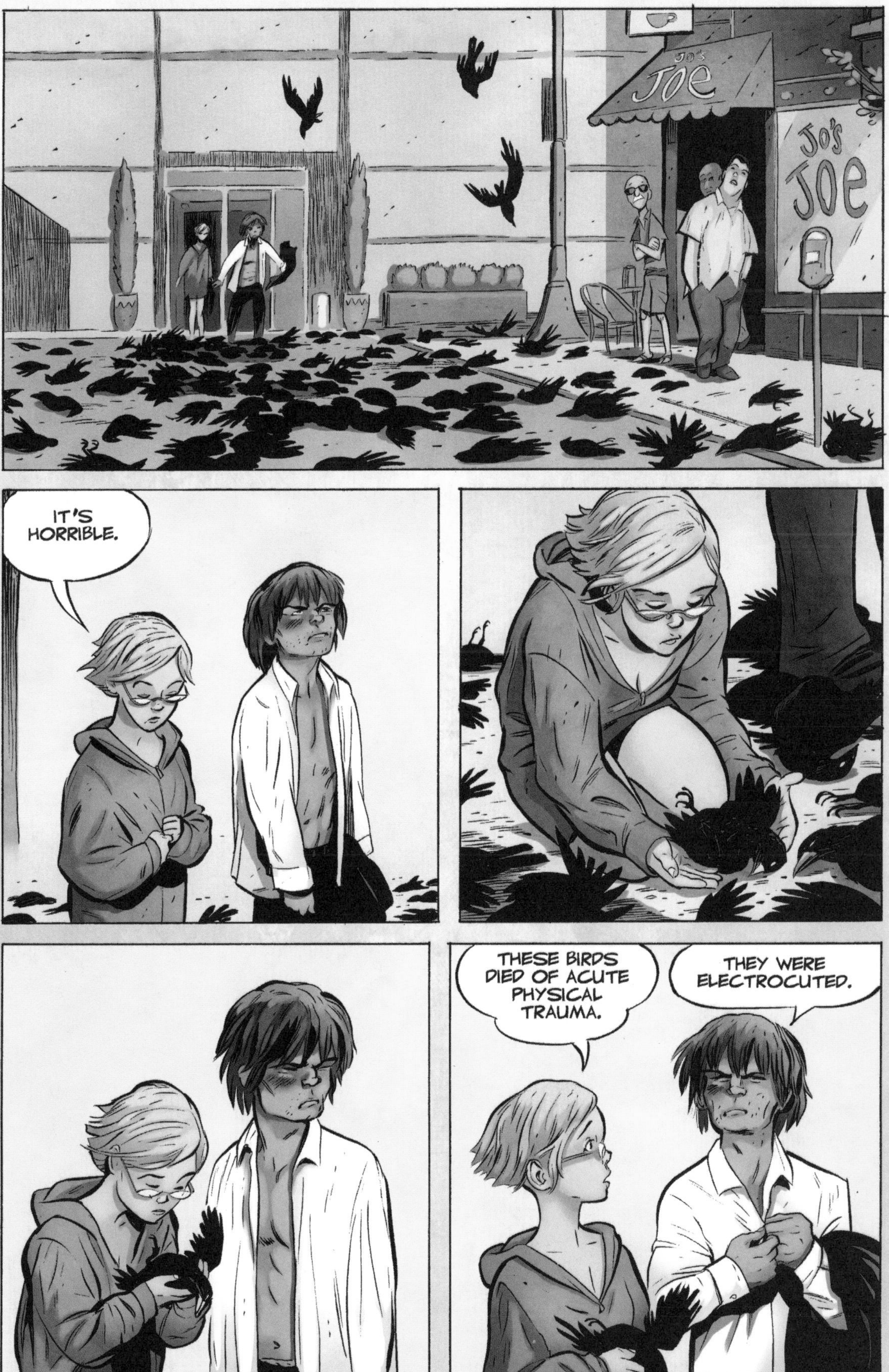
Jo's Joe
Jo's Joe
IT'S HORRIBLE.
THESE BIRDS DIED OF ACUTE PHYSICAL TRAUMA.
THEY WERE ELECTROCUTED.

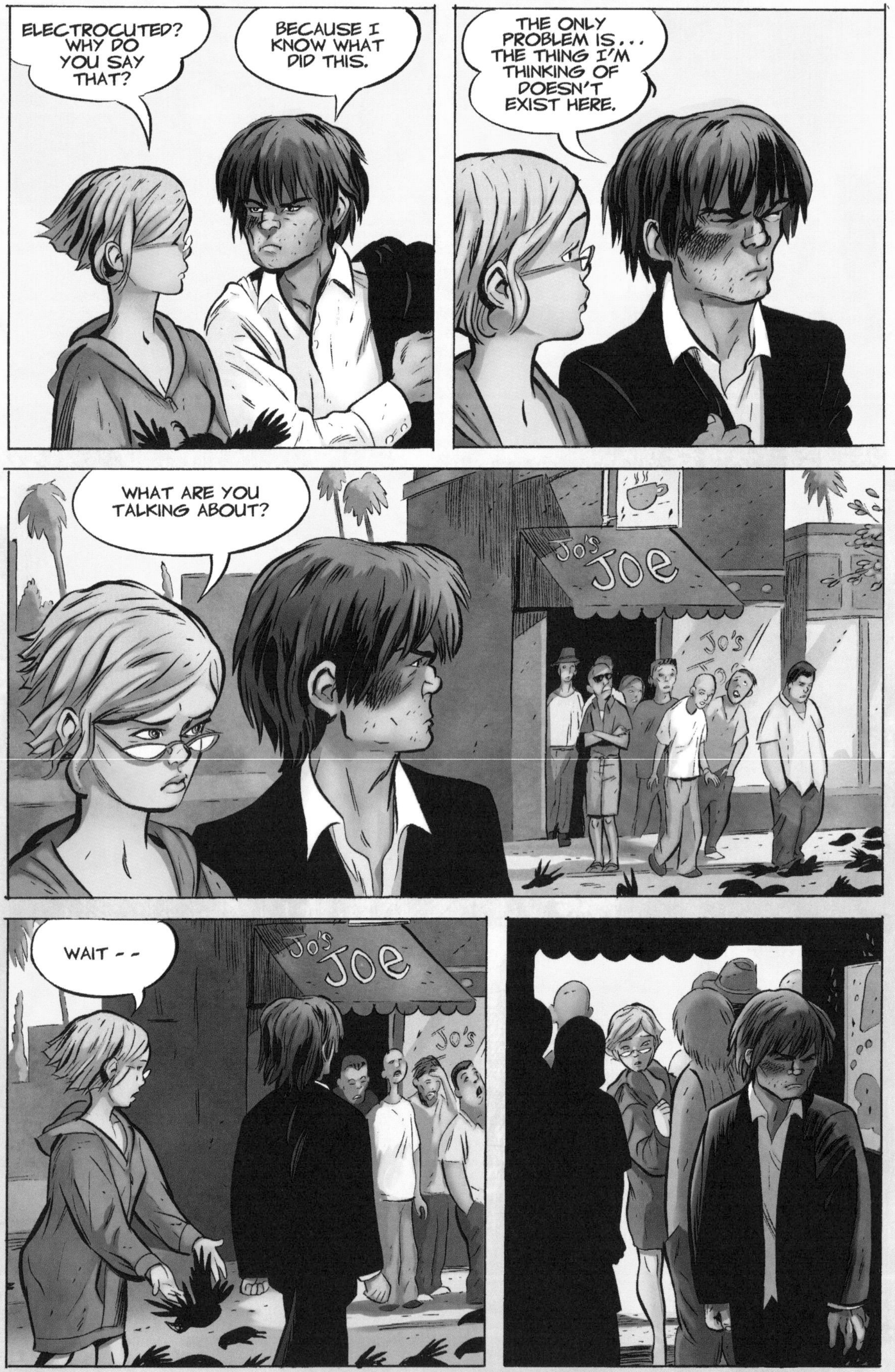

ELECTROCUTED? WHY DO YOU SAY THAT?
BECAUSE I KNOW WHAT DID THIS.
THE ONLY PROBLEM IS... THE THING I'M THINKING OF DOESN'T EXIST HERE.
WHAT ARE YOU TALKING ABOUT?
Jo's JOE
Jo's
WAIT --
Jo's JOE
Jo's

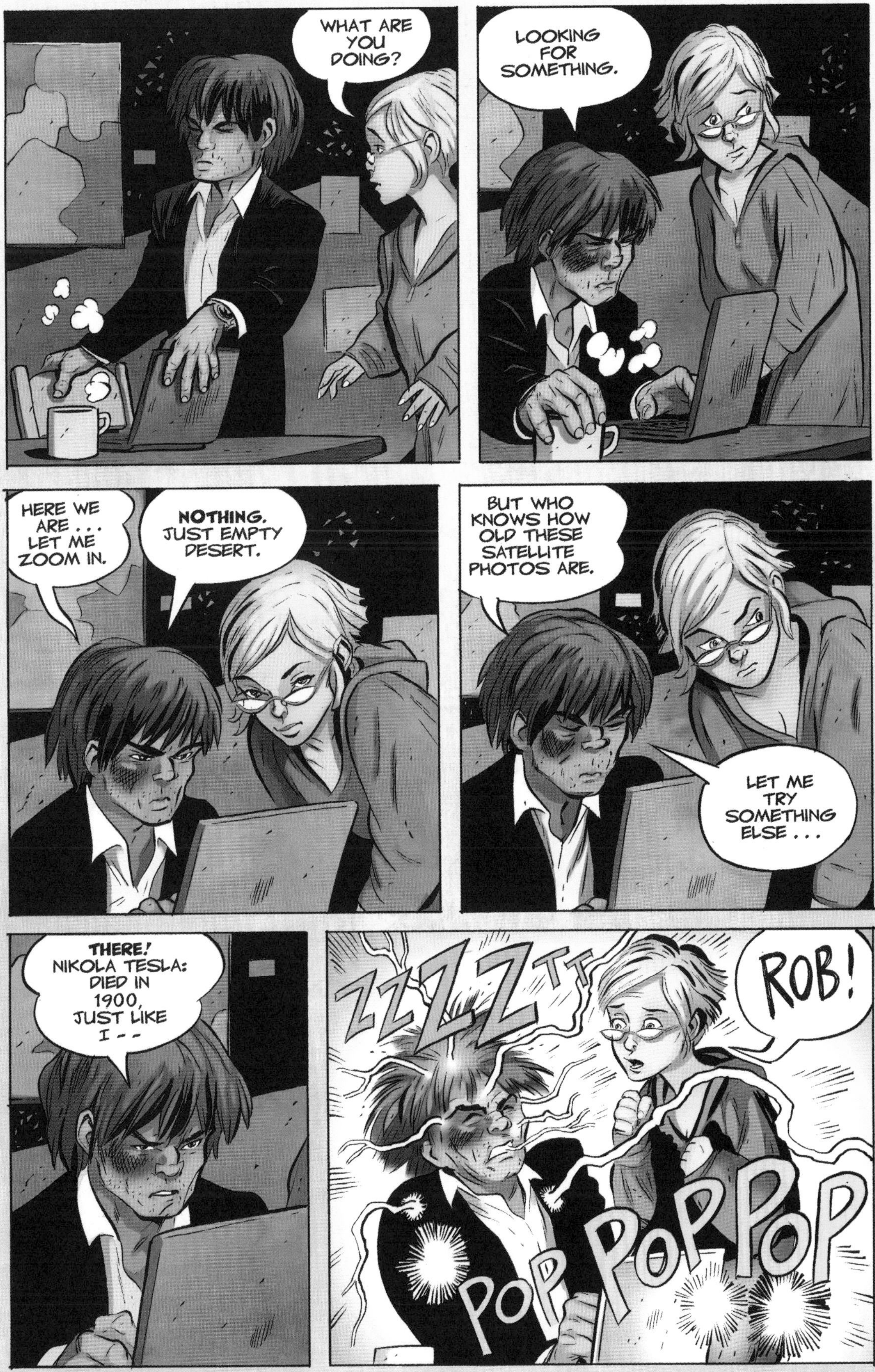
WHAT ARE YOU DOING?
LOOKING FOR SOMETHING.
HERE WE ARE . . . LET ME ZOOM IN.
NOTHING. JUST EMPTY DESERT.
BUT WHO KNOWS HOW OLD THESE SATELLITE PHOTOS ARE.
LET ME TRY SOMETHING ELSE . . .
THERE! NIKOLA TESLA: DIED IN 1900, JUST LIKE I - -
ZZZZTT
ROB!
POP POP POP POP

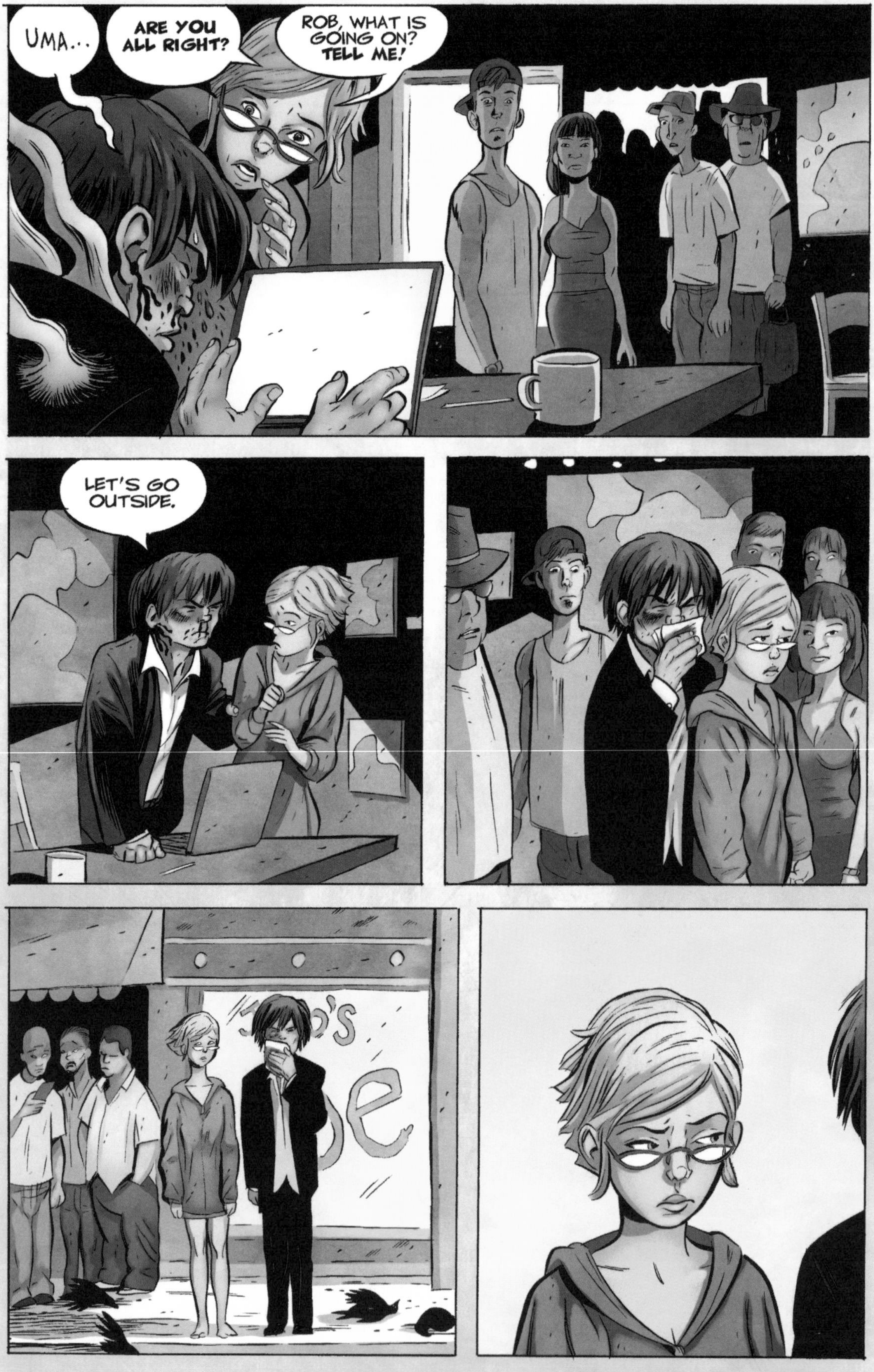
UMA...
ARE YOU ALL RIGHT?
ROB, WHAT IS GOING ON? TELL ME!
LET'S GO OUTSIDE.

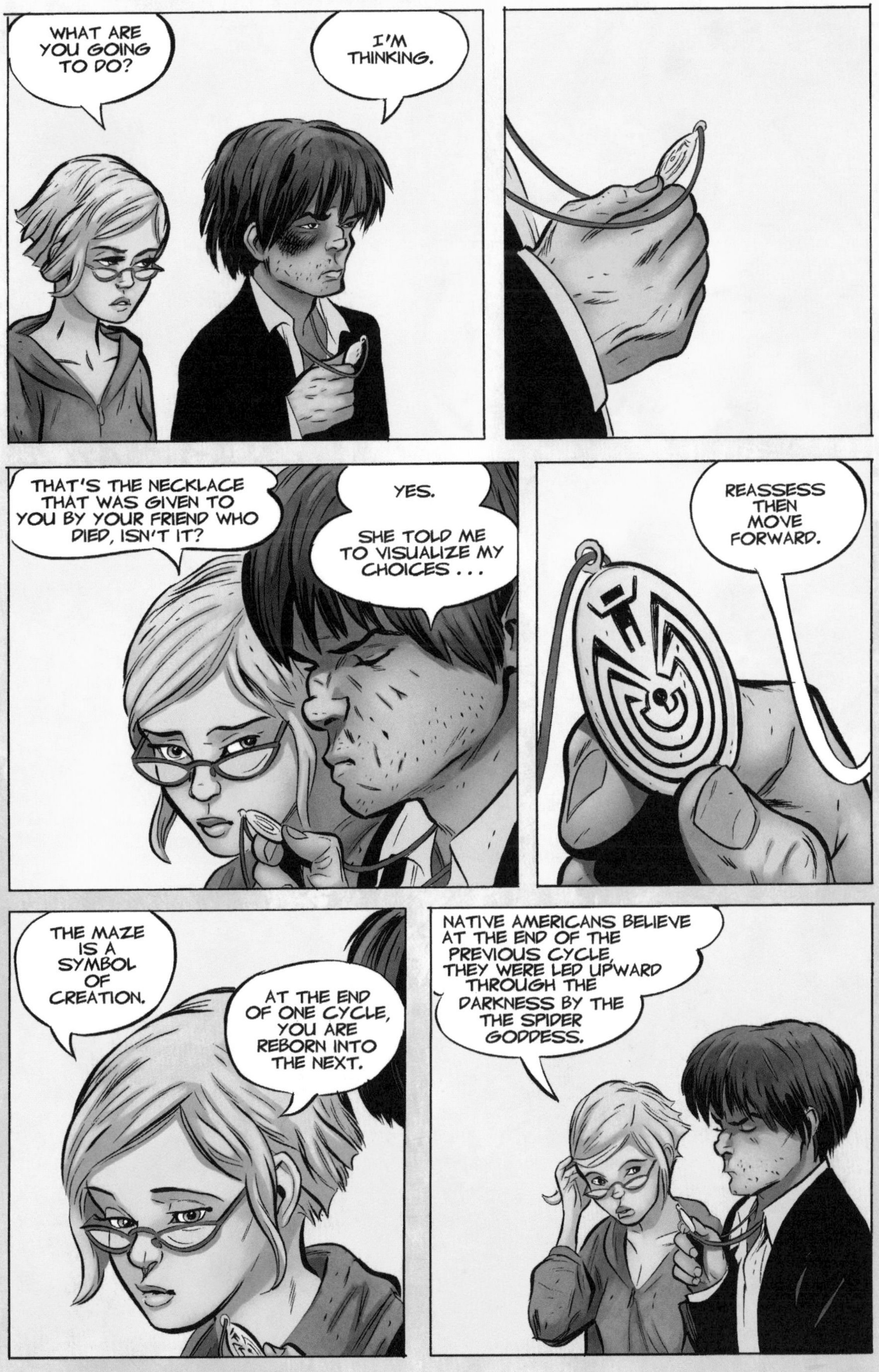
WHAT ARE YOU GOING TO DO?
I'M THINKING.
THAT'S THE NECKLACE THAT WAS GIVEN TO YOU BY YOUR FRIEND WHO DIED, ISN'T IT?
YES.
SHE TOLD ME TO VISUALIZE MY CHOICES . . .
REASSESS THEN MOVE FORWARD.
THE MAZE IS A SYMBOL OF CREATION.
AT THE END OF ONE CYCLE, YOU ARE REBORN INTO THE NEXT.
NATIVE AMERICANS BELIEVE AT THE END OF THE PREVIOUS CYCLE, THEY WERE LED UPWARD THROUGH THE DARKNESS BY THE THE SPIDER GODDESS.

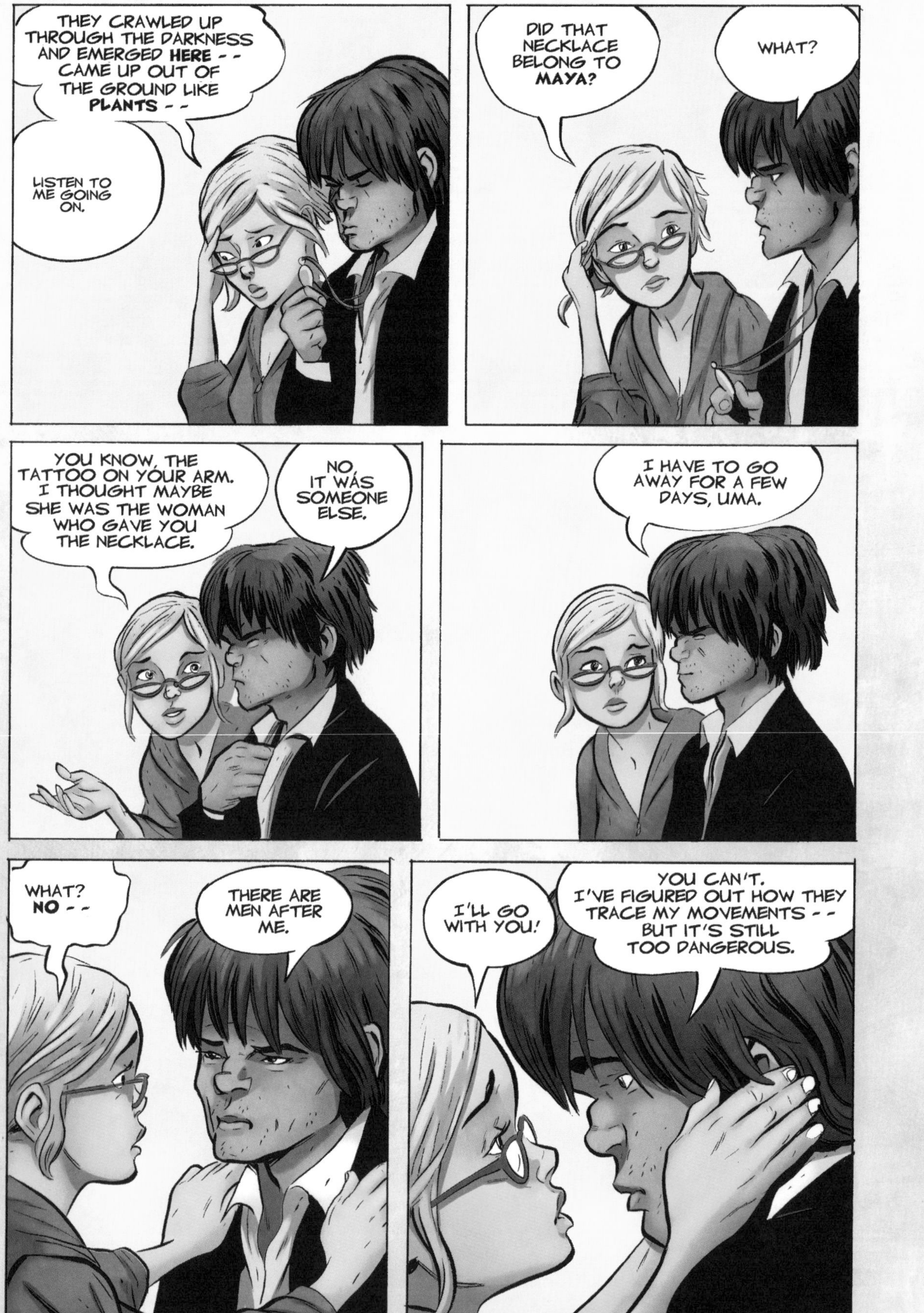
THEY CRAWLED UP THROUGH THE DARKNESS AND EMERGED **HERE** - - CAME UP OUT OF THE GROUND LIKE **PLANTS** - -
LISTEN TO ME GOING ON.
DID THAT NECKLACE BELONG TO **MAYA?**
WHAT?
YOU KNOW, THE TATTOO ON YOUR ARM. I THOUGHT MAYBE SHE WAS THE WOMAN WHO GAVE YOU THE NECKLACE.
NO, IT WAS SOMEONE ELSE.
I HAVE TO GO AWAY FOR A FEW DAYS, UMA.
WHAT? **NO** - -
THERE ARE MEN AFTER ME.
I'LL GO WITH YOU!
YOU CAN'T. I'VE FIGURED OUT HOW THEY TRACE MY MOVEMENTS - - BUT IT'S STILL TOO DANGEROUS.

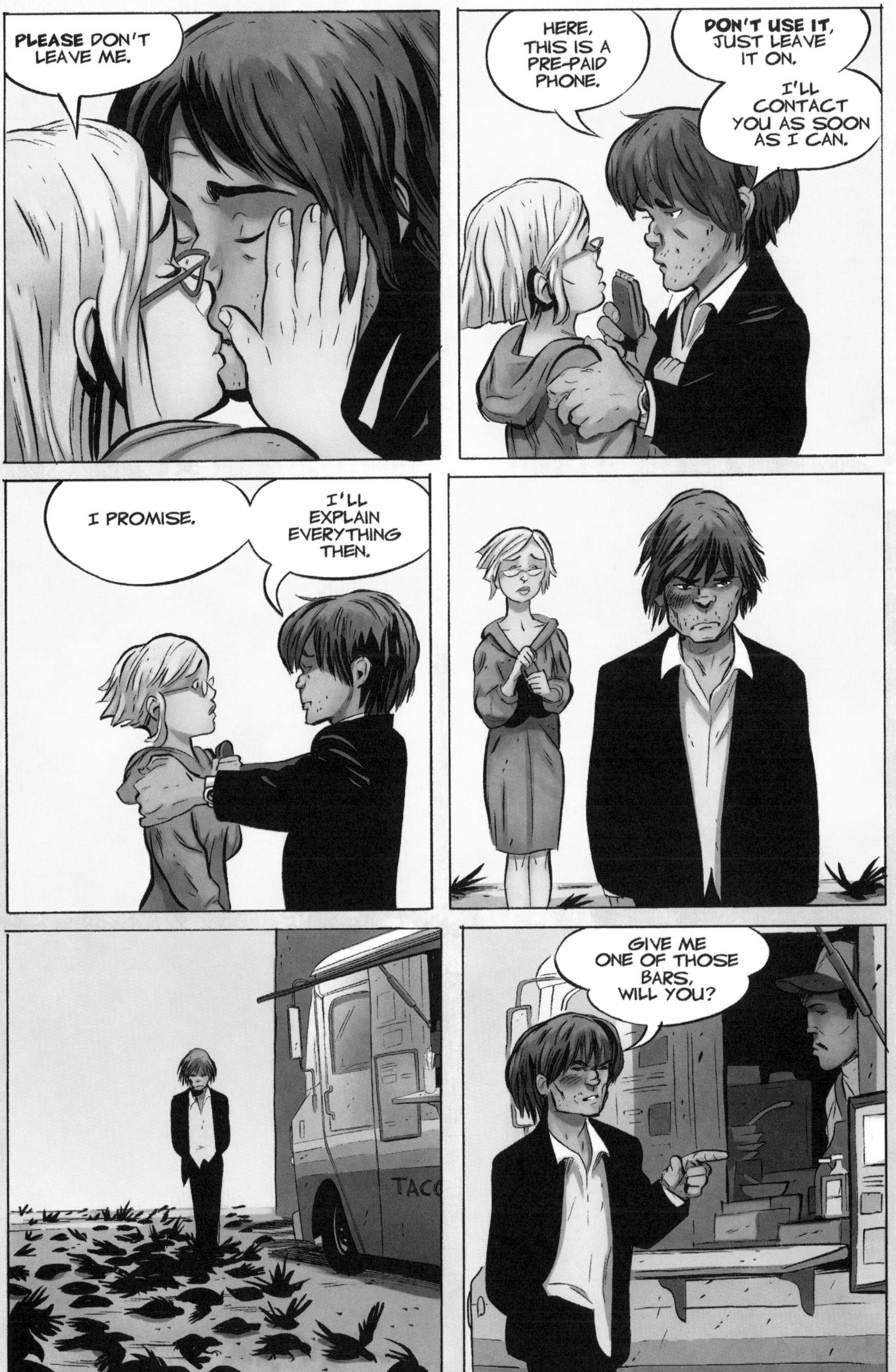
PLEASE DON'T LEAVE ME.
HERE, THIS IS A PRE-PAID PHONE.
DON'T USE IT, JUST LEAVE IT ON.
I'LL CONTACT YOU AS SOON AS I CAN.
I PROMISE.
I'LL EXPLAIN EVERYTHING THEN.
TACO
GIVE ME ONE OF THOSE BARS, WILL YOU?

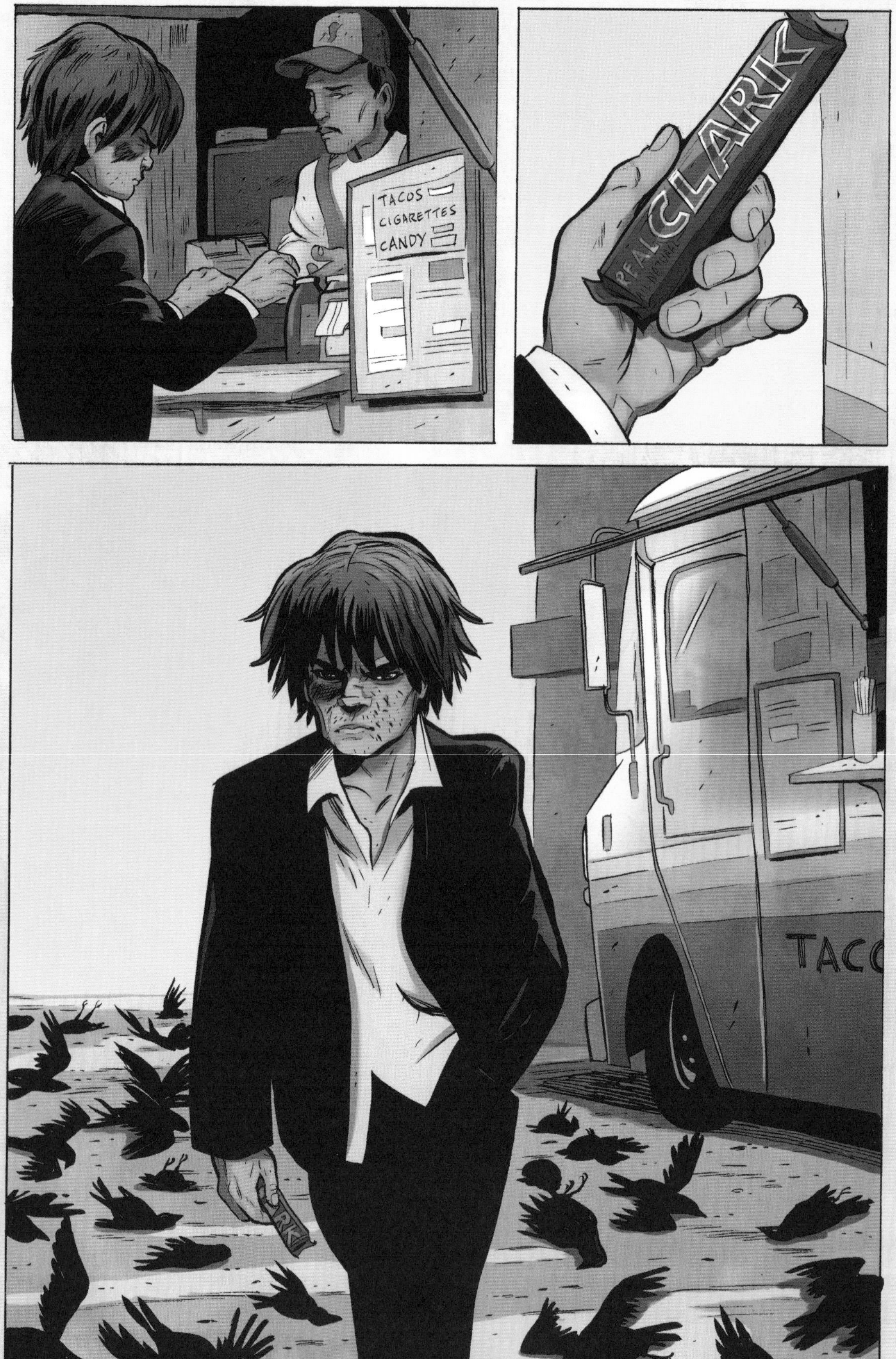
TACOS
CIGARETTES
CANDY
REAL CLARK
TACO

ACT FOUR

THE LOST JOURNALS
OF NIKOLA TESLA

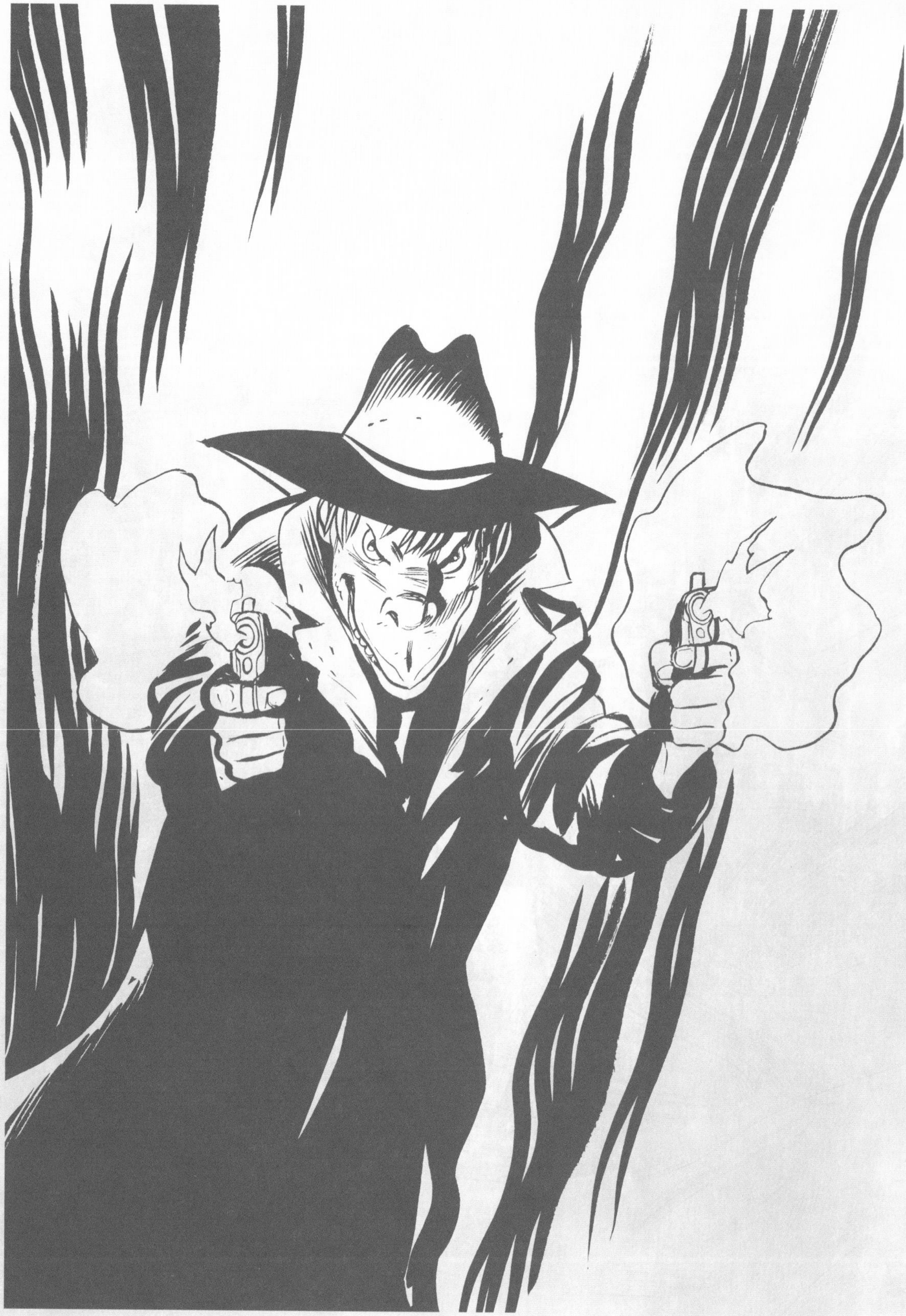

"The day when we know what exactly electricity is, will chronicle an event probably greater, more important than any other recorded in the history of the human race."

"Someday - - but not at this time - - I shall make an announcement of something that I never once dreamed of."

-Nikola Tesla

XII
SYNCHRONICITY

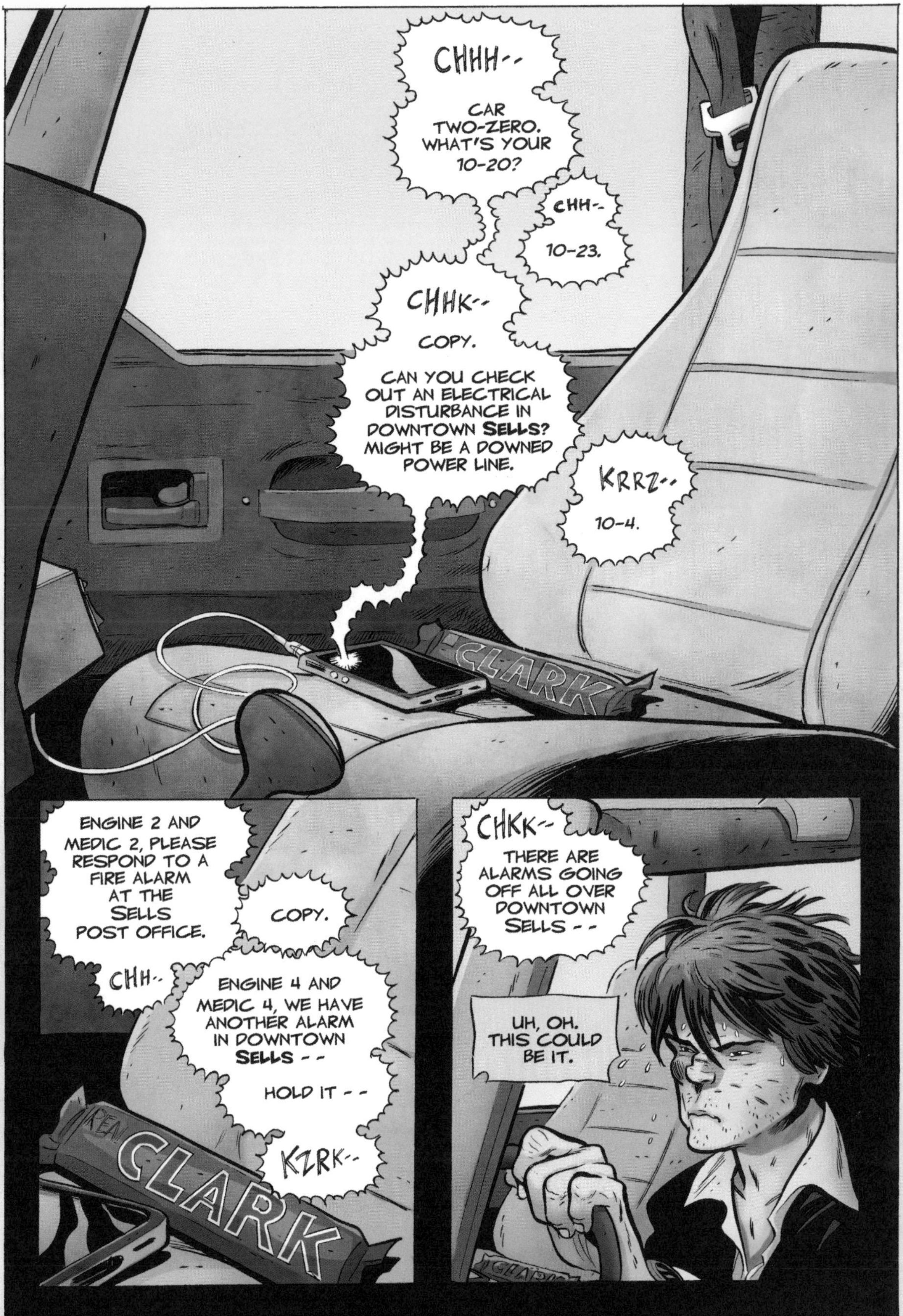
CHHH--
CAR TWO-ZERO. WHAT'S YOUR 10-20?
CHH--
10-23.
CHHK--
COPY.
CAN YOU CHECK OUT AN ELECTRICAL DISTURBANCE IN DOWNTOWN SELLS? MIGHT BE A DOWNED POWER LINE.
KRRZ--
10-4.
CLARK
ENGINE 2 AND MEDIC 2, PLEASE RESPOND TO A FIRE ALARM AT THE SELLS POST OFFICE.
COPY.
CHH--
ENGINE 4 AND MEDIC 4, WE HAVE ANOTHER ALARM IN DOWNTOWN SELLS --
HOLD IT --
KZRK--
CLARK
CHKK--
THERE ARE ALARMS GOING OFF ALL OVER DOWNTOWN SELLS --
UH, OH. THIS COULD BE IT.

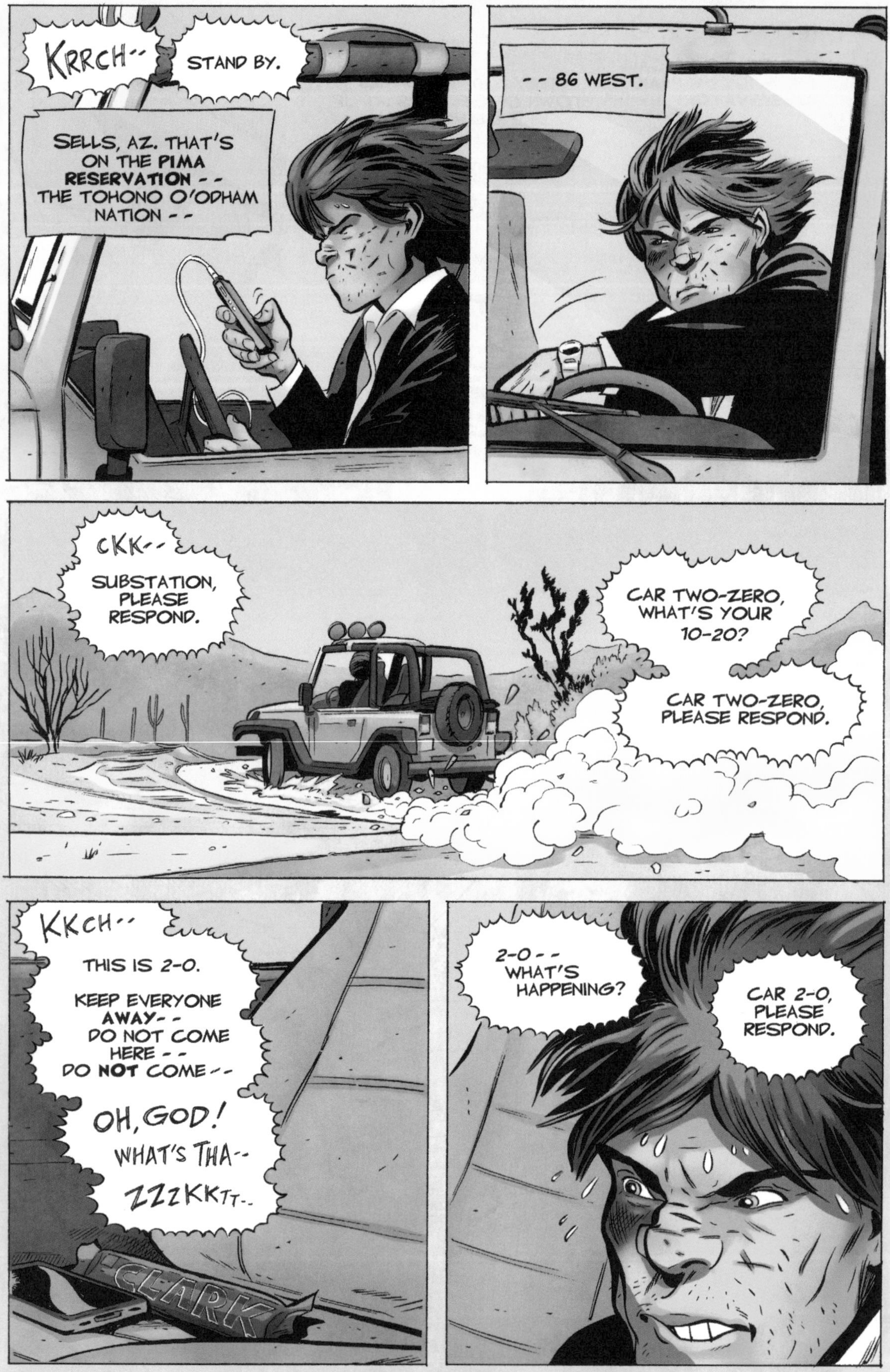
KRRCH--
STAND BY.
SELLS, AZ. THAT'S ON THE PIMA RESERVATION -- THE TOHONO O'ODHAM NATION --
-- 86 WEST.
CKK--
SUBSTATION, PLEASE RESPOND.
CAR TWO-ZERO, WHAT'S YOUR 10-20?
CAR TWO-ZERO, PLEASE RESPOND.
KKCH--
THIS IS 2-0.
KEEP EVERYONE AWAY-- DO NOT COME HERE -- DO NOT COME --
OH, GOD!
WHAT'S THA--
ZZZKKTT--
2-0 -- WHAT'S HAPPENING?
CAR 2-0, PLEASE RESPOND.
CLARK

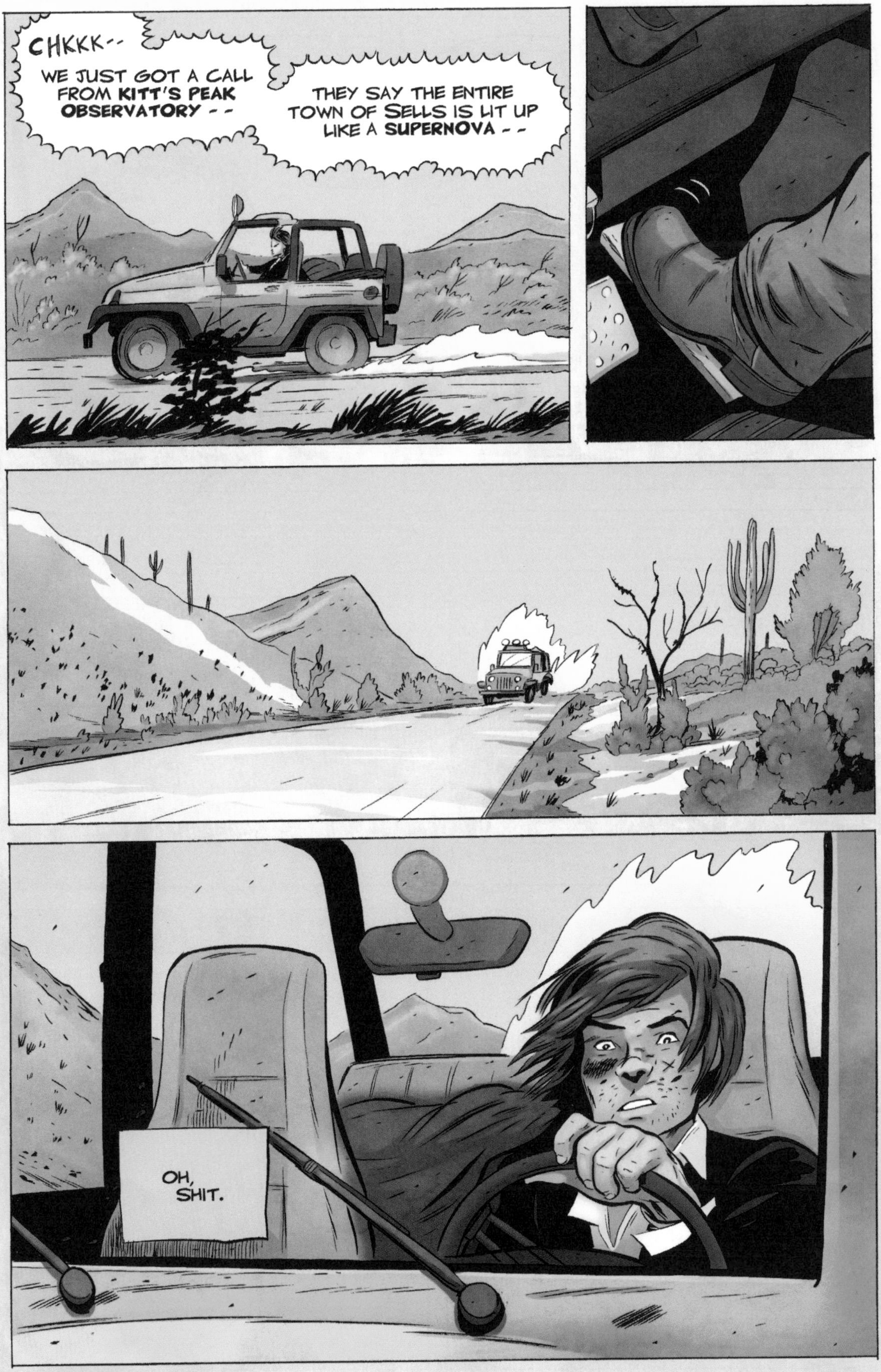
CHKKK--
WE JUST GOT A CALL FROM KITT'S PEAK OBSERVATORY --
THEY SAY THE ENTIRE TOWN OF SELLS IS LIT UP LIKE A SUPERNOVA --
OH, SHIT.

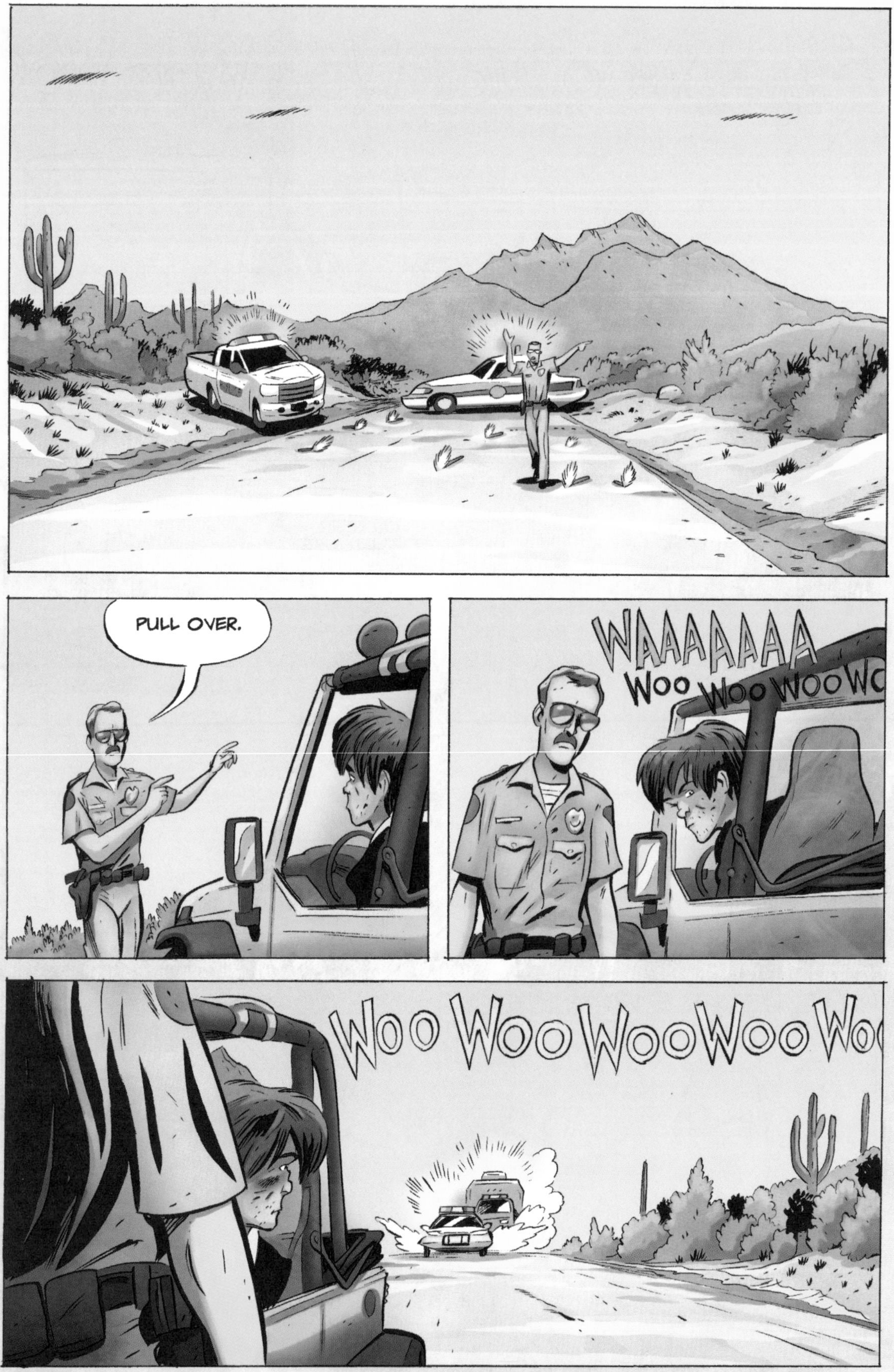
PULL OVER.
WAAAAAAA
WOO WOO WOO WO
WOO WOO WOO WOO WO

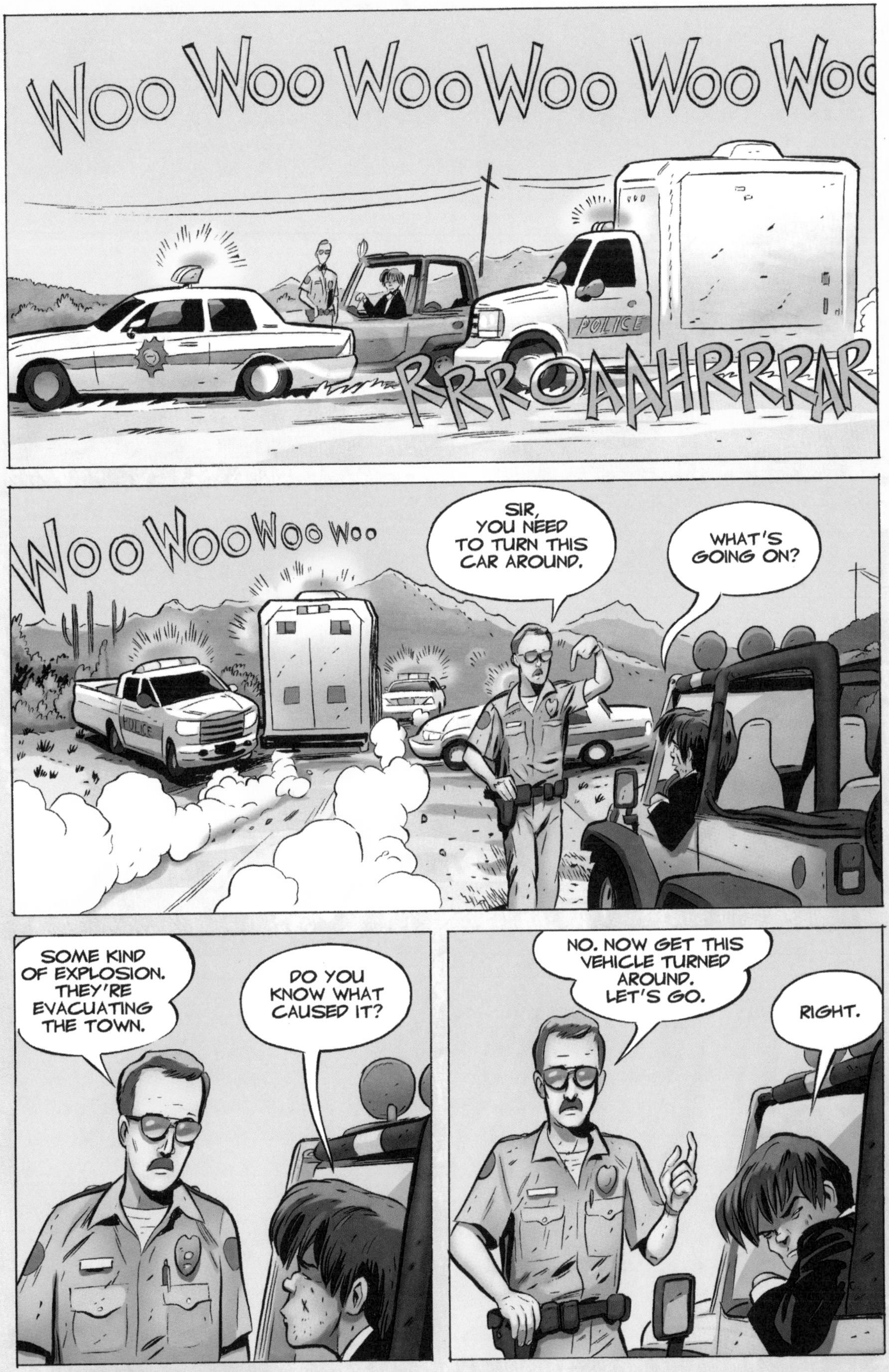
WOO WOO WOO WOO WOO WOO
RRROAAHRRRAR
WOO WOO WOO WOO
SIR, YOU NEED TO TURN THIS CAR AROUND.
WHAT'S GOING ON?
SOME KIND OF EXPLOSION. THEY'RE EVACUATING THE TOWN.
DO YOU KNOW WHAT CAUSED IT?
NO. NOW GET THIS VEHICLE TURNED AROUND. LET'S GO.
RIGHT.

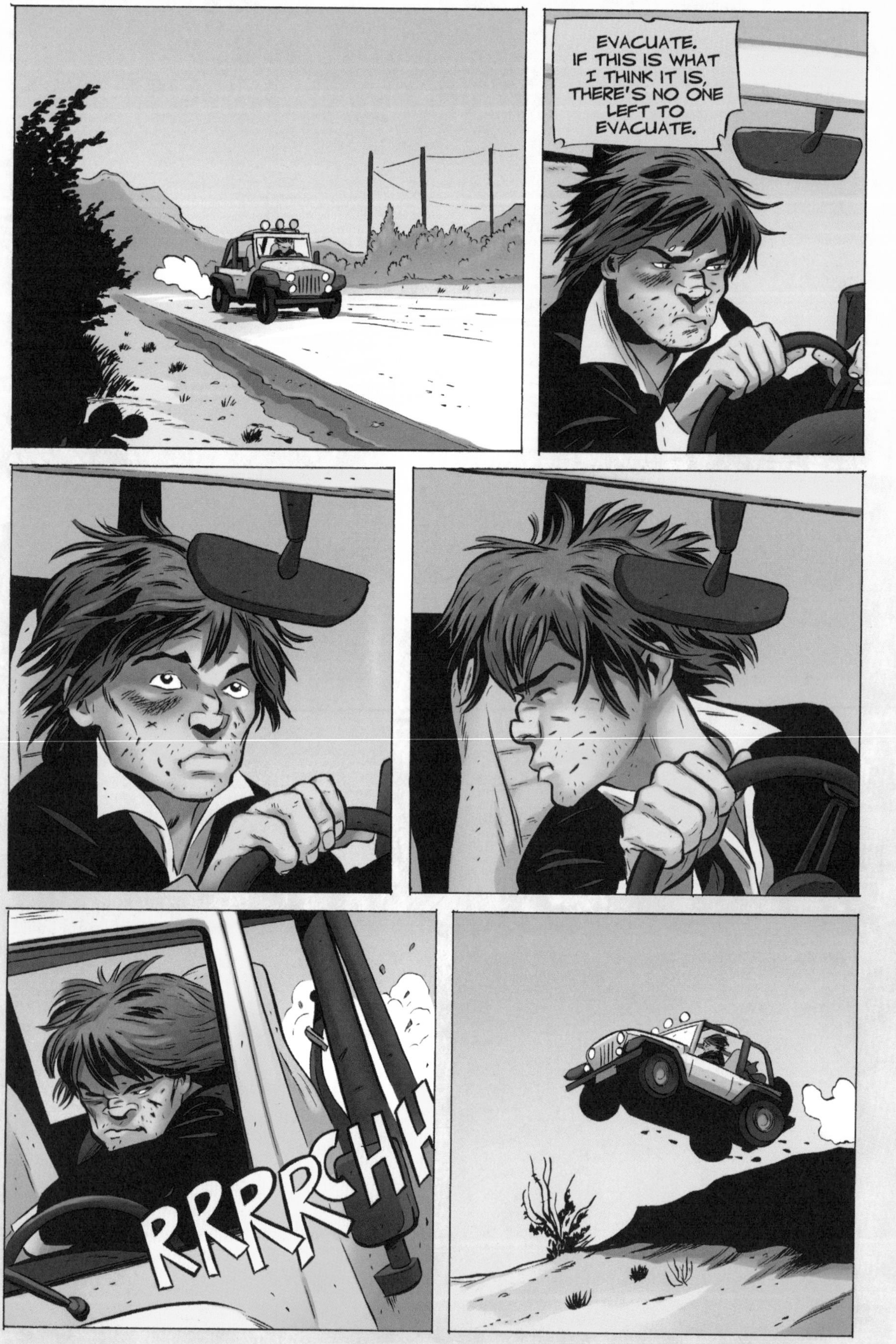
EVACUATE. IF THIS IS WHAT I THINK IT IS, THERE'S NO ONE LEFT TO EVACUATE.
RRRRCHH

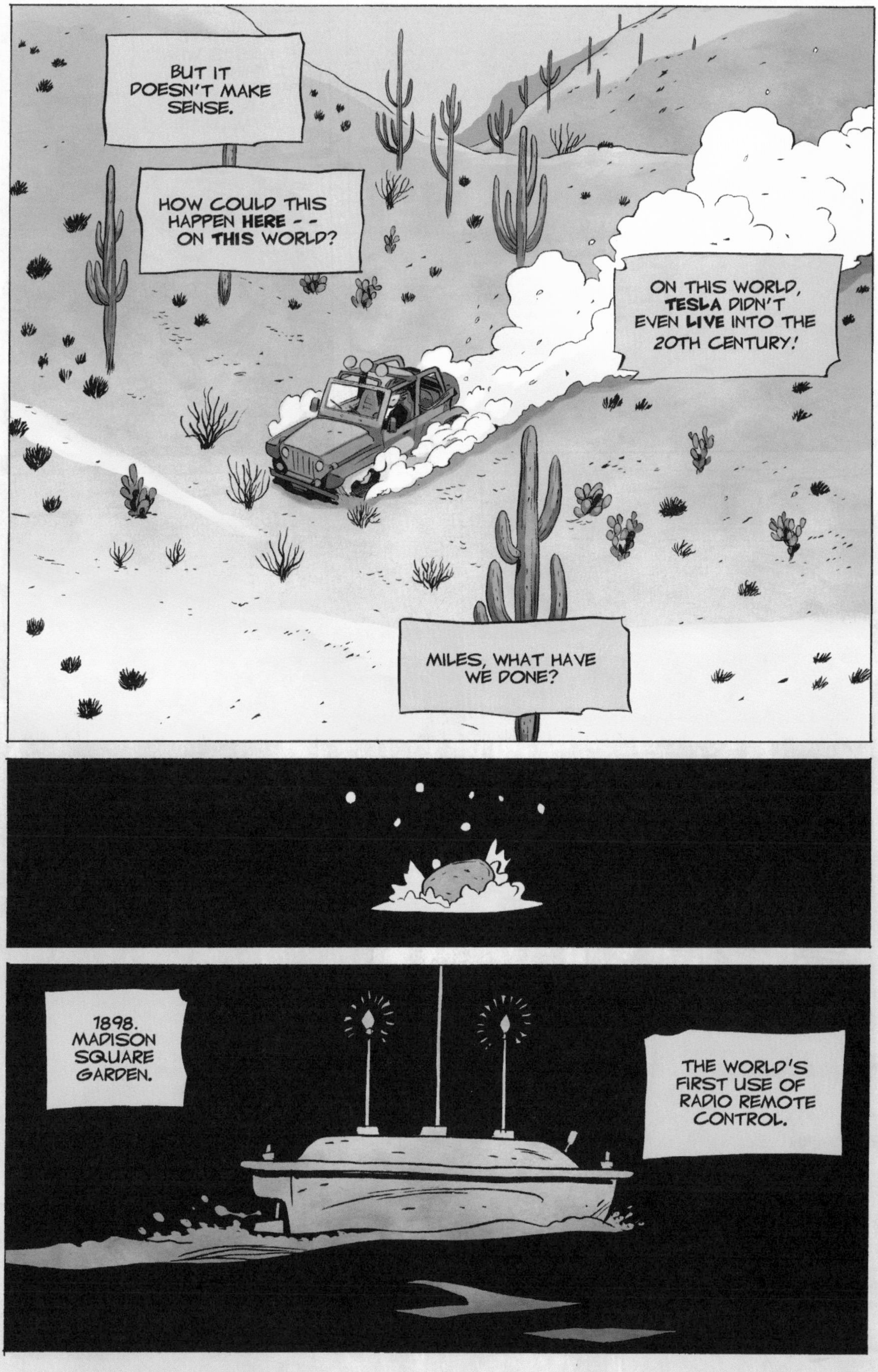
BUT IT DOESN'T MAKE SENSE.
HOW COULD THIS HAPPEN HERE -- ON THIS WORLD?
ON THIS WORLD, TESLA DIDN'T EVEN LIVE INTO THE 20TH CENTURY!
MILES, WHAT HAVE WE DONE?
1898. MADISON SQUARE GARDEN.
THE WORLD'S FIRST USE OF RADIO REMOTE CONTROL.

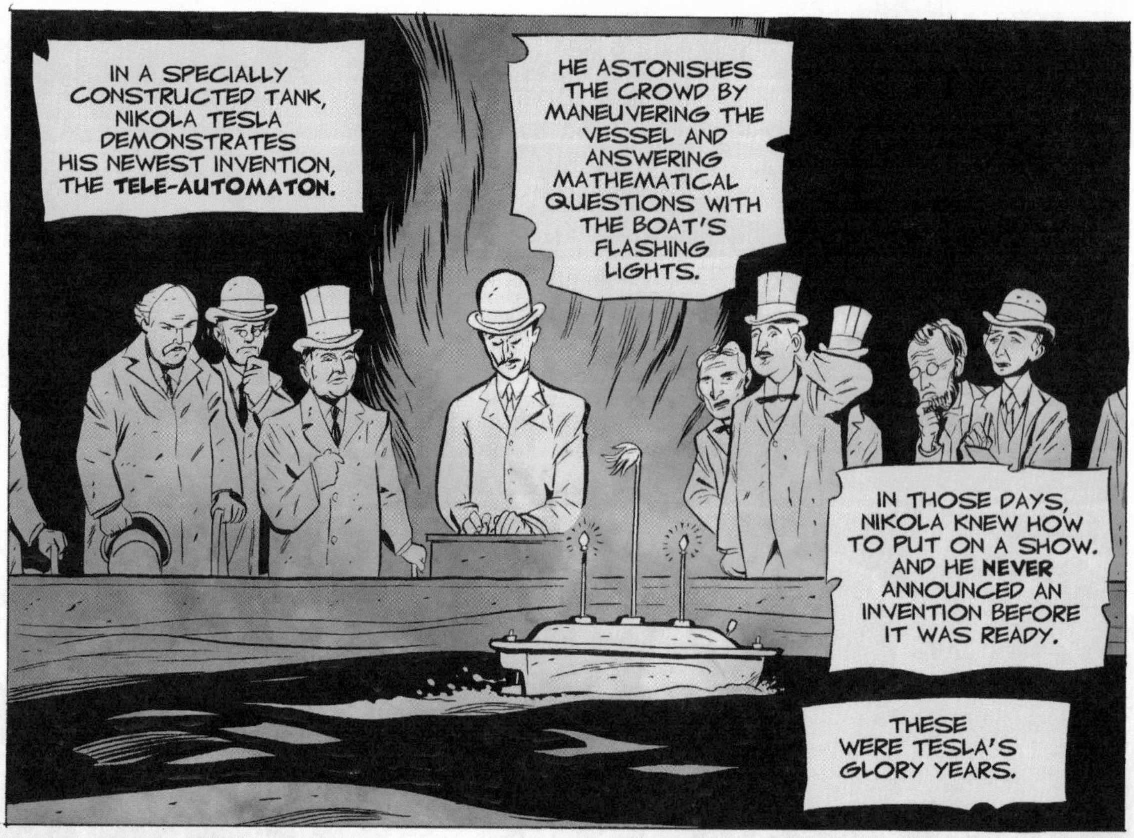
IN A SPECIALLY CONSTRUCTED TANK, NIKOLA TESLA DEMONSTRATES HIS NEWEST INVENTION, THE **TELE-AUTOMATON.**
HE ASTONISHES THE CROWD BY MANEUVERING THE VESSEL AND ANSWERING MATHEMATICAL QUESTIONS WITH THE BOAT'S FLASHING LIGHTS.
IN THOSE DAYS, NIKOLA KNEW HOW TO PUT ON A SHOW. AND HE **NEVER** ANNOUNCED AN INVENTION BEFORE IT WAS READY.
THESE WERE TESLA'S GLORY YEARS.

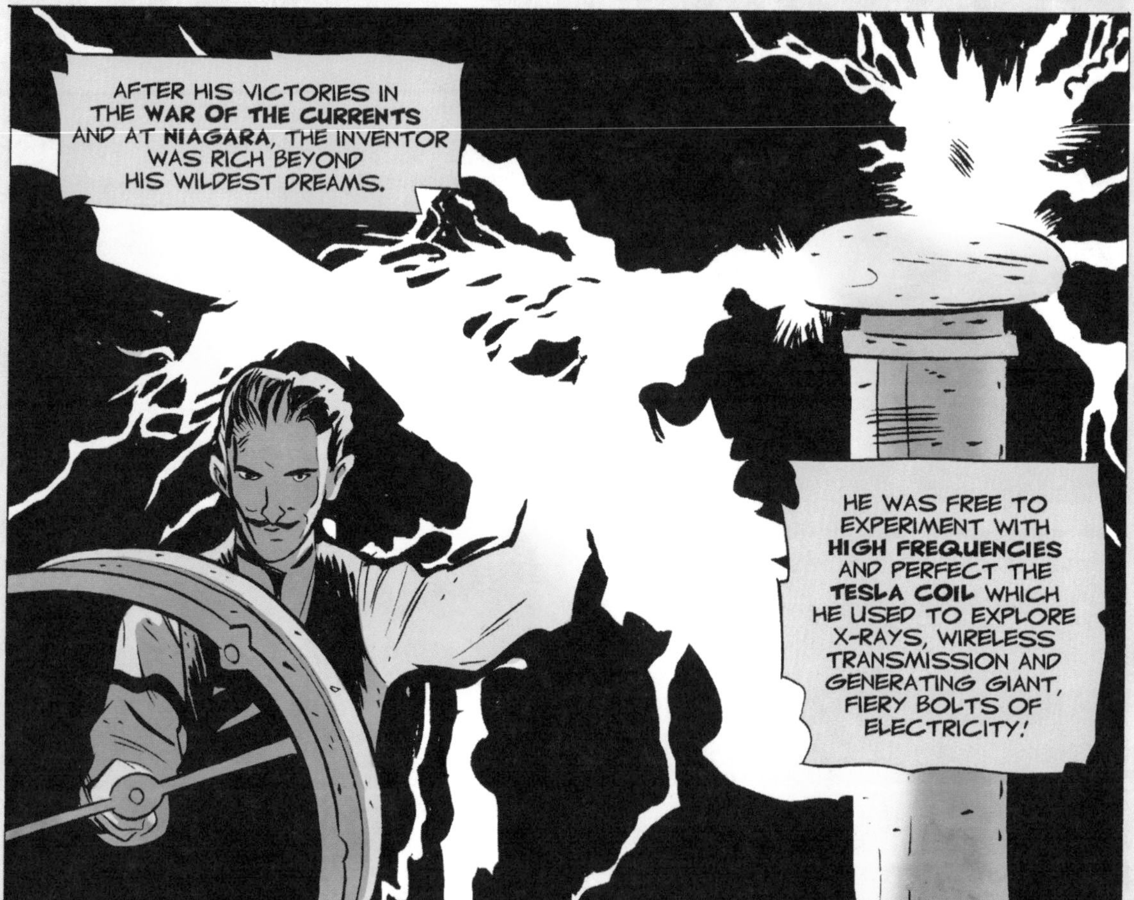
AFTER HIS VICTORIES IN THE **WAR OF THE CURRENTS** AND AT **NIAGARA**, THE INVENTOR WAS RICH BEYOND HIS WILDEST DREAMS.
HE WAS FREE TO EXPERIMENT WITH **HIGH FREQUENCIES** AND PERFECT THE **TESLA COIL** WHICH HE USED TO EXPLORE X-RAYS, WIRELESS TRANSMISSION AND GENERATING GIANT, FIERY BOLTS OF ELECTRICITY!

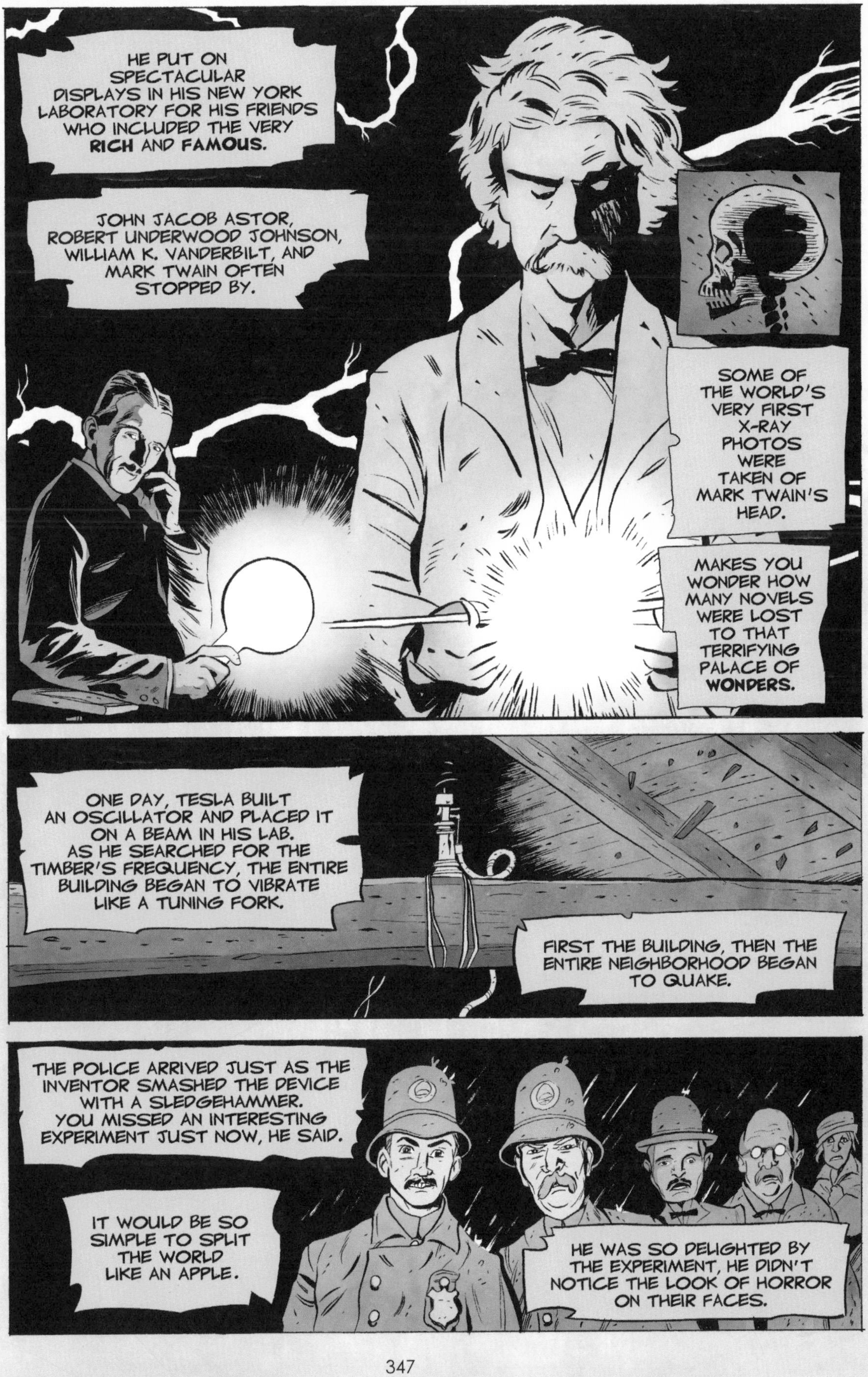
HE PUT ON SPECTACULAR DISPLAYS IN HIS NEW YORK LABORATORY FOR HIS FRIENDS WHO INCLUDED THE VERY **RICH** AND **FAMOUS.**
JOHN JACOB ASTOR, ROBERT UNDERWOOD JOHNSON, WILLIAM K. VANDERBILT, AND MARK TWAIN OFTEN STOPPED BY.
SOME OF THE WORLD'S VERY FIRST X-RAY PHOTOS WERE TAKEN OF MARK TWAIN'S HEAD.
MAKES YOU WONDER HOW MANY NOVELS WERE LOST TO THAT TERRIFYING PALACE OF **WONDERS.**
ONE DAY, TESLA BUILT AN OSCILLATOR AND PLACED IT ON A BEAM IN HIS LAB. AS HE SEARCHED FOR THE TIMBER'S FREQUENCY, THE ENTIRE BUILDING BEGAN TO VIBRATE LIKE A TUNING FORK.
FIRST THE BUILDING, THEN THE ENTIRE NEIGHBORHOOD BEGAN TO QUAKE.
THE POLICE ARRIVED JUST AS THE INVENTOR SMASHED THE DEVICE WITH A SLEDGEHAMMER. YOU MISSED AN INTERESTING EXPERIMENT JUST NOW, HE SAID.
IT WOULD BE SO SIMPLE TO SPLIT THE WORLD LIKE AN APPLE.
HE WAS SO DELIGHTED BY THE EXPERIMENT, HE DIDN'T NOTICE THE LOOK OF HORROR ON THEIR FACES.

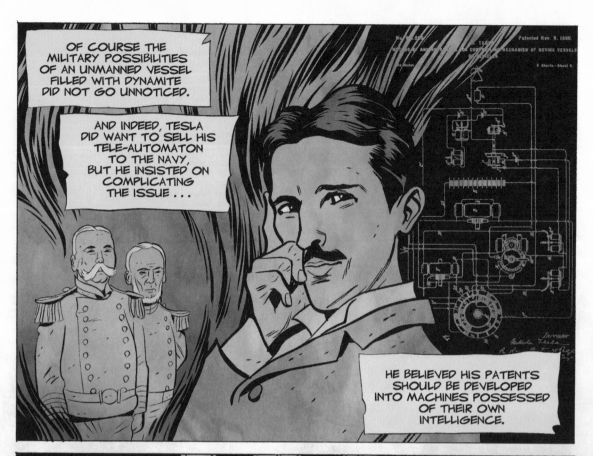

OF COURSE THE MILITARY POSSIBILITIES OF AN UNMANNED VESSEL FILLED WITH DYNAMITE DID NOT GO UNNOTICED.

AND INDEED, TESLA DID WANT TO SELL HIS TELE-AUTOMATON TO THE NAVY, BUT HE INSISTED ON COMPLICATING THE ISSUE . . .

HE BELIEVED HIS PATENTS SHOULD BE DEVELOPED INTO MACHINES POSSESSED OF THEIR OWN INTELLIGENCE.

HE WANTED TO REPLACE THE BOYS ON THE BATTLEFIELD WITH AUTOMATONS THAT COULD ACT AND REASON ON THEIR OWN -- HERALD IN A NEW AGE OF **ROBOT SOLDIERS.**

THE GOVERNMENT CHOSE NOT TO GO INTO BUSINESS WITH HIM AT THAT TIME, BUT THEY WOULD BE KEEPING AN EYE ON MR. NIKOLA TESLA.

THE BEGINNING OF THE END WAS A FIRE THAT DESTROYED HIS LAB.

EVERYTHING WAS LOST. THE WORK OF A LIFETIME GONE IN A FIRE THAT LASTED AN HOUR.

TESLA WAS DEVASTATED AND STAYED IN HIS ROOM FOR WEEKS.

WHEN HE EMERGED, HE REBUILT HIS LAB, AND MADE PLANS TO BUILD ANOTHER ONE IN COLORADO WHERE HE COULD CONDUCT HIGH FREQUENCY EXPERIMENTS IN SECRET.

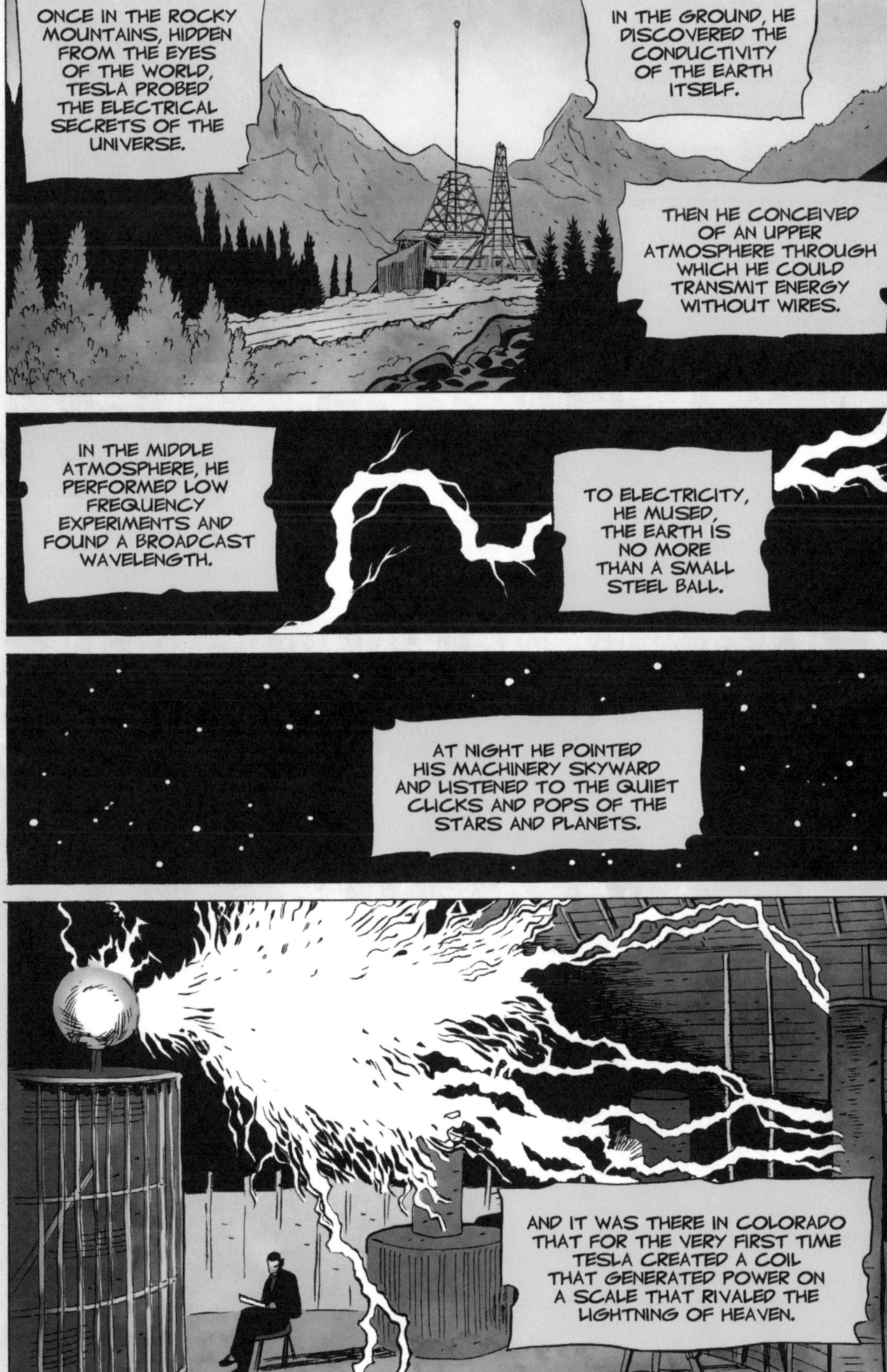
ONCE IN THE ROCKY MOUNTAINS, HIDDEN FROM THE EYES OF THE WORLD, TESLA PROBED THE ELECTRICAL SECRETS OF THE UNIVERSE.
IN THE GROUND, HE DISCOVERED THE CONDUCTIVITY OF THE EARTH ITSELF.
THEN HE CONCEIVED OF AN UPPER ATMOSPHERE THROUGH WHICH HE COULD TRANSMIT ENERGY WITHOUT WIRES.
IN THE MIDDLE ATMOSPHERE, HE PERFORMED LOW FREQUENCY EXPERIMENTS AND FOUND A BROADCAST WAVELENGTH.
TO ELECTRICITY, HE MUSED, THE EARTH IS NO MORE THAN A SMALL STEEL BALL.
AT NIGHT HE POINTED HIS MACHINERY SKYWARD AND LISTENED TO THE QUIET CLICKS AND POPS OF THE STARS AND PLANETS.
AND IT WAS THERE IN COLORADO THAT FOR THE VERY FIRST TIME TESLA CREATED A COIL THAT GENERATED POWER ON A SCALE THAT RIVALED THE LIGHTNING OF HEAVEN.

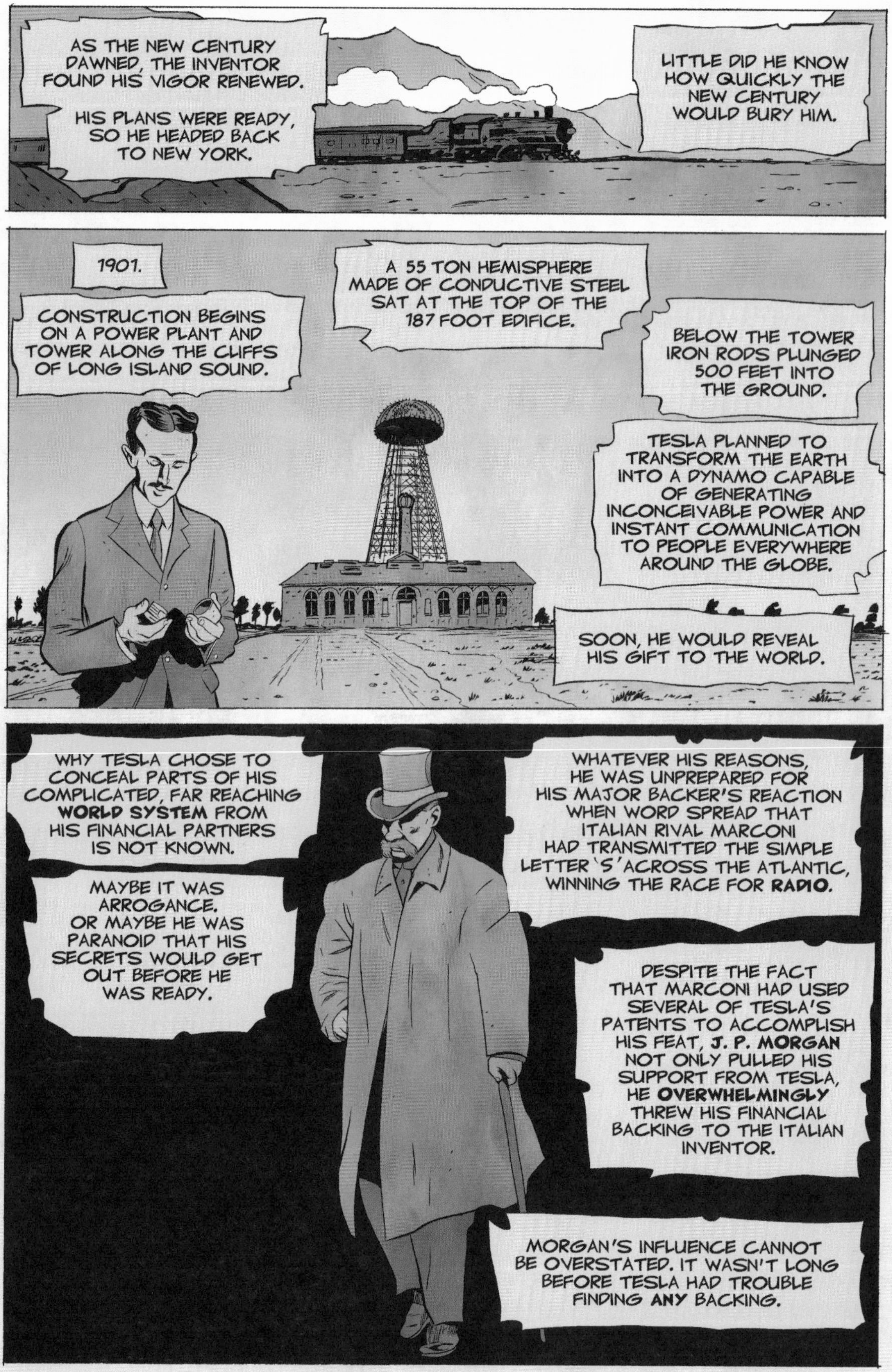
AS THE NEW CENTURY DAWNED, THE INVENTOR FOUND HIS VIGOR RENEWED.
HIS PLANS WERE READY, SO HE HEADED BACK TO NEW YORK.
LITTLE DID HE KNOW HOW QUICKLY THE NEW CENTURY WOULD BURY HIM.
1901.
CONSTRUCTION BEGINS ON A POWER PLANT AND TOWER ALONG THE CLIFFS OF LONG ISLAND SOUND.
A 55 TON HEMISPHERE MADE OF CONDUCTIVE STEEL SAT AT THE TOP OF THE 187 FOOT EDIFICE.
BELOW THE TOWER IRON RODS PLUNGED 500 FEET INTO THE GROUND.
TESLA PLANNED TO TRANSFORM THE EARTH INTO A DYNAMO CAPABLE OF GENERATING INCONCEIVABLE POWER AND INSTANT COMMUNICATION TO PEOPLE EVERYWHERE AROUND THE GLOBE.
SOON, HE WOULD REVEAL HIS GIFT TO THE WORLD.
WHY TESLA CHOSE TO CONCEAL PARTS OF HIS COMPLICATED, FAR REACHING **WORLD SYSTEM** FROM HIS FINANCIAL PARTNERS IS NOT KNOWN.
MAYBE IT WAS ARROGANCE. OR MAYBE HE WAS PARANOID THAT HIS SECRETS WOULD GET OUT BEFORE HE WAS READY.
WHATEVER HIS REASONS, HE WAS UNPREPARED FOR HIS MAJOR BACKER'S REACTION WHEN WORD SPREAD THAT ITALIAN RIVAL MARCONI HAD TRANSMITTED THE SIMPLE LETTER 'S' ACROSS THE ATLANTIC, WINNING THE RACE FOR **RADIO**.
DESPITE THE FACT THAT MARCONI HAD USED SEVERAL OF TESLA'S PATENTS TO ACCOMPLISH HIS FEAT, **J. P. MORGAN** NOT ONLY PULLED HIS SUPPORT FROM TESLA, HE **OVERWHELMINGLY** THREW HIS FINANCIAL BACKING TO THE ITALIAN INVENTOR.
MORGAN'S INFLUENCE CANNOT BE OVERSTATED. IT WASN'T LONG BEFORE TESLA HAD TROUBLE FINDING **ANY** BACKING.

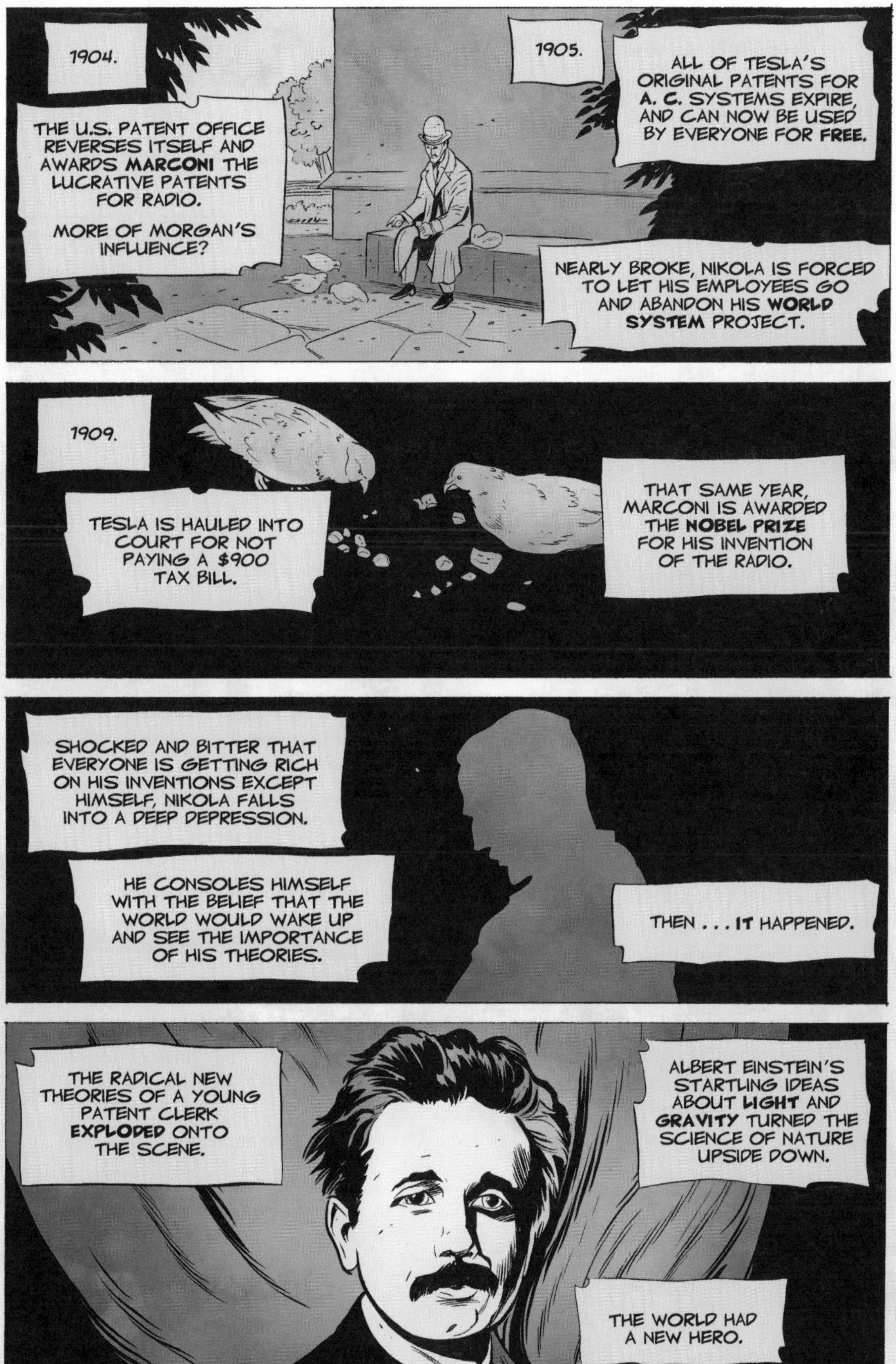
1904.
THE U.S. PATENT OFFICE REVERSES ITSELF AND AWARDS MARCONI THE LUCRATIVE PATENTS FOR RADIO.
MORE OF MORGAN'S INFLUENCE?
1905.
ALL OF TESLA'S ORIGINAL PATENTS FOR A. C. SYSTEMS EXPIRE, AND CAN NOW BE USED BY EVERYONE FOR FREE.
NEARLY BROKE, NIKOLA IS FORCED TO LET HIS EMPLOYEES GO AND ABANDON HIS WORLD SYSTEM PROJECT.
1909.
TESLA IS HAULED INTO COURT FOR NOT PAYING A $900 TAX BILL.
THAT SAME YEAR, MARCONI IS AWARDED THE NOBEL PRIZE FOR HIS INVENTION OF THE RADIO.
SHOCKED AND BITTER THAT EVERYONE IS GETTING RICH ON HIS INVENTIONS EXCEPT HIMSELF, NIKOLA FALLS INTO A DEEP DEPRESSION.
HE CONSOLES HIMSELF WITH THE BELIEF THAT THE WORLD WOULD WAKE UP AND SEE THE IMPORTANCE OF HIS THEORIES.
THEN . . . IT HAPPENED.
THE RADICAL NEW THEORIES OF A YOUNG PATENT CLERK EXPLODED ONTO THE SCENE.
ALBERT EINSTEIN'S STARTLING IDEAS ABOUT LIGHT AND GRAVITY TURNED THE SCIENCE OF NATURE UPSIDE DOWN.
THE WORLD HAD A NEW HERO.

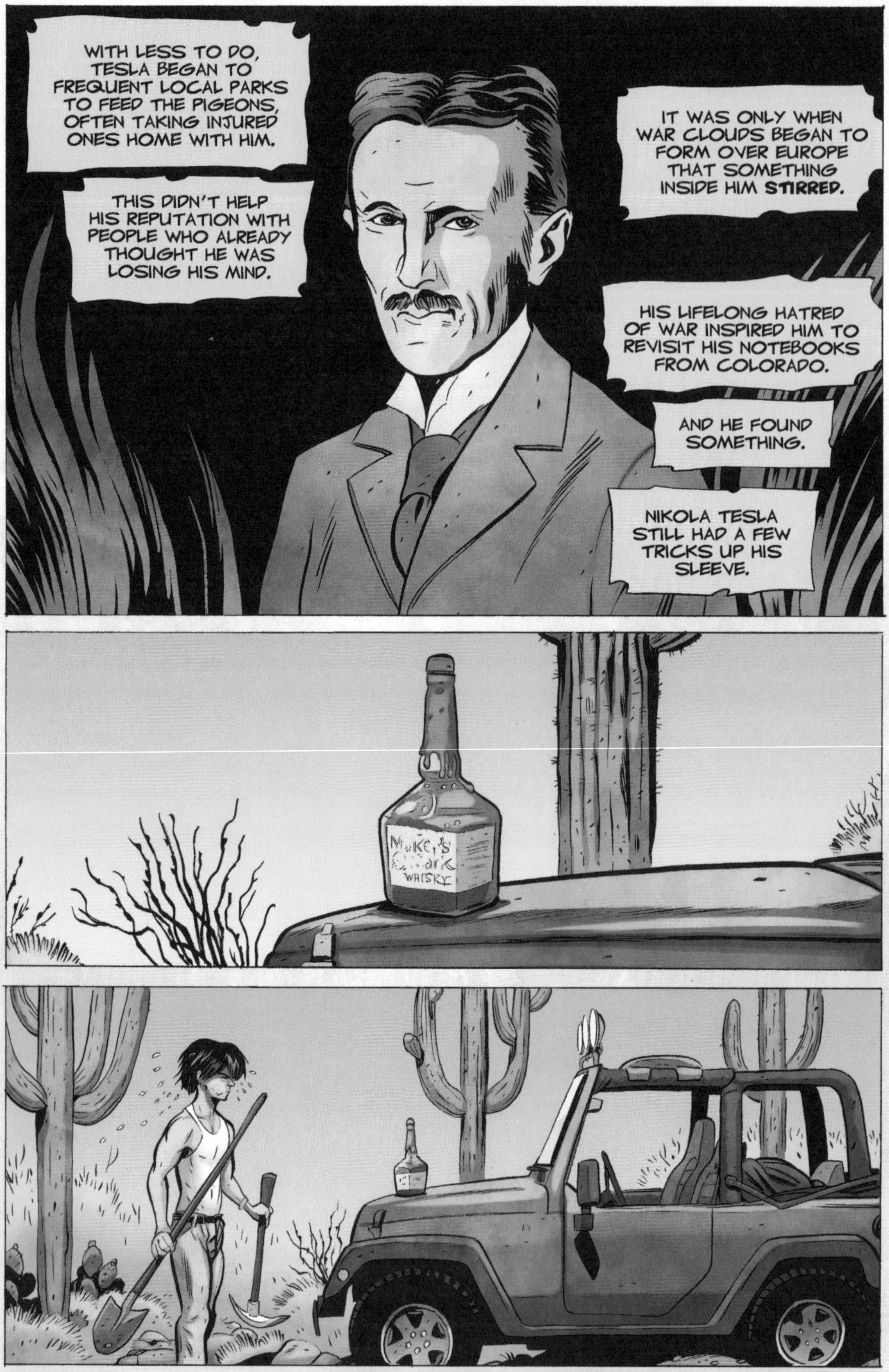
WITH LESS TO DO, TESLA BEGAN TO FREQUENT LOCAL PARKS TO FEED THE PIGEONS, OFTEN TAKING INJURED ONES HOME WITH HIM.
THIS DIDN'T HELP HIS REPUTATION WITH PEOPLE WHO ALREADY THOUGHT HE WAS LOSING HIS MIND.
IT WAS ONLY WHEN WAR CLOUDS BEGAN TO FORM OVER EUROPE THAT SOMETHING INSIDE HIM STIRRED.
HIS LIFELONG HATRED OF WAR INSPIRED HIM TO REVISIT HIS NOTEBOOKS FROM COLORADO.
AND HE FOUND SOMETHING.
NIKOLA TESLA STILL HAD A FEW TRICKS UP HIS SLEEVE.
WHISKY

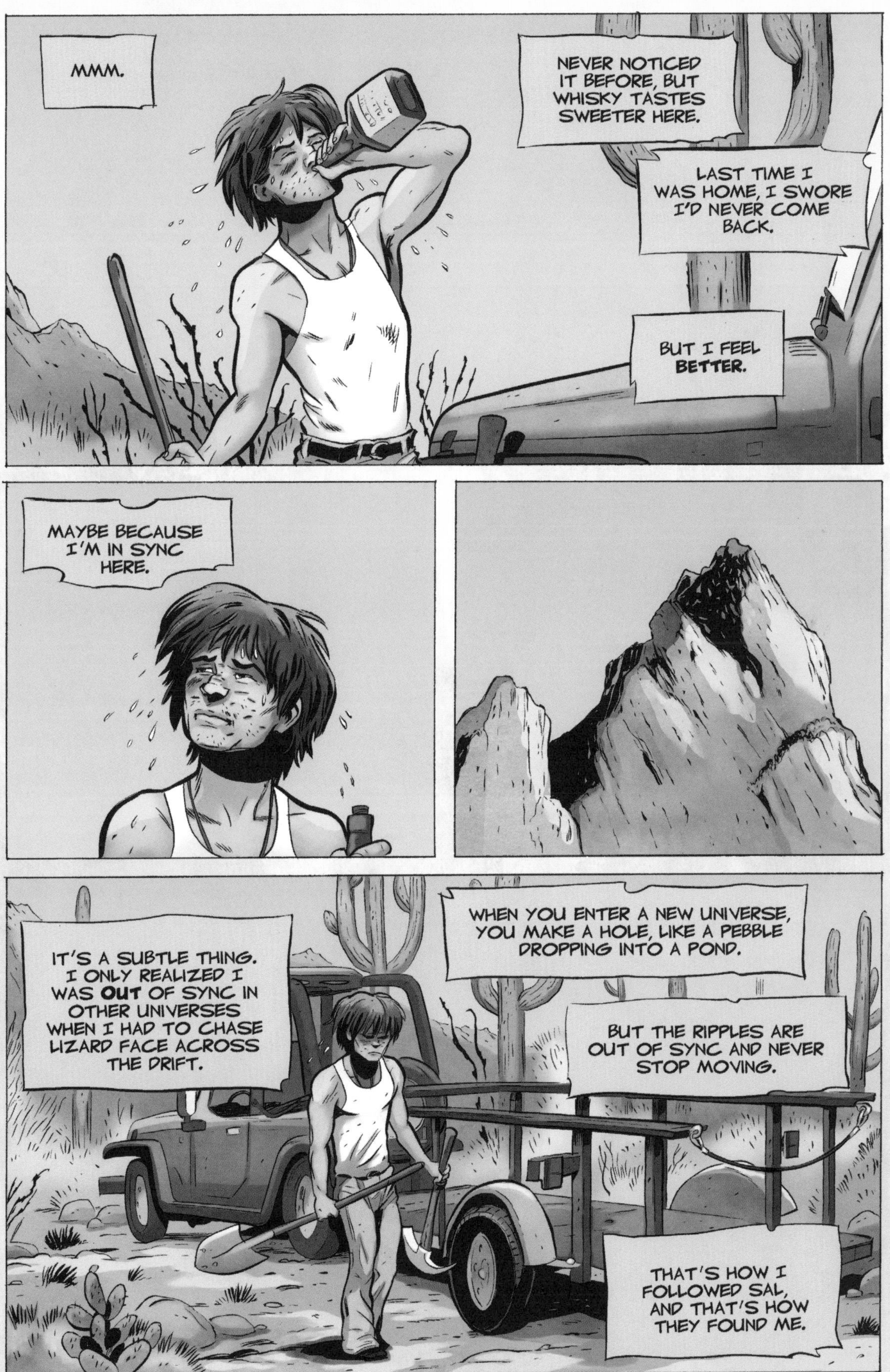
MMM.
NEVER NOTICED IT BEFORE, BUT WHISKY TASTES SWEETER HERE.
LAST TIME I WAS HOME, I SWORE I'D NEVER COME BACK.
BUT I FEEL BETTER.
MAYBE BECAUSE I'M IN SYNC HERE.
IT'S A SUBTLE THING. I ONLY REALIZED I WAS OUT OF SYNC IN OTHER UNIVERSES WHEN I HAD TO CHASE LIZARD FACE ACROSS THE DRIFT.
WHEN YOU ENTER A NEW UNIVERSE, YOU MAKE A HOLE, LIKE A PEBBLE DROPPING INTO A POND.
BUT THE RIPPLES ARE OUT OF SYNC AND NEVER STOP MOVING.
THAT'S HOW I FOLLOWED SAL, AND THAT'S HOW THEY FOUND ME.

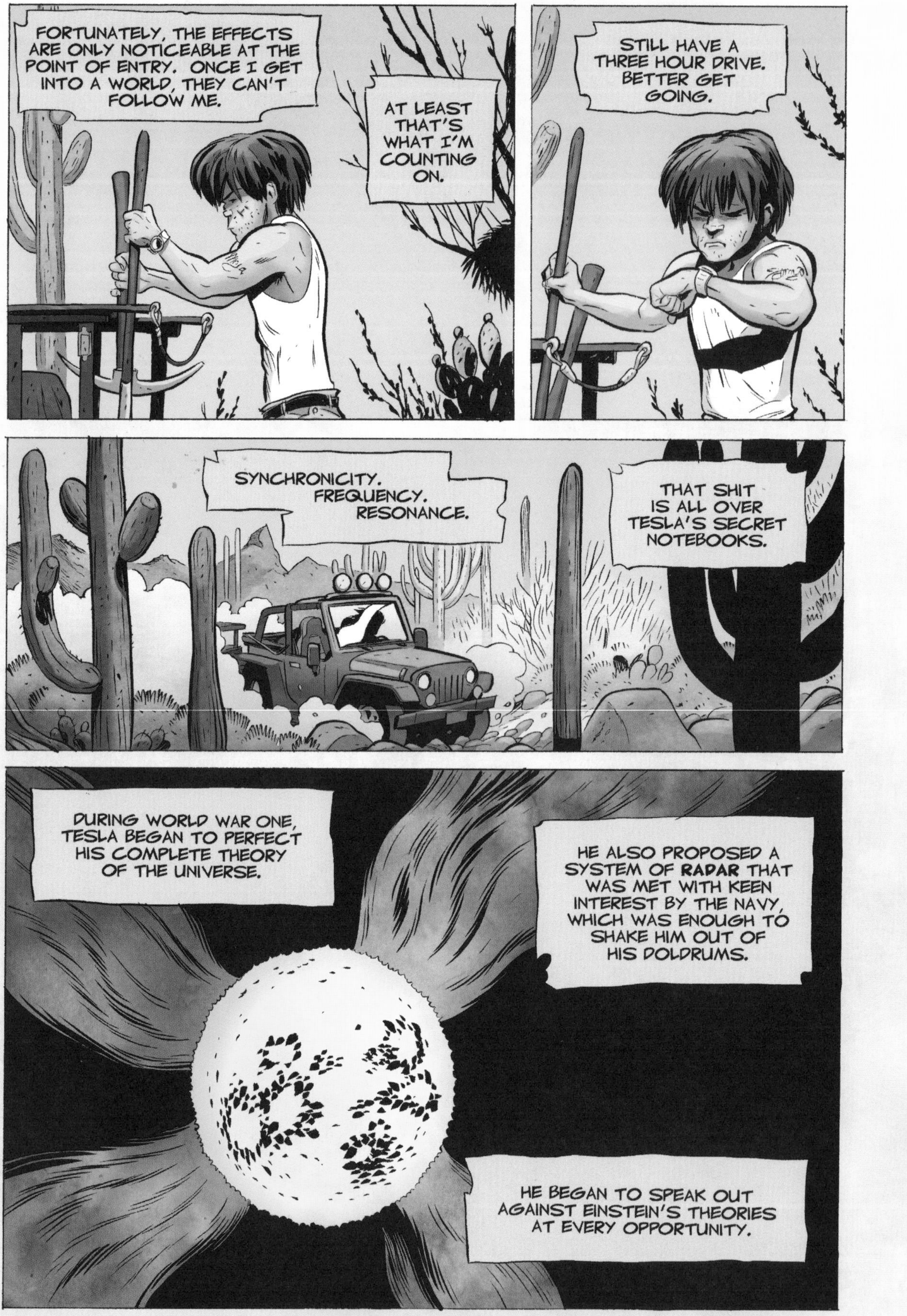
FORTUNATELY, THE EFFECTS ARE ONLY NOTICEABLE AT THE POINT OF ENTRY. ONCE I GET INTO A WORLD, THEY CAN'T FOLLOW ME.
AT LEAST THAT'S WHAT I'M COUNTING ON.
STILL HAVE A THREE HOUR DRIVE. BETTER GET GOING.
SYNCHRONICITY. FREQUENCY. RESONANCE.
THAT SHIT IS ALL OVER TESLA'S SECRET NOTEBOOKS.
DURING WORLD WAR ONE, TESLA BEGAN TO PERFECT HIS COMPLETE THEORY OF THE UNIVERSE.
HE ALSO PROPOSED A SYSTEM OF RADAR THAT WAS MET WITH KEEN INTEREST BY THE NAVY, WHICH WAS ENOUGH TO SHAKE HIM OUT OF HIS DOLDRUMS.
HE BEGAN TO SPEAK OUT AGAINST EINSTEIN'S THEORIES AT EVERY OPPORTUNITY.

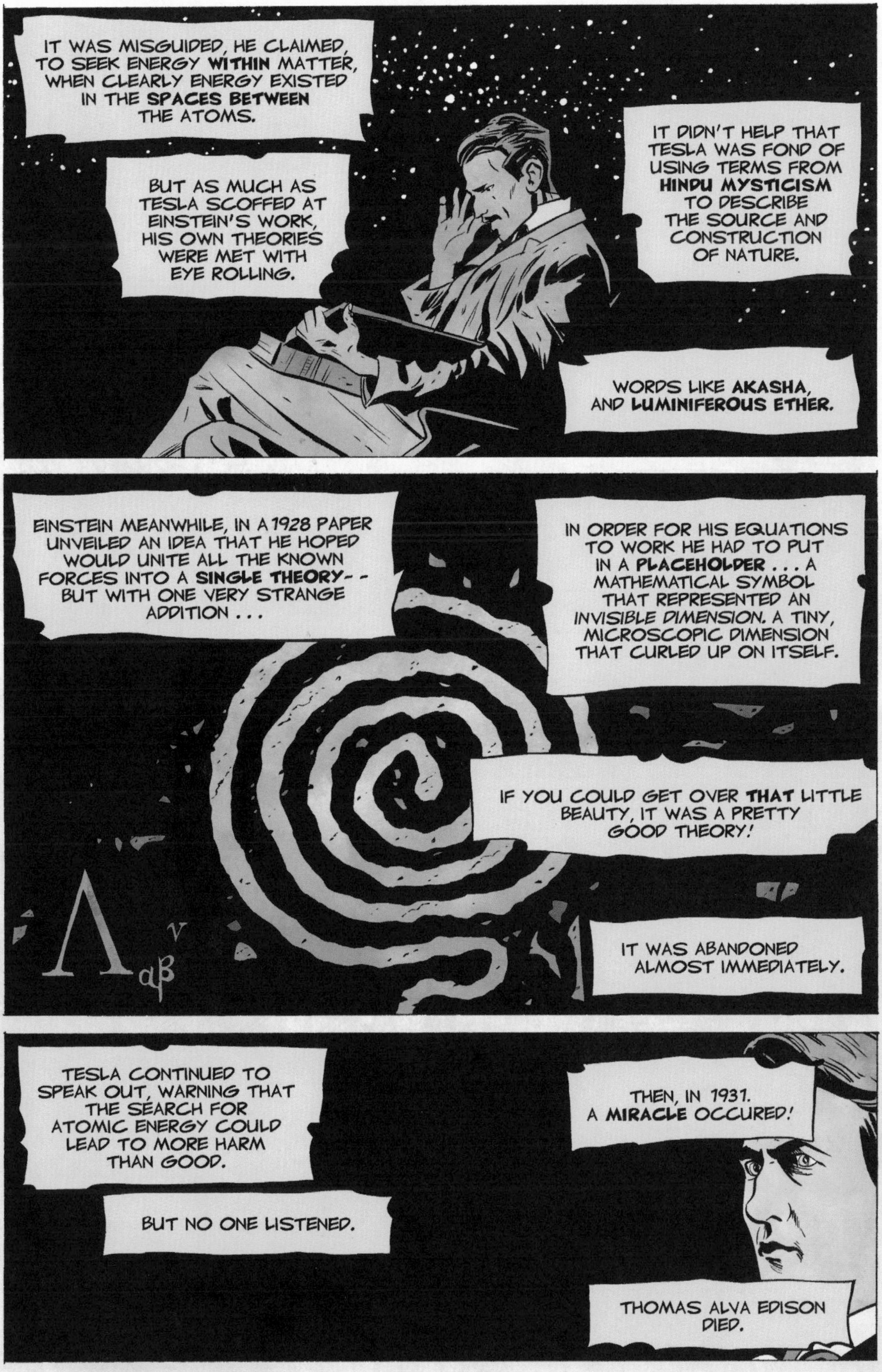
IT WAS MISGUIDED, HE CLAIMED, TO SEEK ENERGY WITHIN MATTER, WHEN CLEARLY ENERGY EXISTED IN THE SPACES BETWEEN THE ATOMS.
BUT AS MUCH AS TESLA SCOFFED AT EINSTEIN'S WORK, HIS OWN THEORIES WERE MET WITH EYE ROLLING.
IT DIDN'T HELP THAT TESLA WAS FOND OF USING TERMS FROM HINDU MYSTICISM TO DESCRIBE THE SOURCE AND CONSTRUCTION OF NATURE.
WORDS LIKE AKASHA, AND LUMINIFEROUS ETHER.
EINSTEIN MEANWHILE, IN A 1928 PAPER UNVEILED AN IDEA THAT HE HOPED WOULD UNITE ALL THE KNOWN FORCES INTO A SINGLE THEORY-- BUT WITH ONE VERY STRANGE ADDITION ...
IN ORDER FOR HIS EQUATIONS TO WORK HE HAD TO PUT IN A PLACEHOLDER . . . A MATHEMATICAL SYMBOL THAT REPRESENTED AN INVISIBLE DIMENSION. A TINY, MICROSCOPIC DIMENSION THAT CURLED UP ON ITSELF.
IF YOU COULD GET OVER THAT LITTLE BEAUTY, IT WAS A PRETTY GOOD THEORY!
$\Lambda_{\alpha\beta}^{\nu}$
IT WAS ABANDONED ALMOST IMMEDIATELY.
TESLA CONTINUED TO SPEAK OUT, WARNING THAT THE SEARCH FOR ATOMIC ENERGY COULD LEAD TO MORE HARM THAN GOOD.
BUT NO ONE LISTENED.
THEN, IN 1931. A MIRACLE OCCURED!
THOMAS ALVA EDISON DIED.

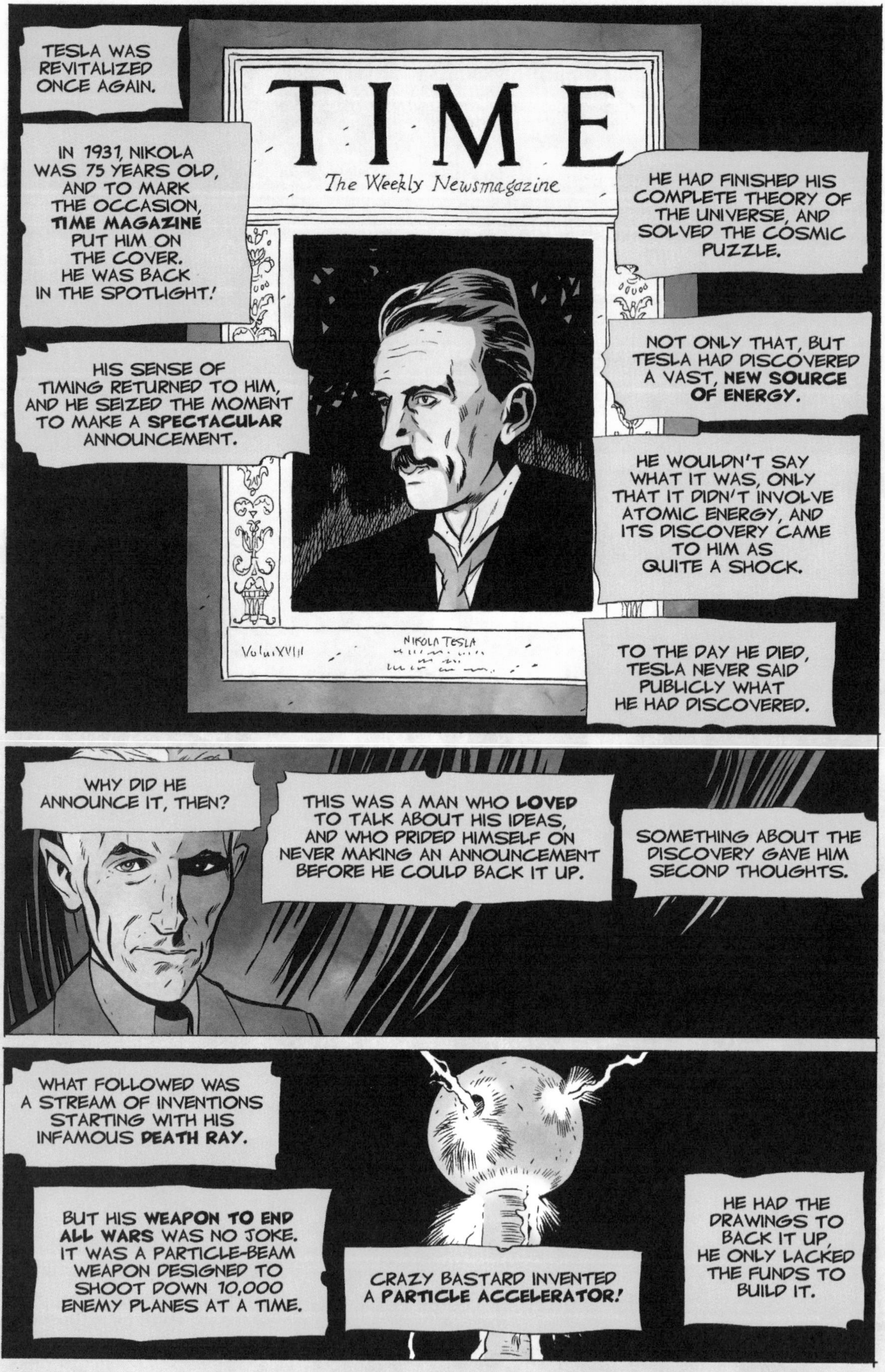
TESLA WAS REVITALIZED ONCE AGAIN.
TIME
The Weekly Newsmagazine
IN 1931, NIKOLA WAS 75 YEARS OLD, AND TO MARK THE OCCASION, **TIME MAGAZINE** PUT HIM ON THE COVER. HE WAS BACK IN THE SPOTLIGHT!
HE HAD FINISHED HIS COMPLETE THEORY OF THE UNIVERSE, AND SOLVED THE COSMIC PUZZLE.
NIKOLA TESLA
HIS SENSE OF TIMING RETURNED TO HIM, AND HE SEIZED THE MOMENT TO MAKE A **SPECTACULAR** ANNOUNCEMENT.
NOT ONLY THAT, BUT TESLA HAD DISCOVERED A VAST, **NEW SOURCE OF ENERGY.**
HE WOULDN'T SAY WHAT IT WAS, ONLY THAT IT DIDN'T INVOLVE ATOMIC ENERGY, AND ITS DISCOVERY CAME TO HIM AS QUITE A SHOCK.
TO THE DAY HE DIED, TESLA NEVER SAID PUBLICLY WHAT HE HAD DISCOVERED.
WHY DID HE ANNOUNCE IT, THEN?
THIS WAS A MAN WHO **LOVED** TO TALK ABOUT HIS IDEAS, AND WHO PRIDED HIMSELF ON NEVER MAKING AN ANNOUNCEMENT BEFORE HE COULD BACK IT UP.
SOMETHING ABOUT THE DISCOVERY GAVE HIM SECOND THOUGHTS.
WHAT FOLLOWED WAS A STREAM OF INVENTIONS STARTING WITH HIS INFAMOUS **DEATH RAY.**
BUT HIS **WEAPON TO END ALL WARS** WAS NO JOKE. IT WAS A PARTICLE-BEAM WEAPON DESIGNED TO SHOOT DOWN 10,000 ENEMY PLANES AT A TIME.
CRAZY BASTARD INVENTED A **PARTICLE ACCELERATOR!**
HE HAD THE DRAWINGS TO BACK IT UP, HE ONLY LACKED THE FUNDS TO BUILD IT.

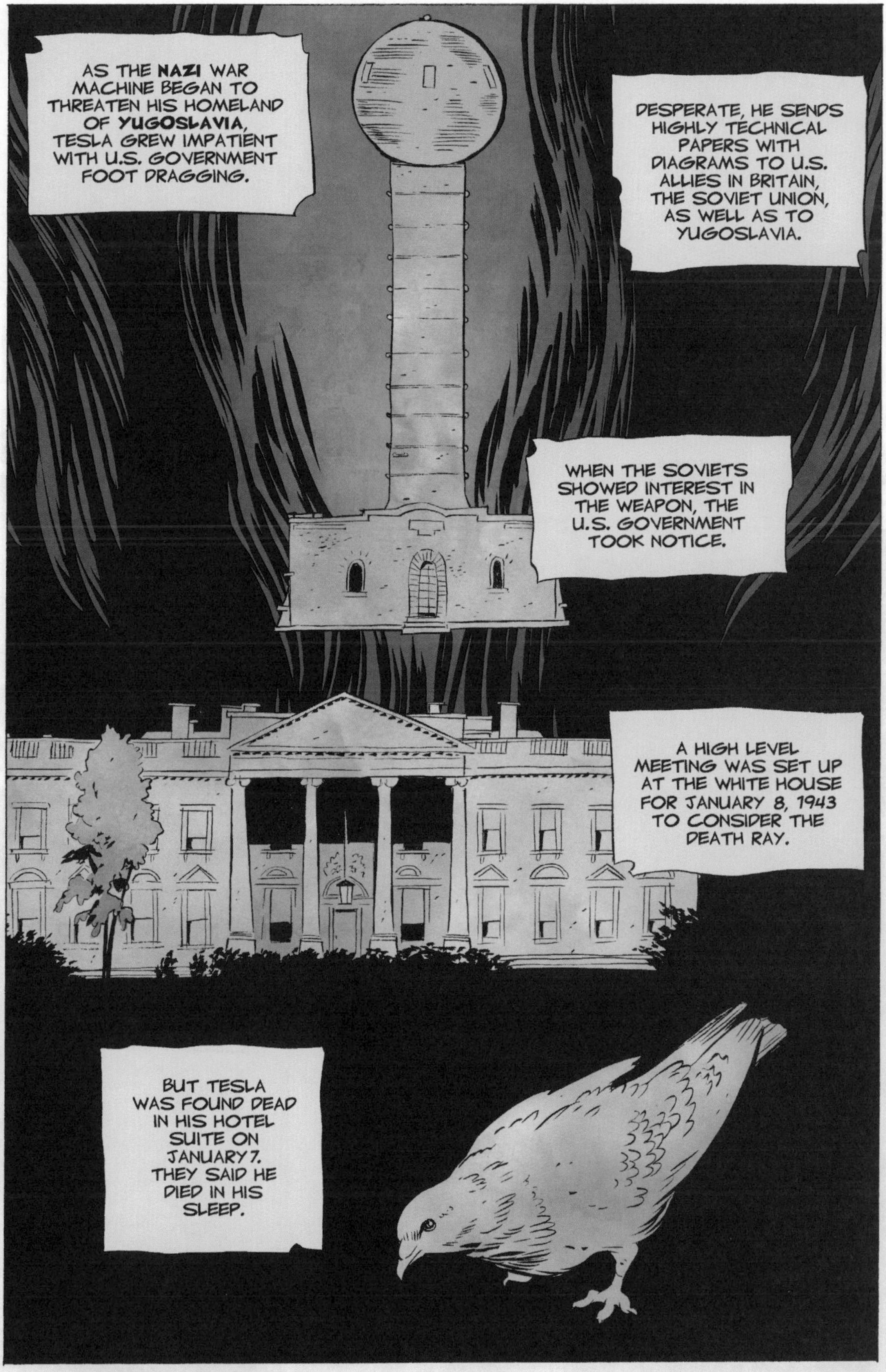
AS THE NAZI WAR MACHINE BEGAN TO THREATEN HIS HOMELAND OF YUGOSLAVIA, TESLA GREW IMPATIENT WITH U.S. GOVERNMENT FOOT DRAGGING.
DESPERATE, HE SENDS HIGHLY TECHNICAL PAPERS WITH DIAGRAMS TO U.S. ALLIES IN BRITAIN, THE SOVIET UNION, AS WELL AS TO YUGOSLAVIA.
WHEN THE SOVIETS SHOWED INTEREST IN THE WEAPON, THE U.S. GOVERNMENT TOOK NOTICE.
A HIGH LEVEL MEETING WAS SET UP AT THE WHITE HOUSE FOR JANUARY 8, 1943 TO CONSIDER THE DEATH RAY.
BUT TESLA WAS FOUND DEAD IN HIS HOTEL SUITE ON JANUARY 7. THEY SAID HE DIED IN HIS SLEEP.

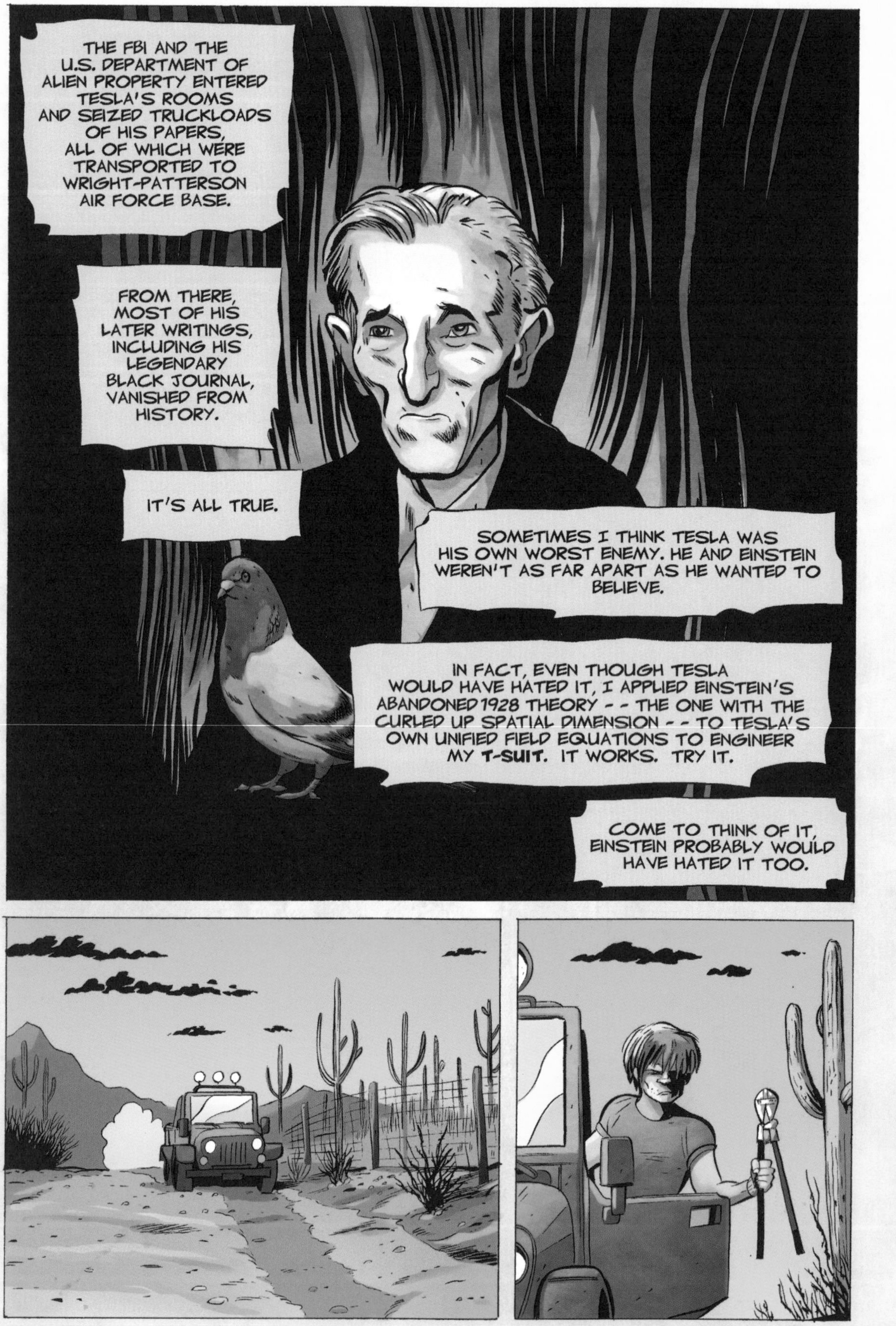
THE FBI AND THE U.S. DEPARTMENT OF ALIEN PROPERTY ENTERED TESLA'S ROOMS AND SEIZED TRUCKLOADS OF HIS PAPERS, ALL OF WHICH WERE TRANSPORTED TO WRIGHT-PATTERSON AIR FORCE BASE.
FROM THERE, MOST OF HIS LATER WRITINGS, INCLUDING HIS LEGENDARY BLACK JOURNAL, VANISHED FROM HISTORY.
IT'S ALL TRUE.
SOMETIMES I THINK TESLA WAS HIS OWN WORST ENEMY. HE AND EINSTEIN WEREN'T AS FAR APART AS HE WANTED TO BELIEVE.
IN FACT, EVEN THOUGH TESLA WOULD HAVE HATED IT, I APPLIED EINSTEIN'S ABANDONED 1928 THEORY - - THE ONE WITH THE CURLED UP SPATIAL DIMENSION - - TO TESLA'S OWN UNIFIED FIELD EQUATIONS TO ENGINEER MY **T-SUIT**. IT WORKS. TRY IT.
COME TO THINK OF IT, EINSTEIN PROBABLY WOULD HAVE HATED IT TOO.

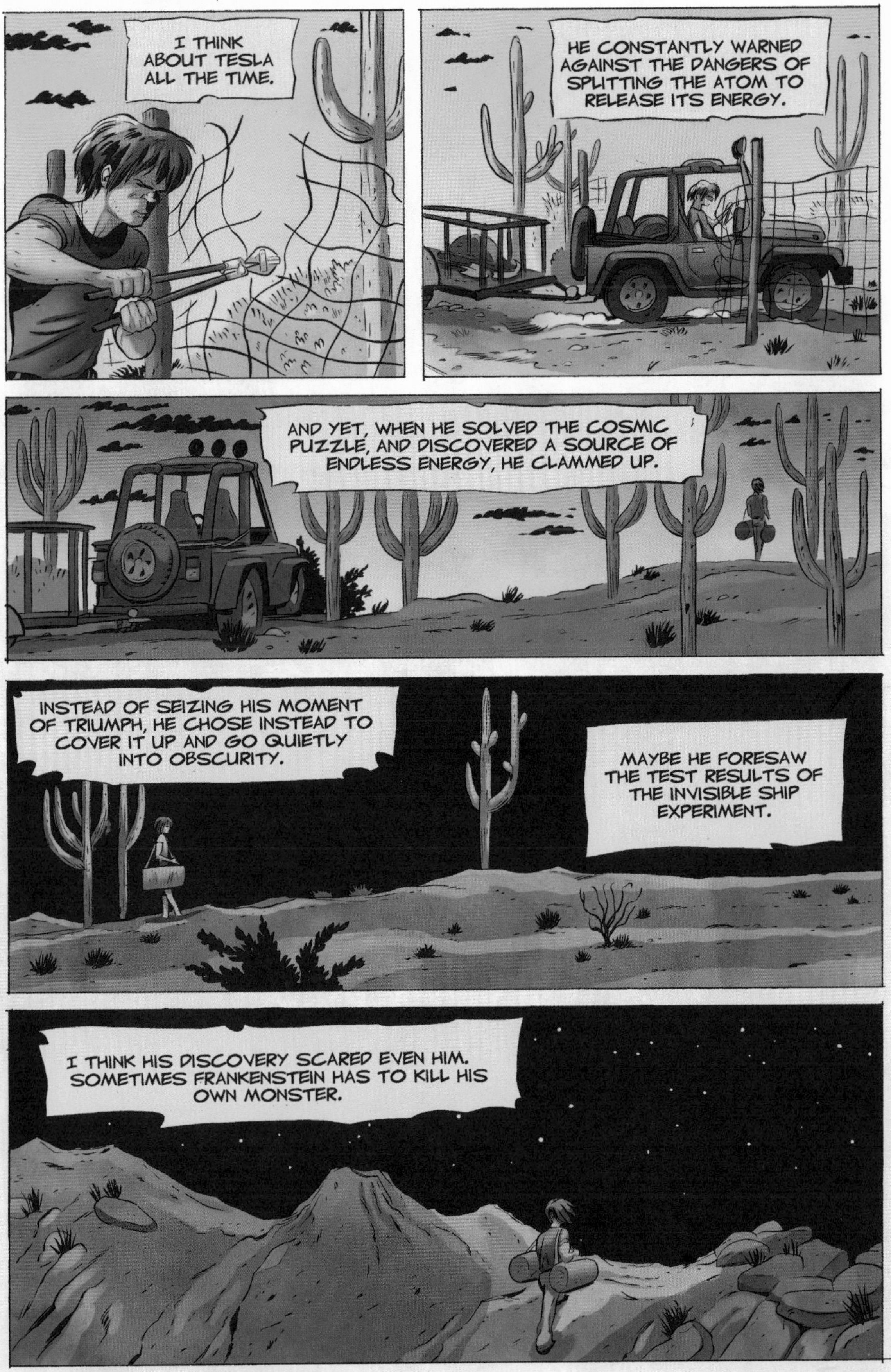
I THINK ABOUT TESLA ALL THE TIME.
HE CONSTANTLY WARNED AGAINST THE DANGERS OF SPLITTING THE ATOM TO RELEASE ITS ENERGY.
AND YET, WHEN HE SOLVED THE COSMIC PUZZLE, AND DISCOVERED A SOURCE OF ENDLESS ENERGY, HE CLAMMED UP.
INSTEAD OF SEIZING HIS MOMENT OF TRIUMPH, HE CHOSE INSTEAD TO COVER IT UP AND GO QUIETLY INTO OBSCURITY.
MAYBE HE FORESAW THE TEST RESULTS OF THE INVISIBLE SHIP EXPERIMENT.
I THINK HIS DISCOVERY SCARED EVEN HIM. SOMETIMES FRANKENSTEIN HAS TO KILL HIS OWN MONSTER.

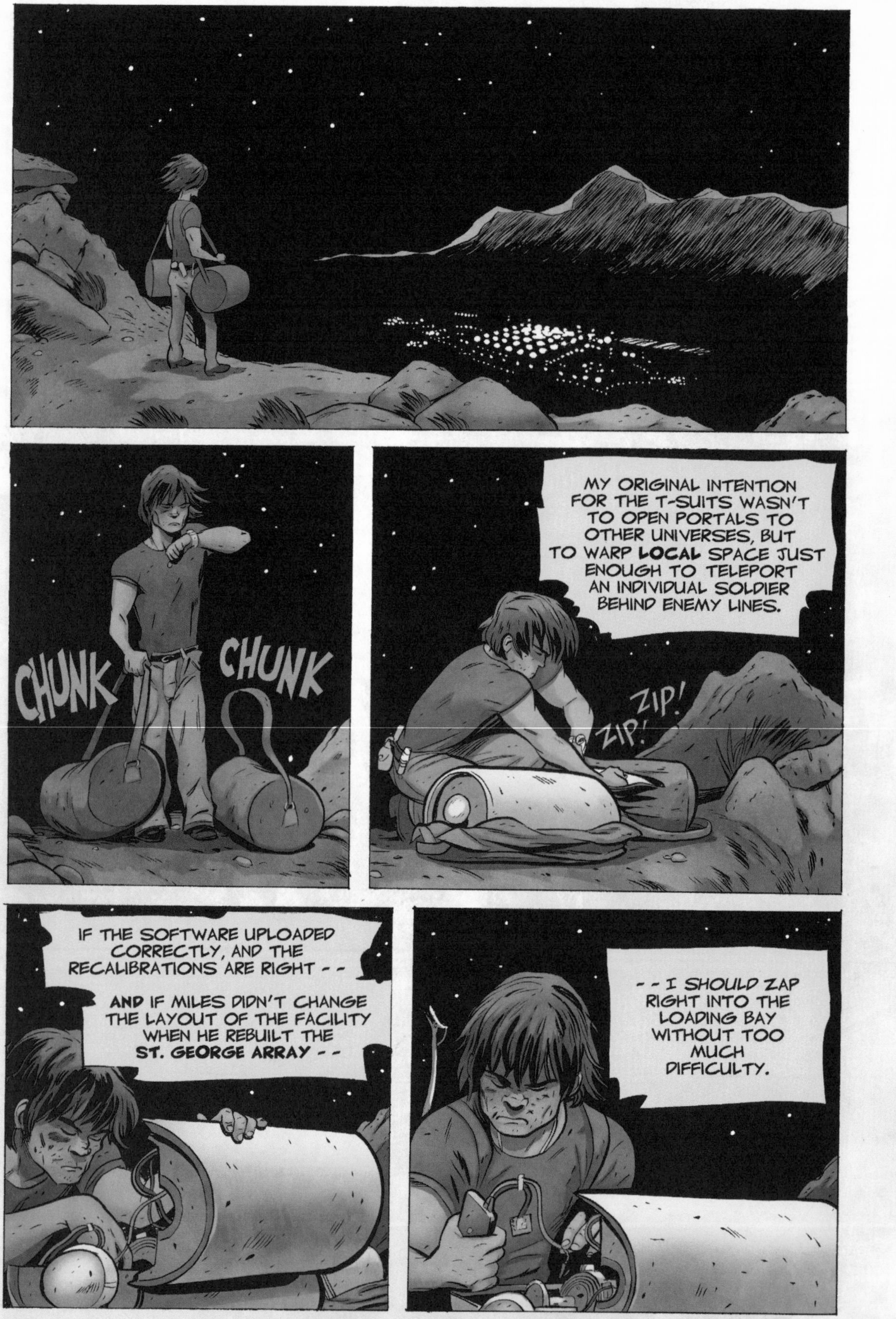
CHUNK
CHUNK
MY ORIGINAL INTENTION FOR THE T-SUITS WASN'T TO OPEN PORTALS TO OTHER UNIVERSES, BUT TO WARP **LOCAL** SPACE JUST ENOUGH TO TELEPORT AN INDIVIDUAL SOLDIER BEHIND ENEMY LINES.
ZIP!
ZIP!
IF THE SOFTWARE UPLOADED CORRECTLY, AND THE RECALIBRATIONS ARE RIGHT - -
AND IF MILES DIDN'T CHANGE THE LAYOUT OF THE FACILITY WHEN HE REBUILT THE **ST. GEORGE ARRAY** - -
- - I SHOULD ZAP RIGHT INTO THE LOADING BAY WITHOUT TOO MUCH DIFFICULTY.

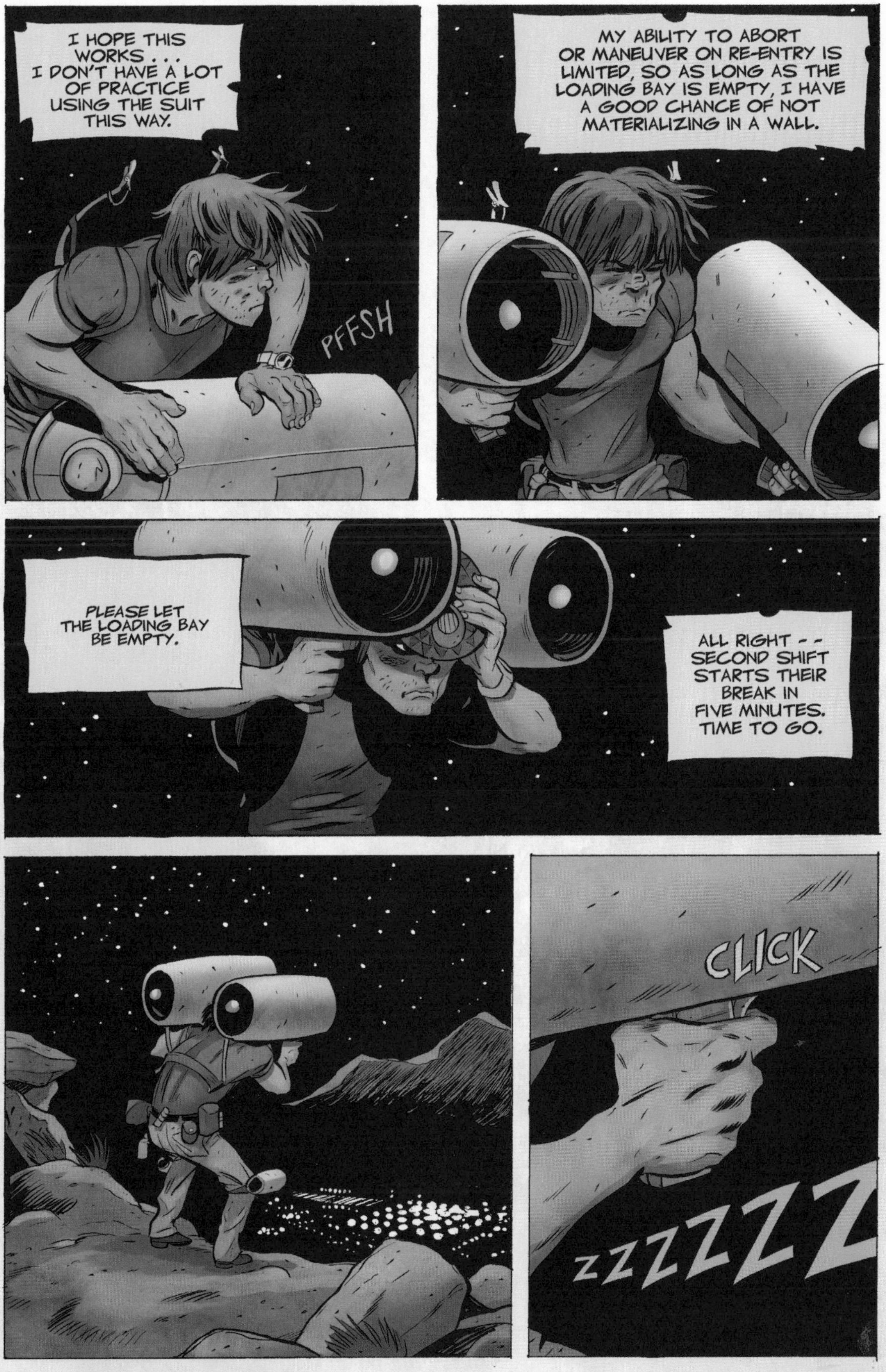
I HOPE THIS WORKS . . . I DON'T HAVE A LOT OF PRACTICE USING THE SUIT THIS WAY.
PFFSH
MY ABILITY TO ABORT OR MANEUVER ON RE-ENTRY IS LIMITED, SO AS LONG AS THE LOADING BAY IS EMPTY, I HAVE A GOOD CHANCE OF NOT MATERIALIZING IN A WALL.
PLEASE LET THE LOADING BAY BE EMPTY.
ALL RIGHT - - SECOND SHIFT STARTS THEIR BREAK IN FIVE MINUTES. TIME TO GO.
CLICK
ZZZZZZZ

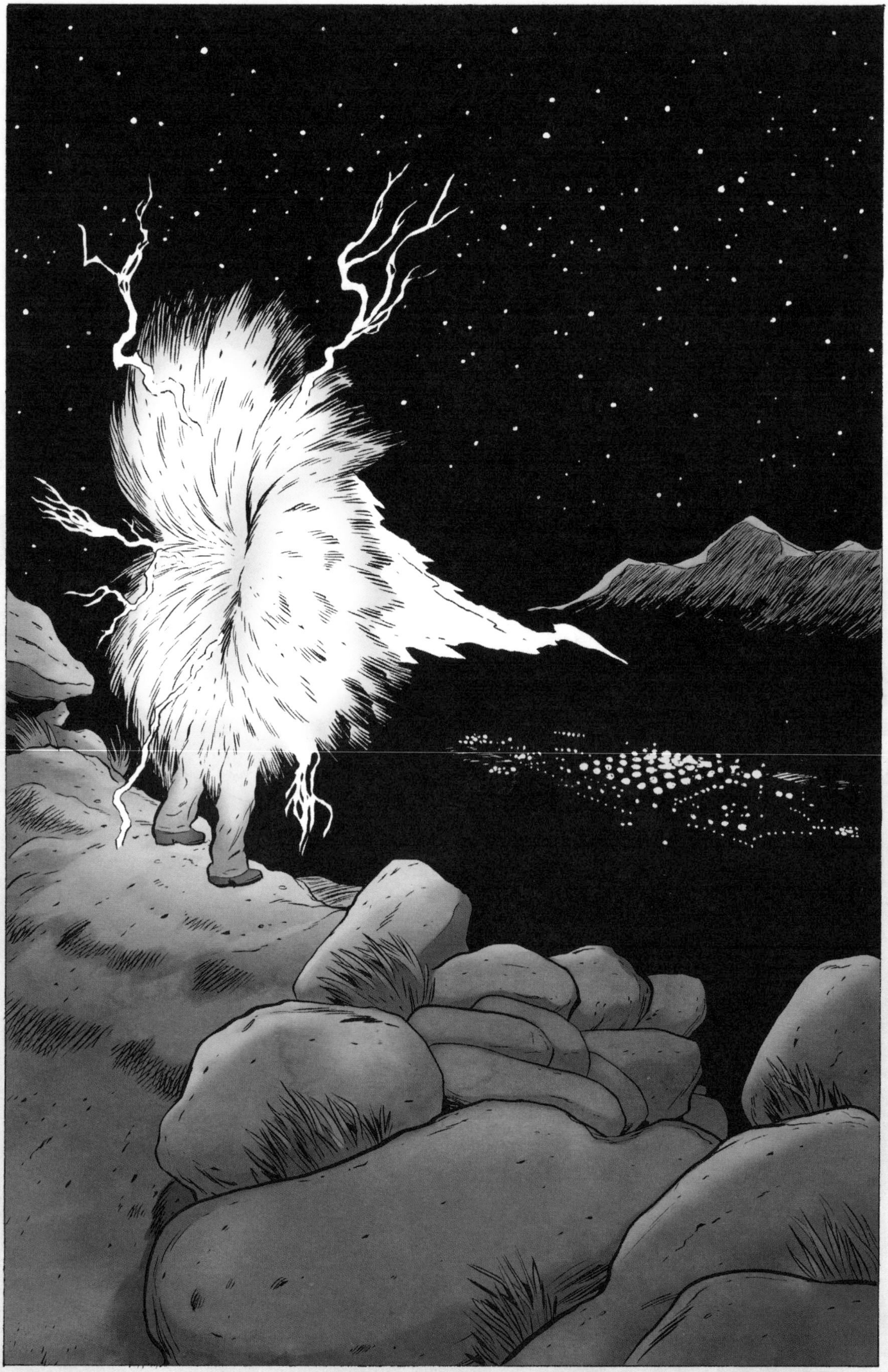

XIII
MILES

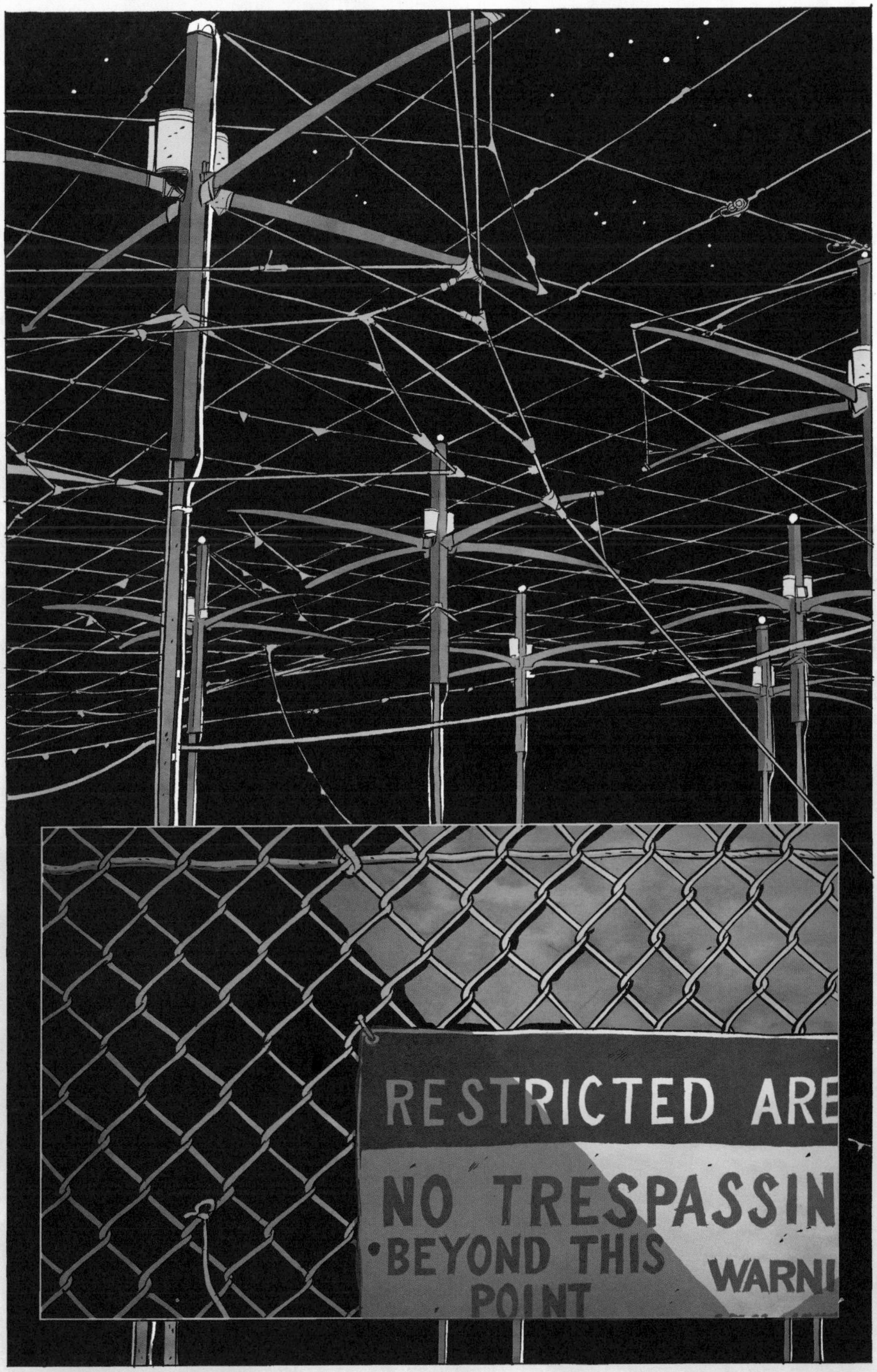
RESTRICTED ARE
NO TRESPASSIN
•BEYOND THIS
POINT
WARNI

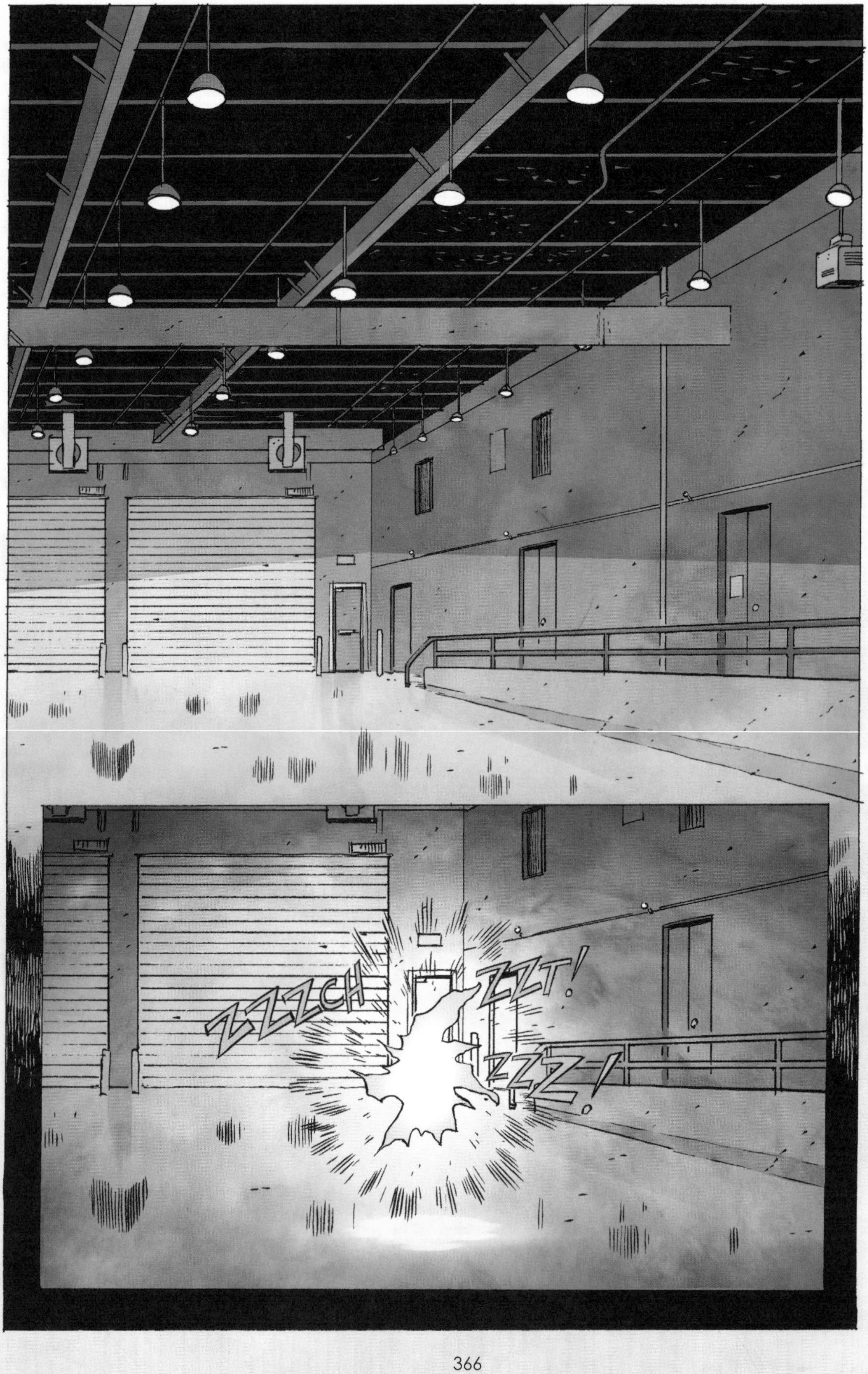
ZZZCH
ZZT!
ZZZ!

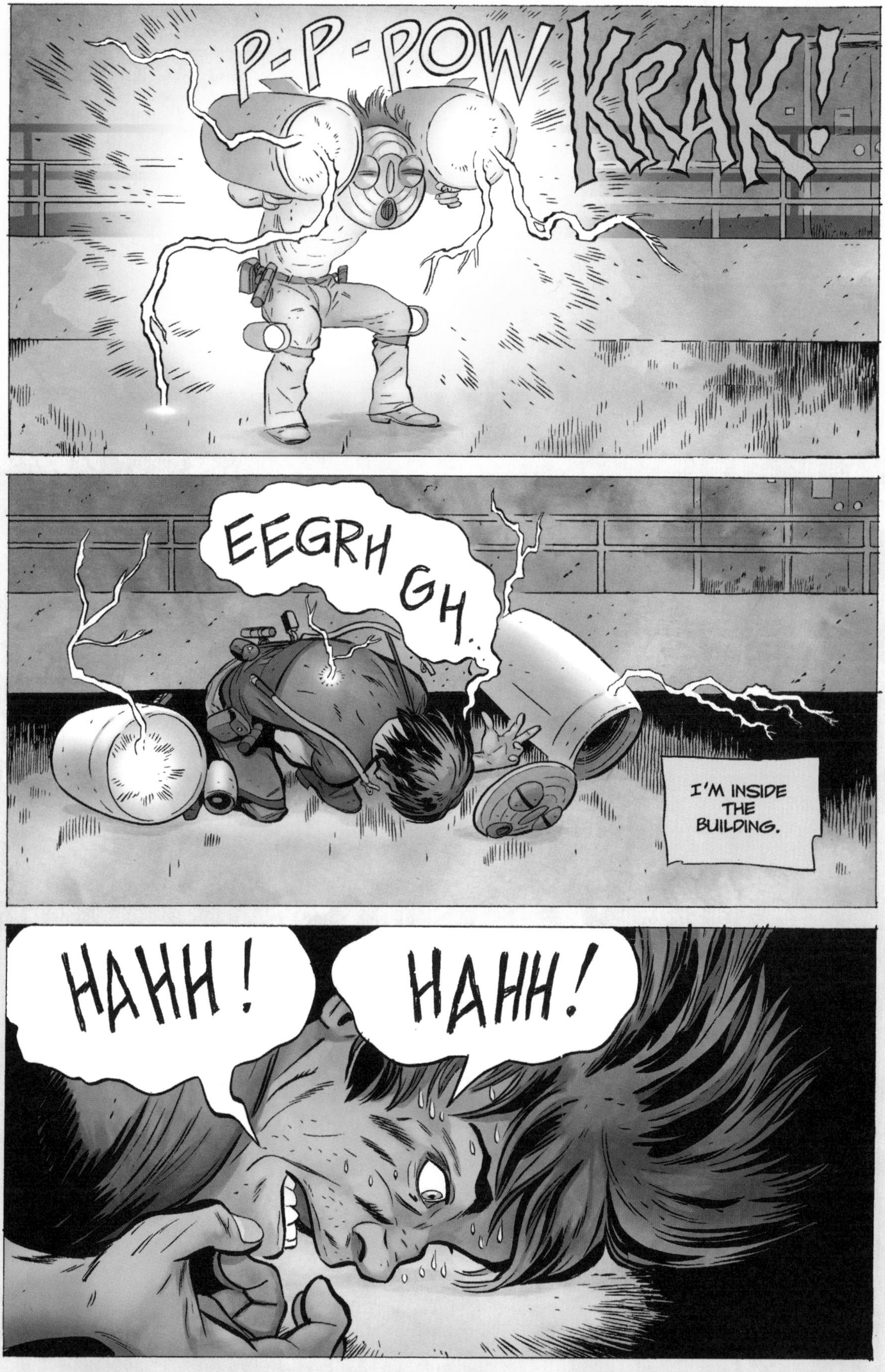
P-P-POW
KRAK!
EEGRH GH.
I'M INSIDE THE BUILDING.
HAHH!
HAHH!

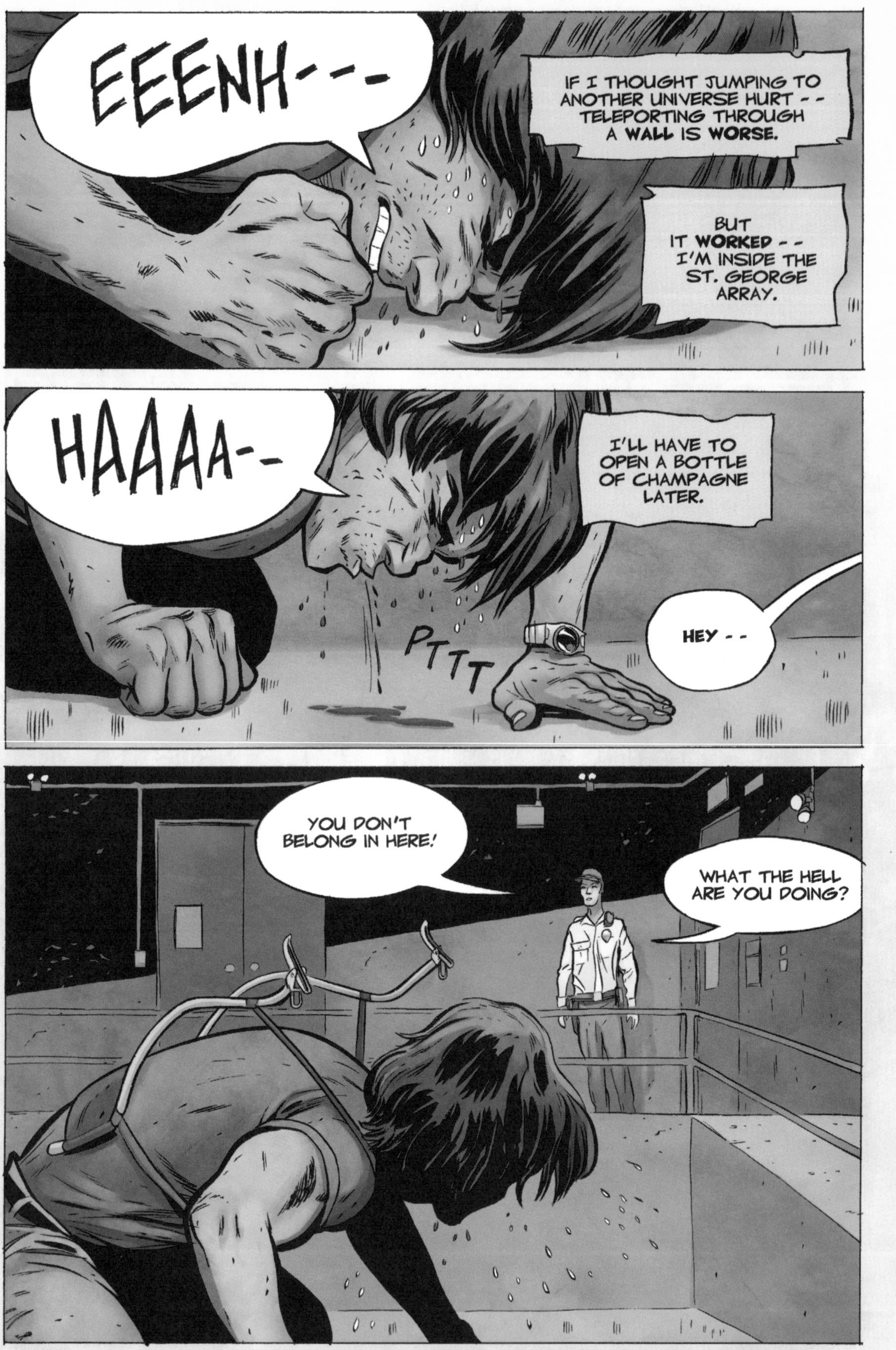
EEENH---
IF I THOUGHT JUMPING TO ANOTHER UNIVERSE HURT -- TELEPORTING THROUGH A WALL IS WORSE.
BUT IT WORKED -- I'M INSIDE THE ST. GEORGE ARRAY.
HAAAA--
I'LL HAVE TO OPEN A BOTTLE OF CHAMPAGNE LATER.
PTTTT
HEY --
YOU DON'T BELONG IN HERE!
WHAT THE HELL ARE YOU DOING?

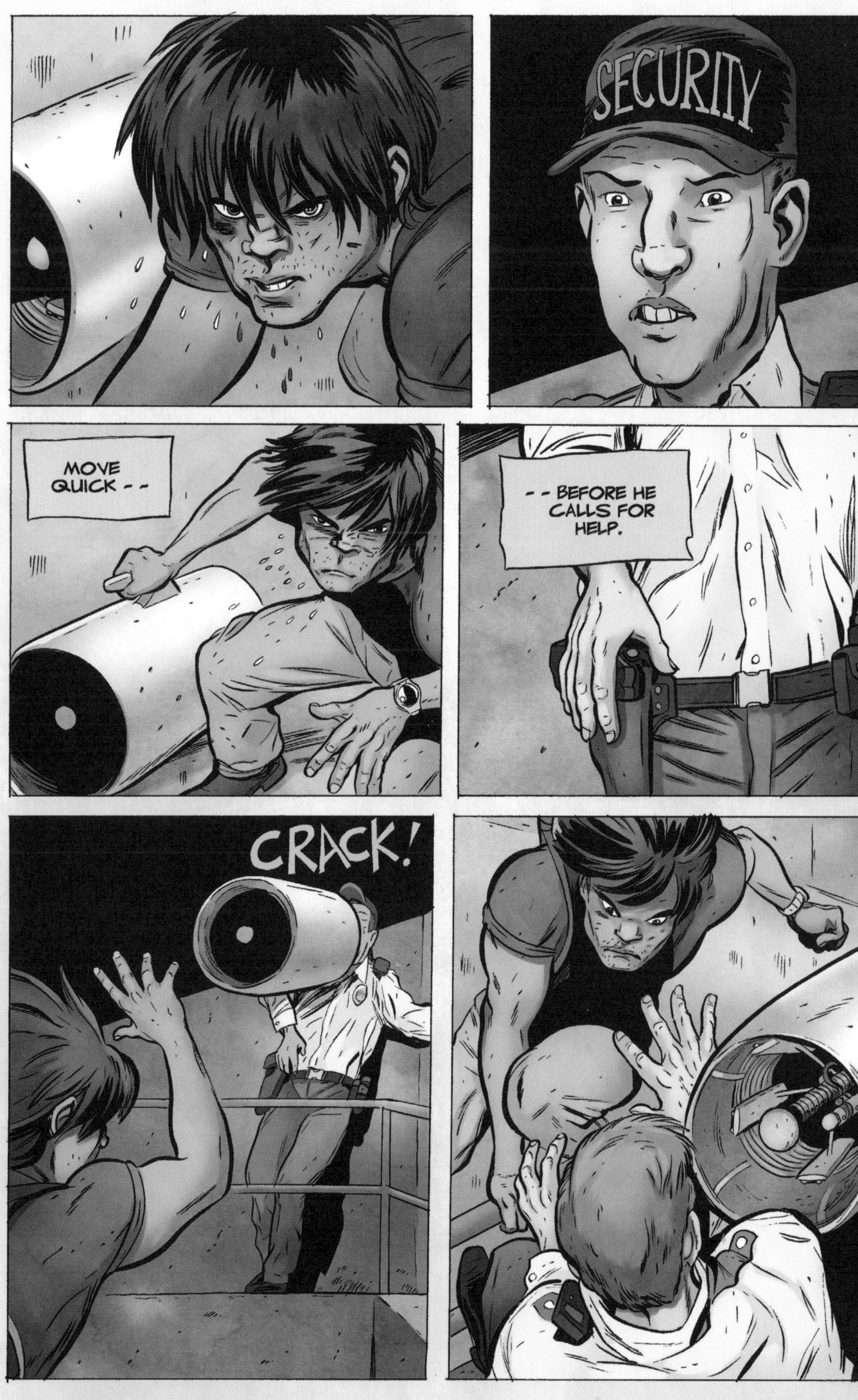
SECURITY
MOVE QUICK - -
- - BEFORE HE CALLS FOR HELP.
CRACK!

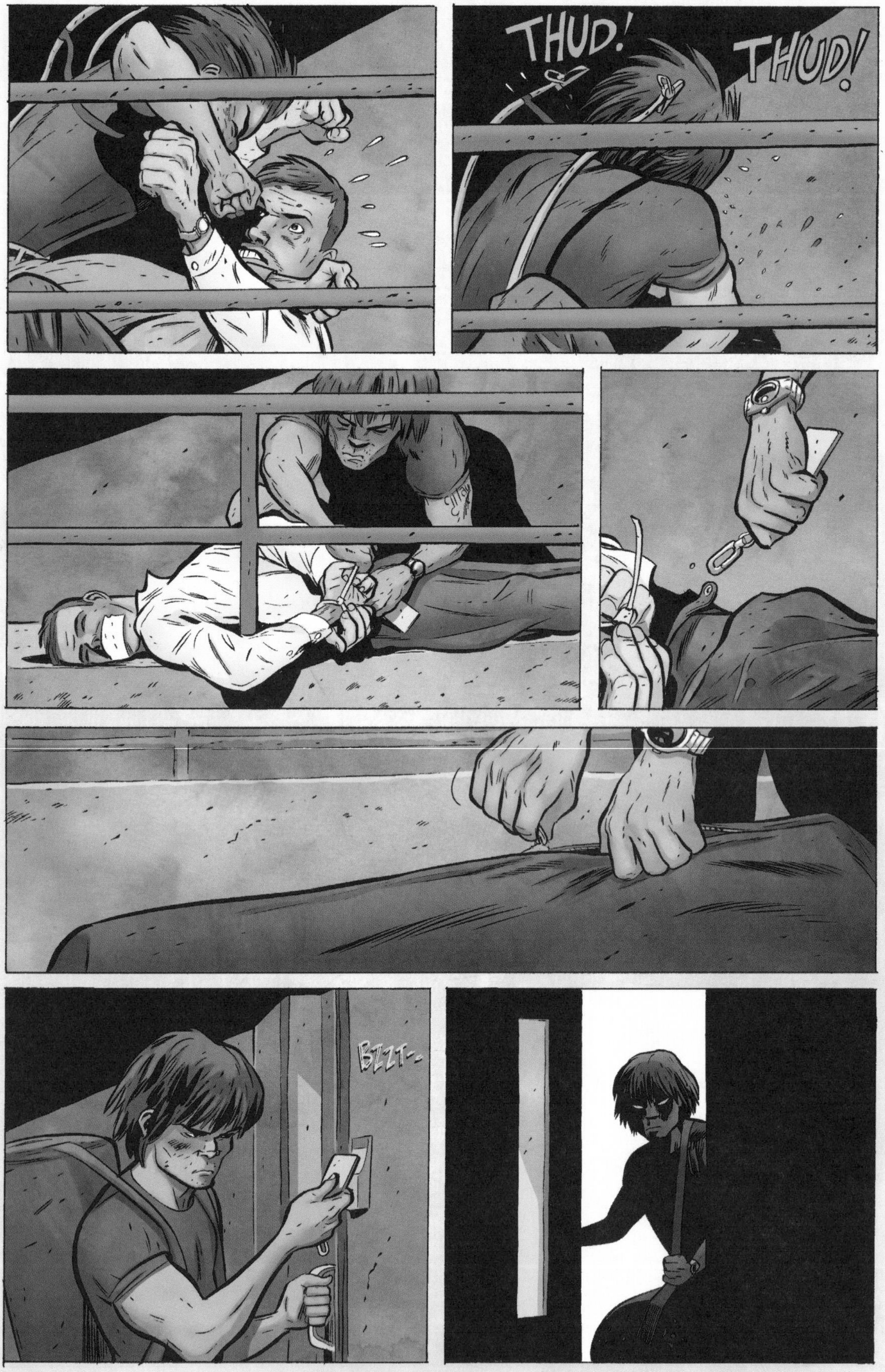
THUD!
THUD!
BZZT--

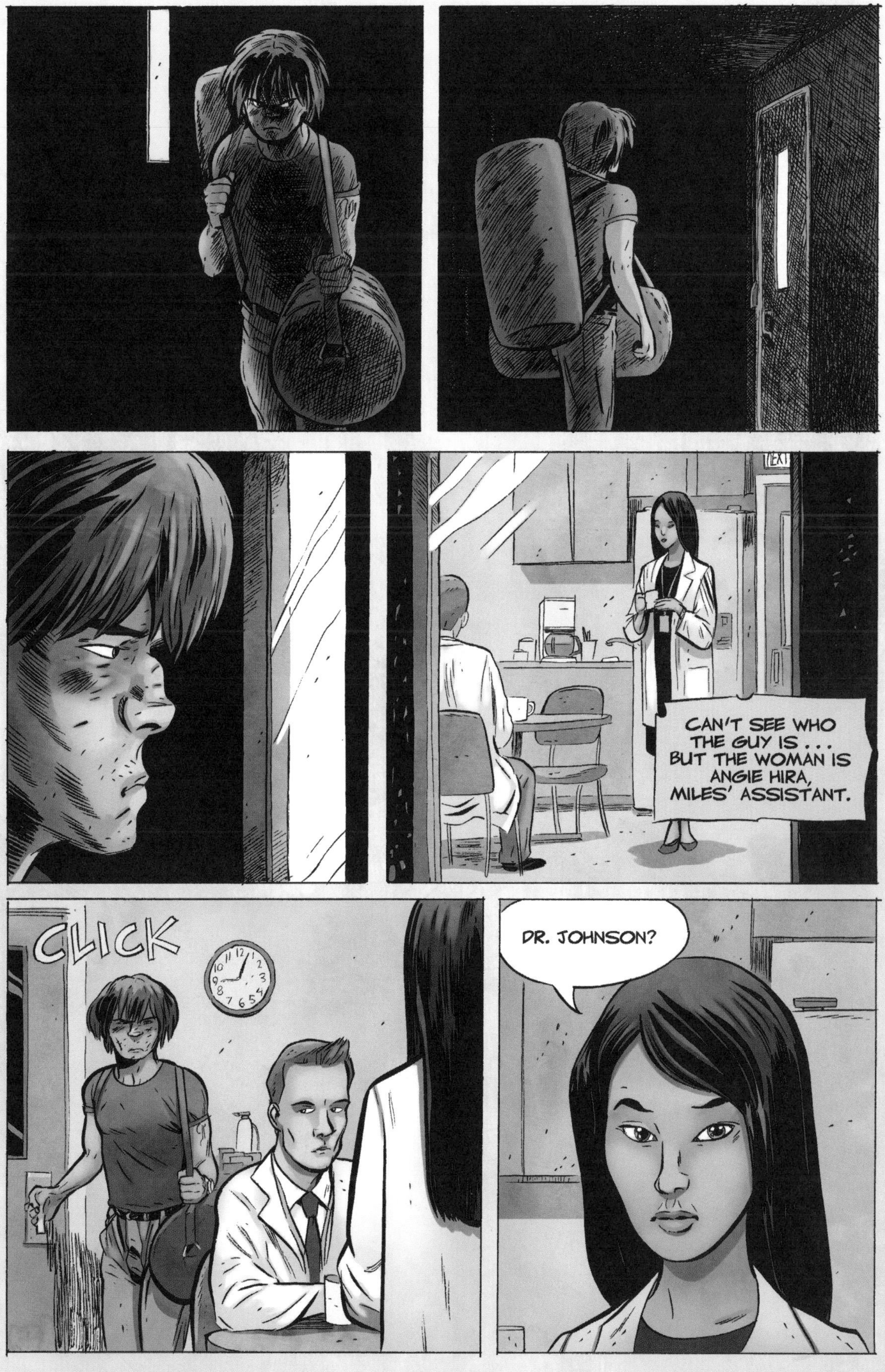
EXIT
CAN'T SEE WHO THE GUY IS . . . BUT THE WOMAN IS ANGIE HIRA, MILES' ASSISTANT.
CLICK
DR. JOHNSON?

ANGIE, I NEED TO GET INTO THE BUNKER. TAKE ME THERE.

WHO ARE YOU? THIS IS A RESTRICTED AREA.

I DON'T KNOW YOU. SIT DOWN.

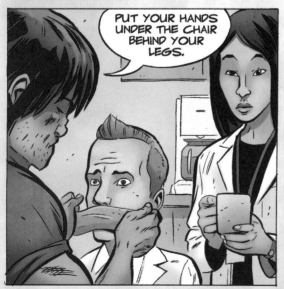

PUT YOUR HANDS UNDER THE CHAIR BEHIND YOUR LEGS.

ANGIE, LISTEN TO ME. I NEED YOUR THUMBPRINT TO GET INSIDE THE BUNKER . . .

WHAT ARE YOU GOING TO DO?

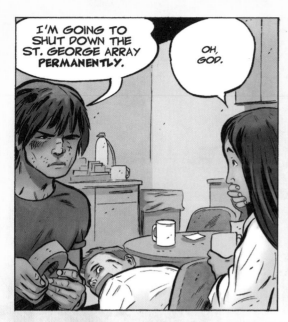

I'M GOING TO SHUT DOWN THE ST. GEORGE ARRAY **PERMANENTLY**.

OH, GOD.

FOUR DAYS AGO, AN ENTIRE TOWN IN THE DESERT WAS **WIPED OUT** --

WHOLE FAMILIES OF MEN, WOMEN AND CHILDREN ALONG WITH THEIR LIVESTOCK --

EVERY LIVING CREATURE IN A FOUR MILE RADIUS WAS **SLAUGHTERED**.

OH, GOD.

DO YOU KNOW ABOUT THAT? DO YOU **KNOW** ABOUT THE DAMAGE THE ARRAY CAUSED?

W-WE RAN A TEST FOUR DAYS AGO, BUT --

NO, YOU DON'T KNOW... TAKE ME DOWN TO THE BUNKER. NOW.

TH - THEY'RE STILL LOOKING FOR YOU FROM THE LAST TIME.

AFTER YOU LET ME IN, YOU CAN HAVE SECURITY EVACUATE THE BUILDING.

NOW.

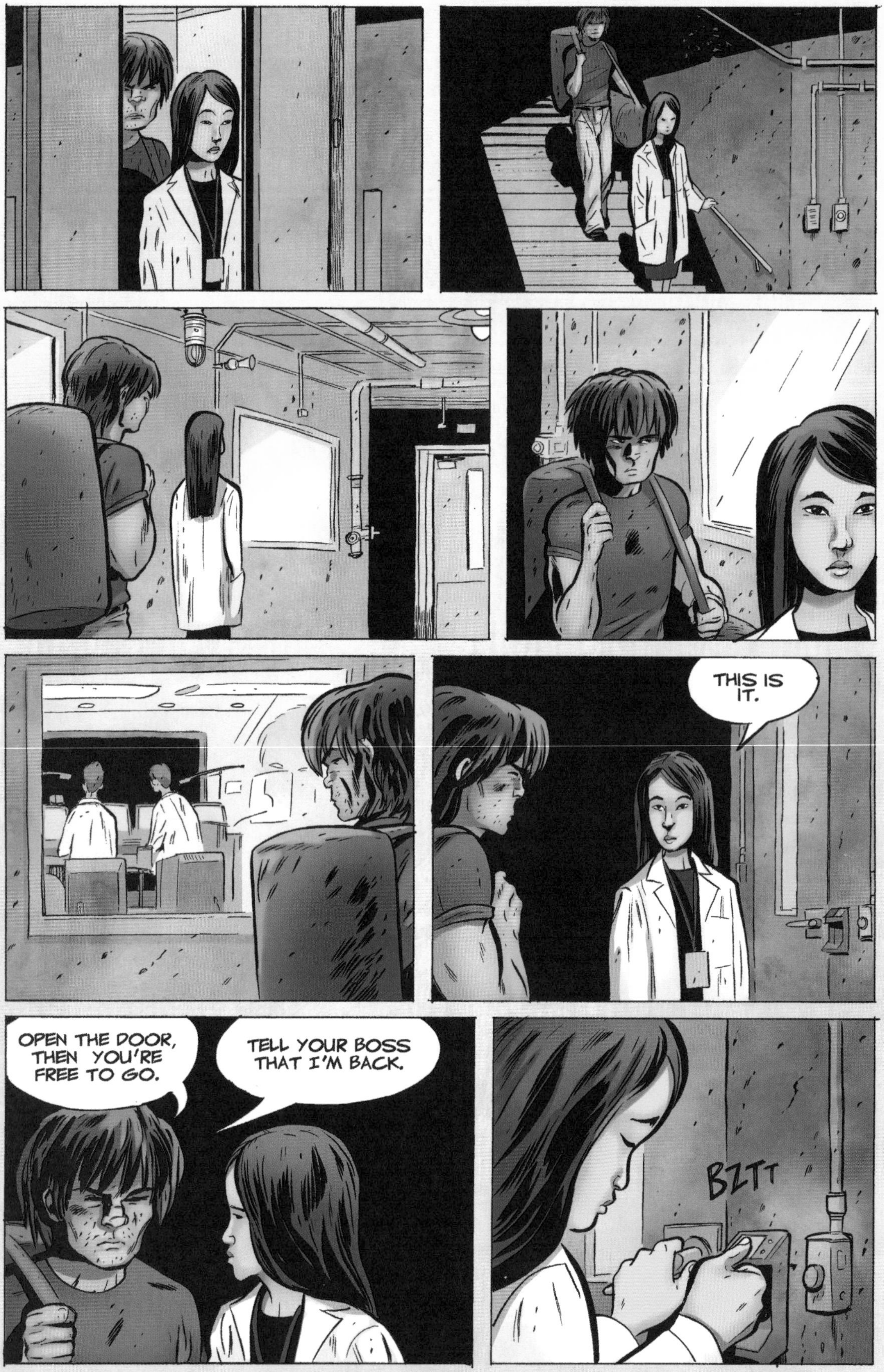
THIS IS IT.
OPEN THE DOOR, THEN YOU'RE FREE TO GO.
TELL YOUR BOSS THAT I'M BACK.
BZTT

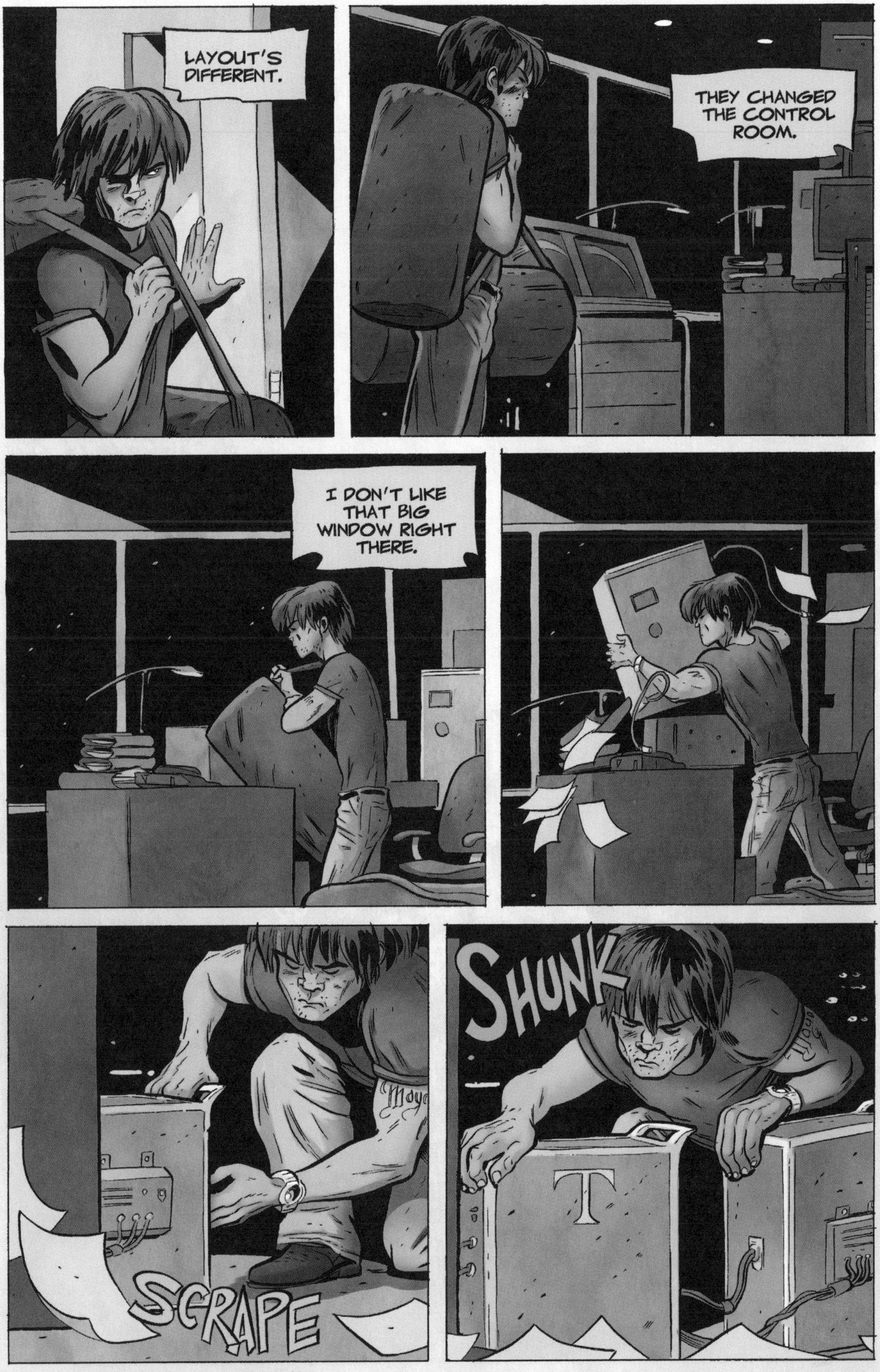
LAYOUT'S DIFFERENT.
THEY CHANGED THE CONTROL ROOM.
I DON'T LIKE THAT BIG WINDOW RIGHT THERE.
SCRAPE
SHUNK

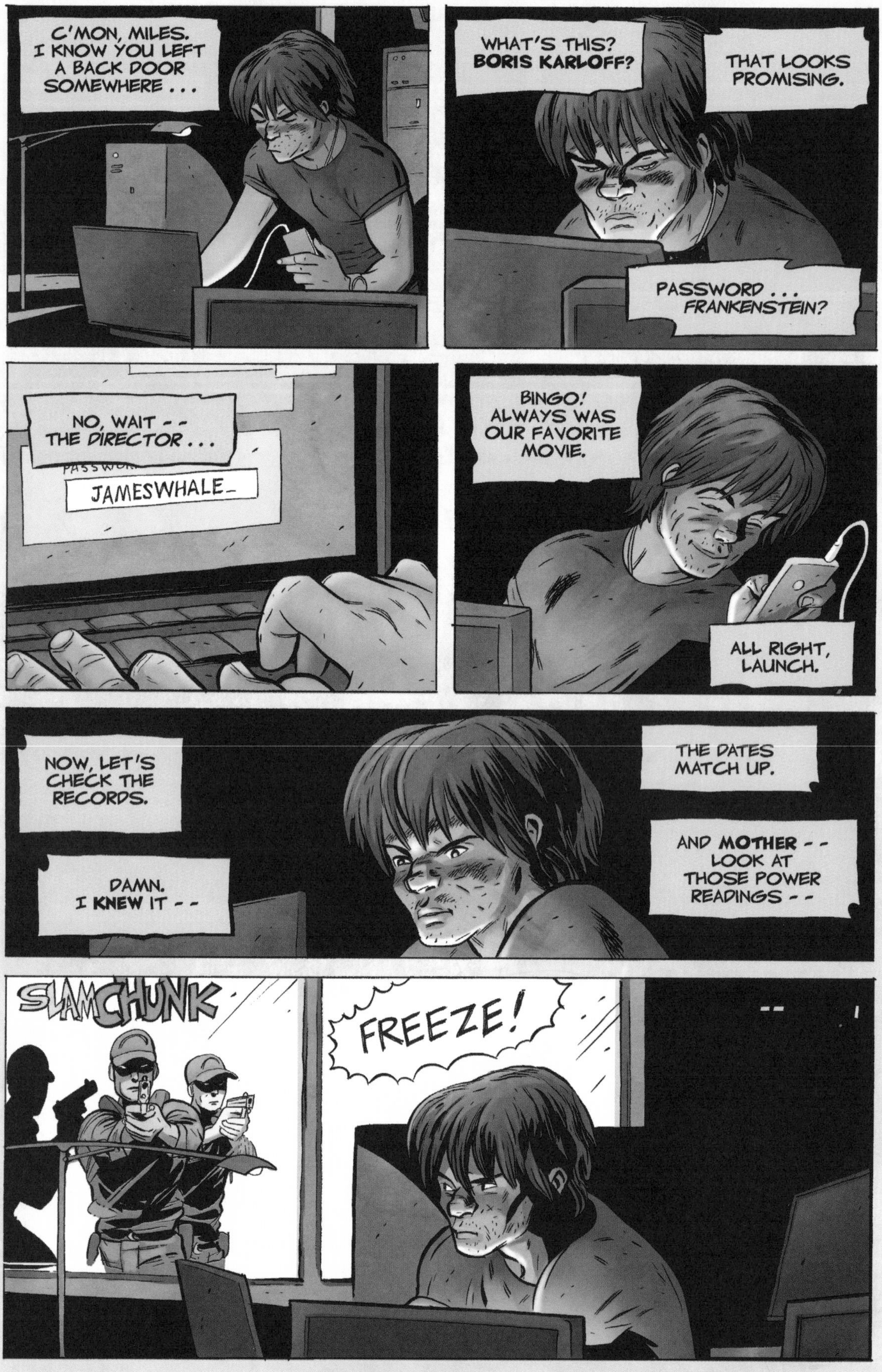

C'MON, MILES. I KNOW YOU LEFT A BACK DOOR SOMEWHERE . . .
WHAT'S THIS? BORIS KARLOFF?
THAT LOOKS PROMISING.
PASSWORD . . . FRANKENSTEIN?
NO, WAIT - - THE DIRECTOR . . .
JAMESWHALE_
BINGO! ALWAYS WAS OUR FAVORITE MOVIE.
ALL RIGHT, LAUNCH.
NOW, LET'S CHECK THE RECORDS.
DAMN. I KNEW IT - -
THE DATES MATCH UP.
AND MOTHER - - LOOK AT THOSE POWER READINGS - -
SLAMCHUNK
FREEZE!

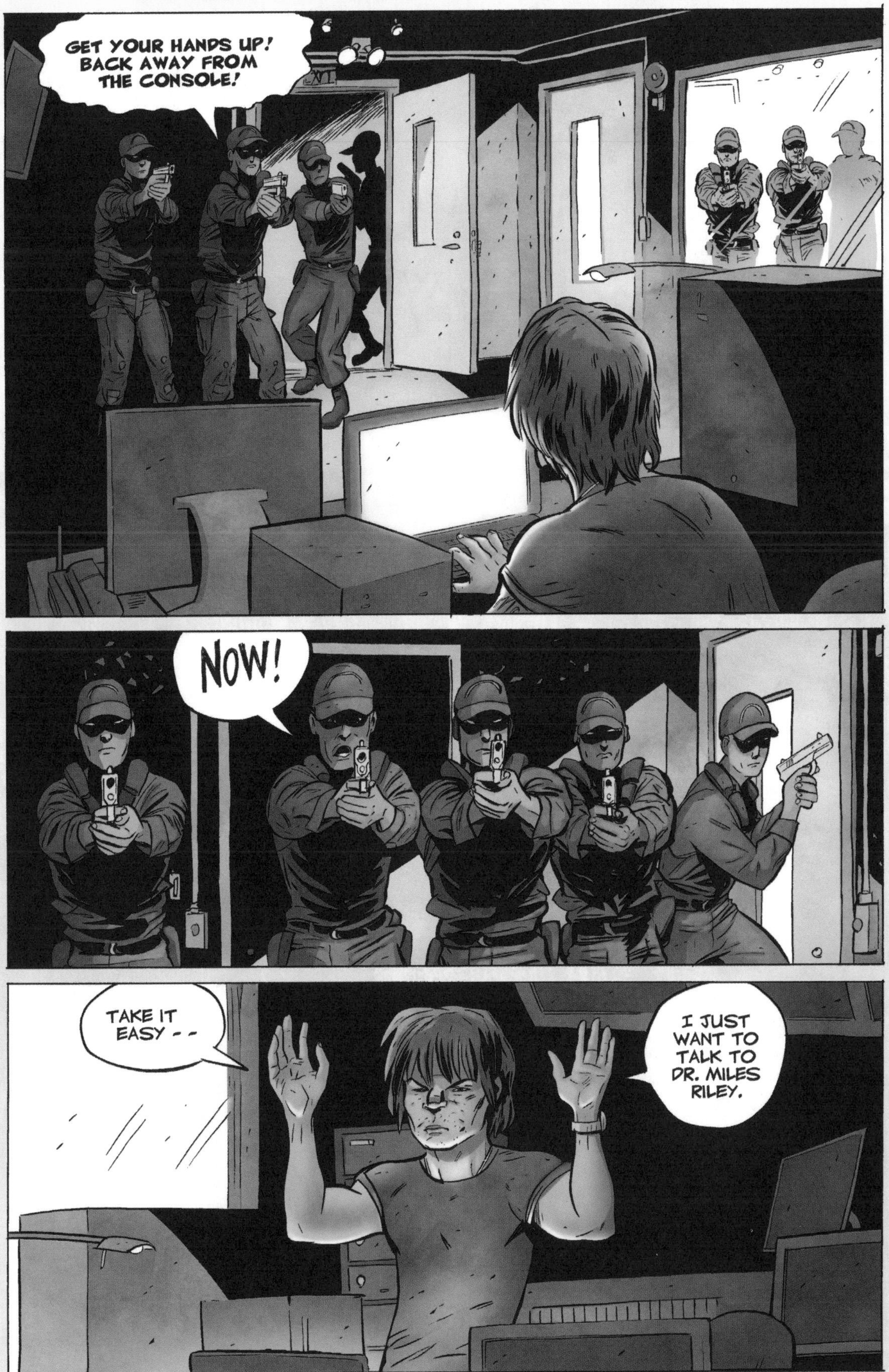
GET YOUR HANDS UP! BACK AWAY FROM THE CONSOLE!
NOW!
TAKE IT EASY - -
I JUST WANT TO TALK TO DR. MILES RILEY.

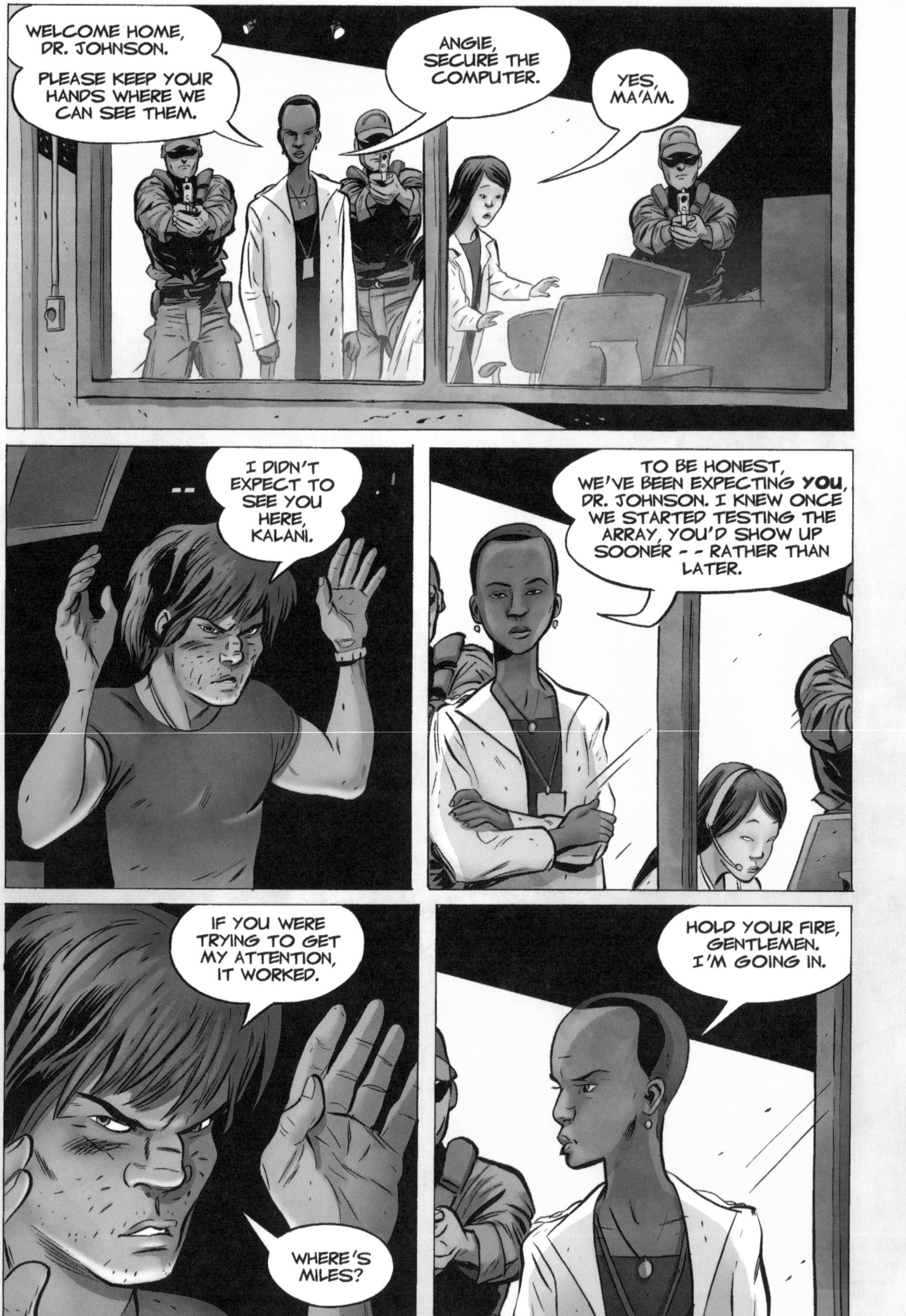
WELCOME HOME, DR. JOHNSON.
PLEASE KEEP YOUR HANDS WHERE WE CAN SEE THEM.
ANGIE, SECURE THE COMPUTER.
YES, MA'AM.
I DIDN'T EXPECT TO SEE YOU HERE, KALANI.
TO BE HONEST, WE'VE BEEN EXPECTING **YOU**, DR. JOHNSON. I KNEW ONCE WE STARTED TESTING THE ARRAY, YOU'D SHOW UP SOONER - - RATHER THAN LATER.
IF YOU WERE TRYING TO GET MY ATTENTION, IT WORKED.
WHERE'S MILES?
HOLD YOUR FIRE, GENTLEMEN. I'M GOING IN.

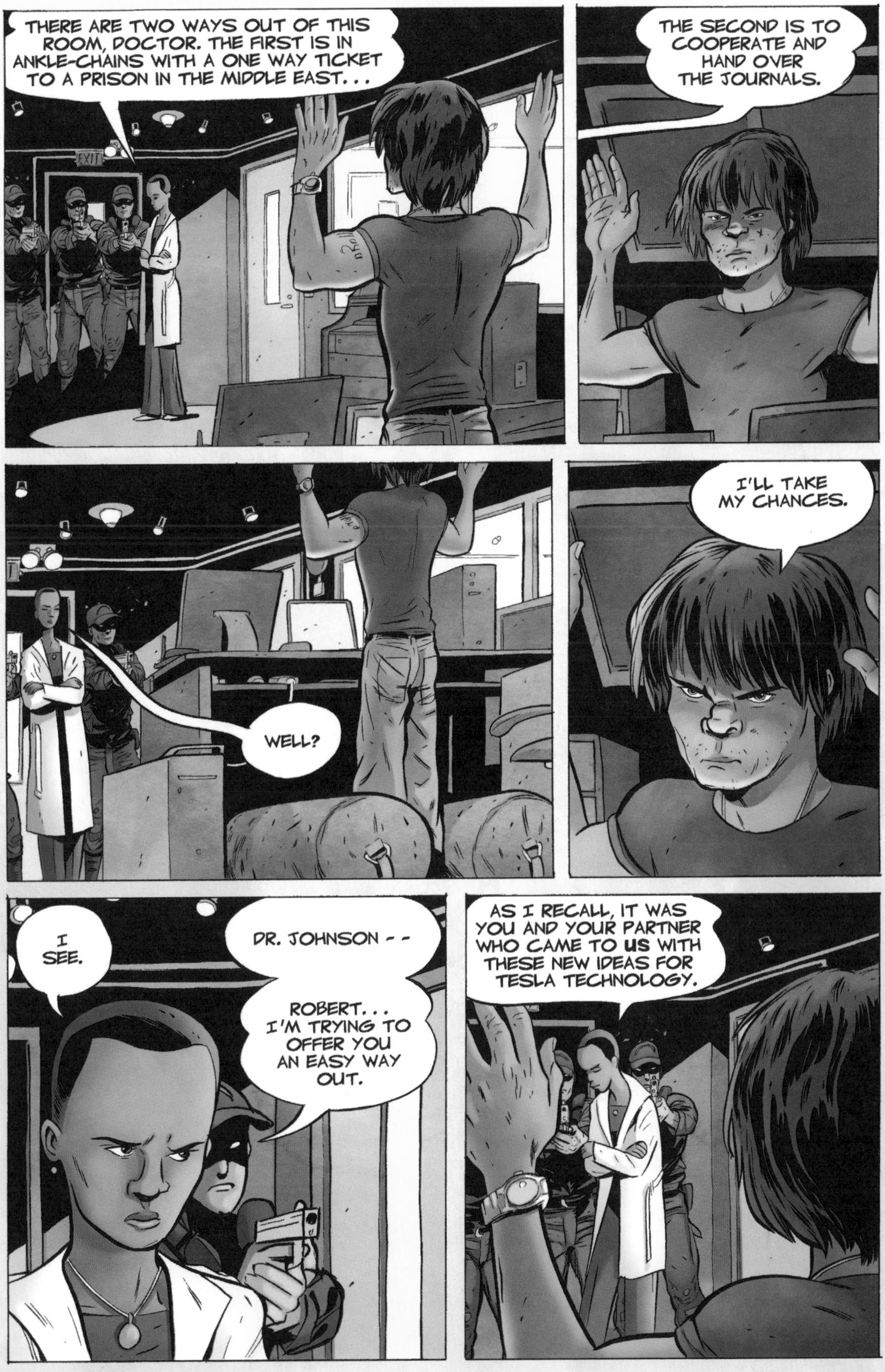
THERE ARE TWO WAYS OUT OF THIS ROOM, DOCTOR. THE FIRST IS IN ANKLE-CHAINS WITH A ONE WAY TICKET TO A PRISON IN THE MIDDLE EAST. . .
THE SECOND IS TO COOPERATE AND HAND OVER THE JOURNALS.
WELL?
I'LL TAKE MY CHANCES.
I SEE.
DR. JOHNSON - -
ROBERT. . . I'M TRYING TO OFFER YOU AN EASY WAY OUT.
AS I RECALL, IT WAS YOU AND YOUR PARTNER WHO CAME TO US WITH THESE NEW IDEAS FOR TESLA TECHNOLOGY.

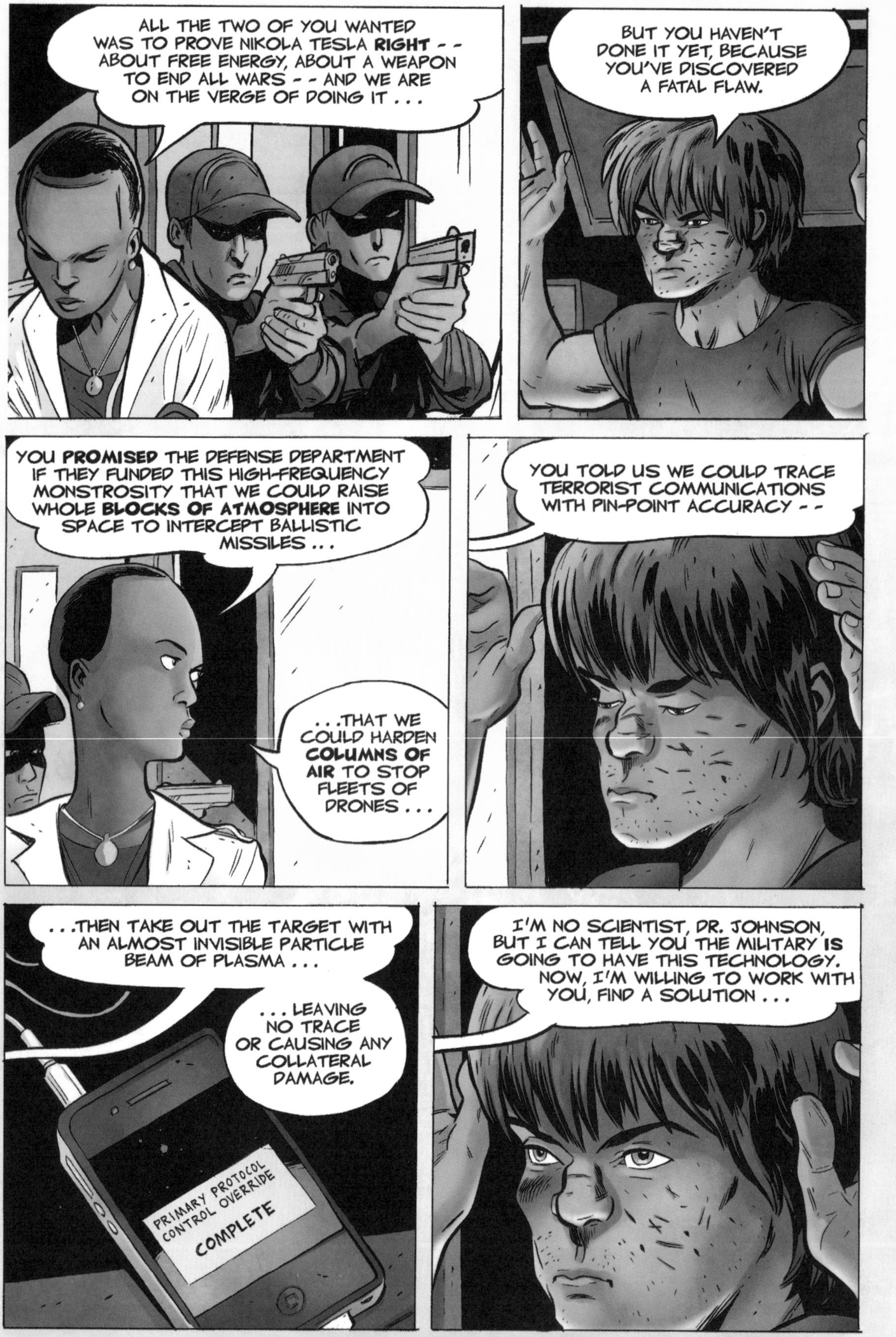
ALL THE TWO OF YOU WANTED WAS TO PROVE NIKOLA TESLA RIGHT - - ABOUT FREE ENERGY, ABOUT A WEAPON TO END ALL WARS - - AND WE ARE ON THE VERGE OF DOING IT . . .
BUT YOU HAVEN'T DONE IT YET, BECAUSE YOU'VE DISCOVERED A FATAL FLAW.
YOU PROMISED THE DEFENSE DEPARTMENT IF THEY FUNDED THIS HIGH-FREQUENCY MONSTROSITY THAT WE COULD RAISE WHOLE BLOCKS OF ATMOSPHERE INTO SPACE TO INTERCEPT BALLISTIC MISSILES . . .
. . .THAT WE COULD HARDEN COLUMNS OF AIR TO STOP FLEETS OF DRONES . . .
YOU TOLD US WE COULD TRACE TERRORIST COMMUNICATIONS WITH PIN-POINT ACCURACY - -
. . .THEN TAKE OUT THE TARGET WITH AN ALMOST INVISIBLE PARTICLE BEAM OF PLASMA . . .
. . . LEAVING NO TRACE OR CAUSING ANY COLLATERAL DAMAGE.
PRIMARY PROTOCOL CONTROL OVERRIDE
COMPLETE
I'M NO SCIENTIST, DR. JOHNSON, BUT I CAN TELL YOU THE MILITARY IS GOING TO HAVE THIS TECHNOLOGY. NOW, I'M WILLING TO WORK WITH YOU, FIND A SOLUTION . . .

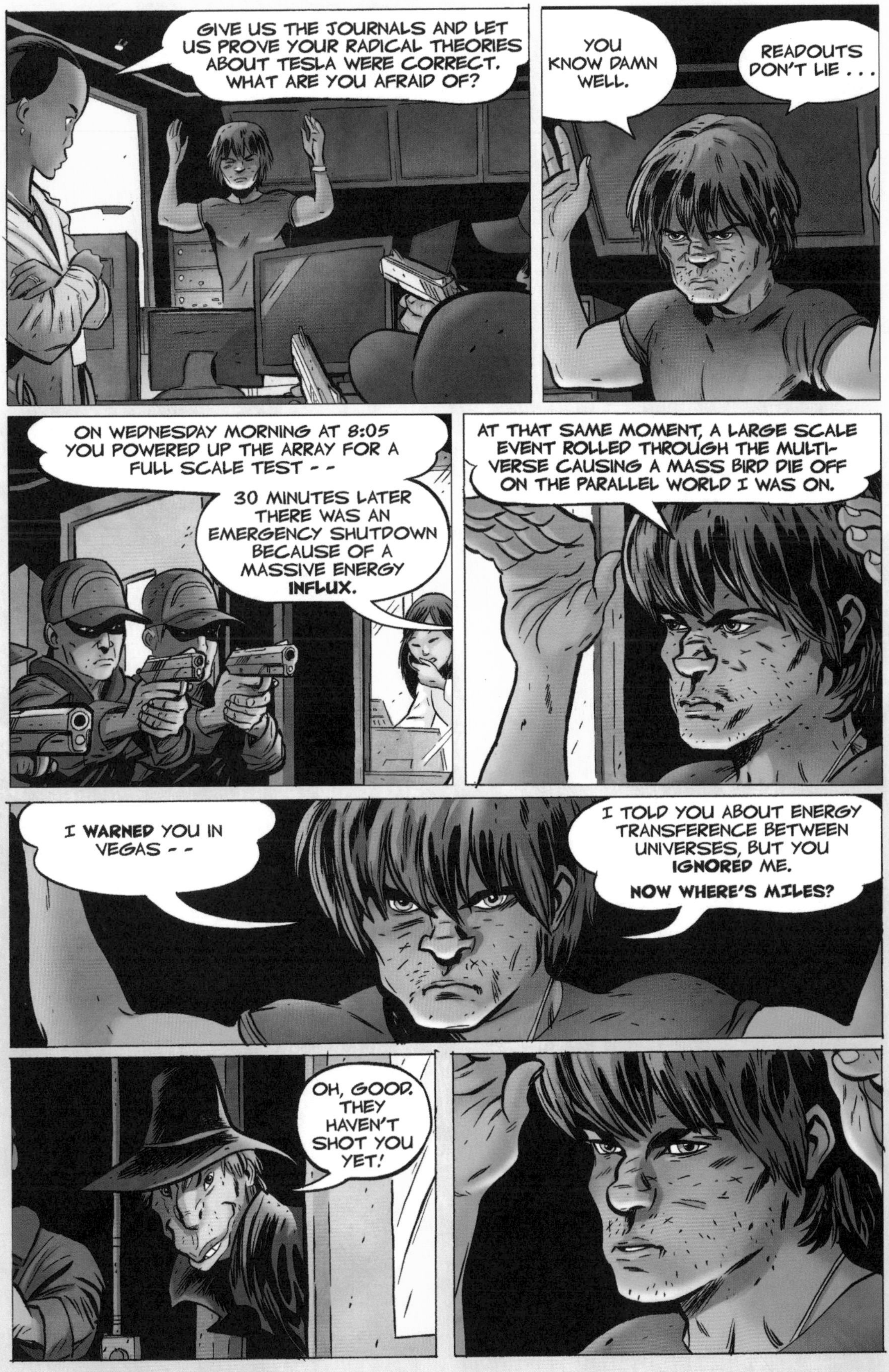
GIVE US THE JOURNALS AND LET US PROVE YOUR RADICAL THEORIES ABOUT TESLA WERE CORRECT. WHAT ARE YOU AFRAID OF?
YOU KNOW DAMN WELL.
READOUTS DON'T LIE . . .
ON WEDNESDAY MORNING AT 8:05 YOU POWERED UP THE ARRAY FOR A FULL SCALE TEST - -
30 MINUTES LATER THERE WAS AN EMERGENCY SHUTDOWN BECAUSE OF A MASSIVE ENERGY INFLUX.
AT THAT SAME MOMENT, A LARGE SCALE EVENT ROLLED THROUGH THE MULTI-VERSE CAUSING A MASS BIRD DIE OFF ON THE PARALLEL WORLD I WAS ON.
I WARNED YOU IN VEGAS - -
I TOLD YOU ABOUT ENERGY TRANSFERENCE BETWEEN UNIVERSES, BUT YOU IGNORED ME.
NOW WHERE'S MILES?
OH, GOOD. THEY HAVEN'T SHOT YOU YET!

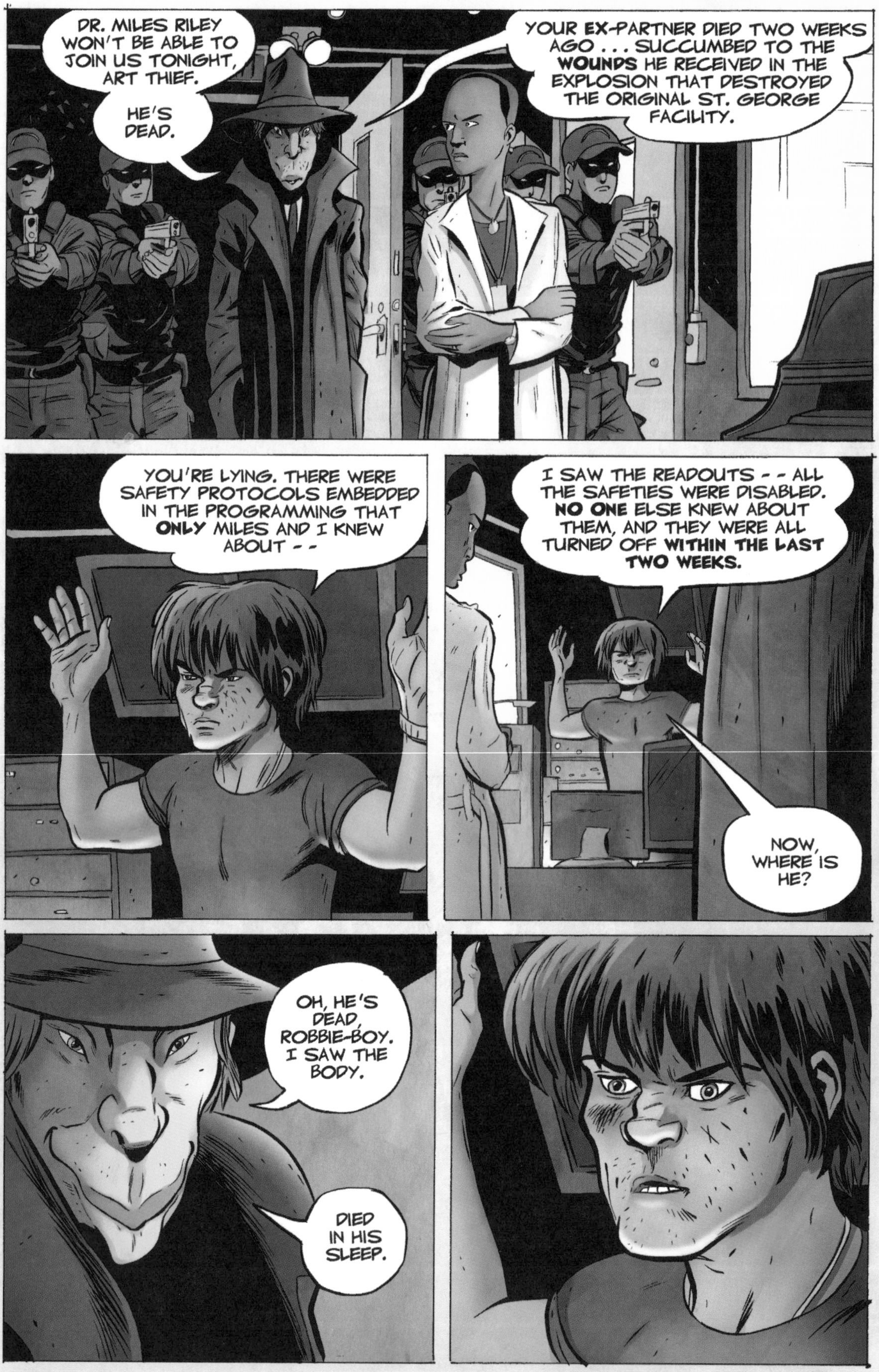
DR. MILES RILEY WON'T BE ABLE TO JOIN US TONIGHT, ART THIEF.
HE'S DEAD.
YOUR EX-PARTNER DIED TWO WEEKS AGO . . . SUCCUMBED TO THE WOUNDS HE RECEIVED IN THE EXPLOSION THAT DESTROYED THE ORIGINAL ST. GEORGE FACILITY.
YOU'RE LYING. THERE WERE SAFETY PROTOCOLS EMBEDDED IN THE PROGRAMMING THAT ONLY MILES AND I KNEW ABOUT - -
I SAW THE READOUTS - - ALL THE SAFETIES WERE DISABLED. NO ONE ELSE KNEW ABOUT THEM, AND THEY WERE ALL TURNED OFF WITHIN THE LAST TWO WEEKS.
NOW, WHERE IS HE?
OH, HE'S DEAD, ROBBIE-BOY. I SAW THE BODY.
DIED IN HIS SLEEP.

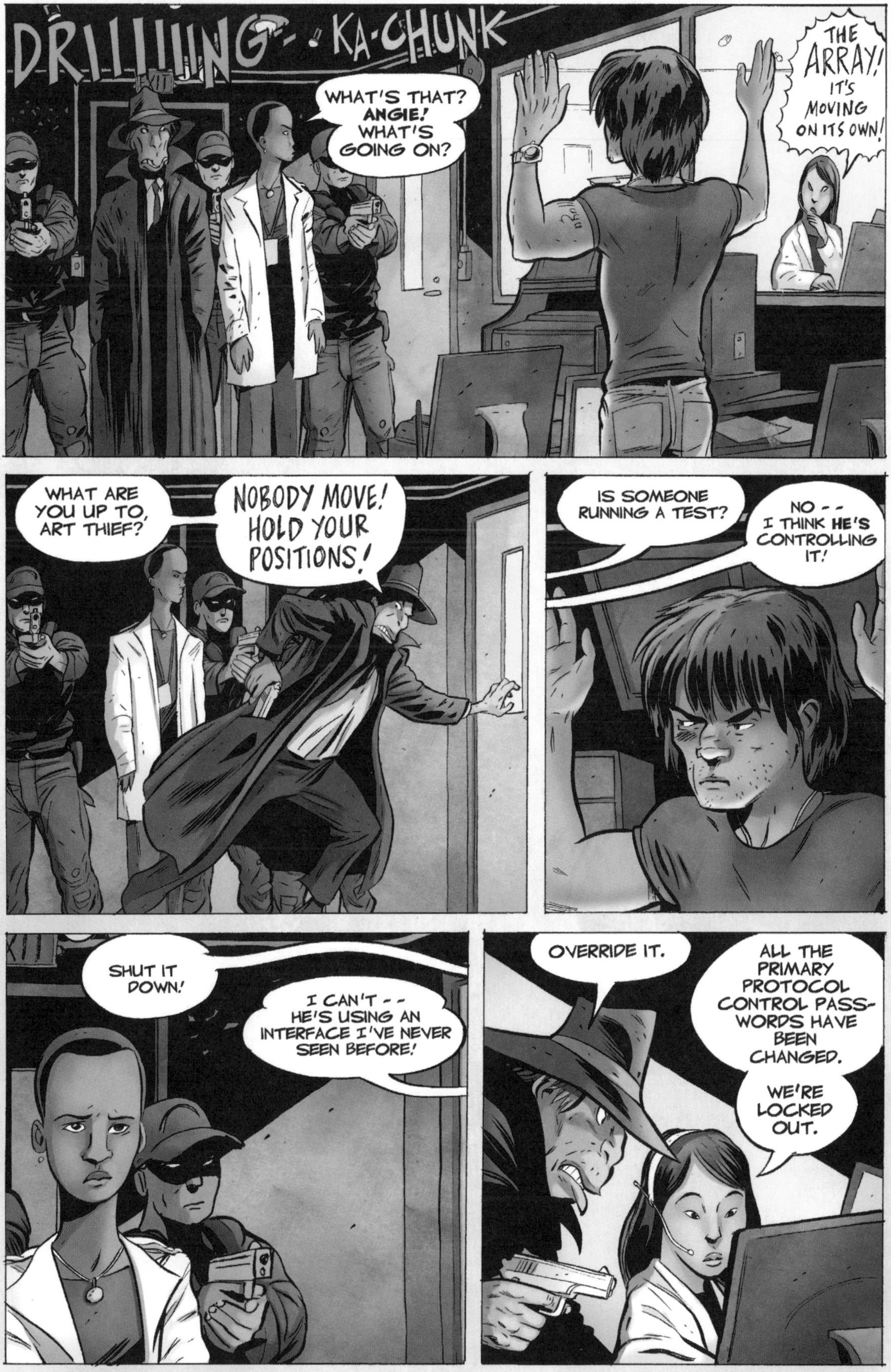
DRIIIIING
KA-CHUNK
WHAT'S THAT? ANGIE! WHAT'S GOING ON?
THE ARRAY! IT'S MOVING ON ITS OWN!
WHAT ARE YOU UP TO, ART THIEF?
NOBODY MOVE! HOLD YOUR POSITIONS!
IS SOMEONE RUNNING A TEST?
NO - - I THINK HE'S CONTROLLING IT!
SHUT IT DOWN!
I CAN'T - - HE'S USING AN INTERFACE I'VE NEVER SEEN BEFORE!
OVERRIDE IT.
ALL THE PRIMARY PROTOCOL CONTROL PASS-WORDS HAVE BEEN CHANGED.
WE'RE LOCKED OUT.

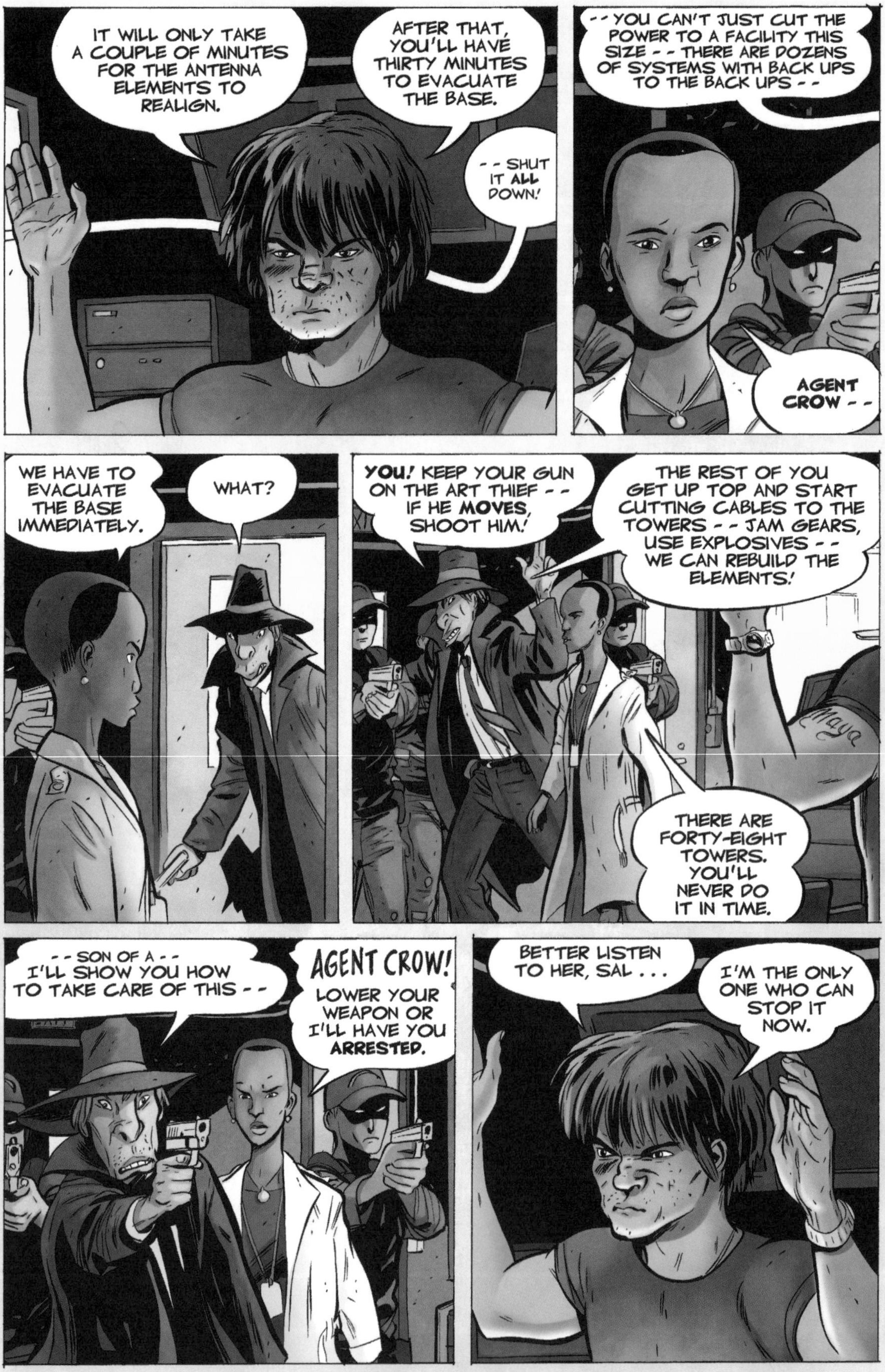
IT WILL ONLY TAKE A COUPLE OF MINUTES FOR THE ANTENNA ELEMENTS TO REALIGN.
AFTER THAT, YOU'LL HAVE THIRTY MINUTES TO EVACUATE THE BASE.
- - SHUT IT ALL DOWN!
- - YOU CAN'T JUST CUT THE POWER TO A FACILITY THIS SIZE - - THERE ARE DOZENS OF SYSTEMS WITH BACK UPS TO THE BACK UPS - -
AGENT CROW - -
WE HAVE TO EVACUATE THE BASE IMMEDIATELY.
WHAT?
YOU! KEEP YOUR GUN ON THE ART THIEF - - IF HE MOVES, SHOOT HIM!
THE REST OF YOU GET UP TOP AND START CUTTING CABLES TO THE TOWERS - - JAM GEARS, USE EXPLOSIVES - - WE CAN REBUILD THE ELEMENTS!
THERE ARE FORTY-EIGHT TOWERS. YOU'LL NEVER DO IT IN TIME.
- - SON OF A - - I'LL SHOW YOU HOW TO TAKE CARE OF THIS - -
AGENT CROW! LOWER YOUR WEAPON OR I'LL HAVE YOU ARRESTED.
BETTER LISTEN TO HER, SAL . . .
I'M THE ONLY ONE WHO CAN STOP IT NOW.

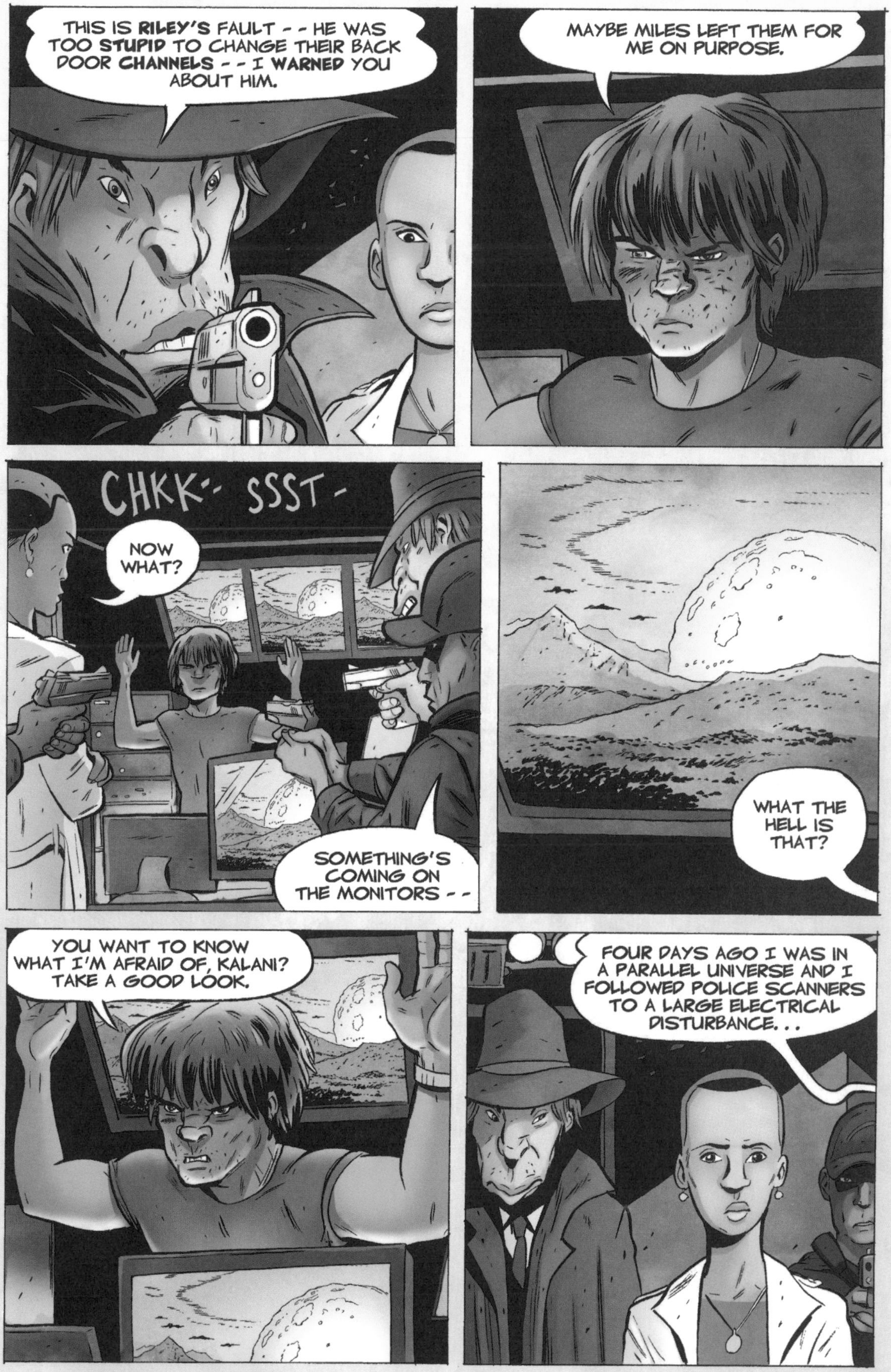
THIS IS RILEY'S FAULT - - HE WAS TOO STUPID TO CHANGE THEIR BACK DOOR CHANNELS - - I WARNED YOU ABOUT HIM.
MAYBE MILES LEFT THEM FOR ME ON PURPOSE.
CHKK - - SSST -
NOW WHAT?
SOMETHING'S COMING ON THE MONITORS - -
WHAT THE HELL IS THAT?
YOU WANT TO KNOW WHAT I'M AFRAID OF, KALANI? TAKE A GOOD LOOK.
FOUR DAYS AGO I WAS IN A PARALLEL UNIVERSE AND I FOLLOWED POLICE SCANNERS TO A LARGE ELECTRICAL DISTURBANCE. . .

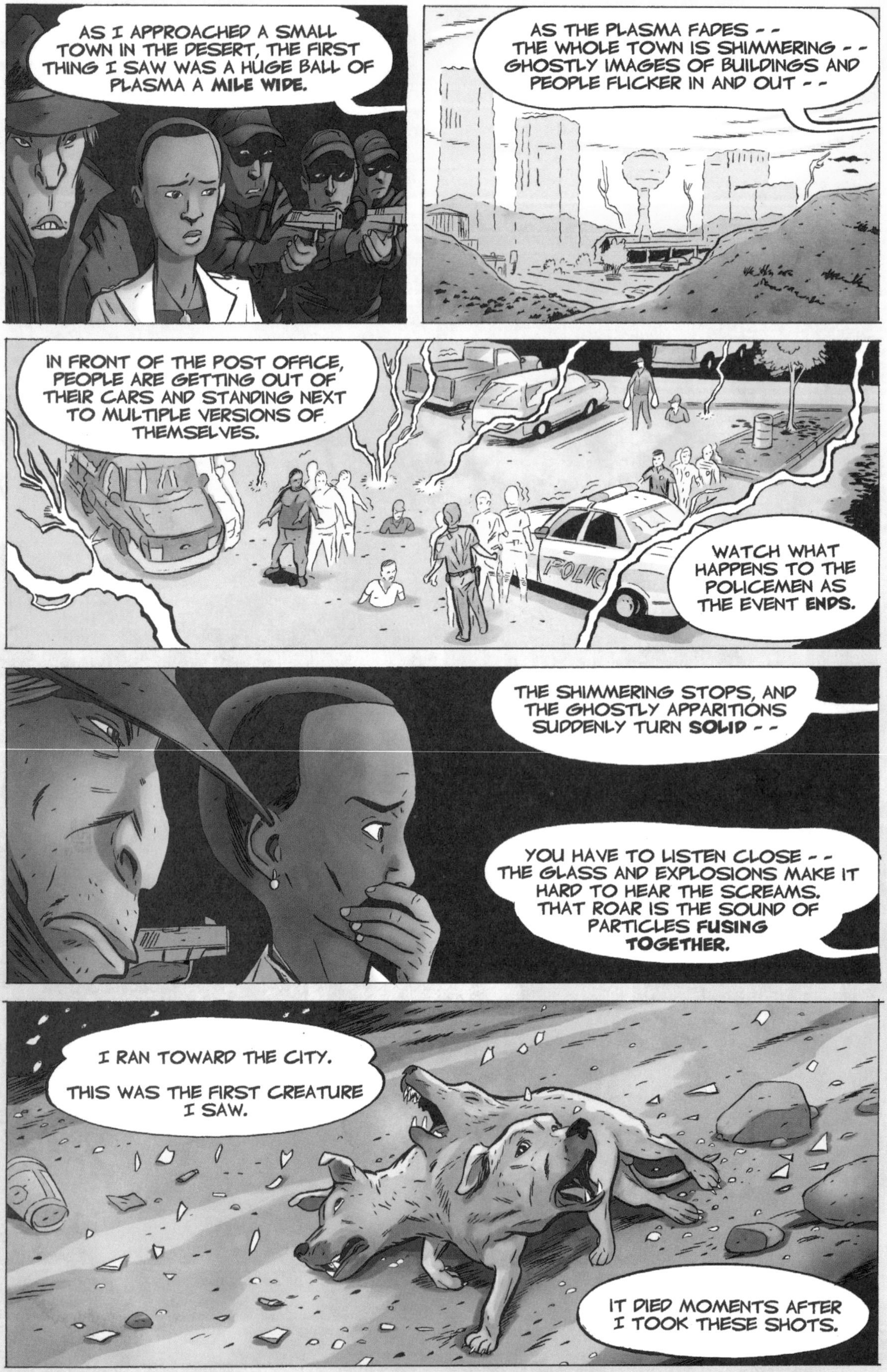
AS I APPROACHED A SMALL TOWN IN THE DESERT, THE FIRST THING I SAW WAS A HUGE BALL OF PLASMA A **MILE WIDE.**
AS THE PLASMA FADES - - THE WHOLE TOWN IS SHIMMERING - - GHOSTLY IMAGES OF BUILDINGS AND PEOPLE FLICKER IN AND OUT - -
IN FRONT OF THE POST OFFICE, PEOPLE ARE GETTING OUT OF THEIR CARS AND STANDING NEXT TO MULTIPLE VERSIONS OF THEMSELVES.
POLIC
WATCH WHAT HAPPENS TO THE POLICEMEN AS THE EVENT **ENDS.**
THE SHIMMERING STOPS, AND THE GHOSTLY APPARITIONS SUDDENLY TURN **SOLID** - -
YOU HAVE TO LISTEN CLOSE - - THE GLASS AND EXPLOSIONS MAKE IT HARD TO HEAR THE SCREAMS. THAT ROAR IS THE SOUND OF PARTICLES **FUSING TOGETHER.**
I RAN TOWARD THE CITY.
THIS WAS THE FIRST CREATURE I SAW.
IT DIED MOMENTS AFTER I TOOK THESE SHOTS.

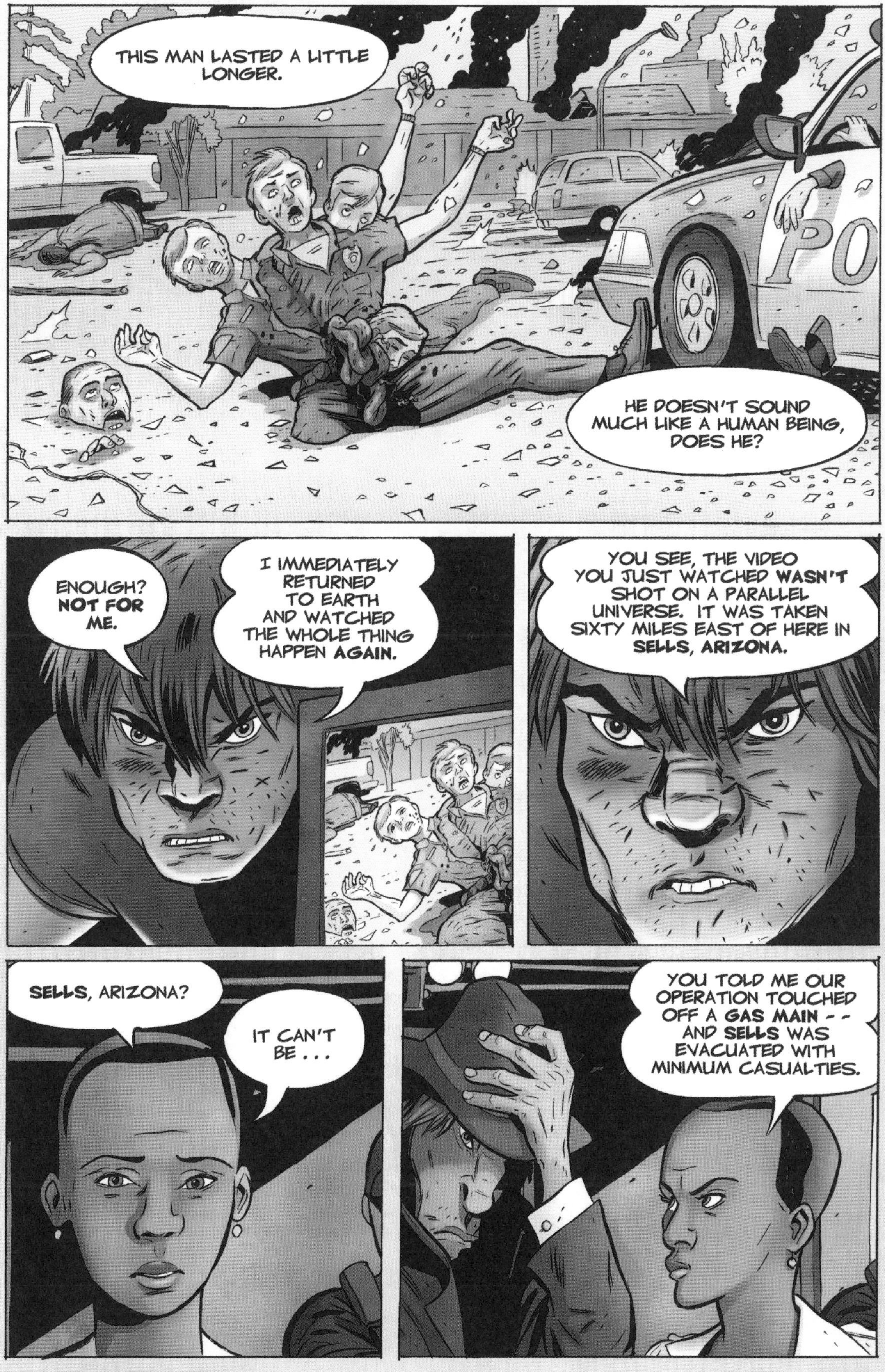
THIS MAN LASTED A LITTLE LONGER.
HE DOESN'T SOUND MUCH LIKE A HUMAN BEING, DOES HE?
ENOUGH? NOT FOR ME.
I IMMEDIATELY RETURNED TO EARTH AND WATCHED THE WHOLE THING HAPPEN AGAIN.
YOU SEE, THE VIDEO YOU JUST WATCHED WASN'T SHOT ON A PARALLEL UNIVERSE. IT WAS TAKEN SIXTY MILES EAST OF HERE IN SELLS, ARIZONA.
SELLS, ARIZONA?
IT CAN'T BE . . .
YOU TOLD ME OUR OPERATION TOUCHED OFF A GAS MAIN - - AND SELLS WAS EVACUATED WITH MINIMUM CASUALTIES.

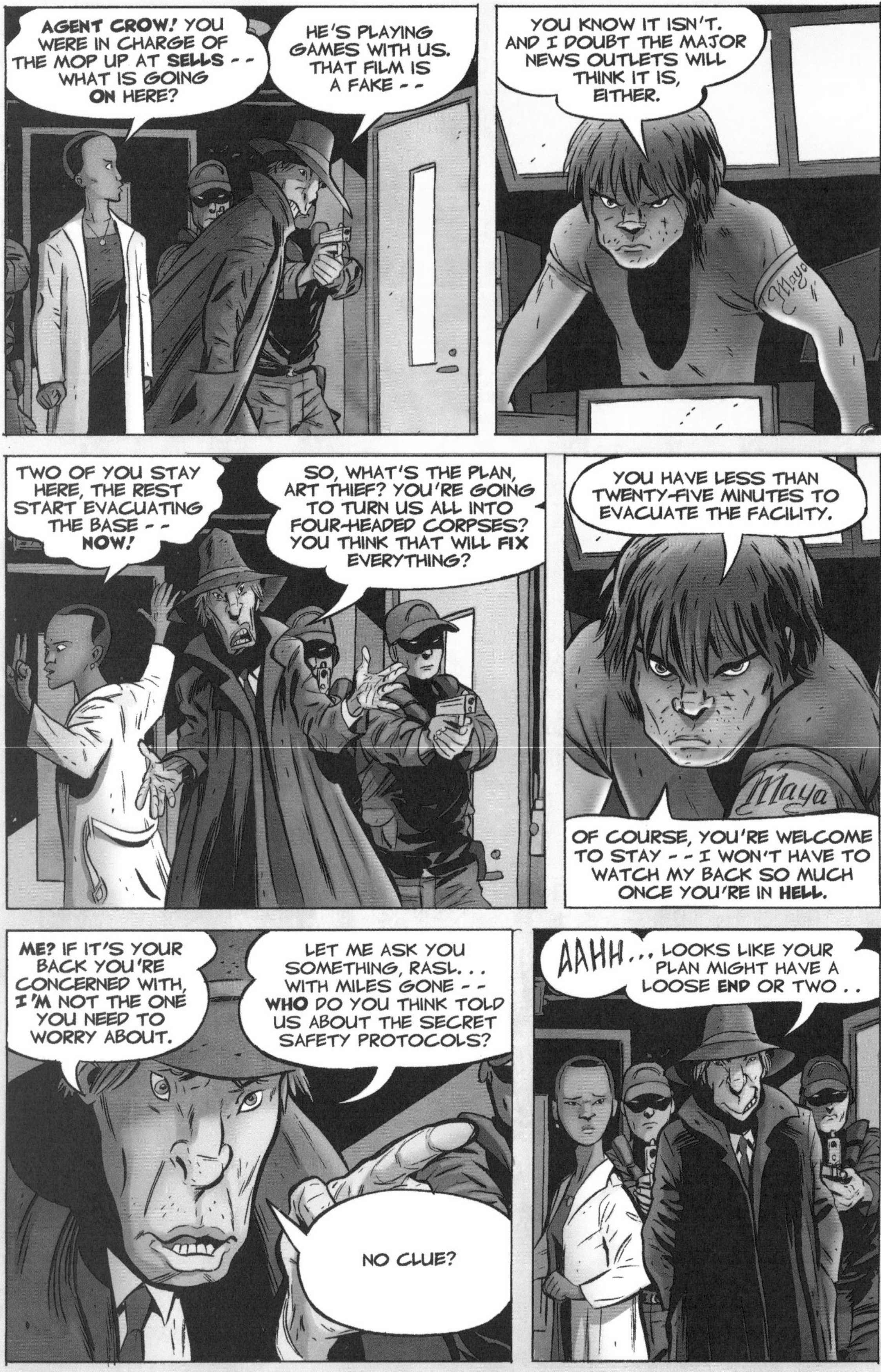
AGENT CROW! YOU WERE IN CHARGE OF THE MOP UP AT SELLS - - WHAT IS GOING ON HERE?
HE'S PLAYING GAMES WITH US. THAT FILM IS A FAKE - -
YOU KNOW IT ISN'T. AND I DOUBT THE MAJOR NEWS OUTLETS WILL THINK IT IS, EITHER.
Maya
TWO OF YOU STAY HERE, THE REST START EVACUATING THE BASE - - NOW!
SO, WHAT'S THE PLAN, ART THIEF? YOU'RE GOING TO TURN US ALL INTO FOUR-HEADED CORPSES? YOU THINK THAT WILL FIX EVERYTHING?
YOU HAVE LESS THAN TWENTY-FIVE MINUTES TO EVACUATE THE FACILITY.
Maya
OF COURSE, YOU'RE WELCOME TO STAY - - I WON'T HAVE TO WATCH MY BACK SO MUCH ONCE YOU'RE IN HELL.
ME? IF IT'S YOUR BACK YOU'RE CONCERNED WITH, I'M NOT THE ONE YOU NEED TO WORRY ABOUT.
LET ME ASK YOU SOMETHING, RASL. . . WITH MILES GONE - - WHO DO YOU THINK TOLD US ABOUT THE SECRET SAFETY PROTOCOLS?
NO CLUE?
AAHH . . . LOOKS LIKE YOUR PLAN MIGHT HAVE A LOOSE END OR TWO . .

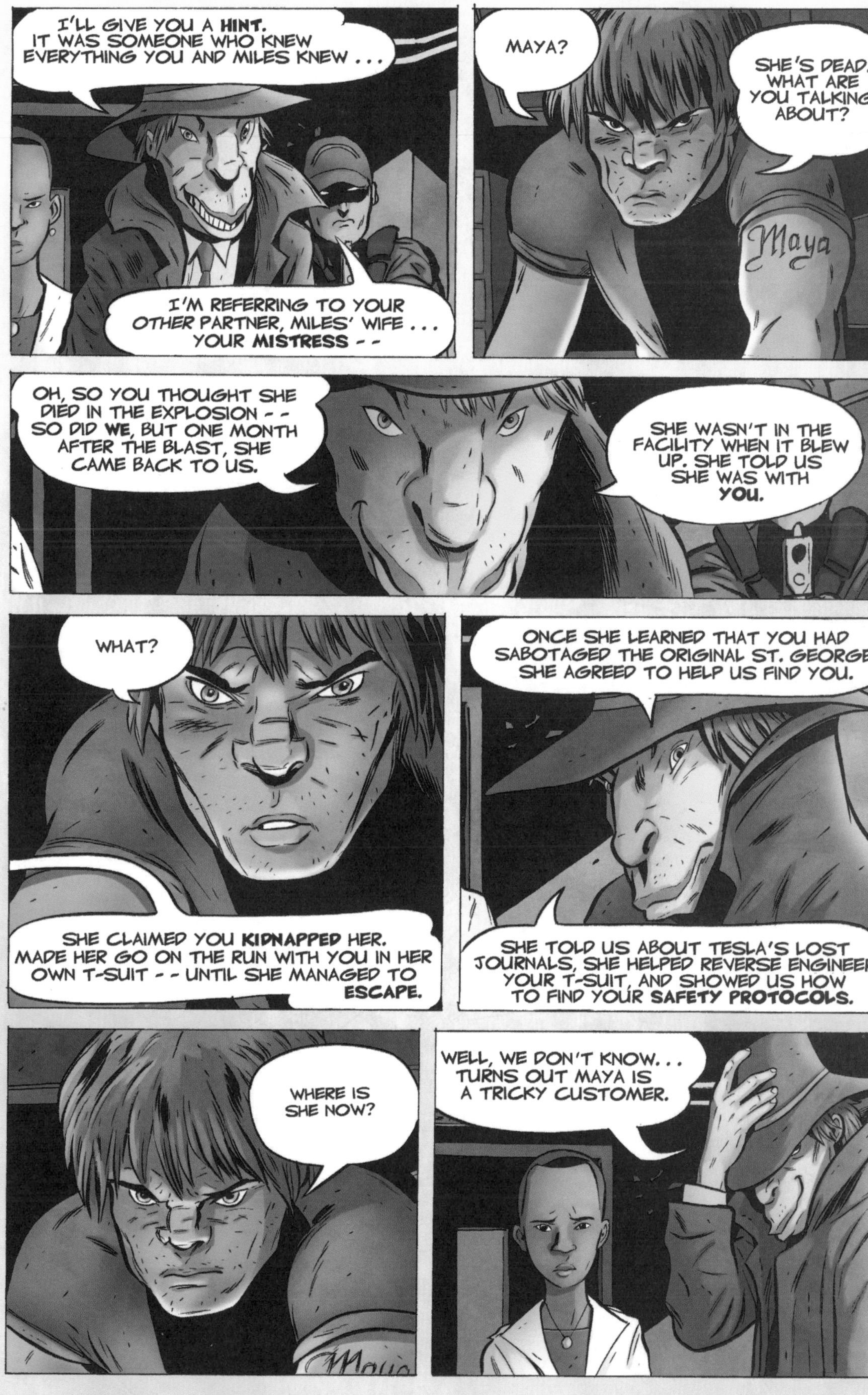
I'LL GIVE YOU A HINT. IT WAS SOMEONE WHO KNEW EVERYTHING YOU AND MILES KNEW . . .
I'M REFERRING TO YOUR OTHER PARTNER, MILES' WIFE . . . YOUR MISTRESS - -
MAYA?
SHE'S DEAD. WHAT ARE YOU TALKING ABOUT?
Maya
OH, SO YOU THOUGHT SHE DIED IN THE EXPLOSION - - SO DID WE, BUT ONE MONTH AFTER THE BLAST, SHE CAME BACK TO US.
SHE WASN'T IN THE FACILITY WHEN IT BLEW UP. SHE TOLD US SHE WAS WITH YOU.
WHAT?
SHE CLAIMED YOU KIDNAPPED HER. MADE HER GO ON THE RUN WITH YOU IN HER OWN T-SUIT - - UNTIL SHE MANAGED TO ESCAPE.
ONCE SHE LEARNED THAT YOU HAD SABOTAGED THE ORIGINAL ST. GEORGE, SHE AGREED TO HELP US FIND YOU.
SHE TOLD US ABOUT TESLA'S LOST JOURNALS, SHE HELPED REVERSE ENGINEER YOUR T-SUIT, AND SHOWED US HOW TO FIND YOUR SAFETY PROTOCOLS.
WHERE IS SHE NOW?
WELL, WE DON'T KNOW. . . TURNS OUT MAYA IS A TRICKY CUSTOMER.

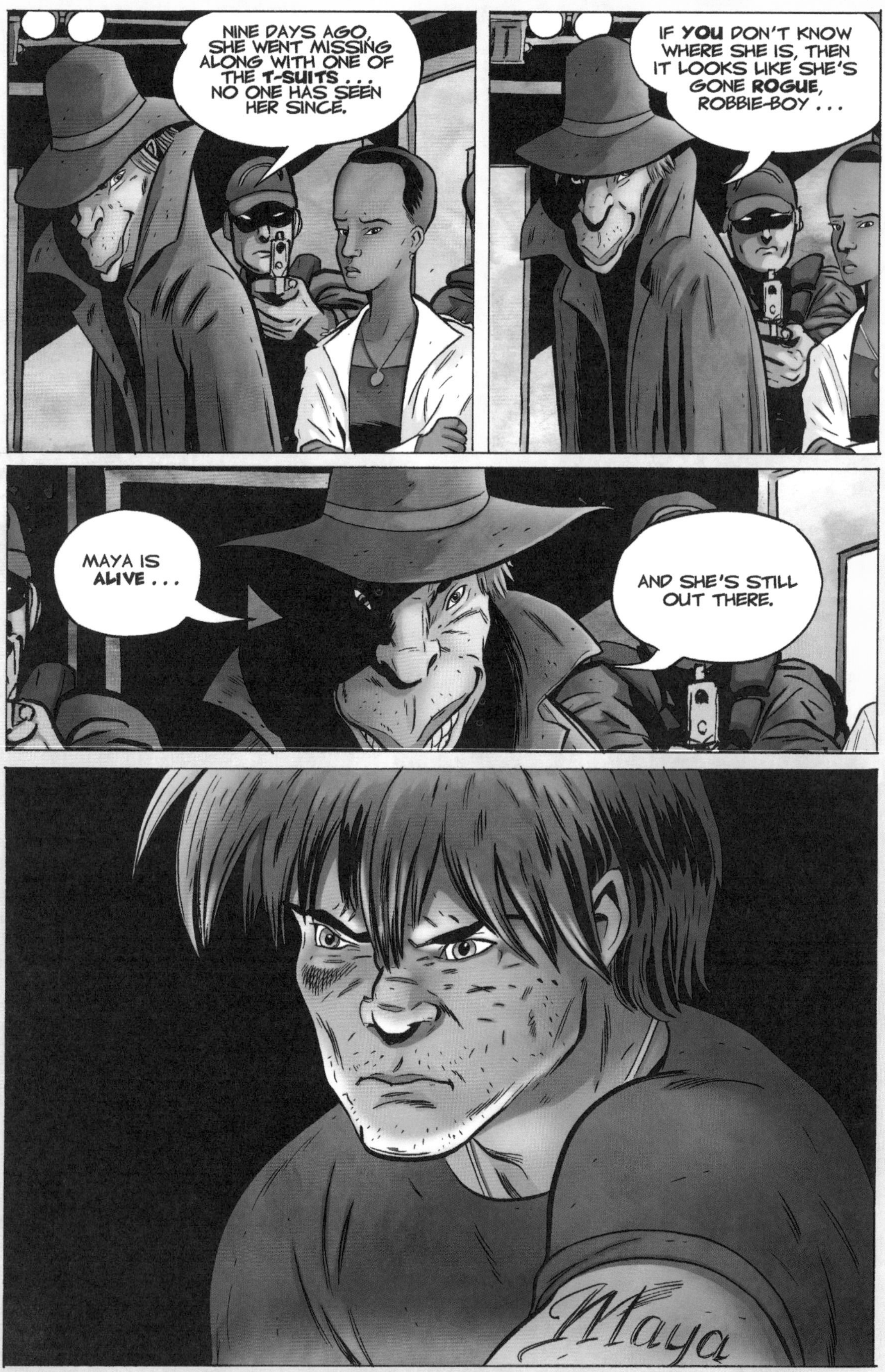

NINE DAYS AGO, SHE WENT MISSING ALONG WITH ONE OF THE **T-SUITS** . . . NO ONE HAS SEEN HER SINCE.
IF **YOU** DON'T KNOW WHERE SHE IS, THEN IT LOOKS LIKE SHE'S GONE **ROGUE**, ROBBIE-BOY . . .
MAYA IS **ALIVE** . . .
AND SHE'S STILL OUT THERE.
Maya

XIV
CLOSER TO THE CENTER

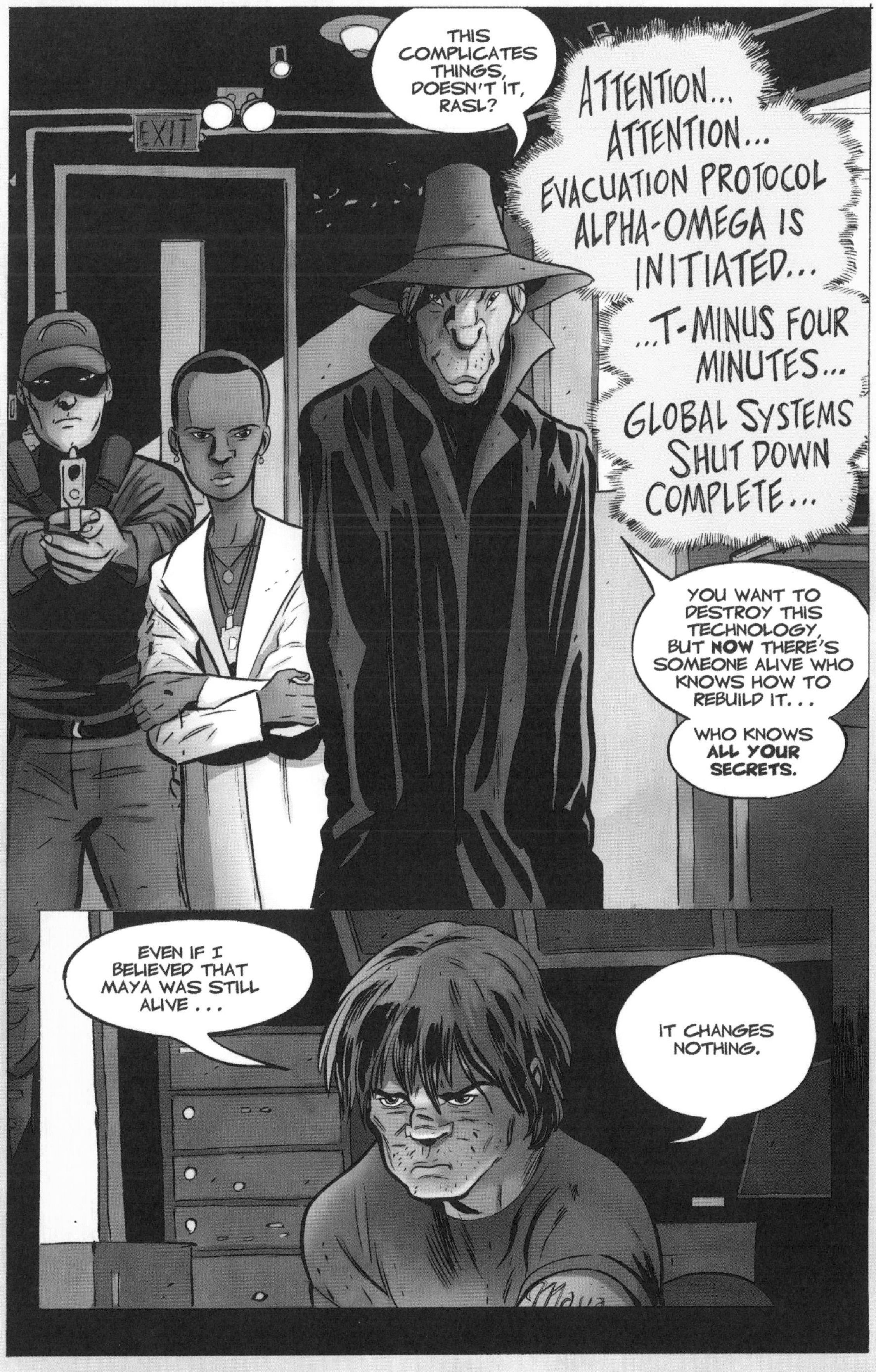
THIS COMPLICATES THINGS, DOESN'T IT, RASL?
ATTENTION... ATTENTION... EVACUATION PROTOCOL ALPHA-OMEGA IS INITIATED... ...T-MINUS FOUR MINUTES... GLOBAL SYSTEMS SHUT DOWN COMPLETE...
YOU WANT TO DESTROY THIS TECHNOLOGY, BUT NOW THERE'S SOMEONE ALIVE WHO KNOWS HOW TO REBUILD IT...
WHO KNOWS ALL YOUR SECRETS.
EVEN IF I BELIEVED THAT MAYA WAS STILL ALIVE...
IT CHANGES NOTHING.

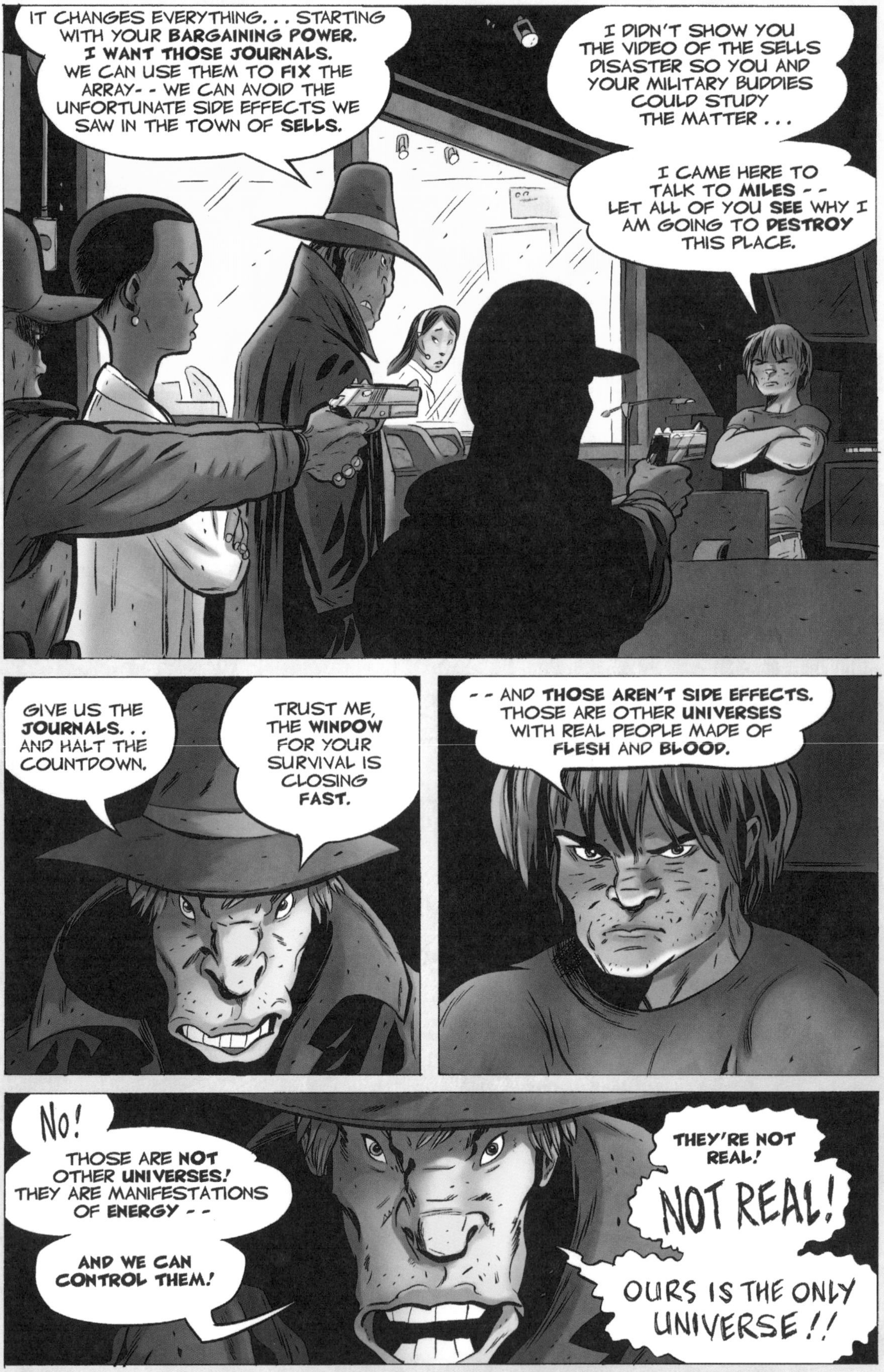
IT CHANGES EVERYTHING. . . STARTING WITH YOUR BARGAINING POWER. I WANT THOSE JOURNALS. WE CAN USE THEM TO FIX THE ARRAY- - WE CAN AVOID THE UNFORTUNATE SIDE EFFECTS WE SAW IN THE TOWN OF SELLS.
I DIDN'T SHOW YOU THE VIDEO OF THE SELLS DISASTER SO YOU AND YOUR MILITARY BUDDIES COULD STUDY THE MATTER . . .
I CAME HERE TO TALK TO MILES - - LET ALL OF YOU SEE WHY I AM GOING TO DESTROY THIS PLACE.
GIVE US THE JOURNALS. . . AND HALT THE COUNTDOWN.
TRUST ME, THE WINDOW FOR YOUR SURVIVAL IS CLOSING FAST.
- - AND THOSE AREN'T SIDE EFFECTS. THOSE ARE OTHER UNIVERSES WITH REAL PEOPLE MADE OF FLESH AND BLOOD.
No! THOSE ARE NOT OTHER UNIVERSES! THEY ARE MANIFESTATIONS OF ENERGY - -
AND WE CAN CONTROL THEM!
THEY'RE NOT REAL!
NOT REAL!
OURS IS THE ONLY UNIVERSE!!

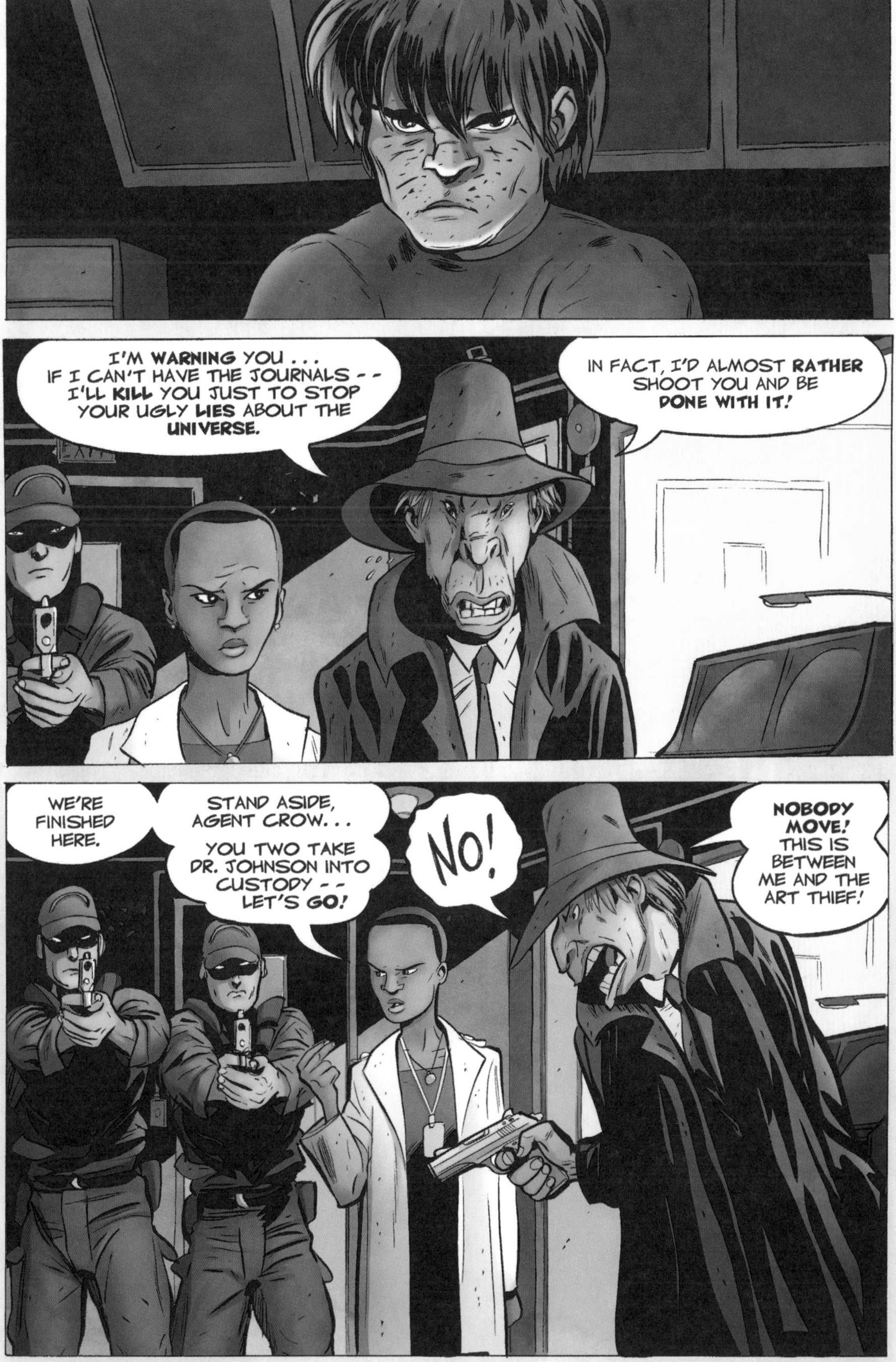
I'M WARNING YOU . . . IF I CAN'T HAVE THE JOURNALS - - I'LL KILL YOU JUST TO STOP YOUR UGLY LIES ABOUT THE UNIVERSE.
IN FACT, I'D ALMOST RATHER SHOOT YOU AND BE DONE WITH IT!
WE'RE FINISHED HERE.
STAND ASIDE, AGENT CROW. . .
YOU TWO TAKE DR. JOHNSON INTO CUSTODY - - LET'S GO!
NO!
NOBODY MOVE! THIS IS BETWEEN ME AND THE ART THIEF!

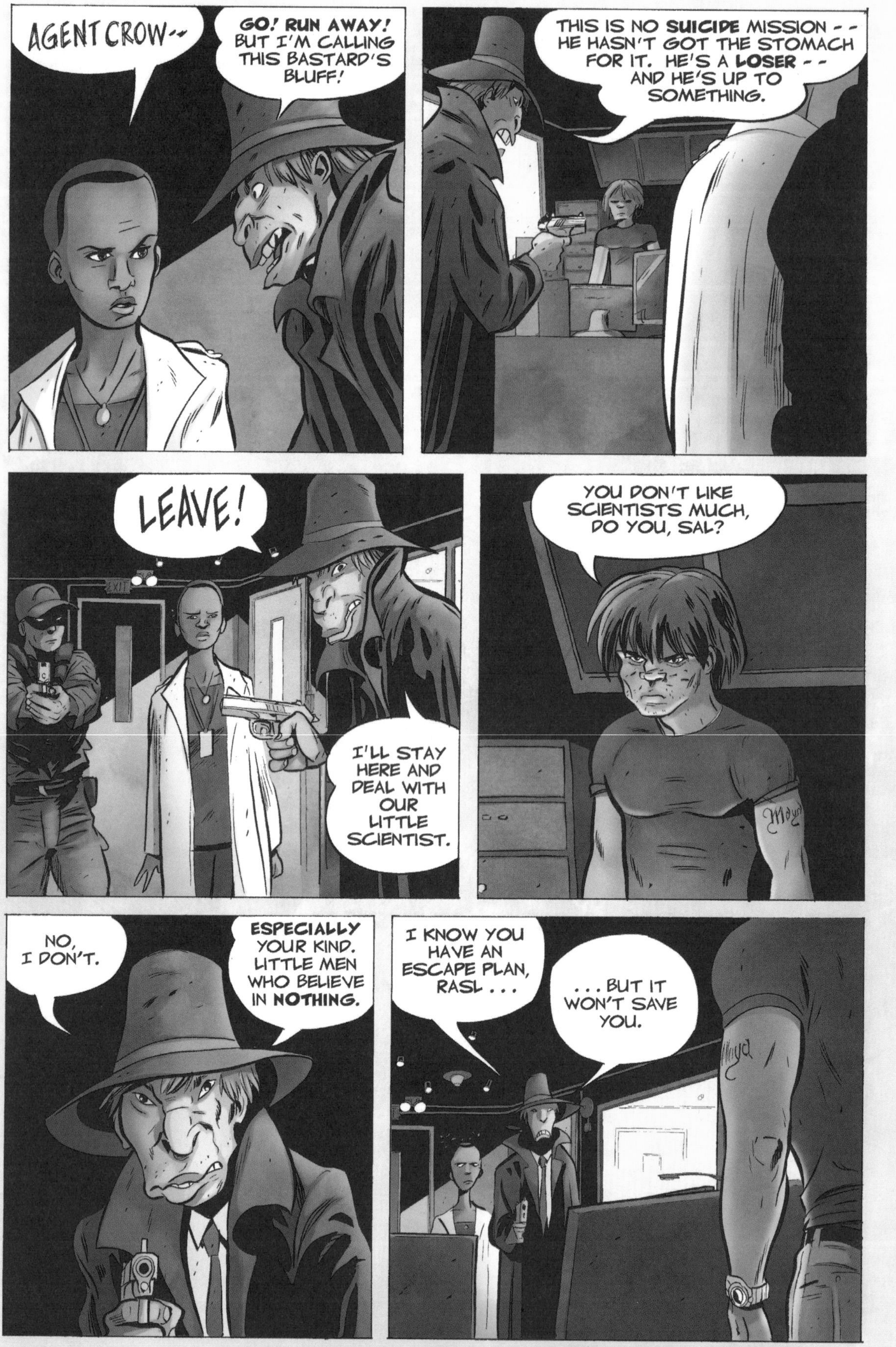
AGENT CROW--
GO! RUN AWAY! BUT I'M CALLING THIS BASTARD'S BLUFF!
THIS IS NO SUICIDE MISSION -- HE HASN'T GOT THE STOMACH FOR IT. HE'S A LOSER -- AND HE'S UP TO SOMETHING.
LEAVE!
I'LL STAY HERE AND DEAL WITH OUR LITTLE SCIENTIST.
YOU DON'T LIKE SCIENTISTS MUCH, DO YOU, SAL?
NO, I DON'T.
ESPECIALLY YOUR KIND. LITTLE MEN WHO BELIEVE IN NOTHING.
I KNOW YOU HAVE AN ESCAPE PLAN, RASL . . .
. . . BUT IT WON'T SAVE YOU.

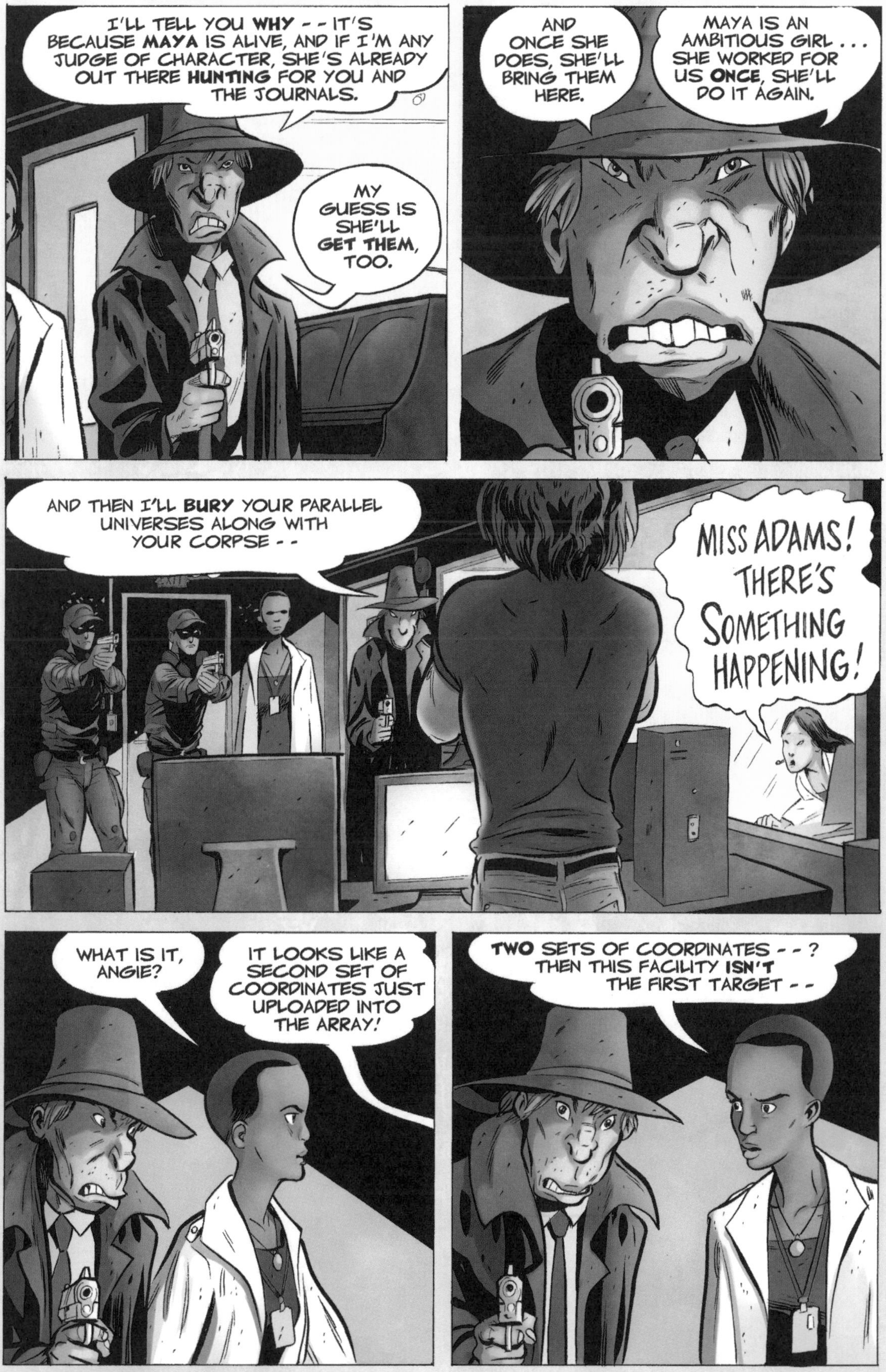
I'LL TELL YOU WHY - - IT'S BECAUSE MAYA IS ALIVE, AND IF I'M ANY JUDGE OF CHARACTER, SHE'S ALREADY OUT THERE HUNTING FOR YOU AND THE JOURNALS.
MY GUESS IS SHE'LL GET THEM, TOO.
AND ONCE SHE DOES, SHE'LL BRING THEM HERE.
MAYA IS AN AMBITIOUS GIRL . . . SHE WORKED FOR US ONCE, SHE'LL DO IT AGAIN.
AND THEN I'LL BURY YOUR PARALLEL UNIVERSES ALONG WITH YOUR CORPSE - -
MISS ADAMS! THERE'S SOMETHING HAPPENING!
WHAT IS IT, ANGIE?
IT LOOKS LIKE A SECOND SET OF COORDINATES JUST UPLOADED INTO THE ARRAY!
TWO SETS OF COORDINATES - - ? THEN THIS FACILITY ISN'T THE FIRST TARGET - -

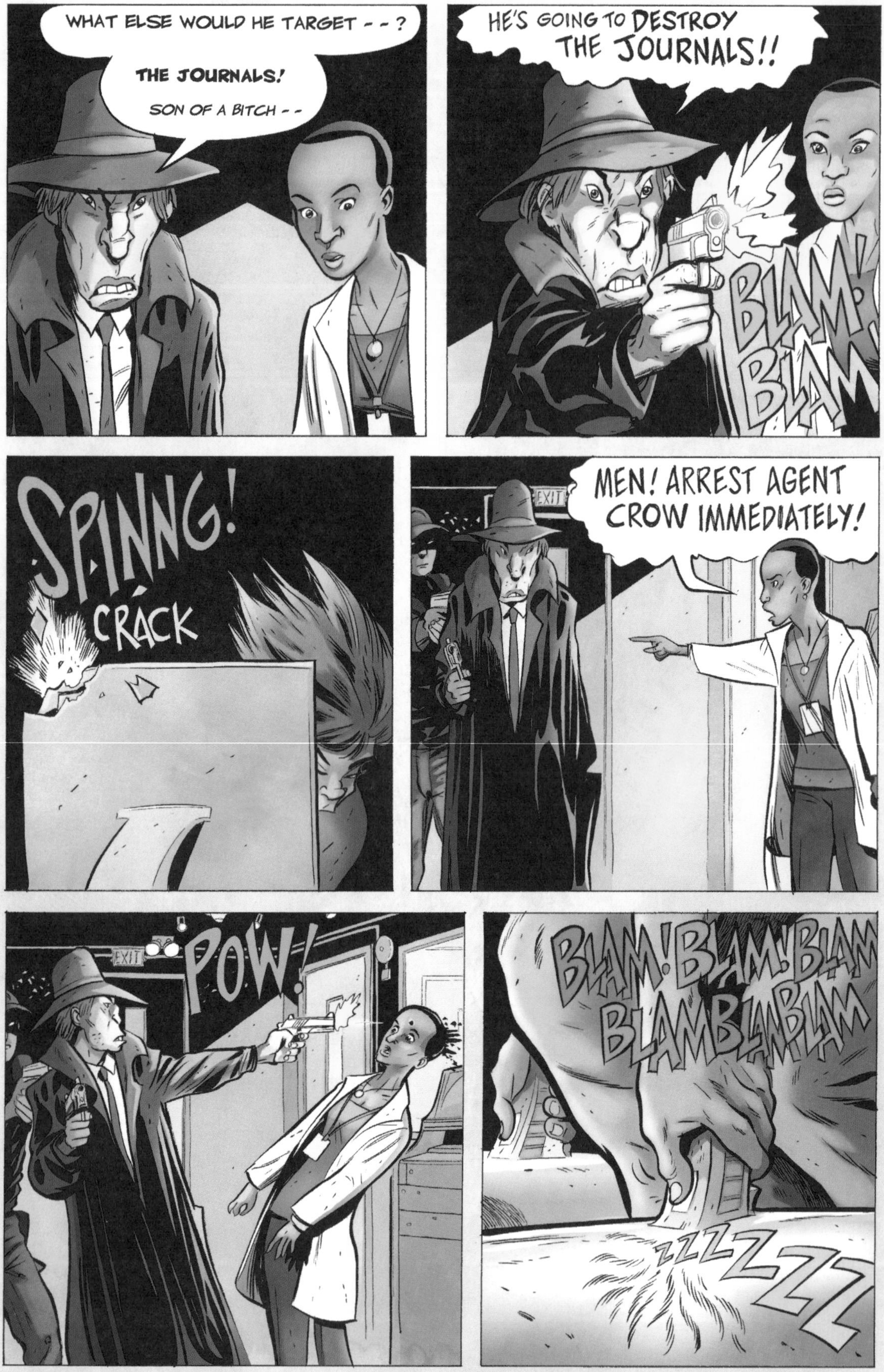
WHAT ELSE WOULD HE TARGET - - ?
THE JOURNALS! SON OF A BITCH - -
HE'S GOING TO DESTROY THE JOURNALS!!
BLAM! BLAM!
SPINNG!
CRACK
MEN! ARREST AGENT CROW IMMEDIATELY!
EXIT
POW!
EXIT
BLAM! BLAM! BLAM BLAM BLAM BLAM
ZZZZZZZ

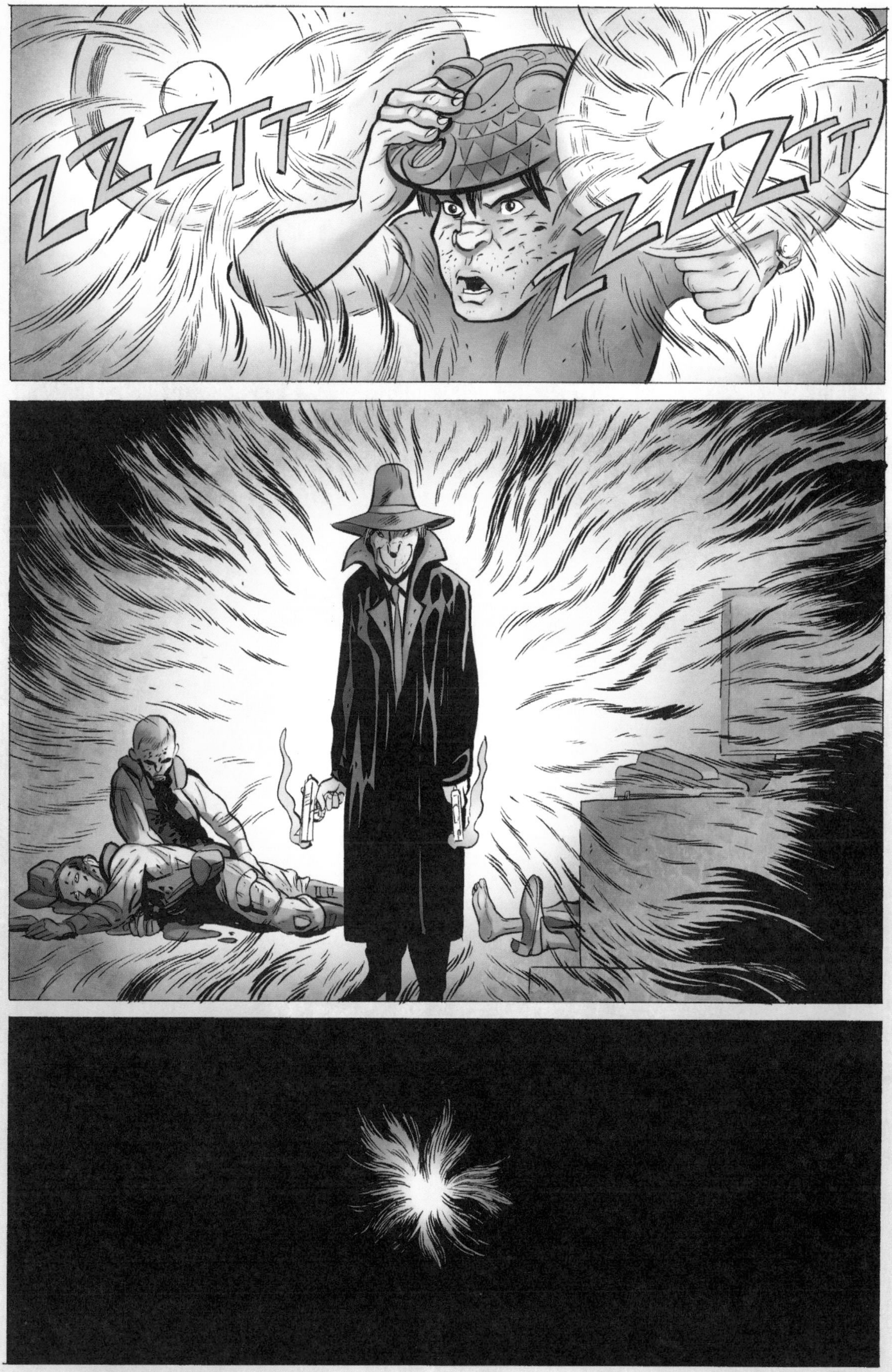
ZZZZTTT
ZZZZZTTT

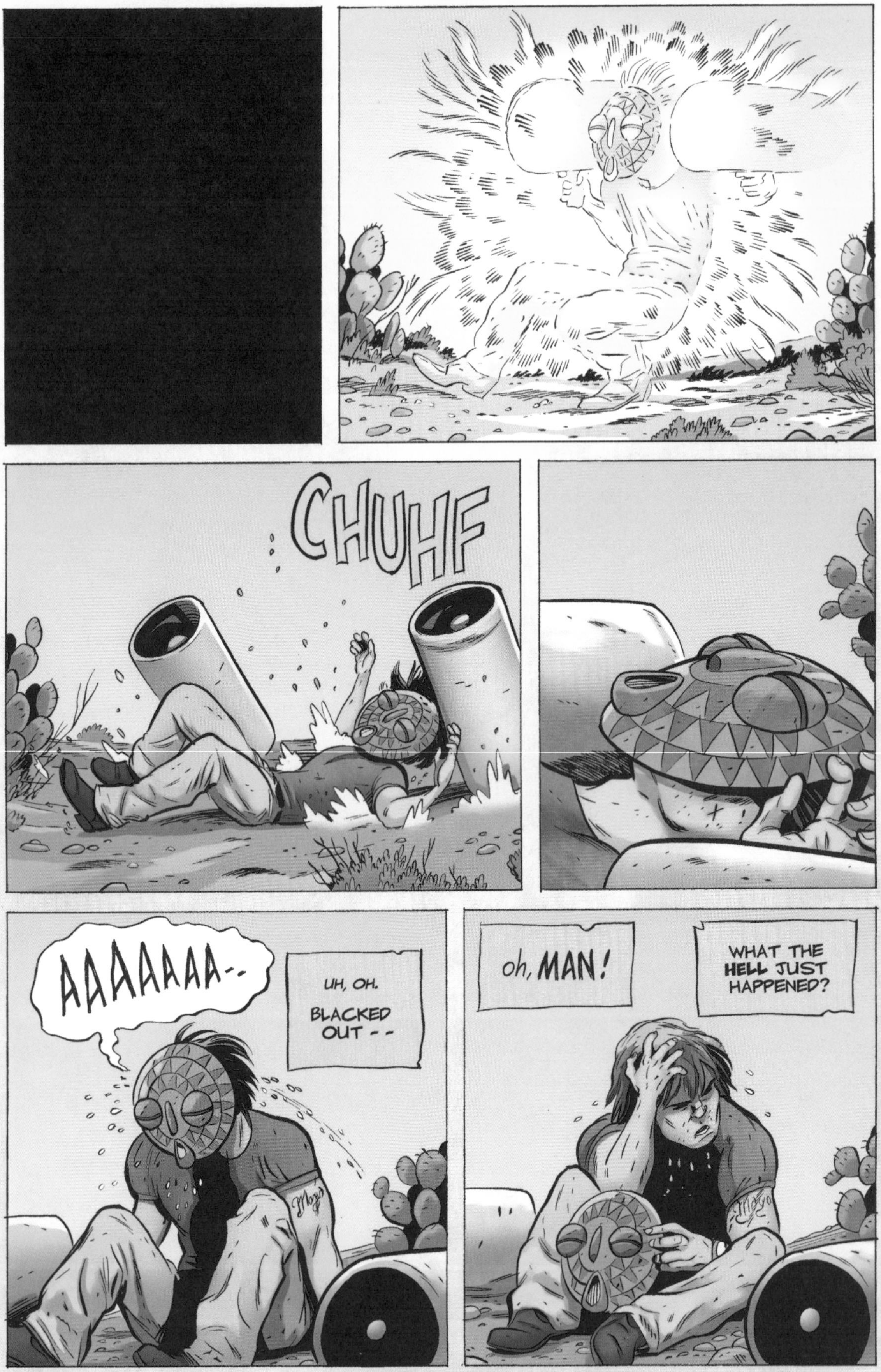
CHUHF
AAAAAAA--
UH, OH.
BLACKED OUT --
oh, MAN!
WHAT THE HELL JUST HAPPENED?

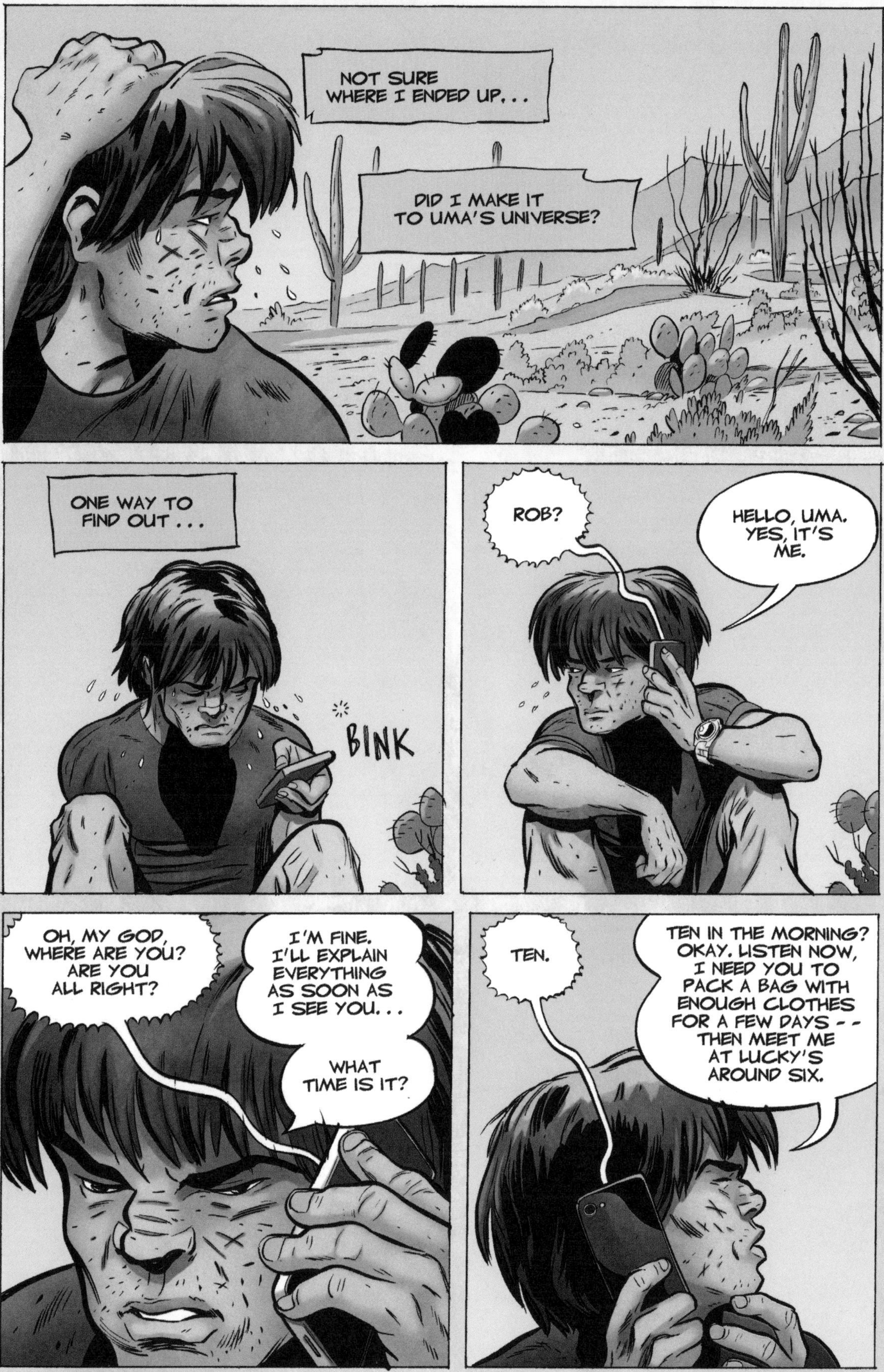
NOT SURE WHERE I ENDED UP...
DID I MAKE IT TO UMA'S UNIVERSE?
ONE WAY TO FIND OUT...
BINK
ROB?
HELLO, UMA. YES, IT'S ME.
OH, MY GOD, WHERE ARE YOU? ARE YOU ALL RIGHT?
I'M FINE. I'LL EXPLAIN EVERYTHING AS SOON AS I SEE YOU...
WHAT TIME IS IT?
TEN.
TEN IN THE MORNING? OKAY. LISTEN NOW, I NEED YOU TO PACK A BAG WITH ENOUGH CLOTHES FOR A FEW DAYS -- THEN MEET ME AT LUCKY'S AROUND SIX.

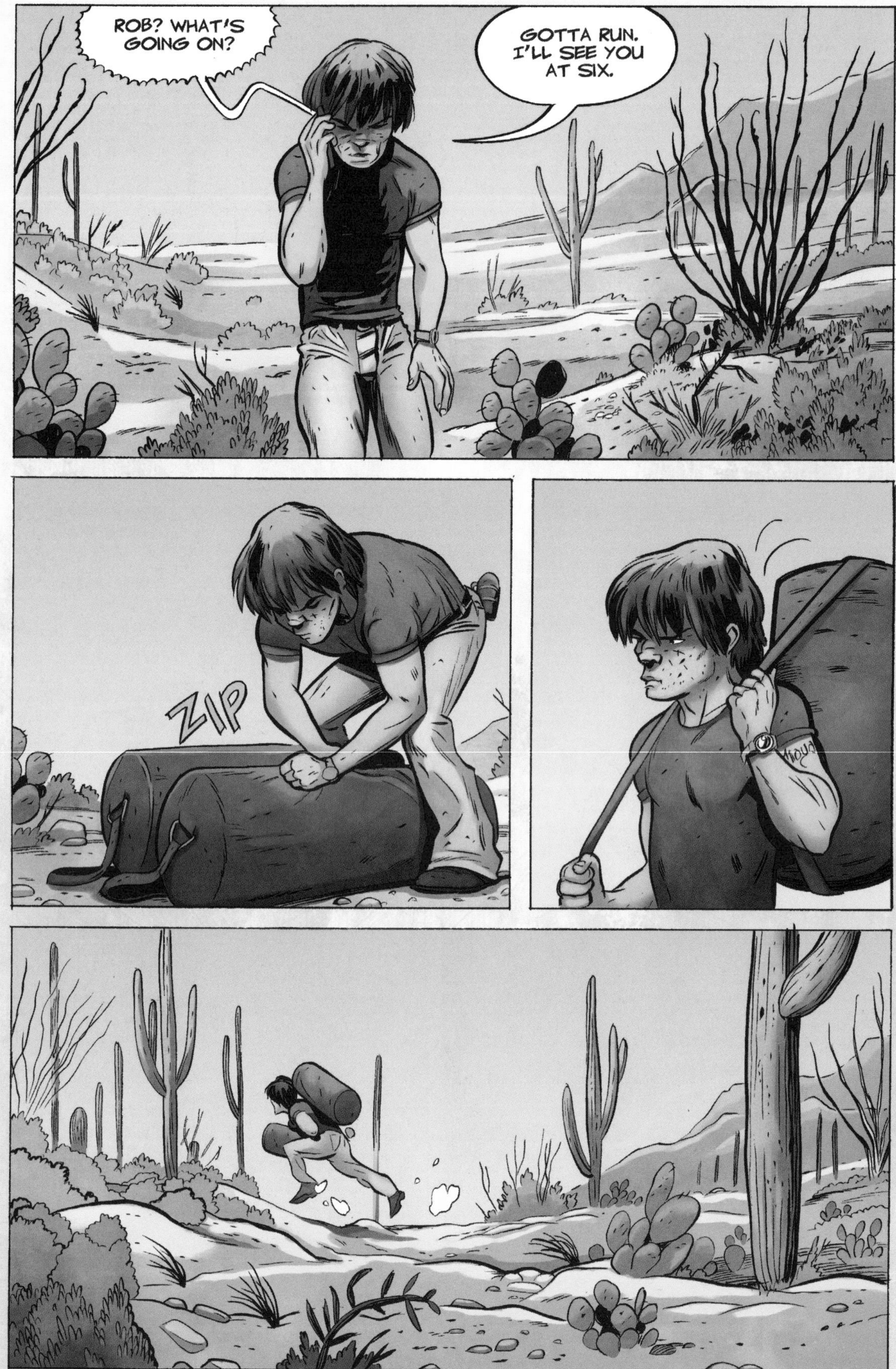
ROB? WHAT'S GOING ON?
GOTTA RUN. I'LL SEE YOU AT SIX.
ZIP

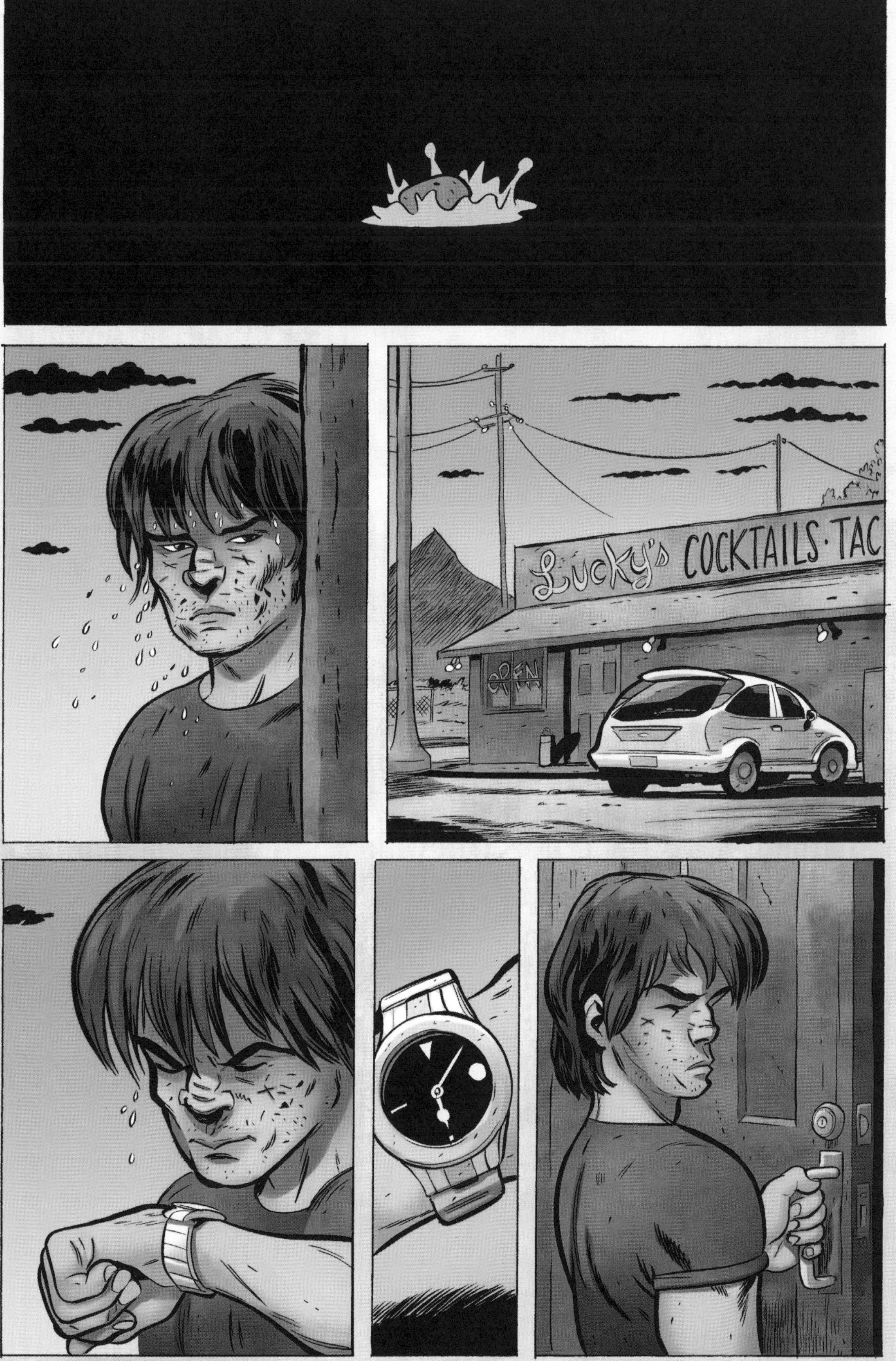
Lucky's COCKTAILS·TAC
OPEN

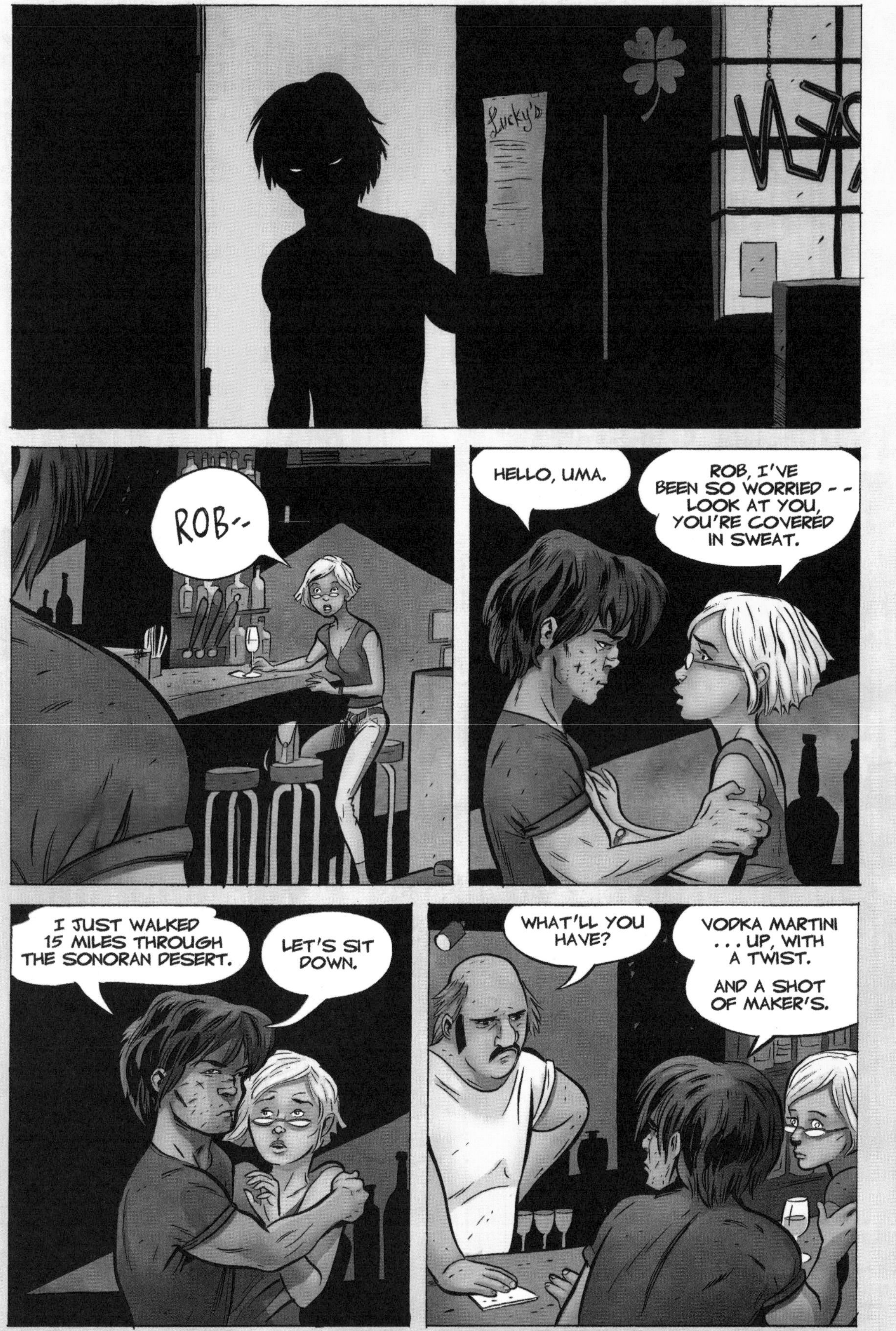
Lucky'D
ROB--
HELLO, UMA.
ROB, I'VE BEEN SO WORRIED - - LOOK AT YOU, YOU'RE COVERED IN SWEAT.
I JUST WALKED 15 MILES THROUGH THE SONORAN DESERT.
LET'S SIT DOWN.
WHAT'LL YOU HAVE?
VODKA MARTINI . . . UP, WITH A TWIST.
AND A SHOT OF MAKER'S.

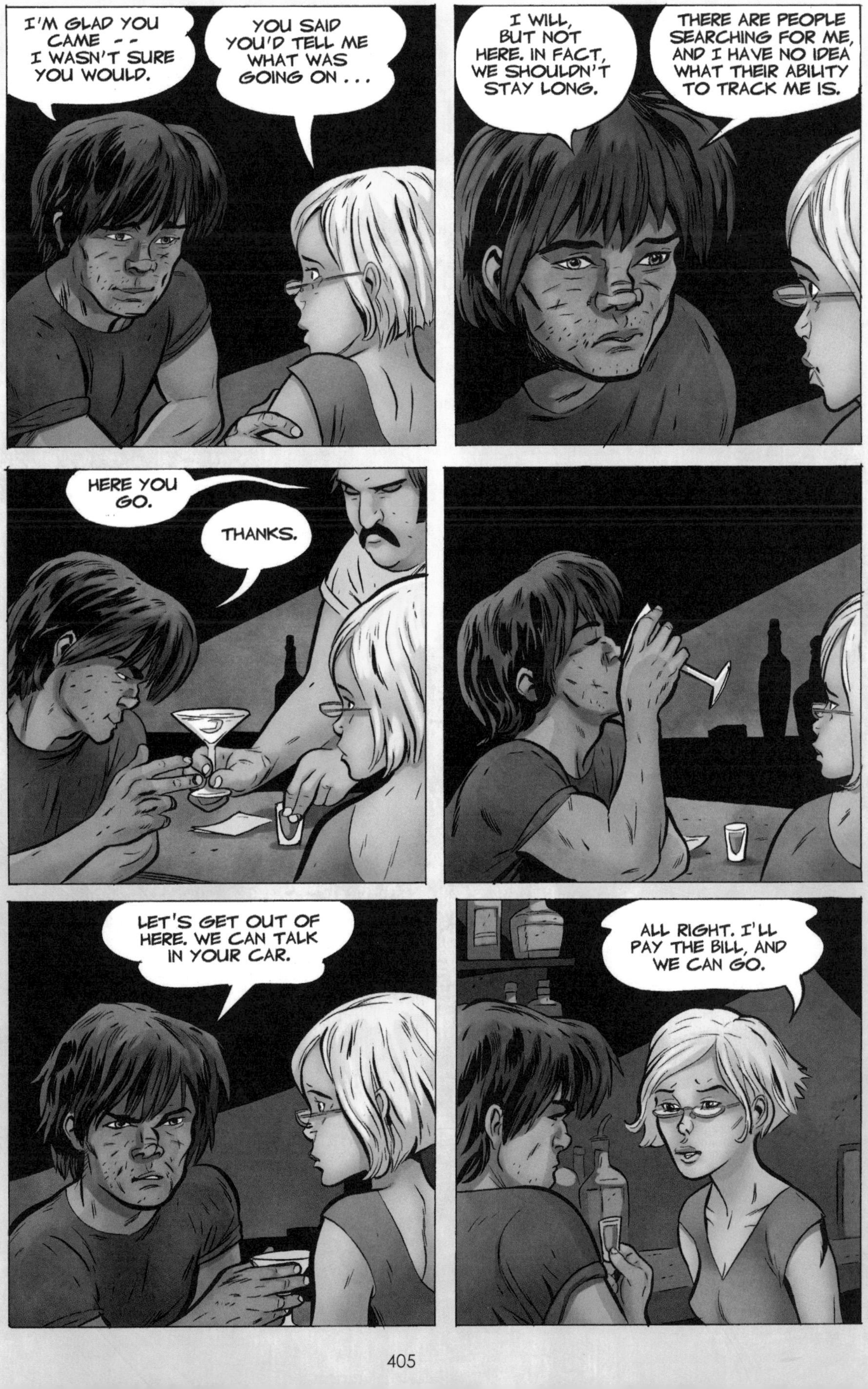
I'M GLAD YOU CAME -- I WASN'T SURE YOU WOULD.
YOU SAID YOU'D TELL ME WHAT WAS GOING ON . . .
I WILL, BUT NOT HERE. IN FACT, WE SHOULDN'T STAY LONG.
THERE ARE PEOPLE SEARCHING FOR ME, AND I HAVE NO IDEA WHAT THEIR ABILITY TO TRACK ME IS.
HERE YOU GO.
THANKS.
LET'S GET OUT OF HERE. WE CAN TALK IN YOUR CAR.
ALL RIGHT. I'LL PAY THE BILL, AND WE CAN GO.

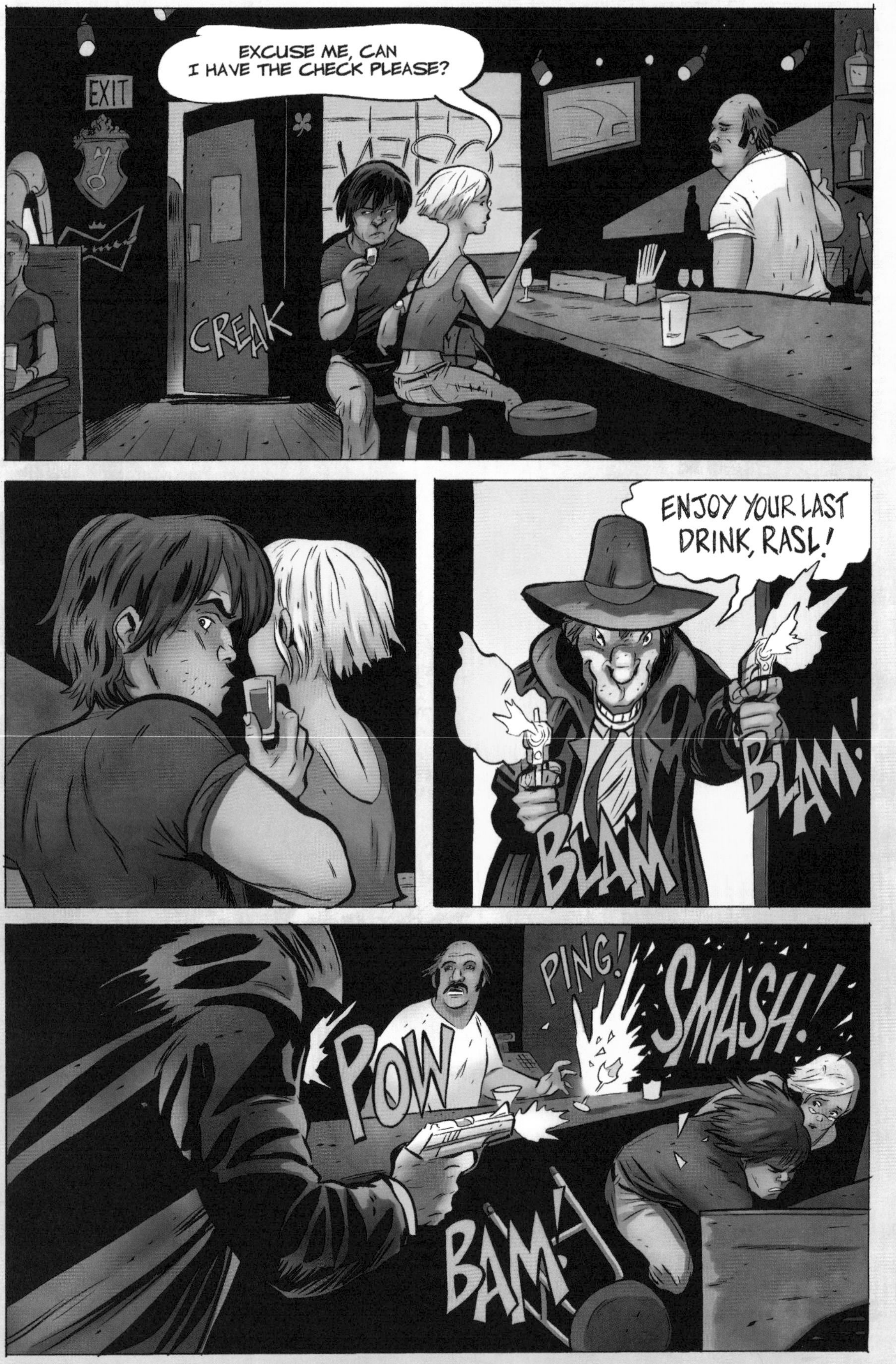
EXCUSE ME, CAN I HAVE THE CHECK PLEASE?
EXIT
CREAK
ENJOY YOUR LAST DRINK, RASL!
BLAM
BLAM!
POW
PING!
SMASH!
BAM!

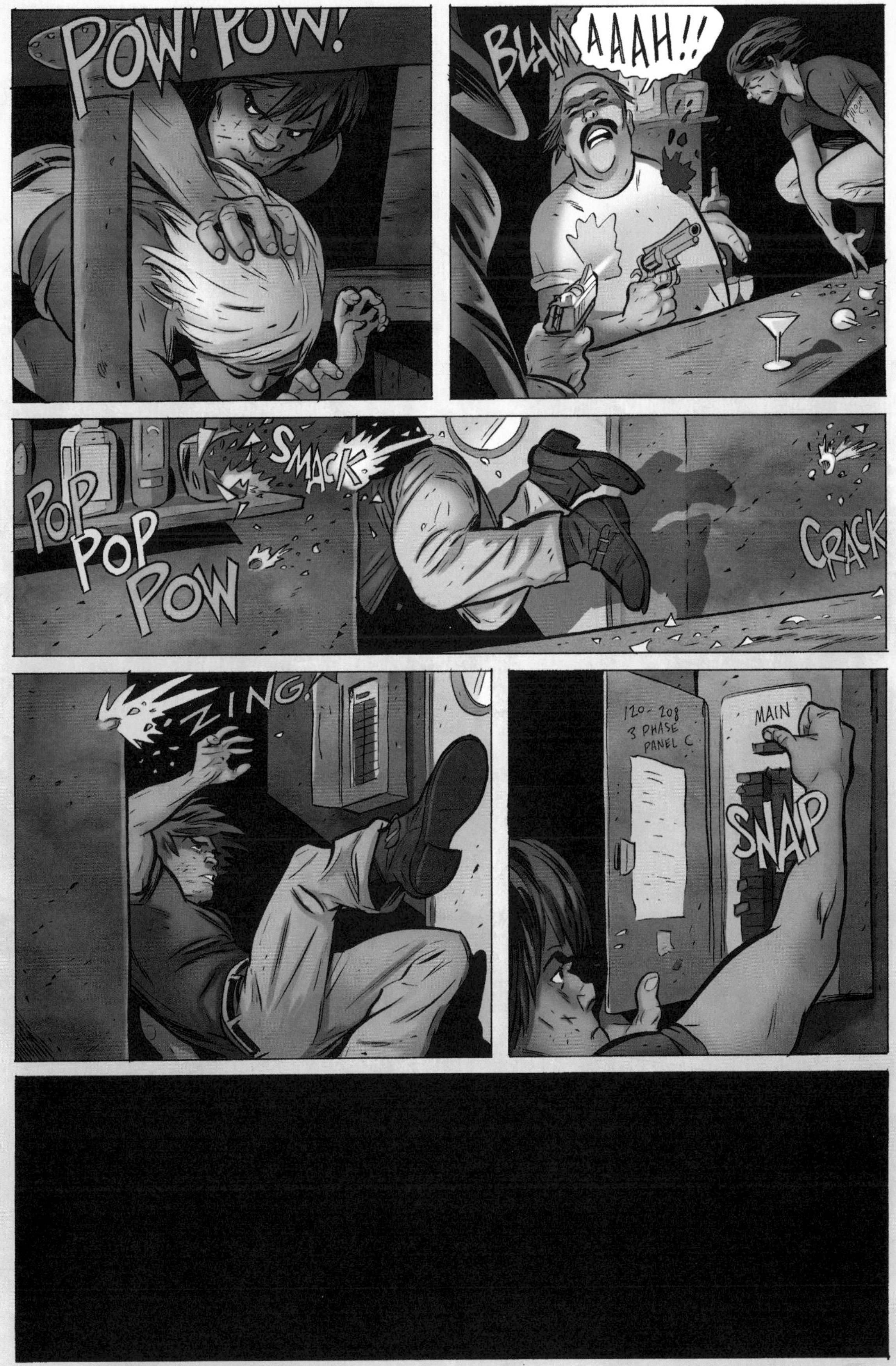
POW! POW!
BLAM
AAAH!!
POP
POP
POW
SMACK
CRACK
ZING!
120-208
3 PHASE
PANEL C
MAIN
SNAP

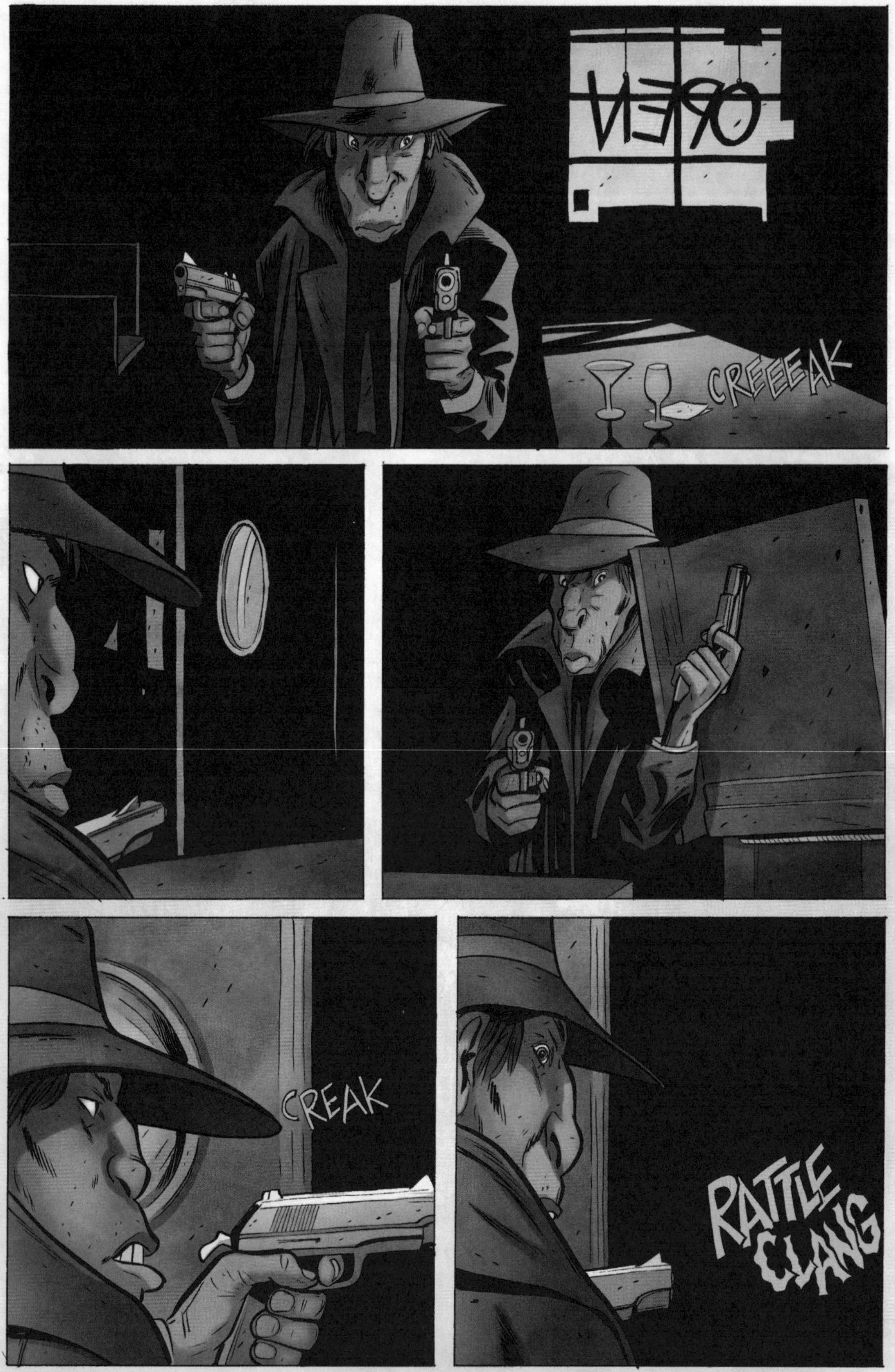
OPEN
CREEEAK
CREAK
RATTLE
CLANG

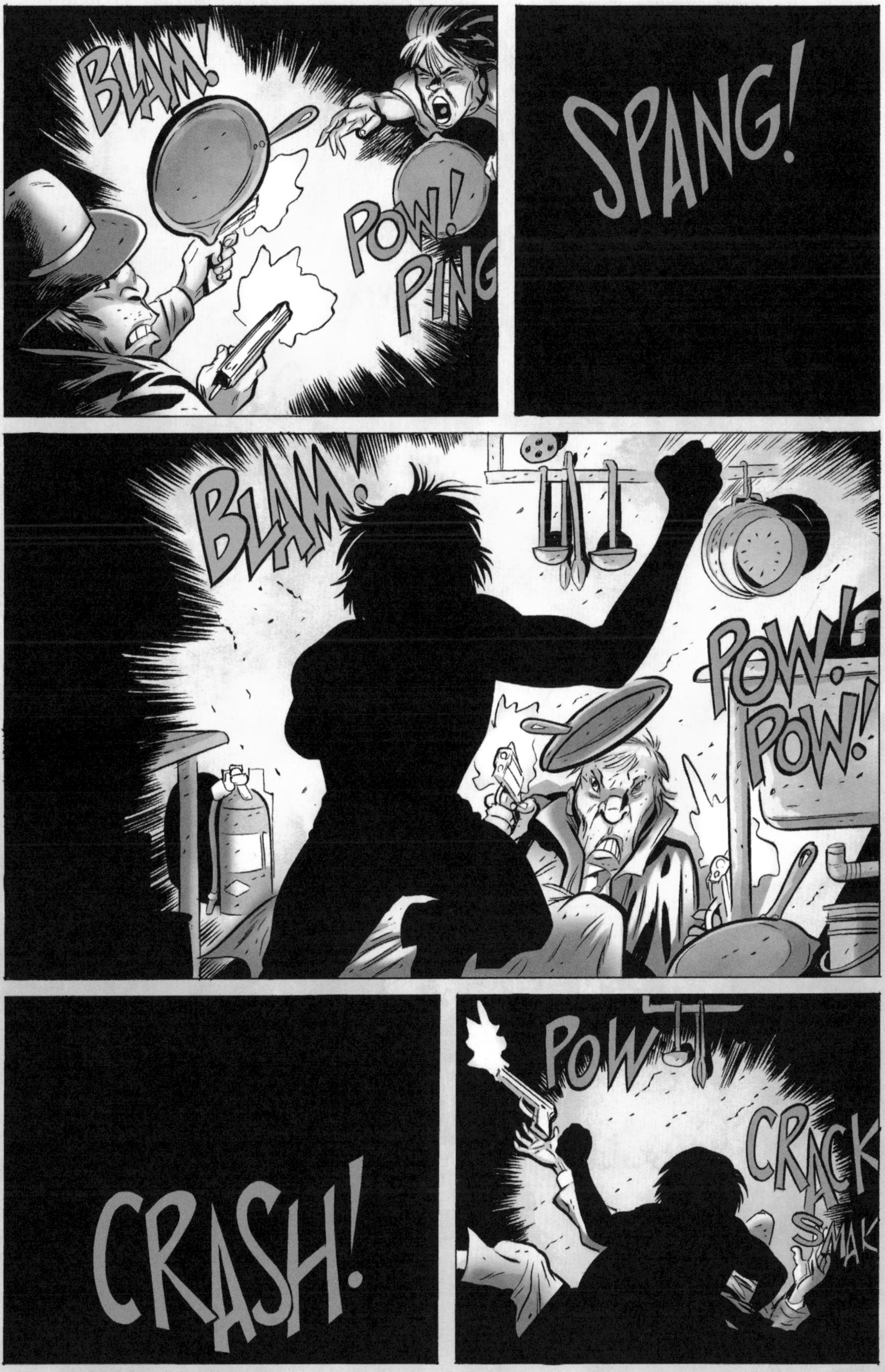
BLAM!
POW!
PING
SPANG!
BLAM!
POW!
POW!
CRASH!
POW
CRACK
SMAK

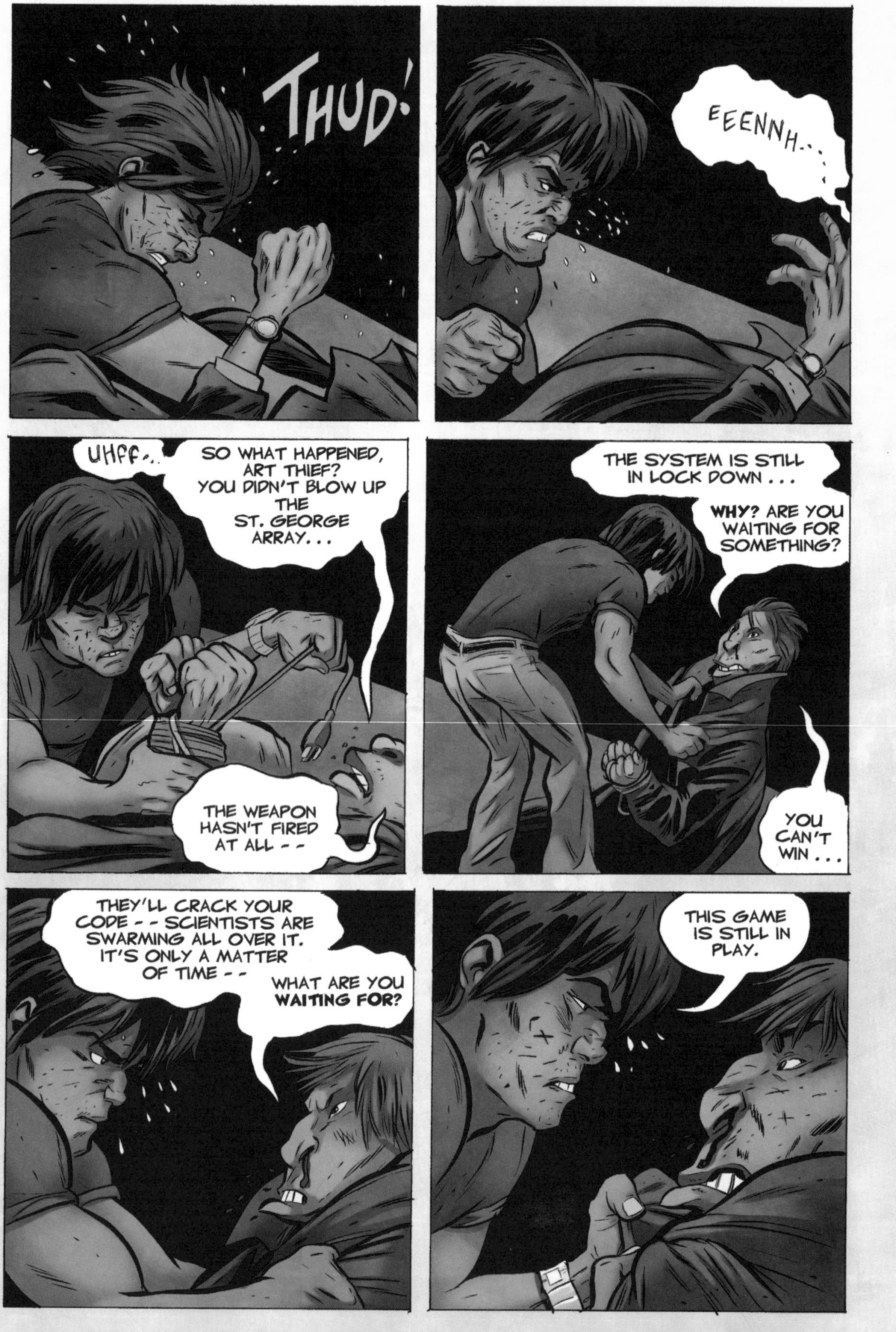
THUD!
EEENNH...
UHFF...
SO WHAT HAPPENED, ART THIEF? YOU DIDN'T BLOW UP THE ST. GEORGE ARRAY...
THE WEAPON HASN'T FIRED AT ALL --
THE SYSTEM IS STILL IN LOCK DOWN...
WHY? ARE YOU WAITING FOR SOMETHING?
YOU CAN'T WIN...
THEY'LL CRACK YOUR CODE -- SCIENTISTS ARE SWARMING ALL OVER IT. IT'S ONLY A MATTER OF TIME --
WHAT ARE YOU WAITING FOR?
THIS GAME IS STILL IN PLAY.

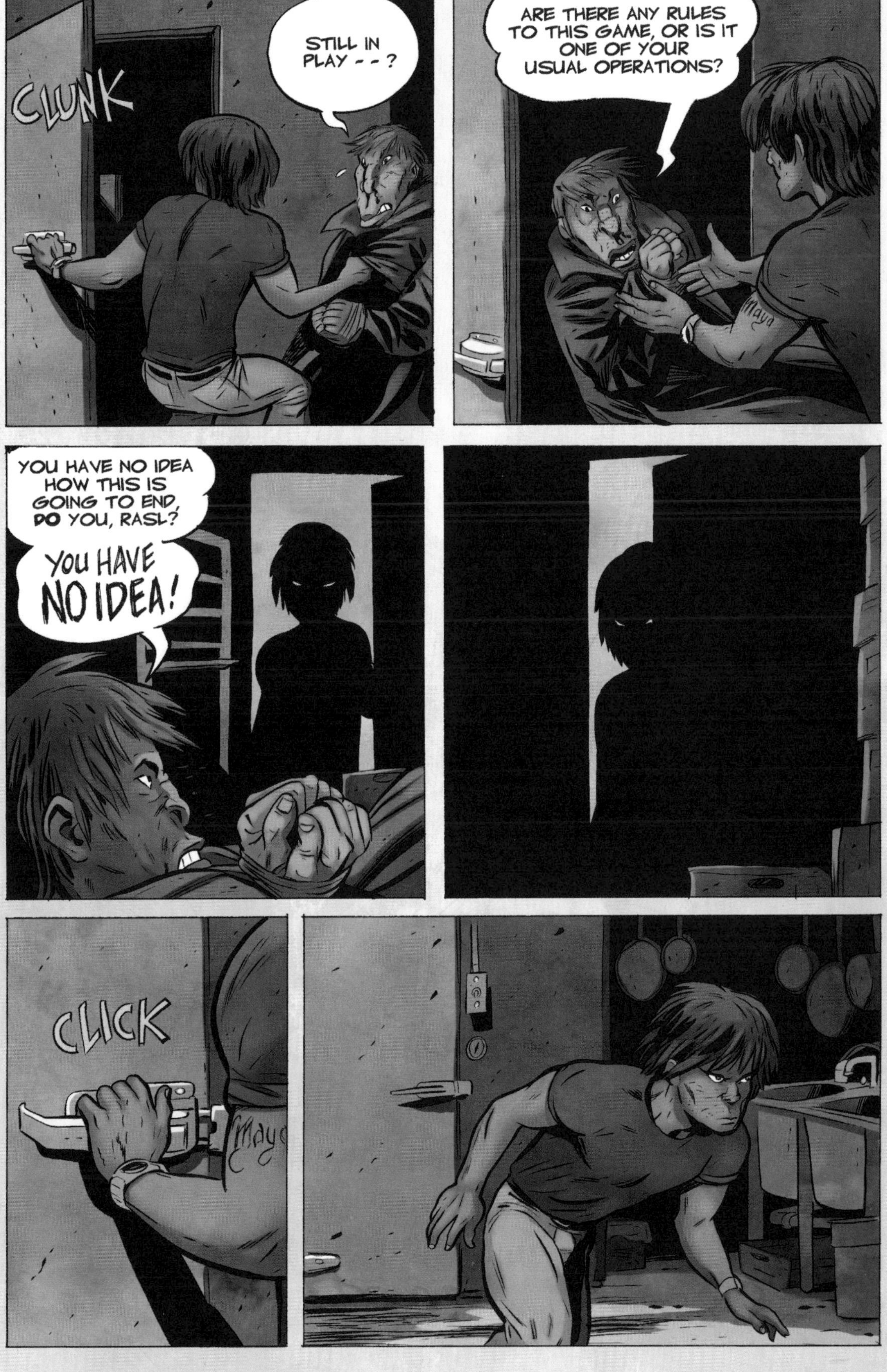
CLUNK
STILL IN PLAY - - ?
ARE THERE ANY RULES TO THIS GAME, OR IS IT ONE OF YOUR USUAL OPERATIONS?
Maya
YOU HAVE NO IDEA HOW THIS IS GOING TO END, DO YOU, RASL?
YOU HAVE NO IDEA!
CLICK
Maya

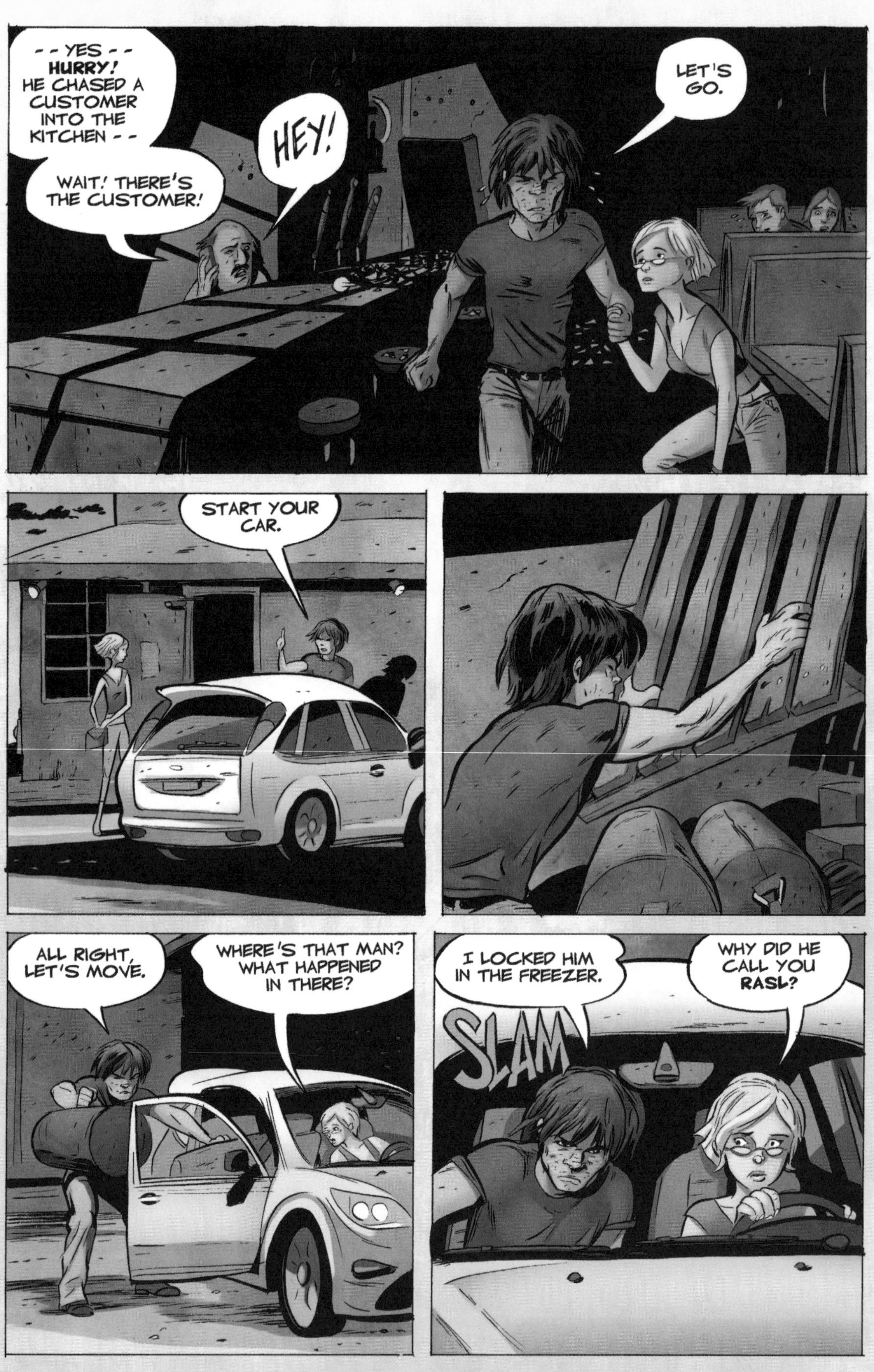
- - YES - - **HURRY!** HE CHASED A CUSTOMER INTO THE KITCHEN - -
HEY!
WAIT! THERE'S THE CUSTOMER!
LET'S GO.
START YOUR CAR.
ALL RIGHT, LET'S MOVE.
WHERE'S THAT MAN? WHAT HAPPENED IN THERE?
SLAM
I LOCKED HIM IN THE FREEZER.
WHY DID HE CALL YOU **RASL?**

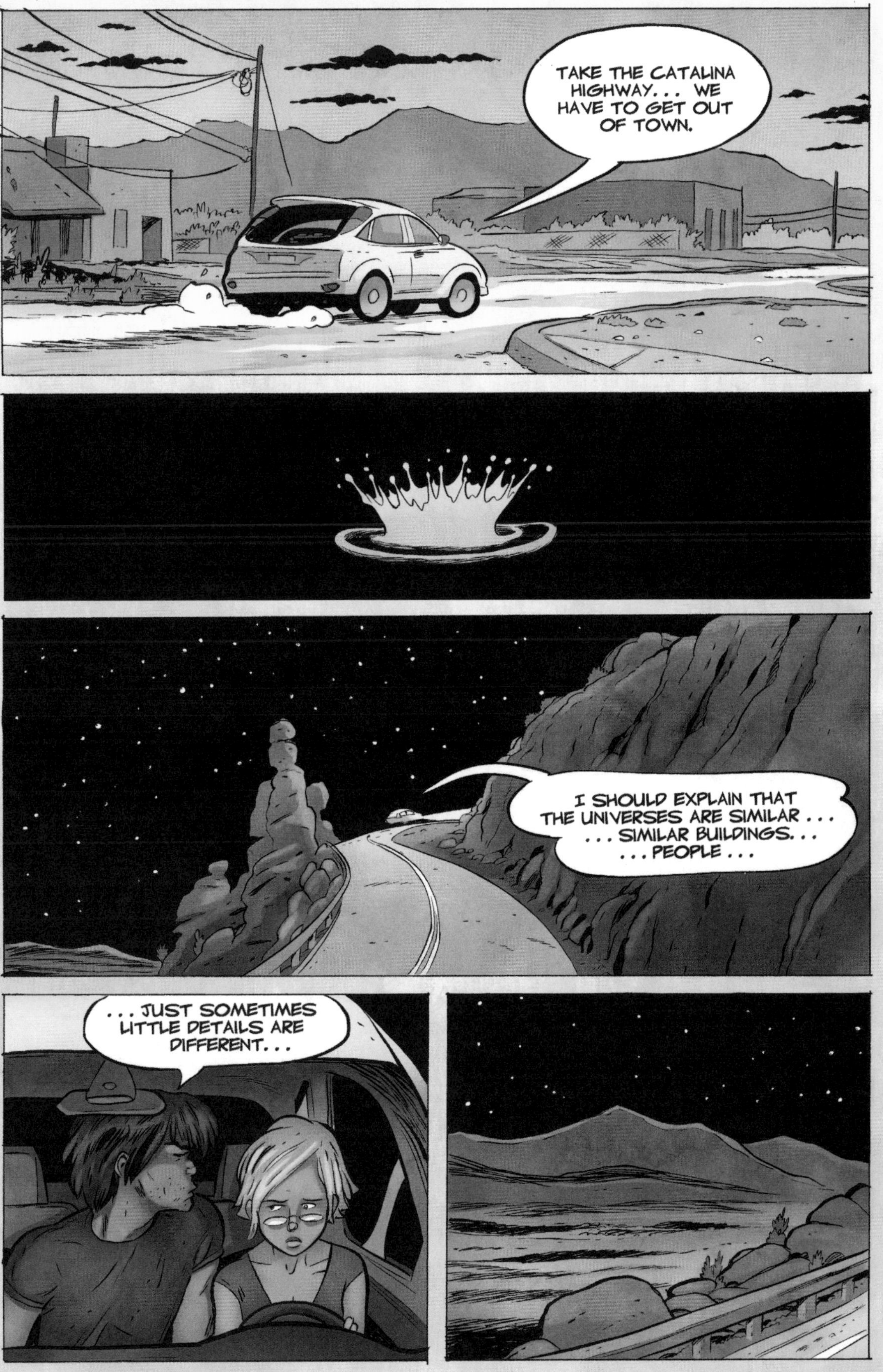
TAKE THE CATALINA HIGHWAY... WE HAVE TO GET OUT OF TOWN.
I SHOULD EXPLAIN THAT THE UNIVERSES ARE SIMILAR... ...SIMILAR BUILDINGS... ...PEOPLE...
...JUST SOMETIMES LITTLE DETAILS ARE DIFFERENT...

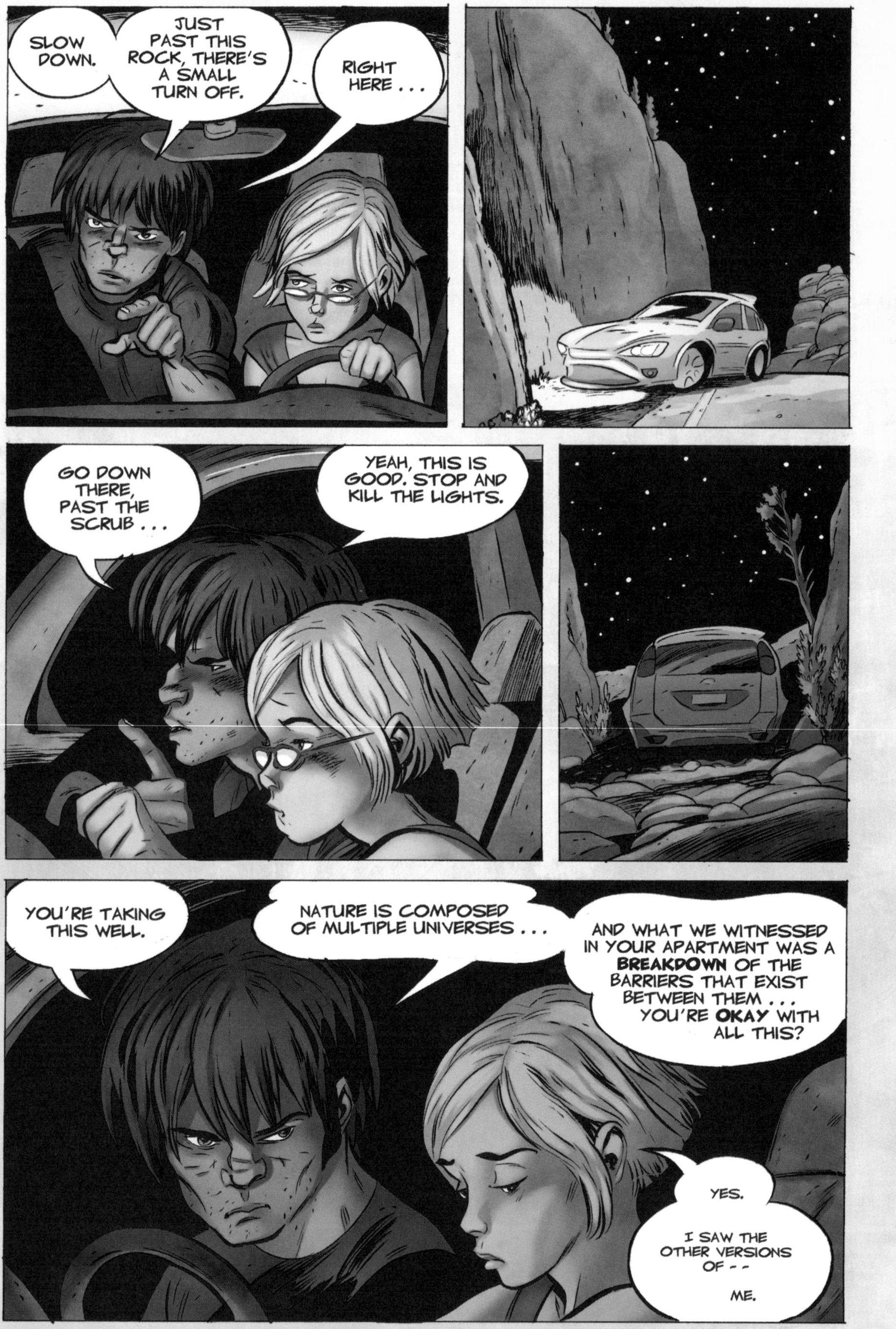
SLOW DOWN.
JUST PAST THIS ROCK, THERE'S A SMALL TURN OFF.
RIGHT HERE . . .
GO DOWN THERE, PAST THE SCRUB . . .
YEAH, THIS IS GOOD. STOP AND KILL THE LIGHTS.
YOU'RE TAKING THIS WELL.
NATURE IS COMPOSED OF MULTIPLE UNIVERSES . . .
AND WHAT WE WITNESSED IN YOUR APARTMENT WAS A BREAKDOWN OF THE BARRIERS THAT EXIST BETWEEN THEM . . . YOU'RE OKAY WITH ALL THIS?
YES.
I SAW THE OTHER VERSIONS OF - -
ME.

IT GETS BETTER . . . AND IT WON'T DO ANY GOOD TO PUT IT OFF.

I'M FROM A PARALLEL UNIVERSE.

THIS **TATTOO**? IT'S THE WOMAN I LOVED ON THE WORLD I CAME FROM. SHE WAS YOUR **EXACT** DOPPELGANGER - - I THINK THAT'S WHY YOU FEEL LIKE YOU KNOW ME.

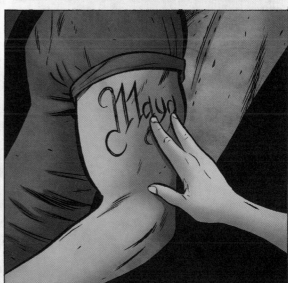

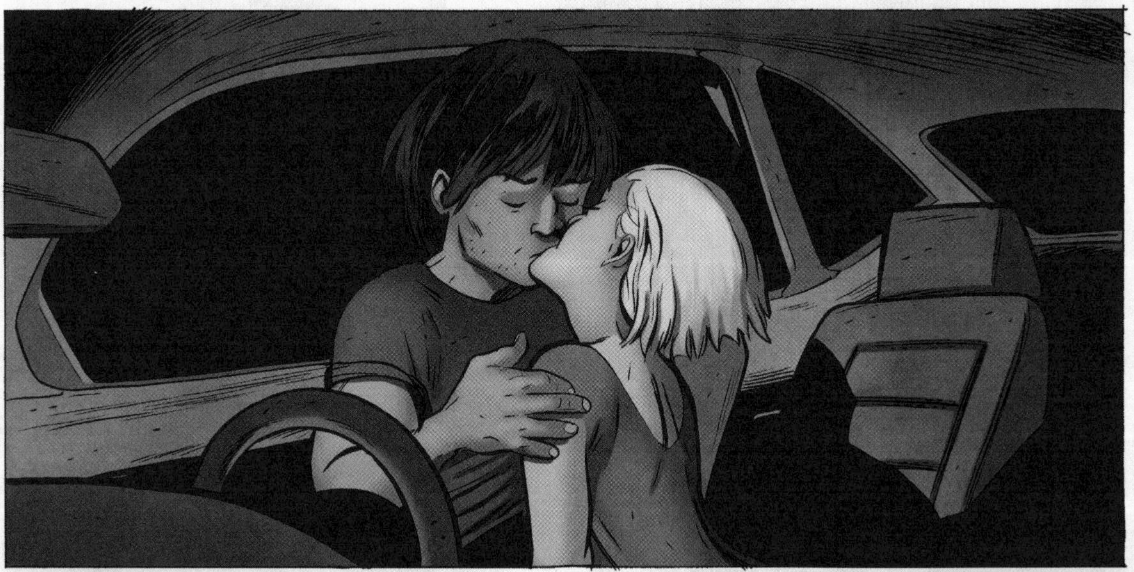

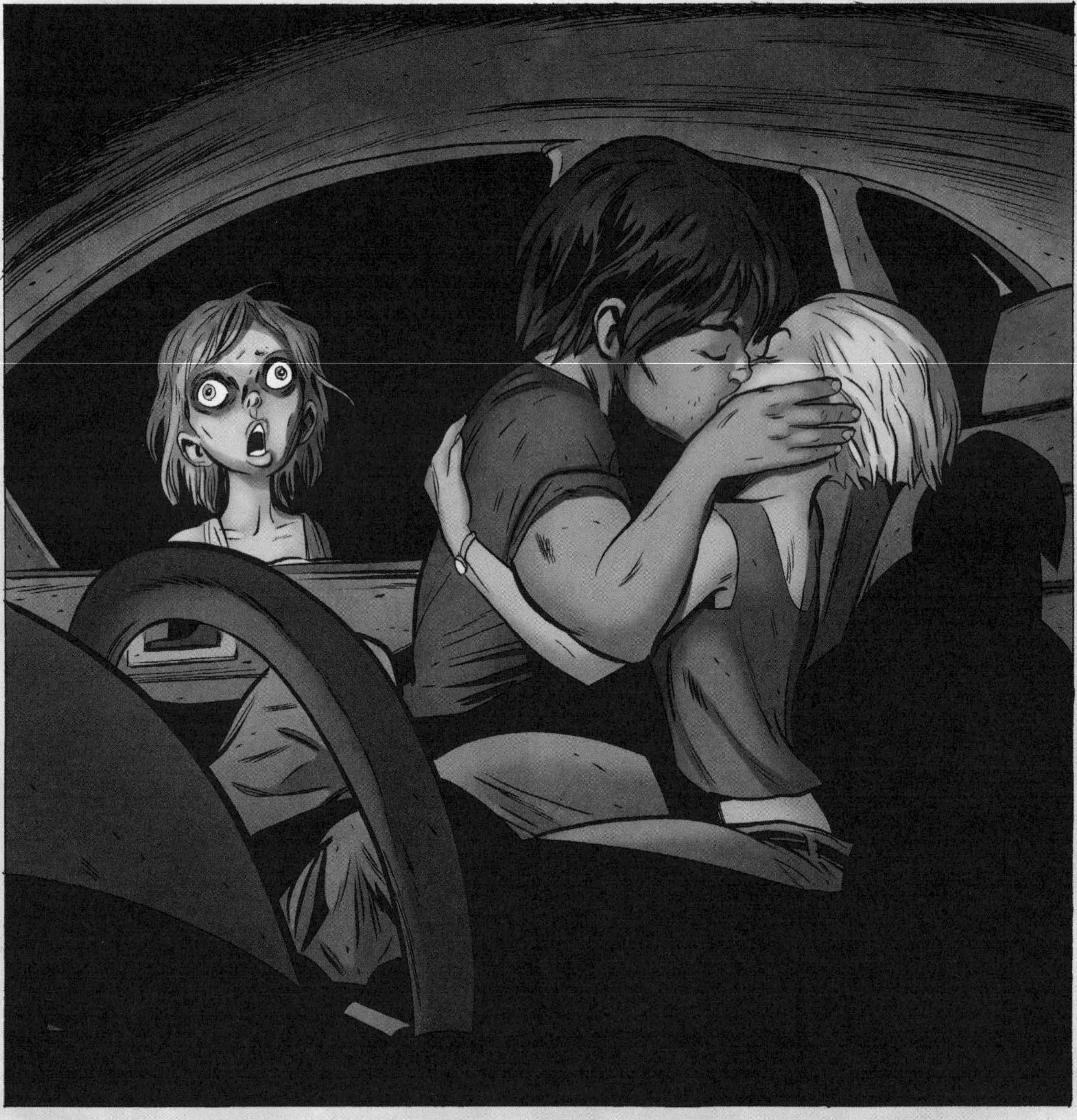

XV
TAKING THE FALL

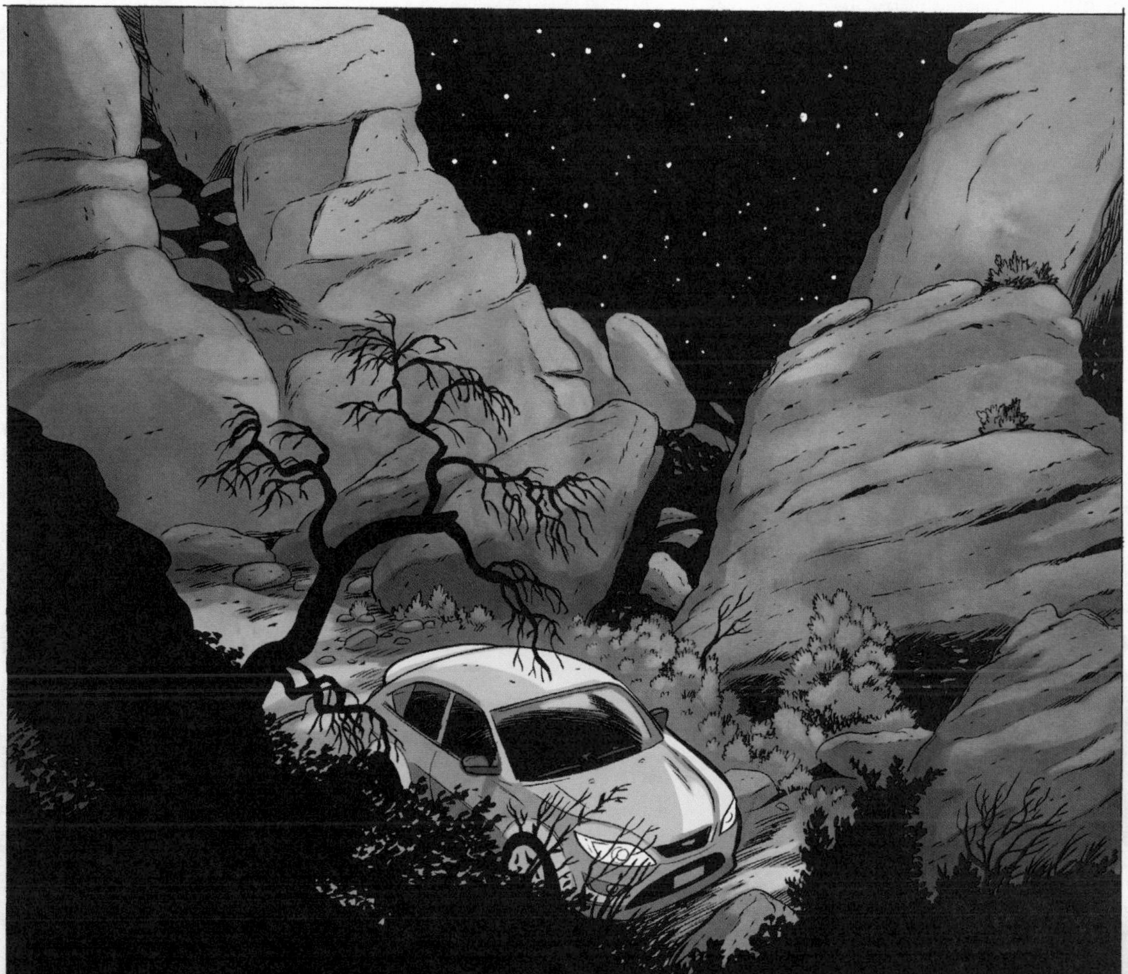

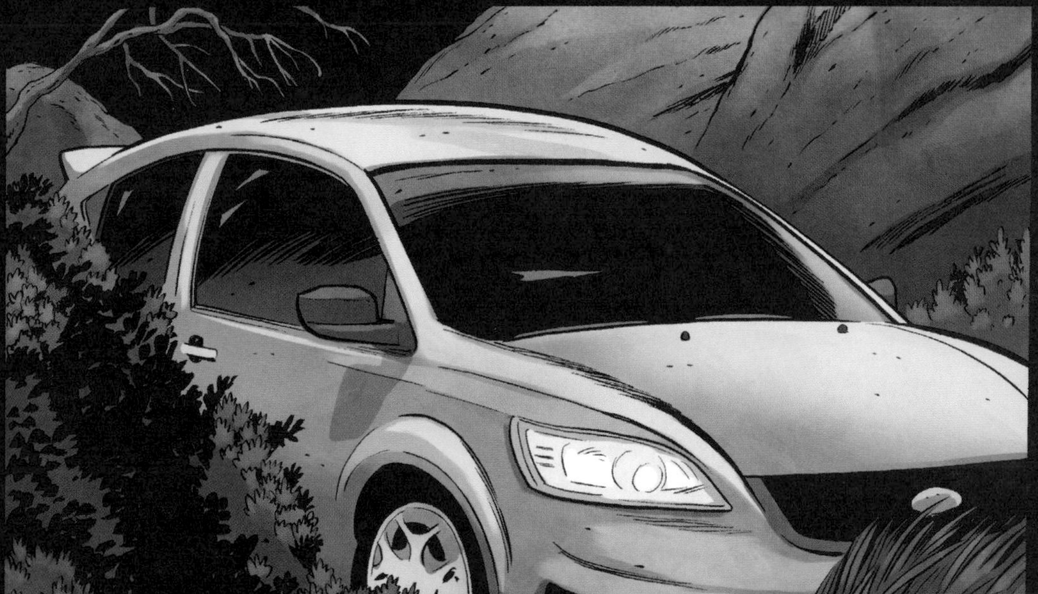

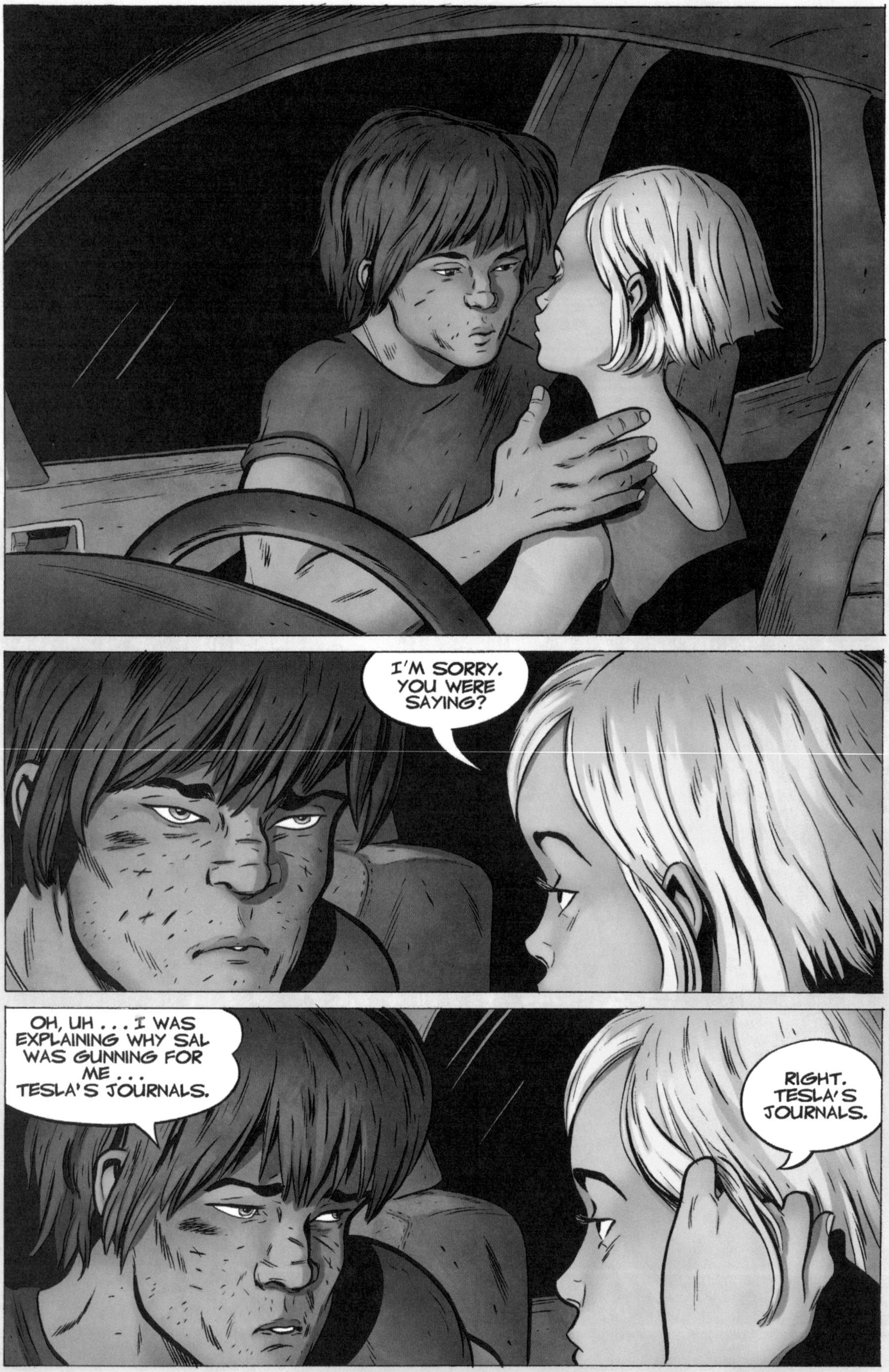
I'M SORRY. YOU WERE SAYING?
OH, UH . . . I WAS EXPLAINING WHY SAL WAS GUNNING FOR ME . . . TESLA'S JOURNALS.
RIGHT. TESLA'S JOURNALS.

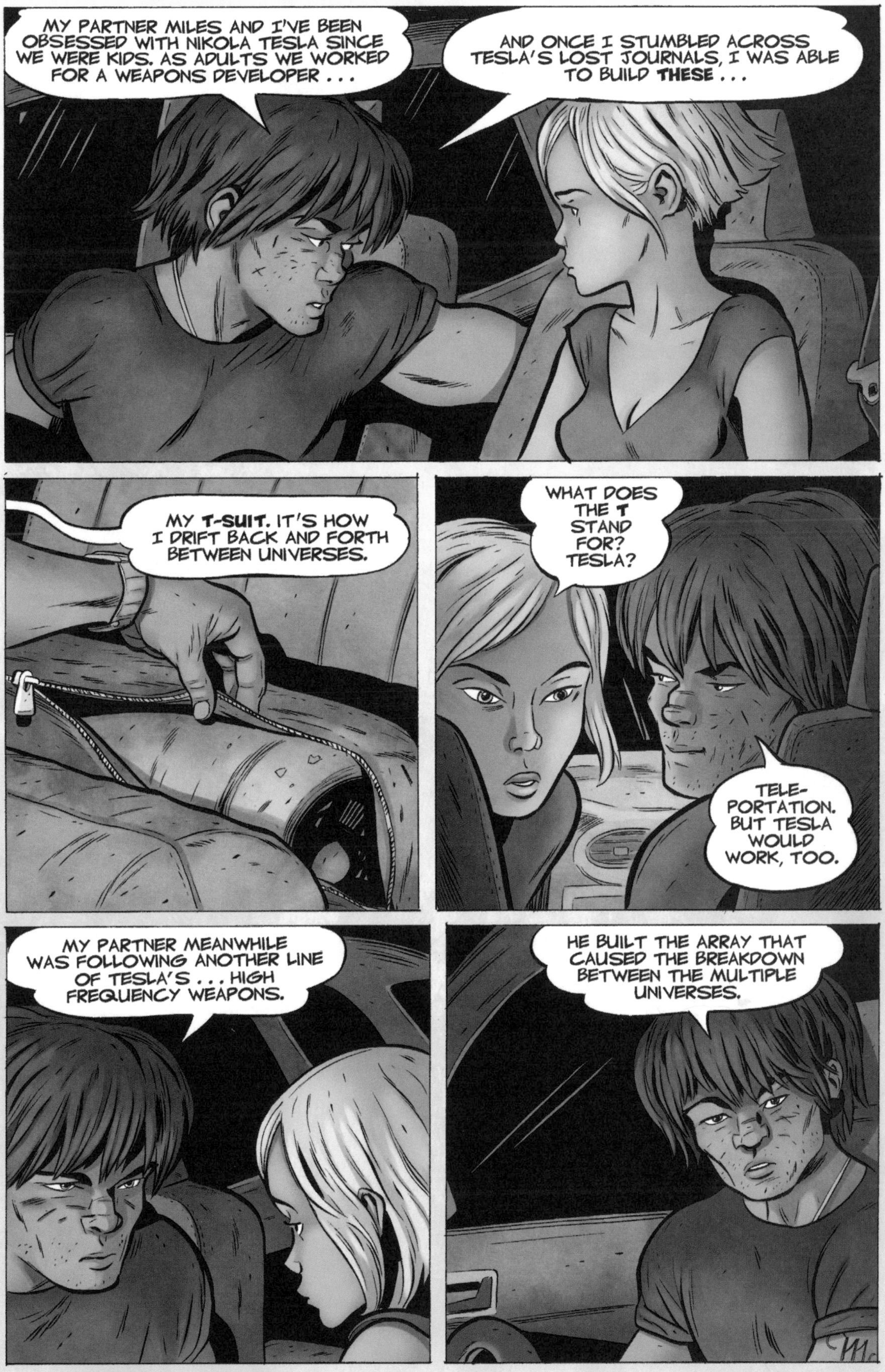
MY PARTNER MILES AND I'VE BEEN OBSESSED WITH NIKOLA TESLA SINCE WE WERE KIDS. AS ADULTS WE WORKED FOR A WEAPONS DEVELOPER . . .
AND ONCE I STUMBLED ACROSS TESLA'S LOST JOURNALS, I WAS ABLE TO BUILD **THESE** . . .
MY **T-SUIT**. IT'S HOW I DRIFT BACK AND FORTH BETWEEN UNIVERSES.
WHAT DOES THE **T** STAND FOR? TESLA?
TELE-PORTATION. BUT TESLA WOULD WORK, TOO.
MY PARTNER MEANWHILE WAS FOLLOWING ANOTHER LINE OF TESLA'S . . . HIGH FREQUENCY WEAPONS.
HE BUILT THE ARRAY THAT CAUSED THE BREAKDOWN BETWEEN THE MULTIPLE UNIVERSES.

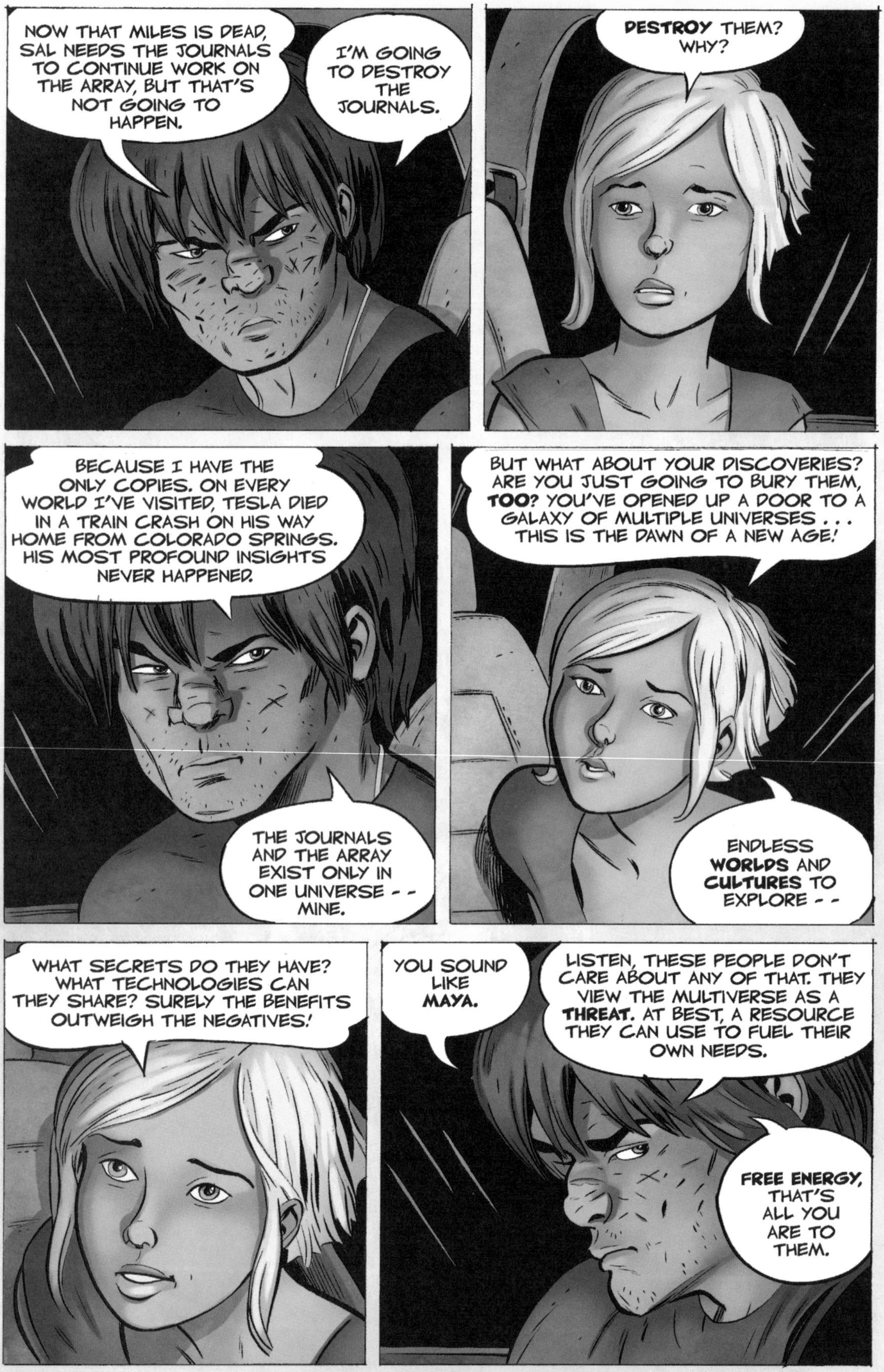
NOW THAT MILES IS DEAD, SAL NEEDS THE JOURNALS TO CONTINUE WORK ON THE ARRAY, BUT THAT'S NOT GOING TO HAPPEN.
I'M GOING TO DESTROY THE JOURNALS.
DESTROY THEM? WHY?
BECAUSE I HAVE THE ONLY COPIES. ON EVERY WORLD I'VE VISITED, TESLA DIED IN A TRAIN CRASH ON HIS WAY HOME FROM COLORADO SPRINGS. HIS MOST PROFOUND INSIGHTS NEVER HAPPENED.
THE JOURNALS AND THE ARRAY EXIST ONLY IN ONE UNIVERSE -- MINE.
BUT WHAT ABOUT YOUR DISCOVERIES? ARE YOU JUST GOING TO BURY THEM, TOO? YOU'VE OPENED UP A DOOR TO A GALAXY OF MULTIPLE UNIVERSES . . . THIS IS THE DAWN OF A NEW AGE!
ENDLESS WORLDS AND CULTURES TO EXPLORE --
WHAT SECRETS DO THEY HAVE? WHAT TECHNOLOGIES CAN THEY SHARE? SURELY THE BENEFITS OUTWEIGH THE NEGATIVES!
YOU SOUND LIKE MAYA.
LISTEN, THESE PEOPLE DON'T CARE ABOUT ANY OF THAT. THEY VIEW THE MULTIVERSE AS A THREAT. AT BEST, A RESOURCE THEY CAN USE TO FUEL THEIR OWN NEEDS.
FREE ENERGY, THAT'S ALL YOU ARE TO THEM.

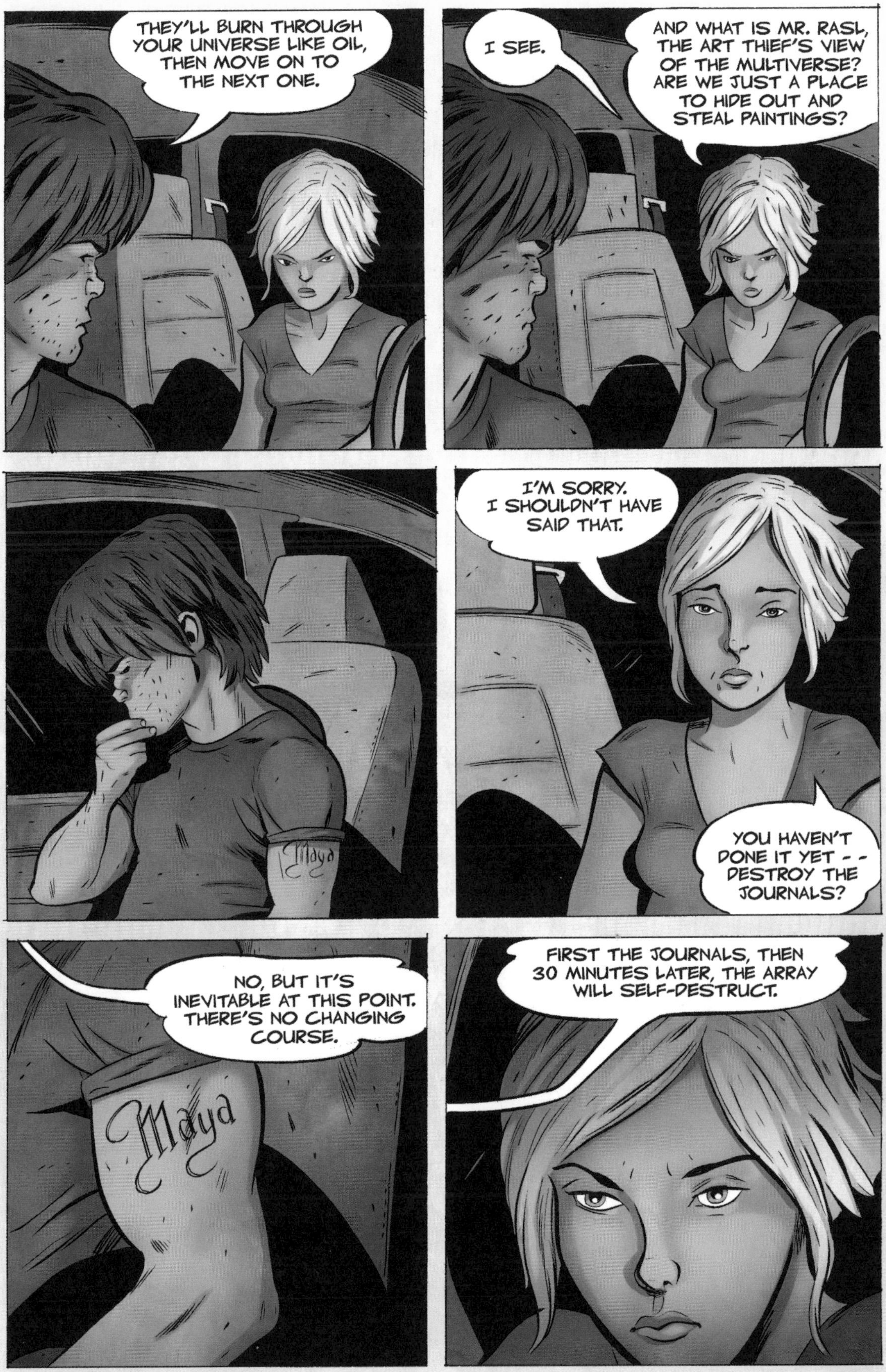
THEY'LL BURN THROUGH YOUR UNIVERSE LIKE OIL, THEN MOVE ON TO THE NEXT ONE.
I SEE.
AND WHAT IS MR. RASL, THE ART THIEF'S VIEW OF THE MULTIVERSE? ARE WE JUST A PLACE TO HIDE OUT AND STEAL PAINTINGS?
Maya
I'M SORRY. I SHOULDN'T HAVE SAID THAT.
YOU HAVEN'T DONE IT YET - - DESTROY THE JOURNALS?
NO, BUT IT'S INEVITABLE AT THIS POINT. THERE'S NO CHANGING COURSE.
Maya
FIRST THE JOURNALS, THEN 30 MINUTES LATER, THE ARRAY WILL SELF-DESTRUCT.

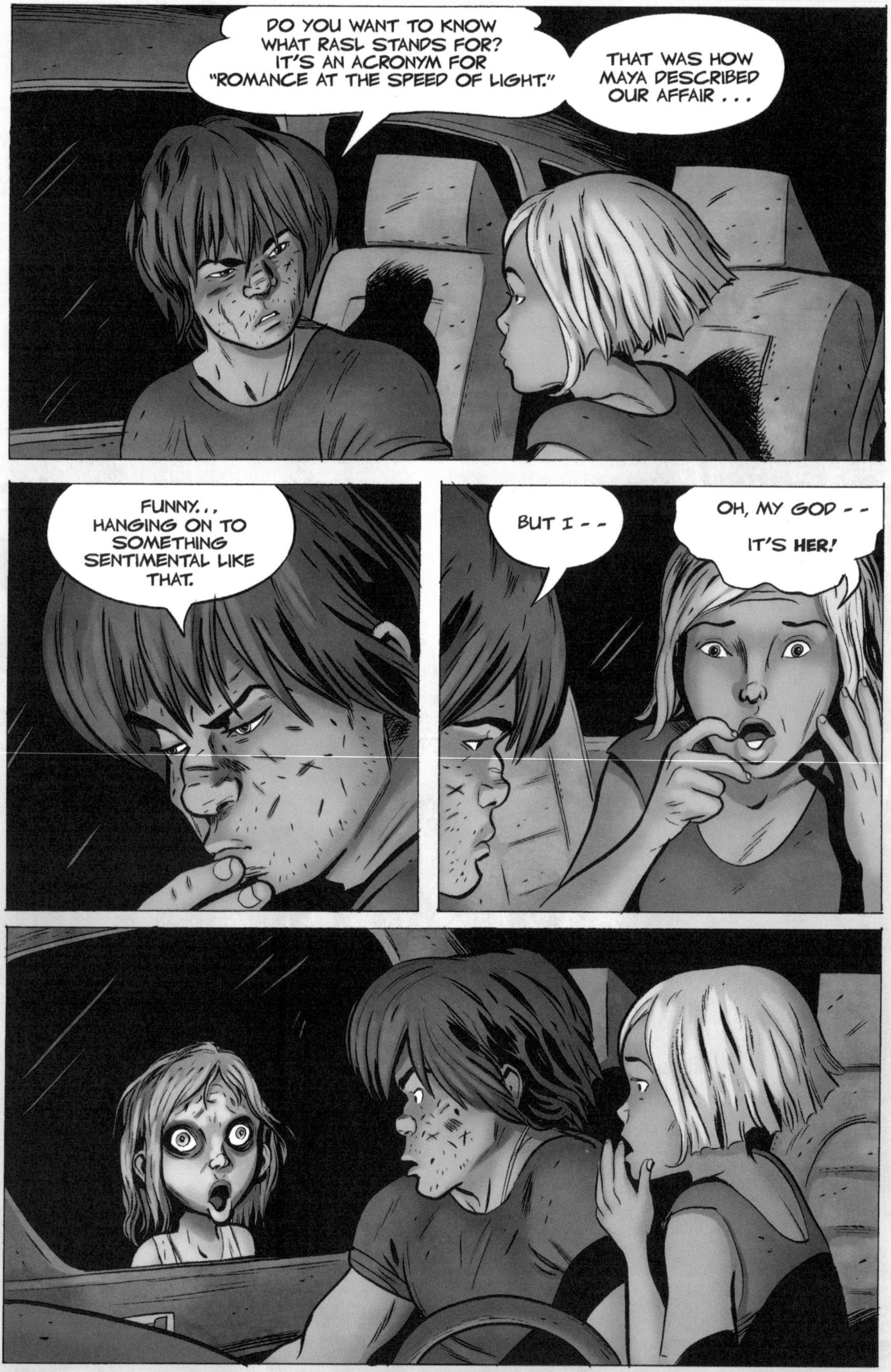
DO YOU WANT TO KNOW WHAT RASL STANDS FOR? IT'S AN ACRONYM FOR "ROMANCE AT THE SPEED OF LIGHT."
THAT WAS HOW MAYA DESCRIBED OUR AFFAIR . . .
FUNNY. . . HANGING ON TO SOMETHING SENTIMENTAL LIKE THAT.
BUT I - -
OH, MY GOD - -
IT'S **HER!**

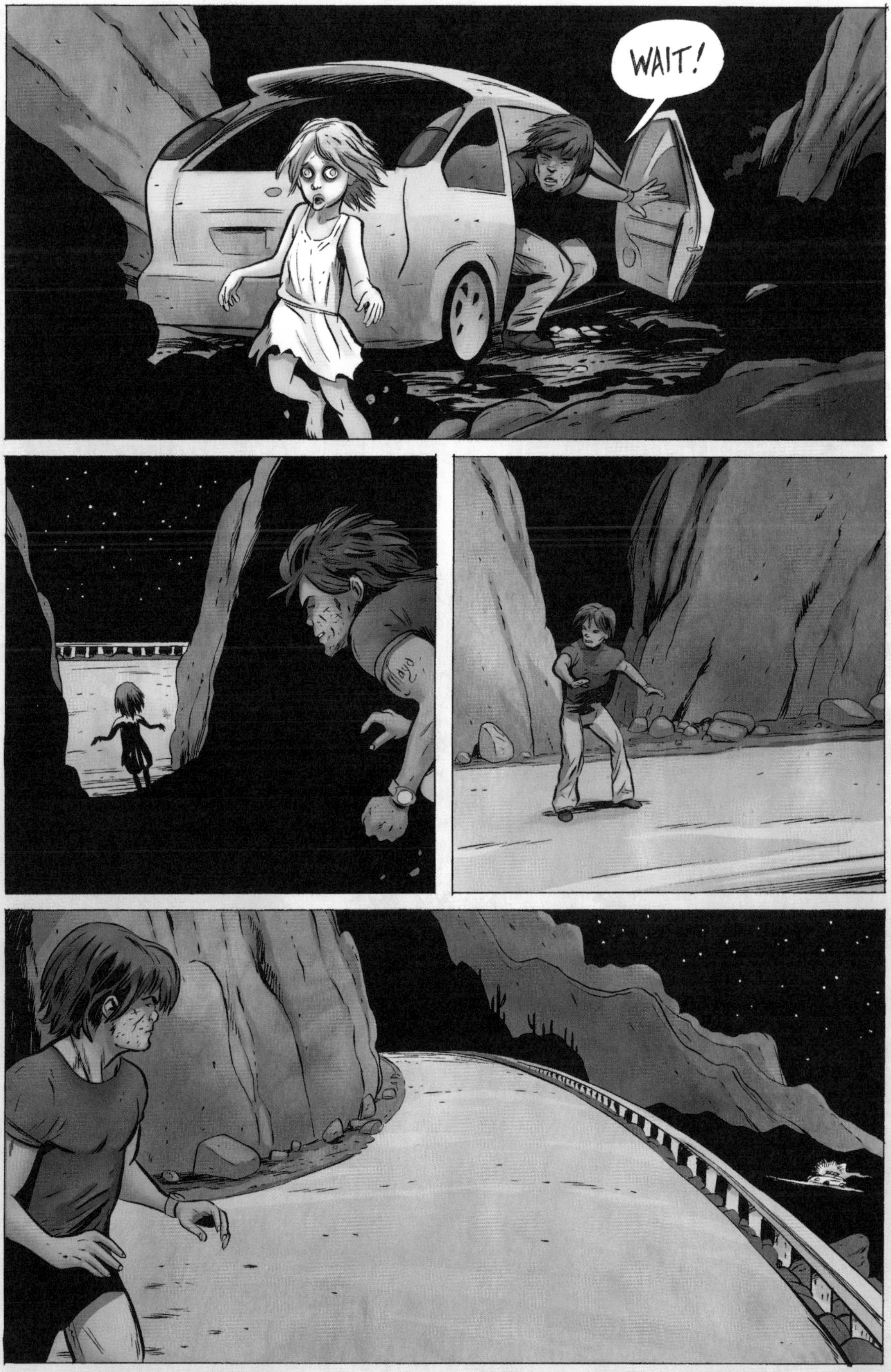
WAIT!

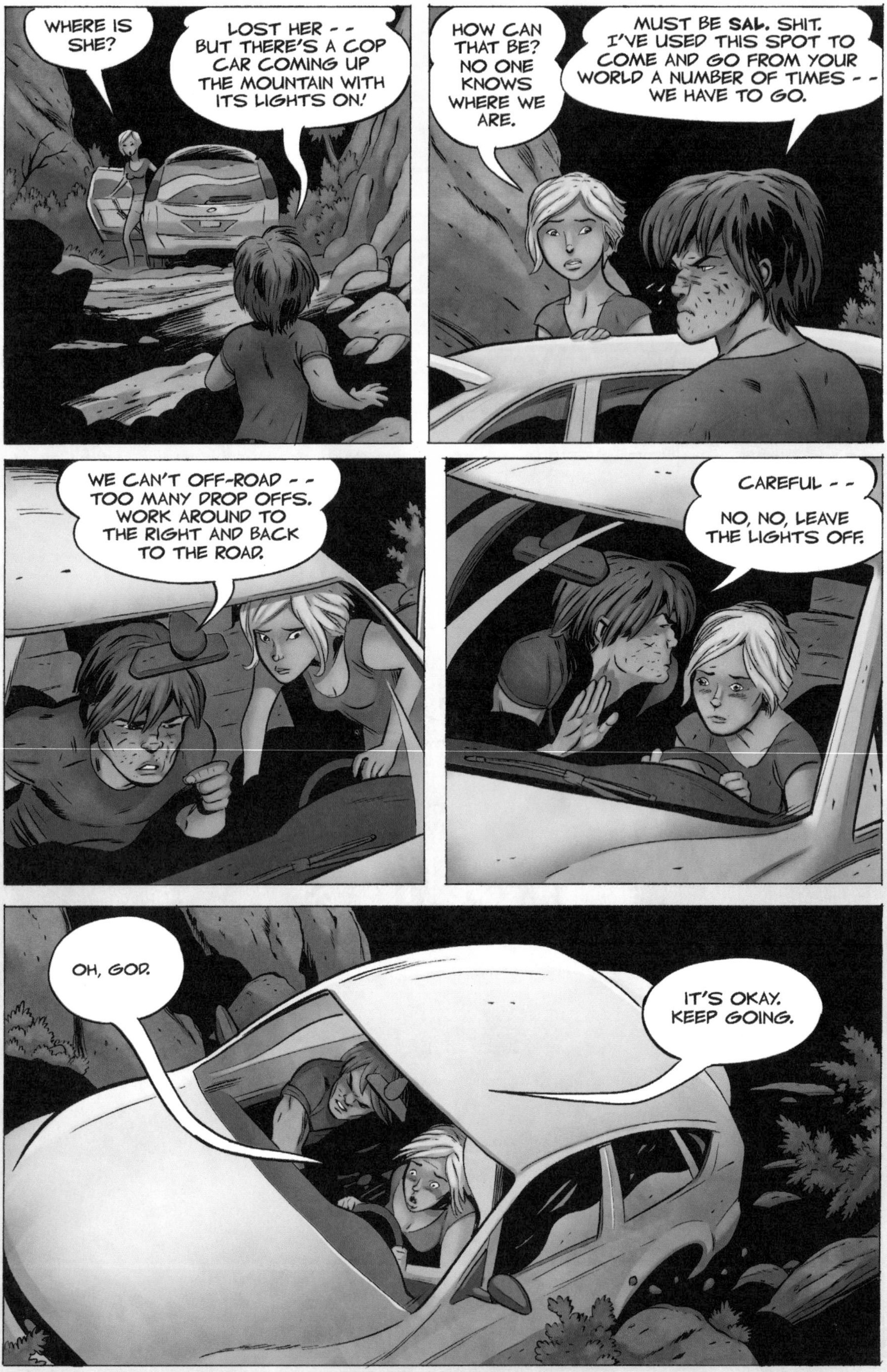
WHERE IS SHE?
LOST HER - - BUT THERE'S A COP CAR COMING UP THE MOUNTAIN WITH ITS LIGHTS ON!
HOW CAN THAT BE? NO ONE KNOWS WHERE WE ARE.
MUST BE SAL. SHIT. I'VE USED THIS SPOT TO COME AND GO FROM YOUR WORLD A NUMBER OF TIMES - - WE HAVE TO GO.
WE CAN'T OFF-ROAD - - TOO MANY DROP OFFS. WORK AROUND TO THE RIGHT AND BACK TO THE ROAD.
CAREFUL - -
NO, NO, LEAVE THE LIGHTS OFF.
OH, GOD.
IT'S OKAY. KEEP GOING.

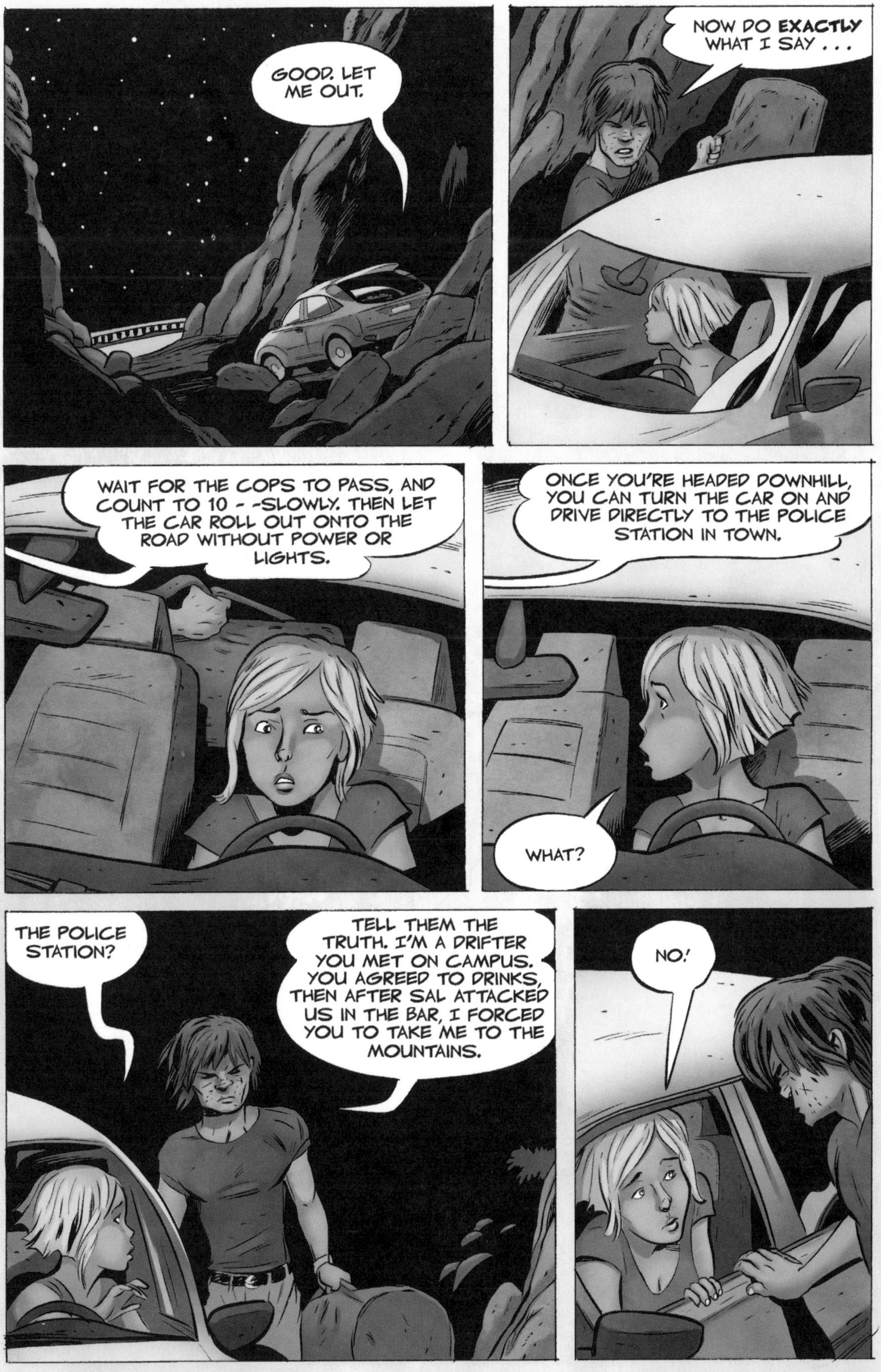
GOOD. LET ME OUT.
NOW DO EXACTLY WHAT I SAY . . .
WAIT FOR THE COPS TO PASS, AND COUNT TO 10 - -SLOWLY. THEN LET THE CAR ROLL OUT ONTO THE ROAD WITHOUT POWER OR LIGHTS.
ONCE YOU'RE HEADED DOWNHILL, YOU CAN TURN THE CAR ON AND DRIVE DIRECTLY TO THE POLICE STATION IN TOWN.
WHAT?
THE POLICE STATION?
TELL THEM THE TRUTH. I'M A DRIFTER YOU MET ON CAMPUS. YOU AGREED TO DRINKS, THEN AFTER SAL ATTACKED US IN THE BAR, I FORCED YOU TO TAKE ME TO THE MOUNTAINS.
NO!

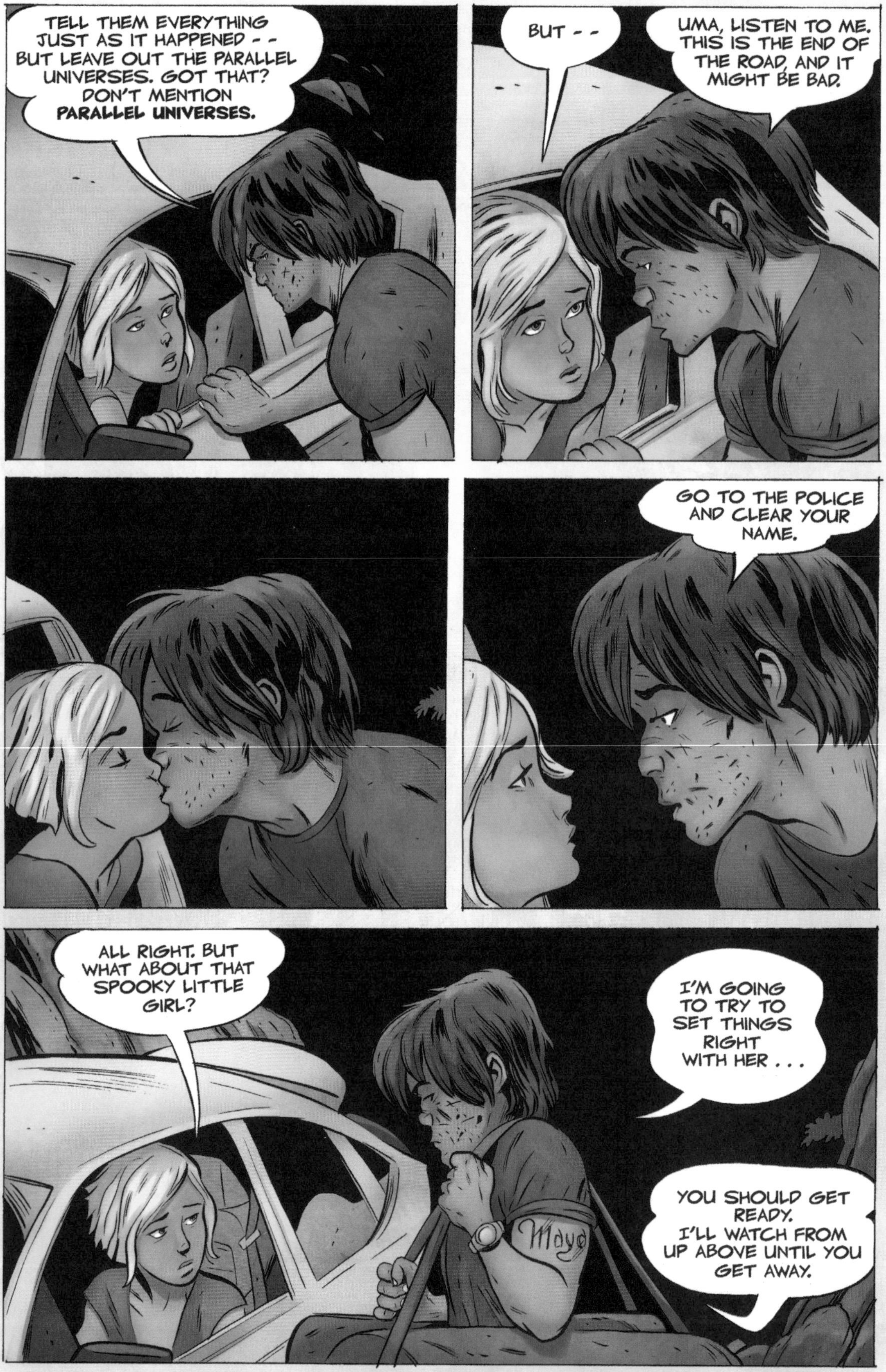
TELL THEM EVERYTHING JUST AS IT HAPPENED - - BUT LEAVE OUT THE PARALLEL UNIVERSES. GOT THAT? DON'T MENTION **PARALLEL UNIVERSES.**
BUT - -
UMA, LISTEN TO ME. THIS IS THE END OF THE ROAD, AND IT MIGHT BE BAD.
GO TO THE POLICE AND CLEAR YOUR NAME.
ALL RIGHT. BUT WHAT ABOUT THAT SPOOKY LITTLE GIRL?
I'M GOING TO TRY TO SET THINGS RIGHT WITH HER . . .
YOU SHOULD GET READY. I'LL WATCH FROM UP ABOVE UNTIL YOU GET AWAY.

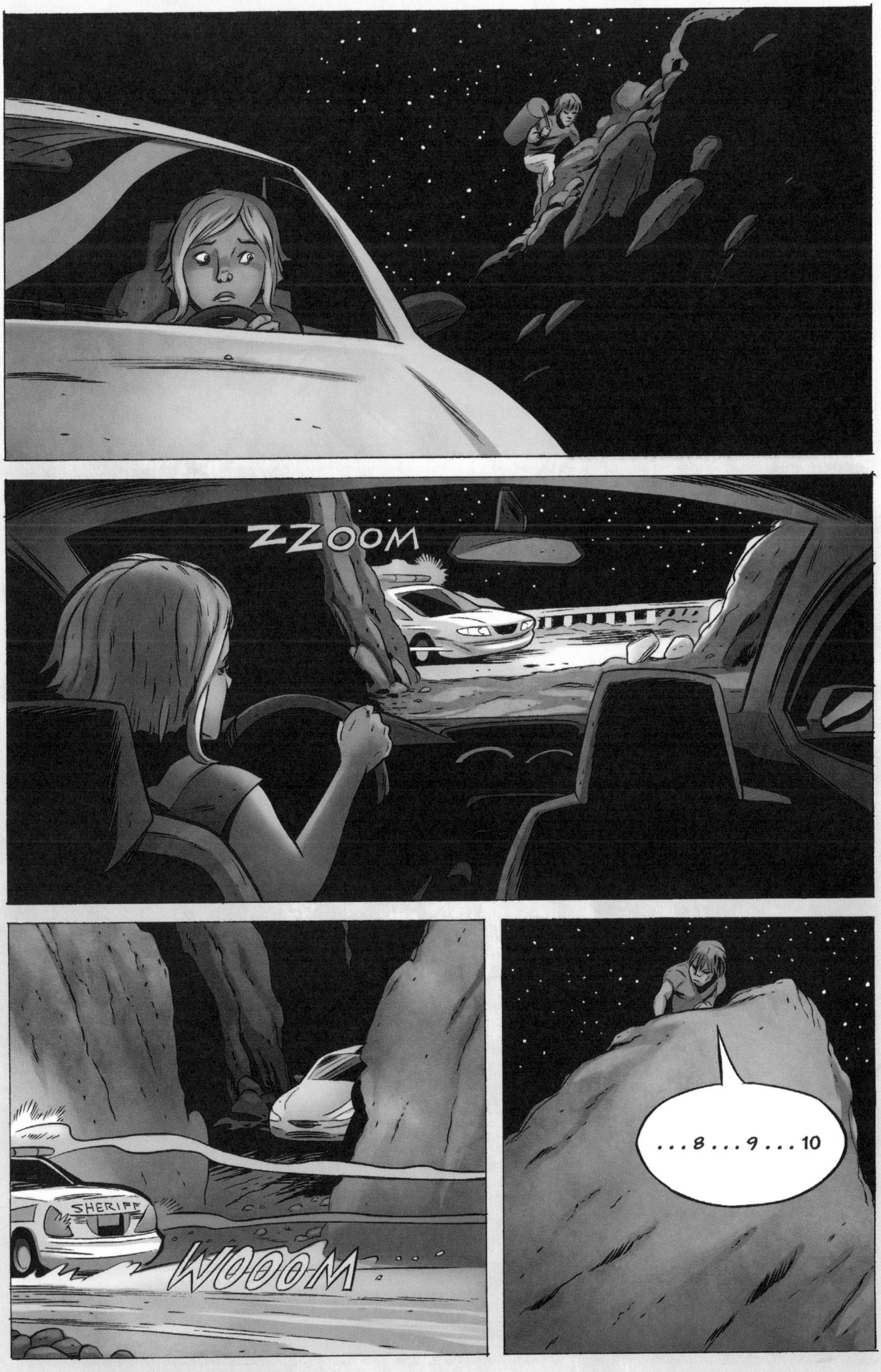
ZZOOM
SHERIFF
WOOOM
. . . 8 . . . 9 . . . 10

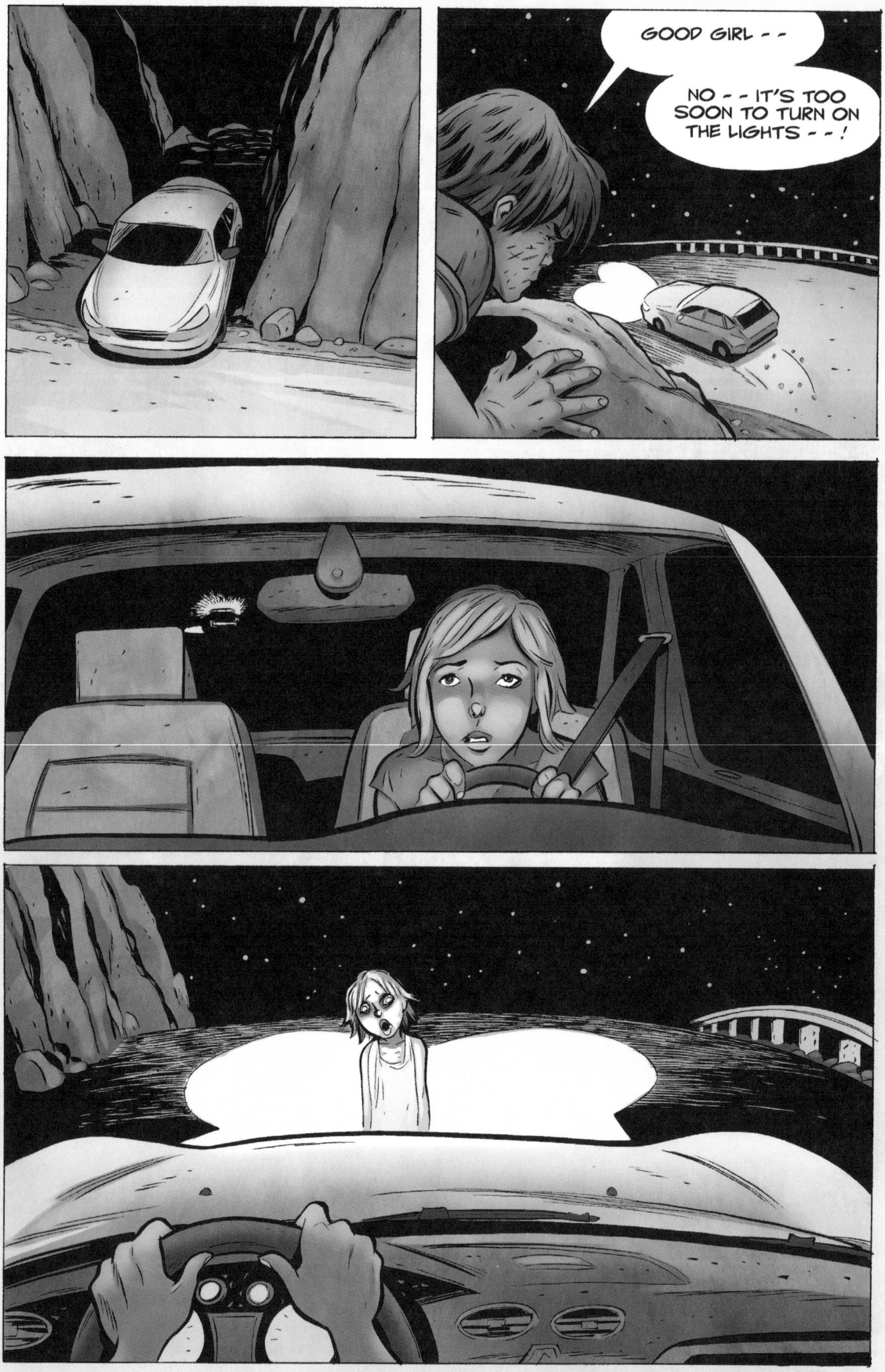
GOOD GIRL - -
NO - - IT'S TOO SOON TO TURN ON THE LIGHTS - - !

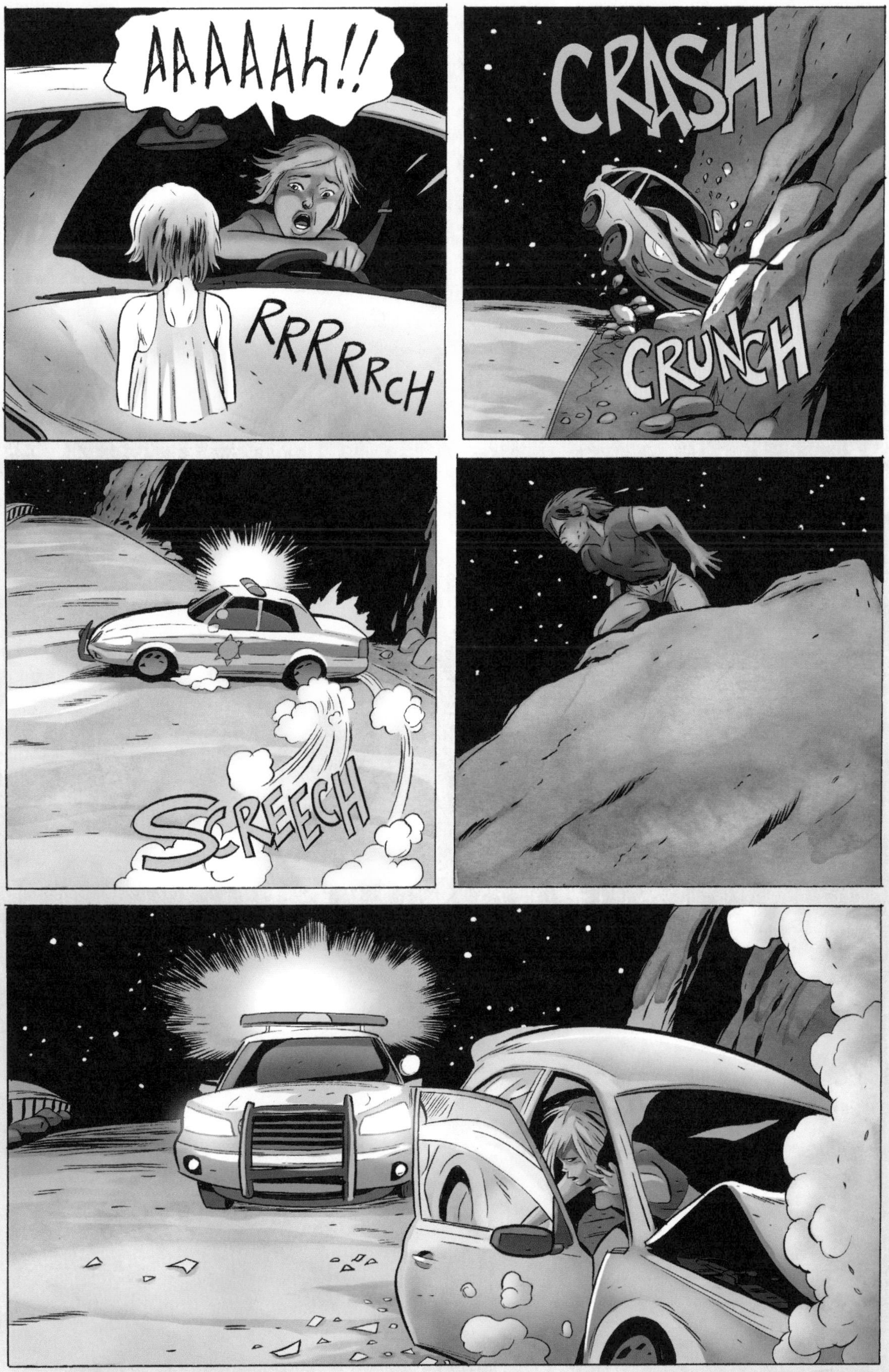
AAAAAh!!
RRRRRRCH
CRASH
CRUNCH
SCREECH

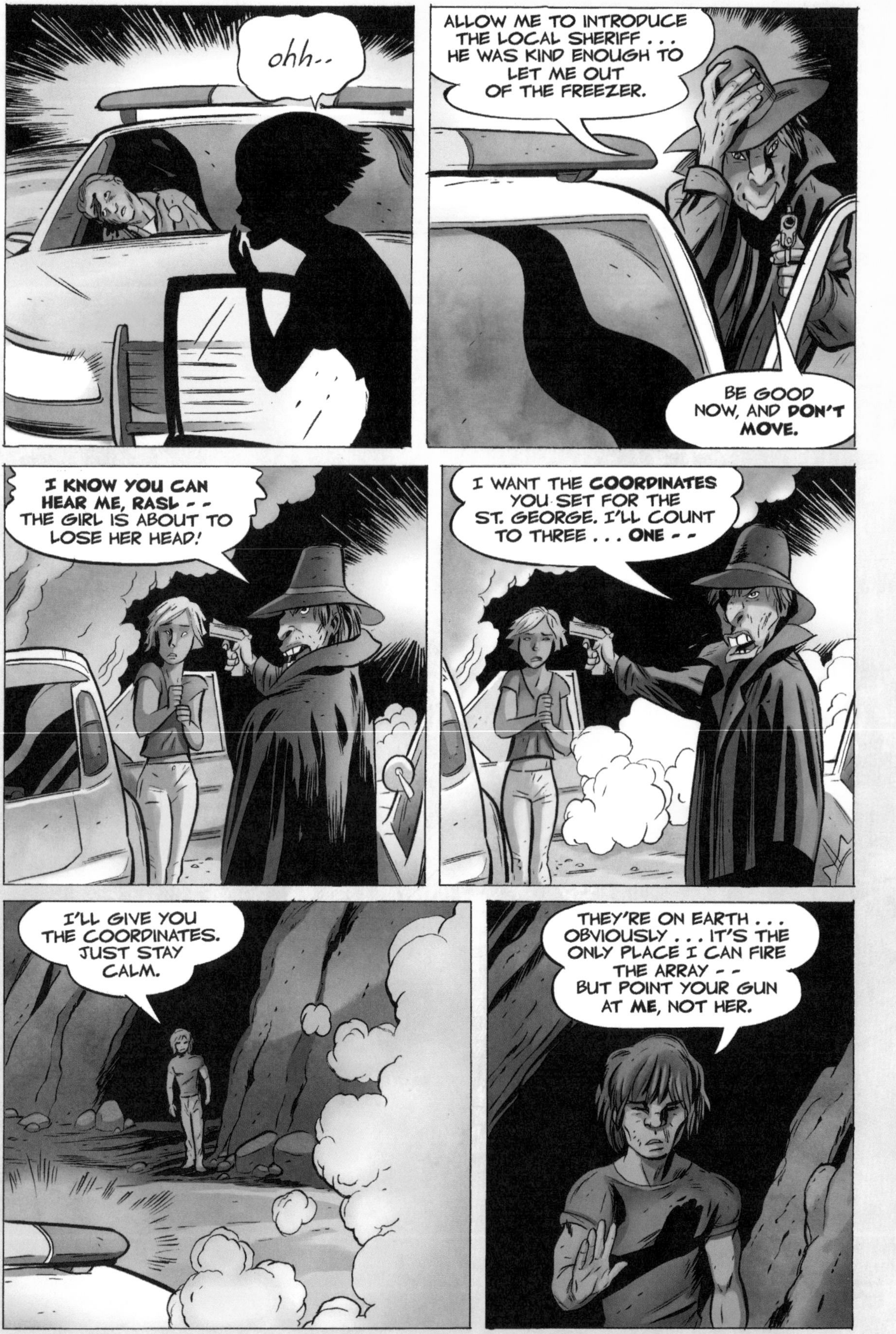

ohh..
ALLOW ME TO INTRODUCE THE LOCAL SHERIFF . . . HE WAS KIND ENOUGH TO LET ME OUT OF THE FREEZER.
BE GOOD NOW, AND DON'T MOVE.
I KNOW YOU CAN HEAR ME, RASL - - THE GIRL IS ABOUT TO LOSE HER HEAD!
I WANT THE COORDINATES YOU SET FOR THE ST. GEORGE. I'LL COUNT TO THREE . . . ONE - -
I'LL GIVE YOU THE COORDINATES. JUST STAY CALM.
THEY'RE ON EARTH . . . OBVIOUSLY . . . IT'S THE ONLY PLACE I CAN FIRE THE ARRAY - - BUT POINT YOUR GUN AT ME, NOT HER.

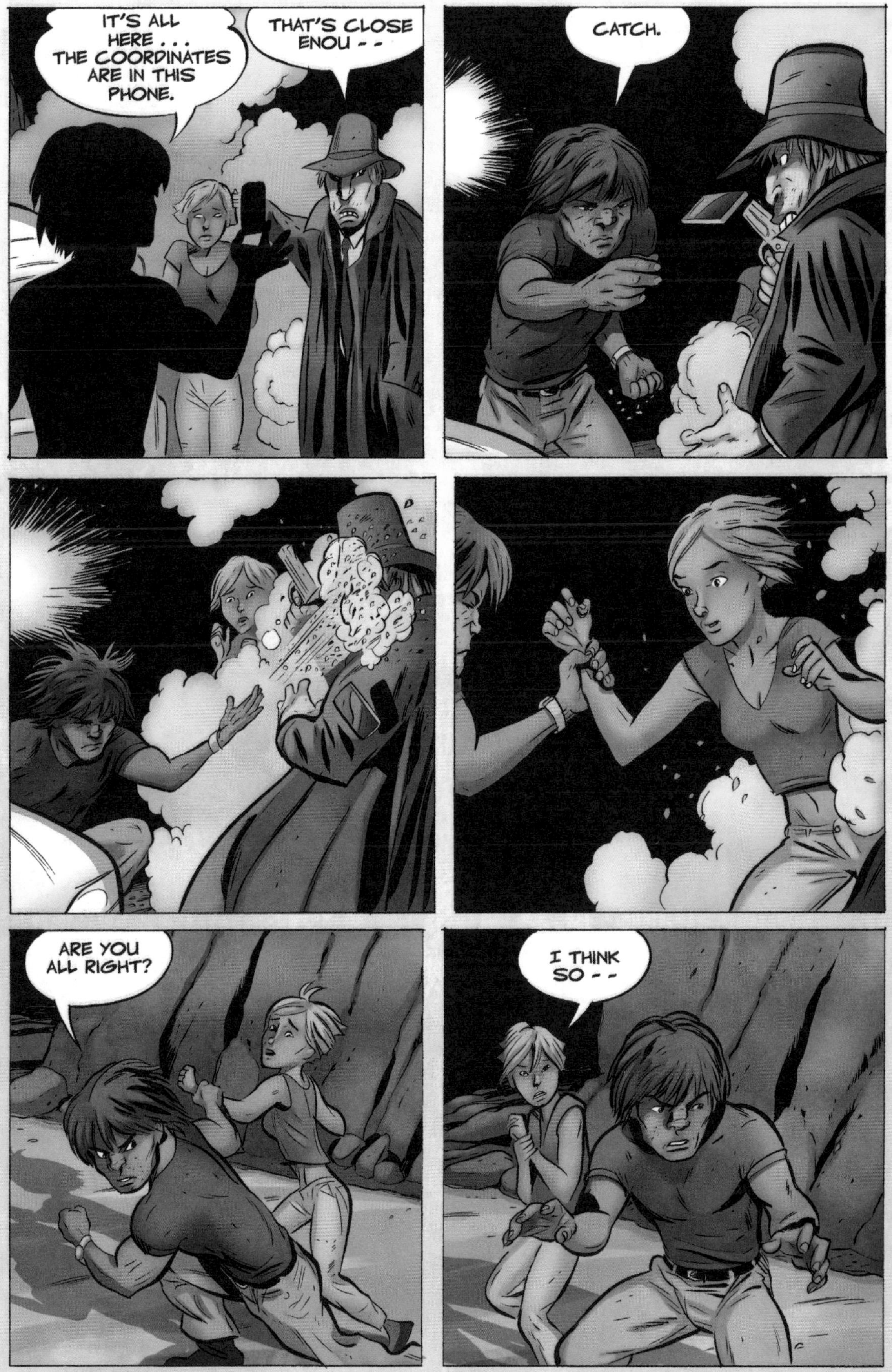
IT'S ALL HERE . . . THE COORDINATES ARE IN THIS PHONE.
THAT'S CLOSE ENOU - -
CATCH.
ARE YOU ALL RIGHT?
I THINK SO - -

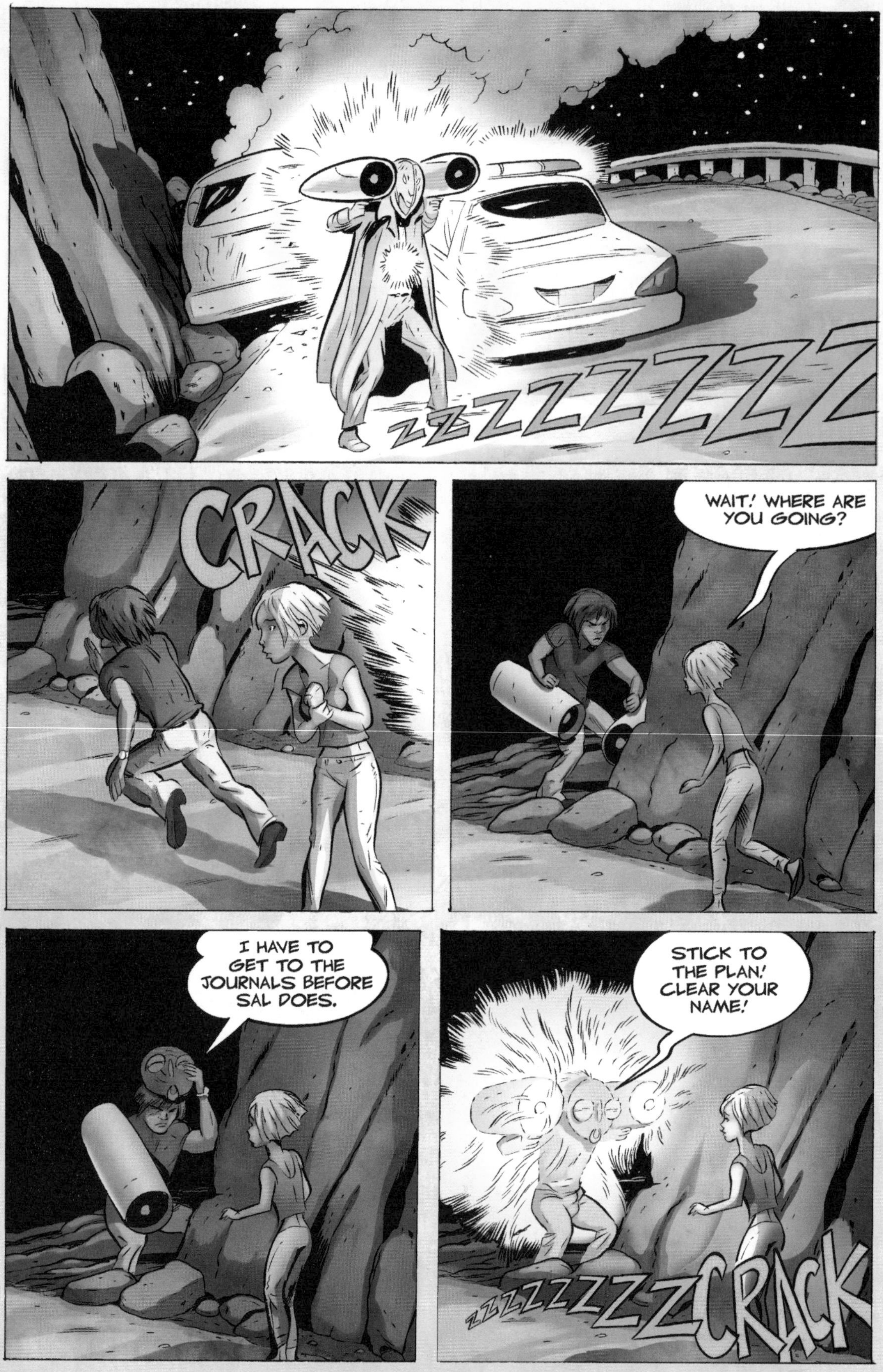
ZZZZZZZZZZZZ
CRACK
WAIT! WHERE ARE YOU GOING?
I HAVE TO GET TO THE JOURNALS BEFORE SAL DOES.
STICK TO THE PLAN! CLEAR YOUR NAME!
ZZZZZZZZZZCRACK

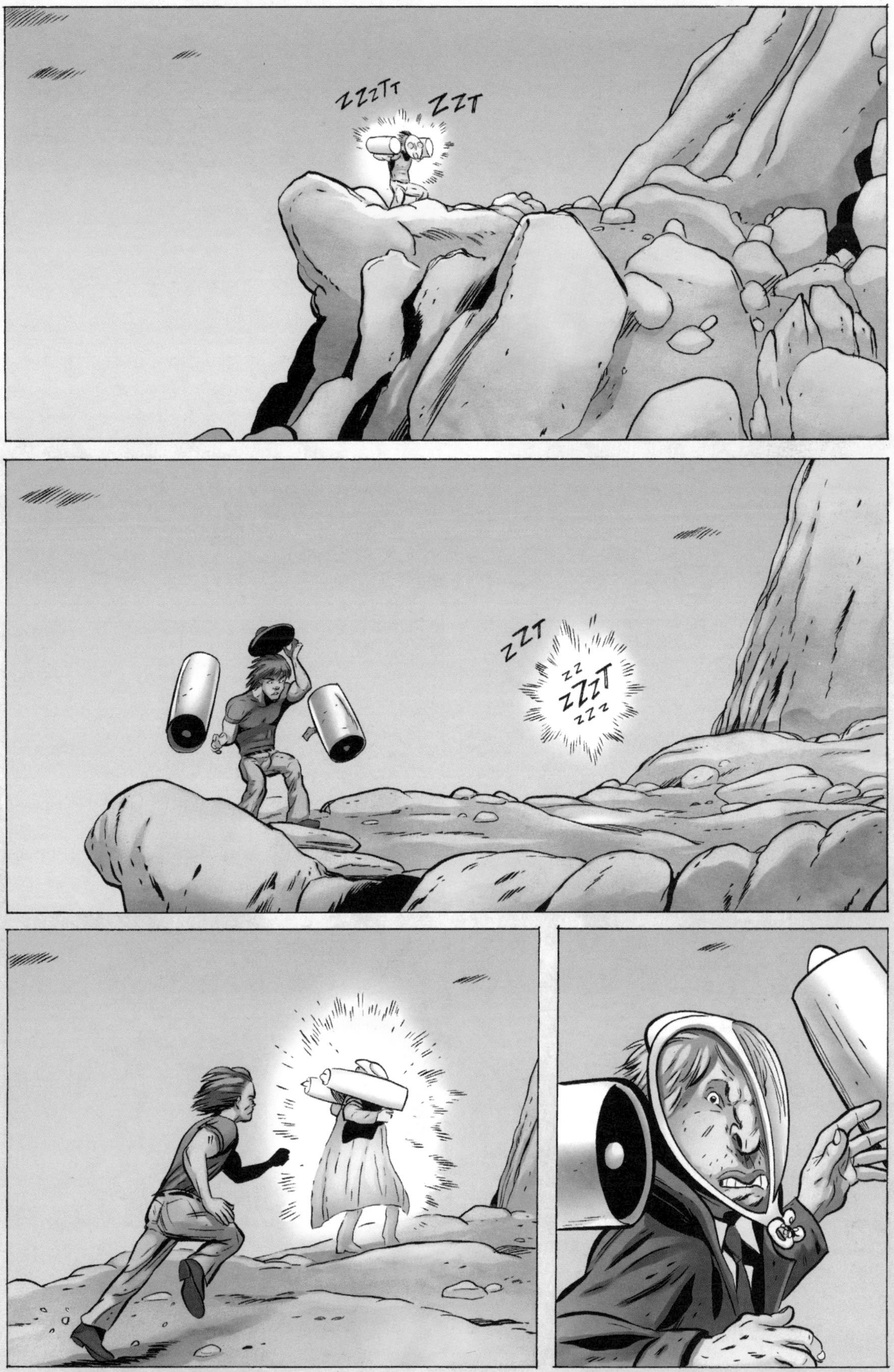
ZZzTT
ZZT
ZZT
ZZzT

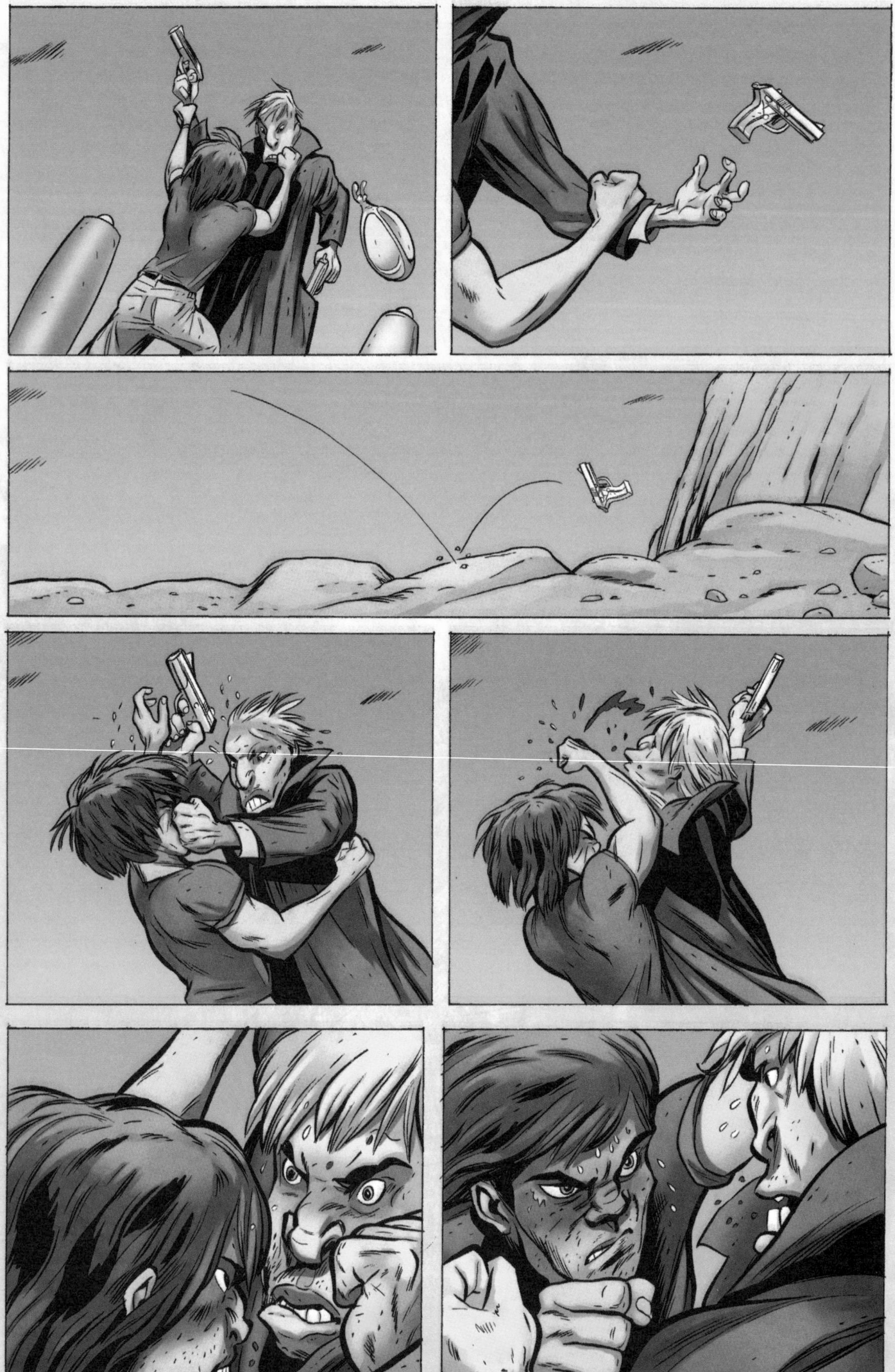

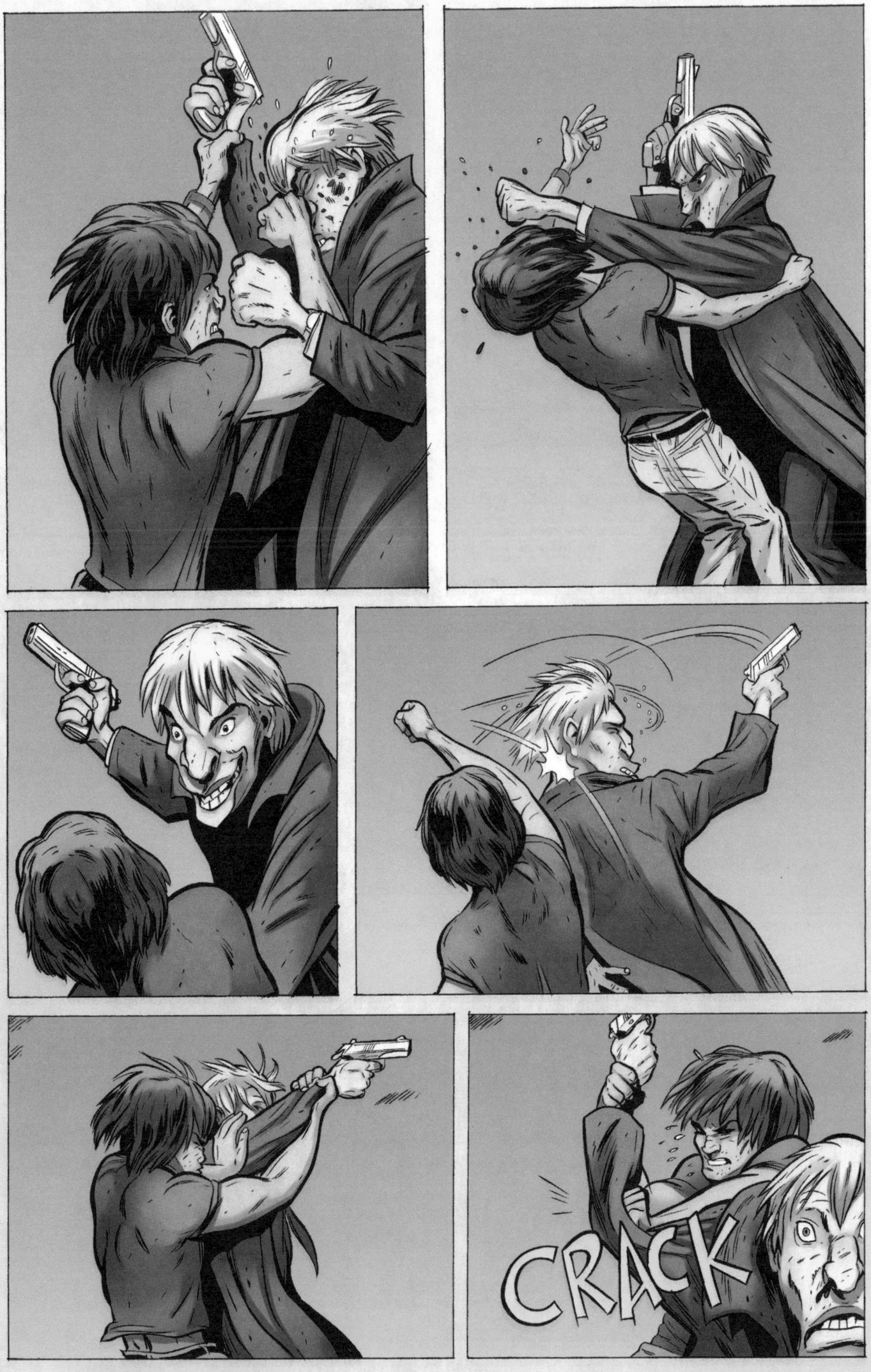
CRACK

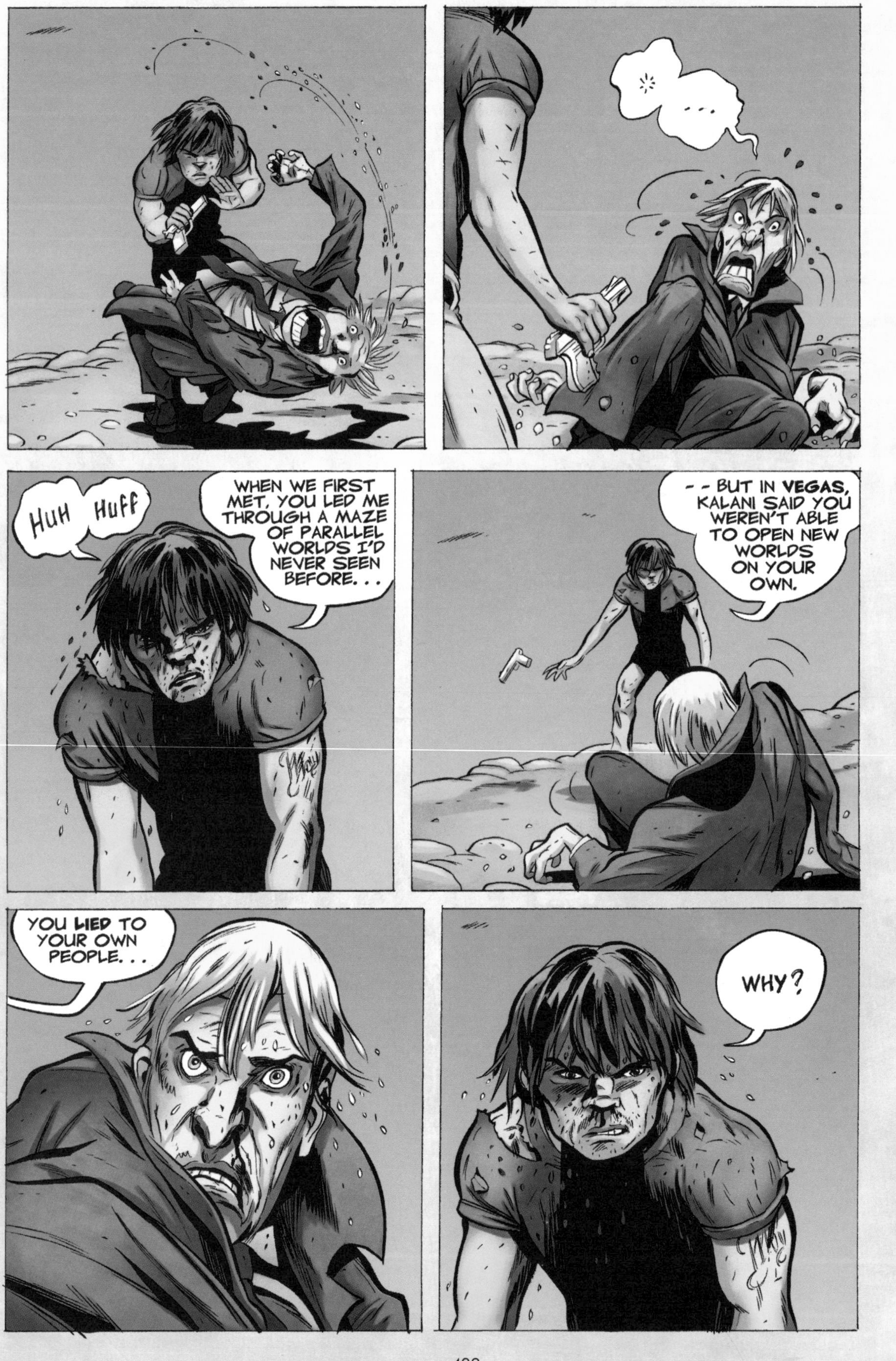
!
. . .
HUH HUFF
WHEN WE FIRST MET, YOU LED ME THROUGH A MAZE OF PARALLEL WORLDS I'D NEVER SEEN BEFORE. . .
- - BUT IN VEGAS, KALANI SAID YOU WEREN'T ABLE TO OPEN NEW WORLDS ON YOUR OWN.
YOU LIED TO YOUR OWN PEOPLE. . .
WHY?

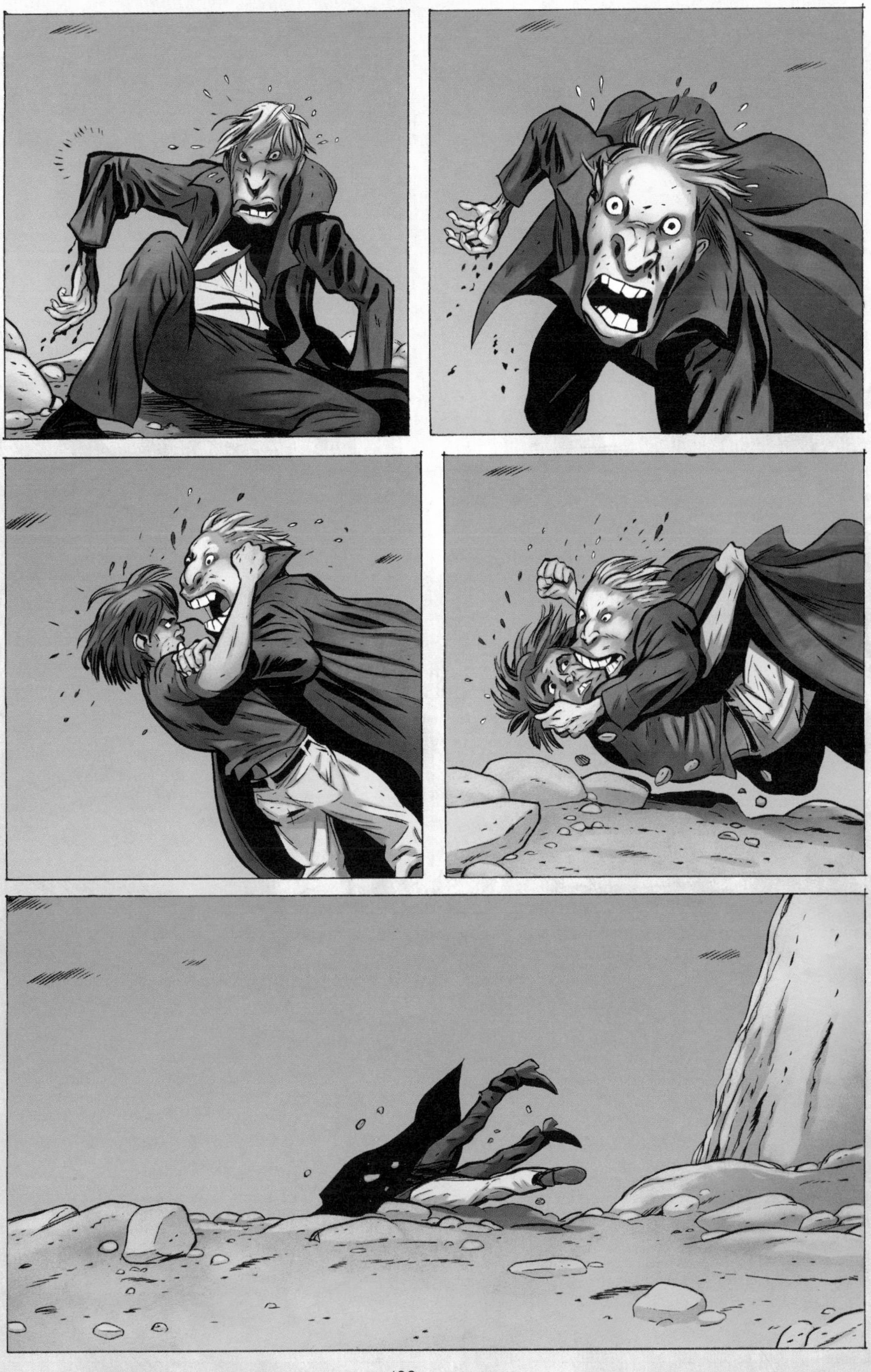

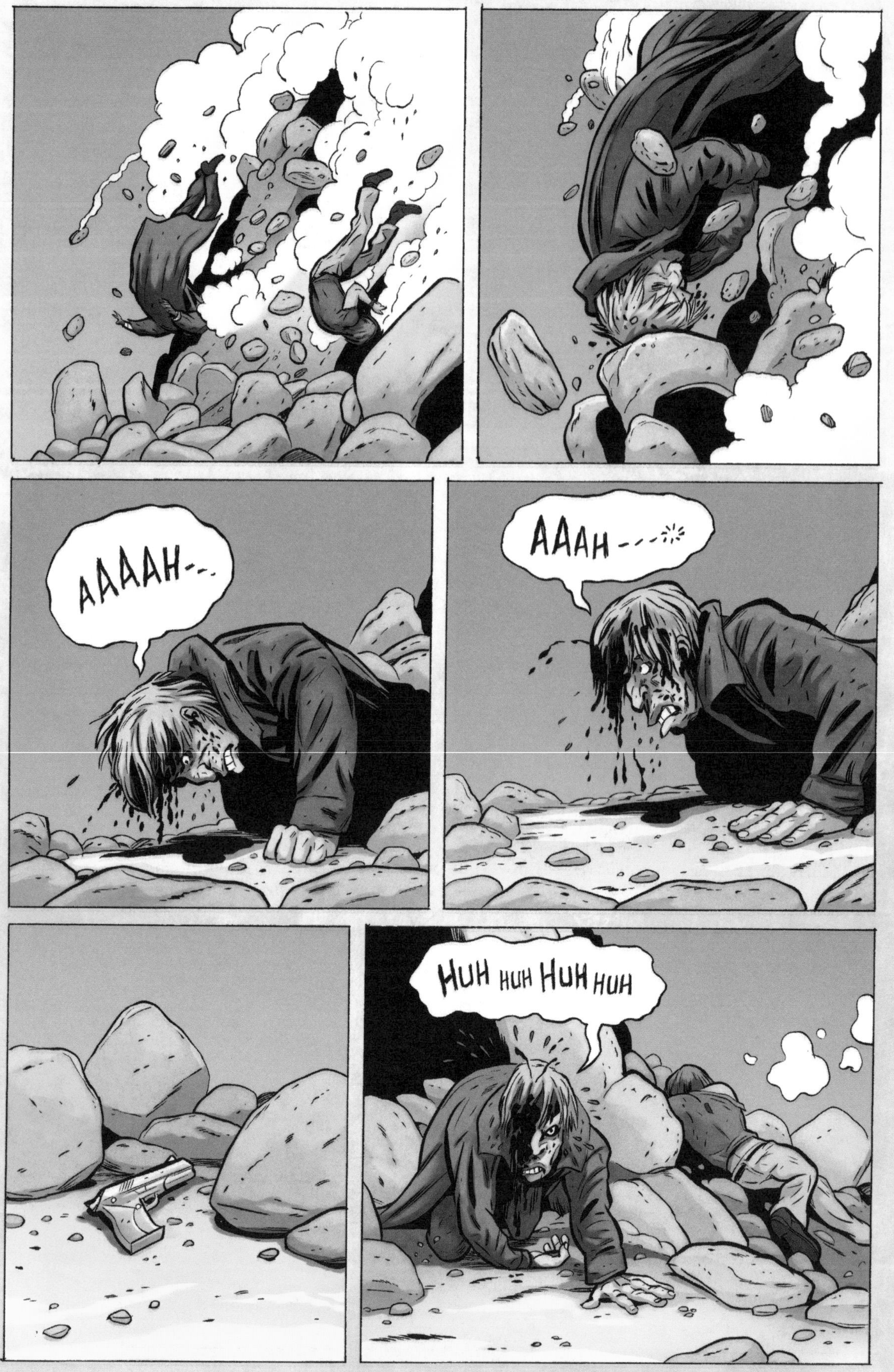
AAAAH---
AAAH----
HUH HUH HUH HUH

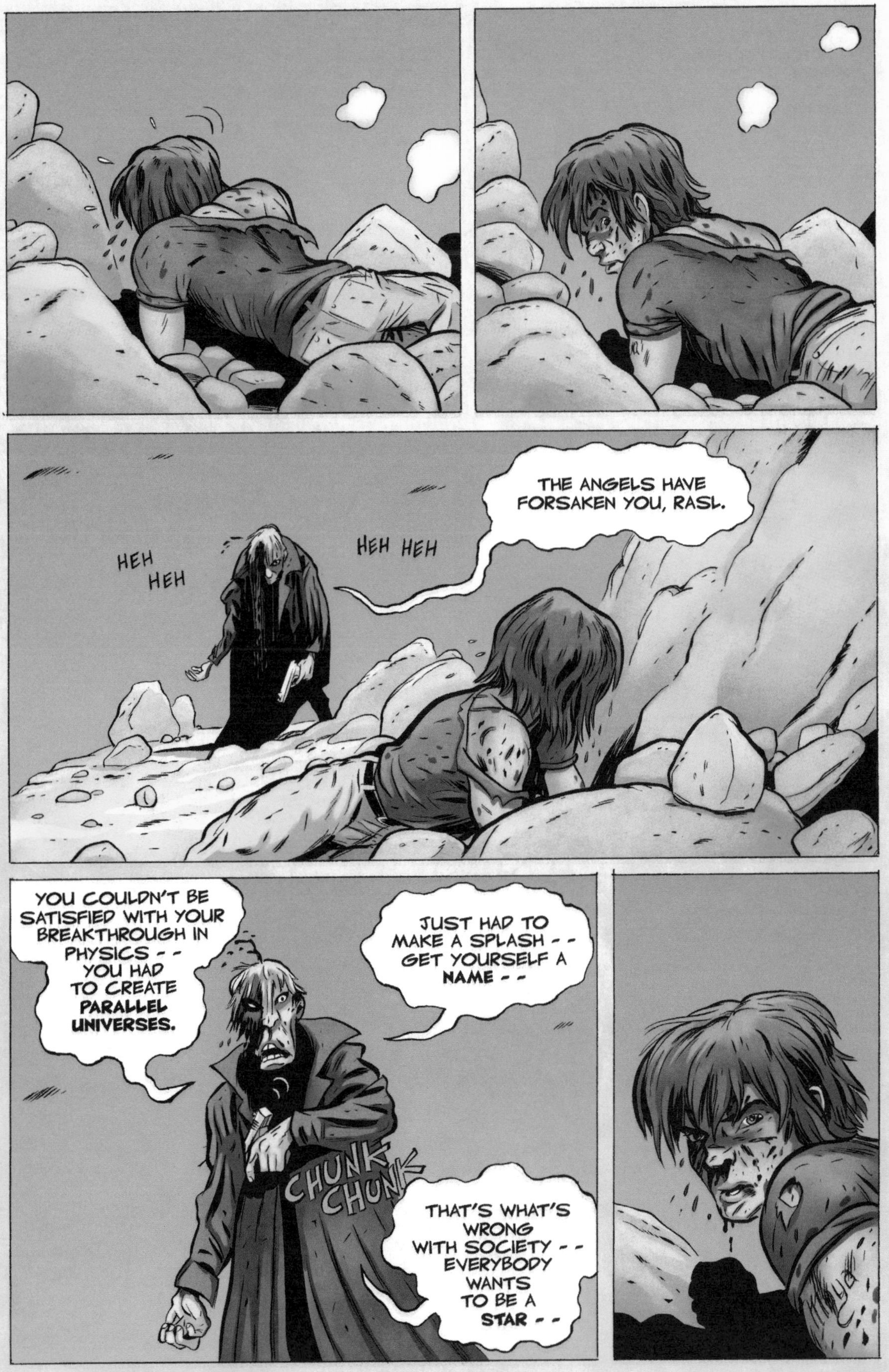
THE ANGELS HAVE FORSAKEN YOU, RASL.
HEH HEH
HEH HEH
YOU COULDN'T BE SATISFIED WITH YOUR BREAKTHROUGH IN PHYSICS - - YOU HAD TO CREATE PARALLEL UNIVERSES.
JUST HAD TO MAKE A SPLASH - - GET YOURSELF A NAME - -
CHUNK CHUNK
THAT'S WHAT'S WRONG WITH SOCIETY - - EVERYBODY WANTS TO BE A STAR - -

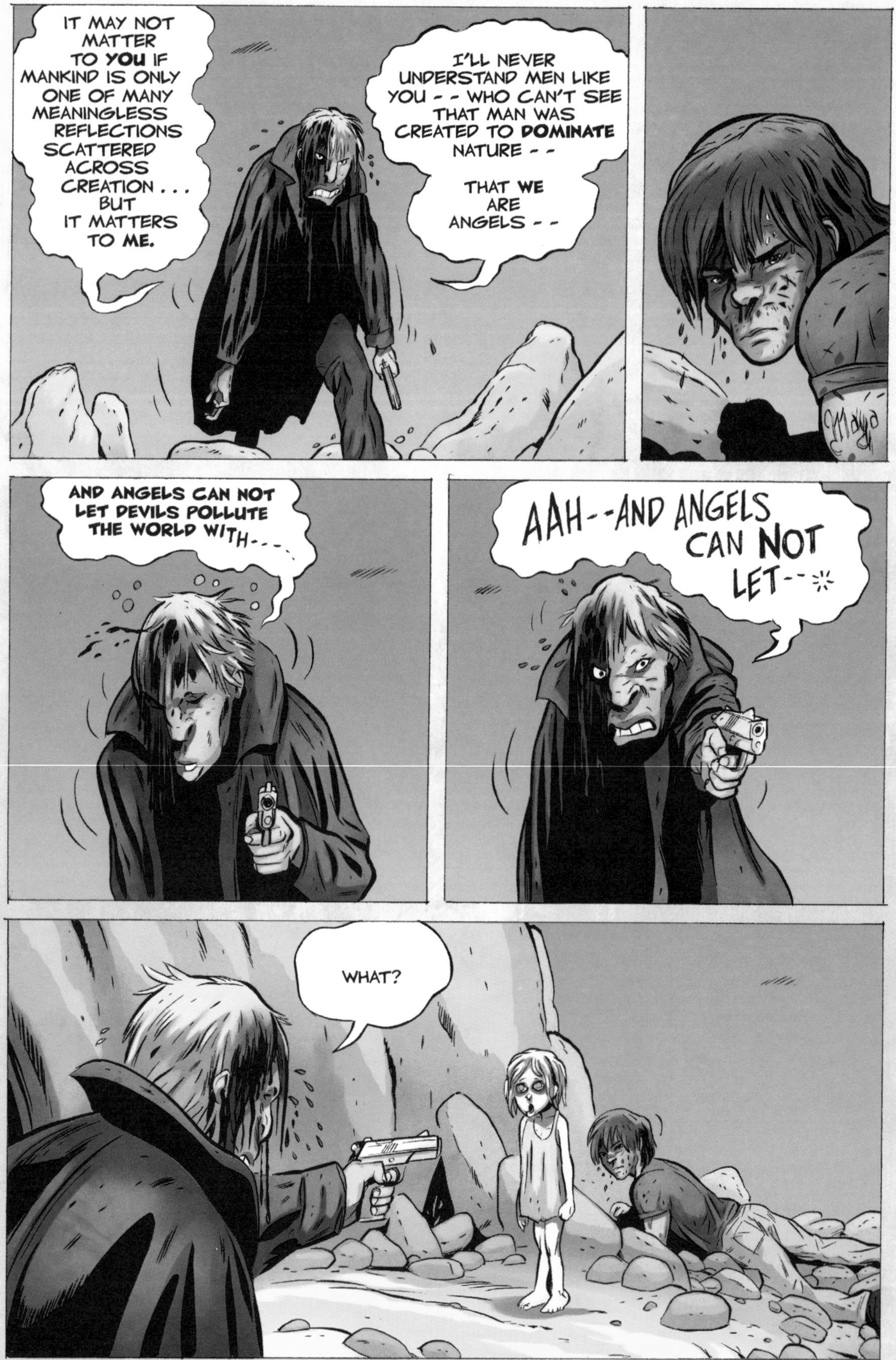
IT MAY NOT MATTER TO YOU IF MANKIND IS ONLY ONE OF MANY MEANINGLESS REFLECTIONS SCATTERED ACROSS CREATION . . . BUT IT MATTERS TO ME.
I'LL NEVER UNDERSTAND MEN LIKE YOU - - WHO CAN'T SEE THAT MAN WAS CREATED TO DOMINATE NATURE - -
THAT WE ARE ANGELS - -
AND ANGELS CAN NOT LET DEVILS POLLUTE THE WORLD WITH- - -
AAH- -AND ANGELS CAN NOT LET- -
WHAT?

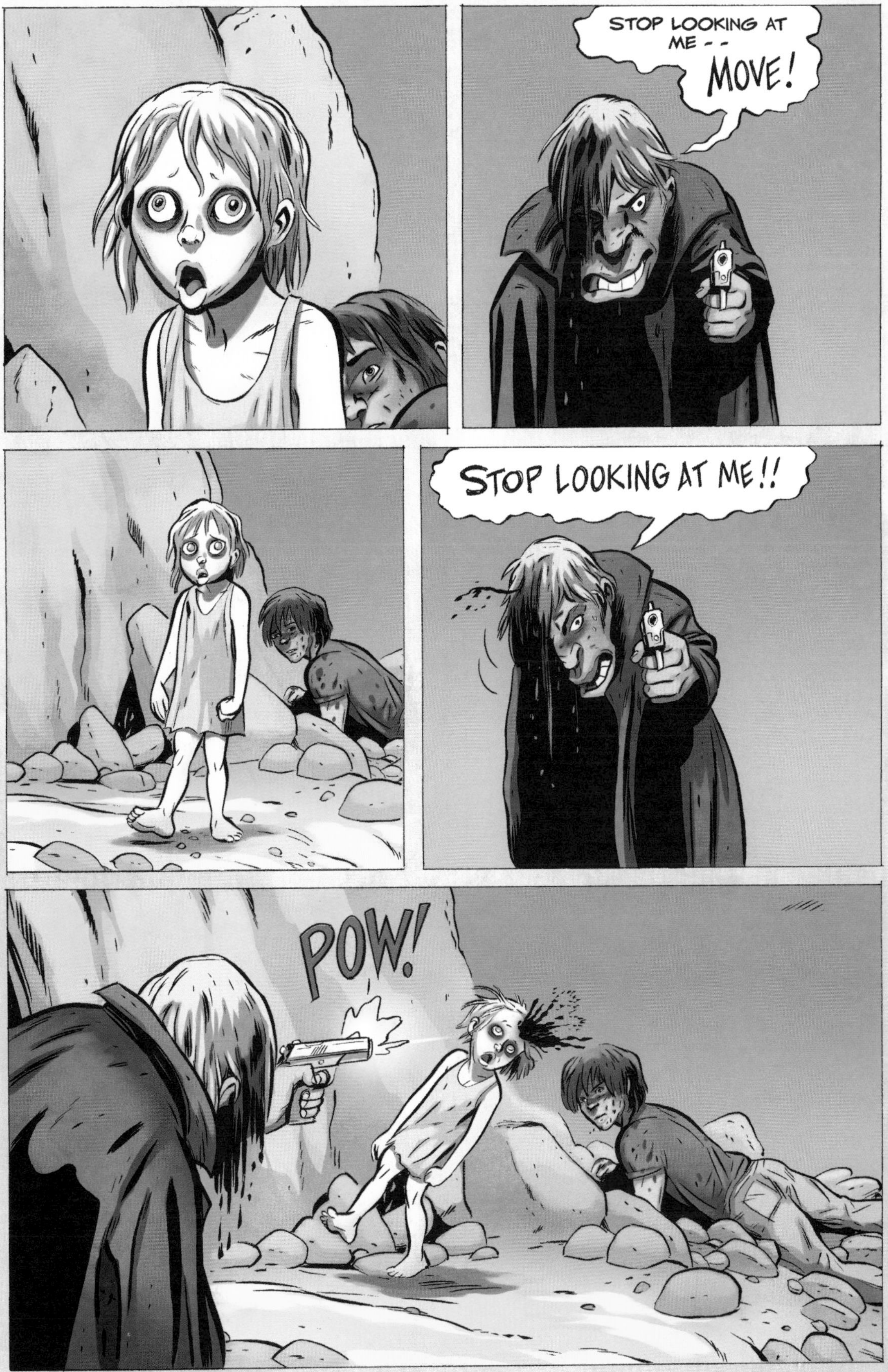
STOP LOOKING AT ME - - MOVE!
STOP LOOKING AT ME!!
POW!

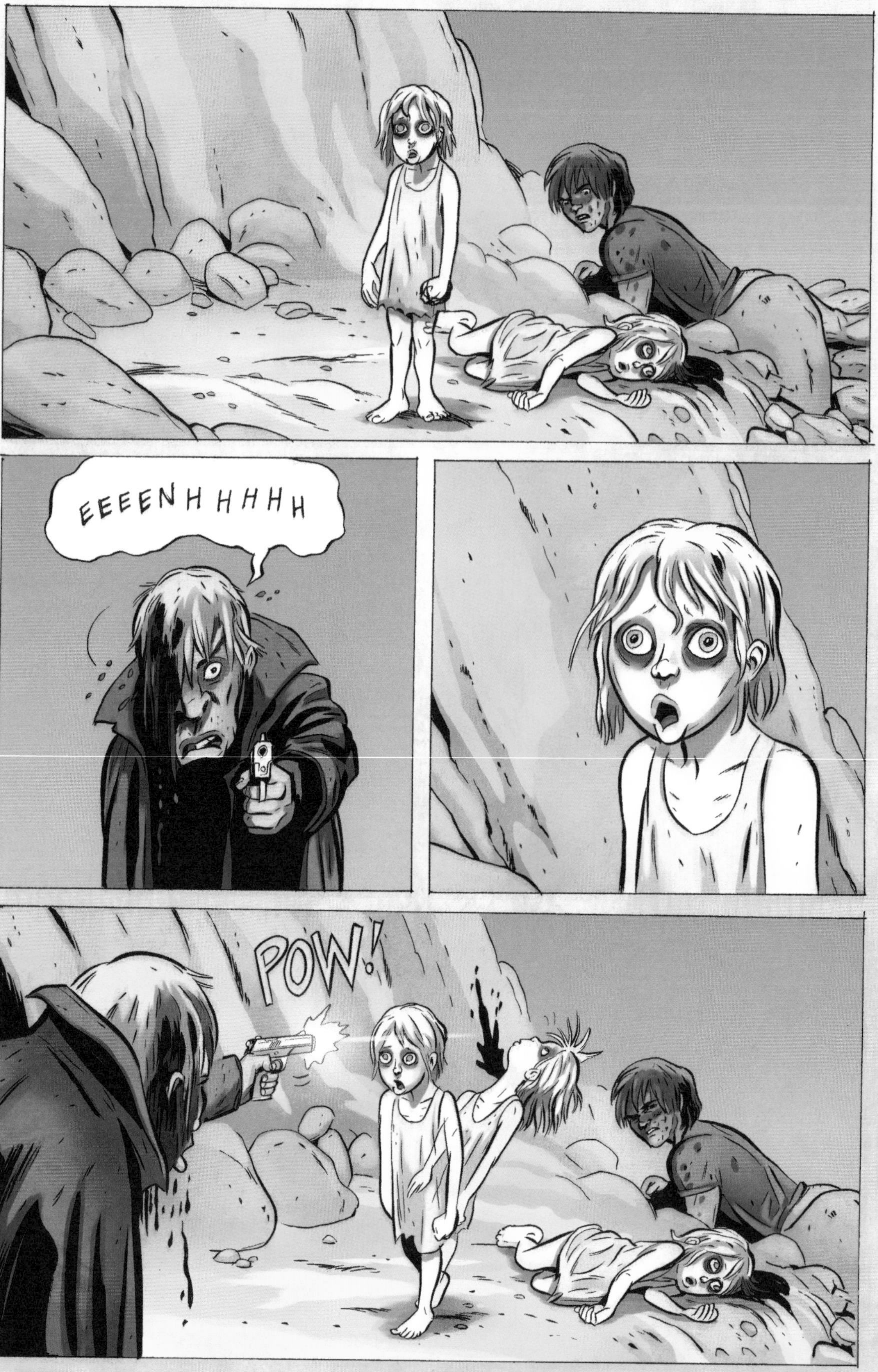
EEEENHHHHH
POW!

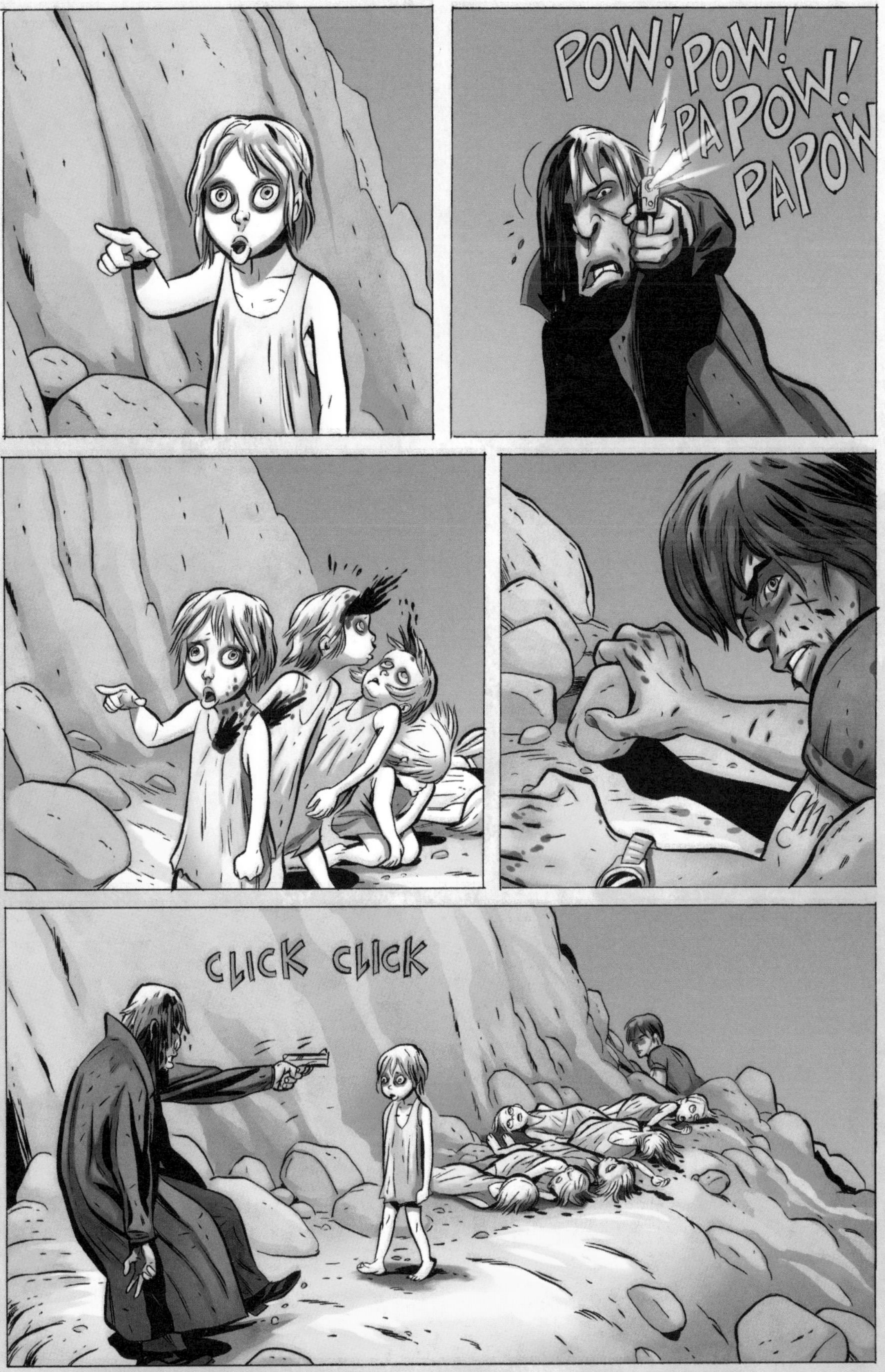
POW! POW!
PAPOW!
PAPOW
CLICK CLICK

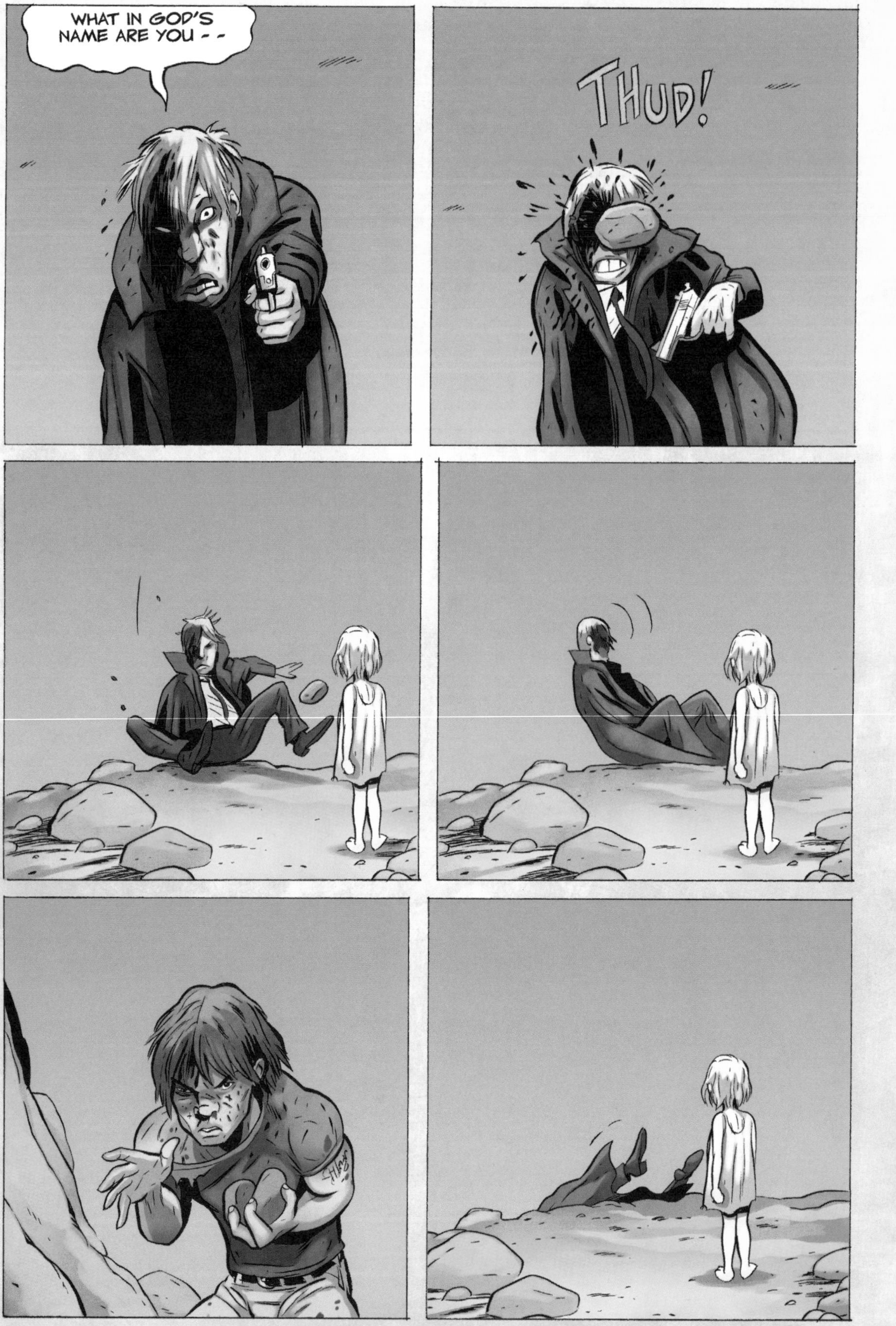
WHAT IN GOD'S NAME ARE YOU - -
THUD!

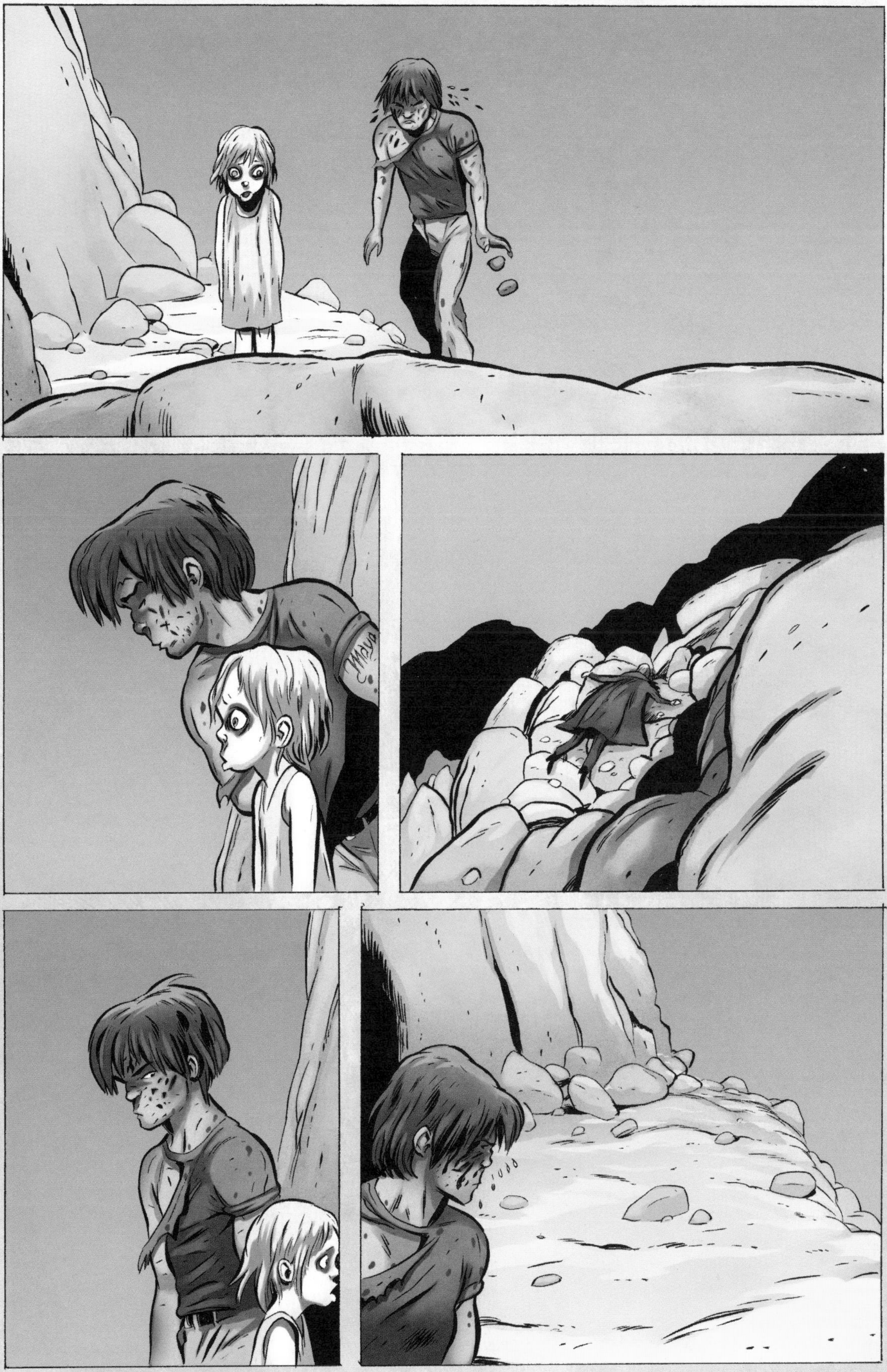

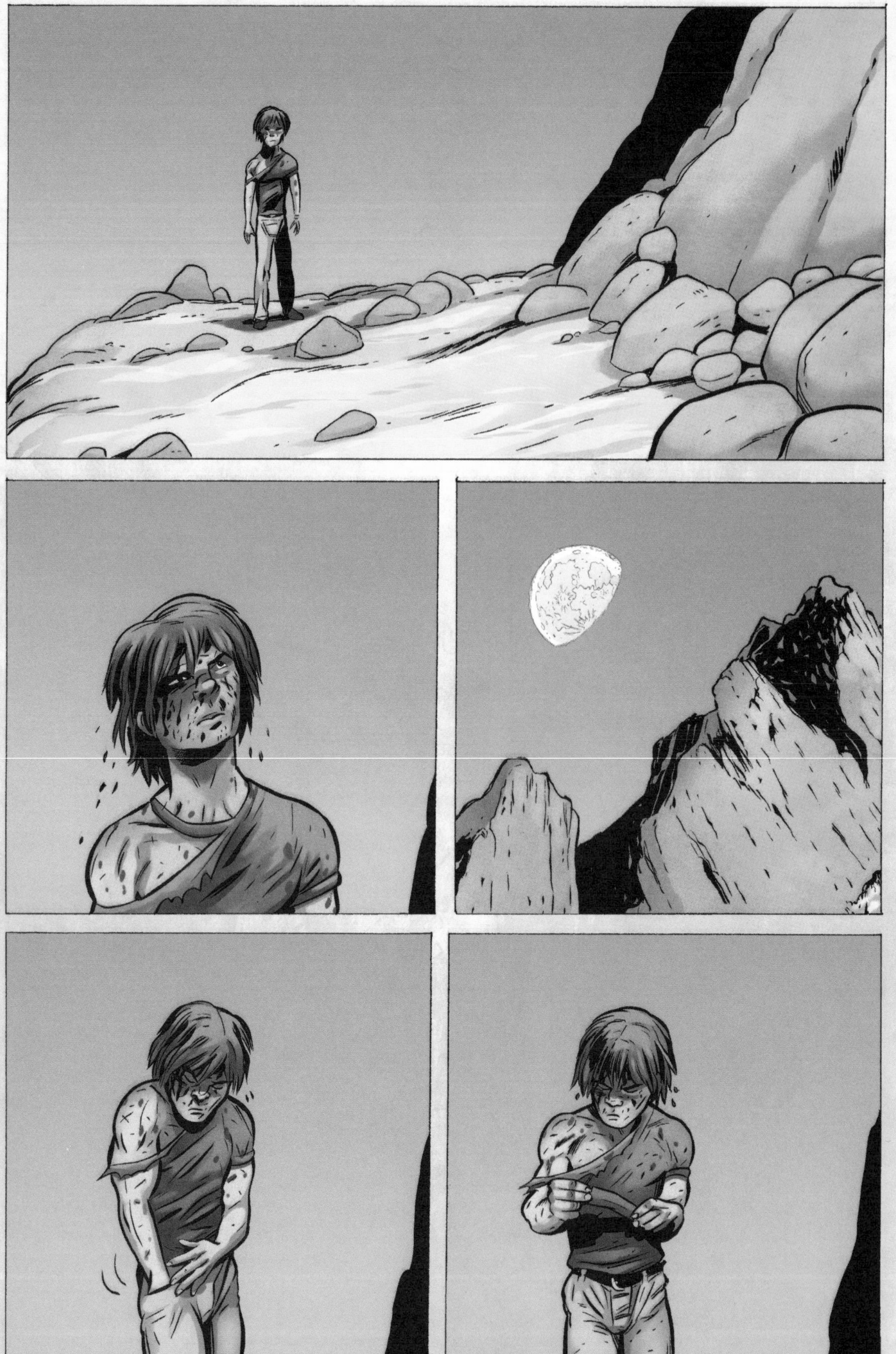

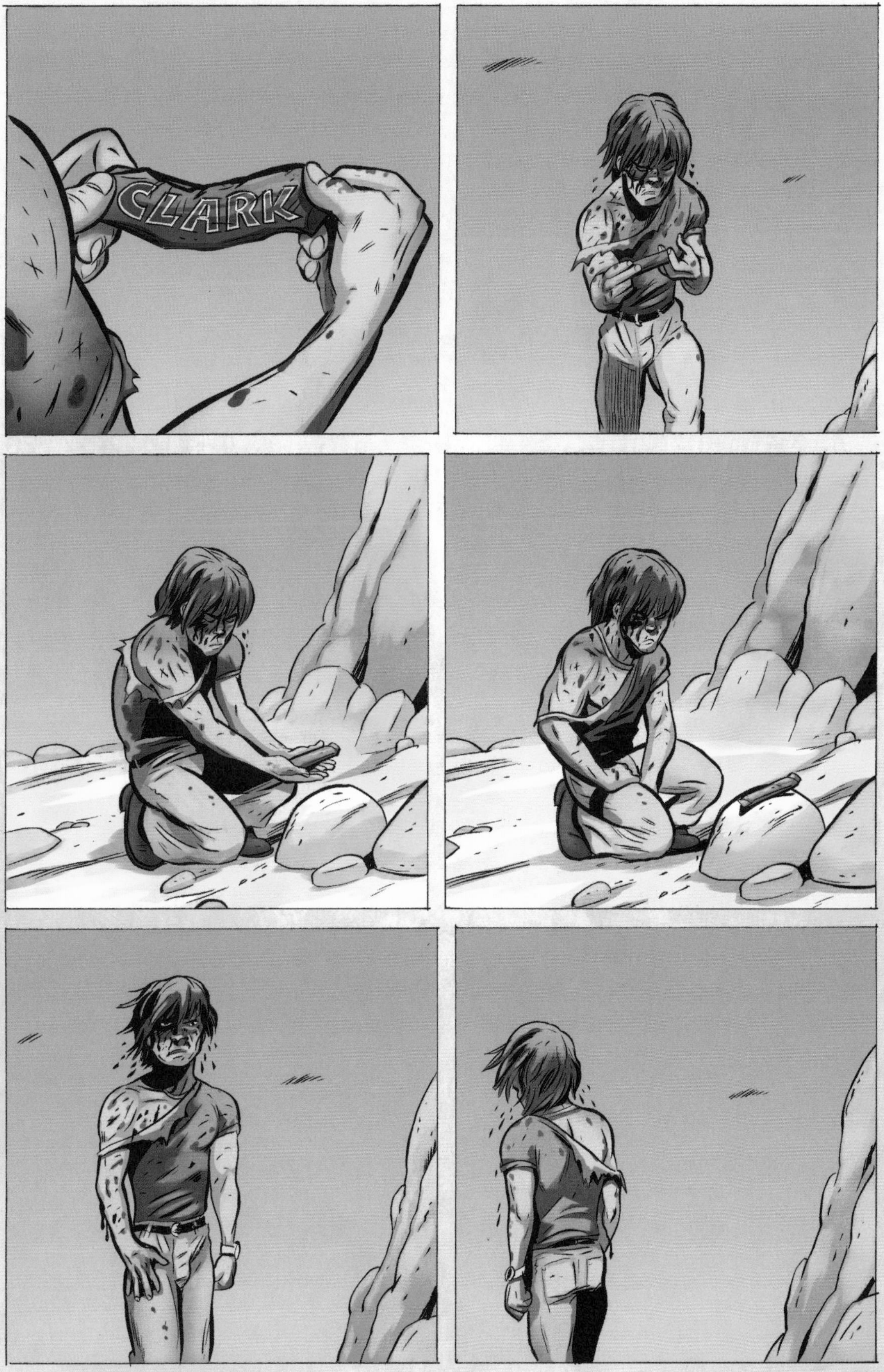
CLARK

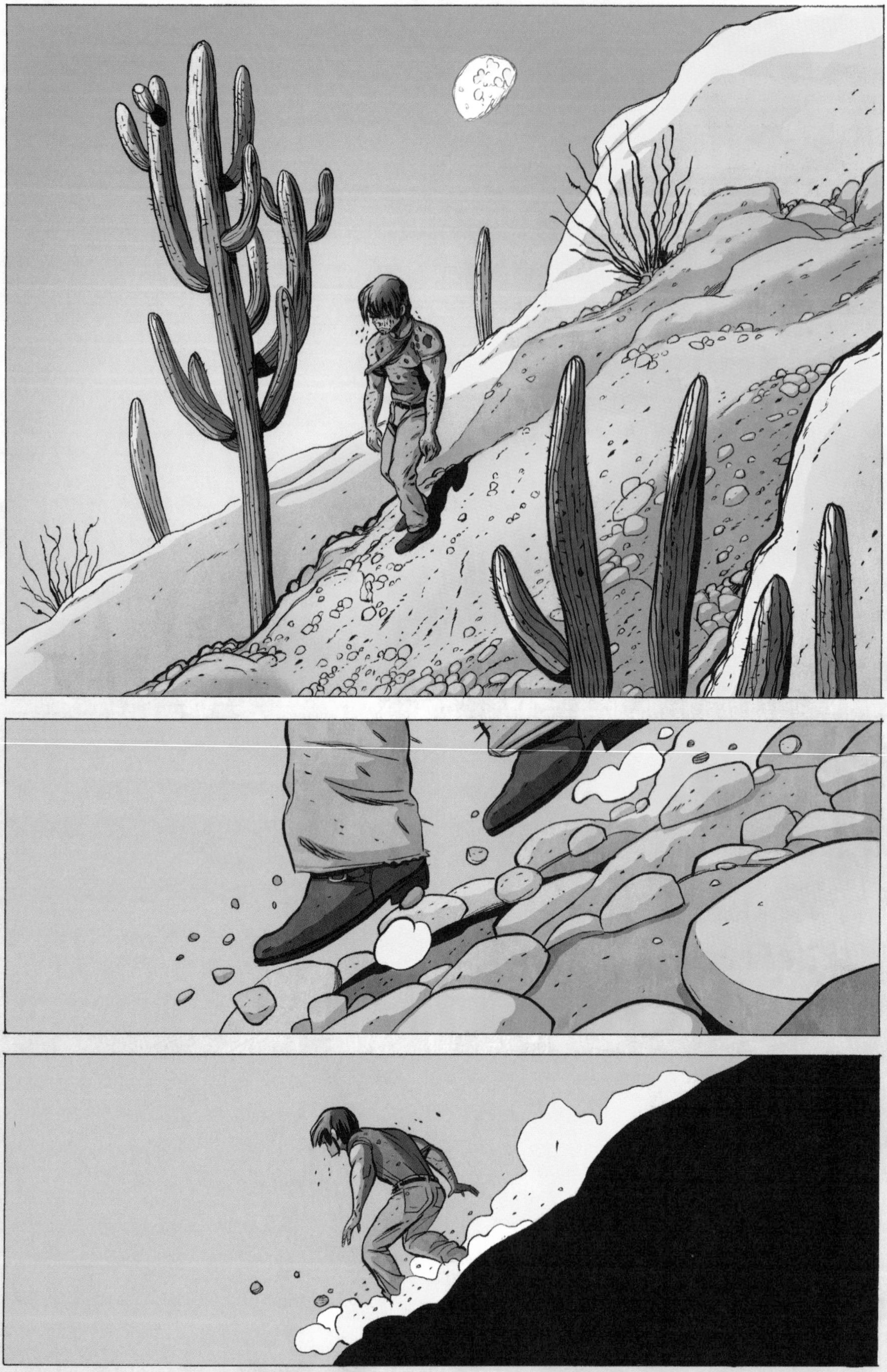

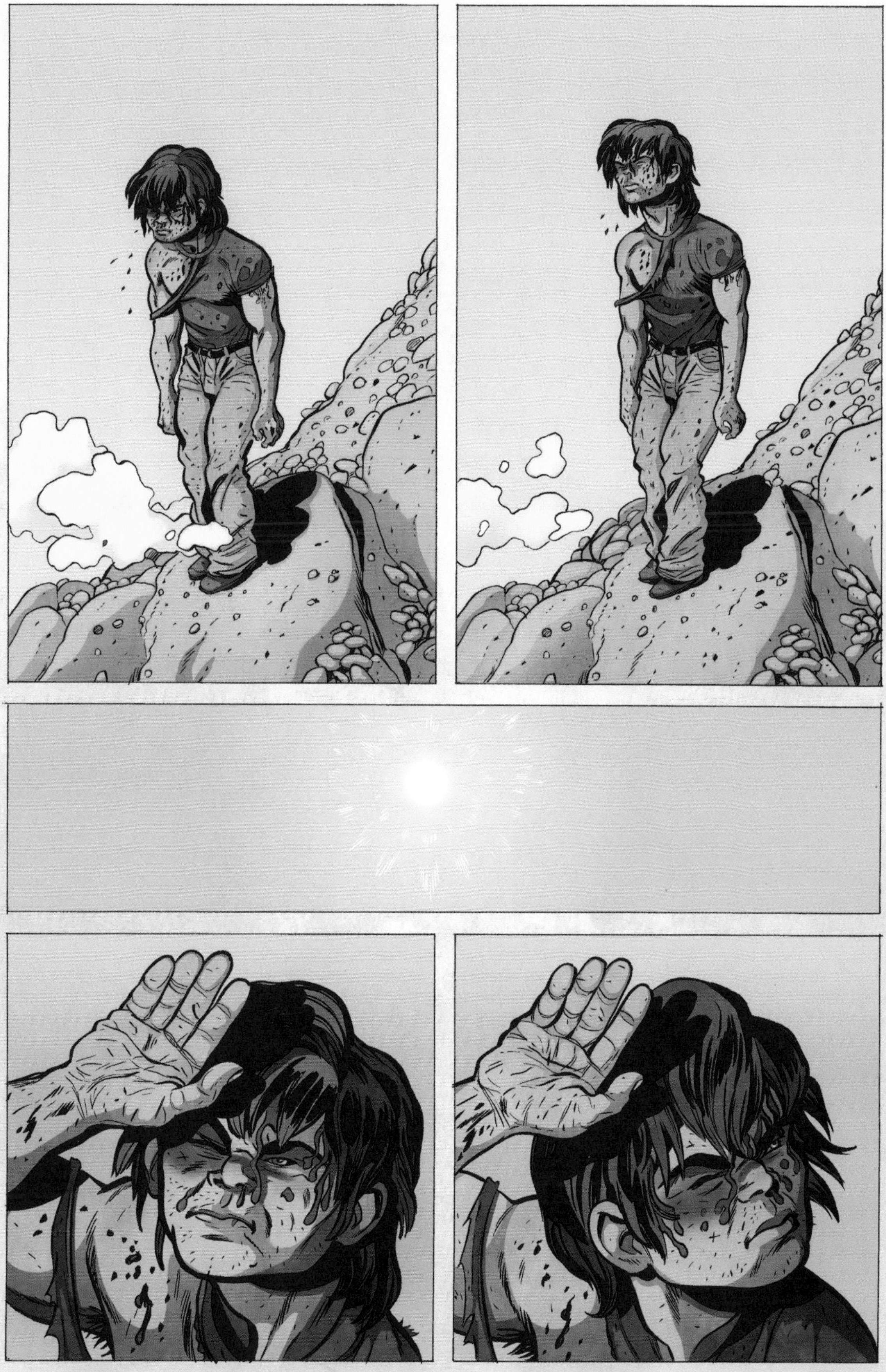

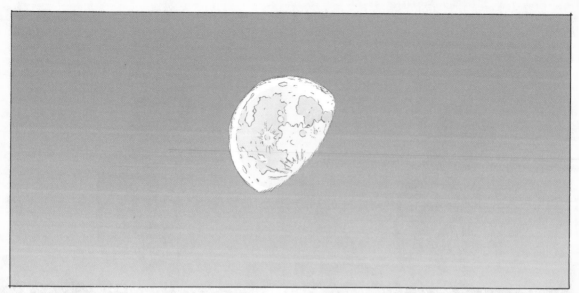

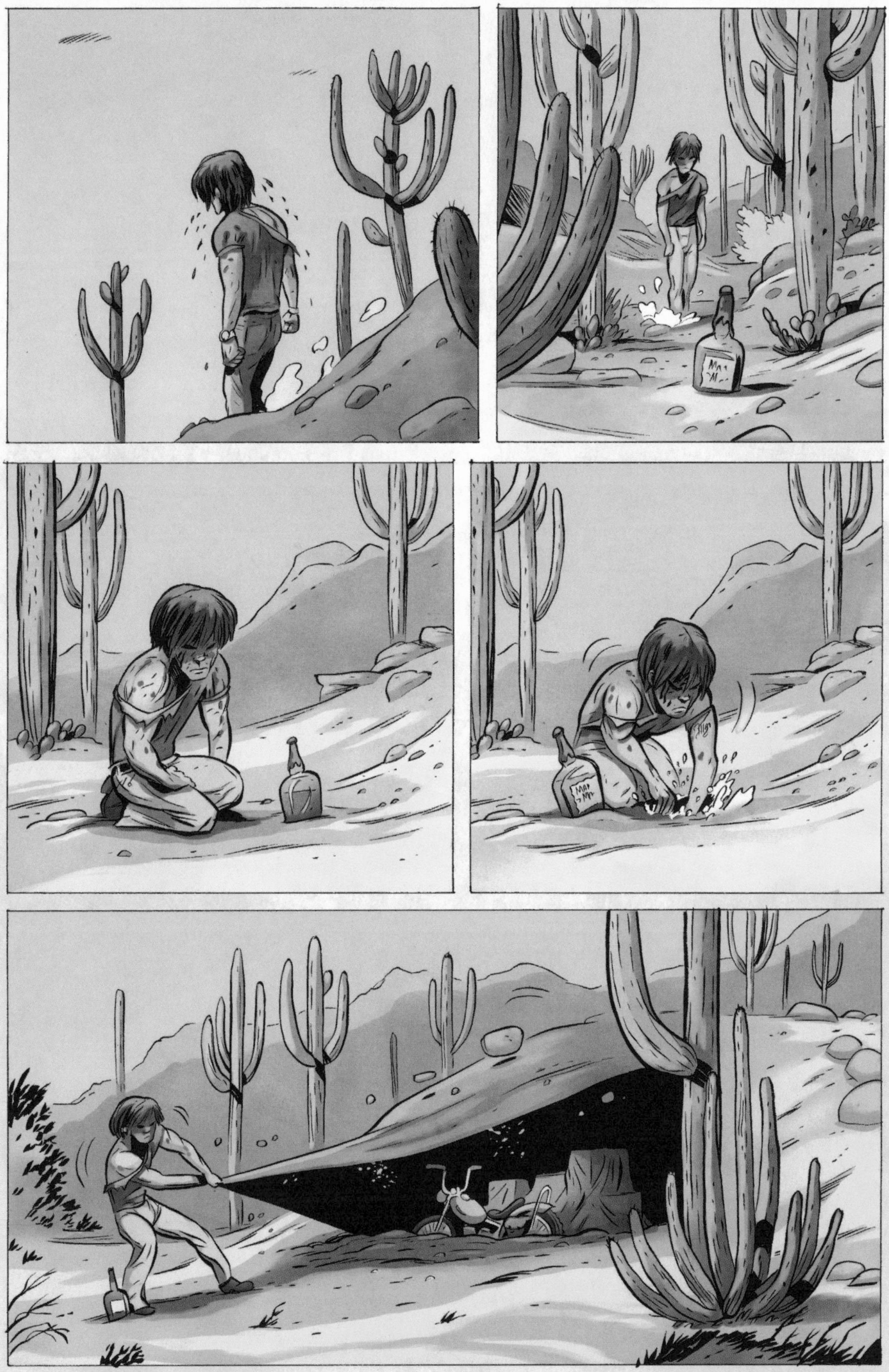

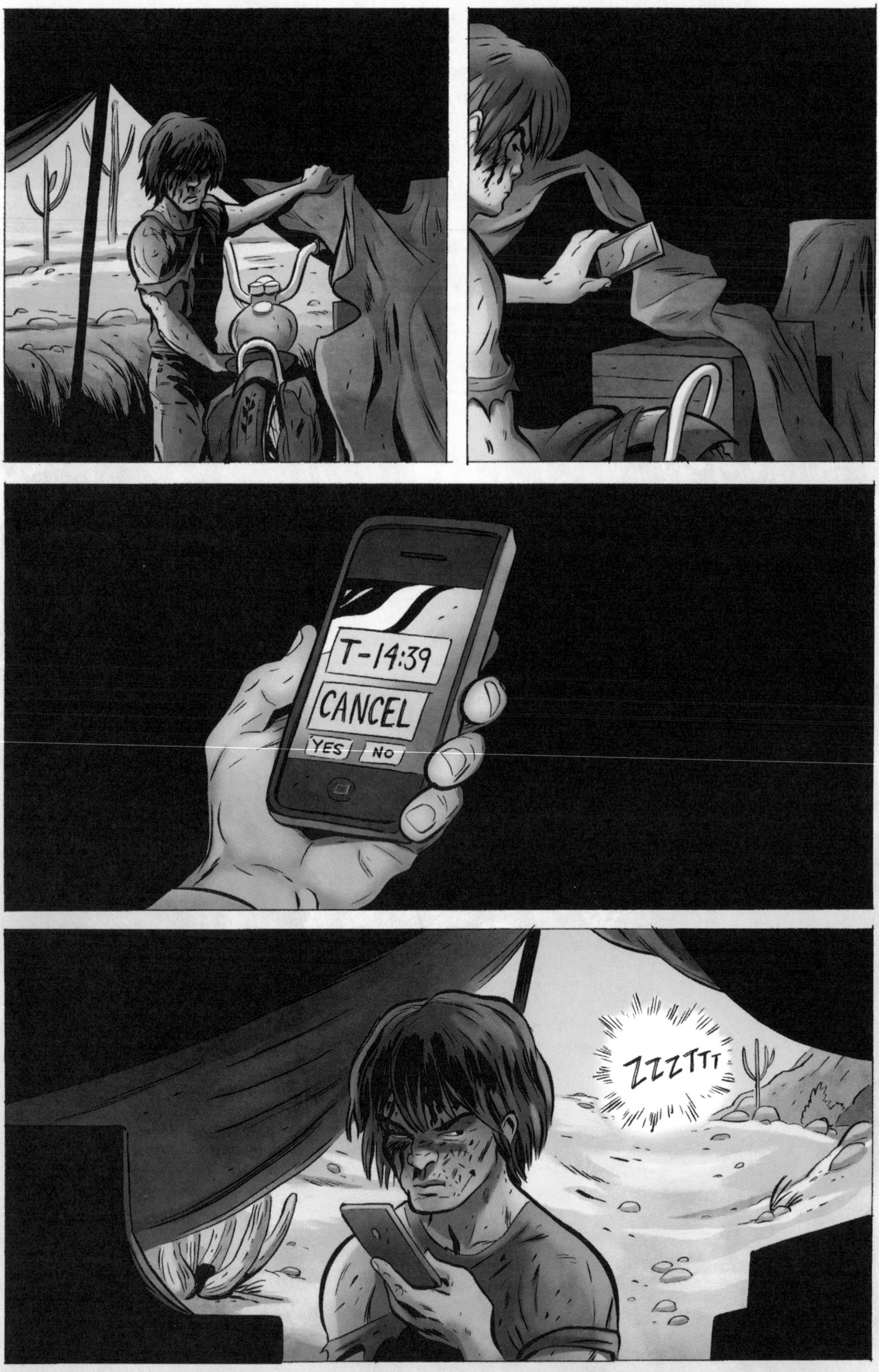
T-14:39
CANCEL
YES
NO
ZZZTTT

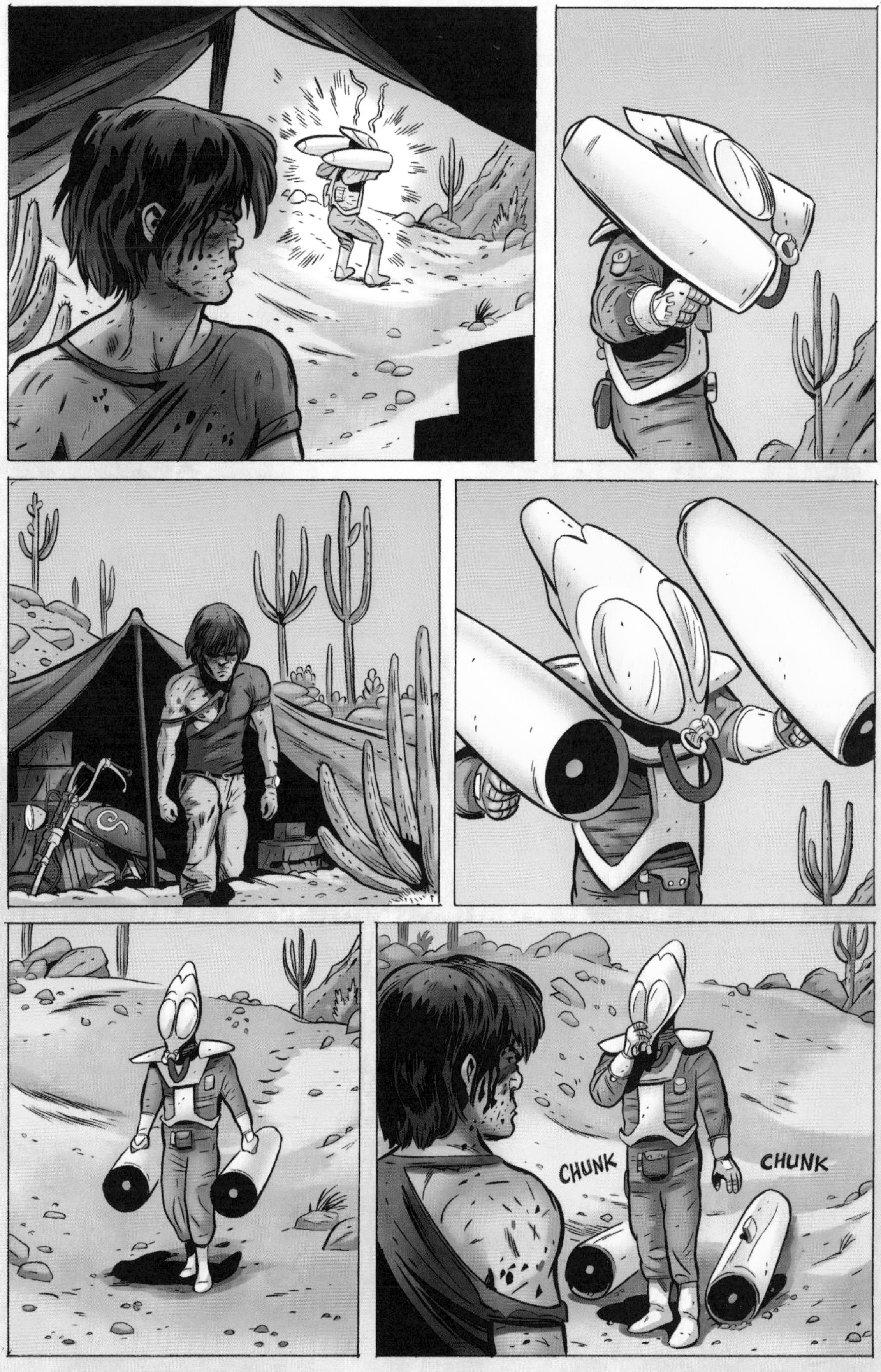
CHUNK
CHUNK

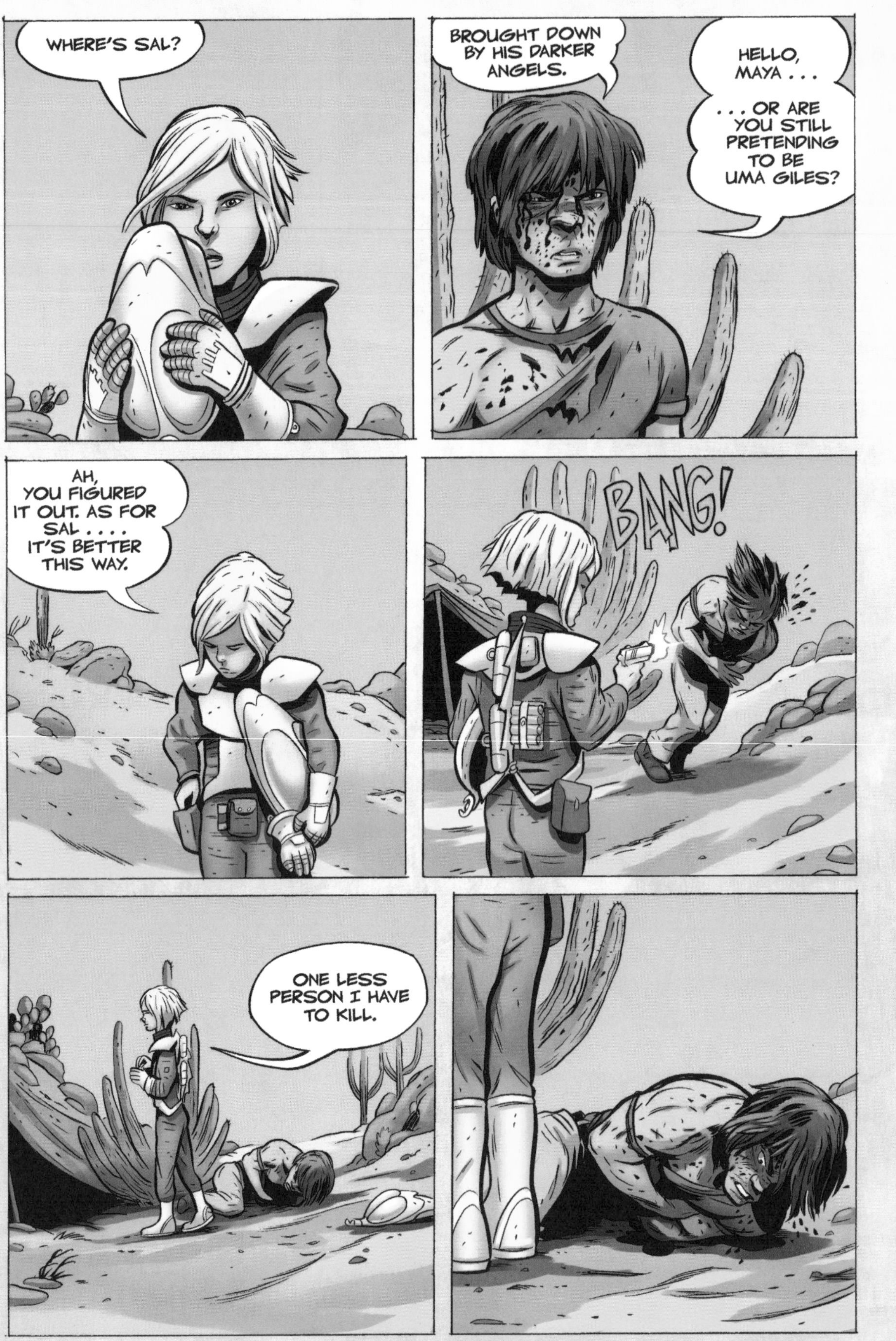
WHERE'S SAL?
BROUGHT DOWN BY HIS DARKER ANGELS.
HELLO, MAYA . . .
. . . OR ARE YOU STILL PRETENDING TO BE UMA GILES?
AH, YOU FIGURED IT OUT. AS FOR SAL . . . . IT'S BETTER THIS WAY.
BANG!
ONE LESS PERSON I HAVE TO KILL.

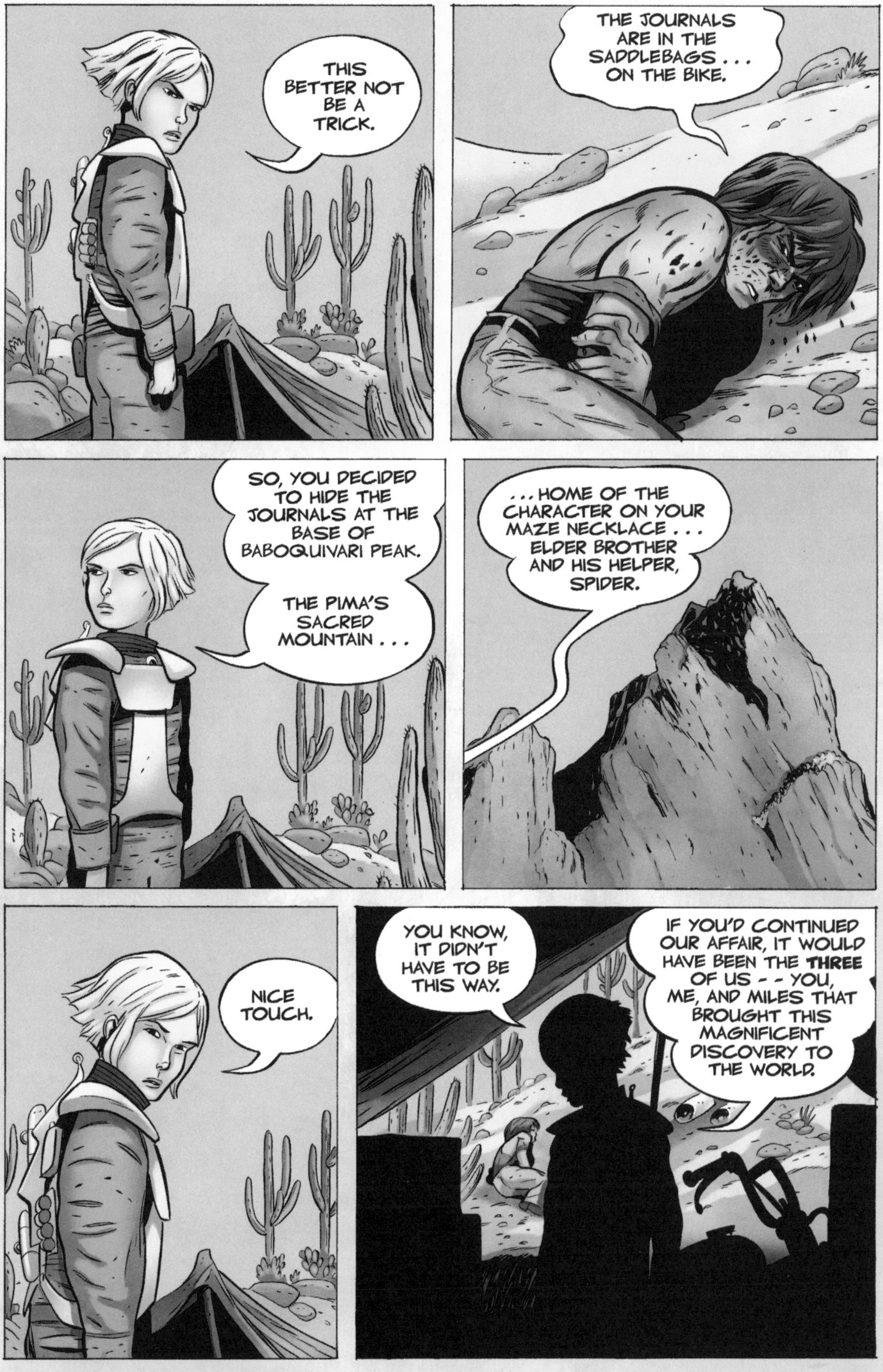
THIS BETTER NOT BE A TRICK.
THE JOURNALS ARE IN THE SADDLEBAGS . . . ON THE BIKE.
SO, YOU DECIDED TO HIDE THE JOURNALS AT THE BASE OF BABOQUIVARI PEAK.
THE PIMA'S SACRED MOUNTAIN . . .
. . . HOME OF THE CHARACTER ON YOUR MAZE NECKLACE . . . ELDER BROTHER AND HIS HELPER, SPIDER.
NICE TOUCH.
YOU KNOW, IT DIDN'T HAVE TO BE THIS WAY.
IF YOU'D CONTINUED OUR AFFAIR, IT WOULD HAVE BEEN THE **THREE** OF US - - YOU, ME, AND MILES THAT BROUGHT THIS MAGNIFICENT DISCOVERY TO THE WORLD.

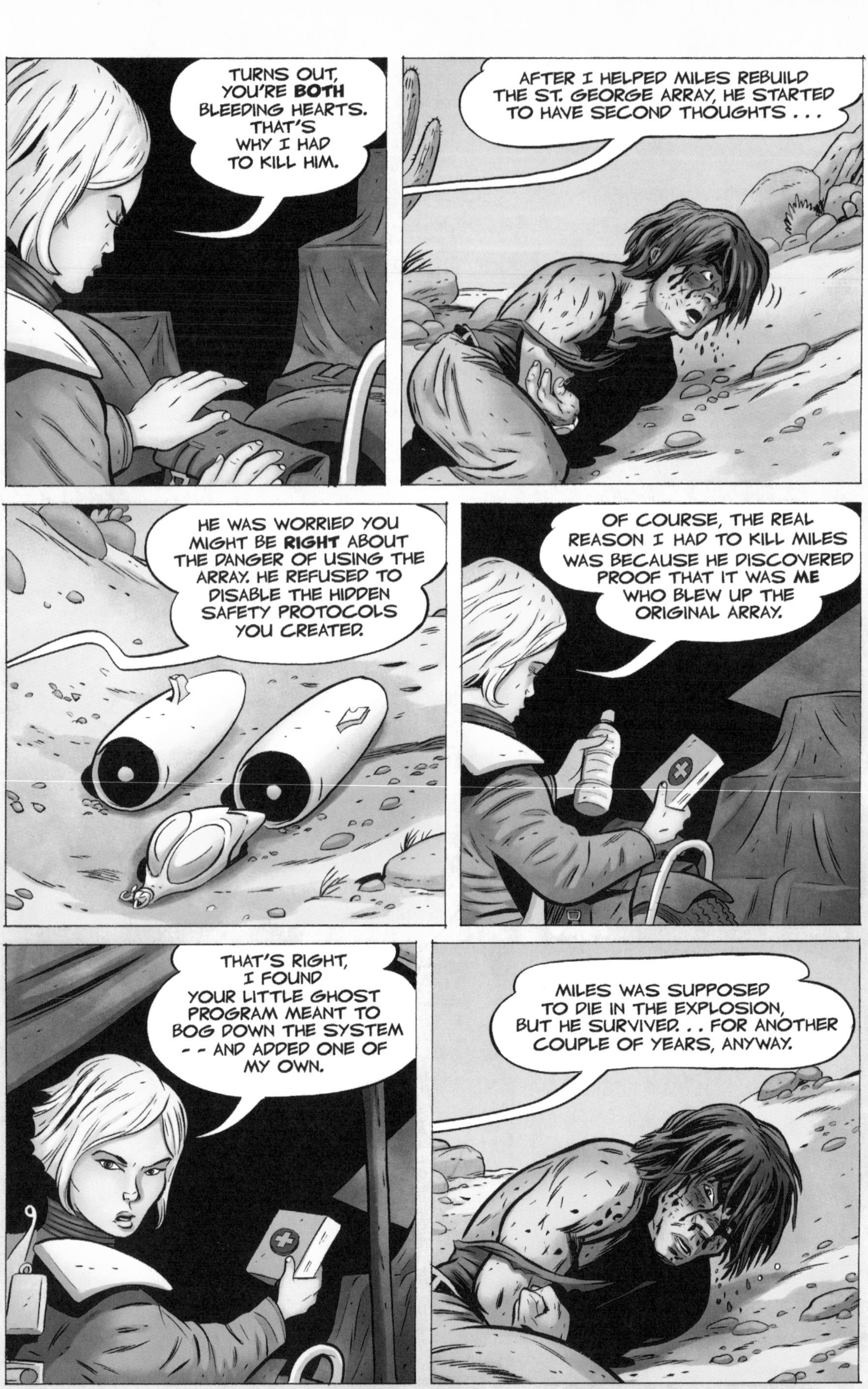
TURNS OUT, YOU'RE **BOTH** BLEEDING HEARTS. THAT'S WHY I HAD TO KILL HIM.
AFTER I HELPED MILES REBUILD THE ST. GEORGE ARRAY, HE STARTED TO HAVE SECOND THOUGHTS . . .
HE WAS WORRIED YOU MIGHT BE **RIGHT** ABOUT THE DANGER OF USING THE ARRAY. HE REFUSED TO DISABLE THE HIDDEN SAFETY PROTOCOLS YOU CREATED.
OF COURSE, THE REAL REASON I HAD TO KILL MILES WAS BECAUSE HE DISCOVERED PROOF THAT IT WAS **ME** WHO BLEW UP THE ORIGINAL ARRAY.
THAT'S RIGHT, I FOUND YOUR LITTLE GHOST PROGRAM MEANT TO BOG DOWN THE SYSTEM - - AND ADDED ONE OF MY OWN.
MILES WAS SUPPOSED TO DIE IN THE EXPLOSION, BUT HE SURVIVED. . . FOR ANOTHER COUPLE OF YEARS, ANYWAY.

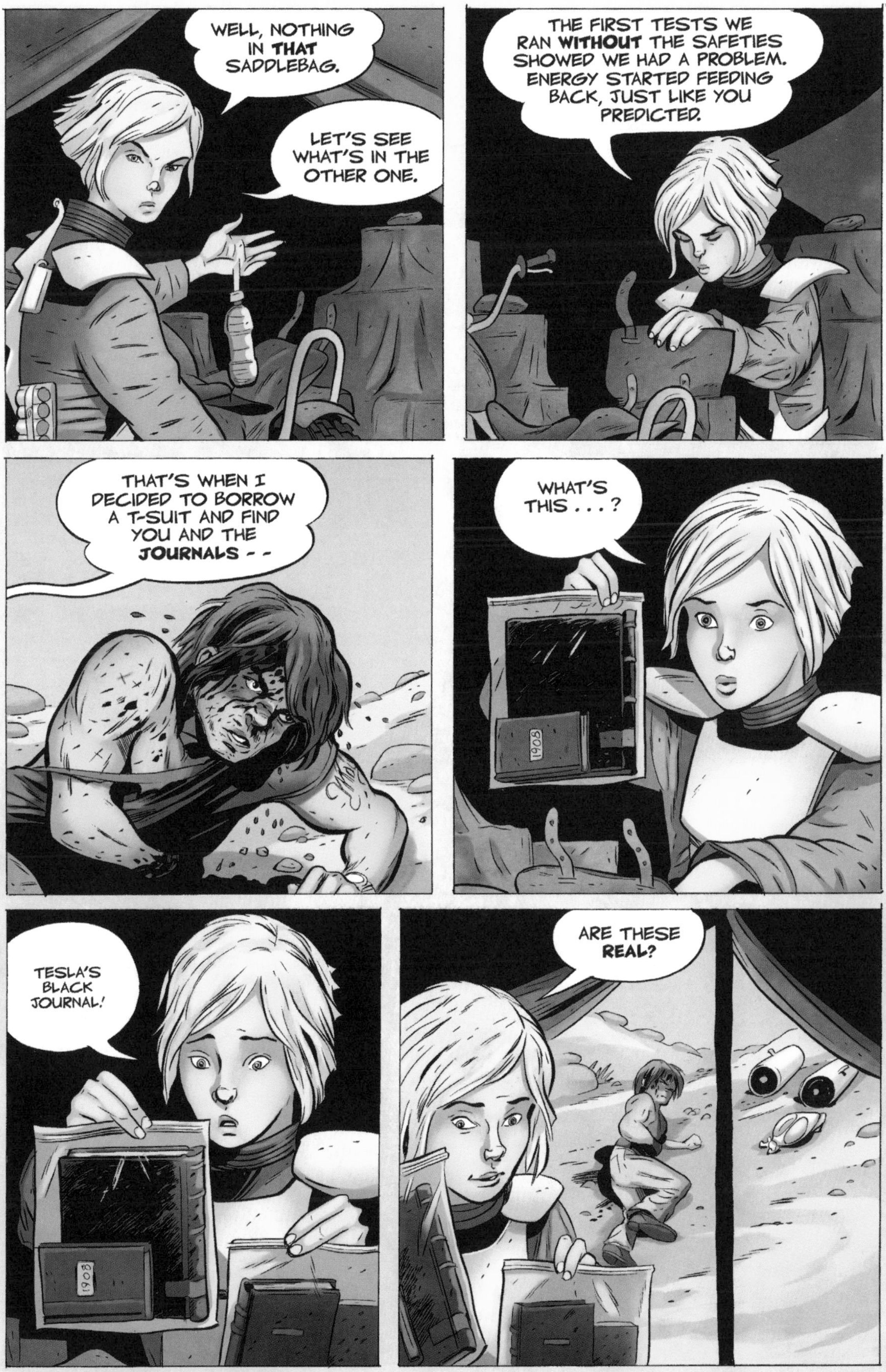
WELL, NOTHING IN THAT SADDLEBAG.
LET'S SEE WHAT'S IN THE OTHER ONE.
THE FIRST TESTS WE RAN WITHOUT THE SAFETIES SHOWED WE HAD A PROBLEM. ENERGY STARTED FEEDING BACK, JUST LIKE YOU PREDICTED.
THAT'S WHEN I DECIDED TO BORROW A T-SUIT AND FIND YOU AND THE JOURNALS - -
WHAT'S THIS . . . ?
1908
TESLA'S BLACK JOURNAL!
1908
ARE THESE REAL?

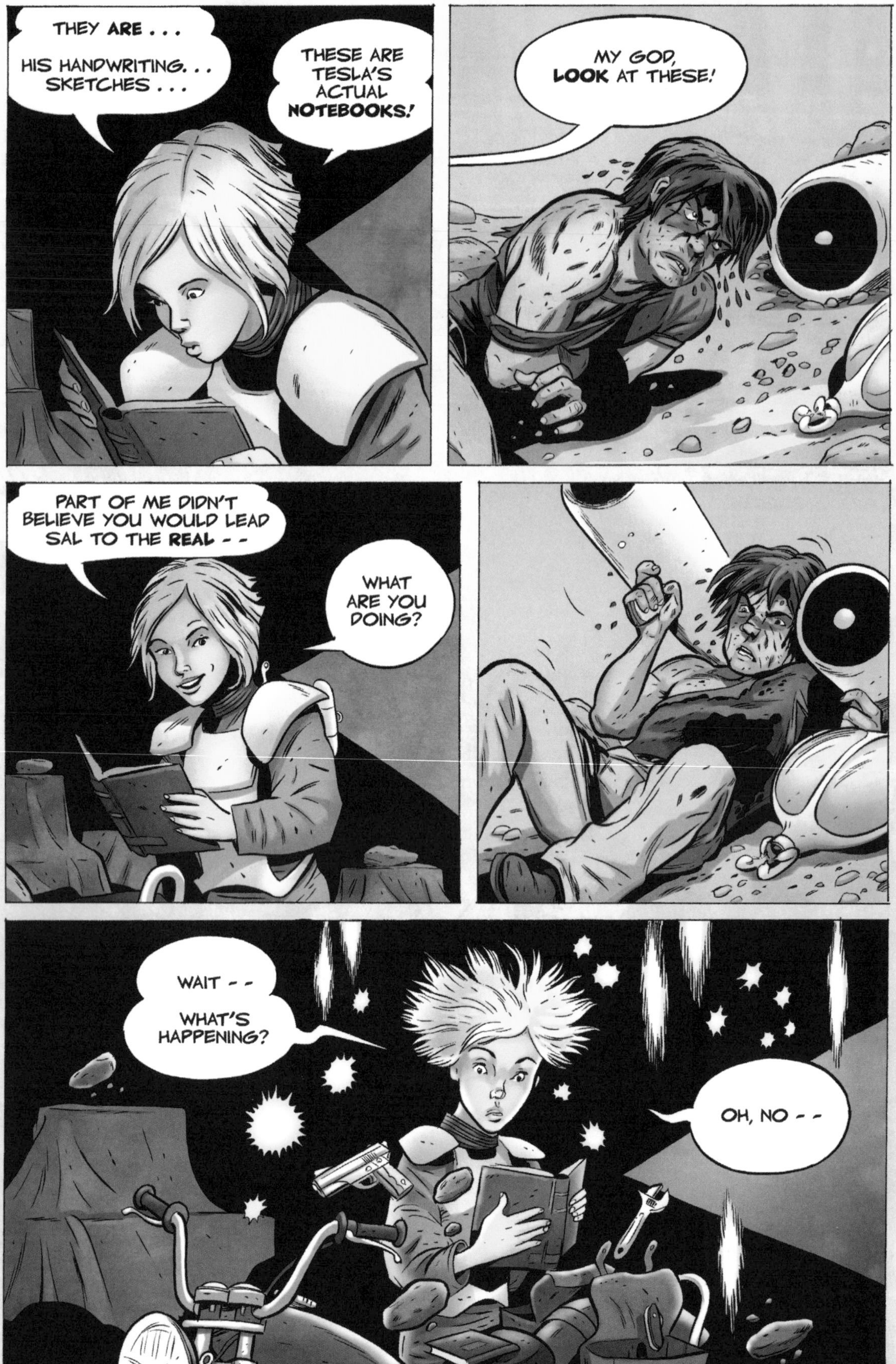
THEY **ARE** . . .
HIS HANDWRITING. . . SKETCHES . . .
THESE ARE TESLA'S ACTUAL **NOTEBOOKS!**
MY GOD, **LOOK** AT THESE!
PART OF ME DIDN'T BELIEVE YOU WOULD LEAD SAL TO THE **REAL** - -
WHAT ARE YOU DOING?
WAIT - -
WHAT'S HAPPENING?
OH, NO - -

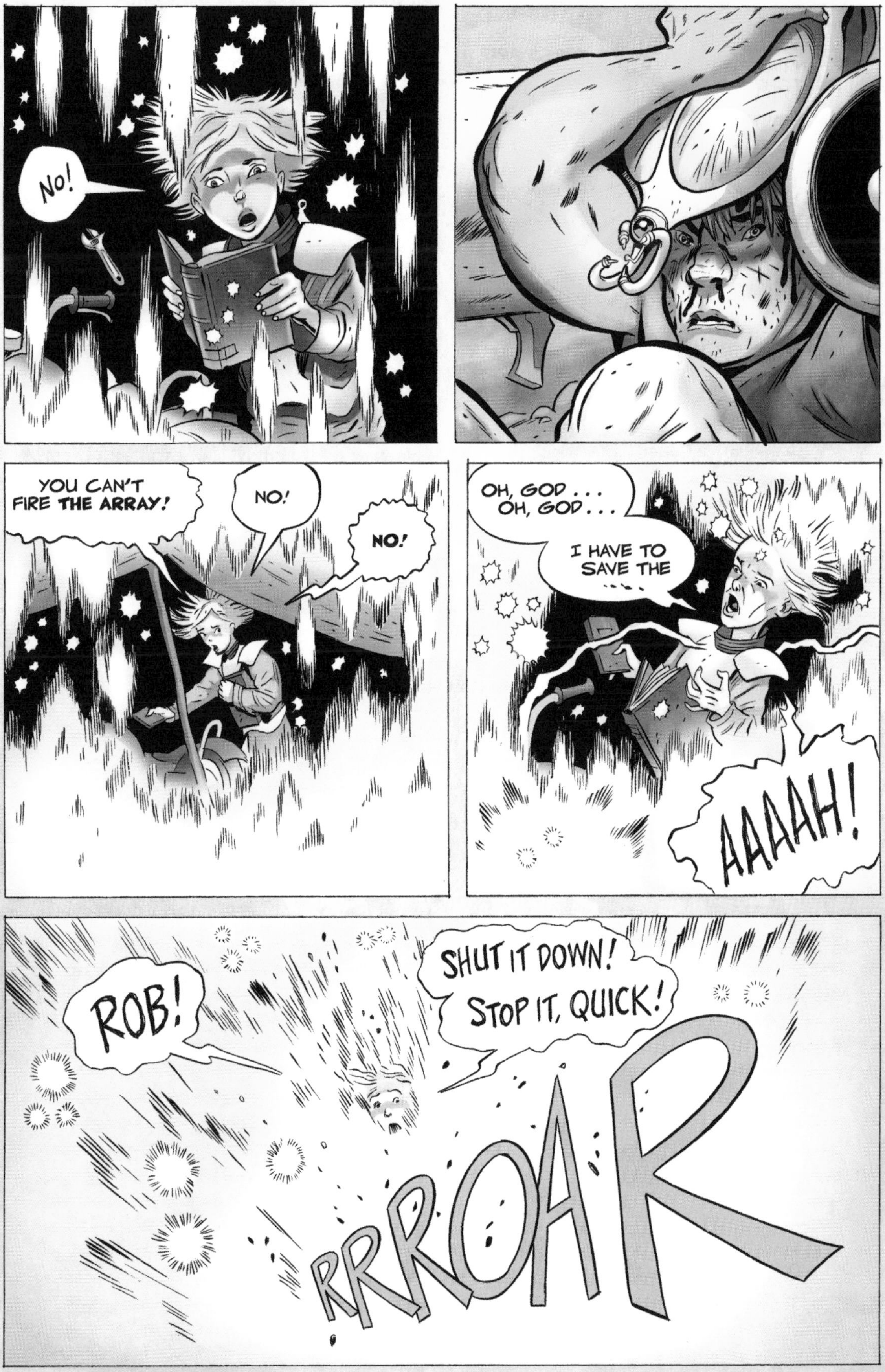

No!
YOU CAN'T FIRE THE ARRAY!
NO!
NO!
OH, GOD . . . OH, GOD . . .
I HAVE TO SAVE THE . . .
AAAAH!
ROB!
SHUT IT DOWN! STOP IT, QUICK!
RRROAR

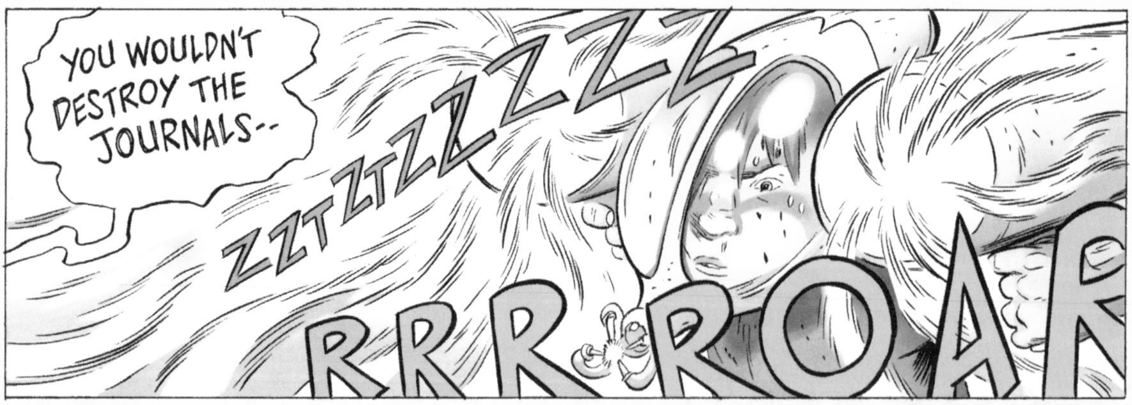
YOU WOULDN'T DESTROY THE JOURNALS--
ZZTZTZTZZZZZZZ
RRRROAR

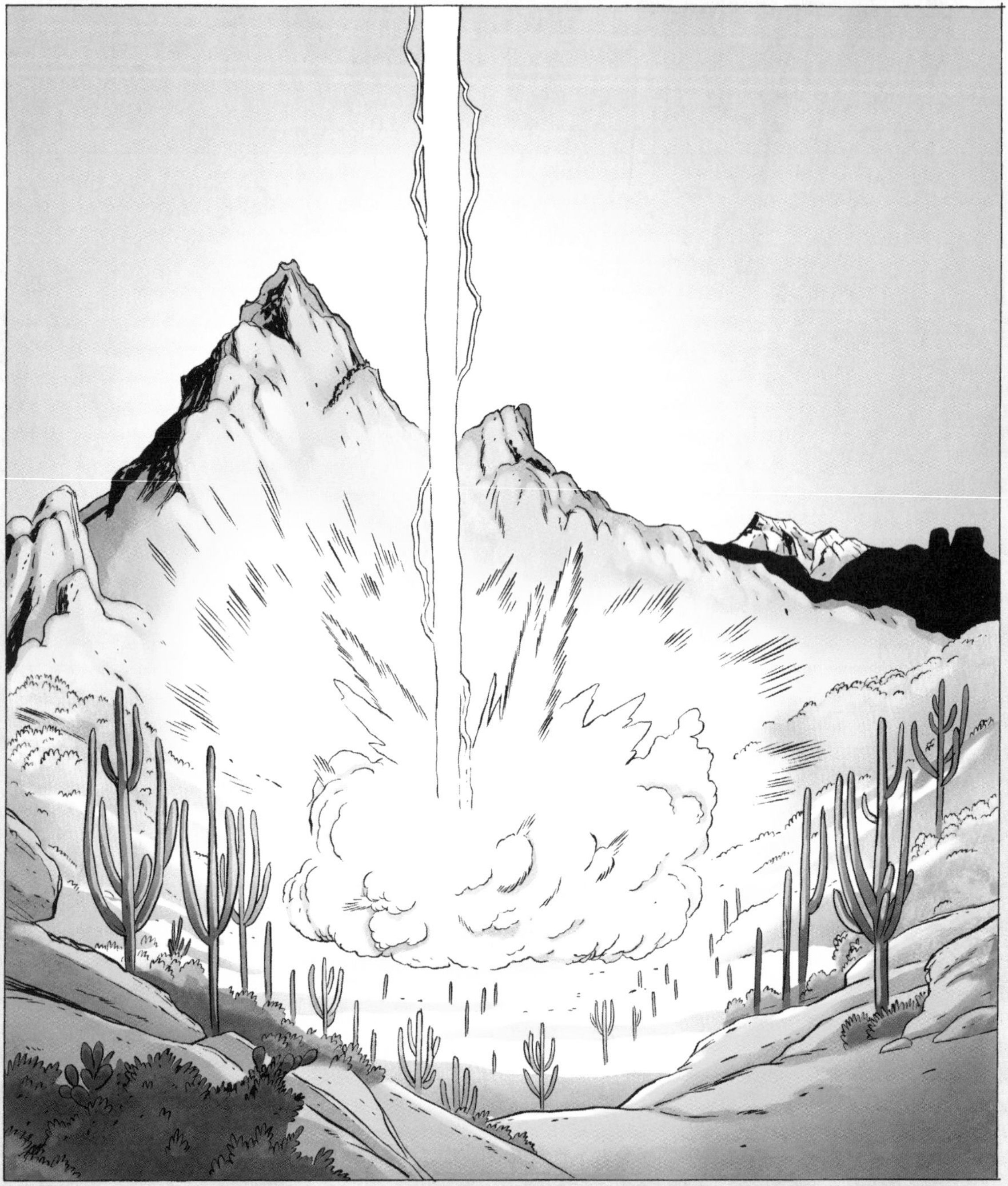

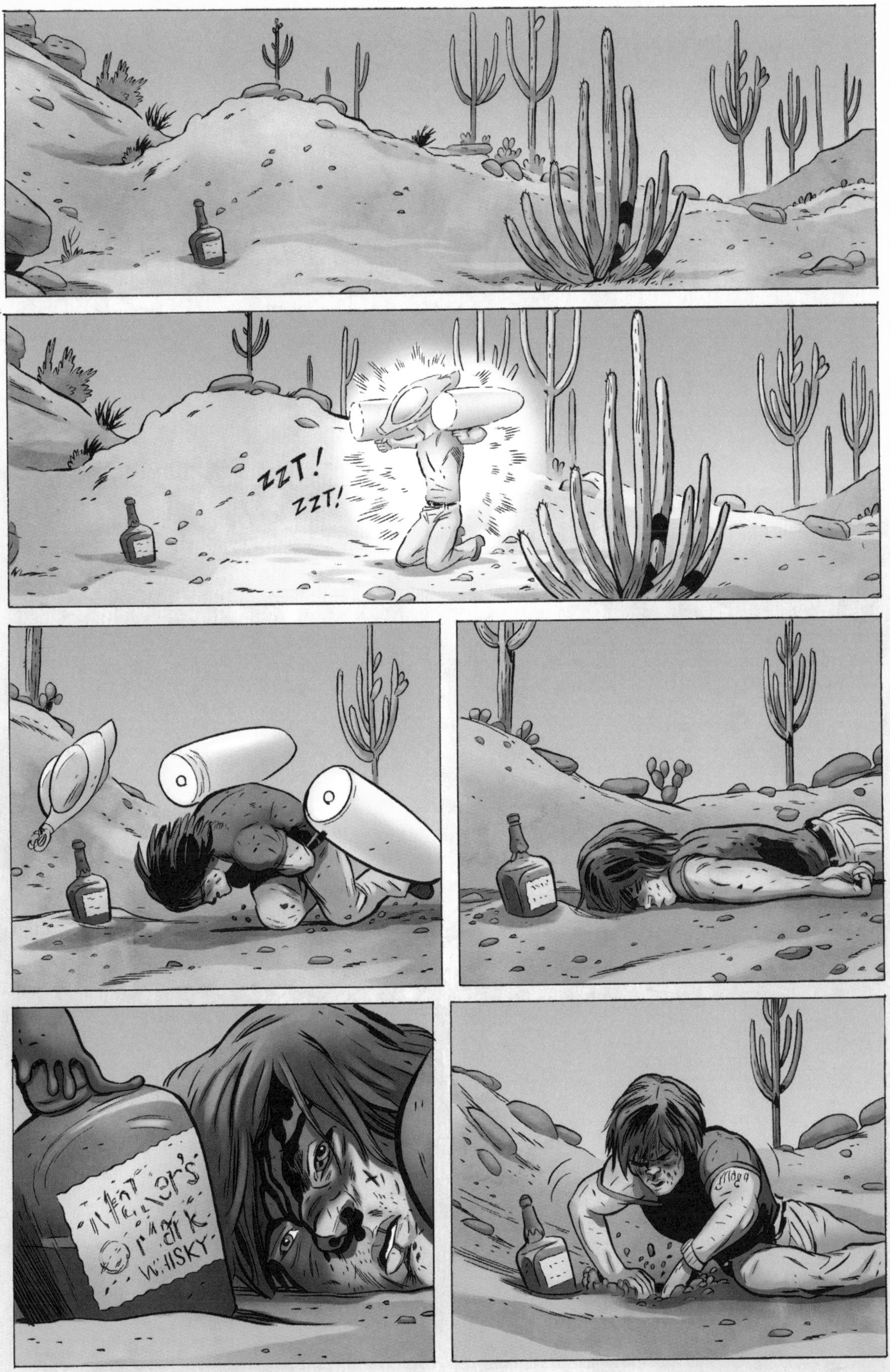
ZZT!
ZZT!

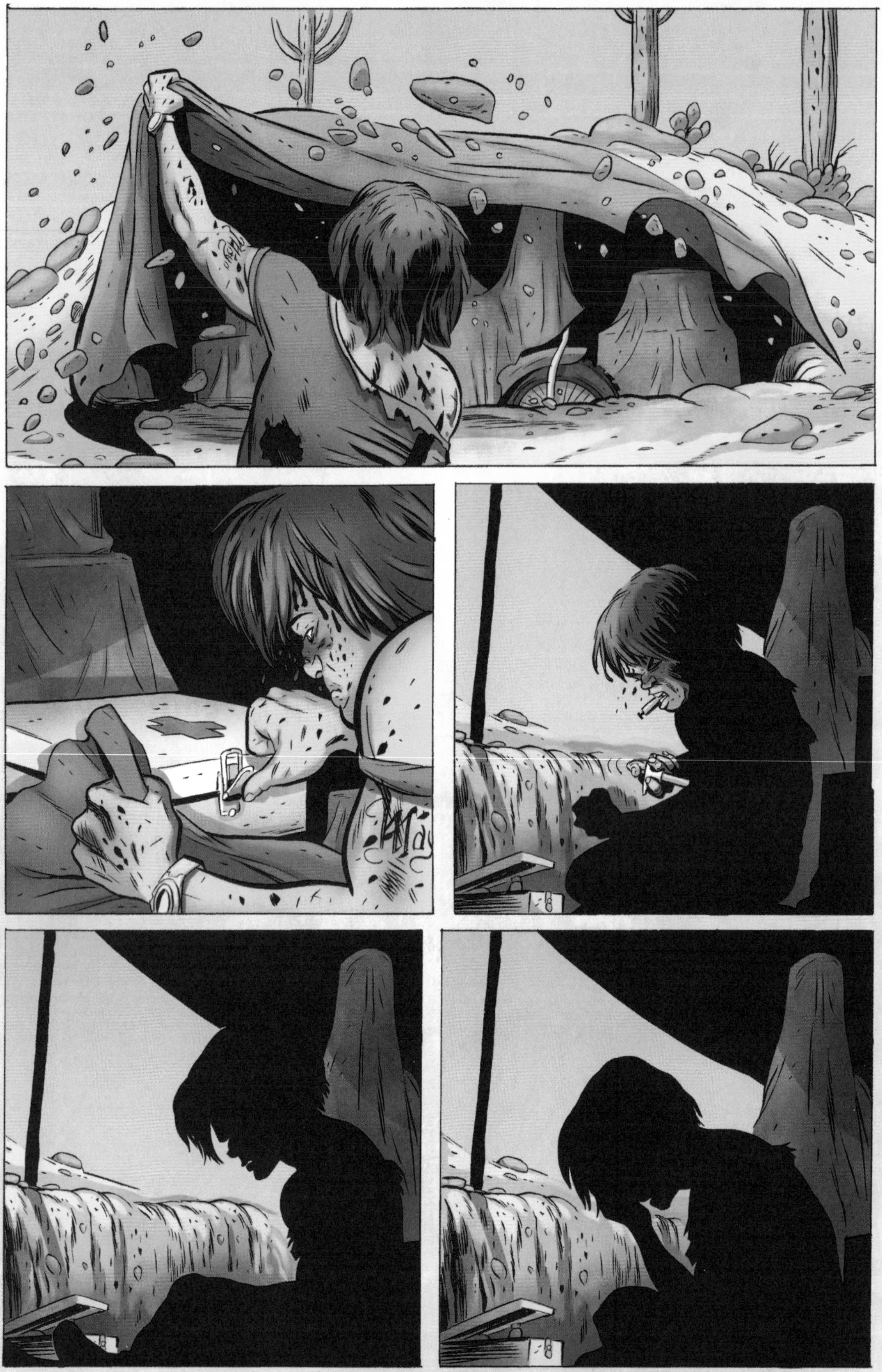

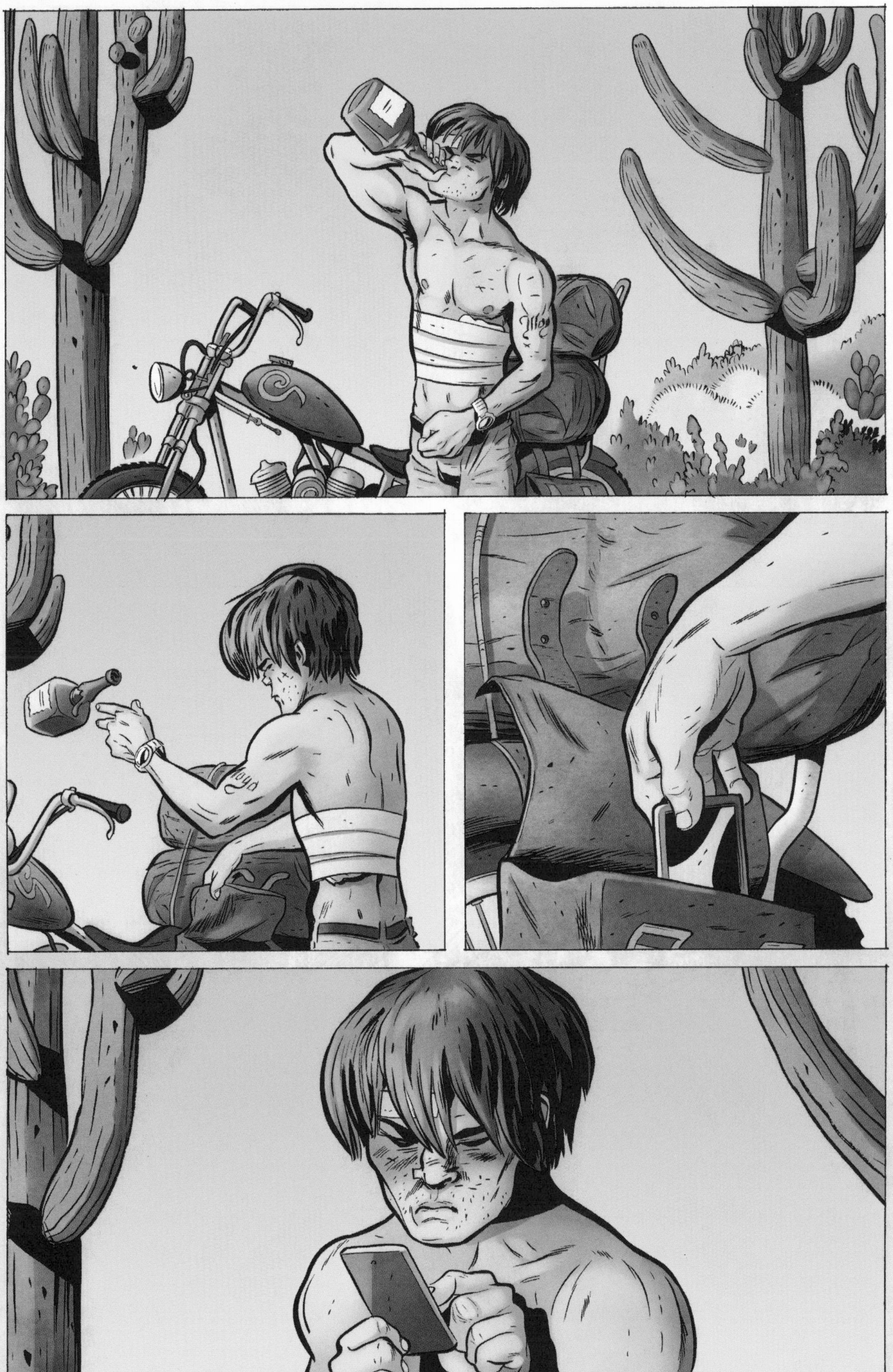

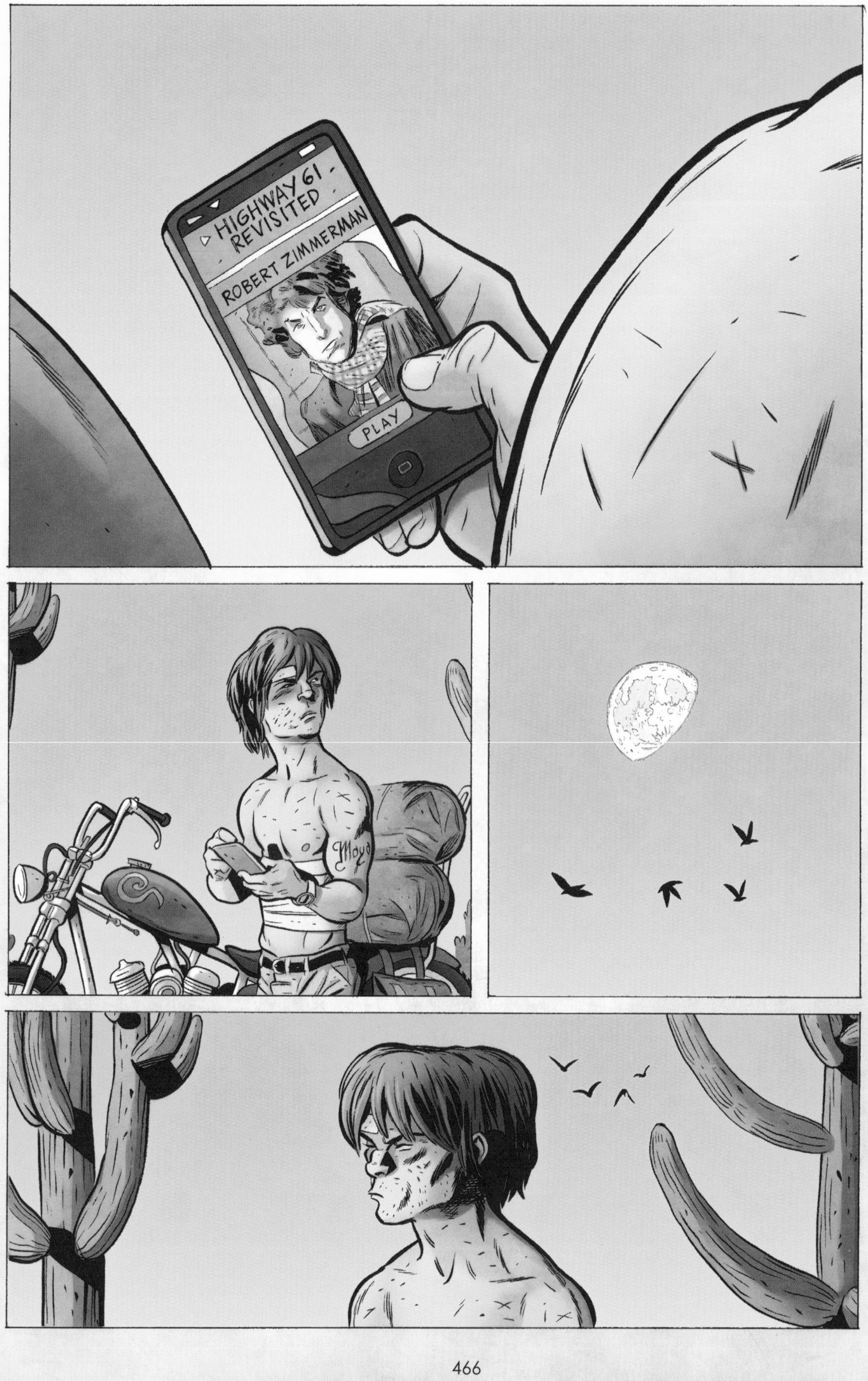
HIGHWAY 61
REVISITED
ROBERT ZIMMERMAN
PLAY

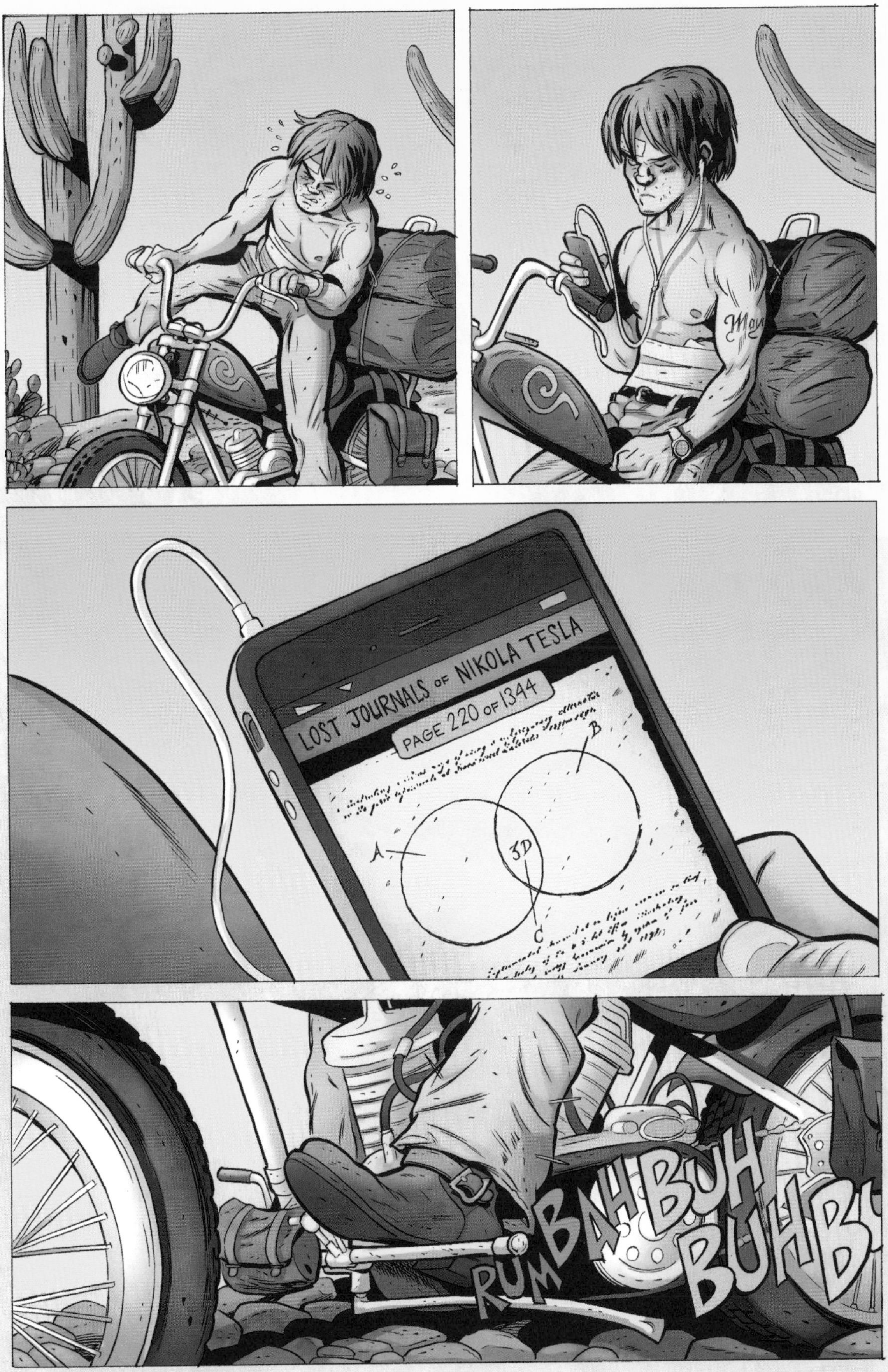
LOST JOURNALS OF NIKOLA TESLA
PAGE 220 OF 1344
A
B
C
3D
RUM BAH BUH BUH BU

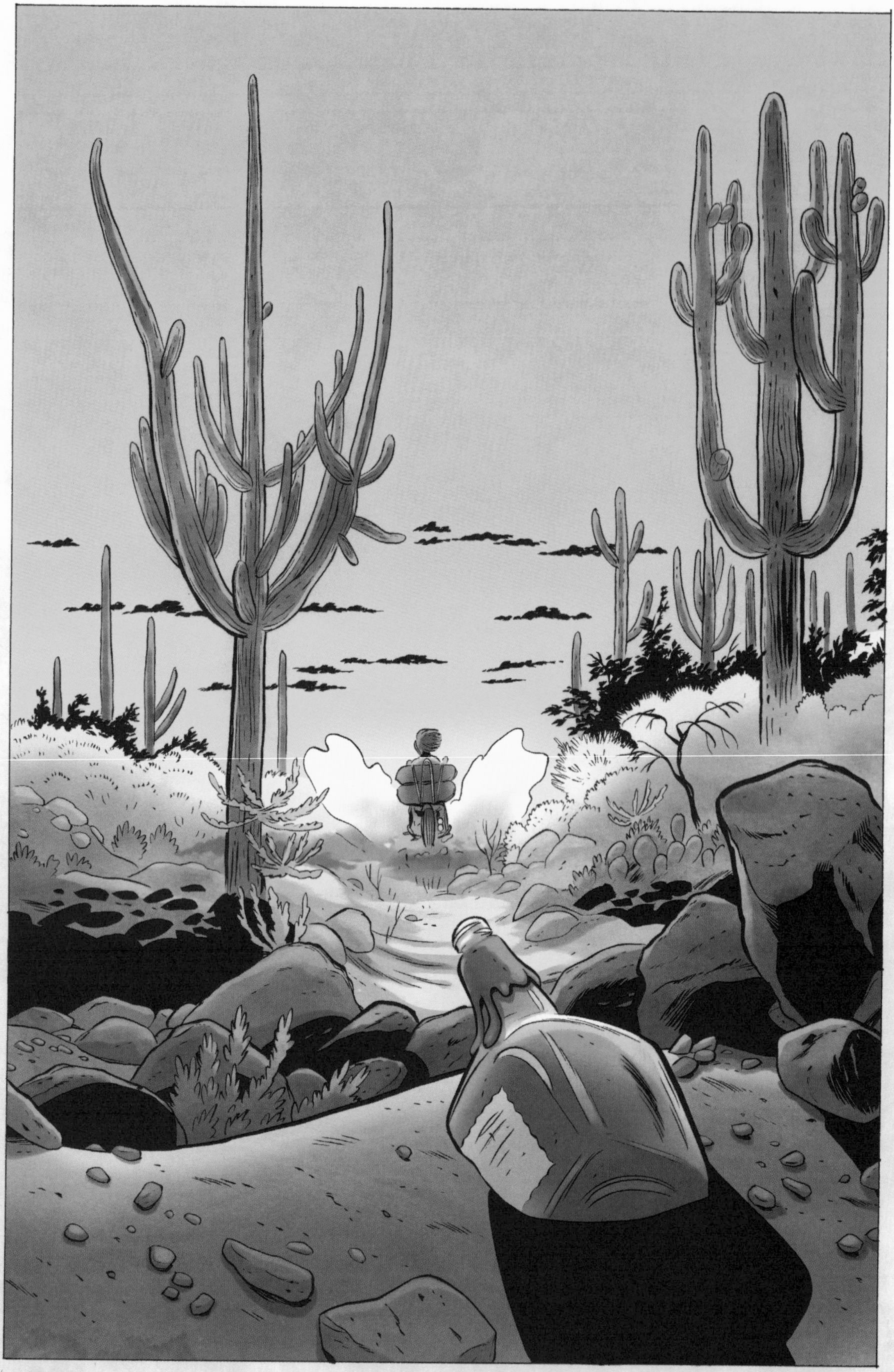

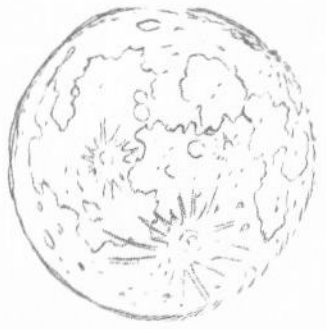

SPECIAL THANKS TO

Howard Fine, Marty Fuller, Jennifer Oliver,
Phil Corrigan, Louis Rios, Tony Murray,
Vijaya Iyer, Kathleen Glosan, Tom Gaadt,
Steve Hamaker, Tom Leckrone, David Filipi,
Paul Pope, Terry Moore, Scott Gaudi, Scott Harbin,
Chris Steele, Larry Medrano, Steve Leland, Phil Falco,
Khari Saffo, Garth Murphy and Mary Cagle
for sharing their expertise,
advice, patience
and
electricity.

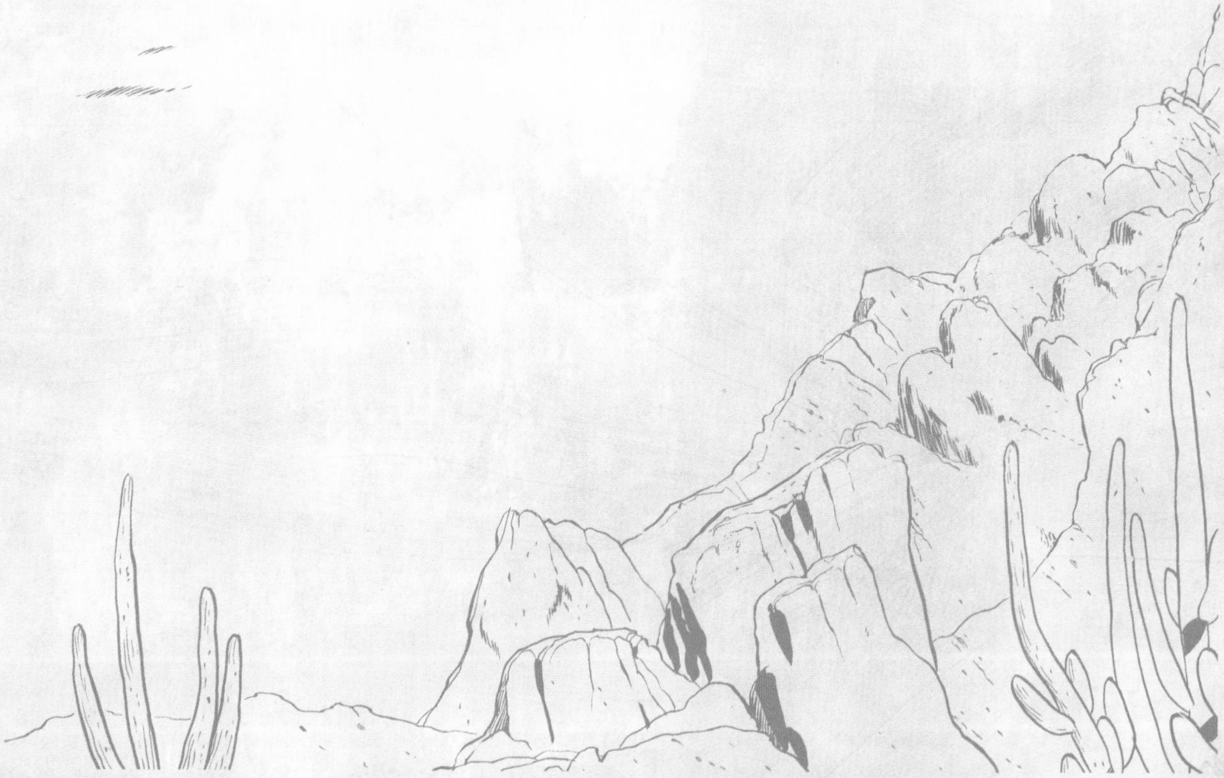

A Brief Bibliography

Books:

Fabric of the Cosmos
by Brian Greene
(Vintage)

Parallel Worlds
by Michio Kaku
(Anchor Books)

Secrets of the Unified Field
by Joseph P. Farrell
(Adventures Unlimited Press)

Paths of Life
edited by Sheridan & Parezo (University of Arizona Press)

The Philadelphia Experiment
by Moore & Berlitz
(Fawcett)

DVDs:

Tesla: Master of Lightning
(PBS Home Videos)

Nova: The Elegant Universe
(WGBH Boston Video)

Cosmos by Carl Sagan
(Cosmos Studios)

Holes in Heaven? H.A.A.R.P. and Advances in Tesla Technology
(NSI)

Frankenstein
directed by James Whale
(Universal Studio)

Google:

Key words: Tesla, H.A.A.R.P., Philadelphia Experiment, Tunguska.
Enter any combination of these words and hold on to your hat!

About the Author:

A co-founder of the 90's Self-Publishing Movement, and an early adopter of the graphic novel format, Jeff Smith is best known as the writer and artist of BONE, an award winning adventure about three cartoon cousins lost in a world of myth and ancient mysteries.

In 2009, Smith was the subject of a documentary called *The Cartoonist: Jeff Smith, BONE, and the Changing Face of Comics.*

Most recently, Smith was guest editor of The Best American Comics 2013, and continues to make and promote comics around the world.

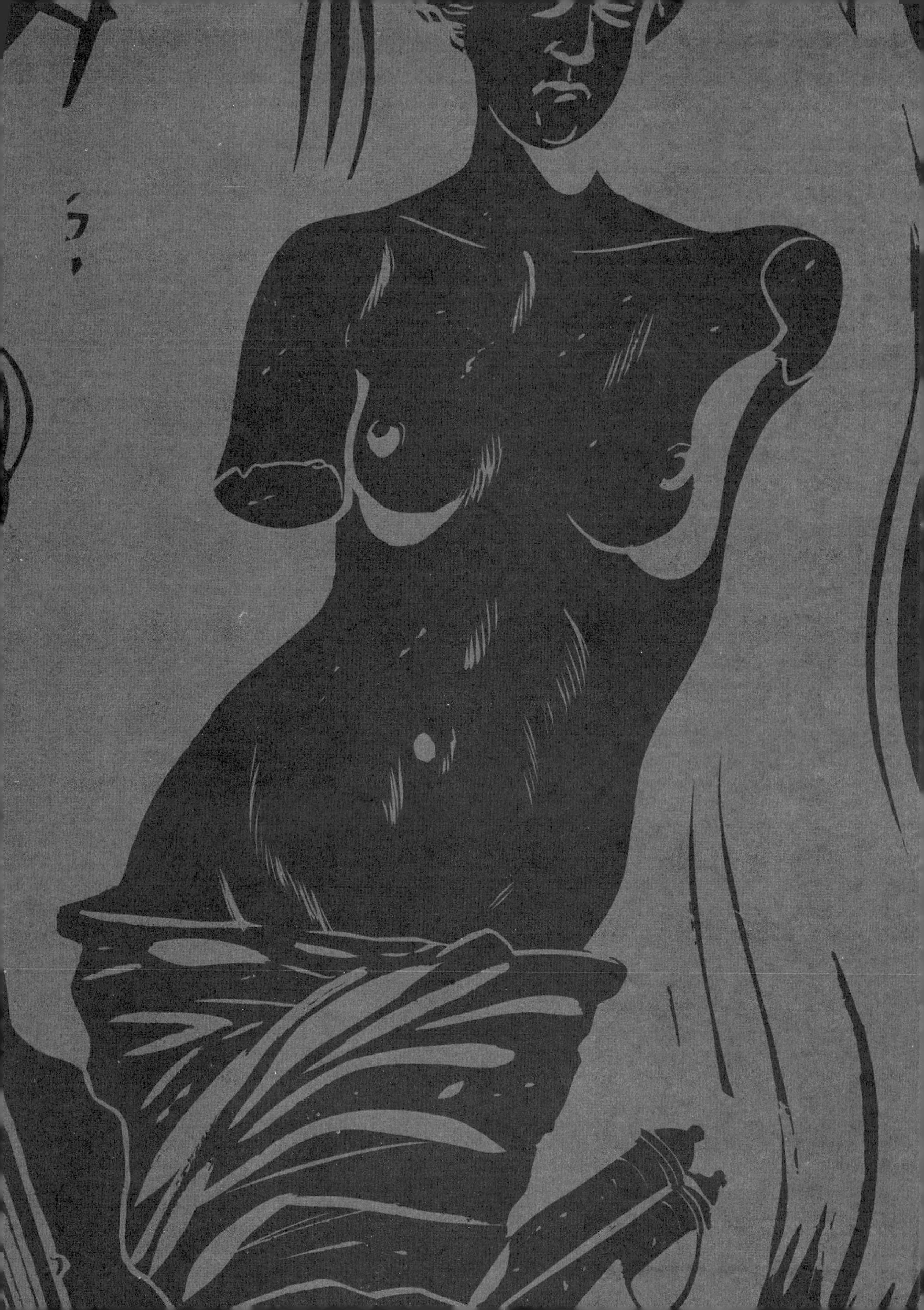